The Small Town in American Drama

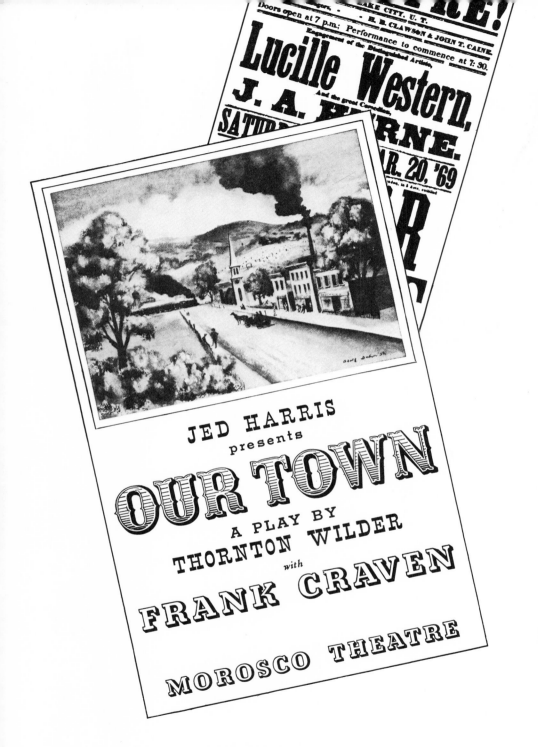

JED HARRIS

presents

OUR TOWN

A PLAY BY
THORNTON WILDER

with

FRANK CRAVEN

MOROSCO THEATRE

SOUTHERN METHODIST UNIVERSITY PRESS
DALLAS, TEXAS

THE
SMALL TOWN
IN
AMERICAN DRAMA

Ima Honaker Herron

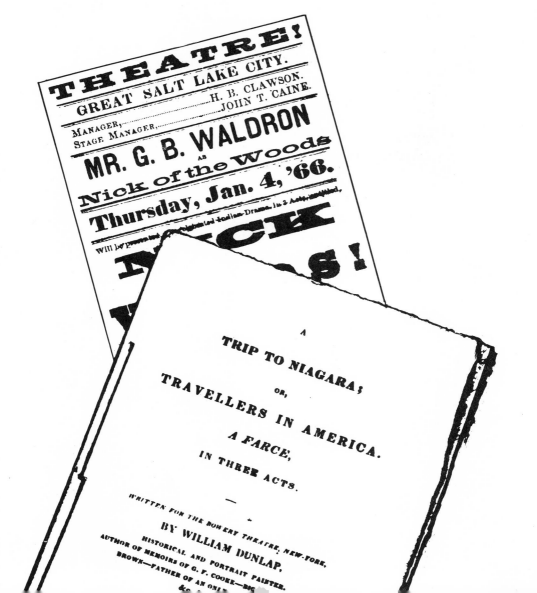

THEATRE!

GREAT SALT LAKE CITY.

MANAGER, ... H. B. CLAWSON.
STAGE MANAGER, ... JOHN T. CAINE.

MR. G. B. WALDRON
AS
Nick of the Woods

Thursday, Jan. 4, '66.

Will be presented the celebrated Indian Drama, in 3 Acts, entitled,

NICK

A

TRIP TO NIAGARA;
OR,
TRAVELLERS IN AMERICA.

A FARCE,
IN THREE ACTS.

WRITTEN FOR THE BOWERY THEATRE, NEW-YORK,

BY WILLIAM DUNLAP,

HISTORICAL AND PORTRAIT PAINTER,
AUTHOR OF MEMOIRS OF G. F. COOKE—BIO
BROWN—FATHER OF AN ONLY

© 1969 : SOUTHERN METHODIST UNIVERSITY PRESS : DALLAS
Library of Congress Catalog Card Number 69-11729

Over: Playbills for 1866 and 1869 performances at the Great Salt Lake City Theatre, from George D. Pyper, *The Romance of an Old Playhouse* (1928); program cover for first-run production of *Our Town* (1938); title page of William Dunlap's farce, *A Trip to Niagara* (1830), first produced at the Bowery Theatre in 1828

In Loving Memory of
William Patrick Herron (1870-1957)
Martha Gene (Wilson) Nicholson (1938-1965)
and
In Tribute to
Beulah Alice (Honaker) Herron
— all staunch upholders of the best community traditions

Preface

IN THE COURSE of more than three centuries of developing literary expression in America, two characteristics have appeared repeatedly: a tendency toward introspection, and a longing for community. Since the late eighteenth century this feeling for community, or interrelationship, has been portrayed so frequently in native plays interpreting the small town and its folk that a sizable body of dramas, diversely expressive of this aspect of our society, has come into existence. Even the agony of aloneness, the torment of estrangement from fellowship and community activity so often interpreted in our dramatizations of folk life, is persuasive evidence of the existence of a strong underlying feeling and need for community.

Play after play among the more than three hundred plays (both widely recognized and relatively unknown ones) surveyed here contains individual characters estranged from normal association with fellow citizens. Interest in, as well as sympathy for, the condition of man in the United States often becomes quite meaningful when associated with the small town, whether real or dramatized. Such concern has been demonstrated repeatedly in a variety of plays ranging from the grim portrayals of Colonial Salem and the little town of Boston (as portrayed in dramatized versions of *The Scarlet Letter*), to humorously pictured Down East villages, to more modern scenes in Faulkner's mythical Yoknapatawpha, Tennessee Williams' strife-torn Delta towns, and Albee's New Carthage. In dozens of plays the small town appears as a social entity wherein the lives of folksy Americans become interinvolved—sometimes comically, again tragically. For decades American drama has helped to preserve this entity and other community patterns.

In an earlier history, *The Small Town in American Literature*, I appraised pertinent poetry, short stories, novels, a few plays, local histories, diaries, notebooks, and autobiographies expressive of how provincial Americans have been written about both as individuals and as members of communities, in different epochs and places. This present study enlarges the scope of the previous history by its detailed presentation of the ways in which many of our American playwrights have held the mirror to village and, later, small-town life.

Sometimes the reflection is clear. Again it is distorted by a romantic glow, or uglified by propaganda or caustic satire. All in all, however, these provincial, or community, plays give ample support to a cogent note sounded by John Dos Passos and Paul Shyre in their dramatized *U.S.A.* (1960):

"But mostly U.S.A. is the lives of its people."

Acknowledgments

DURING MY LONG PREOCCUPATION with both actual and fictional small-town life in the United States, I have incurred many obligations. In the very beginning there were the family stories of a Texas-bound caravan of sturdy German-American pioneers. Disposing of their substantial properties in Russell County, Virginia, these westering folk (including my venturesome great-grandparents and their large family, with some of their freed slaves) endured a three-months' trek to what is now North Central Texas. Here in 1856, in a "sea of grass" located between forks of the Trinity River, they helped build a new town on the virgin prairie. From these forebears I gained an early understanding, through listening to oft-repeated family history, of the ways of pioneer townspeople, their hardships, and their folk aspirations.

In time childhood's absorption in family tales was to yield place to something deeper. In my youth three keen-minded students of American civilization—Professors Jay Broadus Hubbell, the late John Hathaway McGinnis, and Richard A. Hearon—first turned my attention to the significant role of small towns in both actual and literary history. Through the years I have learned well that the diversified literature of the American small town has indeed a recognizable and complex identity. This identity I have tried to explore and signify in various articles and in two histories, *The Small Town in American Literature* (1939; 1959) and the present one.

My more recent research could not have progressed without the benefit of financial subsidy and less tangible help. To the administration of Southern Methodist University and my colleagues in the English department I express warm thanks for a semester's leave, which in the spring of 1958 speeded the initiation of this current project. My special gratitude is extended to the Danforth Foundation, to Southern Methodist University's Graduate Council of the Humanities, and to former Provosts Hemphill Hosford and William L. Ayres (comptrollers of a Shell Oil Company research fund) for several summer grants. I am deeply appreciative of the unexpected subsidy which came from the Southern Methodist University Alumni Association in connection with a 1962 Faculty Achievement Award.

Among librarians, Lois Bailey of Southern Methodist University deserves thanks unstinted for her faithful efforts in securing for me rare copies, microfilm, and photostats of early plays through the Interlibrary Loan Service. Also, the generous assistance of her staff members— Genevieve G. Porter, Elizabeth Glaab, and Elizabeth Julian (curator of the Mary McCord Theatrical Collection)—made research all the more profitable. I am appreciative, too, of the aid given by James Phillips (of the DeGolyer Foundation Library, Dallas), by George Henderson, Fine Arts Librarian in charge of the Margo Jones and W. E. Hill theater collections at the Dallas Public Library, and his assistant, Ann Honea. Paul Meyers, of the Theatre Collection of the New York Public Library (and more recently of Lincoln Center), was unflagging in his assistance. Librarian Stanley Pargellis made available certain rare items in the Sherwood Anderson Collection at the Newberry Library, Chicago. Impersonal references are woefully inadequate as expressions of my thanks to co-operative librarians elsewhere: at Yale University, the University of Wisconsin, Harvard's Widener Library (for microfilm of rare Puritan plays), the University of Georgia (for southern folk plays), the University of Pennsylvania, the University of Texas, and the Library of Congress. Frank Weitenkampf (Curator of Prints, the New York Public Library), Alan Wilcox, and Wilson Duprey ably assisted me in securing photographic reproductions of provincial scenes from the Eno Collection. Benjamin Blom and Yolanda Melniker (of the A&B Booksellers, New York) supplied me with certain rare plays and playbills of yesteryear. Harvey B. Carlton generously shared with me his collection of modern playbills. I am extremely grateful to Rafael de Choudens, William A. Sandberg, and Houston Allred for their courtesies which facilitated the task of research.

I owe much to my inquiring students, notably to those who have found careers in the theater and the field of dramatic criticism. Often their provocative questioning and perceptive criticism heightened my own intellectual stimulation, thus contributing indirectly to the making of this book. Also, the two individuals who worked most intimately with me as informed and industrious secretaries—Beulah M. Mayo and Mary C. Shinn—deserve special commendation for their indispensable aid.

Final obligations deserve fuller acknowledgment than I can make here. My indebtedness to those authors and publishers who have given me permission to quote from their books and to many critics and historians of our native theater and drama is acknowledged, with gratitude, in the text, notes, and foreword listing permissions to quote. Deepest appreciation must go to my family—Thera Patrick Herron, Wallace W. Herron, Anna Belle and Eugene M. Wilson—for their forbearance and co-operation when the long preparation of this book placed domestic burdens upon them. For his warmhearted encouragement and kindnesses I thank Allen Maxwell, director of the Southern Methodist University Press. In Margaret L. Hartley, editor of the Press, I have found a wise and sympathetic adviser. Frances L. Aman of the editorial staff has lent a practiced hand to the labor of correcting galleys and page proofs and other essential chores. To Vicky C. Olmos goes the credit for designing the book.

Thanks are due Mrs. Hartley also, in her capacity as editor of the *Southwest Review*, for permission to reprint portions of this history which first appeared as articles in that journal. Similar thanks go to Crystelle Ferguson, editor of the *Eleusis*, and to Earle Labor, editor of the *CEA Critic*, in which magazines other portions were originally published.

IMA HONAKER HERRON

Dallas, Texas
November 24, 1968

Gratitude is here expressed to the following publishers, authors, and authors' representatives for permission to quote excerpts from the works named.

ATHENEUM PUBLISHERS and EDWARD ALBEE
Who's Afraid of Virginia Woolf? by Edward Albee. Copyright 1962 by Edward Albee. Reprinted by permission of the author and Atheneum Publishers. "Caution: Professionals and amateurs are hereby warned that *Who's Afraid of Virginia Woolf?*, being full protected under the copyright laws of the United States of America, the British Empire, including the Dominion of Canada, and all other countries of the Berne and Universal Copyright Conventions, is subject to royalty. All rights, including professional, amateur, motion picture, recitation, lecturing, public reading, radio and television broadcasting, and the rights of translation into foreign languages are strictly reserved. Particular emphasis is laid on the question of readings, permission for which must be secured from the author's agent in writing. All inquiries should be addressed to the William Morris Agency, 1740 Broadway, New York, New York 10019."

ESQUIRE, INC. (Arnold Gingrich, Editor; Myron D. Davis, General Counsel)
Welcome to Our City by Thomas Wolfe, as published in an abridged form in *Esquire*, XLVIII (October, 1957), 58–82. Copyright 1957 by Esquire, Inc.

PAUL GITLIN (present Administrator, C.T.A., of the Estate of Thomas Wolfe)
KETTI FRINGS (Mrs. Kurt Frings)
Look Homeward, Angel: A Play by Ketti Frings based on Thomas Wolfe's novel, *Look Homeward, Angel: A Story of the Buried Life* (Charles Scribner's Sons, 1929). Copyright 1958 by Edward C. Aswell as Administrator, C.T.A., of the Estate of Thomas Walfe and/or Fred W. Wolfe and Ketti Frings.

HARPER & ROW and THORNTON WILDER
The Long Christmas Dinner by Thornton Wilder. The 1931 copyright

held by Coward-McCann, Inc. has been taken over by Harper & Row.

Our Town by Thornton Wilder. Copyright 1938, 1957 by Thornton Wilder. The 1938 copyright held by Coward-McCann, Inc. has been taken over by Harper & Row.

Preface by Travis Bogard to *Three Plays* and two plays included therein: *The Skin of Our Teeth*, copyright 1942 by Thornton Wilder; *The Matchmaker*, copyright 1955, 1957 by Thornton Wilder. An earlier version of *The Matchmaker* entitled *The Merchant of Yonkers* was copyright 1939 by Thornton Wilder.

THE MACMILLAN COMPANY

"New England." Reprinted with permission of The Macmillan Company from *Dionysus in Doubt* by Edwin Arlington Robinson. Copyright 1925 by Edwin Arlington Robinson. Copyright renewed 1952 by Ruth Nivison and Barbara R. Holt.

NEW DIRECTIONS and TENNESSEE WILLIAMS

27 Wagons Full of Cotton by Tennessee Williams. Copyright 1945, 1953 by Tennessee Williams.

Battle of Angels by Tennessee Williams. Copyright 1940, © 1955, 1958 by Tennessee Williams.

Summer and Smoke by Tennessee Williams. Copyright 1948 by Tennessee Williams.

Camino Real (Foreword) by Tennessee Williams. Copyright 1948, 1953 by Tennessee Williams.

The Rose Tattoo by Tennessee Williams. Copyright 1950, 1951 by Tennessee Williams.

Orpheus Descending by Tennessee Williams. Copyright © 1955, 1958 by Tennessee Williams.

Sweet Bird of Youth by Tennessee Williams. © 1959 by Two Rivers Enterprises, Inc.

The Milk Train Doesn't Stop Here Anymore by Tennessee Williams. Copyright © 1963, 1964 by Two Rivers Enterprises, Inc.

RANDOM HOUSE, INC.

The Days Between by Robert Anderson. Copyright 1961 as an unpublished work by Robert Anderson. Copyright 1965 by Robert Anderson.

Requiem for a Nun by William Faulkner. Copyright 1950, 1951 by William Faulkner.

Requiem for a Nun, a play by Ruth Ford based upon the novel by William Faulkner. Copyright 1959 by William Faulkner and Ruth Ford.

Introduction

AS ROBERT FROST once said, "What makes a nation in the beginning is a good piece of geography." In many ways the mythic vastness of the American land, stretching almost endlessly westward, has been instrumental in the shaping of our national beliefs and character, and in the development of our farms, plantations, towns, cities, and other areas. As acknowledged many times over, our distinctively native way of thought, character, and conduct owes much to the broad land. Many interpreters, furthermore, have associated significant elements of Americanness with the smaller community. For one, the late Sherwood Anderson, in his *Home Town* (1940), expressed his feeling that "the real test of democracy may come in the towns." Also, in his *American Memoir* (1947) Henry Seidel Canby recalled that "life in America began on the farm and continued in the small city or town." As late as "the eighties and the nineties the fathers and mothers of most families had been born in the country," but the next generation (Canby's own) owed "its provenance to the town." For many twentieth-century Americans, including Canby, "It is the small town, the small city, that is our heredity; we have made twentieth-century America from it . . ." Indeed, the small town per se, though its history is long, would be an unimportant scene if it had not been a significant part of the historic development of the United States.

In still another fashion the American small town has had a vital significance. "America," historian Marshall Fishwick observed recently, "is not so much a nation or a people as a search," originating several centuries ago, which has inspired countless imaginative recorders to create "myths and miracles of this broadbacked, boisterous land." This is the obvious truth, but the shaping imagination has created far more than myths and miracles from the raw materials of the land. Among the countless transformations of the ample American world through art, numerous extant plays, of varied types and values and dated from the eighteenth century to the present, attest to the long-lasting appeal of the little town and its folkways for our native playwrights.

The earliest actual, or historic, settlements—glorified as "cities in the wilderness"—as they were in the decades after their founding became for dramatists of the nineteenth and twentieth centuries the symbols of our origins, our struggle, and our eventual growth. In later years the sea-board settlements of Massachusetts Bay Colony and elsewhere came to symbolize for certain playwrights studying our past the circumscribed and cheerless living of seventeenth-century Puritans. As settlement slowly and hazardously extended westward, the small place, appearing first as a crude clearing—a dot upon the virgin land—offered new raw material for regional playwrights. Often their dramatizations represented a mythus —a legend, or symbol, of the opportunity of free men—of the commu-nity way of life in a new land. In the Mauve Decade and afterward, with the receding of once available land on the national horizon, a fencing in —a spreading standardization—increasingly began to have a stultifying effect on the American village and the prevailing attitudes toward it, literary and otherwise. As the patriotic and romantic outlooks of the eighteenth and early nineteenth centuries waned, the village was no longer "Fair Columbia's bower," "a seat of democracy," a "haven," or a "resort of peace," but a commonplace community dulled by mental stag-nation and petty inhibitive forces. Gradually Pleasant Valley and Friend-ship Village yielded place to Gopher Prairie and the far-reaching blights of the "village virus." Scenes of mill towns made ugly by strikes and breadlines, of southern communities torn by racial strife, of New England harbor towns caught in the web of hate and bigotry, began to crowd our stages.

With the approach of "the years of the modern," the pendulum began to reverse itself, as the exodus from the city brought thousands back to provincial areas. As giantism continued to pose problems for the citizens of Megalopolis and even Suburbia, many writers, playwrights included, satirically exposed the corruptions and injustices of the present, while searching for a usable past. And a part of what they have found imaginatively usable in our American heritage has been the small town as a place of escape from urban congestion and other ills. Within recent decades, however, manifold and countrywide urbanization has made of our once peaceful small places virtually a vanishing America. Many small towns, in the judgment of Edward Albee and other dramatists of the absurd, in their present decay and loss of frontier vigor no longer typify a roseate American dream. With the accelerated changes in pro-vincial America, the many dramatizations of native town life, under all sorts of conditions, take on new significance as manifestations of a provincialism long central in our history. Even the crude beginnings of this extended record are intrinsically dramatic.

Actually our drama was born in an air of small community life: of a tiny and rawly new Spanish settlement once called El Paso del Norte.

This frontier beginning turns one's imagination backward to Spanish expeditionary ventures in the late sixteenth century. The drouthy summer of 1598, vividly described in Paul Horgan's *Great River*, was marked by considerable disturbance in the small settlement of San Juan de los Caballeros in the valley of the Rio Grande del Norte. In late August Governor Juan de Oñate, troubled by spying Indians and their lamentations for rain and angered by mutinous soldiers under his command, endeavored to create harmony by ordering a week of community festivities, to be apportioned equally between ecclesiastical and military display. Also, with official zeal, he hurried the construction of a church.

This jubilee in the wilderness was enlivened by the performance of a *comedia*, *Los Moros y Los Cristianos*, an anonymous play customarily attributed to a Sevillian, Captain Marcos Farfan de los Godos. (Earlier, on April 30, at a river grove encampment near El Paso del Norte—the site of modern El Paso—Captain Godos had climaxed a celebration of the Mass by a performance of his hastily composed play dramatizing the coming of the Franciscan fathers to New Mexico.) Designed to impress invited Indian chiefs and expeditioners alike, this summertime diversion was a practical expression of exciting action: a military tournament, heightened by colorful pageantry, lively bullfights, and the firing of gunpowder (without shot), all to simulate the warring between Moors and Christians.

At best only a crude theatrical activity, this *comedia* of 1598 is significant mostly as an experiment with a traditional form of entertainment undertaken by adventuring Spaniards as a proper addition to a religious celebration in one of their New World provinces. During the same era there were comparable theatrical experiments in the burgeoning settlements in other provinces under the rule of the French and the English. Thus our earliest known theatrical art, while only a small part of the rough and strenuous life of a remote, largely unsettled country, was an immediate outgrowth of a raw settlement's emotional and cultural needs and a colonial governor's diplomacy. From such an unprofessional beginning on through many stages of national expansion until the twentieth century, the provincial spirit, later to be associated with the small town, has left its indelible mark on American drama.

Contents

Illustrations

xxiii

The Small Town in American Drama

I. The Puritan Village and
"The Common Madness of the Time"

". . . so intense a light"

IN HIS SATIRE "Puritanism as a Literary Force," H. L. Mencken tartly viewed religious intolerance and prejudice as a traditional barrier to the stimulation of imaginative writing in the United States during the twenties and thirties. Vehemently he protested against a continuing and repressive Puritanism which, he argued, had held in check the imaginative faculties of our modern novelists since the time of Mark Twain, rendering them timid and apologetic—but safe. As to the relation of our playwrights to the restraining force of Puritanism, Mencken had little to say, although notable ones (from James Nelson Barker, in 1824, to Arthur Miller) have created stageable plays variously dramatizing the operation of the Puritan code, usually highlighting its narrowness. He thus left to one side an important phase of the question of Puritanism as a literary force: that of the implications of Puritanism for the first builders of New England's towns in the wilderness, as they have been seen by and have had their effect upon later dramatic interpreters.

Cotton Mather, in the *Magnalia Christi Americana*, saw his own New England as a country "whose interests were most remarkably and generally enwrapped in its ecclesiastical circumstances." Later, Alexis de Tocqueville was impressed by the widespread and continuing influence of religion on American life and thought. He wrote: "On my arrival [in May, 1831] in the United States the religious aspect of the country was the first thing that struck my attention."[1] Moses Coit Tyler, writing in 1878, stated that "in its inception New England was not an agricultural community, nor a manufacturing community, nor a trading community: it was a thinking community; an arena and mart for ideas." The intensity of this mental activity went with Puritan colonials "into everything—piety, politics, education, work, play." Most of all, "it was toward religion, as the one supreme thing in life and the universe, that all this intellectuality of theirs and all [their] earnestness were directed."[2] Today these claims are under dispute. For example, according to Perry Miller and Thomas H. Johnson, Puritanism in America was far more than a state of mind, however intellectual or straitlaced it may have been. From the social and economic viewpoint, it was in the beginning "a philosophy of social stratification," seriously

3

believed in by seventeenth-century Massachusetts theocrats, "auto-cratic, hierarchical, and authoritarian."[3] Aiming at exclusive control of a new environment, early Puritans held that all must be subject to both ecclesiastical and political leaders; hence, the responsibilities of a vested interest.

Before the rise of the force of democracy in the 1770's, then, Puritan-ism symbolized a rigorous autocratic standard characterized by the lead-ership of earnest, bookish clergymen and laymen who, as Tyler noted, favored "a social structure with its cornerstone resting on a book," and the responsive subjection of the less tutored folk. With authority placed in the hands of such oligarchs as John Cotton, the Mathers, and John Norton, Puritanism, dedicated to the achievement of uniformity, de-manded obedience from its nonclerical believers. Throughout the colo-nial period it connoted a mixture of strong moral earnestness, rigor-ous repression of the more exuberant joys of life (as satirized in Hawthorne's "The Maypole of Merry Mount"), a sense of social re-sponsibility, and the sort of piety and even mysticism that later charac-terized Jonathan Edwards. Moreover, Puritanism went beyond being merely a religious creed to become "a philosophy and a metaphysic ... [and even] an organization of a man's whole life, emotional and intellectual, to a degree which has not been sustained by any denomina-tion stemming from it."[4] In short, historic Puritanism, "with roots reaching back into mediaeval life," was the controlling force for the folk, high and low, in seventeenth-century New England's villages and towns and on her farms.

That force had, of course, originated in England, springing in the late sixteenth century from dissidence within the Church of England, as a reform movement of that church which, in the New England colonies, became known as Calvinism.[5] Carl Sandburg, in *Remembrance Rock* (1948), imaginatively re-created the life of Scrooby Village (near York), where as early as 1607 a group of dissenters, led by Elder Wil-liam Brewster and his young neighbor William Bradford, had so "wea-ried of form, ceremonial, the Book of Common Prayer" that they began "hating prayer and worship by compulsion."[6] Seekers of religious lib-erty, the Scrooby congregation held secret and heretical meetings, en-dangering their safety by declaring that "the living heart should confess and petition God." Villager Bradford even daringly hoped that "they may become one small candle to light a thousand and mayhap kindle a nation."[7]

And such zealous and courageous seekers for a faith did kindle a tiny village world in New England's wilderness. In the beginning, these transplanted villagers upheld the principles of a free-spoken liberty of conscience, freedom to worship God as they saw fit, and the right to read the Bible for both instruction and faith. On the other hand,

so intense a light could but cast some deep shadows: suppressing sweetness and gaiety in the human heart; stiffening conscientiousness into scrupulosity, rectitude into asceticism; making punishment a species of retributive vengeance; so stimulating zeal for their own creed that this zeal should become intolerance and even violence toward those who held a creed that was different.[8]

In fact, as the settlements grew, these "stewards of theocracy" adhered more and more strongly and uncompromisingly to the stern tenets of Calvinism. Inevitably such zealots became persecutors. "Toleration," says Tyler, became a scandalous word, even an impiety. And inevitably this intolerance found its mark, the menace to New England's theocracy (later dramatized) of a growing and militant Quakerism. As the Friends, motivated by their faith in the simple life, reiterated their beliefs in "perfection more than in sin, in guidance by the inner light rather than in restraints imposed by the authority of the clergy and magistracy," local differences led to clashes and punishment. Some of the Puritan towns limited the suffrage to church members.[9] In certain places (like the Boston of Longfellow's tragedy, *John Endicott*) Puritan dogmatists resorted to force and severe cruelty to stamp out the Quaker nonconformists whom they called "anarchists," "heretics," and "emissaries of the devil." For the men there were heavy fines, public shaming before the Church Assembly, workhouse labor, branding in the palm of the right hand, cutting off of ears, imprisonment, or even hanging. For the women there were severe whippings, boring of the tongue with a hot iron, or banishment on pain of death.[10]

The most pernicious of all Puritan misconceptions, however, took the form of superstitious Satanism, a concern—at times fanatical in its intensity—with the "evil mysteries" which had terrified people since the Middle Ages.[11] Such fear of the menacing world of demons—of what Cotton Mather called "the wonders of the invisible world"—led many Puritans (even some of the learned, though this charge is contested) into a misconception of nature and a false evaluation of their fellow men.

It is true, as George Lyman Kittredge has pointed out in *Old and New England*,[12] that "our forefathers believed in witchcraft, not because they were Puritans, not because they were colonials, not because they were New Englanders,—but because they were men of their time." It is a fallacy to regard the New England Puritans as a peculiar folk, unaware of continental and British thought and legends. Even the Salem upheaval of 1692, which Kittredge calls "the darkest page of New England history," was not an isolated phenomenon, for by the seventeenth century belief in witchcraft had long been a common heritage, and all kinds of extraordinary happenings were attributed to Satan's activity. At that time, too, the "crime [of witchcraft] was recognized by the Bible, by all branches of the Church, by philosophy, by natural science, by the medical faculty, by the law of England."[13] Prominent non-Puritans—among them Jeremy Taylor and Dr. Henry More, Cambridge scholars, and Oxonians Sir Thomas Browne and Joseph Glanvill—expressed belief in witchcraft. Glanvill's *Sadducismus triumphatus; or, A Full and Plain Evidence concerning Witches and Apparitions*, published in 1681 and with five editions up to 1726, exerted a powerful influence and was well known to the Mathers.[14] The use of talismans, the evocation of evil spirits especially in connection with the orgies of the Sabbat, natural and other magic (such as the raising of a storm or a fire), spell-casting, often associated with the causing of wasting diseases, the sticking of puppets or poppets with pins to hasten bewitchment, the keeping of familiars ranging from butterflies to toads, cats, and dogs, and even belief in lycanthropy were among the forms in which superstition possessed the minds of many men and women.[15] Historically considered, the outburst of hysteria at Salem Village was a mere incident, a transitory episode, in the long history of the terrible but perfectly natural folk reactions to superstition.

Finally, among the harsher aspects of Puritanism which have moved the imagination of playwrights is a view basic in Puritan theology: the doctrines of original sin and human depravity and of God's grace. Sin and limited regeneration helped to frame Puritan thought and to stir the life of New England towns. Of prime importance in the life of the people of Massachusetts was their belief that "men not only inherit the Adamic guilt, they add to it by their innate desire to sin. Thus man's degradation is complete."[16] The dour determinism of so bleak an outlook was, for the Puritans, brightened somewhat by the corollary that man had some opportunity for salvation, depending, of course, upon God's "irresistible" grace, through which sinful man might become "a regenerated creature." Although the manner of its attainment remained a mystery, such salvation, according to covenant theology, was bestowed only upon those achieving the qualifications, involving man's assumption of a moral obligation to abide by the covenant made with God.[17] Strengthened by their faith in God's rightness and justice, early Puritans could more readily confront the tragedies and defeats of their personal and community lives.

On the other hand, for those sinners who remained uncertain as to whether they were to receive God's grace, and thus join the Elect, the loss of peace of mind could but add to the drabness of their daily living.

Such a code of ethics implied, too, that man, with all of his imperfection, must strive constantly to avoid enslavement to his natural desires and passions. Violation of the code, as in the imaginary case of Hawthorne's Reverend Arthur Dimmesdale, subjected man to loss of mental peace and a heightened sense of guilt. Moreover, a still more intense agony of soul supposedly came from the concealment of sin, the familiar human deflection used as the key motif in *The Scarlet Letter* and the several dramas later fashioned from it, such as that made in 1899 by James Edgar Smith. As the branding and public shaming of offenders bearing the "scarlet stigma" of sexual violation indicate, such a stern attitude toward various forms of guilt left little room for mercy. Later Hawthorne was to associate the similar punishment of Quakers by whipping with "The crimson trail [which] goes wavering along the Main-street."

From their study of the strict mores of colonial New England, various novelists (Hawthorne most of all), poets (especially Quaker Whittier), and playwrights have interpreted the Puritan ethic of guilt. Hawthorne pictured pride as the root evil; in his tales and novels many manifestations of pride—spiritual, intellectual, social, family, and the like—are associated with retributive justice. Overweening pride, as used anew in dramatized versions of *The Scarlet Letter* and in Barker's *Superstition*, leads to man's degradation and even death. Morbid introspection, a byproduct of pride, appears in our dramatic portrayals as a force of self-destruction. For example, a criticism of the introspective habits of the seventeenth-century mind is implicit in the private reflections of the prideful Endicott, overbearing religious zealot and governor in Longfellow's *John Endicott*. It may be noted, too, that dramatic interpretations of guilt sometimes parallel confessional entries about sin in early diaries, like those of Cotton Mather and Jonathan Edwards.[18]

Puritan Tragedies

Exactly how has the small place, so significant in colonial New England, been re-created dramatically? By and large, native playwrights inspired by colonial community life, while not neglecting the physical aspects of early towns and their folk, have in common their concern about Puritan attitudes. Generally, too, they have shown more interest in portraying the darker side, sometimes the agony and the evil, of Puritanism. Also, most of these dramatists (from Barker, actively engaged in Jacksonian politics, to Miller, disturbed by modern repressions) themselves have lived in times of extraordinary change, when the principles of freedom and justice have been endangered. Accordingly, the dark past of Salem, Boston, and neighboring villages has offered a more compelling challenge to certain imaginative playwrights than have the brighter aspects of New England life. There are, of course, some exceptions. For instance, Percy MacKaye's humorous Dickon ("a Yankee improvisation of the Prince of Darkness"), in *The Scarecrow*, suggests the lighter side of Puritan living occasionally reflected in Sewall's *Diary*, in the entries about taverns, dancing, and, more personally, the judge's amusing courtship of Madame Winthrop.[19]

In Britain witchcraft outbreaks generally have coincided with times of political excitement or other anxiety. Likewise, the witchcraft delusions in this country, climaxed by the shameful Salem trials, mark a time when Massachusetts colony was just emerging from a political and religious struggle that threatened its very existence.[20]Although from the beginning New England's Puritans had striven heroically to maintain unity, public feeling, even prior to the furor about witchcraft, was marked by uncertainties and disquietude.[21] Fear of the disfavor of the British king, of surprise Indian attacks, of the missionary zeal of heretics, principally ranting Quakers, and of the menacing powers of darkness governed the nervous condition of Massachusetts townsmen and even lonelier farm people.

Such is the public mind dramatized in several of the best village plays. The Indian attack and the routing of the savages by the Unknown in *Superstition*; the hysteria of the trial scene in that play, matched in dramatic tension by comparable trials in the Longfellow and Freeman tragedies of the Coreys and in Miller's study of the Proctors; the superstitious belief in the potency of spells, magic mirrors, and the devil himself, as in *The Scarecrow*; Longfellow's portrayal of Governor Endicott's determined persecution of Quakers—all of these reflect the tense spirit of actual emergencies, such as Indian raids and the Salem arraignments of Giles and Martha Corey, the Proctors, and other victims. In Barker's tragedy ill-fated Mary Ravensworth, fearful and prophetic, senses the mounting perils threatening New England communities as early as 1675: "Fell superstition now had spread around/ . . . [and] the doctrine of the times/ Grew daily still more stern, . . . "

While each dramatist's imaginative approach is individual, each shares with other delineators of the colonial town the quality of historicity. Each has had some acquaintance with contemporary and other valuable sources. Barker, as the first American playwright to deal artistically with colonial history, materialized the little Massachusetts town of his *Super-*

stition (1824) from authentic early records, including Governor Thomas Hutchinson's *History of Massachusetts* (1795) and Robert Calef's *More Wonders of the Invisible World* (1823).[22] Longfellow, during the long composition of *The New England Tragedies* (1868), used sources ready at hand in the Harvard library: Norton's *The Heart of New England Rent* (1659), Mather's *Magnalia* (1702), and Besse's *Sufferings of the Quakers* (1753).[23] Later, both Mrs. Freeman and MacKaye, the latter inspired by Hawthorne's "Feathertop," showed comparable familiarity with records of the seventeenth-century mind. More recently, Arthur Miller, though modifying his source materials somewhat, in a foreword to *The Crucible* speaks of the essential historical accuracy of his tragedy. In studying what he considers "one of the strangest and most awful chapters in human history," the Salem trials, Miller refers to his creative use of Puritan letters, the trial records as kept by the Reverend Samuel Parris, and certain contemporary broadsides.[24] Finally, the authenticity of the various dramatizations of *The Scarlet Letter*, obviously, is traceable to Hawthorne's brooding about and his library exploration of his ancestral past, as it concerned his native "Main Street" (Salem) and colonial Boston. The modern adapters have added little that is new.

These dramatists variously concern themselves with Puritanism as "a philosophy of social stratification." All of their fictionalized towns serve as scenes for different stories of human passions at work under the rigid social conditions of a definite historical epoch, the seventeenth century. Severely Puritan, each town is governed by stern and zealous theocrats, typified by Barker's Ravensworth (suggested by Salem's Reverend Mr. Parris), who "would root out with an unsparing hand, /the weeds that choke the soil," and John Norton (in *John Endicott*) who preached that "Truth is relentless; justice never wavers." Each town, too, has its controlling magistrates and leading citizens: on occasion a governor and a deputy-governor (like Longfellow's Endicott and Bellingham), men of civil eminence (Judge Hathorne and his Salem trial colleagues), merchants, Harvard dons (as in *The Scarecrow*), Puritan squires, and grand dames like Dame Bellingham. Beneath these are the individually unimportant townspeople and strangers who, as in *The Scarlet Letter*, serve much the same purpose as a Greek chorus. Constables and townbeadles, tavern keepers, sailors, children and servant girls like those who "cried out" at the Salem trials, good wives, farmers, certain outsiders (mysterious Tituba from San Salvador, Indians in their savage finery, and badgered Quakers), and other citizens typify both the routine and the occasional excitements of Puritan village life.

In the prologue to an early comedy, *Tears and Smiles*, first acted in

1807, Barker answered Philadelphia's Anglomaniacal "witlings about town" by daring to dramatize American manners, opinions, characters, and scenery, which local "hypercritics" apparently had derided as "hideous, rank Columbianisms."[25] Much later, as he was bringing his dramatic career to a close (shortly after serving as Philadelphia's mayor), Barker produced a blank verse "serious dramatic tale," his eleventh and last play. This dramatically effective arraignment of delusion and religiosity, titled *Superstition; or, The Fanatic Father*, was first played at Philadelphia's Chestnut Street Theatre on March 12, 1824.[26]

Barker's success in this tragedy (the best play written in America up to that time) rests largely on his craftsmanship in unifying various narrative interests.[27] Moreover, his imagination often transforms his more prosaic sources into dramatically appealing scenes and characterizations. The time of the play is about 1675, and the place is a small Massachusetts town whose citizens are terrified by an Indian attack, simulating the actual raid made on Hadley during King Philip's War. Barker, however, shifts the scene to Salem, and he just as freely manipulates actual events to fit artistic demands. For instance, the exile of William Goffe (English Puritan and regicide) in Hadley and near New Haven between 1661 and 1664 is moved forward to 1675, when a mysterious rescuer, The Unknown (actually Goffe), guides the villagers in achieving victory over the Indians. A further sign of inventiveness is the imaginative portrayal of the family relationship between The Unknown, his genteel daughter Isabella, and her son Charles. This family group, according to Barker's biographer, may have been suggested by the *Goldsmith Letters* which Goffe wrote to his wife under the assumed name of Walter Goldsmith.[28]

Throughout five acts Barker displays skill in relating the several narrative threads to the basic issue, the tragic conflict between Puritan fanaticism and cant and the hopes of the young lovers (Mary, daughter of the minister Ravensworth, and the gentlemanly Charles, recently come from England). In Act I Ravensworth's bigotry, but momentarily tempered by the moderation and common sense of his colleague Walford, suggests the general fear that satanic forces are at work in the town. Ravensworth's bent toward moral action determines his decision to battle with "The powers of darkness [which] are at work among us."[29] Isabella and Charles, as nonconforming newcomers acquainted with a more worldly way of life, fail to offer the homage due even a village theocrat. His vanity thus pricked, Ravensworth suspects them of sorcery and evil and uses his position to influence the minds of his parishioners against them. Thus early in the plot a sense of doom is felt.

Isabella's coming to this Puritan village to search for her regicidal father is tied in with Charles's return from college. En route, in a forest, he meets and talks with a strange older man (The Unknown), but the youth is unaware of the traveler's identity as a regicide and as his own grandfather. A lighter aspect of seventeenth-century life is introduced through the witty dialogue of Sir Reginald Egerton and his flippant nephew George, acting as agents of Charles II to discover the whereabouts of Goffe. George, quite bored with Puritan sobriety, makes unwelcomed love to Mary. Charles, as her rescuer, duels with cavalier George, who though merely hurt is believed mortally wounded; hence, the villagers, aroused by Ravensworth's resentment, regard Charles with greater suspicion than ever. It is indeed ironic that Charles's tragic flaw, his humane kindness to George at the end of their duel, hastens his own doom. At this point, the Indian attack offers an interlude. Just as the excited colonials are about to be routed, an unexpected deliverer (The Unknown), assisted by Charles and Walford, valiantly aids the townspeople to defeat the savages and then mysteriously disappears. With characteristic lack of charity, Ravensworth links this strange delivery with the work of the Devil, whose local human accomplices, in the minister's distorted judgment, are the gallant Unknown, Isabella whom he now condemns as sorceress, and the heroic Charles.

From that point on, the somber plot moves speedily toward a climax. In a well-managed scene, Isabella, while urging escape, confesses to Charles a few details about her secret morganatic marriage in England and the reason for her flight to New England. Again Ravensworth, with the tenacity of the fanatic, is determined that "this dark woman" and her son will be called "to the judgment seat." Accordingly, mother and son, charged with practicing sorcery, are ordered before the village examination council, comparable to the actual commissions which met in the Salem church. Charles, however, has an anguished meeting with Mary in her room, where her suspicious father and the court constable find them. This farewell love scene is, for Barker's period, a model of restraint and sincere expression. The stirring climax scene of Ravensworth's branding Charles as "a lewd libertine" offers double evidence of Barker's artistry in portraying tragic love and of his sharp departure from the highly embellished seduction motif popularized in America by Mrs. Rowson's best seller, *Charlotte Temple*, and other similar American and British tales of the period.

The tragic closing scene, the trial in the village meetinghouse, suggests the hysterical 1692 examinations conducted in Salem Village church. As prosecutor, Ravensworth sternly denies Isabella counsel. As a result, like Shelley's ill-fated Beatrice Cenci, she must defend herself against terrible charges. Her eloquence, though refuting Ravensworth, fails to move her already prejudiced accusers. Determined on vengeance, Ravensworth suddenly dooms Charles with triple charges: with George Egerton's murder, with the attempted rape of Mary, and with assisting the supposedly diabolic Unknown. Again, it is ironic that young Charles, trying to protect Mary, refuses to plead, and thus, according to colonial Massachusetts law, all but signs his own death warrant.

Continuing his unmerciful prosecution, even in the midst of a furious storm (somewhat Gothicized), Ravensworth moves spectators to mass hysteria as he speeds Charles's execution, offstage. Tardily but futilely, Mary now pleads Charles's cause, just as his body is brought back into the meetinghouse. Overcome by the horror, Mary suffers a quick mental breakdown and dies. In a grand finale, while the storm rages unabated, the now broken Ravensworth despairs, Isabella dies of grief, and Sir Egerton makes known Goffe's pardon while disclosing that Charles is the son of a king.

All in all, Barker's tragedy is a stirring re-creation of the earlier stages of Massachusetts superstition and delusion. Salem, as it appeared in 1675, seemingly was peopled by unthinking Puritans, easily moved by "the monster prejudice" to "mob hysteria whom bigotry has brutaliz'd" (Charles's words). Further, as Isabella and Walford saw the truth, " . . . such folly,/ When it infects the crowd, is dangerous," because "the frenzy spreads." As portrayed in this tragedy, too few Salemites were willing to listen to the intelligent minority, as represented by Walford's rationalistic explanation of the sources of superstition, or to believe with him the urgent necessity of searching for the truth, even while "frenzy's flame" runs through the minds of men. Walford, symbolizing the man of reason, warns against serious belief in "infant witnesses" whose malice, "childish petulance, e'en idiocy" could "with a hint destroy." Unfortunately he is little heeded, for already almost all of the community had fallen to the mob spirit.

The somewhat localized and sporadic frenzy of the 1670's, in actuality as in fiction, was a sort of prologue for the slowly rising action culminating by 1692 in a drama of terror. Hence, *Superstition* is distinctive as our first dramatic interpretation of early town life under the strain of delusion. Both insignificant and recognized playwrights followed Barker as recorders of the impact of demonology upon the colonial mind. Their diverse talents, all coupled with the lasting literary appeal of Puritanism, have at least left multiple pictures of the wilderness towns of seventeenth-century Massachusetts. Although of negligible literary value, R. P. Smith's two-act tragedy *The Witch* (in holographic manuscript, dated October 1,

1827, in the Harvard library) and H. B. Mattison's *The Witch; or a Legend of the Catskill* (1847) suggest a romantic interest in Satanism and witchcraft, whether associated with New England or New York or a Vosges village. During the slavery agitation of the fifties, when George L. Aiken's version of *Uncle Tom's Cabin* was making a strong emotional appeal on stage North and South, various other plays indicated that in another era of stirring change Puritanism still had dramatic interest. Cornelius Mathews' *Witchcraft or Salem Village* was published in London in 1852, at the same time being released by Samuel French in New York as *Witchcraft, A Tragedy in 5 Acts*. (Mathews' tragedy began its successful stage run in Philadelphia in 1846 under the billing of *Witchcraft; or the Martyrs of Salem*.)

Finally, the notoriety of *The Scarlet Letter* may have motivated the various dramatizations of it which appeared in the years after its 1850 publication. Perhaps A. C. Coxe's scathing denunciation of the novel (printed in the *Church Review* in January, 1851) aroused playwrights to rebut his charge that it was degrading to our literature.[30] At any rate, by 1857 George H. Andrews had written a short version (published in Boston, 1871), with one by Aiken following in 1858. In Boston during 1876 Elizabeth Weller Peck published her poetized *Scarlet Letter: Dramatized*, while during the same year Gabriel Harrison's prose play was printed in Brooklyn. Apparently either the notoriety of the novel was long lasting or its excellence was appreciated, for other interpretations appeared here and abroad. Two British adapters, N. Forbes and S. Coleridge, prepared a "romantic drama in 5 acts," produced at the Royalty on May 9 and June 4, 1888. Also, another version, consisting of a prologue (by C. Charrington) and four acts (by Alec Nelson), was presented at the Olympic, in London, on June 5, 1888.[31] As late as 1899, when what Alice Felt Tyler has called "freedom's ferment" was still manifesting itself through popular interest in animal magnetism, hypnotism, and stigmatization, James Edgar Smith's versified *The Scarlet Stigma* was published in Washington, D.C. In our times mass media— the movies, radio, television, and newspapers—have popularized Hawthorne's novel, as well as the witchcraft crisis in Salem, through a number of presentations.

Of the town societies dependent upon the Puritan way, the parish life of old Salem village (a part of present day Danvers) has been most fully re-created in both versified and prose dramas. Village plays by Mathews, Longfellow, Mrs. Freeman, Arthur Miller, and others of lesser note suggest that the history of Salem witchcraft symbolizes the history of witchcraft in all Massachusetts for about a century.[32] Moreover, Miller's conception of the tragedy implicit in Salem's hysteria is a dramatic linking of past and present, of the frenzied witch-hunting of 1692 with twentieth-century accusations.

Longfellow was our first notable poet to dramatize these superstitious times, both in Salem and in Boston. But his dilatory method of composition delayed the completion of his *New England Tragedies* until sixteen years after a New York editor and minor poet had attracted much attention by his own retelling of the awful purgings at Salem.

Cornelius Mathews (1817-1889), native of Port Chester, New York, was familiar from his childhood with the picturesque country and the folkways of villagers in Westchester County. Later, during editorial work in New York for the *American Monthly Magazine* and the *Arcturus*, Mathews drew upon his early experiences for poetic nature descriptions and provincial characterizations included in some of his various romances, satires, and plays. On at least two occasions, his interest in folkways turned his fancy backward to colonial Massachusetts and New York for historic materials dramatized respectively in his *Witchcraft* and *Jacob Leisler*, both staged during the later forties. The earlier of these, *Witchcraft; or the Martyrs of Salem*, was produced successfully by J. E. Murdock first at the Walnut Street Theatre, Philadelphia, and afterward on tour, as the contemporary praise of Margaret Fuller, in her *Papers on Literature and Art*, suggests. Miss Fuller, impressed by its poetic conception (largely blank verse) and characterization of the "witch" Ambla Bodish (somewhat comparable to Barker's Isabella), thought the tragedy "a work of strong and majestic lineaments." Doomed too often, as she attended New York theaters, to listen to the romantic heroisms, sentimentalism, and stale morality of current offerings, Miss Fuller found in Mathews' treatment of the love of a son, Gideon Bodish, for his mother a motif sufficiently strong to create tragic interest.[33]

From the opening exposition to the tragic aftermath of the Bodish trial, multiple community scenes in *Witchcraft* picture the "gathering of the evil humor to a head" as Salemites and neighboring townspeople in Hadley, Beverly, Lynn, and other affected places engage in witch-hunting. From first to last Mathews links the relentlessness of Puritan leaders with social stratification and the severe penalties for nonconformity imposed in the Salem vicinity. As representatives of the Elect, Deacon Perfect Gidney (his name suggestive of bigotry), Justice Fisk, and jealous Jarvis Dane know quite well that laxity of laws will cause lesser village folk "to slip away into disorder" and thus "raise the devil up in Salem." Deacon Gidney, pharisaically leading Salem covenanters, has learned through his informers that already witchcraft

Has reached Hadley and Lynn, and from the villages
About, a wolf at bay, encompassed in,
Will here, at Salem, tear most bloodily,
The hand that touches it.[34]

He wonders on whose house in Salem the first darkness will fall. At the house of Goody Hubbard, earlier excommunicated by the church? Or on aged Ambla Bodish's isolated cottage? Weren't both Ambla and her son Gideon damned for failing to enter the meetinghouse on the Sabbath? And Justice Fisk, equally a conformist, is cheerfully convinced that, although poor wretches may be burned, hanged, or put in irons, "good shall come out of Salem, yet." On the other hand, the deacon's stooge, Constable Cephas Pudeator, is less interested in community respectability. An animated geiger counter, Cephas runs at night up and down the town keeping an eye on old women, looking through their keyholes, and eavesdropping on their gossip. His local reputation rests upon his discovering a witch somewhere in the neighborhood.

Eventually Cephas' zeal, Gidney's love of power, and the quickening of Jarvis' hatred by young Susanna Peache's idealization of Gideon make Ambla the main target for Puritan persecution. In a succession of somber scenes the balance of a village world is destroyed: by the force of misinterpreted love (mother-son love, the mutual but unfulfilled love of Gideon and Susanna, Jarvis' futile love) and of vengeance (Gidney's, motivated by Ambla's refusal to submit to his theocratic power; Jarvis', directed against the Bodishes), the loss of boyhood friendship (Topsfield's and Braybrook's for Gideon), and the stupidity of the mob (symbolized by foolish goodwives easily swayed by Gidney and Jarvis). Oddly, the protagonist is an aged recluse, Ambla brooding alone on the long-past murder of her husband. (Margaret Fuller, praising Mathews' bold choice of a cronelike heroine, notes the difficulty during the forties of persuading an actress to assume such a role. In her view, however, Ambla's nobility of soul and personal magnetism, before superstition and death ruin her, make for a powerful characterization.)

Like Isabella's dilemma in *Superstition*, Ambla's tragedy rests in part on the varying effects of the natural magnetism of her strong nature. Mostly her influence leads to disaster. Bigoted Gidney, willing to let nothing slip through his fingers, is determined to hang Ambla and Gideon, too, if they continue carrying "their necks so straight,/ And [holding] their heads above us villagers."[35] Naïve Susanna timidly testifies against Ambla because in her simplicity she believes Gideon bewitched by his own mother. (Later, mentally deranged by what she has done, Susanna commits suicide.) Jarvis, moved by the supposed supernatural power which Ambla holds over Susanna, stirs community feeling against mother and son alike. Most crucial is the scene of Ambla's realizing that her beloved son joins all others in distrusting her and regarding her as a witch. Thereafter, the confusion of the trial sweeps Ambla and Gideon to their physical doom but leaves them spiritually united. As Gidney and his henchmen force "this infamous woman" toward the gallows tree, Jarvis, bringing news of Susanna's suicide, incites mob action and runs Gideon down with his sword. But Gideon, before he and his mother die, realizes the truth about Ambla and passionately defies his persecutors:

> "She is no witch,
> But my dear mother still, to whom is due
> All this arm's strength."[36]

As far back as 1839 Longfellow had wanted to write a play about Cotton Mather, but he delayed until 1856 before doing anything. In March of that year the poet wrote that a German friend, Emanuel Scherb, wanted him to treat the Puritans and the Quakers in a poem, possibly as a tragedy. Longfellow's reading in Besse's record of Quaker persecution and other sources prefaced his writing of a scene of a play (tentatively called *The Old Colony*) on April 2, note-taking on May 1-2, and drafting (by August 27, 1857) a tragedy of Quaker martyrdom called *Wenlock Christison*. Continued delays, however, brought changes. This original tragedy, written in prose and printed in but ten copies, did not receive publication until October 10, 1868, and even then as a versified drama titled *John Endicott*. In February, 1868, Longfellow had composed quite hastily a second tragedy, *Giles Corey of the Salem Farms*, which with *John Endicott* was released by Boston's Ticknor and Fields as *The New England Tragedies*.[37]

In a prologue Longfellow refers briefly to his inspiration from books, grants himself freedom in letting characters use mostly the language attributed to them in the records, acknowledges his license in handling dates and events, and admits a moralistic purpose: the teaching of tolerance by reviewing "the errors of an age long passed away." Yet Longfellow does not devote his five acts of *John Endicott* to sermonizing. Probably, although Longfellow protested, his publisher-adviser, James T. Fields, was right in considering both tragedies as sketches, for they lack a sufficiency of audience-stirring scenes and compelling characters. Gentlemanly Longfellow—American Victorian—simply failed to interpret Puritan persecution and bigotry with the passionate indignation which gives verisimilitude to Whittier's fine Quaker ballad, "Cassandra Southwick," and stirs sympathy for the plight of two imprisoned Quakeresses described in his *Margaret Smith's Journal*. Longfellow's tragedies do, however, catch "the acrid spirit of the times" in both Boston and Salem Village. As pictured in *John Endicott*, various classes of Bostonians experience during 1665 "days of fear" as Governor Endicott's lust for more power against Quakers (in his eyes, "persistent and provoking strollers and ranters") and Minister John Norton's relentless intolerance both symbolize the "righteous zeal" of Puritan leaders. (Incidentally, Longfellow tampered with history a bit, for in reality the events which he dramatizes took place in 1656. In July of that year, Master Simon Kempthorn of the *Swallow*, sailing from the Barbadoes, brought Quakeresses Mary Fisher and Ann Austin into Boston harbor. Then, as Rufus M. Jones fully relates in *The Quakers in the American Colonies*,[38] the trouble began.)

The Boston of the successive scenes of *John Endicott* (far less completely re-created than the same little community in *The Scarlet Letter*) appears physically as "a crooked little town," squeezed between an environing wilderness and the great sea. Its narrow thoroughfares and crooked lanes lined with quaint gabled dwellings, shops, meetinghouses with leaden-latticed panes, the imposing terraced house of Governor Endicott, and the busy wharves and shipping of Dock Square typify the more pleasant aspect of Puritan living: the respectable and the prudential. To the Elect, then, the town was a fine Puritan capital, drawing attention to itself by its church assemblies, the governor's halberdiers, the sermons of John Norton and fellow theocrats, its hope for a new mandamus from Charles II giving further power to the theocracy, and the burgeoning wealth which flowed in from the Barbadoes and elsewhere. To the victims of Puritan severity, Boston seemed a cruel, bloody town, in their opinion "the Lost Town," or "the hornet's nest." Accused Quakers had no pride in either town pumps or dignified townhouses; rather, they knew too well the adjacent pillory and stocks, as well as the dismal and dank prison cells. True, the less strict Puritans knew the taverns—the Three Mariners as well as the Three Nuns and Comb—on Dock Square, where they met sailors and ships' captains from afar. In general, the citizens were prudential, concerned with daily routine; yet they gossiped about the mysterious power of Satan and his minions in an invisible world. Even the governor's son John—an imaginary character—longs to escape: "to sail for lands unknown,/No matter whither!" but far away from the "gloomy and narrow," the "grim and sombre" little town. Through this iconoclastic young Bostonian, then, Longfellow early foreshadows the persecution of the Quakers: of Wenlock Christison, his daughter Edith, Edward Wharton, and aged but humane Nicholas Upsall.

Action begins in the Boston meetinghouse, on a Sunday afternoon, with the solemn intoning of hymns by "gospel" members. Then, from the pulpit, Minister Norton, mindful of "the horror in the air," begins vehemently denouncing the "awful and appalling" sin of heresy, abettor of "the mysterious Power of Darkness." At this point his oratory suddenly ceases, and his congregation starts up in confusion as a strange procession slowly moves up the aisle. A barefooted Quakeress, Edith Christison, dressed in sackcloth and wearing her hair loosened, calmly leads a band of Quakers toward the pulpit and there boldly challenges Norton's intolerance. Her daring defiance of the ruling covenanters—"The law of God is greater than your laws"—is thematically significant. Thus in the opening scene begins the collision between equally determined religious antagonists: the small Quaker group, lately from the Barbadoes, struggling against the theocrats and civil authority.

Most of these antagonists—Governor Endicott, Bellingham, Norton, the male Quakers (Christison, Wharton, and Upsall), and Captain Kempthorn—are historical figures. Only Edith and John Endicott are imaginary, although they have historical parallels. Their conflict, like that in *Giles Corey*, resolves itself into a bitter struggle between two opposing ways of belief. In the course of events the helplessness of the individual (Christison, Edith, John Endicott, and even the governor) in the face of the accusing forces of society poses anew the question of what is victory. As Governor Endicott is faced with an ironic situation, the arrest of his own son for sheltering Quakers, victory eludes him. At the end, the real victory, as in most of the Salem tragedies, is neither political nor theocratic, but mental and spiritual. Hence, Edith, though imprisoned and shamed, gains a spiritual victory—a triumph for truth—through reliance on the inner light and the love of John Endicott. And John himself, pondering the stern ways of his father and fellow Puritans, philosophizes: "O soul of man,/Groping through mist and shadow, and recoiling/ Back on thyself, are, too, thy devious ways/subject to law?"[39]

In his second tragedy, also in blank verse, Longfellow reveals (again by prologue) continued interest in

> Delusions of the days that once have been,
> Witchcraft and wonders of the world unseen,
> Phantoms of air, and necromantic arts
> That crushed the weak and awed the stoutest hearts, —
> These are our theme. . . .[40]

More than that, Longfellow, in portraying elm-shaded Salem Village (amid its woods, hills, and sunny farms), dramatizes the sudden burst of "the common madness of the time" upon a peaceful township. In short, his version of the plight of the well-to-do old goodman, Giles Corey, and his spirited, outspoken wife Martha somewhat parallels the tragedies of the persecuted Quakers in Governor Endicott's Boston. Under stresses comparable to the cruel pressures imposed upon the Christisons, the Coreys and other simple farm folk of Salem Village typify the strong resistance of minorities to the power of the ruling theocracy and the will of the majority. As in his *John Endicott*, here Longfellow, though familiar with historical matter (such as the Bridget Bishop case and other trials which he knew from the *Magnalia*), creates little more than poetic sketches. True, he shows a close following of history, in the temper of the times as well as in individuals: in the Indian slave Tituba, the buxom much-married Goody Bishop, the Coreys, John Proctor (a central figure in *The Crucible*), the Walcot(t)s including "afflicted" Mary, John Gloyd (Giles's hired hand and friend to Proctor), prosecutor Hathorne, Cotton Mather, and others. More imaginative touches include Longfellow's making Martha a young wife rather than the sixty-year-old woman of reality, his employment of a dream in which Martha sees Giles's written testimony against herself, his giving Gloyd prominence as a vindictive informer, and his portraying a hearty sea captain and Corey's old-time friend (suggestive of Captain Kempthorn) as the symbol of man's love of freedom and as a foil to stress the true nobleness of old Giles's nature.

As to dramatic interest, Martha Corey's examination and hanging, though intrinsically important, prepare the way for the greater scene of her husband's trial and suffering. Later dramatists, as we shall see, create more compellingly the cross-examination or brow-beating of Martha; yet Longfellow's portrayal of her stubborn, fearless self-defense reveals her as valiantly protesting her innocence and begging, but to be denied, the freedom to pray. But pity never was a Puritan virtue. Earnestly Martha declares: "I never had to do with any Witchcraft/ Since I was born. I am a gospel woman."[41] In answer, Mary Walcot (*sic*), her wildly emotional accuser, shrieks about Martha's power of bewitchment, points out an imaginary yellow bird as Martha's familiar, and wilfully accuses the goodwife of carrying the Devil's book. Poor Giles's blundering testimony against his own wife, together with Judge Hathorne's persistence in favoring "the poor dear girls" while condemning Martha to the gallows, turns attention toward the most significant movement in the tragedy: the eventual accusation of old Giles himself, his tense trial, and his subsequent martyrdom.

The sharp contrast in Corey's nature before and after his trial and condemnation is dramatically effective. An exceptionally sturdy giant of a man (about eighty), Giles in the beginning appears superstitious and at odds with the more pragmatic Martha, who disbelieves in witchcraft. Moreover, he seems befuddled and blundering to the point of inadvertently incriminating his wife, and both stubborn and irascible in neighborly relationship with the Proctors and others. Under duress, however, the old farmer actually grows in character. Contrite over his failure to save his "lass," Giles determines to win a victory for Martha and himself by complete refusal to talk (that is, confess) in the presence of the magistrates and court. His muteness (allowed under Puritan law) and courage prevail. In a desperate effort to force a confession of wizardry, Hathorne mercilessly sentences the mute Corey "to be pressed by great weights until you shall be dead." But Giles, confounding the magistrates, dies a martyr's horrible physical death, but with soul uncrushed and triumphant. And this lone old man's spiritual victory, as a fictionalized Mather declares to Hathorne at the play's end, becomes something greater, a symbol of nonconformity to be feared. "And this poor man, whom we have made a victim,/Hereafter will be counted a martyr."

Once Samuel G. Goodrich (Peter Parley), in reminiscing about his native Ridgefield, Connecticut, said that "towns, as well as men, have their inner and outer life."[42] The outer life may be jotted down in census records or reported in newspapers, but the inner life, comprising the condition and progress of the community at large, is seldom written. Certainly, it is more difficult to re-create. Longfellow succeeded but partially in giving readers glimpses of the inner life of colonial Boston and Salem; accordingly, one must turn to the witchcraft tragedies of later dramatists for more intimate revelations of the living folk and provincial manners to be found in country towns like Salem Village during the seventeenth century.

Mary E. Wilkins Freeman, in her bicentennial prose tragedy of 1892-93, shows considerable insight into the complex nature of the Salem delusion, a community hysteria which, as Giles Corey of her play said in foolish jest, places "this whole land . . . now in bedlam, and the Governors and the magistrates swell the ravings."[43] Mrs. Freeman's realistic retelling of the trouble which started in Salem Village gives evidence of her mature understanding of certain familiar facets of the Puritan mind: its love of unity and display of power, its outbursts of enmity, its ready response to the phenomena of superstition and fear, of trance and hypnotism, and even of insanity. Humanly dramatizing the persecutions of the Coreys—a sort of foretoken or prototype for Miller's modern treatment of a neighboring family, the Proctors—she traces, often in colloquial dialogue, a family's destruction as speeded by their neighbors' unnatural and "unaccountable behaviors."

Throughout the first act of *Giles Corey, Yeoman* plenty of signs suggest that the normal activities in the Corey household are not running as smoothly as usual. A vague sense of uneasiness disturbs each family member, though the routine tasks of cooking, spinning, sewing, and outdoor chores are continued. Nancy Fox, the old and petulant Negro servant, sits by the fireplace paring apples, orphaned Phoebe Morse dutifully does the dreary task of knitting stockings (something expected of even a child), and Olive (Giles and Martha's daughter) industriously works her spinning wheel. But this typical Puritan scene of hard work is broken into by Nancy's rattlebrained gossip about witchcraft and the foolish fancies of the child. Olive tries calming their fears by persuading Phoebe to join in her singing of a spinning song, romantically beginning "I'll tell you a story; a story of one,/ 'Twas of a great prince whose name was King John." But Nancy, like the Parrises' Tituba, is not to be denied her indulgence in magic. At midnight, she lures Phoebe back into the kitchen and tries to initiate the susceptible child into the mysteries of witchcraft by spitefully cursing Bridget Bishop (out of envy because of her silk hood) and teaching Phoebe to use a poppet to curse her own aunt Martha, Giles, and Olive. As an anticlimax, Nancy quaveringly parodies Olive's ballad: "I'll tell you a story, a story of one;/'Twas of a dark witch, and the wizard her son." Earlier the tender love scene between Olive and the unsuperstitious and reasonable Paul Bayley adds a lighter tone, darkened a bit by "afflicted" Ann Hutchins' envy and her malicious accusations that Olive had cast an evil spell upon her.[44] As Paul then was aware, " . . . sometimes danger sneaks at home, when we flee it abroad." All in all, the later tragedy of Olive's parents appears all the more poignant in the light of what they lost: their satisfactory economic status in the township, their domestic happiness, and their very lives. But, as Perry Miller has cogently noted, "Catastrophe, by and for itself, is not enough."[45] Needed, too, are the living folk, such as Mrs. Freeman's artistry has portrayed.

Some think the case of Giles Corey the most tragic in the history of American witchcraft.[46] Certainly the sturdy yeoman emerging from Mrs. Freeman's six acts seems a flesh-and-blood provincial. In younger days, before his conversion, Giles's honesty may have been questionable and his contentious nature the cause of litigation with John Proctor and other neighbors. Slow witted and superstitious, Corey, in this play as in life, became so fascinated by the witchcraft examinations from their outset that, disregarding his wife's advice, he joined the excited spectators in the village's crowded meetinghouse. As landowner, Giles, proud of his physical strength, labored so diligently that frequently he created ill will among his supposedly overworked helpers. In revenge, laborer John Gloyd proved himself a loudmouthed malefactor by "crying out" against his employer. Giles too was quick to feel resentment, but this was not a deep part of his nature. For instance, the pique aroused in him by Martha's bossy ways was but superficial, though it was to move him to blundering public testimony that helped sentence her to Gallows Hill. Actually, his love for both wife and daughter, at first undisplayed, was to prove deep. And during his extreme test the tortured old fellow—scorned by Judge Hathorne to the last as "an unlettered clown, and tavern brawler" endured with amazing courage until death. But let Giles furnish a self-portrait in the words he addressed to Master Bayley just before he was carted from the dreary Salem jail to the field where he was pressed to death:

"... you see before you Giles Corey. He be verily an old man, he be over eighty years old, but there be somewhat of the first of him left. He hath never had much of the power of speech; his words have been rough, and not given to pleasing. He hath been a rude man, an unlettered man, and a sinner. He hath brawled and blasphemed with the worst of them in his day. He hath given blow for blow...."

In the last of his confession, Giles, long since a man of the covenant, rises to a kind of nobility. Granting his lack of nimbleness of speech or wisdom to save his life, he knows that "he hath power to die as he will, and no man hath greater."[47]

The Goody Corey of Mrs. Freeman's realistic characterization closely resembles Salem's stalwart country wife victimized during the historic frenzy of 1692 as a "gospel witch." Practical and unsuperstitious by nature, Martha caused gossip among neighbors in the farm lands by freely jesting about witchcraft and twitting the more gullible Giles for believing. In the village, where she was known as "a stout professor of faith," Martha's outspoken skepticism concerning the ethics of witch-hunting was remembered during her trial, when court and spectators alike branded her as heretic. Then, they remembered little of her thrift, practicality, and loving kindness as a goodwife; rather as a community, gathered for "righteous" judgment, these gospel folk aired her dictatorial ways with Phoebe and old Nancy, her opinionated talk, and her uncanny ability to anticipate what one was about to say. Thus, during the emotional excitement of her trial, villagers momentarily forgot her piety and neighborly help. They were swayed by the malicious spite of neurotic Widow Hutchins and the screeching of the girls, who according to Giles's imprecations were nothing more than despicable "lying hussies" and "ill favored little jades, puling because no man will have ye." Certainly these emotional weaklings and the blinded magistrates, in utter disregard of her goodness, ruined Martha beyond redemption. Ruthlessly righteous Hathorne and vacillating Jonathan Corwin (ineffectual prosecutors suggestive of Irving's satirized "little great men") were not much better than Martha's pastor, pusillanimous Samuel Parris. As for the latter, in Mrs. Freeman's portrayal, Giles's bold vilification, "Ye lying devil's tool of a parson that seasons prayer with murder," seems deserved.[48]

Too late, after the jailing of Olive and her subsequent stripping and searching for witch marks, and following Mercy Lewis' hysterical crying out against Giles himself, he remorsefully tried to make atonement for his indiscreet remarks about his wife. Equally futile was Martha's long and rational speech of defense (matched by Isabella's pleas in *Superstition*).[49] When she had been branded as a "gospel witch" and sentenced to hang on Gallows Hill, then, again too late, Giles heatedly blurted out a frantic assurance of her decency: "Think ye Goodwife Martha Corey gallops a broomstick to the hill of a night, with her decent petticoats flapping?"[50] But his peppery plea is to no avail and Goodman Corey comes to the slow realization that had he remained silent Martha might have been saved. Accordingly, he decides, in full respect for her good name, to remain mute at his forthcoming trial. His guilt complex thus leads him to repay Martha and to save for her daughter Olive and the son-in-law Paul the considerable property which otherwise would have been confiscated by the authorities.

In this tragedy, as in her more familiar short stories, Mrs. Freeman has delineated a narrow, primarily unlovely provincial world. Picturing largely unromantic, even grim, actualities of Salem's past, she re-creates ably a special crisis, which for some skeptical folk in Salem Village signified that rigid theocratic control over the minds and destinies of men is not right. A gradually increasing dissatisfaction with the horrors of the trials led some to question cautiously, as did Giles, "Who is safe?" This sense of the new beginning of things boded ill for fanatical Parris, the judges whose righteousness was becoming spotted, and the jittery wenches who had had their day with their shrieks of yellow birds, black beasts, the Devil's book ("*black* with blood-red clasps"), and wild Sabbat dancing. And Giles, though not a deep man, had more wits than the villagers dreamed of when he spoke to Paul of his own striving to understand "that which is at the root of things." His faith in a force beyond human ties led him into believing that "not only old Giles Corey . . . lies pressed to death under stones, but the backbone of this great evil in the land shall be broke by the same weight."[51] At the end of the sixth act, the marriage of Olive and Paul (at Giles's urgent request) romantically symbolizes the coming of a new year, with uncontrolled commotion ended and the plowing started again in Salem Farms.

On February 3, 1850, Hawthorne completed the writing of *The Scarlet Letter*, whose early sales were good enough to warrant in 1852 the release of an advertisement in which his publishers (Ticknor, Reed, and Fields) quoted the number sold as currently being in its "sixth thousand."[52] Accordingly, comedian Andrews' adaptation of the novel for presentation in the Boston Theatre on December 28, 1857, and Aiken's version for Barnum's New Museum (New York) on February 24, 1858, were, if not artistic, well timed "to catch the trade."[53] In several respects Andrews, familiar with practical problems of the theater, set up a pattern which influenced later adapters, though each made modifications suitable to the form of dramatization chosen—familiar or formal prose or verse. Generally these adapters, while using the main characters of *The Scarlet Letter*, freely add minor ones, or show more theatricalism in portrayals than did Hawthorne. For instance, Andrews' "Molly" Hibbins, reputed witch, and Harrison's cronelike Hibbins, frenzied leader of a conference of Indian witches and wizards, obviously are cruder and more theatrical characterizations than the outwardly respectable Mistress Hibbins, sister to Governor Bellingham, in the novel. An oddity among the dramatis personae of the several *Scarlet Letter* plays appears in *The Scarlet Stigma*. Here, throughout Act III, Scene 3, a quite histrionic Satan, who appears to Dimmesdale—Dimsdell in this play—as a hallucination, furnishes the conflict. In general, too, each adapter's reliance on *The Scarlet Letter* led to his reproducing its general plan, "a drama of moods superimposed upon a background of village life." Except for individual touches, each adaptation, like the original, presents "a colonial tale of remorse, sorrow, and despair enfolded between two vividly pictured community scenes: the earlier public execution of the magisterial sentence and, at the close, the public holiday of the election ceremonies."[54] Much, however, is lost. All in all, little skill is shown in transferring to the dramatic medium either Hawthorne's artistic use of symbolism, his deep insight into the soul's agony, or his fine creation of the drab circumstances of life in the village of Boston and the environing Puritan world.

All of the plays examined re-create scenes in Puritan Boston and the nearby forests; yet there is little agreement as to the exact time, since Harrison, Smith, and Andrews respectively date the action 1650, 1668, and 1680, while Miss Peck indicates no particular year.[55] Moreover, each version, except *The Scarlet Stigma*, opens with Hester Prynne's public shaming in the market place, thus at once creating the somber atmosphere of Puritanism. Factually paralleling Hawthorne's first chapter but lacking its artistry and complexity, each initial scene presents the motley crowd gathered on the grass plot before the prison. These dramatizations, whose dialogues range from folksy speech to blank verse, are similar in their portrayals of the avid and mostly malicious interest of Boston commoners in the trial and subsequent shaming of a gentlewoman for bastardy. Pitiless goodwives (Mistress Gossip and friends clamoring for the hanging or the hot iron branding on the forehead of the beautiful "malafactress"), bearded townsmen generally more compassionate, an officious town-beadle, soldiers, rough sailors (often contemptuous of the Puritans), curious Indians (in Harrison's version individualized by such bizarre names as Swamp-fox, Spear-head, Blighted-trunk, and Fleet-wing), other typical Puritans, and a lone travel-stained stranger (Roger Chillingworth, of course) restlessly await Boston's inquisitorial magistrates and the "brazen hussy" who has brought scandal "to our godly New England." In each play a differently named informant—Harrison's Master Townsman, Andrews' Hezekiah Parkins, and the like—reviews for the inquiring Chillingworth known details contrasting Hester's respectable past in England and Amsterdam with her present humiliation. Each opening, too, stresses the irony of the situation, so effective in *The Scarlet Letter*, in which Arthur Dimmesdale must question Hester as to the identity of her paramour. From that scene on to the election holiday and its tragic events, these several adaptations, with the exception of *The Scarlet Stigma*, dramatize scenes corresponding loosely to the familiar episodes in Hawthorne's plot.

According to historian Alice Felt Tyler, "The Spiritualism that swept over the United States in the mid-nineteenth century was remarkable only for its vigor and for the large numbers of men and women who became deeply interested in it."[56] A comparable popularity was enjoyed by various cults and fads, as different as diet reforms and slum work by debutantes. In spite of ridicule, zealous advocates turned to mesmerism or hypnotism, phrenology, hydropathy, animal magnetism, and stigmatization. Small wonder, then, that theater managers and some playwrights responded dramatically to faddism. Among the playwrights was James Edgar Smith, who discovered in *The Scarlet Letter* the leitmotif (Arthur Dimmesdale's autohypnotic trance, or ecstasy) for a four-act prose and blank verse tragedy, delineating theocratic Boston, in 1668, as "a town run mad." Smith's interest centers not on Puritan village life per se, but upon the slow mental breakdown of one of its highly respected intellectuals, the secretly distraught "Arthur Dimsdell, a youthful divine." Generally the townspeople serve as a chorus of informers, first introduced in an un-Hawthornesque scene, a tavern (with settles on the porch) and the street in front of it. The sailors and irreverent citizens, smoking and drinking, suggest that the ruling Puritans were not exercising full control. And the passage where Captain Butts leads the drinkers in a chantey sinks to the level of burlesque.

> The Margarey D was a trim little ship,
> The men could man, and the skipper skip;
> She sailed from her haven one fine summer day,
> And she foundered at sea in the following way,—
>   To-wit:

> *All.* A-rinkety, clinkety, clink, clank, clank.
> The liquor they bathed in, the spirits they drank;
> A sailor at sea with three sheets in the wind
> Can hardly be called, sirs, quite sober.

> The captain was thirsty, and so was each man
> They ladled the grog out by cup and by can,
> The storm it was stormy, they knew not the place,
> And they sang as they sank the following grace,—
>   To-wit:

> *All.* A-sinkety, sink, sank, sunk;
> Our captain is tipsy, our mate is quite drunk,
> Our widows we leave to the world's tender care,
> And we don't give a damn for the Devil![57]

Emboldened by tipsiness, Captain Butts defies Satan's power, his roistering "swabs" disrespectfully toast "the mousey Puritan lasses," tavern keeper "Mother" Carey (the image of Salem's Bridget Bishop) fills their cups with "stingo," and Ursula, waitress, adds her bit of tavern gossip about her recent service as midwife to a genteel adulteress whose trial has set Boston tongues wagging. As she serves Captain Butts, who leaves, and later, a solitary stranger (Roger, still incognito), Ursula repeats the woeful tale of Mistress Prynne, but three years past a passenger on the captain's boat out of Amsterdam. Bitterly Ursula now condemns the cruelty of "those proper Bostonians" who shunned Hester like a plague. After the delivery, "None came near/But pious Master Dimsdell." With full contempt, Ursula denounces her fellow citizens as "serpents, all of them . . . they have double tongues to hiss, but ne'er a hand to help."[58] Using his favorite technique of the soliloquy, Smith characterizes Roger as sentimentally recalling his long bachelorhood devoted to science—another dramatization of Hawthorne's motif of social isolation

—and his belated attraction to Hester's lovely beauty ("a hawthorn in its pink of youth") and her ladylike manner. Smith, incidentally, places more stress upon Hester's position as a gentlewoman than do the other adapters. Scene 2, again a soliloquy, offers an early glimpse into the young minister's tortured mind and prepares for his later stigmatization. Is it better to confess and be disgraced as Hester's paramour, or to suffer silently the pangs of conscience? Thus, Arthur's warring natures swung backward and forward between two magnets. The path of righteousness leads to Heaven, but "the broad and easy road of Sin" will "Lead on to Hell!"[59]

Thereafter, each act shows Smith's response to current audience interest in autohypnotism. Arthur endures a private hell, ever worsening. Meanwhile, Chillingworth, as vengeful leech, diagnoses his patient's illness as the "soul's sickness." His persistent, subtly sadistic efforts to glimpse the secret that "leecheth" Arthur's life push the action toward theatricalism. Structurally the entire third scene of Act II (set in the minister's gloomy bedroom) is a soliloquy, a dramatic transcript from Dimsdell's diseased consciousness. The hallucinatory presence of the "Prince of Hell," taunting horrible archangel with bat wings; the impress of the stigma, a glowing scarlet A, on Dimsdell's breast; the phantasmagoric images of Hester changing from a figure, with babe in arms and clothed in pure white to one wearing the scarlet letter on her gown, all symbolize the culmination of Arthur's autohypnotic ecstasy. In Act IV, in a melodramatic scene for the gallery, Arthur suffers a second cataleptic trance, falsely identifies Roger with Satan, chokes the now sinister doctor to death, and strides out as a madman to deliver his Election Day sermon (ironically about man's destiny), confess his sin, disclose the stigma, and die after begging Hester's forgiveness. Before the curtain Hester histrionically casts off her own scarlet letter so that Arthur's soul may rest in peace.

Finally, relatively full directions accompanying each of these *Scarlet Letter* plays mark the increase of realistic technique in American stage design and costuming during the seventies and later. Gabriel Harrison (1818-1902), once a recognized elocution instructor in Brooklyn,[60] in his notes for the staging of the opening scene, describes a painted flat (suggestive of William Dunlap's earlier sets) to represent the exterior of the old-fashioned wooden prison. Wooden steps, iron crossbars on a huge door, a rosebush in full bloom at the right side of the door, iron-barred windows, and a high rough stone wall on either side of the building are painted, in effective contrast, on a black background. Harrison's practical knowledge of artistic lighting is typified by his explicit notes for the staging of Hester's first entrance, stipulating a ray of light (in relief against the black background) which must fall across her head and shoulders. Calcium lights are used to create the effect of moonlight in the wild forest scene of the witches' conference. His directions for the construction of the pillory platform and later properties suggest a set of instructions for stage carpenters. Other flats represent Arthur's library and study—a wainscoted apartment with bookcases and a painted window scene of village houses and steepled church—and Hester's small white cottage near a cove in Boston harbor. Smith's directions in *The Scarlet Stigma* are similarly detailed, though different. Since he dramatizes Hester as occupying a house secretly the property of Roger Prynne, Smith indicates that the furniture used shall be Dutch-English, the handsome window drapes scarlet fringed with scarlet crosscords simulating the letter A, and rich needlework displayed in the hangings and accessories. Each playwright suggests realism in costumes.

We have seen, in these various imaginative portrayals of seventeenth-century folkways, different treatments of the devious practices used in fighting off the devil in Salem Village and neighboring towns. But the real ordeal of the 1670's, and after, has evoked later and even more artistic unmaskings of the Salemites and nearby townspeople by the late Percy MacKaye (1875-1956) and Arthur Miller. Apparently both professional playwrights discovered in the records of Massachusetts townships a fine folk quality not always fully realized by their predecessors. As the late Montrose J. Moses once said about the literary misuse of our "native stuff," "Drama is not folk speech; it is folk passion, and in contemplating the peculiar way of expressing that passion, one gets to the bone of local life and outlook."[61] Neither MacKaye nor Miller has shown any inclination to let such native material go to waste. Rather, as *The Scarecrow* and *The Crucible* prove, both have dramatized veritable congeries of the passions, tensions, and reactions of Massachusetts folk under strained conditions, and made them universal.

Percy MacKaye's two-volume *Epoch*, though ostensibly the biography of his versatile father, Steele MacKaye, offers valuable intimate glimpses of the son's growing up with the theater.[62] Moreover, *Epoch* incidentally reveals significant influences which held the younger MacKaye to the world of the theater: the father's Scottish ancestry with a Celtic strain responsible for the son's delight in fantasy; further family ties with early New England; his Harvard studies under Professor George Pierce Baker, with graduation in 1897 before the English 47 Workshop; later study in Italy and Germany (1898-1900); his pre-Harvard playwriting and composing of chorals for his father's *Columbus*; the influence of his father's enthusiasm for community masques and singing; and, finally, his own continued study and travel, quickening his realization of the dramatic value of our national backgrounds. In fact, it was this strong historical sense which prompted Percy MacKaye's enthusiastic turning to New England's history for the material of his one-act *Yankee Fantasies* and *The Scarecrow*.

The Scarecrow (first staged by the Harvard Dramatic Club, December 7, 1909) has been widely produced in the United States and in other countries, including Russia.[63] MacKaye, in the preface to the first edition, 1908, explains his attitude toward his colonial material and analyzes his literary source, Hawthorne's "Feathertop," stressing its ironic presentation of a scarecrow (the creation of Mother Rigby, "one of the most cunning and potent witches in New England"). The goody's "darling," in MacKaye's opinion, is "the imaginative epitome or symbol of human charlatanism, with special emphasis upon the coxcombery of fashionable society."[64] Based on this thematic idea, "Feathertop" becomes "a satire upon a restricted artificial phase of society." MacKaye thought, however, that colonial Massachusetts society, with all of its stratification, deserved "a development far more universal, than such satire." In fact, as early as 1903 he was planning a drama (later much revised) to begin at the point where Hawthorne closes his tale, with Mother Rigby's ironic portrayal of Feathertop as "a superficial fop" unequal to another chance, for, she says "His feelings are too tender—his sensibilities are too deep." Earlier Hawthorne's witch had wondered cynically if her wretched puppet was able "to take his chance among other men of straw and empty fellows who go bustling about the world." On this note MacKaye imaginatively begins his play as "The Glass of Truth: A Tragedy of the Ludicrous." By contrast, his scarecrow, masquerading as a Lord Ravensbane, becomes far more than a sorry "emblem of human pathos." Bitterly experiencing in Puritan society "the agony of being ridiculous," Ravensbane at last sacrifices his existence to free his beloved Rachel, but glories in the manly image of himself belatedly reflected in the glass of truth. Thus, as MacKaye's Dickon ("dickens" or devil) pseudo-philosophically chants, "The ideal —*the beau ideal*, dame—that's what we artists seek. The apotheosis of scarecrows!"[65] But the magic of witchcraft still disturbs Rachel, who closes the play with a query: "Was it a chimera, or a hero?"

Outwardly Ravensbane, as Dickon said, impresses the village as a waistcoated "macaroni" though actually he is a scarecrow "that's decidedly local color." A wonderful "Yankee masterpiece," *"Filius fit non nascitur,"* a fantastic manikin, magically created by Goody Rickby to Dickon's incantation of

Pulse, beet;
Gourd, eat;
  Ave Hellas!
Poker and punkin,
Stir the old junk in:
Breathe, bellows![66]

And MacKaye's story presents a medley: a delightful fantasy, a romance, and a satirically humorous drama of the effects of demonology on a Massachusetts town, where in the late seventeenth century "witchcraft is catching and spreading like the small-pox." As action progresses, the meaning deepens. One small community, the background of Ravensbane's "essential tragedy of the ludicrous," becomes "a place in the outer limits of the human soul." MacKaye's thoughtful conception, expressed in the most felicitous diction, is impishly summed up by Dickon: "Nay, Jacky [Ravensbane], all mortals are ridiculous. Like you, they were rummaged out of the muck: and like you, they shall return to the dunghill."[67] Thus tutored by the evil Dickon, Ravensbane at first is merely the pipe-smoking, pumpkin-headed instrument of Blacksmith Bess's revenge on her former lover, Justice Gilead Merton, now respected in his village world and honored by Harvard dignitaries and other officials. Tricking the Justice into thinking that gentlemanly, handsomely attired Ravensbane is his son, Dickon begins a devilish deception that ends with the "apotheosis of scarecrows."

In every respect *The Scarecrow* is far more than an outward chronicle of a small town under the spell of witchcraft. It is actually a reflective play on the identity and destiny of man, whose wisdom is measured by his ability to know—to understand—his own face mirrored in a glass. After the climax (at the close of Act III), when Ravensbane, seeing himself imaged as a scarecrow, loses love, he soliloquizes at length (as Act IV opens) on his condition. Gazing at his image and musing in much the same skeptical manner as Carlyle's Teufelsdröckh and Mark Twain's two arguers in "What is Man?", Ravensbane questions "What am I?" and "What's a man?" A pretty phantom? A scarecrow? A "tinkling clod" utterly contemptible and superfluous? Then realization comes that though he be monstrous, ludicrous, and but a "breathing bathos," he, at least, can now know himself and, by laughing at himself, find comfort.

If *The Scarecrow* has been linked with the progress of poetic and imaginative drama in the United States, similarly *The Crucible* is the ultimate treatment among the many dramatic probings into superstition and injustice which began in 1824 with Barker.[68] Most of all, Miller, while evaluating anew the many-faceted tensions of Salem Village, in this play directs our interests toward the universality of folk delusion, injustice, and "diabolism," his term for the fear and hatred of opposites.[69] If such fear is organized, as Miller discovered in Salem's records, the community and region at large may suffer manifold evils. The awful result of mass hysteria has been fictionalized effectively by Jay Williams in *The Witches* (his 1957 novel of sixteenth-century Scottish diabolism), in which he affirms that hysterical trials, fearfully intertwining the forces of religion, politics, and demonology, may spread fears and drag in the innocent. " . . . the danger to men," Williams contends, "lies not in destroying the guilty, but in such frantic terror that a hundred innocent are destroyed lest a single guilty man escape."[70] This is the force (comparable to the "blind custom"—living, hard, cruel—once denounced by young Shelley) which Miller evokes vividly, suspensefully, and somberly out of the authenticated documents of old Salem.

Generally, in these Puritan plays the same family and community relationships appear and reappear, somewhat in the fashion of Galsworthy's moving certain Forsytes from novel to novel in his *Forsyte Saga*. From different points of view we watch village folk—the Parris, Hathorne, Putnam, Nurse, Walcott, Lewis, Hale, Bishop, and other families, or their fictional counterparts—lose their neighborly trust or forbearance and, with the outbreak of smoldering hatreds and spread of new fears, tragically victimize themselves or their neighbors. In *The Crucible* some of the citizens presented earlier reappear, amid the same atmosphere of suspicion and hysteria; and the same inquisitorial tactics doom innocent Salemites to Gallows Hill. There are, however, differences. Miller's protagonist and his wife, John and Elizabeth Proctor, are younger than either their historical prototypes or their equally independent neighbors, the ill-fated Coreys, and thus have more to lose. Further, Miller's tragedy, modern in technique, belongs to the history of sociological ideas more than do its forerunners. The temptations of contemporary diabolism (of opposites); the dramatic linking of sex, sin, and the devil during the craze of 1692; the enthralment of the popular mind by current concepts of Satanism, all typify the more speculative and, as reviews indicate, controversial qualities of *The Crucible*. In short, Miller dramatizes one of the "crimes" of the Proctors, their supposed consorting with the devil, as guilt by association, interpreted by some critics as a link with contemporary "security trials." In a recent reference to such a parallel, Joseph Wood Krutch says that "its validity depends upon the validity of the parallel and those who find it invalid point out that, whereas witchcraft was pure delusion, subversion is a reality, no matter how unwisely or intemperately it may be combatted."[71]

Since his University of Michigan days in the late thirties, Miller's interest in Salem witchcraft has apparently moved him to deep regard for the "moral size" of those unfortunate Salemites who, though suffering defeat and death, "didn't whimper." Furthermore, as a craftsman familiar with Aristotelian principles, Miller discovered in the happenings of 1692 an organic wholeness which appealed to him. As he has recently said, "Salem is one of the few dramas in history with a beginning, a middle, and an end." Their stubborn beliefs and hysteria brought months of terror; yet the Salem folk, says Miller, "saw the errors of their ways quite soon after the tragedy occurred." (Actually, there was a slow return to reason in response to a growing public protest against the trials. The realization that no one was safe was, indeed, a sobering thought.) Their devotion to Puritan ideology, their knowledge of why they struggled, and, when some were charged, their strength to struggle so valiantly that they did not die helplessly made these New England villagers, in Miller's opinion, fit characters for drama.[72] As we have seen, Longfellow and Mrs. Freeman made some creative use of this quality of Puritan nature in their scenes dramatizing the ultimate triumph of the Coreys. All in all, Miller, by concluding John Proctor's struggle on a note of self-realization and affirmation, seems through this tragedy to challenge those of his contemporaries overly insistent on dramatizing modern man as driven into a dark little pocket of frustration and defeat. Miller's search for a more positive approach to man's dilemma turns our thoughts backward to the forties when Van Wyck Brooks was on a similar quest. Even then, our writers no longer possessed "the mood of health" which Brooks associated with great literature. For the writers of 1941 Whitman's once promising invitation, with the challenge "Allons, the road is before us," had lost its cogency. Instead, a mood of desperate unhappiness seemed to reign in the world so widely that the temperamental cards of the forties were stacked in favor of a sterile despair.[73] Unlike these and contemporary pessimists, Miller has acknowledged that in using the Salem episode he hoped to move "a step toward an assertion of a positive kind of value in contemporary plays."

Critical opinion has tended to contrast O'Neill's and Tennessee Williams' psychological probing into character with Miller's primary concern for man's sociological status in an unfriendly or even evil world. Some recent critics, including George Jean Nathan, point toward Ibsen's "social" plays as powerful stimulants to Miller's intellectual interests and express regret that *The Crucible*, with little warmth of character, has so much of "dialectic chill" and "wayward sense of propaganda" that the characters themselves become "documentary mouthpieces." His realistic

technique, they also complain, is slanted too much toward ideas, especially the thematic one that Salem's community-wide hysteria (an outgrowth of superstition, ignorance, fear, hatred, and bigotry) brought
tragedy to the innocent.[74] On the other hand, certain changes in the new
production, restaged by Miller himself on January 22, 1953, six months
after the New York premiere, created better audience effect. A cyclo-
ramic and light-flooded scene, the meeting place for John Proctor and
infatuated Abigail Williams (once their servant), gives more plausibility
to the girl's later "crying out" against the Proctors and establishes the
motif of infidelity which neither man nor wife could ever forget.[75] Another technique, not too favorably viewed by critics, is the use of several ex-
pository devices: a prologue or overture (belittled by Nathan as "largely
only discourse" rather than effective drama) portraying the start of the
witchcraft delusion in the Reverend Samuel Parris' own household; interpolated essays ("extended documentation," says Nathan) describing the
village and its Puritan ways, squabbles between the Nurses and the Putnams, the egotism and irascibility of minister Parris, the Reverend Mr.
Hale's study of demonology, and other aspects of colonial town life; and
an epilogue ("Echoes down the Corridor") suggesting how the mania
died down, leaving the power of theocracy in Massachusetts broken.
Through such technical means Miller re-creates a small-town society's
use of the easiest ways to get revenge, best shown by the false charges
brought by Abigail and the Putnams; the repression of freedom by bigoted and fear-paralyzed magistrates; the victimizing of minorities offering
threats to Puritan unity typified by Proctor's and Giles Corey's proud
and bitter struggles to preserve their identities; the pettiness of man's egotism, as personified by the pusillanimous Parris; and "land-lust" sancti-
fied by morality, shown in Thomas Putnam's avarice.

A whole community and, eventually, a whole colony were affected by
Salem's delusion; yet no one playwright, unless he resorted to folk
pageantry or spectacle, could very well present all of the townspeople. In
fact, certain principal victims, such as notorious Goody Bishop and
Rebecca Nurse (a pious matriarch long respected as a humanitarian and
as one of the "new" gentry), never have been portrayed as protagonists,
though they have been celebrated in history and poetry and occasionally
dramatized as minor figures. Rose Terry Cooke, for example, has
sketched with much humaneness the carting of Goody Nurse to the sum-
mit of Gallows Hill, where she was hanged on July 19, 1692. "They
hanged this weary woman there,/ Like any felon stout,/ Her white hairs
on the cruel rope/ Were scattered all about."[76] In his turn, Miller has
facilitated his ideological conception of the life implicit in Salem's records

by portraying but a few chosen groups of Puritans. First, the vested interests of the Puritan theocracy and magistracy are represented, by and large, by resentful, twisted, or narrow-minded souls: the contentious Parris, whose ineffectual ministry at Salem had been marred by social friction; the Reverend John Hale, from nearby Beverly, an intellectual interested in witchcraft, whose manly efforts to bring moderation "to stop the whole green world from burning" are thwarted by his own vacillating —his own "fever of guilt and uncertainty"; gullible Deputy Governor Danforth (enacted superbly by Walter Hampden) fumbling in his conduct of a special court; Judge William Hathorne, worried by problems of conscience and the Puritan suppression of all opposition; Ezekiel Cheever and Herrick, "eager beavers" as town clerk and marshall respectively.

Secondly, as in earlier plays the "afflicted" girls—timid Mary Warren, Susanna Walcott, childish Betty Parris, fat Mercy Lewis, a sly servant girl of eighteen—all show an almost hypnotic obedience to Abby Williams, outwardly pious as Parris' niece, but actually a liar and a whore. The next group is as historically true as the others, except for Miller's using the name of John, rather than the historic one of Israel, for Proctor and making both of the Proctors relatively young (in their thirties rather than middle-aged as in reality). Here, too, are Salem's landowners, accusers (like grasping Putnam and his sarcastic wife Ann, neurotically attributing the loss of her children to Rebecca Nurse and other local "witches") as well as the accused, ranging in social status from respected farm folk—aged Francis and Rebecca Nurse, the Proctors, and Corey, stalwart at eighty-three—to disreputable old Sarah Good and Parris' slave woman, Tituba, versed in the voodooism of her native Barbadoes.

Miller's stress on marital conflicts, activated by mutual distrust and infidelity, is a facet barely touched upon in the Longfellow and Freeman characterizations of the Coreys. Conflicts within conflicts disturb John, Elizabeth, and Abby, as each struggles against the others, with self, and against society. The unhappiness of the Proctors—their sense of a growing separation—stems largely from John's lusting for Abby and his impatience with Elizabeth's illness, her reticence and coldness, her suspicious manner, and her determination to keep John for herself alone. Accordingly, their incompatibility early turns John toward their voluptuous maidservant. Elizabeth, understanding psychological problems better than John, intuitively knows that Abby yearns to be his new wife, for there is "monstrous profit." In turn, Abby, derisively branding Elizabeth, in John's presence, as "a cold, sniveling woman," envisions the fulfilment of her desires through Goody Proctor's death. (Here, the hatred—the diabolism—of opposites!) Ironically, Elizabeth herself hastens the finale of their tragedy by urging John to break his promises to Abby. His contrition does move him to renounce Abby. Fearlessly but tactlessly he accuses Abby of possessing a whore's "lump of vanity" and threatens to tell the court of their fornication. Abby, angered at being cast off, achieves vengeance in the easiest way: by "crying out" against Elizabeth. There is grim irony in her eventual loss of John.

Their domestic entanglement links the Proctors with the madness gripping the town. Though but a farmer, John (like Corey) acts with a dangerous self-reliance and a shocking nonconformity. His heated swearing that "my wife will never die for me!" catapults him into "civil disobedience." His vehement, but futile, denunciation of the floundering magistrates and even of the rigid Puritan view of God are daring rebuttals to Deputy Governor Danforth's specious reasoning and the cries of the "bewitched" girls. By daring to speak his own mind, John subjects himself to imprisonment and the death penalty, but maintains his own identity. In short, his bitter mental struggle to reassert the prime importance of the individual, in the face of theocratic control, brings the comforting realization that, as Emerson was to say later, the self-reliant man "must take himself for better for worse as his portion." Resisting ministerial pleas to confess to participation in witchcraft, John refuses to lie or compromise. At the last he chooses death but maintains his goodness and integrity. Thus, without hindrance from Elizabeth (saved from the gallows because of pregnancy), John Proctor triumphed in his severe test, his crucible. To the finale, Miller stimulates thought about a cosmology "gripped between two diametrically opposed absolutes," good and evil.[77] His record of Salem closes with the reaffirmation that the town's delusion, like all human dilemmas, had run its natural course. As the final drumroll crashes for her husband, Elizabeth, by her prison window, feels "the new sun . . . pouring in upon her face, and the drums rattle like bones in the morning air."[78]

MacKaye and Miller, then, suggest that the plight of the individual under the yoke of an inhibitive Puritanism may well typify the threats that constantly endanger Everyman. But defeatism, they imply, is not the only way. Freedom and peace may be achieved, provided each protagonist succeeds in voicing the things buried deep in his soul. Catharsis, therefore, often comes from what Poe, in *Eureka*, terms "self-cognizance."

II. Yankee Villagers and Other "Hempen Homespuns"

"Unlettered Philosophers"

THE VIEW that "literary fashion has been a distorter of history"[1] is but partially true in relation to that phase of American drama portraying Puritan small towns. Representative dramas, as we have seen, follow a fashion of dramatizing the sterner aspects of colonial village life to the extent of overshadowing happier phases of the Puritan way. On the other hand, this fictionalized picture is not so much a marked distortion as a sharply selective portrayal with considerable verisimilitude. For a more comic and distorted dramatization of the New Englander, as well as of other provincials, one may turn to numerous native comedies reflecting changes in the democratic environment, from the post-Revolutionary era until the close of the nineteenth century. At the very time when Barker, himself a Jacksonian, was composing his tragic *Superstition*, Andrew Jackson's political principles were stimulating our playwrights, as they were nondramatic writers, such as Bryant, Cooper, Hawthorne, Emerson, Irving (but temporarily), and Whitman. As a national democratic spirit developed from the 1820's onward, playwrights turned repeatedly to native grounds for appealing eccentricities and regional humor implicit in contemporary problems and folk philosophy. Consequently, certain "figures of earth," with all of their shrewdness and rude energies, sobriety, prudence, and paradoxical naïveté, slowly emerged as comic representatives of farm and village life and caught the fancy of theater audiences throughout the Union. These humorously exaggerated portrayals of Yankee farmers and shopkeepers, small planters (like Major Jones of Pineville, Georgia), eccentric village lawyers and squires (often the local political leaders), woodsmen and hunters, Yankee and southern "gals," and comparable community types suggest how our comedy, under the influence of early nationalism and Jacksonian democracy, turned in the direction of regional folk humor, quirks, and quiddities. Along the wide front of the cultural revolt during this era the new theatrical fashions for melodrama, farce, minstrels, caricature, and other forms freely adapted—perhaps distorted—social history to suit the tastes of the audiences, the talents of comedians, and the box office needs of managers.

Small-town ways of antebellum times, North and South, were amusingly if not artistically portrayed in comedies of manners known to the Placides, Sol Smith, James H. Hackett, Dan Marble, Edwin Forrest, and many other troupers, or strollers. Quinn has recorded that "the stage histories are crowded with names of plays which indicate their light, often trivial, and often imitative nature."[2] Comedies and characters which proved theatrically successful were imitated quickly by ingenious playwright-adapters, actors capable of improvising, and money-minded managers. Examinations of the authentic histories by Seilhamer, Quinn, Rusk, Hornblow, Carson, Hoole, Pyper, MacMinn, Hodge, and others, of their checklists and playbills relating to productions in St. Louis, Charleston, Salt Lake City, San Francisco, and other places, and of the autobiographies of Sol Smith, Joseph Jefferson, and fellow players supply plentiful evidence that the comic and homespun characters not only had wide appeal but characterized popular intelligence as well. Thus, as "one world was passing away, while another was struggling to be born,"[3] comic versions of the Yankee and similar plain people were enlivening the American stage. Curiosities they may have seemed to the intellectuals, to the Brahmins (Lowell and Holmes excepted); yet such homely critics of affairs, originating in oral tradition, were created in response to the democratic tastes of the time. Moreover, as the "Golden Day" dawned and lengthened, Emerson, Whitman, and other leading idealists felt that "the only future for a powerful native literature, dealing fearlessly in truth and reality, seemed to lie in the bold exploration of the possibilities of democracy."[4] If, in the long struggle for a national literature, American small-town comedy failed to contribute artistry and cogent ideas, it did promote an early rediscovery of America which antedated *The Biglow Papers* (1848, 1867) and the local color movement at the turn of the century. Long before Emersonian dreams of the self-reliant man helped pattern our "American Renaissance," spinners of yarns, comic versifiers, newspaper and almanac editors, and especially popular playwrights and comedians recognized in plain countrymen and villagers the stuff of comedy.

Certainly the concept of nativism fostered the creation of a Yankee villagedom for the American stage, with parallels localized down South and·in the frontier West. To various stage Yankees and other homespun commentators, thoroughly democratized and usually caricatured for theatrical appeal, were attributed familiar American characteristics earlier foreshadowed in Crèvecoeur's portrait of the eighteenth-century settler as "a new man, who acts upon new principles," who must "entertain new ideas, and form new opinions." Although not truly "the first American[s]," these comic figures, in their turn, were the "new birth of our new soil." Their horse sense—their gumption and down-to-earth thinking—their rustic truisms, their outward conformity to the demands of conscience, and even their stupidities and antics (often as ludicrous as Major Jones's awkward attempts at courting) appealed mightily to American audiences who respected the intelligence and enterprise of the self-made man. In fact, these theatrical characters had long popularity largely because they embodied some of the qualities which Americans always have admired most in their folk heroes. According to Dixon Wecter, in the chronicle of American hero-worship women have had but a small share; but few artists, scholars, or professional people, except lawyers, have become national idols; and no saint or physician has won popular recognition. What kind of hero, then, has been most frequently chosen? Mainly, our favorite hero has been self-respecting, decent, honorable, blessed with mother wit and resourcefulness, with self-confidence in leadership (typified by Davy Crockett's "Be always sure you're right, then go ahead!"), shrewdness (mostly for a good cause, though there has been some admiration for rustic rascality), neighborliness and manliness as shown through bravery, honesty, and strength of character, and a strong sense of duty. Also, the folk mind has favored men with a love of the soil, tinkering, and other activities expressive of the atmosphere of small towns.[5] Since our truly American hero usually wore the "halo of rugged individualism," the independent folksy characters on our stages became great favorites.

Brander Matthews, looking backward from the seventies when the vogue for stage provincials was in its decadence, recalls that the most successful early comedies in our American theaters featured "native sons": legendary Rip Van Winkle, stalwart Davy Crockett of the West, Colonel Mulberry Sellers (southerner), easterner Judge Bardwell Slote, and many others.[6] The fashion for foreign plays—adaptations from the French, English, and German—was but ephemeral as contrasted with the long popularity of "the cheaper and less artistic homespun." Dion Boucicault (guilty, as Matthews felt, of giving "a smart setting for a half-truth") tartly satirized American audiences (from about the 1780's to 1870's): ". . . all that the Americans seem to recognize as dramatic here is the caricature of eccentric character, and that is what the successful plays are—caricature of eccentric character set in a weak framework." Generally, such American folk comedy succeeded not so much as expressions of comic truth but as "realistic farce." Moreover, this striving on the part of eighteenth- and nineteenth-century playwrights to make comedy "a mirror of manners, to reflect human nature as affected by its American environment, has at all times been visible on the stage of our nation ever since it was a nation."[7] Among these singular "homespun oracles" the dominating figure was the Yankee, whose myth grew as our comedies grew. Assuredly, Constance Rourke's delightful relation of the developing myth of a many-sided Yankee brings to life an upcountry character fashioned by "many hands, from the South, from the West, even from New England."[8] As peddler, sailor, wood carver, wool dealer, itinerant tutor, and practical joker, this "wry triumphant portrait was repeated again and again, up and down the Atlantic coast, over and over in the newly opened West, where its popularity had a quirk of oddity."[9] Originating during the Revolution, this comic countryman, as Brother Jonathan, "wandered through doggerel, anecdote, and stage caricature. For forty years he clumped about in the lowest reaches of literature."[10] In addition to comedies, Western almanacs, joke books, newspapers, and other popular media provided, in slow process, numerous characterizations of the Yankee, some youthful, some old. On the other hand, "no Yankee drama ever attempted a realistic psychological study of theYankee, nor did the Yankee plays extend into the era of realism."[11]

This variform portrait had an early literary beginning in a dramatized picture of a blundering, genial Down Easter away from his native village and farm. On the sixteenth of April, 1787, the American Company presented at New York's John Street Theatre a five-act comedy by witty William Clark (Royall) Tyler, later Chief Justice of the Vermont Supreme Court. This "Revolutionary fable," familiarly known as the first comedy written by an American to be presented in this country, was *The Contrast*, which owed its initial success largely to the "inimitable humour" of the British comedian, Thomas Wignell. In the role of the homespun Jonathan, Wignell, although not quite natural in his pronunciation of the Yankee dialect, drew "the unceasing plaudits of the audience." So it seemed to at least one critical spectator, alias Candour. Reporting in the *Daily Advertiser* for April 18, Candour responded with enthusiasm to the challenging prologue spoken by Wignell on opening night:

> Exult each patriot heart!—this night is shewn
> A piece, which we may fairly call our own; . . .

Candour, while deploring the overuse of farce, applauded the nationalistic theme, "our native worth" and manners as opposed to the fashionable aping of the Chesterfieldian conduct of London's beaux and belles. "Nothing," Candour rejoiced, "can be more praise-worthy than the sentiments of the play throughout."[12]

In spite of its resemblances to *The Spectator*, Richardson's novels, *The School for Scandal*, and the letters of Lord Chesterfield, *The Contrast* is essentially American in spirit and rather well localized in New York City. Primarily, it is an amusing ridicule of the absurdities of eighteenth-century decorum which, as satirized at its fashionable best in America, was really but pseudo-Chesterfieldian and, in Jonathan's eyes, little better than a "School for Scandalization." Beaux with lily-white faces; giggling, simpering, flirtatious belles constantly thinking of "Man! for whom we dress, walk, dance, talk, lisp, languish, and smile"; socialites—male and female—with extravagant wardrobes a la mode, whose chitchat was usually about balls, playhouses, Battery promenades, and backbiting gossip; and sentimental Maria languishing over her reading of *Clarissa Harlowe* and other "weepy" fiction: all of these, and other social leaders, people the fashionable world which Jonathan had come from small-town New England to see. A comic villager he was, gawking along Broadway or blundering into the theater ("Where they played *hocus pocus* tricks")—the prototype of the roving Yankees of later comedies.

Even when engaged in seeing the sights of New York, this self-designated "true blue son of liberty" chats freely with his new acquaintances ("thick as mustard"). His Yankeeisms suggest the peaceful life "back home," where there is little class distinction. In his socially democratic village, Jonathan, though one of seven sons on an upland farm, is as much respected as farm-owning Colonel Manly. His delight in "bussing" the "gals" is climaxed by his pledging his troth with his "true-love" (Deacon Wymen's daughter, Tabitha), each of them keeping a half of a broken coin. The Deacon himself was "pretty dumb rich," allowing Tabitha a dowry of "twenty acres of land—somewhat rocky though—a Bible, and a cow." Sometimes Jonathan and other "Bunker Hill sons of liberty" enlivened things a bit in the village by play parties, singsongs, and other rural amusements. Mostly the villagers sang "go to meeting tunes," and Jonathan himself apparently enjoyed singing "Old Hundred" and other psalm tunes. Also, he knew "Yankee Doodle," although he confessed to knowing but "a hundred and ninety verses; our Tabitha at home can sing it all." But an experience far more exciting than intoning psalms or playing "Hunt the Squirrel," a rural game of pursuit, was his bussing the citified Jenny. His expressive Yankeeisms tell this story: "Burning rivers! cooling flames! red-hot roses! pig-nuts! hasty-pudding and ambrosia!"[13]

Once Woodrow Wilson, in evaluating the character of democracy in the United States, reiterated that from the beginning "Our democracy, plainly, was not a body of doctrine; it was a stage of development."[14] Obviously, a strong force motivating this development has been freedom of thought. In *The Contrast* such freedom becomes one of the leveling forces operating in Jonathan's village. Jonathan's own mental independence, in fact, is one of the motifs governing the action of the comedy. Also, his emphatic declaration, "No man shall master me," not only describes freedom-loving townsmen of the Age of Enlightenment, but is expressive of one of the principles quickening the favorable response of early audiences to the independent Yankee. To the last, "Jonathan the First" was a self-reliant villager in spirit. To illustrate, when Jenny slapped him, after he kissed her, Jonathan, unintimidated, proclaimed his village loyalties: "If this is the way with your city ladies, give me twenty acres of rock, the Bible, the cow, and Tabitha, and a little peaceable bundling."[15]

Through such sentiments as these the Yankee rustic, who was to hold the boards intermittently until after the Civil War, was brought to popular attention. Tyler's queer-looking Down Easter certainly was not designed as a main character; yet he quickly appealed to colonial audiences as a symbol of what patriots considered was of real importance in our slowly developing national character. Jonathan's patriotic fervor, his loyalty as orderly ("waiter") to Colonel Manly, his common sense and battle of wits with silly, foppish "Anglo-maniacs," his puritanic attitude balanced by his delight in rustic frivolity (in "sparkin' " and "girl huntry" rather than in Jessamy's foppish "gallantry"), his drawling and "nat'r'l" speech, even his stupidities and honest acknowledgment of his blunder in mistaking the theater for "the devil's drawing room" all helped establish this shrewd yet uncultivated New England villager as that odd mixture of reality and romanticism, the stage Yankee. Further, although Colonel Manly typified native culture and probity, Jonathan amusingly symbolized the sincere and independent American way, a sharp contrast to Dimple's British dandyism and Maria's sentimentality. In short, *The Contrast* expresses the nationalistic temper of its era. It was "in its own sphere a spiritual Declaration of Independence" and "the first dramatic presentation of the concept of American cultural self-consciousness and self sufficiency."[16] As such, *The Contrast* and similar comedies following it are most significant in calling attention to a growing body of folk material which, as noted earlier, got its start through comic songs and anecdotes of oral tradition.[17]

William Dunlap, recording theatrical history in 1832, remembered that the reaction of readers to Wignell's subscription edition of *The Contrast* (in one thousand copies) was cold.[18] He recalls, too, his own return to New York from England in the late summer of 1787 when he discovered that Tyler's comedy, though the talk of the town, "was already put on the shelf of the prompter, or buried in his travelling chest."[19] Actually, the stage run was unusually successful for so new a venture, although there is recorded but one revival (1789) in New York after its first season. Five New York performances, in quick succession, were followed by presentations in Baltimore (1787, 1788), Philadelphia (1790), Boston (1792, with advertisement as a "Moral Lecture in five parts," and 1795), Charleston (1793), and Richmond (1799).[20] Several factors, according to Dunlap, may have attributed to such relative success. First, Jonathan—"strictly speaking, the only character"—provided Wignell with the big hit of his career. Second, the local dramatic situation, where the comedy "was read to critics as young and ignorant [of dramaturgy] as the author, and praised to his heart's content," furthered both the rise of nativism and the reception of Tyler's first effort. This, thought Dunlap, was a bad beginning where mere localism, rather than a national drama, was the preference of the day. "Mr. Tyler, in his *Contrast* and some later writers for the stage seems to have thought that a Yankee character, a Jonathan, stamped the piece as American, forgetting that a clown is not the type of the nation he belongs to." Third, Dunlap implies that Tyler, a Harvard-educated and patriotic Massachusetts gentleman, became better acquainted with the American folk character through his early legal and military activities in Maine and Vermont.[21] (His eventual change of residence to Brattleborough, Vermont, "then a *new* country," did not occur until 1801.)

Dunlap's pleas for a national drama are in accord with that prolonged "paper war" which reached a climax in 1837 with Emerson's urging Harvard "scholars"—the Phi Beta Kappas—to be satisfied no longer with "the sluggard intellect of this continent." The American scholar, as *Man Thinking*, must help bring to a close "Our day of dependence, our long apprenticeship to the learning of other lands, . . ." Actually, neither the sporadic though fervid protests by American idealists nor the unrestrained diatribes of foreign critics, like outspoken Sydney Smith, immediately curbed the craze for things foreign: dress, social manners, plays, novels, and the like. True, Smith's caustic taunts probably were hurtful to the pride of those uncritically boasting of America's greatness. His insulting insinuations must have aroused their ire, if they noted in the January, 1820, issue of the *Edinburgh Review* this string of damning questions:

In the four quarters of the globe, who reads an American book? Or goes to an American play? Or looks at an American picture or statue? What does the world owe to American physicians and surgeons? What new substances have their chemists discovered? What new constellations have been discovered by the telescopes of Americans? What have they done in mathematics? Who drinks out of American glasses? Or eats out of American plates? or wears American coats or gowns? or sleeps in American blankets?

Reportedly, his scornful questions dumbfounded Brother Jonathan and angered those American orators and newspaper "scribblers" whom he belittled for their fatuous glorification of themselves and their fellow countrymen as "the greatest, the most refined, the most enlightened, and the most moral people on earth."[22] Smith's depreciatory remarks showed clearly that, long after *The Contrast*, the task of creating a vigorous national literature was still a difficult one. Certain powerful deterrents worked against the steady progress of an emerging drama and theater. As late as 1820 hostile criticism from abroad, a lack of discriminating native reviewers and of financially successful literary magazines (especially in the South), inadequate provision for copyright laws, high postal rates on newspapers, magazines and books, a limited reading public, technical difficulties hampering the artistic development of native materials, and a general chauvinistic spirit, set in motion by the Revolution and the War of 1812, deterred the writers of our struggling literature.[23] Their search for stabilizing national and literary ideals affected drama, as well as other forms. Under these conditions there was, in the years following *The Contrast*, a lull in the stage presentations of the Yankee which lasted until the 1820's.

During this interim a few dramatic efforts, mostly without real artistry, suggest flickers of popular interest in village worlds and native traits. Apparently a small number of comedies, produced at scattered intervals, entertained with such theatrically appealing themes as the satire of foppishness (as in Barker's *Tears and Smiles*), political trickery, and the peculiarities of American rusticity. In imitation of *The Contrast*, some of these turn-of-the-century comedies are primarily comic, even farcical, portrayals of city life; yet their incidental pictures of roving villagers, usually obscure Yankees, are precursors of the greater vogue for provincial comedies developing from the 1820's onward. Typical incidental village portraits include that of a Yankee servant in Dunlap's unpublished "The Modest Soldier" (1787); a "Yankeeish" rustic in the 1788 *The Politician Outwitted* ("by an American," presumably Samuel Low); a New Yorker in Yankee disguise, as well as the Negroes—West Indian types—in J. Robinson's farcical two-acter, *The Yorker's Stratagem, or Banana's Wedding*, produced by the Old American Company on April 24, 1792; another Jonathan (a seller of apples, cider, potatoes, dried onions, and cheese), together with the Negroes Harry and Phillis, in A. B. Lindsley's *Love and Friendship; or Yankee Notions* (at New York's Park Theatre, 1807, though not published until 1809); the Yankee Humphry Cubb and the Negro, Caesar, in Lazarus Beach's *Jonathan Postfree; or, the Honest Yankee* (1807); and Nathan Yank, in Barker's *Tears and Smiles*, first acted on March 4, 1807, in Philadelphia—a new Englander in his "proper, native light," who resented the nickname of "Yankey Doodle."[24] From 1794 to 1796 three popular village plays—William Macready's *The Village Lawyer*, Irish John O'Keeffe's *World in a Village*, and Isaac Biggerstaffe's *Love in a Village*—were seen in regular and benefit productions, featuring Hallam, Hodgkinson, Macready, and others, in New York, Boston, Philadelphia, Annapolis, Newport, Providence, and Charleston.[25]

Miss Rourke has sketched the Yankee as a restless soul, adventuring alone and surviving by native cleverness, even in remote countries. "Scratch the soil in China or Tibet or North Africa, and up would spring a Yankee, exercising his wits."[26] Washington Irving's nondramatic burlesque, *A History of New York . . . By Diedrich Knickerbocker* (1809) prepared the way for later dramas of traveling Yankees. His mock-heroic scene exposing William the Testy's determination to "conquer by proclamation" the disturbing and "daring aggressions of the Yankees" in New Amsterdam is a masterpiece of hilarity. In 1819-20, *The Sketch Book's* caricature of the transplanted Yankee, in the person of Master Ichabod Crane, unforgettably satirized the Yankee's "itch for travel." Irving's good-humored fun poked at the clash of cultures (the Dutch, Swedish, and Yankee ways of long ago) has some parallel in two representative plays of the Yankee's response to foreign manners.

David Humphreys, an aide-de-camp to General Washington who later served as minister to Portugal and Spain, offers another example of the American public official who once turned playwright. His published *The Yankey in England* (*c.* 1815) furthered the growing tradition of the Yankee villager as traveler through a comic servant, Doolittle, and the better-educated Newman.[27] Both an appended glossary of Yankeeisms and a critical introduction, relating his characters to real-life prototypes, offer the fullest presentation to date of the traits constituting the stage Yankee.

He is made up of contrarieties—simplicity and cunning; inquisitive from natural and excessive curiosity, confirmed by habit; credulous, from inexperience and want of knowledge of the world; believing himself to be perfectly acquainted with whatever he partially knows; tenacious of prejudices; docile, when right-managed; when otherwise treated, independent to obstinacy; easily betrayed into ridiculous mistakes; incapable of being overawed by external circumstances; suspicious, vigilant, and quick of perception, he is ever ready to parry or repel the attacks of raillery by retorts of rustic or sarcastic, if not of original and refined, wit and humour.

"Varmounter" Doolittle, adventuring sailor and later unwilling footman to a *nouveau riche* countess, is full of some of these "notions." His pride in being "a free-born American" from "pritty ancient stock" is strong enough to dispel "the Gothic night" and prevailing "Anglomania," which, according to Humphreys' prologue and epilogue, are intruders on "Columbia's stage." If, as he sarcastically says, Doolittle has brought his "pigs to a fine market" (that is, to an English seaport, scene of the comedy), he remains to the last a wholly unawed "Yankey doodle dandy," who plays his Jew's harp and fiddle and sings "Yankee Doodle" with spirit:

> Let what will cum, it shall be borne,
> I will not cry and snivil—
> I'd better have my breeches torn,
> Than dealings with the Divil. (Act V, p. 78)

Earlier (p. 33) Doolittle had declared to Newman that "I'd rather be in rags, than feel my blood bile so [at being called a servant]; or go the world stark naked, then be imposed upon." All in all, Doolittle, far more amusing than Newman, is "an independent, honest fellow with all of his oddities."

The many hostile accounts of America published by British travelers after the War of 1812 motivated the addition of Jonathan Peabody to the gallery of Yankee portraits. Versatile James Kirke Paulding, one of Irving's New York friends, replied to the prejudiced British through diverting allegory and satire suggestive of Swift's techniques. His allegorical *Diverting History of John Bull* (1812), *John Bull in America* (1825), *The Lion of the West* (his long-lost frontier farce, first played in 1831), and *The Bucktails; or Americans in England* (written shortly after the War of 1812 but published in his *American Comedies*, 1847) reveal the long persistence of Paulding's nationalistic ideas.[28] The satiric theme of *The Bucktails*, as suggested by the title, ridicules the traditional British as smugly viewing all Americans as the most primitive of aboriginals, who, in Miss Obsolete's distorted opinion, are copper-colored "wild men." She has been assured that "they wear copper rings in their noses—eat raw meat—paint one-half their faces red and the other black—and are positively half naked."[29] Throughout this early international comedy Paulding's admiration for homespun American villagers is balanced by his satirically expressed dislike of Tory England. Henry and Frank Tudor, young American visitors in Bath, and their servant Jonathan typify a land where, in Obsolete's thinking, "Everything is new and detestable; and the very rocks, they say, were made but yesterday."[30] But Jonathan, modeled on the pattern of Tyler's Jonathan the First, is unperturbed by England's traditionalism. He merely gapes, often somewhat stupidly, at the sights of Bath, cheerfully whistles "Yankee Doodle," and speaks the same picturesque dialect as that associated with the Down East towns of humorous literature.

From the 1820's onward, beyond the "fabulous forties," unusually popular comedians and minstrels provided impetus for native comedy by their amusing impersonations of Americans indigenous to the soil and the village. By their arts of mimicry Alexander Simpson, Henry Placide, G. H. ("Yankee") Hill, Danforth (Dan) Marble, James H. Hackett, Joshua S. Silsbee, John Edmond Owens, and others not only brought cash to the tills of many theaters, but also put new life into various characterizations of antic countrymen and villagers. It is thought that much of the comic acting of that day "must have been akin to horseplay, to buffoonery, except where a genius heightened the characterization, and made it human."[31] Such comedians usually did have a bag of tricks to heighten the appeal of their chosen roles. Among these gifts was their mastery of dialect. Dan Marble, for example, discovered his talent for New England dialect "by imitating his landlady's daughter so inimitably that she, herself, called him down into the best parlor one evening to entertain her guests by 'mocking' her."[32] The fame of George Handell Hill's impersonations rested largely upon his understanding of the language and other peculiarities of the real Down Easter—"the pure, unadulterated 'Yankee' of the lower class."[33] Owens enriched the meager original part of teamster Solon Shingle (in *The People's Lawyer*) by his voice, which, according to his wife, seemed to "ruralize."[34] As ample stage directions and extant portraits suggest, costume intensified the appreciation of provincial characters. For instance, actor William Warren in the role of the Yankee politician from Cranberry Centre, Mr. Jefferson S. Batkins, was costumed in a blue swallowtail coat, a high stiff collar, a yellow vest, gray trousers, and boots. He wore a high-crowned black hat and displayed a large watch chain with seals. A dark overcoat and umbrella completed the costume.[35] Such a typical Yankee costume, as Moses has noted, seemed "a mixture of atmospheric truthfulness and cartoon humor." Also, our comedians, familiar with the new theatrical form popularized through comic circus songs and Negro minstrelsy, knew certain tricks of singing and dancing to enliven roles calling for the singing of "Yankee Doodle" and other lyrics.[36] Finally, foreign influences quickened American interest in singing and dancing. A significant influence was the popularity of John Gay's *The Beggar's Opera*, which lived on long after its first London performance and printing in 1728.[37] By the 1820's the popularity of Gay's social satire and lyrics and of other English pastiches, like Bickerstaffe's widely performed *Love in a Village*, had helped create a vogue for native operatic plays, including John Howard Payne's romantic *Clari* (1823) with its sensational lyrical hit, "Home, Sweet Home." Both the songs and the characters in Micah Hawkins' *The Saw-Mill* (1824) and Samuel Woodworth's *The Forest Rose* gave new opportunity to those comedians gifted in portraying American provincials.

The Saw-Mill; or a Yankee Trick, both written and composed by Hawkins, is a two-act comic opera, "performed at the Theatre, Chatham Garden, with distinguished success," on November 29, 1824.[38] Whereas the earlier Yankee comedies highlighted pecularities of provincial character, *The Saw-Mill*, though not bypassing Yankee characterization, offers a somewhat realistic picture of a small town itself. The slightly shifting scene, changing from Rome in Oneida County to Oneida Creek, New York, is one of burgeoning town-building and industrial speculation activated by rumors of the opening of the "Grand Canal" (that is, the Erie Canal).[39] In fact, this animated scene of the growth of a new town, as eager investors, sawmill operators, mill hands, carpenters, cooks, canal lockmen, and other settlers throng into Oneida County, is a ballad opera version of contemporary economic development. (In some ways it early foreshadowed certain modern novels, like Conrad Richter's *The Town*, picturing the amazingly fast growth of towns in the wilderness.) Business of all sorts, honest and dishonest, accounts for the hubbub in Rome and Oneida Creek. And the busiest of all the speculators are Richard Bloom and Gat Herman. In disguise as Yankee millwrights, they assume the ridiculous names of Ezeakiel Amos and Zebedee Freelove Petteepague, supposedly from "a small townd of Kinnettiket," that is, "Stuningtownd" (Stonington). Both seem so skilled in trickery that, according to Bloom, ". . . in ten minutes' time we can be either Yankee, Turk, or Indians." On this occasion they try for easy money by inveigling rich Baron Schaffderduval (really old Van Brumstael) into a sawmill scheme. All in all, Hawkins' plot is of less interest than his gifts for social satire, often expressed lyrically as in Herman's song, "Our Yan-

kee Girls," and the parody, "The Yenkeetutels," sung by Stoduff, a
satiric Dutchman aged eighty-one:

> Yenkeetutels come to town
> For to puy molashes—
> Make Bungkin Pies
> An' Shingerspread,
> Sweet as sugar-candy—
> Yenkeetutelstantee.—

While Herman, with Yankee whine, objects that "You'm the sorts Tue
make fun of us Yankee doodles," Jacob, Bloom's cook, sings the finale:

> And long may this saw-mill saw;
> Yet never saw asunder
> THE tale of its origin—
> A YANKEE TRICK—and
> BLUNDER.

One of the most popular American plays before the Civil War was
the third one written by a versatile Massachusetts journalist, Samuel
Woodworth (1785-1842). *The Forest Rose; or, American Farmers*
furthered the vogue both for native "pastoral opera" and for the stage
Yankee. Also, from its October 7, 1825, opening at Chatham Garden,
Alexander Simpson gained recognition as "one of our best native low
comedians"[40] for his realistic portrayal of Jonathan Ploughboy, a New
Jersey village boy. Woodworth, in a published note of thanks to the
personnel of the Chatham (October 18), praised Simpson as in "every
way equal to my hopes and wishes."[41] But Yankee impersonation alone
did not create the pastoral atmosphere. Before its later discontinuance,
the music by John Davies, consisting of an elaborate descriptive overture and some fifteen songs, must have added much to the New Jersey
village scene.[42] In the opening directions for Act I, the overture is
described as expressing various sounds heard at dawn in the country,
even the ticking of the village clock, striking four, and the noises of
the first movements of the villagers, the singing of the birds, and a
distant hunter's horn. In short, and as shown again in the opening
trio, here are "scenes of sweet seclusion,/Far from bustling crowds."
Descriptions of the "stage house at the sign of the Spread Eagle," the
neat cottages, and the farmyards add to the picture of a quiet village
in the "Jarseys."

Unfortunately, the homely materials of the village background are
weakened by the use of stereotyped characters and the loose construction of a double plot, concerning several sets of lovers. Harriet, a
volatile village coquette suggestive of Mrs. Hardcastle, yearns to

escape to New York's "polite world," with its fashions, the Park, the Battery, Castle Garden, the circuses, the gaslights, waterworks, fireworks, and other attractions. But remembering that a "sprightly girl of sixteen/Ne'er spurns a saucy lover," Harriet pretends simplicity to attract a foppish Londoner, Bellamy, who thinks her "a charming Forest Rose." With affected naïveté, she listens to his supercilious impressions of New York, where his sensibilities were shocked by "The geese . . . flocking around a marble house in the park. . . . The calves and donkies are principally found in your Broadway, . . . The pigs, I believe New York's the only place where they enjoy the freedom of the city."[43] To Harriet's sly inquiry as to whether "donkies" and "dandies" are the same, William, her village lover, retorts that the words are from the same root. "The real genuine dandy, however, is an imported animal; and the breed having been crossed in this country, the fullblooded bucks command but a low price in the market at the present time."[44] Harriet's love of fun prevails. When Bellamy proposes an elopement, Harriet impishly tricks him into a rendezvous with a Negro servant, Black Rose, instead, and for herself chooses honest William. In a very thin subplot another pair of lovers—weepy, languishing Lydia and romantic Blanford—eventually are united.

Frolicsome Sally and Jonathan, the third couple, provide the humor according to the comic conventions of the time. Jonathan, a compound of stupidity and shrewdness, introduces himself as "a little on the merchant way, and a piece of farmer besides." A Yankee shopkeeper—formerly in Taunton, Massachusetts, but now in the "Jarseys"—he bargains with the natives, selling them "everything, whiskey, molasses, calicos, spelling-books, and patent gridirons."[45] Like other stage Yankees, Jonathan plays a Jew's harp, blushes when kissing the girls (especially on the occasion when Sally tricks him into bussing Black Rose), uses Down East lingo ("a darnation queer kind of a time," "see what your drift is," "calculate," and "don't care three skips of a flea for you"), and idealizes the village lass who "can milk a cow, make a cheese, and boil a pudding."

The literary significance of *The Forest Rose*, as well as of other "faded favorites," outweighs its obvious defects. Woodworth's importance extends a bit beyond his composition of the widely sung "The Old Oaken Bucket." In fact, in Ploughboy he created "the first stage Yankee who attained anything like general popularity or length of days." Comedians Simpson, Hill, Silsbee (appearing in London for more than one hundred consecutive nights), and Henry Placide advertised far and wide, even to California, the American qualities of the opera's provincial scenery, sentiments, and episodes.[46] The responses of American and British auditors to such a musical dramatization of a bucolic agricultural village further highlight the ascendancy of the sentimental mind during what Herbert Ross Brown has called the "Sentimental Years: 1820-1860."[47] *The Forest Rose* and comparable stage successes of long ago, with their sentimental interpretations of the small town as "too peaceful a microcosm to be disturbed," must have created in their auditors what Brown calls that "handkerchiefly" feeling. In Woodworth's comedy, however, there is a striking contrast to its mood of sentimentality, especially portrayed in Lydia's "moon calf" languishing for her lover. Its reflections—in Harriet's discontent and Jonathan's moving from his native Massachusetts to New Jersey— of the nineteenth-century shifts in village populations, usually city-ward, link romantic escapism not only with the glorification of the pastoral village but with economic trends as well.[48]

Several factors possibly stimulated others to turn to village patterns which Woodworth helped popularize. The drama began reaching larger audiences as more theaters were built. In New York, for example, the 1821 opening of the Second Park Theatre, seating 2,500, and the 1826 opening of the Bowery, with a seating capacity of 3,500, affected the cultural rise of the common man. For his taste, too, design painters (Dunlap included) began decorating stages with spectacular and garish dioramas and panoramas.[49]

Perkins Howes's *New England Drama* is another village play of 1825. With its treatment of a variety of elements—sentimentality and moralizing, religiosity, melodrama, and Yankee self-sufficiency—and a cast of more than twenty-five villagers, the play is something of a medley; the small-town atmosphere is, however, rather well sustained. Though but a little place, Becket Village has definitely marked social gradations, with at least one local philanthropist, a Quaker respected for his contributions to a school and other charities. Tart chitchat of three selfish sisters suggests a stock citizenry with familiar social attitudes. Mrs. Convers, with "neither religion nor scruples," prates about the cost of educating her daughters as ladies a la mode. Her babbling about their costly merino shawls, fashionable hats, prunella shoes, and silk stockings ends with her boast that they have private dancing and music masters. Sister Doggett, proud of her membership in the "Foreign Missionary Society" and her contribution—for public show—to the schooling of young Cherokees, is a prototype for Sinclair Lewis' Widow Bogart, outwardly a Good Influence, piously moralizing and spreading scandal. And canting Mrs. Wilson, affecting scorn of dancing schools, disciplines her unwilling children by the rigid Calvinism of their ministerial heritage. Howes further satirizes the "female" mind through the religiosity of a missionary-spirited Methodist, old maid Mary Hull, who berates the three sisters as hypocrites for their lack of charity for their orphaned niece Jane.

At the opposite pole of the social scale is a large family of Yankee mountaineers, who sell their wares in nearby Becket. The self-reliant father, a sort of fictional Thoreau who drawls that "as long as a man has his wits, he has something to work with," sees no need for hard farm labor. Leisure is more important. He has easy business enough supplying chance travelers from his home stock of cakes, beer, and "tansy bitters—a nice trade for a cold stomach." Between times he tinkers at making wooden bowls and dishes, which he peddles in the town once or twice a year. He is so persistent a trader that "there is not an old wife, or a young one either for the matter of that, but I can coax them to buy a dish or two; I take my pay in provisions of clothing; all the cash I get, is by the beer and cake; . . ."[50] His Yankee conscience moves him to pay "my minister's tax and my school tax, as reg'ler as any of them." Yet he is unorthodox to the point of disliking "Deacon Hollister's funeral surmon. Too much hell-fire."

Finally, this Yankee trader is, as he says, "a little notional about names." In his family there are his wife Tempe, Desdemony who scatters her "victuals" of milk and porridge, Velorus, Oclary, and Rodolphus (their lazy hound). But he met with disappointment in naming the baby. Usually he found plenty of names in a peddler's book, which he got from a hawker who was "going over the mountain with tin-ware and brooms, and books and pamphlets, and one notion and another."[51] Obtaining his book by swapping some wooden dishes, the mountaineer straightway found therein the name of Sophronius; but as his wife's father died about that time, he had to name the baby Solomon Wheeler after him.

All in all, Howes's inclusion of Gothic terrors—melodramatic scenes of thunder, lightning ("full of brimstone"), and imprisonment—his preachments about moral conduct, and even the tall-tale yarning of the Yankee mountaineer suggest that in this medley he kept abreast of the literary fashion of his times. But his many-faceted satire of the provincial mind and his sketching of another type of Yankee, however incompletely achieved, look forward to a later period of village characterizations before and after the Civil War. For example, his satiric exposure of the shallowness of the female mind anticipates Mrs. Mowatt's hilarious portrayal of Mrs. Tiffany (in *Fashion,* 1845) and

Lowell's witty appraisal of Cooper's stereotyped heroines, in *A Fable for Critics* (1847-48): "And the women he draws from one model don't vary,/All sappy as maples and flat as a prairie."

Mrs. Mercy Otis Warren's dramatic satires, begun in 1773 and set against the exciting background of the Revolutionary struggle, constituted a gentlewoman's daring dramatization of current events and participants therein. But during the decades following the appearances of her satires, few American women turned playwright; in fact, only one, Mrs. Mowatt, "the Lady of Fashion," achieved distinction as both playwright and actress. Of lesser note, Mary (Clarke) Carr, self-advertised "Authoress of the Fair Americans, Clermont, Herbert, &c.," published in Philadelphia (February, 1823) a five-act comedy, *The Benevolent Lawyers, or Villainy Detected.* Dedicated to "the Gentlemen of the Bar," her "effusion of the imagination" purported to prove that "in the United States, at least, a Benevolent Lawyer is not a phenomenon," a thematic idea rhymed in the prologue, thus: "A Benevolent Lawyer! The lady is mad!/A phenomenon sure that is not to be had." But this lengthy comedy, except for slight portrayals in dialect of Darby, an Irish porter, and a Pennsylvania Dutch money-lender, adds little to the dramatic records of the small town. Rather, it is her very early comedy, *The Fair Americans* (played in 1789, but published in Philadelphia in 1815), which romantically reproduces village scenes near Lake Erie, the region described in *The Saw-Mill.*

As another link in the development of early social satire, Mrs. Carr's *Fair Americans*, with its lyric interludes, reflects the once prevailing notions on the partisanship stirred by the War of 1812. Her solicitude for "Columbia's fame" typifies the currents of interest in the distinctively American nationality after the war, when the new republic was struggling toward fulfilment. Alas for nativism, the mixed group meeting in Erie Village—sailors, soldiers, officers (American and British), and the townspeople—seem little more real than Howells' familiar "cardboard grasshopper." The opening scene introducing the villagers as "rich and happy," picturing Lake Erie, at sunrise, as "beautifully romantic," and glorifying soldiers as dashing lovers (in young Anna's song, "A soldier is a lady's man") keynotes, in minute circumstantiality, "the smiling aspects of American life." The Fairfield family, all too wooden symbols of the American way of happiness through industry, are known throughout the village for their constant bustling around in their "domestic bliss" of cooking abundant meals, baking bread, churning and molding butter, pressing cheese, brewing beer, weaving, milking, and feeding their pigs, turkeys, geese, and ducks. But such

"smiling peace" in the village ends suddenly with the news of war
with England. The arrival of a recruiting party, whose sergeant scorns
the civilians as "a set of cowardly rascals," and rumors that Indians
will attack for the British arouse fears that "our flourishing village will
be laid in ruins; our smoking hamlets, serve but to light their dis-
tressed inhabitants in their flight."[52]

Further offsetting Mrs. Carr's inept romanticism is a somewhat
realistic talkfest (Act III) enjoyed by "armchair oracles" sententiously
weighing the advantages of the war. Yankee practicality and nativism
turn their folksy comments into a strongly anti-British vein. They
"argufy" that the fighting will prove that "we are not the poor, mean,
pusillanimous nation" derided by British critics. Their rosy prophecies
for village and nation envision the improvement of American manu-
factures through natural resources, the fuller development of our
native ingenuity, and the disuse of imported luxuries. Exemplary
Dame Fairfield, however, wonders about the fate of the ruined American farmers. Jesting about her skepticism, Fairfield retorts that "we
will run you for President." Others, more optimistic about the military
victories of the provincials, glorify the flag made by the Erie "ladies"
and favor the "use of bonfires, feasts, rejoicings, balls and tea party's
for a month."[53]

Early theatrical managers, while responding to the demand for
romantic foreign plays, also made way for presentation of American
themes, especially those concerning patriotism. Such a native play was
Samuel Benjamin H. Judah's *The Battle of Lexington*, whose second
performance on July 6 marked the close of the 1821-22 season at the
Park Theatre.[54] In his flowery three-act attempt to dramatize Matthew
Prior's phrase, "The wounds of patriots in their country's cause,"
Judah most obviously found in the actual affray at Lexington, on
April 18, 1775, a ready-made groundwork. Unfortunately, the idea was
far better than what he made of it. Acknowledging his close reliance
on source materials, Judah confesses in prefatory apologies that he
hastily planned and in four days wrote his comedy for Mr. Simpson
of the Park, where, he boasts, its first performance on the evening of
July 4, 1822, was received with "unbounded applause." Actually, Judah
does very little in this comedy to lend credence to his assertion that
plays of a national character based on the Revolution "should be the
first and most desirable subject for an American dramatist." Even his
subtitle—"A National Comedy, Founded on the Opening of the Revolution"—is an echo of the literary nativism of the time.

The least preposterous delineation is that of patriotic Adam Bothel, "humble American farmer" whose anger is aroused "when the king's troops come under the sanction of rulers who wish to make us slaves." Urging the citizens to stand up for their rights, Adam encourages "Captain" Parker as he drills hastily armed townsmen and farmers on Lexington Green. When Major Pitcairn's grenadiers begin firing and plundering the homes of Lexington, old Adam rallies his neighbors but is himself brutally assaulted. A further effort at realism takes a more humorous turn in the sketching of two Lexington scouts, as well as of the drinking soldiers Ambuscade and Haversack. Talkative, pedantic Grimalkiah Sheepshanks and the more silent Sampson, Yankee in outlook and speech, offer some comic relief. Forever quoting the Scriptures and scraps of Latin, parson Grimalkiah is a canting, mock-serious figure antedating by five years Cooper's ridiculous scientist, Doctor Battius of *The Prairie* (1827). Also, there is a suggestion of the pedantry which amiable Lowell was to satirize in the *Biglow Papers*, in the person of that long-winded Jaalem villager, the Reverend Homer Wilbur. Unfortunately, Judah's tale, with its poverty of original matter, presents thinly charactered village folk. ("But what can one expect of a man who names his hero Osbyn Ethelinde?" or of a heroine "singing like Ophelia, or prophesizing like Meg Merrilies?" asks Odell.) Its real significance is mostly extrinsic: the revelation of continued dramatic awareness of the lasting implications of the Revolutionary fight for freedom. Nevertheless, this turgid comedy called the attention of Park Theatre patrons of the twenties to the spirited reaction of Massachusetts villagers during a crisis threatening their liberties.

"One reason for the enormous popularity of historical fiction is that it satisfies many tastes."[55] During our "Golden Day," popular taste contributed to the perennial vitality of suspenseful, melodramatic plays of military glory and patriotism comparable to Judah's comedy. Perhaps continued audience demand accounts for the fact that one of America's "lost plays," although produced eighteen years later, is quite similar in patriotic theme, military action, Yankee characterization, and romantic style to *The Battle of Lexington*. At any rate, the Judah play has a near duplicate in *The Battle of Stillwater; or the Maniac*, a Revolutionary comedy attributed to H. J. Conway and first staged at the National Theatre in Boston on March 16, 1840. Odell's damning criticism of Judah's hasty composition is matched by a recent evaluation of Conway's "moralized melodrama" as "a turgid melodramatic mixture of patriotism, rustic humor, and a sensational love plot, climaxed by the surrender of Burgoyne on October 17, 1777, and a pageant of the 'Genius of liberty.' "[56]

Like Judah, Conway weakened authentic Revolutionary matter by ridiculous embellishments borrowed from Gothic romances and tales of seduction. These timeworn motifs include Julia Cotton's secret marriage to an enemy, British Captain Valcour, his subsequent desertion of Julia and her child, and her return to her father's house, near Stillwater village, as "a manaic from grief." Conway's unoriginal elements of romanticism include further Valcour's disguise as one Edward Singleton, a patriot, his attempted kidnapping and seduction of Rose Cotton (Julia's sister), Julia's melancholy songs of false love, and old Adam Cotton's recognizing Singleton as a British spy. Fortunately there is the saving grace of Yankee humor, apparently Conway's chief interest. The rusticity of New Hampshireman Uzzial Putman, patriot volunteer, follows a familiar pattern, including the usual shrewd Yankeeisms, his courting Lucy (ironically the pretty daughter of a stiff puritanical sergeant, Azariah Lambson), and his nostalgic gossip about his native village, near Baker's River, New Hampshire. Uzzial's songs, which he tauntingly sings as near the British lines as possible, include such folksy "varses" as these, on occasion used as patriot passwords:

> Cape Cod is all afloat,
> Marblehead is sandy,
> Charlestown is a spunky place,
> And Boston is the dandy.
>
> Corncobs twist your hair,
> Cart wheels surround you,
> Fiery dragons carry you off
> And mortar pestle ground you![57]

When he is taken prisoner, along with his cart of pumpkins and squash, and interrogated by General Burgoyne, Uzzial serves the plot as a connecting link between the British and American forces. Unabashed in the presence of the general, Uzzial, with characteristic Yankee pride, boasts that the New Hampshire volunteers "can live on the feed of a mule and carry more than a horse when their dander's up . . . They can eat granite and drink a mill stream." A good teller of yarns, Uzzial describes one of his fellow volunteers as "a real roarer" who can "hit a squirrel on the full gallop with his rifle ball." Later, after he has overheard talk about Valcour's plot to abduct Rose, Uzzial escapes through the lines to inform Rose and Adam that ". . . some confloberated varmints [are] a coming here to do a little outrageousness," and his Yankee reaction to that mischief is, "I'll be antidolrollified into a crab apple jam . . ." Most of all, Uzzial, who will be "twenty-six year old next grass," possesses true Yankee independence. As he says, ". . . you'll find us raw Yankees just as quiet as kittens, only let us alone; but just git their ebenezers a little riz—and then, Jehu! They'll have satisfaction if they cross the Atlantic on a raft of grindstones!"

Uzzial's quick-witted yarning about his New Hampshire village, to all willing listeners, follows a stereotyped pattern which Conway adapted to at least two later Yankee comedies. *Hiram Hireout; or, Followed By Fortune* (1852) offers a one-act treatment of a farcical theme, a Yankee villager's ridiculous and futile attempts at marrying for a fortune. More mirth-provoking, though hackneyed, are the servant Hiram's tall-tale reports about *his* village affairs, including a noisy New England town meeting and a lively Fourth of July celebration, when "a hull lot o' chaps, got on a kind of spree, down at Uncle Josh's."[58] (The description of Josh's dog, whose "tail curls so tight his hind legs can't reach the ground," is matched, almost verbatim, by Hiram Dodge's yarning— in Barnett's *The Yankee Peddler*, p. 7—that "Hopeful Parkins used to keep a dog with such a curly tail that it couldn't keep its hind feet on the ground.") In *Our Jemimy; or, Connecticut Courtship* (1853) Conway uses the unusual approach of featuring a vivacious New England girl (instead of the usual countrified youth), who is less Yankee in her actions than in her colloquial speech.

During the thirties, when actual small places (such as Concord and Cambridge) were in the limelight, village plays continued in popularity. Even bare lists—available in Quinn's history and elsewhere—suggest both popular interest and managerial response to small-town dramatizations.[59] *Down East; or, The Militia Training*, possibly by James H. Hackett, was performed in New York at the Park, April 17, 1830. S. E. Glover's *Banished Provincials; or, Olden Times* was staged at the American Theatre in New Orleans, April 29, 1833. An anonymous play of a resort community, *The Moderns; or, A Trip to the Springs* was a Park production of April 18, 1831, while an anonymous dramatic echo of Seba Smith's popular Downing letters, *Major Jack Downing; or, The Retired Politician* was on the boards, at the same theater on May 10, 1834. It was, indeed, a propitious time for a professional such as William Dunlap to publish his *A Trip to Niagara* (1830), another resort town comedy which, however, was staged earlier (November 28, 1828) at the Bowery Theatre.

Cooper, with insight into our struggles for cultural nationalism, repeatedly tried through fearless, but often tactless, criticism to evaluate our complex national traits and to warn his countrymen against an extreme provincialism, in his view our greatest social evil. Typically frank, *A Letter to His Countrymen* (1834), castigates "a custom peculiar to

America," the quoting of foreign opinions.[60] Too much deference, he cautioned, was dangerous to our institutions and destructive of our self-respect and manly mental independence. Defenders of our national system deserve fair play, so that, among other things, "a useful stage can exist" with our playwrights free "to delineate the faults of society."[61] Certainly, as we have seen, Dunlap gave impetus to literary nationalism through his dramatic criticism, his social satire, and even his painting of theatrical dioramas on historical and other native subjects. As to the satire, he notes in his *History* (p. 362) that "The last piece I wrote for the stage was a farce called *A Trip to Niagara.*" While Dunlap further declares that his "main intention . . . was to display the scenery," actually he aimed at a genial enough ridicule of traveling Londoners (en route to see the scenic wonders at Niagara Falls), who typify the British habit of applying the prejudices of their more conservative society to everything American. The snobbish "hero" Wentworth, with few convictions of democracy, is exceptionally rude in expressing his dislike of American scenery, Yankee cant, and the "republican insolence" evident—to him, at least—in the free and easy manners of Americans.

To cure Wentworth of his prejudice, another Englishman, John Bull (suitor to Amelia Wentworth), assumes *several* disguises, Dunlap's use of an old trick in a new way. As a Frenchman and then as a Yankee (called Jonathan, of course), Bull so berates the American way to Dennis, an Irishman, that Wentworth must speak out in its defense. Actually, the greatest interest in Dunlap's farce lies in his five caricatures of national types found in various early plays: the British, Yankee, French, Irish, and Dutch. The impersonations of the Negro (in "high falutin' " Job Jerryson, porter) and Leatherstocking (in dress described in *The Pioneers*) suggest that this farce "makes pretensions to no higher character." In fact, Dunlap acknowledges that it was written at the request of the managers of the Bowery, who wanted only "a kind of running accompaniment to the more important product of the Scene-painter."[62] Accordingly, the most graphic elements of localism appear in the moving diorama, whose eighteen scenes, in the manner of Thomas Cole and other Hudson River artists, represent the picturesque sights seen by boat passengers en route from New York harbor to Catskill-landing. A series of nonmoving drops—a night scene in the barroom of the Pine Orchard Inn in the village of Catskill-landing; State Street in the larger town of Albany, with the Capitol, Mohawk Falls, and the "great canal" in the distance; resort hotel scenes at Buffalo and Niagara (on the American side)—simulated representative scenes of provincial life which moved Amelia to prefer America's "flourishing towns, with laughing inhabitants, [rather] than the ruins of barbaric Castles or the tombs of their guilty and tyrannic lords."[63]

Finally, though Dunlap's main dramatic interest was entertainment through the farcical exposure of "Yankee-land" scorners, several passages descriptive of the American small town present, for their time, significant social ideas. John Bull's mock-serious argument, spoken in imitation of Yankee lingo, reminds one of Cooper's dilemma reflected in his attempts to reconcile—in *The Pioneers* (1823) and *The Prairie* (1827)—the dichotomy of the freedom offered by the wilderness and the order of civilization. As Bull (i.e., Jonathan) satirically protested,

"But these curst creeturs [New Yorkers] have spoilt all that [i.e., the virgin land]. What with their turnpike roads, and canals, they have gone, like tarnal fools that they are, and put towns and villages, gardens and orchards, churches and schools, and sich common things, where the woods and wild beasts and Indians and rattlesnakes ought to have ben."[64]

Also, Wentworth's astringent "John Bullism" about village conformity offers a very early approximation to the "village virus" diagnosed in Lewis' *Main Street*.

"So, this is Buffalo! . . . And what do I see after all. A town like other towns, water like other water, and people like other people—only made worse by democracy. I have not seen a well-behaved man since I came into the country, only a wild half Indian [i.e., Leatherstocking]."[65]

As certain writers and comic actors continued to experiment freely with the Yankee genre, "the gathering of the forces" interpretive of our "native roots" gained momentum. Leaders among these specialists of the later thirties and forties included Dr. Joseph Stevens Jones (1809-1877), Cornelius Ambrosius Logan (1806-1853), and most of the comedians mentioned earlier—such as Hill, Marble, Hackett, Silsbee, and Owens—whose popularity had grown with the increase of their repertories and their mastery of mimicry. Of these, energetic Dr. Jones assisted materially in enlarging the possibilities of the Yankee characters. Successively, he was an actor, a genial proprietor and manager of Boston's National and Tremont theaters, a prolific playwright (author presumably of more than 150 plays, mostly ephemeral but some very popular), and after his 1843 graduation from the Harvard Medical School, an honored physician and scientific lecturer in Boston for many years. First and last a Bostonian, he contributed variously to the cultural institutions of his native city.

From the beginning his play titles gave evidence of Dr. Jones's love for New England and his interest in folk types. For example, in his first successfully staged play, *The Liberty Tree, or Boston Boys in '76* (Boston, 1832), he himself impersonated a Yankee, Bill Ball. His eventual meeting with Hill and Marble, in the course of his theatrical activities, gave new reason for Jones's creation of other New England characters. To illustrate, Hill, with his broad Down East accent, inspired the characterization of a Yankee farm hand in *The Green Mountain Boy*, the role of Jedediah Homebred, which he played first at the Chestnut Street Theatre, Philadelphia, on February 25, 1833.[66] Jones again featured New England localism in the 1839 melodrama dealing with witchcraft, *Moll Pitcher, or the Fortune Teller of Lynn*. On May 6 of the same year, at Boston's National Theatre, Jones produced a conventional village tale of dishonesty and vengeance called *The People's Lawyer*. Oddly, a minor character named Solon Shingle, a New England teamster, eventually became, by virtue of several stage changes, one of the most popular provincial roles on our stage.

Originally but a meager role for G. G. Spear, Hill, Hackett, and Silsbee, the rustic teamster of their impersonations was a young New Englander, "a sort of Yankee juvenile Paul Pry," says Hutton. Later, when F. S. Chanfrau, young New York comedian in the Mose the Fireman series, was managing the National Theatre, his stage manager was Charles Burke, gifted actor and half-brother of Joseph Jefferson. One day Chanfrau, looking through a lot of manuscripts, discovered Jones's *The People's Lawyer*, which he called to his partner's attention. Burke, sensing the realistic possibilities in the role, changed Solon Shingle into "an old and simple-minded Massachusetts farmer intent on his 'bar'l o' apple-sass.' " On stage Burke's keen understanding and versatility, highly praised by Jefferson, led to such a successful presentation of Solon that John E. Owens tried the role in 1854 at the Baltimore Museum. Thereafter, especially in the 1860's, Owens achieved the greatest successes through his individualized interpretation of Solon Shingle.[67] According to Brander Matthews, Owens' clever acting left with spectators "a direct and simple picture of a homely New England farmer, loquacious, inquisitive, shrewd in a measure, full of his own importance, . . . a picture not sufficiently ideal to call out the first qualities of the actor, but real and distinct to an extraordinary degree."[68]

The comic interludes of Solon Shingle; the jail sentence of a falsely incriminated young clerk, stubbornly honest Charles Otis; his widowed mother's humiliations because of her "honest poverty"; the perjury of John Ellsley, fellow clerk and thieving spendthrift; merchant Winslow's forgery; the double identity of Robert Howard, "the people's lawyer";

and various additional and melodramatic elements (mostly absolutes of good and evil) all but overshadow the town background. Small-town ways are, however, linked with plot and characterization. Winslow's general merchandise store, a village dance, Grace Otis' feminine interest in drawing and painting, snobbish Mrs. Germain's ridiculous pretensions to culture (on a level with the determination of Gopher Prairie's Mrs. Ezra Stowbody to expose the good ladies of the Thanatopsis Club to English literature—from *Beowulf* to Thomas Hardy— within forty-five minutes), and local constables are familiar symbols of the people and the ways of the small community. Social conflicts, between caste and class in a New England town, are keynoted in Mrs. Otis' meeting with rich Mrs. Germain, as well as in the courting of Solon's daughter Nabby by John Ellsley, son of the town's rich man. Finally, the Boston court scene, during the progress of Charles's trial, reintroduces the symbol of the traveling Yankee. Like Tyler's Jonathan and Mrs. Mowatt's Trueman, Solon, a stranger to metropolitan customs, has a countryman's natural distrust of city people.

Having dozed during the trial proceedings, Solon suddenly awakes in great confusion. He is under the delusion that a thief is being tried for stealing "apple-sass" from the back of his wagon that morning. On the stand, Solon, although typifying justice and common sense, rattles on about his own dilemma. At last, realizing the truth, Solon drawls, in Yankee dialect, that ". . . if ever anybody catches me inside of a court house agin, I'll agree to be proved non pompus—and that means a tarnal fool, according to the law books. Jest so."[69] Disgusted, but by no means intimidated, by his mistake, Solon is ready to part company with the Bostonians:

"These city folks will skin me out of my old plaid cloak, that I bought ten years ago; hat, boots, and trowsers, tu, far as I know. I've been here long enough. I'll . . . find my Nabby, buy a load of groceries, and get home as quick as my team will go it. When I'm in this 'ere Boston, I get so bewildered I don't know a string of sausages from a cord of wood. Jest so."[70]

By this straightforward outburst, Solon reveals his character anew. He continues talking until the finale. Cautioning Mrs. Otis not to mind his talking, he tells her that "you might as well try to back a heavy load, as stop my thoughts coming right out in homely words."

The "Clyde Fitch of his day," Dr. Jones in 1852 created another repeatedly staged success in his last printed comedy, *The Silver Spoon*, whose opening performance on February 16 at the Boston Museum helped make actor William Warren famous, but primarily satirized the shortcomings and intrigues of the members of the "Great and General Court of the Commonwealth of Massachusetts."[71] Once again an entire play was popularized when a comic Yankee was given the spotlight. The traditional cleavages between town and country appear in comic interpretation when Mr. Jefferson Scattering Batkins (impersonated by Warren), member of the "General Court from Cranberry Centre," follows the instructions of his constituents to vote "agin the Boston klink." Protesting that he is no politician but merely a member of "the Honest Men's Independent Party," Batkins is proud of his political heritage. He boasts that his father, back in Cranberry Centre, "was a real Demicrat; he put Jefferson in my name. Scattering come next, after my father, who periodically run for Selectman of Cranberry Centre, and come in on the scattering list."

Batkins, still a bachelor, considers himself "an old greeny" as to city ways. The old-fashioned ways of Cranberry Centre, where folks like "flap jacks with molasses," suit him better. But he is adaptable to new conditions, as he demonstrates when his Yankee pragmatism prompts him to combine political duties with the sale, in Boston, of homemade ax handles, hoop poles, and poultry. As he says with some shrewdness, "I can learn my duty to my country as I go along, and do some little chores for myself and relatives." Observing the extravagance of Bostonians, villager Batkins, with the folk wisdom of Franklin's Poor Richard, remarks that ". . . the most fashionable people borrow the most money." As an independent rustic delegate, Batkins is not afraid either to oppose all Boston politicians fighting against his agricultural interests or to declare, in the presence of Hannah Partridge (his former sweetheart in the Centre), his dislike of forward women. ". . . I don't believe in hens in politics," he says, "or women wearing spurs, or riding war-horses." Taken as a whole, the rather realistic episodes featuring the Cranberry Centre folk show that the Honorable Jefferson Batkins and his friends, for all their Yankee self-reliance and solvency, were not born with silver spoons in their mouths. Such fortune, described in conventional scenes, belongs to another youth, the overly romanticized inheritor of an old-fashioned heavy-chased silver spoon, symbol of his family's prestige since their Plymouth Rock landing!

Sol Smith once ridiculed the hastily composed "sensation Plays" of his time as "made up of escapes from trains, burning steam-boats or sinking ships, negro jigs, and banjo-playing," enacted by actors and actresses "hired by the job." His fellow comedian and trouper on the western circuit, "Old Logan," offered in *Yankee Land* and *The Vermont*

Wool-Dealer neither sensational jigging nor banjo-playing; yet both comedies seem today but a potpourri of farce, melodramatic mysteries, and confused identities. In each the nearest approach to realism is seen in the Down Easters, again the earthy spokesmen for the manners and morals of small-town society and the life of the environing farmlands. The printed version of the two-act *Yankee Land*, replete with extremely detailed costume notes and listings of the casts playing from 1834 to 1854, shows that from its opening at the Park the main Yankee role of young Lot (Launcelot) Sap Sago appealed to Hackett, Spear, and Silsbee.[72] (Dan Marble once played the minor role of the countryman, Joe.) Lot's specified costume—drab long-tailed coat, broad striped vest and odd striped trousers, straps and boots, yeoman crown hat, and bright cravat—must have achieved an amusing effect of rusticity. A sort of New England version of untutored Hareton Earnshaw of Wuthering Heights, Lot moves in his uncouth way in and out of the action, at last to be recognized as the long-lost illegitimate son of Sir Cameron Ogleby. Actually, the play's title seems a misnomer. True, the action does take place in the Yankee village of Cantine and on nearby farms; yet there are among the characters so many transplanted Britishers—high and low—that much of the scene, by way of flashbacks, seems associated with international entanglements, largely picaresque adventures in England.

The theme of "honorable poverty" in conflict with "grasping cupidity" impinges upon the mystery about Lot's parentage. Intensely disliking his foster father, Malson, who forced him to serve as a kitchen maid, Lot uses typical Yankeeisms: "—a purty kind of raising it was tu—he says he found me in an apple orchard, and I wasn't no highern a corn cob." Though inured to farm chores, Lot grows up "a young bear," good at skunk hunting, fishing, and pranks, but so awkward in "sparking" that he declares ruefully: "A pretty kettle of chowder I've made. I wish I was adrift on a hencoop." His prankish nature displays itself most humorously when, in a scene comparable to Tony Lumpkin's scaring the wits out of Mrs. Hardcastle, he places Manikin, a city surveyor, astride two oxen and sends him "galumphing" down Slush Lane. Later he puts Manikin on a "regular snorter," with the warning that if the horse proves too hard to manage "you must let go of the bridle, hold on to the mane, stand on your knees, and put your legs up behind, and by the time you get through your journey, you'll look jest like a crumbled johnny cake." But this horse, as Lot reported, gave "one loud snort, and set off full chisel." Lot's cure for the victim is the ultimate in his prankishness: "I stowed him away in a bunk in the bar room at the tavern, and told the landlord [at the Cantine hotel] to give him a strong dose of pepper sarce and molasses to settle his internals—that's the last we shall see of him."

The one-act farce, *The Vermont Wool-Dealer*, which opened at the Bowery on April 11, 1840,[73] apparently rivaled in popularity the "weepy" temperance plays—*Fifteen Years of a Drunkard's Life*; *The Drunkard, or The Fallen Saved*; and *Ten Nights in a Bar Room*— which Samuel French was advertising (within the covers of *The Wool-Dealer*) for fifteen cents each. Logan, by the creation of an aphoristic wool dealer, Deuteronomy Dutiful, as impersonated by Marble and Burke, added to recorded localism another "doodle" and his invented village, this time in "Varmount". Once more, then, the Yankee "doodle"—customarily the "simpleton, noodle, silly, or foolish fellow"—travels not to Boston "with a load of ax-handles, hoop-poles, and other notions for sale" but to Saratoga Springs.[74] Once more, too, the Yankee represented the country and village as opposed to the "smartness" of the city. En route Dutiful becomes acquainted with fashionable Amanda ("Miss Mandy" to him), who uses him "a leetle damned scurvy" to promote her flirtation with Captain Oakley. She had not, however, counted on the Vermonter's "quick humor and his indomitable perseverance." Dutiful is determined that he "will court the gal, by grasshopper! 'Cause she's got $55,000 . . . Roll me into pig iron, if I don't." Although Logan rather crowds his stage with native characters—Americanized Con Golumby, "stupid Irish waiter" at a Saratoga hotel; a Negro servant ("a dacent lad, cuffee,[75] you are"); and a mulatto maid—Dutiful's dialect is the most colorful and studded with folk sayings. He has the same delight as Mrs. Malaprop in high-sounding, almost sesquipedalian words, such as "Conglomerate the fools!," "approximate you[r] bombastical rotundity," and, to Amanda, "By scrumsky! . . . [I have] roused the ramifications of your rampant sensibilities . . . and rouse[d] up your sanguine sensations." His similes are earthy: "I'm hungry as a juvenile hippopotamus, and as dry as a squash bed in April," or "Why, you look out of your eyes like a catfish with cholic," or "like the Cape Cod sea sarpant in convulsions." Like Batkins, Deuteronomy Dutiful shows great pride in his pioneer family, his grandfather having been "one of the first settlers in our part of the country—bought up pretty nighly one third of the hull country." Further typifying the rise of the common man, grandfather Michael, after his marriage to "as like a gal as ever drove a pair of oxen," eventually was sent to the state legislature.

Versatile Dan Marble, even during the years of his amusing portrayal of Deuteronomy Dutiful, turned his comic gifts to other Yankee roles. For example, on September 18, 1841, in Buffalo, Marble acted the leading role in Lawrence La Bree's one-act farce, *Ebenezer Venture; or, Advertising for a Wife*, written expressly for the comedian's peculiar talents. Possibly Marble's personative powers gave life to the stereotyped adventures of a raw New Hampshire youth, Ebenezer Venture, who journeys from his village in Rockingham County to "the tarnallest place—this ere New York." The timeworn battle of the wits between townsman and countryman reappears in La Bree's reliance upon a hackneyed plot to trick Ebenezer, supposedly gullible, into believing that his city cousin is the future wife for whom he has advertised in a New York paper. La Bree adds little to the human image, for, as with many previous village characters, Ebenezer is the theatric Yankee still. His anecdotal style, marked by familiar Yankeeisms, helps re-create his origins, as folksy as those of his stage predecessors. "I was born," he declares, "down East, in Rockingham County, New Hampshire, and that was about the first that was hearn of me." Like Tyler's Jonathan, Ebenezer has "come down to New York to see the place, and tell the folks a thing or two. . . ." He is most amazed by the crowds ("All sorts of folks here tu—niggers, a nation on 'em—foreigners by the bushel. Guess Europe are unpopulated, now—. . . .") and the ignorance of city folks about small-town ways ("these New Yorkers . . . the most ignorantest nation of people ever I did see. . . ."). Back home in New Hampshire Ebenezer's family seems, to use Van Wyck Brooks's words, to have been "bound with the brass fetters of the Philistines." Although the village "school marm" called him "her little genus, . . . it didn't make me proud; my father was select man of the town, my mother was President of the Benevolent Society, and Secretary of the Foreign Board of the Charitable Society . . . ; my Aunt Nabby, she was a snorter—a screamer—she conducted the singers in the core [chorus] of the meeting house, Sabbath days; . . ."[76] Self-sufficient to the point of being "a team by myself," Ebenezer exhibits the happier side of the stage Yankee: "I can play on the jewsharp, fiddle, fife, drum and bugle horn, the sweetest; I can dance anything, from the college hornpipe, to Jim Crow—I can read loud, sing, and sometimes make poetry."

Homespuns Down South

As early as 1770, even before *The Contrast*, the everyday village world down South found unique dramatic representation through the talents of a Virginia planter and colonel, Robert Munford. Later, from the twenties through the fifties, sporadic dramatizations of southern small-town ways paralleled, both as to time and as to literary approaches, the conscious movement toward realism in the urban East which, as we have seen, popularized the comedy of native provincials. During this same period, "in the good old times of muster days and quarter racing, before the camp meeting and the barbecue had lost their charm; when men led simple, homely lives, doing their love making, as they did their fighting and plowing, in a straight line,"[77] there was in the South and the Old Southwest—Georgia, Alabama, Mississippi, and Tennessee—a brief, but definite, literary movement manifesting itself in humorous, spontaneous sketches and a few dramatizations of contemporary life. Here, before the Civil War had despoiled earlier traditions, provincial conditions favored the frontier humorist and local colorist. With their material ready at hand, these humorists, themselves an integral part of the simple life they undertook to depict, formed a picturesque group of writers which "flourished in bar-rooms, on law circuits, on steamboats, and in the wide, open spaces. They were not professional humorists, but debonair settlers engaged in various tasks: lawyers, newspaper editors, country gentlemen of family and fortune, doctors, army officers, travelers, actors—who wrote for amusement rather than for gain."[78] These waggish young men (emergent figures all), playing on local minutiae with grotesque exaggeration of peculiarities of speech and custom, made their contemporaries aware of the commonsense, unromantic aspects of community life. Often their droll treatments of rustic character and incident of the "flush" times occasioned uproarious mirth.

While Colonel Munford satirized the foibles of the eighteenth-century planter aristocracy of the seaboard, these later humorists—Judge Augustus Longstreet, William Tappan Thompson, Joseph Glover Baldwin, Johnson Jones Hooper, and others—wrote of small towns bearing all the marks of the rough democracy of the backcountry which flourished not too far distant from the Tidewater plantations. As story after story appeared in the newspapers and periodicals of the lower South, or in William T. Porter's popular humorous journal, the New York *Spirit of the Times* (1831-46), new scenes, newly conceived comic rustics, countless anecdotes, local satirists and small-town observers all helped set up a unique pattern in the literature of southern village and rural life. To Colonel Munford's and James Brice's Tidewater towns were added the agricultural villages of Middle Georgia, where "no impassable chasm shut off the 'po whites' "; isolated village communities of the great Smokies; Alabama and Mississippi towns of the "flush" times; and others.

In village and country at circuit courts, revivals, weddings, infares, quiltings, corn shuckings, fish frys, shooting matches, militia drills, horse races, cock fights, and informal gossipy gatherings at local doggeries [grocery stores] the daily doings and local life were sufficient to produce anecdotes, community legends, and tall tales and furnish inspiration for humorous provincial figures: for shrewd Captain Simon Suggs, whose favorite aphorism was "It is good to be shifty in a new country"—at the expense of others; Ovid Bolus, Esq., whose "reputation stood higher for lying than for anything else"; practical jokester, Ned Brace; Sut Lovingood, "a queer looking, long legged, short bodied, small headed, white haired, hog eyed, funny sort of genius"; and Major Joseph Jones, Esq., from Pineville, Georgia.[79]

These typify the rough-and-ready characters created by southern fun-makers (a few playwrights included) whom Donald Wade once described as "the court-jesters of a homogeneous culture," which faded with the entrenchment of cosmopolitanism.

In 1798 a Petersburg, Virginia, printer issued for a Mecklenburg County planter-poet, one William Munford, a memorial volume of plays and poems written by his father, witty and distinguished Colonel Robert Munford, who had died fourteen years earlier.[80] From this motley collection of pastoral, patriotic, and humorous poems, a translation of Ovid's *Metamorphoses,* and sundry items, two satiric plays—*The Candidates; or, the Humours of a Virginia Election* (a three-act comedy) and *The Patriots* in five acts—best display, according to his son's preface, Colonel Munford's understanding of "the true points of ridicule in human characters" and his drawing them "with great accuracy and variety." A gentlemanly planter but no professional writer, Robert Munford wrote for amusement rather than for publication. In his son's words, *The Candidates* was "intended to laugh to scorn the practice of corruption and falsehood" and "to teach our countrymen to despise the arts of those who meanly attempt to influence their votes by any thing but merit." *The Patriots* (1776), described by William Munford as "a picture of real and pretended patriots," is a better play, offering an early dramatization of the then rising tide of nationalism. Our interest here, however, is in *The Candidates,* as a dramatically presented exposure of the conduct of a small-town election in Tidewater Virginia about 1770.

In Hubbell's evaluation, *The Candidates* has greater historical interest than *The Patriots* "because it is among the very firsthand sources of information about elections in eighteenth-century Virginia." The opening sentence points toward the composition of the comedy shortly after the death of "good old Governor Botecourt" on October 15, 1770. The prologue (pp. xi-xii of the 1798 collection), written "By a friend," perhaps by request of William Munford, suggests not only that

Colonel Munford wrote with stage production in mind, but that he had considerable satiric power as "Virginia's first and only comic son":

> Ladies and gentlemen, tonight you'll see
> A bard delighting in satiric glee;
> In merry scenes his biting tale unfold,
> And high to Folly's eye the mirror hold:
> Here eager candidates shall call for votes,
> And bawling voters louder stretch their throats:
> Here you may view in groups diverting, join'd
> The poor and wealthy rabble of mankind.
> All who deserve the lash, the lash will find.

The successive scenes in *The Candidates* bring to life the entire citizenry of a colonial Virginia town, but not in the manner of the highly descriptive, romantic picturing which John Esten Cooke, in his *The Virginia Comedians* (1854), gives of the Golden Age of Williamsburg, when that little town was the capital of a far-flung plantation area. Yet, for the occasion, Munford's pictured town is as teeming a place as Cooke's Williamsburg, with its citizens and visitors moving through the streets, crowding the legislative chambers, drinking convivially at the Raleigh tavern, or applauding at the New Theatre the efforts of Hallam and his English troupers. Rather, *The Candidates*, antedating Goldsmith's and Sheridan's comedies by some seven or more years, is a remarkably early American comedy of manners. As such, it offers some hilarious scenes of Tidewater townspeople in characteristic action during a spirited election campaign. As the different candidates, each with persuasive followers, electioneer for the several places in the General Assembly, their "antic strivings" seem even today ridiculously funny, yet realistically expressive of the lively nature of colonial town political rallies.[81]

Occasional bits of stilted dialogue, typified characters, and a thinly developed plot fail to obscure the verisimilitude of the town scenes: the candidates' treats, their bountiful barbecues and breakfasts, with barbecued bullocks and pigs, whiskey and rum; tavern guzzling bouts; election betting; whispering campaigns by each faction; and falsely glorified promises, handshaking, and insincere personal inquiries made by glib candidates to squeeze votes from the freeholders. First in class distinction are the wealthier planter candidates, Worthy and Wou'dbe, and the convivial toper, Sir John Toddy, "that fine beast of a gentleman." Of lesser distinction are gentleman justices, appropriately named Mr. Julip and Mr. Paunch, and such property-holding candidates as conceited Strutabout and horsey Smallhopes. Freeholders Guzzle, Twist, Stern, and Prize—a noisy, rum-drinking lot—accept the then prevailing notion that the gentry best represent their county in the House of Burgesses. Their gossipy, and sometime drinking, wives apparently concur. Of these uninhibited freeholders the most loquacious is the weak tippler and ignoramus, Guzzle, whose wife also drinks but claims she is sick from eating gingerbread. Guzzle, wholly unaware of the real qualifications for a reputable member of the House of Burgesses, loudly declares to his fellow tipplers that all a Williamsburg delegate needs is "to tell some damned lie." ("To convince you, eating, drinking and sleeping are three; fighting and lying are t'others.") His loudmouthed protest against sham promises, always unfulfilled, has the ring of truth: "Yes, damn it, you all promise mighty fair; but the devil a bit you do perform; there's Strutabout, now, he'll promise to move mountains. He'll make the rivers navigable, and bring the tide over the tops of the hills, for a vote."

Of course, other Virginians—country girls and village belles, the folksy wives of the freeholders whose loyalty is bought by gifts of ribands and shoebuckles, political stool pigeons, and servants—variously complete Munford's dramatization of a town in a holiday mood. Of these, Ralpho, as the farcical servant to burgess Wou'dbe, is of some significance in dramatic history. In him, as Hubbell and Adair have noted, the Negro comedian made his first appearance in any play, European or American; but the portrait is scarcely realistic and suggests little of the modern pattern of the "stage Negro." On the other hand, Ralpho, years before Mrs. Malaprop's oddities of language convulsed theatergoers, delighted in "highfalutin" words as much as in showy clothes ("a little decreation") to attract the "gals" among the pre-election throngs. For all of the artificiality of his characterization, Ralpho, adding a bit of local color, completes the roster of caste and class in a predominantly aristocratic society.

Munford gives much attention to his own cultivated class, using the gentry to symbolize community leadership. Worthy and Wou'dbe, eventually successful at the polls, are blessed with the social and intellectual capacities for maintaining social stability, as were their historical counterparts. By contrast, Sir John Toddy, devoted to his bottle, dog, and pot-companions (including Guzzle, who whispers the names of the voters, whom addlepated Sir John then addresses as old friends), is bitingly satirized as the hiccoughing "Sir John Blockhead." Apparently only Worthy and Wou'dbe, however lofty, have insight enough to recognize the social significance of the freeholders' bold demand for lighter tax levies, free ferryage across the river, and stricter supervision of "the damn'd pickers" who habitually condemn the tobacco of the small planters for their private use. Wou'dbe, with full candor, concludes the comedy with a lament concerning the perils of one's being a public servant: ". . . in order to secure a seat in our august senate, 'tis necessary a man should either be a slave or a fool; a slave to the people for the privilege of serving them, and a fool to himself, for thus begging a troublesome and expensive employment." But in the finale, where the sheriff announces to the crowds in the courthouse yard the election of Worthy and Wou'dbe, Munford truthfully portrays the spirit of independence becoming to Virginians in the casting of their ballots. And Wou'dbe, as "the *fittenest* man," rises to the challenge of leadership in a few moralistic couplets:

> The prudent candidate who hopes to rise,
> Ne'er deigns to hide it, in a mean disguise.
> Will to his place with moderation slide.
> And win his way, or not resist the tide.
> The fool, aspiring to bright honour's post,
> In noise, in shouts, and tumults oft is lost.

After Munford's time, when theaters and actors became more and more a part of the southern scene, small-town affairs and characters —political, social, and amatory—continued to find dramatization, largely in the popular form of farces and burlettas. Further realistic scenes satirizing punch-drinking candidates and their constituents at another county election in Virginia and ridiculing the gullible persons fooled by confidence men appear in *Blackbeard* (1824), an amusing farce by Lemuel Sawyer of North Carolina.[82] Munford's Sir John Toddy has a successor in Turpis, a common people's candidate for representative to the state assembly who wins the election by distributing jugs of whiskey to his constituents. ". . . I want no better friend than this jug," he says, "with what little I can put in slyly between drinks. The bottle's the best electioneer, after all. . . ." Also, a few years before Longstreet's lively sketches in *Georgia Scenes* (1835) pictured a closely knit world of farms, smaller plantations, crossroads stores, trading villages, and larger towns like Augusta, James F. Brice in *A Country Clown, or Dandyism Improved* (1829) ridiculed, with some sting in his humor, the pretensions of village "society."[83] Brice's satire concerns the ridiculous efforts of a greenhorn, Arable, to transform himself into a dandy. Having inherited an estate, Arable comes "to town [apparently Annapolis] to be the tip of the mode." The slapstick action centers at a village tavern, where landlord Tapster, with the assistance of his waiters, the local barber, tailor, cobbler, and hatter, and his daughter

Flirtilla, schemes to fleece the "country clown." But they are mistaken in thinking Arable an easy mark. To them he is a simpleton, a "rustified gentleman" who wants his hair cut "a la mode" but who cannot distinguish between a Parisian "tonsore," which he thinks is food, and a roasted canvasback duck; yet, when he senses that the townspeople are making a fool of him, Arable throws soapy water in the barber's face and otherwise demonstrates that a country clown, like certain stage Yankees, has plenty of horse sense.

A Cincinnati lawyer's 1833 evaluation of the cultural promise of the West applies somewhat to southern village and rural life of the thirties and later. The most promising themes for an original literature, so wrote Isaac I. Jewett long before Mark Twain's time, were the picturesque Mississippi boatmen and the "ludicrous anomalies" of avaricious peddlers swindling an untutored people.[84] Certainly the stage Yankee, often a most peripatetic cuss, peddled his wares down South. In 1839-40, at Boston's Tremont Theatre, Morris Barnett's *Yankee Peddler or, Old Times in Virginia* began more than a decade of bookings, with Dan Marble, "Yankee" Hill, and H. F. Stone starring as the peddling Hiram Dodge in St. Louis (1841), Louisville (1845), and Chicago (1853) respectively.[85] In this one-act farce, Barnett apparently was not so much interested in small-town life per se as in the "Old Times" in general in an undesignated section of Virginia where existed a closely integrated provincial world of a crossroads tavern, surrounding plantations and racecourses, and a town not too far distant.

As in Munford's eighteenth-century town, here, too, class distinctions form a stratified society. The gentry are represented by planter Fuller —a stock character delighting in mint juleps, imported "segars," and the success of his prize mare at the fall races—and his daughter, Maria. A more democratic place than the plantations is the community around the tavern, where Cowpens, the keeper, advertises "Entertainment for Man and Beast." Of the provincial folk, ranging from the local gentry to their "darkies," who come to the tavern from far and near, the most individually colorful is Hiram Dodge, a very adaptable Yankee peddler ever ready to double-cross any gullible person crossing his path, if he senses a business profit for himself. Two interests determine his "destiny": his delight and skill in gulling and his suddenly awakened love for Jerusha (Jerushy), a pert Yankee girl attached to Fuller's household. Hiram's own sales cry, delivered in characteristic lingo, reveals his business acumen; "Fancy Ware! Fancy Ware! ghee who-ghee whoop! Ger long you pesky critter, now travil—who-a— . . ."

Entering the tavern with his basket in hand, Hiram further expresses himself to the company at large: ". . . that ere hoss of mine is troubled with nervous agility. . . . Fancy Ware! Fancy Ware! It was bout these parts that I made considerable money last spring, on Jamakee rum, inions, wooden cheese, Leather Hams, Pepper cannisters, Sossingers, mustard, Pocket-books, and Rat-Traps. Fancy Ware! Fancy Ware!" Last year he sold Squire Fuller—"a dreadfully riled old chap"—a Canadian pony whose tail "was only glued on." But Hiram, interested in a quick sale, "don't feel a bit consarned about that." He is, however, much concerned about the success of his courting, even to the point of giving Jerusha "a hull string of sassingers for nuthin.'" Having convinced her that "I'm yourn till death," Hiram, in a finale, begs Fuller and his neighbors to "overlook the Yankee dodging of Hiram Dodge, and well wish success to Mrs. Dodge, and all the little Dodges." Mostly, Barnett's picture of old-time Virginia is focused on the antics of this quick-witted but broadly caricatured peddler disposing of his shoe pegs, "Omnipotent mo-lasses candy," and other notions.

This epoch of growth for native plays saw the staging at Philadelphia's Walnut Street Theatre, on October 12, 1839, of one of the most realistic political comedies since *The Candidates*, James E. Heath's *Whigs and Democrats; or Love of No Politics*. According to Heath's nationalistic preface, his three-act comedy represented his effort to show that American playwrights, instead of forever imitating unsuitable foreign models, should at once recognize that the United States "furnishes ample material for drama." Believing that "dramatic interest may be sustained by the delineation of simple, natural, every day circumstances, without the aid of wild and extravagant incidents," Heath scorned the exaggerations of foreign romanticism. Rather, he purposed to "hold up to ridicule the despicable arts of demagoguism" in an attempt to check its current practice and insure the safety of our free institutions.[86]

Again the citizens of a Virginia town, with its tavern and streets full of Whigs, Democrats, and sundry merrymakers, are portrayed as experiencing the excitement of an election day. Amusingly satirizing the campaign methods used in a country town, Heath (apparently a Whig) uses a rather lifelike local boss as a means of ridiculing current "bossism." The crude, boastful proprietor of Hickory-Tree Tavern, "Major" Roundtree, swaggers among the voters, expertly electioneering for General Fairweather, Democratic candidate for Congress. Freely soliciting votes by bribes and liquor, Roundtree knows that "on election day a Major of Militia is as good as a Congress general."

Although Fairweather is in a close contest with the Whig candidate Manly, Roundtree recognizes the power of influence, as both a valuable friend and a formidable foe. And his own influence over "the boys hereabouts" stems from his good training of them. "I can make them wheel to the right or to the left with as much ease as I muster my battlion," he says. "I've only to blow a horn, and the rogues swarm around me like bees in summer time." Accordingly, the Major orders his "scouts" and "file leaders" to "beat every bush" and to "clap fire on every democratic terrapin's back in the precinct" and arranges for "hired expresses" to bring in election results. Such well-controlled methods, he feels, will entitle him to put in a claim "one of these days for a bite at the public crib." After all, he has gained local recognition as "a whole hog-drag-out republican,—the real grit."

Comic contrasts to the Major's loud boasting about his influence and social equality—". . . at the Hickory-Tree Tavern, and on election day . . . I am as good as you [the General] or any other man"—are his henpecked responses to his sarcastic wife. Like Mrs. Hardcastle's ridiculous aping of "the refinements of London," Mrs. Roundtree's social airs are the target for hilarious satire about "female eddication." Her nagging about the necessary town "eddication" of "Our poor dear Kate" forces the irritated Major to "question the good of it all." Protesting that his wife had sent Kate "away to a Whig town to be corrupted," Roundtree regrets the transformation of "a snug tidy country girl" who could make a pudding and mend a stocking into nothing more than "a town flirt, with her head cram'd full of aristocratic notions, about botany, natural philosophy, and all that." But Mrs. Roundtree, scorning the cruder taste of the Major, glorifies her affected daughter as "an accomplish'd young lady, who can talk French,—play on the piany,—dance like a top,—draw pretty landscapes, and understand all about the natur' of flowers." She finds full confirmation in the praise of that educated sycophant, Supine, who is caricatured as a snuff-taking, Latin-quoting country schoolmaster. *"Excellentissima puella!"*—that's Kate, exalted beyond recognition.

Finally, Heath's references to the "Bank monster" as "a great enemy to Democracy" and to the tariff as "a monstrous mischievous thing— a sort of sea sarpent"—may not be of perennial interest. On the other hand, the racy gossip about these and other issues helps create a town picture with realism. Likewise, further electioneering practices, such as handshaking, inquiries about the welfare of voters' families, and newspaper propaganda, the rather realistic speech of the Negro characters, and the bipartisan conflict in the town between the Whiggish families of "the old school" and the Democratic "upstarts" all suggest Heath's observance of real town life in antebellum Virginia.

The popularity of *Georgia Scenes*—from the 1835 Augusta edition through the ten Harper editions, 1840-97—influenced the humorous studies of small communities by other southern interpreters. Earliest among these was Ohio-born William Tappan Thompson (1812-1882), witty printer-journalist once associated with Longstreet in editing the Augusta *State Rights Sentinel*.[87] With the useful background of a legal apprenticeship in Florida and of further newspaper work in other Georgia towns, Thompson won acclaim during the forties and fifties, here and abroad, by some amusing sketches and letters, supposedly by a thoroughly rustic villager and farmer, Joseph Jones, dubbed "Major" solely because of his position on the Pineville, Georgia, militia drill team.

The first of these chatty sketches appeared anonymously in June, 1842, in the Macon *Family Companion and Ladies' Mirror*, of which Thompson was coeditor. The unexpected popularity of this early sketch and Thompson's move, in August, to Madison to start the weekly *Southern Miscellany* led to further informal letters to the editor, "sketches of rustic life and character [which, as Thompson wrote later,] were written to give variety and local interest to the columns of a Georgia country newspaper."[88] His original purpose was to portray the Georgia cracker, a class of provincial people whom he knew well, "with no more exaggeration than was necessary to give distinction to the picture." To achieve this purpose he used the patois peculiar to the small plantation area of Georgia; yet he made the Major a respectable slave-owning farmer rather than a cracker. These early letters, together with later sketches in the collected editions and a dramatization, present a genuinely realistic miscellany of rural, small-town, and larger-town life in Georgia. As to the provincial nature of the locale, the different scenes, so Watterson once noted, "might possibly be laid in Tennessee or Alabama, but not in Virginia or Mississippi."

Of the several series in book form, the very popular *Major Jones' Courtship* (1843) is the source of a domestic comedy, *Major Jones' Courtship or Adventures of a Christmas Eve, By Major Jones*.[89] This diverting dramatization of provincial scenes and homespun Georgians chiefly concerns Major Jones's amatory adventures during one Christmas season. It has a two-act development with little obstruction, no formal plot, and no villain more formidable than Crotchett (alias Wiggins), "a pretended exquisite, a runaway barber from N. York," whose plan to swindle the Pineville folks fails. Joseph—"a simple, yet shrewd, straightforward, honest Georgia lad"—opens the comedy with a long soliloquy describing the way he feels. Obviously "flustricated," he admits having "a sort of hankering after Miss Mary Stallings," but, uncertain about her attitude, is afraid "to pop the question." Actually, Mary, a Pineville belle just home from Wesleyan Female College at Macon, returns his love; but she joins with her sisters Caroline and Kesiah in teasing the kindly, naïve Major. Her mother, a plain old country lady, approves of the match, since Joseph, though uneasy about his "grammer" and "retorick," is well-to-do "and he knows a thing or two" (including politeness to old women).

In the comedy, as in the original letters, Joseph has the faculty of making himself ridiculous, especially in his clumsy attempts to gain the favor of "the darlinest gal in the county." His credulity and innocence add to the difficulties of his courting. The worst trouble, of course, comes from his lack of self-assurance and sophistication. For instance, when he faces a socially changed "Miss Mary," Joseph is addled by her high talk of the Wesleyan Female College. Her new "schoolmarm" manners puzzle the Major, as does her conversation about the male companions she had at Macon. At his side of the Stallings fireplace, Joseph seems miles away from his beloved Mary; so, in an effort to make conversation, he timidly asks about her experiences in Macon. In his ignorance he thinks Mary's chitchat regarding her course of study refers to her Macon beaux: Matthew Mattics, Philo Sophy, Trig O' Nometry —"town chaps" with "lots of gab." Joe thinks these are Irishmen who were with Mary day and night. When Mary explains, Joe hitches up his chair, spits into the fire, and tries to "pop the question." But when he cannot say a word, Mary thinks he may be having another "magnetic attack." (Earlier some jokesters, boasting of their powers of magnetism, have tried to trick Joseph into believing that he is suffering from such an attack.) Joe's spitting puts out the fire as he tries desperately to make his proposal. Mary, in the dark, leaves the room, with Joe finally calling for her in vain. In trying to get out, Joe upsets the tea table and mistakenly gropes his way into the girls' bedroom, grumbling, "But that's always the way with me. Ther's everlastingly something a happenin to upset all my calculations."

Mary's desire to test the fidelity of "my dear, good, bashful Joseph" inspires her to make false promises of elopement with two other suitors: Crochett (interested solely in her "snug little fortune") and Dr. Peter Jones, a Pineville fop and "affection'd ass." Unexpectedly, their pseudolearned talk about phrenology, magnetism, and "spasmodic convulsions" makes the Major "monstrous mad." He denounces Crochett as "an infernal vagabones" going "through the country feelin young lady's heads and talkin all sort of nonsense in ther ears." Best of all, he swears a folksy oath to end his dillydallying:

> This night I'll bring Miss Mary to the pint,
> Or put my nose completely out of jint.

And he has help from mischievous Caroline and Kesiah, who hasten the long delayed proposal by the trick of persuading Joseph to conceal himself in a large bag suspended from the porch beam and on Christmas morning to offer himself as a gift to Mary.

Thompson's plot, then, is little more than a simple domestic tale. On the other hand, the homely idiomatic dialogue contains many references to other phases of small-town life in early nineteenth-century Georgia, which not only add variety to Major Jones's courting experiences but also show that Thompson, like Longstreet, was a realist who saw in many commonplace situations a humorous aspect. The growing importance of "female" finishing schools; the excitement of a Christmas play party (of folk games like "Blind Man's Bluff," "Button, button, who's got the button?" and "Hunt the Slipper"), country dances, and an occasional cotillion; curiosity about "the new ologies and isms" (phrenology and magnetism); the usual gossip, especially about occasional visitors from the outside; a rather democratic relationship with the Negro servants; muster drills; the power of the local law men" (constables); and other realistic features of town life form the homespun stuff out of which Thompson creates the little community of Pineville, Middle Georgia.

The Decline of Homespun Comedy

The numerous changes quickened by the Civil War and the years of reconstruction are but later manifestations of the forces which Emerson saw destroying the peace of an earlier day: "Things are in the saddle, /And ride mankind." Out of a welter of newness—the tremendous growth of our cities, multiple economic developments, renewed curiosity about the West and the Southwest—emerged more modern literary forms. The rise concurrently of the social novels of Mark Twain, Howells, and contemporary naturalists, the international novels of Henry James, countless local color stories, and realistic poetic experimentation gradually diminished the vogue for comic rustics and village oddities. A few homespun plays lingered on the boards, and a few others were written or adapted by later interpreters, mostly stage folk like John Augustin Daly and James A. Herne. By and large, however, the national trend toward conformity and the disappearance of some of the most popular comedians lessened the appeal of comic stage villagers of different types.

The realistic romancer Thomas Bailey Aldrich summed up this situation well in his 1883 admission that a serious accident connected with the running of the first train over the Eastern Road from Boston to Portsmouth, New Hampshire, during the late fifties affected his own portrayals of town life. The accident, occurring in the crowded station at the Portsmouth terminus, was unobserved at the time. "The catastrophe was followed, though not immediately, by death, and that also, curiously enough, was unobserved. Nevertheless, this initial train, freighted with so many hopes and the Directors of the Road, ran over and killed—LOCAL CHARACTER."[90]

But a few more comedies, variously expressive of community ways, found their audiences. Some of these linked the small town with national issues, such as the antislavery movement and the Civil War. For example, John Townsend Trowbridge's *Neighbor Jackwood*, produced at the Boston Museum on March 16, 1857, serves to illustrate the popularity of the stage Yankee until the opening of the war. As a dramatization of a novel of propaganda, this comedy centers around a Vermont provincial and abolitionist, Jackwood, who ministers to the needs of fugitive slaves. His neighbors—speculating Enos Crumlett, crotchety Grandmother Rigglesty (with a "crick in her back"), and others, such as fretting Mrs. Jackwood and Camille, an octoroon runaway from Louisiana—all represent provincial reaction in Vermont against the Fugitive Slave Law. A mixture of provincial realism and melodrama related to the tragedy of mixed blood, *Neighbor Jackwood* has a parallel in a southern play of slavery, Mrs. J. C. Swayze's *Ossawattomie Brown or, The Insurrection at Harpers' Ferry*, acted at the Bowery on December 16, 1859. A great deal of the action takes place at Brown's house on Pottowottomie Creek, other farms, and a nearby tavern. The three acts are chiefly devoted to John Brown as a rash old man, a ringleader fomenting trouble, "a wild fanatic." His rashness, of course, leads to the attack on Harpers Ferry. There is considerable melodrama; yet the pictures of Brown's sons—Frederick, Oliver, Watson, and Lewis—of Frederick's marriage to Julia, of Brown's forces stationed outside the Armory and the hotel at Harpers Ferry, of street fighting, and of Brown on a prison cot are fairly realistic scenes of a town during a warlike crisis.[91]

Fifteen years after Harriet Beecher Stowe's *Uncle Tom's Cabin*, her clergyman brother, Henry Ward Beecher, tried unsuccessfully to picture a localized Yankee village during New England's Golden Day. His novel, *A Legend of Norwood, or Village Life in New England* (1867), by no means equals his sister's effective Oldtown stories of the same period, but gives a wooden, didactic interpretation of a Connecticut River town both before and during the Civil War. Although Beecher wanted "to give a real view of the inside of a New England town, its brewing thought, its inventiveness, its industry and enterprise, its education and shrewdness and tact,"[92] he failed in this purpose by using too large a canvas. His story wanders from Norwood to college scenes at Amherst, to Boston and Washington, and to the horrors of Bull Run and Gettysburg. Mostly lay figures, his Yankee villagers (even Hiram Beers, a rather realistically portrayed teamster and local oracle) move like puppets through artificial actions and philosophical arguments. Deficient though the novel is, Augustin Daly saw theatrical potentialities in its war scenes, already familiar to readers through the serialization of the novel in Bonner's New York *Ledger* during 1867. At any rate, Daly's four-act adaptation while not too successful in its production at the New York Theatre on November 11 of the same year, at least was recognized as the earliest stage version of the Battle of Gettysburg. Daly, more than Beecher, focused attention (in his third act) on the action at Gettysburg, where the hero, young Cathcart, and his fellow Yankee villagers share in the fighting. Daly's first two acts, however, follow the novel closely in language and realistic presentation of New England small-town life before the outbreak of war disturbed its peaceful local character. Both the novel and the play show how provincialism, long undisturbed, weakened before the newer force of war and industrial progess. Thousands of soldiers, before the war farmers, small townsmen, or untraveled students, were suddenly shifted from their native, and often isolated, locales into strange regions of ever changing scenes and contacts. Whole regiments of young provincials, akin to Cathcart and Daly's drummer boy "from Hardscrabble," swarmed from remote hill towns, prosperous valley towns (like Norwood), ports, and farms throughout New England to the South, a virtually new country to many of them, and measured themselves against men from the southern plantations and other areas.

If Daly realistically dramatized the Yankee villager fighting amidst the horrors of war at Gettysburg, two experienced actors—Denman Thompson (1833-1911) and James A. Herne (1839-1901)—achieved considerable realism in the last notable portrayals of comic, homespun New Englanders. Both Joshua Whitcomb of Thompson's *The Old Homestead* (1886) and Nathan'l Berry of Herne's *Shore Acres* (1892) mark the Yankee's eventual entry into the realm of more realistic comedy. Each play, incidentally, was much rewritten.

A native Pennsylvanian but a New Englander by adoption, Thompson came to Boston in 1850, later drifting with theatrical troupes to other cities, including Toronto. Thus familiar with theatrical custom, Thompson experimented in Pittsburgh during 1875 with the writing and staging of a variety sketch of provincial Yankees, the source for his 1876 comedy, *Joshua Whitcomb*, written in collaboration with George W. Ryer. An even later expansion, or sequel, also written with the help of Ryer, took the form of a four-act comedy called *The Old Homestead* which was produced at the Boston Museum on April 5, 1886. This final version provided in "Uncle" Josh, "hard as a hickory nut and spry as a kitten at sixty-four," an exclusive role in which Thompson delighted audiences until shortly before his death on April 14, 1911. While the plot is too meandering and the tone too sentimental to suit modern tastes, *The Old Homestead* records the simple village ways of yesterday as localized in Swanzey, New Hampshire, and the nearby town of Keene. Thompson's use of homely details in background scenes (as in the set for the Whitcomb living room, with its large fireplace in which hickory logs are crackling, its old clock ticking in a corner, and bunches of corn, strings of dried apples, and slices of pumpkin decorating the walls), in his pictures of lively village customs (a New Year's party of relatives and friends, with country fiddling for the dancing of the Virginia Reel, and a sleighing party) and in the creation of old Joshua possibly influenced, as did Herne's provincial folk, "the great vogue of rural plays in the last decade of the century."[93]

Herne's relationship with Thompson, perhaps mutually beneficial, and with zealous leaders—notably Howells, Hamlin Garland, editor B. O. Flower, and Mary E. Wilkins Freeman—in the then radical crusade for realism moved him not only to dramatize the folk with realism but fearlessly to publicize (in Flower's *The Arena*, February, 1897) his critical credo in "Art for Truth's Sake in the Drama." Believing that "truth is the essential of all art," Herne seriously considered the truthful play, at its best a perpetuation of the life of its time, to be based on the principles of selectivity and of what he called realistic "character *business*." While Herne's adherence to truth appears most convincingly in *Margaret Fleming*, his 1890 drama of marital infidelity, then a bold fictionalization, his Uncle Nat Berry and fellow villagers of *Shore Acres* point toward the imaginative use which he made of a real town: Lemoine, a small place on Maine's Frenchman's Bay, where he and Mrs. Herne (Katharine Corcoran, gifted actress) summered.[94] Out of his friendly association with the Lemoine folk and later with Long Island villagers Herne developed two comedies of coastal towns, *Shore Acres* and the less successful *Sag Harbor*, his last play.

Originating in 1888 as *The Hawthornes*, this first folk comedy gradually changed after Herne personally associated with the people at

Lemoine. While none of his characters are drawn directly from the Lemoine villagers, all are easily recognizable by their local wisdom and prejudices as realistic representatives of the Down Easters of the 1890 era. (Katharine Corcoran Herne inspired the creation of Ann Berry, whose husband Martin was based on the lighthouse keeper at Berry Village.) The best characterization is that of wise and sympathetic Uncle Nat Berry, Martin's elder brother, a role played successfully by Herne for five years. A kindly, Christian bachelor, Nat serves as a self-sacrificing mediator, both within the troubled Berry household and in the village at large. Losing the girl he loved, and the family property as well, to Martin, Nat finds happiness in assisting others. Nat's broadminded views, sharply contrasted with Martin's intolerance, enable him to assist in the elopement of Helen, his niece, with "free-thinkin'" Dr. Sam Warren; to thwart Martin's grandiose schemes for real estate speculation with "Shore Acres," the family land, which includes their mother's burial plot; and eventually to save the lives of the eloping lovers. Greatly angered at his daughter's elopement, Martin, in a melodramatic scene, tries in vain to prevent Nat's lighting the beacon to guide Captain Ben Hutchins, on whose boat, the *Liddy Ann*, Nat had helped Sam and Helen to take passage.

Though it has the same Dickensian heart appeal that dominates all the Herne plays, *Shore Acres* reveals its author's once daring modernism and his progress as a playwright of ideas, deeply moved by the discussions of the group of "radical" intellectuals with whom he sympathized. Herne's daughter Julie reports that at their family dinner table the animated talk between the Hernes and their guests ranged far and wide, including fictional art, socialism, impressionism, evolution, the nebular hypothesis, Ibsen, heredity, and Henry George's theory of the Single Tax. Thus Herne's best plays reflect various ideas current during his time. For example, *Shore Acres*, unusual for its time, connects the hazards of young love with serious social problems affecting even village life: the land boom and speculation in the lighthouse village of Berry, near Bar Harbor; the rebellion of youth asserting its rights to work out its own destiny unobstructed; religious narrowness; and liberal thinking about evolution.

Herne's emphasis on ideas (a technique too seldom used in the Yankee plays) and on realism of character is coupled with verisimilitude in stage directions and in presentation of small-town ways characteristic of the Frenchman's Bay area along the Maine coast. If he fails to show the influence of the region on character, still Herne effectively portrays such small-town characters as a grass widower, the postmaster and storekeeper, the skipper of the *Liddy Ann* and his crew, plain folk, like hired girls who "kinder work around," Martin as keeper of Berry Light and speculator, and "upper crust" villagers such as Squire Andrews. Uncle Nat, sixty but sturdy of frame, is the ultimate in the long line of stage Yankees. Of the soil, he nevertheless has "an inherent poise and dignity about him that are typical of the men who have mastered their environment."

Herne's interest in village ways continued through his final play, the four-act *Sag Harbor* (1899), named after the picturesque old whaling port not far from Herne Oaks, his Long Island home. Accordin to Miss Herne, the quaint sayings and little human touches of this comedy are based upon her father's daily experience. "While sailing his boat on Great Peconic Bay, he became interested in the hardy 'bay-men' . . . who earn their livlihood 'scallopin' winters and sailin' comp'ny summers." Frequently he talked with a local skipper, and often he would anchor and visit one of the little bay towns, where he discovered a village life so much like that of New England, yet so distinctive in its own right, that for this final effort he used the background and the atmosphere "of a drowsy Long Island of twenty-five years ago [i.e., from 1895 to 1897], its leisureliness, its vivid interest in other people's affairs, its utter peacefulness."[95]

Sag Harbor, a reworking of the popular *Hearts of Oak*, not only dispenses with melodramatic episodes such as those which weaken the plot of *Shore Acres*, but further exemplifies Herne's striving for truth. From its first production at Boston's Park Theatre in October, 1899, with Herne as Cap'n Dan Marble, retired sailing master, the comedy appealed to large audiences in Boston, Chicago, and New York largely because of the simplicity and utter naturalness of the Sag Harbor background and its independent "fisher folk."[96] A familiar triangle situation—Martha Reese's marrying Ben Turner, though she really loves his younger brother Frank, a sailor—is less effective dramatically than the realistic scenes of the nautical townspeople busy with workaday chores in Ben Turner's picturesque "little country shipyard," by the wharves, or in shops along Sag Harbor's main street. The village women, young and old, are especially well drawn as they go about their household duties in their small, quaint homes, sing in the choir on Easter Sunday and at other times, or wait at the wharves for their seafaring men. Between Uncle Nat Berry and tanned, fiftyish Cap'n Dan, cheerfully singing chanteys, there are close resemblances. Alike in speech, manner, and character, both are the last of our notable "hempen homespuns" responsible for the longevity of our folk comedy.

Each is of the soil and is well versed in regional folklore. Each, though possessing comic appeal, has far more poise, dignity, and tenderness than preceding stage Yankees and other rustics. Moreover, each, blessed with folk wisdom and tolerance, acts in the role of community arbiter, a sort of local "do gooder". In these, as in other stage creations, Herne went beyond the achievements of his predecessors in establishing, among our stage folk types, believable realism of character.

Ostensibly from the New England and Middle States to the lower South, in the long period from 1770 until after the Civil War, a hardy substratum of American humor brought entertainment to readers and spectators alike through a multiplicity of lighter plays. During these years the repeated demand for an American literature, one facet of the nationalistic movement which had its start in the eighteenth century, produced varied and popular dramatizations of ordinary scenes, of provincial characters never before staged, and their colloquialisms. William Cullen Bryant, speaking on the art of poetry before members of New York's Athenaeum Society during April, 1826, ended his third lecture with the thought that if our poetry should fail to rival that of Europe, "it will be because Genius sits idle in the midst of its treasures." Certainly Genius was not at work in the production of our Yankee plays and their parallels; yet the early literary discovery of the commonplace revealed public interest in "the Real and the Present—in local manners and dialects, in larger cultural patterns inherent in the ceaseless push westward."[97] Without doubt, the stage Yankee, however much distorted, owed much of his lasting popularity to his personification of our cherished trait of self-reliance. Stage figures could be matched easily with real personalities. "If I were asked to select a model Yankee," wrote Dr. T. L. Nichols in 1864, "I should take the late Horace Greeley," who, as a young New Hampshireman just arrived in New York, "was tall, lanky, near-sighted, awkward, with a large head, white hair and eyebrows, a very white complexion, and scarcely any beard." Dressed "in a suit of blue cotton jeans," Greeley was "the owner of two brown shirts, and had five dollars, his entire savings, in his pocket. But he knew his trade, . . ."[98] And there is no mistaking the regional identity of Emerson's choice of the self-sufficient American: "A sturdy lad from New Hampshire or Vermont, who in turn tries all the professions, who teams it, farms it, peddles, keeps a school, preaches, edits a newspaper, goes to Congress, buys a township, and so forth, in successive years, and always like a cat falls on his feet, is worth a hundred of these city dolls."[99]

III. Idealized Rusticity

Romantic Vogues Influencing Village Dramas

FOR ALL ITS OVERUSE of the ludicrous, the Yankee theater in its heyday succeeded in celebrating native small-town and farm characters—Down Easters, Georgians, Virginians, and their counterparts in other states—as stage versions of democratic and free people. Concurrently, romanticism stimulated some of our native playwrights to follow, in the dramatization of native materials, a many-faceted approach which included themes of the idyllic village. Apparently early theater patrons enjoyed the vogue for picturesquely scenic villages, for "seats of rural felicity," and for the thrills, even the horrors, of Gothic supernaturalism, as much as they did Yankeeisms, Negro and cracker dialect, and the dramatized exploits of Davy Crockett, Colonel Sellers, and other applauded heroes. Appearing on our stage were village types, often used as symbols of "the rising glory of America," which personified rural ease and happiness, together with appealing re-creations of American legendary figures—the most successful example being the several characterizations of Rip Van Winkle and his fellow villagers.

If advertisements of current plays may be taken as one limited gauge of popular taste, the printed lists of play titles once issued by enterprising William V. Spencer, Boston bookseller and publisher, partially record the romantic tastes of nineteenth-century American playgoers and readers. For example, his 1855 bargain list, advertising 703 plays at 12½¢ and 25¢ each, includes many adaptations of romantic foreign novels and original dramas. Such titles as *Rob Roy Macgregor, Bride of Lammermoor*, and *Guy Mannering* suggest that Scott's American popularity had not waned, even as Walt Whitman began sounding his "barbaric yawp over the roofs of the world." Moreover, Dickens' *Old Curiosity Shop*, the *Witch of Windermere, Belphegor, Bombastes Furioso, Mary Queen of Scots, Lady Godiva*, Otway's *Venice Preserv'd*, the Byronic *Sardanapalus*, and Bulwer's *The Lady of Lyons* (in which Mrs. Mowatt starred as Pauline) all indicate the popular clamor for sentimentality, romantic love, the supernatural, and heroic tragedy. Certain plays, such as Charles Dance's *The Victor Vanquished* and John Madison Morton's *Our Wife; or, The Rose of Amiens*, reprinted in Spencer's Boston Theatre series, are romantically foreign rather than

American in their settings and characters.[1] Perhaps spectators enjoyed a sort of escapism as they viewed spectacular drops picturing a Swedish baron's Gothic chamber, a picturesque villa in the English Lake District, a French shop in the time of Cardinal Richelieu, a rocky place on the Cornwall coast, a small town *shebeen* (tavern) in Galway, and Rhine landscapes with grotto baths and Gothic halls.[2] The few village titles which intrude in Spencer's list seem all but lost in his larger advertisement of plays with more picturesque or exotic settings. These provincial titles, however, though as generalized as *A Village Tale* and *Miller of Mansfield*, do suggest the variety of our early theatrical fare. And one must also consider the fluctuations of public taste, wavering then between Francomania and other vogues for foreign romanticism, farces about the "common man," and idyllic representations of our villages, conventionally romanticized as rural haunts of the American muse or as peaceful, smiling havens "rising on the green."

The idyllic interpretation of the American village had a broad background in the other arts which influenced the drama. In poetry, Philip Freneau's *The American Village: A Poem*, originally published in New York in 1772, is the first village poem, so far as is now known, to be written by a native poet of exceptional promise. In trying to fit village scenes of his own new world and disturbed era into the pastoral pattern of pre-Romantic tradition, especially Goldsmithian in design, Freneau pioneered in providing conventional bucolic pictures whose counterparts were to be found, shortly thereafter, in native romantic plays. Timothy Dwight's *Greenfield Hill*, written in 1787 but not published until 1794, idealizes our village society, picturing it as blessed with every virtue. These and other early appearances of the romanticized village in American poetry were significant mainly as a sign of the times; they contributed to a romantic trend which affected early playwrights as well as poets.[3]

By 1790, in New England as in adjoining regions, about 85 per cent of the entire population lived in towns of less than three thousand inhabitants, and by the close of the "Golden Day" thousands of small communities dotted all regions east of the Mississippi.[4] Such communities attracted the attention of note-taking travelers, native and foreign, whose published descriptions often featured the more appealing aspects of the little town. In 1838, for example, Harriet Martineau, in her *Retrospect of Western Travel*, which followed by a year her critical *Society in America*, wrote: "The villages of New-England are all more or less beautiful. . . . They have all the graceful, sweeping elm; wide roads overshadowed with wood; mounds or levels of a rich verdure; white churches, and comfortable and picturesque frame dwellings."[5]

And Washington Irving confessed, in "The Author's Account of Himself," which formed the first part of instalment No. 1 (May 15, 1819) of *The Sketch Book*, his youthful delight in spending holiday afternoons rambling through the Hudson countryside, near his New York home. The fertile little valleys, the encircling mountains, the deep Hudson, and the glorious skies left him with the impression that "on no country have the charms of nature been more prodigally lavished."

But early "passionate and romantic creations" of the village, as well as of the land itself, were not confined to words. Landscape painting added still further to the vogue for the romantic. As early as 1800, when romanticism had already brought new life to the arts of Europe, a few American artists gradually began "to succeed to the inheritance of European landscape painting."[6] Among the American romantic painters was English-born Thomas Cole, friend of William Cullen Bryant[7] and founder of the Hudson River School. His paintings stirred the imagination by their depiction of shadowy glens and contrasting sunlight on mountain tops, delicately leaved trees, mossy oaks, and gnarled decaying treetrunks; the upland clearing and rustic hut above a rushing waterfall; and rocky gorges and poetized figures.

The genre painters, a somewhat later group of artists, served as a link between the early Hudson landscapists and the later realists. Two of these, like others less well known, extended the geographic limits of American landscape painting, George Caleb Bingham by his graphic scenes of river life on the Missouri and the Mississippi and the people on the farms near these rivers, and William Sidney Mount by his provincial Long Island materials. Each regionalist caught the spirit of American democracy in paintings of the ordinary activities of the common man, in town, farm, or river environments. Paralleling small-town political dramas, Bingham's "The Verdict of the People" truthfully interprets the holiday exuberance of voters during an election celebration.

More appealing than any paintings to popular taste and pocketbook were the great number of Currier & Ives lithographs, dated from 1834-35 to 1898, which, sometimes garishly and sometimes sentimentally, recorded innumerable phases of mid-nineteenth-century life in the United States. The partners, Nathaniel Currier and James Merritt Ives, disliking empty landscapes, published prints crammed with details of many phases of American life: outdoor work and sports, such as farming, trapping, hunting, fishing, and whaling; city activities, such as fire fighting, horse racing, driving through Grand Central Park and other amusements; shipping, railroading, and politics; American dwellings, from the castellated Hudson mansion to the log hut in a western clearing; and many other aspects of the changing national scene.[8] In 1868-69 the firm issued a series of prints romantically picturing modest homes in rural or village settings as typifying the American dwelling and "the plain, solid common life of the people." These seasonal views of different homesteads proved to be best sellers, and did much to popularize the romantic concept of the American home.

Finally, architecture and landscape design developed during the same period in ways consonant with the vogue for the romantic. During the mid-eighteenth century the most popular architectural style, embodied in the imposing homes of northern merchants and southern planters, had been that borrowed from Renaissance English Georgian. Then an entirely new trend grew out of Colonial admiration for the villa and palazzo architecture of the Italian Andrea Palladio.[9] By the early nineteenth century a growing interest in smaller Italian villas affected British domestic architecture. By 1816 John Haviland, a British architect-author, had come to Pennsylvania, where he carried out commissions in different styles, including Greek Revival details and Italian designs. The various architectural experiments of another Philadelphia architect, John Notman, included designs for an orientalized version of the villa. But there were also those who battled against the inappropriate use of borrowed styles. In 1848 Louisa C. Tuthill of New Haven published her *The History of Architecture*,[10] in which she argued that "domestic architecture [and gardens] in this country must be adapted to the circumstances and conditions of the people."[11] Picturesqueness, she maintained, should be blended harmoniously with utility, whether applied to a farmhouse, a village cottage, or a "charming country-seat."

At mid-century, too, Andrew Jackson Downing, son of a nurseryman of Newburgh, New York, was influencing public taste by books and articles on horticulture, landscape gardening, and rural and village architecture. Downing's spirited and lively books and articles gave new impetus to Italianism during the 1840's and 1850's. As a landscape gardener, he acquired patrons belonging to the richer classes; yet in his popular *Rural Essays*[12] he spoke out boldly against exclusiveness in America. In 1841 he published *A Treatise on the Theory and Practice of Landscape Gardening Adapted to North America*, in which he insisted that harmony between the country house and its setting was an important factor in planning. Ideally the terrain should match the design. Rolling country with trees was, he thought, more appropriate to the Greek Revival style, whereas the more picturesque Gothic Revival was better adapted to uneven or rocky backgrounds. Irregular adaptations of the Italianate villa could be fitted somewhere between these extremes.[13] Widespread interest in Downing's ideas as expressed not only in this book but also in *Rural Essays* and *Cottage Residences* (1842) furthered the vogue for landscape gardening. And his interest in developing a sense of local attachment, security, and repose among his naturally restless countrymen, through his designs for flower beds, lawns, hedges, trees, and arbors, parallels the idealized portrayals of village felicity in contemporary drama. His principle of harmony appealed, in its simplicity, to the imagination of those playwrights who wished to picture the peaceful village or quiet country town.

"Seats of Rural Felicity" and Other Romanticized Villages

Simultaneous with these idealized interpretations of native scenes and people in the various other arts was the creation of an incipient drama expressive of a wide range of romantic tenets.[14] From Barker's tragic *Superstition* (1824) until the Civil War, both comedies and tragedies embodying romantic themes, scenes—foreign and native— and plots enjoyed a stage vogue. The playwrights in this brief display of literary creativity made use of many motifs: court intrigue and ill-fated love, as in George Henry Boker's artistic *Francesca da Rimini* and other plays of foreign background; the lively escapades of royalty illustrated by Washington Irving and John Howard Payne's comic *Charles the Second*; military and athletic triumphs, typified by Edwin Forrest's vigorous enactment of the role of Spartacus in Dr. Bird's spectacular *The Gladiator*; the romantic Indian princess and Powhatan's village stronghold of Weorocomoco as interpreted in G. W. P. Custis' *Pocahontas*; and the varied struggles of the common man, or woman, as in the *nouveau riche* Tiffanys of *Fashion*, in old Febro of Bird's *Broker of Bogata,* in Willis' usurious Tortesa, and in the most unfortunate Zoë of Boucicault's *The Octoroon*. In contrast to this imposing array of romantic plays, and many more besides, there were only a few dramas idealizing the American village and its surrounding countryside; yet each is a contribution, however ephemeral, to the romantic vogue in our theaters. The cult of the picturesque left its mark on a few plays set against various backgrounds of pastoral hamlets and long-established villages rich in folklore. Most such plays appearing before and during our "American Renaissance" pictured the East, since that area, with the wilderness beginning not too far west, was then almost synonymous with American civilization.

Pastoralism flourished quite early in the drama of native village life. Throughout those Yankee plays describing the antics of rustic lads adventuring in the city, the contrast between metropolitan society, with its many excitements, and peaceful village and rural ways is a familiar motif. Also, rustic simplicity and sentiment, at first British in tone and subject, in popular imported plays enabled the Hallams, John Hodgkinson, Isaac Bickerstaff [e], William Macready (after 1820), and other entertainers and promoters to catch the fancy of American audiences. Allardyce Nicoll, describing British taste, during the last years of the eighteenth century, for plays featuring dingy caverns, moldering graves, and rococo ruined castles, notes that "The sentimentalism, the medieval atmosphere, and the bold treatment of unusual themes were all apparent in England before ever Kotzebue and Schiller reached our shores; . . ."[15] He might have added another strain of feeling, actually a phase of sentimentalism, associated with these pre-Romantic trends: the delight in rural simplicity. British plays featuring village worlds proved popular with our colonial spectators.[16] John O'Keeffe's comic opera, *The Poor Soldier*, for example, was so popular in this country that repeated performances were given from December, 1785, until 1787, when it was published in Philadelphia.[17] Typical of the vogue for the simple life are O'Keeffe's *World in a Village*, Bickerstaffe's *Love in a Village*, William Macready's *The Village Lawyer, or Ba! Ba! Ba!*, Thomas Morton's sentimentalized *Speed the Plough* ("hovering on the borderline of serious comedy and frank melodrama"), together with his *Town and Country, or Which is Best?* (a great favorite with Charlestonians), and Benjamin Nottingham Webster's *The Village Doctor*.[18] In addition to these repeatedly performed plays, others on the boards celebrated village sports, country girls, love in humble life, and comparable aspects of community fun and happiness. Evidently the dramatic appeal of the bucolic, from the 1780's until after the Civil War, was uniformly strong in Boston, New York, Philadelphia, Annapolis, Baltimore, Charleston, and elsewhere.

One of the earliest American plays shaped in accordance with popular British models and devoted primarily to the agricultural village is aptly entitled *Rural Felicity* (1801). Its author, New Yorker John Minshull, is remembered mostly as a once industrious writer of farces, which were rejected by the management of the Park Theatre. Angry at such exclusion, Minshull associated himself with the Summer Theatre in Bedlow Street, where *Rural Felicity* was introduced to the public —for one performance—on January 15, 1805.[19] No doubt Minshull's moralistic theory of the drama, as stated in the preface to this comedy, was reason enough for his lack of success with the Park manager. Describing *Rural Felicity* as a dialogue in rhymed couplets and prose, Minshull envisions the theaters of his day as mirrors for reflecting virtue and vice to divert the mind from "the bottle, cards, or dice"— amusements "Oh! horrible to think of." His aim seems to be to prove "the effect of deviating from the general principle." ("Oh! view with horror! then blush who game,/ When by your conduct destroy your fame.")

Using the then popular device of a prologue, Minshull gives a brief exposition of his village scene and plot:

> Preludes vary at the Author's pleasure,
> This pictured scene is drawn from rural treasure;
> Where virtue guides and prudence leads the way,
> The village comic scenes we here display.
> The country blossom charms the city blade;
> Join'd in wedlock's interest, they invade
> The arrogant foe. . . . [20]

This, obviously, is a "conduct" play, centering around Mr. and Mrs. Clover, their daughter, Clara, who is in love with the visitor Constant, and their son George, who sings love lyrics to Constant's sister, Juliana. In the Prelude a father-son dialogue, patently modeled on the advice Polonius offers the departing Laertes, concerns the son's adopting a moral code of conduct. Minshull includes a dig at "critics who destroy" in his reference to the youth's composition of a drama and his fear of public censure. In her turn, Mrs. Clover advises Clara to "be distant, or blame/ Your own conduct [and suffer] blushes of shame." The most realistic note in the play, aside from another Yankee Jonathan's futile courting of his ladylove with a vigorous rendering of "Yankee Doodle," is revealed in Clara's spirited rebellion. "An old maid," she declares heatedly, "is as useless as a china figure on a mantel-piece." Accordingly, she boldly uses the speediest means possible to insure her own "rural felicity." Her plan, in fact, seems quite modern: "Then can you blame me? *Neck or nothing*; I'll have my man as mama had before—." Minshull completes his pattern of idyllic happiness with a further note of moralizing from Clover, urging George to devote his leisure to reading Laurence Sterne, possibly his sermons rather than the fiction, and Bishop Young's *Night Thoughts*, this advice being another echo of Minshull's prefatory plea for "rational literary amusement" as a tool against "the vice and folly of the age."

Although Minshull was but one man in his time and an insignificant playwright at that, it may be that his *Rural Felicity*—or perhaps it was merely the spirit of the 1840's—prompted J. B. Buckstone, the British comedian whose mannerisms were studied by Joseph Jefferson, to produce at the New Charleston Theatre on May 4, 6, and 12, 1840 a play entitled *Rural Felicity, or Life in a Country Town*. Was this comedy an adaptation of the Minshull play, or was it a new composition by Buckstone, who seems to have been industrious both as a traveling comedian and as a playwright? Perhaps the latter is true, for William S. Hoole, in his *The Ante-bellum Charleston Theatre*, lists twenty-six plays attributed to Buckstone, while Jefferson found him important enough to justify his devoting space in his *Autobiography* to a criticism of his talents as comedian and including a full-page portrait.[21]

Irving begins "The Pride of the Village," one of the romantic tales of *The Sketch Book*, with a description of an excursion he once made to a remote English shire: "I had struck into one of those cross-roads that lead through the more secluded parts of the country, and stopped one afternoon at a village, the situation of which was beautifully rural and retired. There was an air of primitive simplicity about its inhabitants not to be found in the villages which lie on the great coach-roads." Such a village, with its spacious green, its towered church and adjacent graveyard, modest houses, and agricultural pursuits, can be matched in American romantic drama. Mrs. Mary Carr's *The Fair American*, published in 1815, is such a play. Except for certain realistic treatments of war episodes, the play, by and large, is romantic in its idealized re-creation of "one of those sequestered spots" along Lake Erie which charms by its picturesqueness. Erie Village, until disturbed by skirmishes during the War of 1812, was indeed a pleasant country town, with its simple rural pleasures and holiday pastimes. Mrs. Carr's directions for painted backdrops of the lake and the village, as well as her use of lyric interludes, tend to glorify humble life, especially in connection with the ordinary occupations of the villagers. Her simple folk, rich in their happiness and their picturesque situation on the shore of "beautifully romantic" Lake Erie, are extolled for their exemplary domestic industry. But the "fair Americans" (village girls and their rustic heroes alike) suddenly lose their "smiling peace" with the killing of the folk and the burning of their homes as British regulars and their Indian allies attack the village. Here, indeed, is dramatized pastoralism, with "rural quiet and village simplicity" coupled with war episodes, typifying, in Irving's words, "the present rage for strange incident and high-seasoned narrative."

For the opening scene of *The Forest Rose; or, American Farmers* (1825), Samuel Woodworth gives explicit directions for a romantically designed backdrop, suggestive of a landscape painting in its distant view of a small place in New Jersey, beautified by surrounding woods and fields. The plate, or face, of the not too distant village clock, a substantial farm cottage at the edge of the town, and its neatly fenced yard are the precise details for the painted design in place at curtain rise, when musical exposition—the overture by John Davies described in Chapter II—enhances the effect of a quiet, rural atmosphere. Following the overture, a trio sung by the principals, Lydia, Harriet, and William, contrasts the city's "bustling crowds" with rural New Jersey's natural beauty, where "in rich profusion,/ Autumn's yellow bounties swell." Such rusticity prevails throughout the comedy and suggests country and village scenes lithographed later in the more sentimental prints by Currier and Ives.

During the period from the 1740's until the early nineteenth century British pre-Romantics, by their poetized emblems of death, as in *Night Thoughts* (1742) and *The Grave* (1743), and their weird imaginings of dismal mansions, ruined and haunted castles, murky corridors and caverns, and moldering graves—popularized by *The Castle of Otranto* (1764), *The Mysteries of Udolpho* (1794), and other tales of terror —set in motion a vogue for the fantastic, replete with aids to melancholy, medieval machinery, and supernatural terrors. The effects of this new sensation were so far-reaching as to influence, with native modifications, the growing spirit of romanticism in American poetry, the novel, the short story, and eventually the drama. Edward Young's and Robert Blair's melancholy and macabre poetry had an imaginative American counterpart in Freneau's visionary "The House of Night; Or Six Hours Lodging with Death," powerful verses first published in August, 1779, in the initial volume of *The United States Magazine*, of which Freneau was editor.[22] The opening lines of the first version of the poem—"Let others draw from smiling skies their theme./ I sing the horrors of the house of night"—reveal the poet's serious reaction at this time against his own youthful pastoralism. Freneau's lurid, yet imaginative, vision was a poetic prelude to native imitation of a foreign fashion, the Gothic romance, during our Federal Era (the 1790's and later). Like British readers, some Americans apparently found thrills in eerie descriptions of hooting owls, yawning trapdoors, ghosts in armor gliding along stone floors with spectral clank, damsels swooning on secret staircases (as in *The Mysteries of Udolpho*), balls of fire rolling around the best-regulated houses, sinister figures in black cloaks waiting at dark corners to waylay impetuous gallants, imprisoned maidens (victims of parental cruelty) secluded in isolated convents or even ruined abbeys, and other stock properties of Gothicism.[23]

Gothic combinations of strangeness with terror, most bizarrely manifested in William Beckford's *The History of the Caliph Vathek* (1783, 1786), were reflected, but with considerable modification, in Charles Brockden Brown's novels, the first American ones of any literary value. From his first published novel, *Wieland, or The Transformation* (1798) through 1801 when the two-volumed *Jane Talbot* ended his brief career as novelist, Brown tested his own abilities at revamping British and German formulae.[24] Moreover, he combined foreign motifs with native materials, such as the Indian and the frontier matter in *Edgar Huntly* and the indigenous second subtitle, *An American Tale*, of *Wieland*. His selection of ordinary homes in familiar native settings, his use of unusual wonders of nature scenically expressive of the "western wilderness," and his emphasis on certain pseudo-supernatural powers—ventriloquism, the spontaneous combustion of the elder Wieland's body, sleepwalking, and others—are typical of his ways of molding or reshaping foreign Gothic patterns to suit his American materials. Also, his graphic descriptions of primitivism—rugged mountains, ravines, waterfalls, savage Indians, and wild animals—long antedating Cooper and his contemporary landscapists, early quickened public interest in the romantic representation of natural American wildness. Brown set the romantic stage for the American "renascence of wonder" which appeared in Irving's delightful folktales and culminated in the Gothicized settings of Poe's stories.[25] And along the way, as this trend of romanticism gained momentum, a few playwrights portrayed the American village as affected by supernaturalism and kindred elements accountable for the popularity of the Gothic novel.

Out of a profusion of early nineteenth-century tragedies and melodramas, often scenically staged in keeping with the vogue for spectacular panoramas and dioramas, a few plays romantically re-created the American village at some historic phase. As we have seen, a number of such plays interpreted the life of Puritan towns or of other villages under the impact of war. Often the action took place against a romanticized background of primitive nature and supernaturalism. Barker's *Superstition* with its village setting, a lonely spot in the midst of a wilderness, uses the menacing power of nature as a romantic device to heighten the atmosphere of supernaturalism, evidenced in the general fear of "the powers of darkness." In the tragic finale (Act V) a wood shown with darkened stage, a raging storm with thunder and lightning effects, and the confusion of the trial within the church, now arranged as a hall of justice, serve to dramatize further the supernatural horrors of witchcraft. Comparable romantic effects are achieved in Cornelius Mathews' *Witchcraft; or the Martyrs of Salem*, a later drama of terror whose first staging (Philadelphia, 1846) coincided with romantic developments in landscape painting and garden designing. In his presentation of the tragic destiny of accused Ambla Bodish and her son Gideon, Mathews creates interest by contrasting the harmony and seasonal beauty of nature with the evil supernatural properties attributed to natural phenomena by superstitious, deluded Salemites. Ambla's cottage, on the outskirts of the village, harmonizes well (in the Downing manner) with a beautiful natural panorama of nearby woods, fields, and meadows. Gideon, under normal conditions a lover of the out-of-doors, is a romantic solitary roamer through the woods and meadows near the village. Thus, although primarily Mathews is dramatizing Salem's witchcraft craze, he manages to cast an aura of romantic pastoralism, so popular during his own time, over the Puritan community of his tragedy.

Contemporary with *Superstition*, Judah's *The Battle of Lexington* and its 1840 counterpart, Conway's *The Battle of Stillwater*, as well as Howe's *New England Drama*, variously portray Gothicized disturbances within the framework of American small-town life. Secret marriages, seductions, mysteries heightened by disguises, lovely but crazed village Ophelias (sweetly singing songs of lament), cottage homesteads usually remote from other village dwellings, and even one scene of mountain wildness—these motifs, properties, and stage designs create from play to play a semi-Gothic atmosphere for tales of familiar American village environments. The intrusion of such popular, or debased, romanticism is well illustrated in the mountain scenes in *New England Drama*. Here Howes places a realistically imagined Yankee trader, with his large family, against a painted backdrop of a romanticized mountain retreat high above a center of trade, the village of Becket. His village pictures, Yankee realities contrasted with Gothic displays of lightning (superstitiously feared as hell's brimstone) and reverberations of thunder, typify the long-continued and popular practice of superimposing Gothic elements, however incongruous, on dramatized interpretations of our little towns.

One romantic play of the late thirties was based on a poem portraying a Massachusetts witch. In 1832 Carter & Hendee of Boston published *Moll Pitcher*, Whittier's first long poem in book form, which was republished in 1840 as *Moll Pitcher and The Minstrel Girl*.[26] Long interested in New England legends, Whittier chose for this poem an unusual heroine, a Yankee witch (not to be identified with a similarly named female cannoneer of Revolutionary times) who disturbs a young girl by falsely foretelling her lover's disaster at sea. Consequently, in 1839 when energetic Dr. Joseph Stevens Jones hastily composed his sensational "tale of the 1790's" called *Moll Pitcher; or The Fortune Teller of Lynn*, the legend of Moll had already been publicized through Whittier's poem. According to his own testimony, Dr. Jones produced a hit in his four-act melodrama, which after its initial performance, on May 20, 1839, at Boston's National Theatre, was "played in every State of the Union in which theatrical exhibitions have been given; and, with one or two honorable exceptions, from stolen and mutilated copies of the original."[27] Jones defines the nature of his action-filled play by calling it a "stage drama," depending for its success "more on what is *done* than *said*."

"This hectic glow and these melo-dramatic screamings"—thus, in *Democratic Vistas*, Whitman decried the spectacle of our national life in 1871, whose low moral, cultural, and political tone appalled him. In its earlier time, Jones's *Moll Pitcher*, primarily a series of melodramatic episodes, is a theatrical display of a "hectic glow." Its widespread popularity, brought about by the demand during the thirties for farces and melodramas, would have been viewed by Whitman as a cheapening of public taste. Almost nothing is presented of the old harbor town of Lynn, on Massachusetts Bay, and its venerable craft of shoemaking. Certainly in this play there is nothing as emblematical of Essex County's manufacturing progress as Emerson's symbols (used in "The Poet") associated with a political parade of New England towns, where "Lowell goes in a loom, and Lynn in a shoe, and Salem in a ship." To Jones, however, the world apparently was not emblematic, as it seemed to Emerson. In *Moll Pitcher* romantic action, at times Gothicized, is paramount. Lynn, nearby Nahant, and Boston are presented largely by picturesque backdrops. Scenes presenting a moonlight view of Egg Rock at Nahant, a landscape of Lynn, Moll's house, a deserted mansion, and the old Charlestown bridge in Boston create a romantic atmosphere for this tale of the 1790's.

Moll Pitcher, the pivotal character, is "an old hag" whom superstitious sailors consult about their voyages. Moll's usual costume—a dark bodice, red petticoat, an old red cloak thrown carelessly over her shoulders, an iron-gray wig topped by a mobcap and a sailor's hat, her crutch and spectacles—contributes much to her witchlike appearance. Appearing and reappearing mysteriously at crucial moments in the action, Moll, for both good and evil, affects the fortunes of Lynn's townspeople and of certain strange pirates and smugglers.

Both the witch and her cottage are familiar sights to the people of Lynn and to the sailors. The latter, desiring her blessings, flock to Moll's cottage to have their fortunes told. The natives are convinced that Moll is

"Satan's agent" familiar with the tricks of necromancy. Jotham Hook, Jr., witty son of a local constable and shoemaker, says that "She'd look a fat hog into consumption in five minutes." Even her leaving and returning home are under Satan's control, for, says Jotham, when Moll's away "the old cat's tail sticks out, sou-and-by-east." The fate of any townsman who stoned the cat was dreadful. Peter Wilson, guilty of throwing a stone, experienced multiple evils. "His pigs died, his hens laid rotten eggs, his potatoes never got ripe, and all his children afterwards were marked with a black cat as nat'ral as death."

Jotham's Yankeeisms furnish a humorous evaluation of Moll's supposedly satanic powers; her own soliloquies give insight into her vengeful personal nature. In one such outburst of cynicism, when by eavesdropping she has learned of a smuggling and kidnapping plot, Moll expresses her contempt for men and reveals that the "devil" which helps her in a private warfare against them is knowledge of their secrets. What the witch knows about her fellow citizens, for good or evil, motivates much of the plot. Here are Gothic thrills galore: shipwrecks, a young lover's double identity, threats of piracy and smuggling, a haunted mansion with secret passageways to the sea—in Jotham's description, "the terror of the town" with its "Groans!—ghosts!—and dead men . . . Midnight horrors"—and the disturbing mystery of Moll Pitcher's past life. For a grand finale Jones furnishes a revelation about Moll's birthplace, a foreign (possibly Italian) village once plundered by ruthless invaders whose leader seduced Moll. And now in her old age, Moll (really Mary Diamond) recognizes and exposes as her seducer of long ago the rich smuggler Maladine, who has renovated Lynn's haunted mansion as a center for his activities.

Whitman, pleading for a superior national literature for the United States, had much to say about the tastes of audiences. "Books too reflect humanity *en masse*, and truly show them splendidly, or the reverse, and prove or celebrate their prevalent traits . . . "[28] Certainly the popular interest in Gothic embellishments, even for village plays, was not conducive to the development of the strong American literature envisioned by Whitman; yet it does attest to one of the vogues, then prevalent, a delight in supernatural theatricalism.

"The Regnancy of Rip Van Winkle"

"Of village architecture we have never had any in the country worthy of the name. There is not a village in the land whose streets, so far as their buildings are concerned, would ever tempt a painter of discernment to linger and make drawings." This quotation could well be from some of the spirited debunking which marked the modern "revolt from the village" during the 1920's. Not so; rather, it is a caustic report by Charles H. Moore, a critic during the Gilded Age, who in 1899 found the raw materials for landscape art in the United States generally unpromising. Fortunately, he made a few exceptions, granting somewhat grudgingly that

In the old Dutch settlements of New York, a substantial though rude style of building prevailed in which there were attractive elements of the picturesque. Houses wrought of native stone, with roofs of tile, having hospitable porches shaded by creeping vines or climbing roses to shelter their doorways, with bright bits of garden hard by, and groups of embowering trees, — all bespeaking an ameliorated and contented life, — existed in numbers along the banks of the Hudson a quarter of a century ago, and some of them still remain.[29]

Fortunately, too, it was such a picturesque Dutch community, rediscovered on a memorable rainy day of reading Irving's quaint story of Rip Van Winkle, that assured Joseph Jefferson of the end of his search for a stage character especially suited to his talents. During that summer vacation of 1859 the young actor and his family were boarding "at a queer old Dutch farmhouse, at the foot of Pocono Mountain, in Pennsylvania." And on that drizzly day the wild scenic valley harmonized with his thoughts as he lay on the hay in the barn loft reading *The Life and Letters of Washington Irving*. Finding, with a thrill of pleasure, a passage where Irving mentioned seeing him in a comic role at Laura Keene's theater, Jefferson suddenly recalled the magic name of Rip Van Winkle. But his quick rereading of the tale proved disappointing. For the actor the theme was interesting, but it was not dramatic. The rich description of the "silver Hudson" and of "the quaint red roofs and queer gables of the old Dutch cottages [which] stand out against the mist upon the mountains" was most appealing, but, alas, Rip spoke not ten lines. "What," Jefferson mused, "could be done dramatically with so simple a sketch? How could it be turned in to an effective play?"[30]

Actually no dramatization of the story has approached Irving's unforgettable "Rip Van Winkle" either in artistry of style or in the vividness of the village and Catskill scenes. According to theatrical history, however, ". . . it is the actor, rather than the dramatist, who has vied with Irving in the vitality of characterization and in the romantic ideality of figure and speech."[31] The refashioning of Irving's kindly but sottish old Dutch ne'er-do-well, derived from German folklore of the Harz Mountains and from old wives' tales, into the very appealing role of the Boucicault-Jefferson version is decidedly a dramatic evolution. Various playwrights and comedians, ranging from hack writers to comic artists, contributed successively to the complex history of Rip's dramatization. John Kerr, Charles Burke, James H. Hackett, James A. Herne, and, most memorable of all, Jefferson and Boucicault, added version by version to an evolution which stemmed from *The Sketch Book* (1819-20) and ended in 1865. Moses, noting the sharp difference between the mechanical framework of the Kerr version and the living portrayal by Jefferson, is right in saying, "It was only when the dry bones were clothed and breathed into by the actor's personality that the dramatization has lived."[32]

Jefferson's toying with the idea of new dramatic possibilities in the Van Winkle sketch led first to a stopgap, a disappointing three-act interpretation which he composed and shortly thereafter presented in Washington. Further work on the play was pushed aside for almost five years of wandering and acting, years which included a successful Australian tour. In 1865, as Jefferson arrived in London by way of Panama, his ideas about a better play began to crystallize when he learned from the crotchety manager, Benjamin N. Webster, that his engagement at the Adelphi depended upon his offering a new play. His meeting at this point with Dion Boucicault was most fortunate, for Webster had turned down Jefferson's Washington version of "Rip Van Winkle." Overcoming Boucicault's objections to the staleness of the Van Winkle story and consenting to his introduction of Rip as a "young scamp, thoughtless, gay," Jefferson finally agreed with Boucicault's proposals for a fresh dramatization. The result was eminently successful for "the transatlantic kid," as Jefferson was nicknamed by an Adelphi comedian. The new play, with Jefferson giving an inimitable performance as Rip, opened at the Adelphi on September 4, 1865, for a run of 170 nights. (It was not produced in New York until September 3, 1866—and then at the Olympic—or in Boston until May 3, 1869.) This composite drama was the culmination of long continued, and generally bad, experimentation with Irving's materials, some versions of which Jefferson remembered from his boyhood.

The origins of *Rip Van Winkle* as a play are obscure. As William Winter once wrote, "It is, perhaps, impossible to ascertain who made the first play that was ever acted on the subject of 'Rip Van Winkle.' "[33] Today, however, any reader curious about the genesis of Jefferson's reconstruction should turn to the detailed research of Winter, Moses, and Quinn.[34] The earliest known version of the tale of the North River Dutchman was a dramatized sketch, *Rip Van Winkle; or, The Spirits of the Catskill Mountains* (by an unnamed adapter, possibly a local citizen), produced on May 26, 1828, at the South Pearl Street Theatre in Albany. Thomas

Flynn, a friend to the Booths, starred as Rip, while Mrs. Flynn, for whose benefit the performance was given, appeared as Rip's daughter Lowenna and Charles B. Parsons as Derrick. In this early sketch, as in the later Kerr and Burke versions, the love affair of Knickerbocker, the village schoolmaster, and Alice, Rip's sister, was featured.

Probably Parsons, the actor-clergyman in the Albany production, used a stock characterization typical of early American theatrical practice when he appeared as Rip in Cincinnati in 1829. The theatrical manager Noah M. Ludlow notes a Louisville performance on November 21, 1831, and records further that as early as the summer of 1828 he bought from an actor friend in New York an anonymous manuscript copy of *Rip*, which he produced the next season in Cincinnati.

The talented Jeffersons are brought into the limelight quite early. On October 30, 1829, at the Walnut Street Theatre, Philadelphia, Elizabeth and J. Jefferson supported William Chapman in his role as Rip.[35] There is doubt, says Moses, as to whether the play was Ludlow's or a first draft by the British-born John Kerr, himself an actor. Winter and Quinn, however, offer evidence in favor of Kerr's authorship.[36] A public announcement, cited by Winter, features a supernatural element in a Gothicized title: "Positively for the last time, a new melodrama, founded on Washington Irving's celebrated tale of *Rip Van Winkle, or the Demons of the Catskill Mountains.*" This title tallies with that on the Lenfesty edition noted by Quinn. On the title page of that undated version may be found the imprint of the Lenfesty Circulating Library of Philadelphia (active until 1835); a patriotically appealing second subtitle, *A National Drama*; and a notice of authorship, "Two Acts, by John Kerr."

Jefferson's most popular predecessor in the character of Van Winkle was Hackett, who acted the role, based on the Kerr play, as early as April 22, 1830, at the old Park and again on August 10 at the Bowery. It was about this impersonation that Sol Smith wrote in his *Theatrical Management*, "I should despair of finding a man or woman in an audience of five hundred, who could hear [his] utterance of five words in the second act, 'But she was mine vrow' without experiencing some moisture in the eyes."[37] Later, during a visit to London in 1832, Hackett became familiar with an adaptation by W. Bayle Bernard, possibly a revamping of Kerr's play for the British actor, Frederick Henry Yates (1795-1842). The uniqueness of this version, as Jefferson mentions in his *Autobiography*, is that Rip dies. On his return to New York, Hackett used this Bernard dramatization at the Park on September 4, 1833, in the same season in which John Hewitt's three-act interpretation was presented in Baltimore, starring the third Joseph Jefferson as Van Winkle. Years later, in 1887, Hewitt recalled the singularly Gothic aspects of his adaptation, especially manifest in his introduction of the "Mountain Spooks"—Captain Hendrick Hudson, Hans Dundervelt, and an eerie elfin crew. Also, Hewitt staged the bowling game amid properly Gothic noises: "sheet-iron thunder, rosin lighting, and weird music." The managers, he recalled, were "unable to raise a chorus of dwarfs"; accordingly, they expediently picked up at a Baltimore wharf a ship's crew of "jolly jack-tars" to sing the chorus accompanying the noisy game.[38]

By mid-century Charles Burke (1822-1854), "natural born comedian" familiar with earlier versions, turned his critical attention to the Irving tale and to the possibilities of adapting the role of Rip Van Winkle to his own talents. Studying most of all the Kerr reconstruction, but having familiarity also with the pieces played by Flynn and Parsons, Burke eventually produced his own two-act play, which was announced at the New National—or New Chatham—in New York, January 7, 1850.[39] As his title suggests, Burke's "Romantic Drama" presents the legendary aspects of Irving's story.[40] At the National, Burke, as Rip, appeared in company with his half brother, Joseph Jefferson the fourth, as Knickerbocker, ex-schoolmaster of the Dutch village. During the summer of 1850 at the Arch Street Theatre, Philadelphia, Burke impersonated Rip, but Jefferson took the role of Seth Slough, the innkeeper in the new town to which old Rip at last returns.

In his autobiographical criticism of the successive Van Winkle dramatizations, Jefferson wrote "that Burke's play and performance were the best . . . " After Burke's untimely death Jefferson, remembering the "deep and strange affection between us," praised his brother's many gifts: his subtle, incisive, and refined effects in acting, his range from the most natural comedy to pathos, and his expressive eyes and features, as well as "a voice that seemed to come from the heart itself, penetrating, but melodious." His "rarest histrionic genius," Jefferson recalled, was marked further by his excellent taste in singing, his other musical talents, and his achievement of dramatic effects more from intuition than from study.[41] On the other hand, as Jefferson confessed, " . . . nothing that I remembered gave me the slightest encouragement that I could get a good play out of any of the existing materials." Actually, although Jefferson and Boucicault finally evolved a more ideal and universal interpretation, they were to owe credit to their predecessors, notably Kerr and Burke.

The Kerr, Burke, and Boucicault-Jefferson versions, however varied, all have one thing in common: their picture of the community of Sleepy Haven—the Dutch *Die Slâperig Hafen*—at the mouth of the Pocantico, at Tarrytown. (The name of Sleepy Hollow, originating with the

English, is now applied to the whole valley of the Pocantico.) Moreover, all three make dramatic use of the picturesque mountains of the Kaaterskill, which were as familiar as the village itself to Irving's Diedrich Knickerbocker, the ostensible author of the original story who gave sly hints about "a little German superstition about the Emperor Frederick de Rothbart and the Kypphauser Mountain."[42] (Local belief long persisted that a certain rocky gorge marks the spot where Rip is supposed to have slept.)[43] In all three plays a peaceful Dutch village during the reign of George III (up to 1783) comes to life in both public and domestic scenes. Both Kerr and Burke people the village and the wild and isolated mountain area with a relatively large number of identified villagers and supernatural beings, while the Boucicault-Jefferson version reduces the chief characters to ten, with the demons or dwarfs and unidentified villagers as extras. All supply essentially the same stage directions, pictorial enough to suggest the old-time ways of Dutch provincials. For example, Kerr, in Act I, scene 1, offers these stage details: "A straggling village with a small house of entertainment, bearing a sign with the Head of George the Third, whose name is underwritten. A rustic table and three chairs in front. Vedder, Knickerbocker, and Rory at table, drinking and smoking." To a similar scene of happy rusticity Boucicault and Jefferson give a romantic place name, the "Village of Falling Waters, set amid familiar and unmistakable Hudson River scenery, with the shining river itself and the noble heights of the Kaatskills visible in the distance." This description and others, especially the mountain scene for Act II, bear the Jefferson stamp and are closely linked with the versatile actor's avocation of landscape painting, in which he excelled to the extent of having several public exhibitions in Washington.[44]

In these plays the supernatural is introduced theatrically against a backdrop of mountain wildness. In each action Rip departs voluntarily for the freedom of the Catskills to escape his scolding "frow." Lured beyond familiar ground by taunting laughter and weird voices calling his name, Rip ventures at last into a lonely, moonlit glen. Here, to his amazement, are grotesque Dutch figures—in Burke's case some of the "demons" are personalized as Swaggrino (The Imp in Kerr), Gauderkin, and Icken (Kerr's Sprite)—engaged in diverse entertainments: bizarre dancing by the sprites, drinking from flagons, smoking, card playing, and playing Dutch ninepins and battledore and shuttlecock. The stunted trees, fragments of rock, and rising moon all contribute to the supernatural atmosphere of "this wild recess." The awesome silence is unbroken except for a chorus sealing Rip's fate: "Twenty years in slumber's chain,/ Is the fate that we ordain."

At the beginning of the second act, Rip, after awakening from his strange sleep, expresses his confusion in a somewhat colloquial and long prose monologue. Scene 2, against the background of the new town of 1783, dramatizes the change in Lowenna's (Lorenna's) emotions from happiness over Gustaffe's return from voyaging to despair over the harsh stipulations of the marriage contract. Kerr dramatizes her loneliness since her mother's death and her dependence upon the Knickerbockers. Burke adds humor through a different situation. The former shrew, Dame Van Winkle, now the wife of irascible Nicholas Vedder, appears as thoroughly subdued and miserable. Another of Burke's additions, a verbal parallel to Bingham's "The Verdict of the People," is Act II, scene 3, dramatizing the economic aspect of town growth (the change of the romantic village of 1763 into a populous town) and the rowdy excitement of a local election.

Almost identical pictures of eighteenth-century merrymaking in the Sleepy Hollow community open the spirited action in the Kerr and Burke versions. A simple set, the serving area fronting a small house of entertainment, accentuates a gay aspect of Dutch conduct. Here at Rory's tavern easygoing burghers relax, smoking, drinking, singing, dancing, and gossiping. At curtain rise Rory's companions loudly chorus a drinking song in praise of the wine of the Rhineland. Their merriment—"So laugh, ha, ha! and dance the hours away"—sets the tone for the first appearance of Rip Van Winkle, changed from his former prosperous position into "one of the laziest, good-tempered, idle, drunken, careless, best hearted fellows that ever lived," according to Kerr's Clausen. (Burke's Vedder merely refers to Rip as "a thirsty soul," always on hand when there's a cup of good liquor.) In each play young Knickerbocker, now clerk to Burgomaster Derrick Van Slous (Deidrich Van Slaus in Burke's cast) and the lover of Alice, Rip's sister, warns the merrymakers to "cut no jokes on Rip."

Before Rip's belated arrival, however, introductory exposition about Dame Van Winkle portrays her as a waspish hausfrau, a proper dramatic foil for her indolent and genial spouse. All of Kerr's first characterizations of "mine frau" tally with Rory's condemnation of her as "a she-devil" and Knickerbocker's belittling of her as "Beelzebub in propria persona" and a termagant deserving to be sold to the first bidder, if such a daring soul exists. Burke's Rory—"the dame's tongue is a perfect scarecrow"— and Nicholas Vedder—"The sound of her voice sets them running just as if she were one of the mountain spirits, of whom we hear so much talk" —while seeing the dame as a natural enemy to all who love a jollification, early introduce the supernatural motif. And in each version

Knickerbocker resents the shrewish dame's objections to his courtship and her calling him "a long, scraggy, mongrel-bred, outlandish animal . . . [looking] like two deal boards glued together." In short, Dame Van Winkle, as portrayed by Kerr and Burke, lacks the refinement of the Boucicault-Jefferson characterization. With vociferous expletives (typified by "Odds bodikins and pins!"), she rants at husband and neighbors alike in the slapstick style often found in Yankee comedies and burlettas of the period.

Her shrewishness rises to new eloquence when the improvident Rip saunters in most naturally, with gun and empty game bag. Highlighting Rip in favor of his own acting and singing abilities, Burke features him as singing, in dialect, a satiric song warning all single fellows against matrimony. (Somewhat later in the action Kerr portrays Rip as singing, to the accompaniment of his wife's cursing, "When the wife once wears the breeches.") Kerr heralds Rip's initial entry by offstage singing. Then Rip enters with careless walk and at once jests about his idling, drinking, and ruination of his good intentions. Vedder had been afraid that "some of the elfin goblins of the mountains had got hold of you." But Rip responds genially by drinking his usual health to the village families: "Here is your goot-hell ["go-to-hell" in Burke], unt your family's, unt may you all live long and [prosper]." Both adapters enliven their scenes with the tall tales of local folklore, Kerr stressing Rip's familiarity with ghost tales about "old Daddy Hudson's ghost" and a pirate who, in order to save his cache of gold in the Catskills, bargained with the devil to return every fifty years. And Rip's exaggerated report on his hunting trip, dramatizing his shooting "one old bull" (rather than a duck for the family pot) and the enraged animal's sending the luckless hunter "flying more as a mile high," is hilarious tall tale yarning which was well suited to Burke's comic talents.

Both plots progress similarly as the result of a tricky marriage contract drawn by the embezzling burgomaster, Derrick Van Slous (Derric Van Slaus), and signed by the unwitting Rip. If within twenty years Rip does not disclaim their mutual agreement, his young daughter Lowenna (Lorenna) then will marry the burgomaster's son Herman, or forfeit to him her inheritance from a wealthy aunt. Also in each plot, after the passage of the twenty years Knickerbocker (then Alice's husband as well as the present burgomaster and a prospective legislator) uses his political influence to assist the aged Rip, but that day returned, in thwarting Herman's design to carry out his dead father's contract. Each playwright resolves the conflict by a court trial during which Rip identifies himself in various ways and restores his daughter to her worthy lover Gustaffe, a native villager but now a sailor. Burke's enactment of old Rip's bewilderment and almost futile efforts to establish his identity has been highly praised, especially in his speaking of Rip's notable line: "Are we so soon forgot when we are gone?" (Boucicault incorporated this passage later in his version.) John Sleeper Clarke, a fellow comedian who heard Burke deliver this entire passage, gave unqualified praise:

> . . . no other actor has ever disturbed the impression that the profound pathos of Burke's voice, face, and gesture created: it fell upon the senses like the culmination of all mortal despair, and the actor's figure, as the low, sweet tones died away, symbolized more the ruin of the representative of a race than the sufferings of an individual: his awful loss and loneliness seemed to clothe him with a supernatural dignity and grandeur, . . ."[45]

Boucicault and Jefferson, combining talents, produced a three-act revision of moderate excellence, but one admirably suited to Jefferson's wide range of histrionic power. In every respect their play was a vitally improved variation in a long tradition; yet "the regnancy of Rip Van Winkle, the fact that the character has become a part of actual life, is due to the stage."[46] Indeed, when "our incomparable Jefferson" bestirred his imagination the happy-go-lucky vagabond of tradition became an essentially new character, which in the second act assumed poetic qualities. In fact, Jefferson's impersonation (by 1882 performed 4,500 times) created the illusion, says Winter, that the bewildered Rip "is a dream-like, wandering poet of the woods."[47] During Boucicault's week of hard rewriting and improving the Burke version handed him by Jefferson, the latter suggested artistic changes and additions.[48] The characterization of Rip in both young manhood and old age has been mentioned earlier. Other suggestions made by Jefferson included the creation of the second act devoted to Rip's experience in the Catskills, the maintaining of an awesome silence by the specters during the midnight meeting on the mountain, and the idea that in this eerie scene only Rip should speak. Boucicault accepted Jefferson's ideas, but himself favored a second marriage for Dame Van Winkle, as Burke had done, and adapted the recognition of Cordelia, in *King Lear*, to a scene of pathos when Rip's daughter (here rechristened Meenie) is reunited with her long absent father. Moreover, Boucicault gave Dame Van Winkle both "a local habitation and a name" when he called her Gretchen and, in early scenes, described her cottage. Such varied revision resulted in a sensationally successful village play, a domestic tale, marked by "the sweet, tender humanity and the weird spirituality" lacking in all the earlier versions.

Repeatedly critic-spectators of Jefferson's performances mentioned his genuinely empathic portrayal of the changing images of the Dutchman. His rare powers of representation apparently showed best in his ability to catch the tricks of Rip's power of thought—to measure his mental capacity. Spectators remembered Jefferson's understanding of the physical and the inner differences between the young and the old Rip— the differences in costume, gestures, action, and language. He pictured young Rip as a good-humored, careless, affectionate, loitering, yet shrewd fellow, with children hanging all about him and dogs following. The children give the key to the man and actually plead for him, in the midst of his idleness and maudlin folly so exasperating to Gretchen. "Shiftless, reckless, drunken he may be," recalled one spectator, "but not bad . . . . He, after all, is a child."[49] (The pathos of Rip's love for his daughter culminates in the third act in his fearful consciousness that Meenie does not know him.) And the speech of this hearty, solid, large-framed villager is colloquial; his actions are lazy and commonplace. His fondness for his dog is commonplace enough. For one theatergoer, "No wholly imaginary object was ever more palpably real than the dog Schneider. And he is made so by a word or two from Rip [that is, Jefferson]."[50]

Still another contemporary spectator felt that the part of Rip was "a profound study in language and movement," as Jefferson himself realized.[51] In his introductory note to the play, Jefferson tells of his insistence, as Boucicault was writing, that the old Rip of the mountain—"the guest of ghosts"—must not be prosaically portrayed. After Rip's encounter with the mountain spirits, in the third act, "the play drifts from realism into idealism and becomes more poetical." And with this change comes a shift to a more dignified and reflective language. After the awakening Rip appears withered, shrunken, white-haired, tattered, but still something of his former self.[52] His patient effort to comprehend, without the least tendency to suspect the truth, and his intolerable sense of desolation—the wish that he were somewhere else—are offset by a calm self-reliance, albeit mixed with simple awe in the presence of the "demons." Through Jefferson's histrionic skill, Rip displays a constant wary mastery of situation, though he talks incessantly, never loudly or hurriedly, as if the sound of his voice reassured him. Such was the impression which Jefferson gave, without declamation but with varying natural tones and looks, of a simple townsman who, under strain, displayed something of heroic human nature.

Certainly the Van Winkle material seems to have been regarded, for several generations, as common property. But Jefferson, with Boucicault's assistance, suggested the potentialities of the Irving legend, enriched the romantic aspects of colonial village life among the Catskills, and offered an individualized character study divested of all staginess or sensationalism. This retold story of a sleepy Dutch community along the Hudson touches upon things basic in human experience. Thanks to Jefferson's art, "fact and fancy; youth and age; love and hatred; loss and gain; mirth and sadness" became convincing in his exposition of "a humorous, cheering, romantic, restful human character."[53] In other words, the regnancy of Rip Van Winkle is due largely to "the triumphs won/ By our incomparable Jefferson!"[54]

And the legend of Rip Van Winkle, however much revised and recreated, has continued to appeal to the artistic mind, even into the twentieth century. Early in 1919, Cleofonte Campanini of the Chicago Opera Association arranged with Percy MacKaye and Reginald DeKoven for an operatic version of the Van Winkle story and its production in Chicago, New York, and elsewhere during the 1919-20 season. Allowed entire freedom in the treatment of their material, both the poet and the composer completed the text and music of a three-act folk opera within a few months.

In devising this opera, MacKaye felt the same liberty as his predecessors "to develop the ancient legend in accordance with the nature and needs of the new work in hand . . . " Thus readers or spectators, in comparing this folk opera with Irving's original tale or its various dramatizations, will find more differences than resemblances. As MacKaye has noted, he made two contributions which modified the old legend: "the creation of a new character, Peterkee [a dreamy girl who delights in accompanying Rip when he goes fishing] and the introduction of a new element in the plot, the Magic Flask." While referring to his changes as differences, MacKaye has admitted that these really are not set apart but spring directly "from that initial wonder of feeling which the images of Rip and Hendrick Hudson — and the echoes of summer thunder in the mountains — have never ceased to stir in me since the early, absolute belief of my childhood."[55]

MacKaye, with able assistance from DeKoven, gives the poet's imaginative handling of an old story. His Shelleyan nature lyrics—such as "Kaaterskill,/ Cloud on the Kaaterskill!" and "The King of the Mountain sleeps"—the humorous Dutch work songs and Dirck's lusty chanteys, the deep-toned choruses of the "Shadow Sailors" of Hudson's *Half Moon*, the dim Fairy Shapes (with "soft, child-pitched voices") peeping at the slumbering Rip, and the numerous villagers "clad in Dutch garb of the Eighteenth Century" are presented against picturesque backdrops.[56] There are seven of these, depicting village, forest, and mountain scenes. In keeping with Irving's familiar descriptions, the Dutch community of Acts I and II presents an effective study in contrasts, with the same scene altered somewhat by the lapse of time. The little town to which Rip returns, after his supernatural adventure, has none of the drowsy quietude of the old-timey village green, shaded by an immense elm, of Act I, but bustles with a new energy. Life in "the blue-green river-valley" has undergone as much physical as social change. The quaint porched church of long ago still stands but is partly overgrown with ivy. The "tree which shades the Inn is visibly larger; over the door of the Inn floats a flag, with thirteen stars, and a new swinging sign—painted with a crude portrait of an officer in uniform—shows the lettered inscription: 'The General Washington Inn.' "[57] Even the children are different. The fun-loving youngsters who were Rip's fishing companions in the long ago are replaced by a hooting and jeering crowd of children, who mock the outlandish Rip Van Winkle (now an "old, tattered, graybeard form") with their antics, while they shout in shrill chorus:

> Tatter-taggle-twitch!
> Dump him in the ditch!
>   Lodge him with a moor-mouse,
>   Board him in a bag o' stuffin',—
>   Ragamuffin! ragamuffin!—
>   Pack him to the poor-house!
> Witch! Witch! Witch!

Some of our early romantic stage portrayals of the small town have much kinship with the once popular "town and country biographies of the nineteenth century [which] reflect a kind of never-never land of wealth and gentility that never, alas, quite existed. The editors had but one style, the adulatory, for paying subjects, which transformed every struggling farmer into a 'prominent agriculturist' and every village law-giver into a Pericles."[58] But whether their playwrights were given to over-glorification or to some show of realism, the plays just surveyed, representative of but one cycle of dramatized rural and small-town life, imaginatively re-create a flourishing countryside with many small farms and reconstruct different types of romantic villages. Puritan towns, Revolutionary villages disturbed by war, legendary Sleepy Hollows, and busy little agricultural centers, sometimes vitalized by small industries, all reflect some form of village felicity. By and large, these romantic plays, mostly comedies, are reflections of current social and cultural interests. As Brander Matthews has said, such dramas

seized and concentrated certain of the floating characteristics of the many atoms of American life, presenting them before us with the rigor and the vigor of a photograph,—sometimes the pose has been chosen with more taste, sometimes the photograph has been more skillfully manipulated than at others; at best, the result is mechanical and lacks the "freedom of art."[59]

Nevertheless, the "exquisite art" of Joseph Jefferson transformed the familiar scenes of Sleepy Hollow into something memorable and Rip Van Winkle into one of the most appealing of our folk types.

IV. "To the West! to the West!"

" . . . of beginnings, of projects, of vast designs and expectations"

"A FEW GENERATIONS ago," wrote naturalist Stewart Edward White in 1905, "wilderness exploration, wilderness taming, was one of the world's great needs."[1] This questing temper, this outreaching spirit, refusing to take things for granted or accept them ready-made and insisting on constructing a new way of life directly from raw materials, had its most dramatic manifestation in the ample physical wilderness of the American West. To the west "the naked forces of life" fanned the frontiersman's "inextinguishable passion to go on, to explore, to see what is beyond."[2] By the mid-1820's trappers, scouts, such as Jedediah Smith, Joseph Walker, and Kit Carson, and other hardy adventurers had pioneered beyond the Rockies into California. Afterward diverse caravans pushed westward from Independence, Missouri, and other places of departure toward the Pacific. During the early forties other adventurers, braving Mexican rule, ventured into California along the routes blazed by lusty Mountain Men. In increasing numbers emigrants moved either by the Oregon Trail with some branching off, by Sublette's Cut-Off, to Salt Lake, or followed along the east side of the Sierras and crossed the mountains by way of Walker Pass.[3] Others chose the southerly overland route across Texas, while hundreds cut short the tedious and dangerous passage "round the horn" at the Isthmus of Panama and, there disembarking, endured the arduous trek through jungles to the Pacific. By these and other established routes, so many came that as early as the mid-forties crude and isolated settlements, lonely markers in a vast and mysterious land, appeared as symbols of the American pioneer's adaptability and hardihood. From the Mississippi to the Pacific these hastily built little towns represented something more than a mere prospecting for resources. As Lewis Mumford has said, the long-continued "westering" which brought them into being "was an experimental investigation of Nature, Solitude, The Primitive Life; and at no stage of the journey, however much the story may be obscured by land-booms and Indian massacres and gold rushes, did these things drop out of the pioneer's mind."[4]

But the western frontier experience, a stirring dramatization of personal experience as national experience, proved far more realistic than a vague dream of solitude and freedom deep in the minds of a westering people.[5] As migration increased, slowly the pioneers' dreams of new Utopias were reshaped by the immensity and the variety of the land itself. Indeed, the physical shapes taken by the wilderness beyond the Mississippi were as numerous as the travel routes and the varied pioneer types who passed over them—Anglo-Americans, Europeans, Mexicans, South Americans, Australians, and Chinese.

Stretching from Texas to North Dakota and westward to the Rockies, the vast plains country—monotonous in its levelness—offered the first challenges to the overlanders. Its light rainfall, causing alternately turbid streams and mere dwindling threads of water, its immense stretches of coarse, short grass eventually broken by gray sage-brush plains and tracts of strangely shaped and colored Bad Lands (in summer sun-scorched wastes and in winter a bitterly cold, desolate area), and its scarcity of trees were all natural symbols of agricultural sterility which had to be met with prodigious labor and sacrifice. Once beyond the monotonous plains, the emigrant saw the formidable Rockies, their slopes covered by forests of varying density, their streams, rivers, and cataracts turbulent, and their highest peaks snow covered. Southwest of the Rockies the far-stretching alkaline deserts—"mere waterless wastes of sandy plain and barren mountain, broken here and there by narrow strips of fertile ground"—were for the homesteader, however glorified his dream, more menacing than promising, except falsely during mirages.[6] Fortunately, beyond the deserts surviving pioneers found "the sunny sierras of California, with their flower-clad slopes and groves of giant trees; and north of them, along the coast, the rain-shrouded mountain chains of Oregon and Washington, matted with the towering growth of the mighty evergreen forest."[7] Such was the wilderness to the west of the Mississippi, beckoning first intrepid white hunters, trappers, and scouts, and stirring the imagination of throngs of settlers and adventurers of all degrees following after. By the 1850's, thousands had risked hazardous overland treks or journeyed by sea far from the comforts of the East.

As each frontier wave lapped westward, sporadic communities were left in its wake. Although such towns, small and usually flimsily built, were all but lost amidst limitless vistas and varied grandeur, they typified a rapidly expanding country "of beginnings, of projects, of vast designs and expectations" which Emerson associated with Young America. In the development of American drama, they served as prototypes for the town scenes, realistic and romantic, produced by a motley group of playwrights, whose appeals to the imagination were as varied as the towns themselves. In the drama, as in reality, there were the stockaded forts, or presidios, scattered along a wide front; busy trading-post set-tlements along the Platte and elsewhere; riotous and usually ephemeral mining towns from Colorado to Nevada to California and Oregon; older Indian and Mexican villages along the Rio Grande in Texas and New Mexico, as well as in California; bustling port and river towns such as San Francisco, or Yerba Buena, and Sacramento, where thousands out-fitted themselves for the diggings; the lusty cow towns of Kansas, Wy-oming, Montana, and Texas; and the later "sod-busting" communities adapted to dry farming, a mode then altogether new. In the actual soli-tary outposts, all products of the wilderness nearly a continent removed from the eastern seaboard, both the more settled villagers and the ad-venturing transients had to meet life face to face. And so it was with certain dramatized western townspeople, the realism of whose portrayal depended upon each playwright's actual experience, or lack of experi-ence, with pioneering and other problems of the early West.

With pioneering came speculation, first in California during the Gold Rush. As wagon trains and boats brought in more and more newcomers, boom-time practices became the order of the day. Dramatist Alonzo Delano, himself a widely known forty-niner, shared in the excitement. "Speculation in towns and lots was rife; and on every hand was heard 'Lots for Sale'—'New towns laid out'—which looked as well on paper as if they were already peopled." His observations, recorded twenty years earlier, closely resemble the satire of *The Gilded Age* (1873), in which Mark Twain and Charles Dudley Warner attacked the wild specu-lation prior to and following the Civil War. According to Delano's satire on the spirit of the forties, a similar speculative mania then spread over the land, "and scores of new towns were heard of which were never known, only through puffs to newspapers, the stakes which marked the size of the lots, and the nicely drawn plot of the surveyor." Dreams of a New Eden dissipated as other confusions arose. "Not a single [Cali-fornia] town," Delano wrote, "was laid out where the title was indis-putable; . . . litigations were frequent. Squatting followed, which resulted, in many cases, in riot and bloodshed." Nevertheless, Delano actually saw certain towns—notably Sacramento and San Francisco—rapidly become "the abode of civilized man." In fact, most of these new towns were scenes of enterprise, notwithstanding the gambling, robberies, and murders which frightened the fainthearted. By 1850 Delano saw Sacra-mento as "a city indeed," with substantial wooden buildings replacing the original cloth houses. There was immense business in miners' sup-plies. The river was lined with ships. The streets were thronged with drays, teams, and busy pedestrians. The stores were large and well filled with merchandise; and long halls, well lighted and decorated with showy pictures, were equipped with magnificent bars and gambling tables. To Delano, recently returned from the diggings, it seemed that "even Aladdin could not have been more surprised at the power of his wonderful lamp, than I was at the mighty change which less than twelve months had wrought, since the first cloth tent had now grown into a large and flourishing city."[8]

Delano, a journalist, was among those New Yorkers who got "the fever of mind for gold" and experienced painful trials in crossing the plains and reaching the California diggings. His graphic travel notes, his letters to the Ottawa (Illinois) *Free Trader* and the *New Orleans True Delta*, his mining town comedies, and various editorial jottings all reflect the harsh realities of trekking westward and of sharing in the recklessness and excitement of the Golden Era. From April 5 until September 21, 1849, when his wagon train halted near the mushrooming river port of Sacramento City, Delano and his fellow Argonauts endured a tortuous, exposed way of travel and saw sights quite at variance with Whitman's romantically imaged "flashing and golden pageant of California." By October 1, when he set out with his load of provisions for the "upper diggings" of the Feather River, Delano was already wise in the ways of pioneering, familiar with its hardships, but hopeful about the promise of "golden California."

His second book, *Life on the Plains and Among the Diggings* (1854), is a vivid review of his experiences.[9] As an Argonaut, he learned all of the formidable perils of the overland crossing: the deep sands of the barren desert, exposure to furious snowstorms, desert heat, floods, hunger and thirst, ague fever and cholera, the perils of the stupendous heights of the Sierras, Indian forays, attacks by wolves, and other dangers. Once in the "Promised Land," Delano—as miner, storekeeper as he had been in Ottawa, and journalist—quickly discovered that the California of 1849-50 was truly "the land of incidents, for you can scarcely make a journey of twenty miles without meeting some adventure."[10] Within a few years, as he gained recognition in the guise of the genial, whimsical "Old Block," Delano, in *Pen-Knife Sketches*, recorded his adventures in the mushrooming towns of San Francisco, Sacramento, Marysville, Grass Valley, Stringtown, and other places where gold and quartz were mined. Playfully claiming "a lineal descent from the great family of Blockheads, so numerous in our community," long-nosed Old Block wrote descriptive "chips" of western town-building, with an authentic flavor of considerable value. These "pen-knife sketches" are Pickwickian notes, mostly humorous, portraying the boom activities of the Gold Rush. "The human circus" which he saw in "the hurly-burly, yearling cloth city of Sacramento," amidst the "Babel of San Francisco," in the quartz-mining village of Grass Valley (in the mountains sixty-five miles northeast from Sacramento), and in other boomtowns is dramatized with remarkable spontaneity in Old Block's rollicking chronicles.[11]

Still another factor was to influence western small-town drama, especially in its scenic design. The varied social conditions out of which these frontier towns grew had their effect on the physical appearance of western homes and other buildings. With the advance of civilization into the wilderness, "roughs among the rough," motivated by a strong desire to own property, usually displayed astonishing energy and force. As Delano observed in booming Sacramento, their "hardy intelligence," their "pluck, energy, and practical knowledge," became evident when the emigrants "planted cities and established civil order upon virgin soil in less than thirty days." Means were speedily adapted to ends. To meet the emergencies of frontier life, townsmen throughout the West hastily erected homes, stores, land and assay offices, saloons, banks, hotels or taverns, churches, occasional theaters, and other structures. Generally such buildings were bad art, expressing the crude artistic aspirations of ingenious homesteaders. Thus, as an eastern architect complained in 1889, in these frontier towns there was a good deal of "architectural masquerading."[12] Since there were no inherited community traditions and townspeople often came from various regions and countries, their buildings were frequently "carelessly compounded of exoteric and heterogeneous elements." Town plans, however, varied from area to area. When Delano arrived in California in 1849, he observed but "few dwellings in the country and those of the most frail and unsubstantial character." The great mass of Argonauts passed a terrible winter in tents or cloth houses. Many, carrying their bed rolls from place to place, slept on the ground. But villages speedily arose. Within that year, in fact, the few adobe huts at Nye's ranch, near Marysville, were added to so fast that when a town was laid out it grew rapidly to over a thousand inhabitants, "with a large number of hotels, stores, groceries, bakeries, and (what soon became a marked feature in California) gambling-houses."[13] Even remote mining camps in the High Sierras (later pictured in *The Danites*) boasted of their saloons. Joaquin Miller once dramatized the miners of one such "New Eden" as crowding "thick as men could stand" around the crackling logs blazing in the fireplace at the Howling Wilderness, a log cabin serving as "battle-field, prize-ring, dead-house, gambling-hell, court-house, chapel, every thing by turn."[14]

A somewhat later journalist, Londoner George Augustus Sala, in making "a grand tour" by rail in 1883 from Chicago to San Francisco, found that the wilderness along the "road to Eldorado" had sprouted "smiling villages, swiftly to ripen into flourishing cities."[15] As he moved westward, meeting en route some of the "roughs," who dubbed him "a dude," and glimpsing isolated towns on the plains and in the foothills, Sala saw more than his lively imagination and the tales of earlier travelers had led him to anticipate. Surprised continually at discovering, on "the threshold of the savage world," signs of a cultured life, he observed plenty to write home. A Missouri town, though content with its status of village, had "a public hall fitted up with a stage and scenery for theatrical entertainments, a daily newspaper, two churches, and three hotels." Council Bluffs, where pilgrims halted on their exodus from Nauvoo, impressed Sala by its Mormon tabernacle. Flourishing Omaha, then established only twenty-six years, promised to be one of the "Cities of the Future."[16] Sala's increasingly strong impression was that Americans tended to make their towns, even at the planning stage, "big things." Unfortunately for such "juvenile American towns," too often "the era of Promise is not always succeeded by the era of Performance."[17] Western streets, he grumbled, "are of monstrous breadth," in the summer "dusty desert" and in the rainy months "a Slough of Despond." Town architecture, "a jumble of all styles," actually had "no style at all." Typically the energetic drygoods merchant erected "a stupendous five-storeyed structure of brick or iron, painted white to resemble marble." But next door to this obvious example of "architectural falsehood" a petty saloon-keeper, or a small grocer, carried on business in a wretched shanty. Then nearby Sala beheld "the colossal granite, or brownstone, or cast-iron premises of the Runnamucca Insurance Company, the Kickafew Express Agency, or the Potawotomic Bank—superb in mansard roofs, Renaissance *loggie*, and 'Corinthian fixings.' " His ridicule of western pretensions to "architectural grandeur" extended further to churches in "the Bedlamite-Byzantine style" and to other falsely decorated structures such as Masonic temples, Odd Fellows' halls, and Hibernian rotundas. Each one was made all the more offensive by nearby advertisements of quack nostrums like Professor Diafoirus's Pulmonic Plugs, and Old Dr. Cure-all's Liver Persuader.[18]

Such strictures about "the face of America," along and beyond the Mississippi, actually represent only the fleeting impressions of a lone British traveler, who in further copious notes about San Francisco, Salt Lake City, and Ogden praised community interest in lectures, concerts, art exhibits, and theatricals, including performances at San Francisco's Chinese theaters and Mormon sponsorship of stage entertainments.

Further records by other chronic sightseers suggest that native and foreign travelers crossing the Mississippi into areas where prairie settlements were already established, or arriving by boat in San Francisco, were not lost in an altogether culturally arid wilderness.[19] For example, as early as 1815 the frontier metropolis of St. Louis, the point of departure for annual swarms of emigrants, was, although isolated in "a vast sea of Wilderness" something of a "tiny island of civilization." On January 6 of that year a few amateur actors, the Thespians, and their friends "witnessed the birth of the [English] drama in the vast territory west of the Mississippi." As reported in the local *Gazette* on February 4, certain young gentlemen of the town, "having raised a dramatic corps, made their debut in the performance of the School for Authors, with the farce Budget of Blunders."[20] Although St. Louis was little more than an isolated, roughhewn town of about two thousand citizens, mostly French and American, amateur theatricals continued there sporadically. It was not until 1818, however, that a professional company, managed by British William A. Turner, arrived. Other managers and actors followed: Noah M. Ludlow, Samuel Drake and family, picturesque Sol Smith, and other troupers. By June, 1827, when James H. Caldwell opened the Old Salt-house Theatre (a reconditioned warehouse) with a popular comedy, Tobin's "The Honey Moon," the cultural tone of the town was rather high for such a frontier place. Some comfortable houses with good furnishings, well-dressed ladies and gentlemen in attendance at balls and other social affairs, and a growing interest in schools, churches, private libraries, the fine arts, and science offset Ludlow's splenetic contention that St. Louis was "surprisingly primitive."[21] So it was also in other progressive towns of the new country, which made rapid and varied cultural advancement in spite of the privations of frontier life. From the forties onward, the "booster" spirit and speculation—in furs in St. Louis, gold and silver in California and Nevada, cattle in the Southwest, and land everywhere—helped to create an optimism which dramatically accelerated the physical growth, as well as the cultural progress, of western towns.

Often in these new towns primitivism, including violence, and the amenities of civilization went together—dependent, of course, upon the nature of the local settlers. During his youth in Oregon and California Joaquin Miller, playwright and poet, felt that western folk fell into two groups. The "noble pioneers," like his own Quaker parents (for many years Miller's father was a schoolmaster and judge in frontier Ohio, Indiana, and Oregon), were generally industrious, honest, and "steady as oak; devout people, who always insisted on building a church and school house, however humble, the very first thing." A contrasting group, "the most depraved and evil element that ever took human form," the convict class from the British penal colonies, "ticket-of-leave men," came pouring in through the Golden Gate.[22] Earlier, Francis Parkman, during his memorable journey of 1846 along the Oregon Trail, saw striking contrasts in the struggling village which had grown up around Fort Leavenworth. On the one hand were the wretched, indolent Indian loungers in calico shirts and red and blue blankets, with their decorations of brass earrings and wampum necklaces. By contrast, neither the manners nor the appearance of the local trader showed any of the usual roughness of the frontier, and his little green and white cottage was tastefully "furnished in a manner we hardly expected on the frontier." Parkman, surprised at the trader's well-filled bookcase, nevertheless took supercilious note of certain tokens of "the rather questionable civilization of the region." A loaded pistol lay on the mantelpiece, and "through the glass of the bookcase, peeping above the works of John Milton, glittered the handle of a very mischievous-looking knife."[23]

Theodore Roosevelt, who experienced the strenuous life long before writing "Ranch Life in the Far West" (1888), sketched most vividly both the wild lawlessness and the more civilized aspects of a "true 'cow town,'" Miles City, at the time of an annual meeting of the Montana Stockraisers' Association. It would be impossible, he noted, to find a more typically "cowboy land" assemblage. "Then the whole place is filled to overflowing, the importance of the meeting and the fun of the attendant frolics, especially the horseraces, drawing from the surrounding ranch country many hundreds of men of every degree, from the rich stock-owner worth his millions to the ordinary cowboy who works for forty dollars a month."[24] Townsmen and visitors jostle one another as they saunter to and fro along the wooden sidewalks, or ride down the dusty streets, or "lounge lazily in front of the straggling cheap-looking board houses." Sullen, watchful hunters in buckskin shirts and fur caps, greasy and unkempt; self-reliant but surly teamsters, "with slouch hats and great cowhide boots"; seamy-faced stage drivers, proud of their high standing in the community; trappers and "wolfers"; desperadoes: gamblers, horse thieves, and even murderous badmen; strong lumberjacks, rough-looking miners and packers; and Indians, too, stalking silently among the others—all have come to do business or to seek "the coarse, vicious excitement" of the town's "flaunting saloons and gaudy hells." If in such early towns of the cattle country men had not then "adjusted their relations to morality and law with any niceness," they held strongly, as Roosevelt had seen, to certain rude virtues. In fact as in the fiction of

Bret Harte and other western playwrights, "Many of the desperadoes, the man-killers, and road-agents have good sides to their characters."[25]

Van Wyck Brooks once claimed that ". . . it is the American village that most betrays the impulse of our civilization . . . "[26] Considering this significance of our small towns, one is astonished that the Anglo-American's impulse to move westward and to adapt himself to the new and often hard demands of life in hastily constructed frontier settlements has failed, to date, to inspire any but a relatively small number of genuinely artistic playwrights. On the other hand, beginning with the Gold Rush era numerous writers, motivated by their own western experiences or acceding to the demands of theatergoers, dramatized nineteenth-century community life in the West. The most notable of these interpreters— Delano, Thomas Dunn English, Bret Harte, Mark Twain, David Belasco, Joaquin Miller, and Charles H. Hoyt—wrote of the exciting life they themselves had experienced as forty-niners or had learned about later as journalists or actors. Indiana-born William Vaughn Moody and Pennsylvania-born Owen Wister, both Harvard graduates, knew the West largely as travelers, while Augustin Daly—a native southerner who won success as a New York playwright and producer—romanticized the West in response to the audience interests of the seventies, as well as in the hope of improving the fading fortunes of the Olympic Theatre, then owned by his father-in-law.[27] During the seventies the Pittsburgh journalist Bartley Campbell, who knew Bret Harte and Joaquin Miller in San Francisco, wrote several dramas of the California frontier. St. Louisan Augustus Thomas is remembered for a series of plays with various state backgrounds, three of which dramatize life in the Midwest and the West. New Yorker Clyde Fitch produced, at the turn of the century, several insignificant melodramas based upon secondhand western materials. In more recent times, with the growth of interest in regionalism, some limited dramatic use has been made of Mormon materials and of various settlements in the early Southwest, as in the Oklahoma plays of Lynn Riggs and in Maxwell Anderson's *Night Over Taos* (1932). Finally, miscellaneous "grass roots" plays—quite apart from the stereotyped Western of radio, cinema, and television—suggest, at least, that regional consciousness still motivates some of our playwrights. Even so, the rich variety of actual western towns remains today only partially pictured in the realm of artistic play-making.

"The full madness of the Rush"

In 1851 Alonzo Delano predicted that "when the history of California shall be written, after time has mellowed the asperities of passing events, the occurrences of the present day will form a singular and strange chapter . . . "[28] As we have seen, Delano was himself one of the most colorful and warmly human raconteurs of the Gold Rush era. A dramatist as well as journalist, Delano was the author of two comedies enlivened by boomtown and mining camp speculation, Indian fighting, and homely philosophy expressed in folk dialogue. His characters include the high and the low: scholars, scientists, lawyers, ministers, merchants, strolling players, prosperous gamblers, faro dealers, prostitutes, vociferous stage-drivers, half-wild hunters, and Indians. Miners, whom Delano did not romanticize, often appear as illiterate and shabby fellows, sometimes victimized by local thieves, drug addicts, and even murderers. One of the earliest of the Western plays, *The Frontier Settlement; or, Scenes in the Far West* (1846) is more descriptive of real pioneering than the several-times-produced *Fast Folks; or, Early Days in California* (1858) by Joseph A. Nunes.[29]

In print three years before Delano turned Argonaut, *The Frontier Settlement* probably grew out of his boyish restlessness in Aurora, New York (his "quiet little outsided, one-horse village" and birthplace), and his subsequent adventuring, from his fifteenth year, in frontier towns in Ohio, Indiana, and adjoining areas. For some years "he sharpened his wits and his appreciation of the American comedy while 'counterjumping' in the 'whiskey towns' of the raw Middle West . . . "[30] Old Block reports that "the itch of [his] inquiring nose led him westward," until by the early forties Delano, by then married, was running a general store at South Bend. It is not known how, or when, Delano first showed his bent toward writing. It is probable, however, that during his years as storekeeper he adapted his own youthful adventures to current rumors and travelers' tales of the Far West, thus composing *The Frontier Settlement*.

The opening wilderness scene, while designated as "a new village in the Far West," could represent the "march of civilization" into frontier South Bend and nearby Indiana communities just as well as into California. The initial backdrop realistically features a small clearing with log houses of simple design and one larger dwelling belonging to a prosperous landowner, Atwood. Later sets simulate a nearby Sioux village, with rude lodges grouped around a larger council house, and a guarded river fort in the vicinity. The remaining sets are more romanticized. Wild forest scenes, replete with waterfalls, dense woods, skirmishing Sioux and Pawnee braves, and their prisoners suggest Delano's dramatic response to the vogue for the Leatherstocking Tales and kindred narratives of frontier adventure.

The villagers, and others, reflect Delano's growing concern with various problems and gradations of border society. Such social appraisal is most convincing in his portrayals of a migratory and improvident gambler's dislike for industrious Atwood; of villagers along an agrarian frontier, afraid of menacing bands of Sioux and Pawnee; of ladylike Alice Atwood and her friend Betty, symbols of village striving for "culture"; of the peripatetic pedant and supercilious Boston pedagogue Nicholas Adverb, the butt of ridicule from anti-intellectual townsmen; and of Captain Sellman, whose soldiers at the Fort may have been suggested by the personnel of presidios along the emigrant trails. Among these characters Adverb typifies the "learned fool," ridiculed because he differs from his neighbors. This "master of all learning" indicates Delano's kinship with Cooper, whose pedantic Dr. Battius (in *The Prairie*) is caricatured for his cocksure reliance on reason and his unswerving faith in scientific classification. Adverb, passionately interested in "the science of grammar," regards the village as "the most ungrammatical place I ever saw." Deploring the degenerate times, he is chagrined that his fellow citizens in "this land of disjunctive conjunctions" mock his efforts at "trying to civilize and teach [them] the rudiments." All that is left to him is preaching "to the half-civilized settlers . . . in the log school-house"; but to no avail, for at sermon's end Adverb's congregation joyously gather in the public square to engage in "unholy sports" of target shooting, quoits, wrestling, and ballplaying.

Delano's most comic character is "a live Hoosier," the boastful hunter and guide, Jacob Jumblejacket. The crude folk sayings and earthy ballad singing of this Hoosier Leatherstocking provoke Adverb to classify him as an unteachable "biped" and "a specimen of primitive simplicity." Jacob's sharp retort reveals quite a different social outlook: "Any man's a fool who thinks he can come here to teach larnin', when he can neither take sight on a rifle nor tell the difference between a coon's track and a woodchuck's. He's parfictly ignorant of human natur'." In the manner of yarn-spinners Jacob claims to "out hunt, out scalp, out jump, knock down and drag out the best man in the settlement." His most drawn-out song, which expresses the spirit of frontier boasting in the exaggerated tone of tall tales, is the best explanation of why Adverb had to renounce his "doctrine of civilizing the uncivilized in the western wilds" and flee to Boston.

> I'm a hunter of Kentucky,
> A roarer from Blue Licks,
> The devil cannot scare me
> With any of his tricks.

With a horn full of powder
And with bullets in my cot,
If I fur to meet 'auld sooty'
I hope I may be shot.

I'm a bull dog at a bear fight,
A screamer at an election,
I can argufy a stump speech
To the height of perfection;
I can grin [shin] down a white oak
Or an ash as well as not
If I can't skin an alligator
I hope I may be shot.

I can lick my weight in wild cats,
I can drink a river dry,
And I can raise a harrycane
In the twinkling of an eye;
I can swallow whole an Indian,
Or a logheap burning hot,
If I can't eat a mammoth
I hope I may be shot.

Delano's second comedy, *A Live Woman in the Mines; or, Pike County Ahead!* (1857) grew out of his own arduous crossing of the plains and his experiences as a forty-niner in Sacramento, Stringtown, and other camps.[31] Hence, his realistic portrayal of these 1849–50 boomtowns (largely tent settlements), with their adventuring throngs and action "founded on fact," somewhat offsets his lack of fine dramatic craftsmanship. Some of the picturesque Californians introduced earlier in the *Pen-Knife Sketches*—Old Swamp, Pike County Jess, High Betty Martin, and others—reappear in *A Live Woman*.[32] Much folk humor comes from a pair of rustic lovers: Pike County Jess, "an open, generous, offhand, uneducated, south and western man—copied from a character I met in crossing the Plains in '49," and mannish High Betty Martin, "a back-woods, western Amazonian." Like the real pioneer women known to Delano, Betty (or Carolina Betsey) is portrayed as "indomitably persevering, brave under difficulties, yet with a woman's feelings when danger is over." The Judge, Stokes, and other miners were Delano's "messmates" at Stringtown, just as the small-town printer Jones is "a true character in name, adventures, and vocation."[33]

The petticoat scene, a side-play of mining camp humor, is mostly true. As reported in "The Miner" (one of the "chips" in the *Pen-Knife Sketches*), the peace of an early Sunday morning in Stringtown was suddenly broken by the firing of a musket and the stentorian shouting of one of Delano's fellow miners:

"Turn out, turn out! new diggins, by Heaven! a live woman came in last night."

"A woman? oh, git out, you're joking."

"No, it's true as preaching. I was prospecting round the camp, and I'll be ———— if I didn't see a petticoat hanging on a limb by a new tent on ———— Bar. I want to raise a company to go and take a look at the animal, for hang me if I've pluck enough to go alone."

In the comedy Pike County Jess praises Mary Wilson as "the prettiest speciment of a live woman I've ever seen in Californy" and tells her of the need for "a live woman for Stringtown." Later, as he is to guide his pack mules down the slippery Feather River trail to Stringtown, Jess wants Mary's petticoat to prove to the miners that he intends bringing "a live woman" to camp. Unfortunately, they doubt his word; yet Old Swamp, while busily frying flapjacks, sentimentally sings (in Act I, scene 6):

> A petticoat flag is the miner's delight
> It awakens sweet thoughts of our mothers at home;
> Our sweethearts and wives to dear memory bright;
> All the girls we will welcome whenever they come.

Although this incident gives the comedy its title, the main plot dramatizes rather sentimentally the misfortunes and eventual success of John and Mary Wilson, whose history parallels that "of hundreds who have come to California." At curtain rise the travel-worn Wilsons, new arrivals in booming Sacramento on this August day of 1850, aimlessly join the excited crowd along J Street. Penniless from mercantile speculation, John and Mary pity themselves as "beggars in a land of splendor." Their dejection makes them "easy pickings" for two rowdy gamblers (Cash and Dice), who try to abduct Mary and pistol John. Suddenly Jess runs up, yelling ". . . let 'er go! no jumping another man's claims in these diggins." Offering them the use of his tent in J Street, Jess persuades the Wilsons to accompany him to the distant Feather River mines and promises to start by daylight with "three mules and a jackass, a greenhorn, and a live woman for Stringtown."

Scenes 2 and 3 repeat the stereotyped rescue motif, with Betsey Martin saving Sluice, a miner who earlier in the J Street Round Tent has been fleeced by Cash and Dice and pushed into a gutter. Revived by a night watchman, he guides Betsey to the post office, actually in operation in 1850, where he reads her Jess's folksy letter urging her to join him at his Stringtown claim. Betsey immediately employs Sluice as her wagon driver to the "diggins."

From this point to the final scene all action takes place in a raw mining town amid the wild, romantic mountains and the deep ravines along the South Fork of Feather River. Stringtown itself is realistically dramatized as "a tent town on the pinnacle of Stringtown Hill," in the opinion of printer Jones "the cussedest hill in all Californy." The realistic sets depict various interiors—the inside of a miner's log cabin and the gloomy interior of the supply store and post office, a lounging place for "the boys" wholly in accord with the primitive background. These scenes of the "diggins" are true to life, for Delano had been there. By contrast, too much sentiment weakens the denouement. Gold is found on the claims which the miners had generously donated to Mary; Jess claims his Betsey ("a true California woman, grit to the backbone"); and Cash and Dice, flogged by the Stringtown miners, are sent to Sacramento to be tried on a murder charge. Yet the sentiment displayed here, as in many other early plays of western town life, is actually typical of the forties. As De Voto once noted, the American consciousness of the forties, in contrast with our modern temper, lacked the sense of tragedy. It had achieved, he wrote, "only pathetics." The popular response to "My Old Kentucky Home," "Oh Susanna," and other favorite lyrics by Stephen Foster, the universal delight in Christy's Virginia Minstrels and various "melodists," "serenaders," and "harmonizers," and the wide appeal of the artistry of Dan Emmett and kindred performers all help explain Delano's turning to sentiment. All in all, says De Voto, "The emotions of the forties were simpler than our own, more limpid, more absolute, and more forthright."[34]

The "Mormon Craze"

Delano pioneered creatively, as well as actually, by bringing into the American theater characterizations drawn largely from the real folk of California's Golden Era. His thoroughly westernized miners, the "live women" of Stringtown, boomtown storekeepers, bartenders, and printers, mule whackers, swindling gamblers, and marauding Indians helped turn the attention of other playwrights to the new towns of the West. As dreams of a gardened desert more and more became a part of the national myth and our western wayfaring spread in various directions beyond the Mississippi, other types of frontier towns came into being. Among these, the Utah and California settlements made by the Mormon Saints and the raw little towns of the vast cattle kingdoms stirred the imagination of a few contemporary playwrights. Dr. Thomas Dunn English (1819-1902) gained much popularity during the forties and later for his ballad "Ben Bolt" and some fifty plays, all mostly forgotten except a three-act comedy, *The Mormons; or, Life at Salt Lake City*. One of the more successful of the "specimens of impudence" caricaturing Mormonism, *The Mormons* apparently was effective enough in its initial production at Burton's Theatre, New York, on March 16, 1858, to warrant "a considerable run at Maguire's Opera House [in San Francisco] in the early summer of 1858."[35] The production at Maguire's, a mixture of caricature and Mormon history, featured thirty-two individualized characters and numerous unnamed Mormons (including the "Destroying Angels" or fanatical Danites), Gentile emigrants, soldiers, guides, and Indians, as well as western folk songs, tableaux, and soliloquies—notably one by Brigham Young describing Mormonism as "a religion which gratifies both veneration and sensuality."[36]

At curtain rise, a moonlit tent settlement in cottonwood timber is enlivened by the joyous singing of Elder Farley P. Pratt and other encamped Mormons. Hopeful that in one more day they will be in sight of "Zion of the Mountains" (Salt Lake City), the Saints confidently sing of their ultimate victory over Gentile foes:

> The Gentiles rage, the Gentiles swear,
> The Gentiles curse us everywhere;
> But soon the Saints will reign alone,
> And Gentile power be overthrown.
>
> Sing, Mormons, sing
> Sing away, with hearts so gay,
> As we travel on the road to Zion
> Shout, shout! brothers, shout.
> Sending the devil to the right-about.[37]

From this opening the melodramatic action revolves around another rescue motif, the attempt to save a youthful Mormon convert, Ambrose Woodville, his wife Lucy, and their friend, orphaned Mary Blanford, "from the wiles and iniquities of the Saints." Hovering near Elder Pratt's campfire are the trapper "Eagle Eye"—actually Mary's Gentile lover, wealthy Walter Markham—Whisky Jake, "a Scout of the Plains," and Chief Dahcomah of the Kiowa tribe, all scheming to rescue Mary and the Woodvilles. Jake shrewdly guesses that Elder Pratt is "makin' up to the gal, too." In fact, English, catering to a public already disturbed by reports of Mormon polygamy and by accounts of rapine and murder by the Danites, unjustly characterizes Pratt as a rascal whose scheme to hang Eagle Eye fails because of the interference of Dahcomah and Jake.[38]

With the second-act shift of scene to Salt Lake City, Jake complains about the Mormons' glorification of their "beautiful Zion," which appeared to him "about ez ugly a plaist as uvver I clapt eyes on. Mean looking cabings, an' scattered at that. 'Taint like no city of any account, I've seed. Whar's the five story housen, an' steeples, and cupolasses, like they have at St. Louis?"[39] Probably Jake's view is in accord with reality, for Captain Richard F. Burton, a visitor in the town during 1862, describes Main Street as "the centre of population and business, where the houses of the principal Mormon dignitaries, and the stores of the Gentile merchants combine to form the city's only street which can be properly so-called. . . . New Zion has not yet built for herself a bazaar or marketplace."[40] Another character from the play, Chatterina Noggs, the first wife of Timothy Noggs, "an impudent, scheming, meddling reprobate," loudly protests against "the deviltry of the place," which makes the town "the nearest approach to the bad place there is in this world." By contrast, Noggs, a ludicrous Gentile with thirteen wives who is determined "to outscheme the wily Mormons," looks upon the new settlement as the town of opportunity. Noggs, a prototype for Mark Twain's Beriah Sellers, optimistically assures Brigham Young and other Mormon hierarchs that he "can put money into your pockets." Arguing for co-operation, Noggs insists that Salt Lake offers opportunities for enriching contracts in railroad building, street paving, city lighting, and other community projects.

Acts II and III, cluttered with episodes of Danite violence, disparagingly picture the City of the Saints as the new capital of scheming Mormon elders bent on empire-building at any cost. The rashly impulsive Pratt is overshadowed by Brigham Young, satirically dramatized as shrewd, calculating, and even dishonest in his handling of public funds. In the tense ritual scene (Act II, scene 2) Young is portrayed with considerable historical accuracy as an imposing high priest, white robed in the center of hooded elders assembled in the Endowment House for Woodville's initiation into the priesthood. Later, when Lucy boldly stops the rites, thus freeing her husband, Young angrily and imperiously threatens death to both of the Woodvilles. But since English was writing comedy on the basis of its emotional appeal to audiences of biased Gentiles, the machinations of the "peculiar people" prove futile. After implausible adventures, the Woodvilles and Mary Blanford are saved from wrathful "Bigamy Young" and the violence of his Danites. The several rescuers—Eagle Eye, Whisky Jake, and Dahcomah—aided by the opportune arrival of a party of U.S. soldiers—triumph over the Danites, while within the town itself thirteen disgruntled wives threaten to tar and feather Timothy Noggs.

Another resourceful playwright who responded to the "Mormon

Craze" was Joaquin Miller. His Oregon and California experiences familiarized Miller with the Mormon War of 1857–58, when Gentiles were ordered to leave Mormon Territory, with the once widely circulated vilifications against Brigham Young and his Elders, and with the shocking tales spread about polygamy, Danite cruelties, and other forms of supposed Mormon fanaticism.[41] By the 1870's, when plays about the West became the vogue, Miller recognized the dramatic possibilities of his *First Fam'lies of the Sierras* (1876), a collection of sketches about the riotous mining towns of the Sierras. Accordingly, with the assistance of P. A. Fitzgerald, a Philadelphia playwright, his *First Fam'lies* was changed into a four-act melodrama, *The Danites, or, the Heart of the Sierras.* At once, from its opening at the Broadway Theatre on August 22, 1877, *The Danites* proved amazingly popular, mainly because of the recurrence of ill feeling against Mormonism stemming from lurid newspaper reports about the illness and the death, on August 29, of Brigham Young. In May, 1878, Thomas Maguire sponsored a not too successful performance of the play at Baldwin's Academy of Music in San Francisco.[42]

The play's melodramatic action, all the more suspenseful because of the relentless search by "The Sons of Dan" for the Gentile murderers of a band of Mormons, takes place, oddly enough, against a realistic setting: a crude gold-rush town high in the Sierras. A few "avenging angels" from the Mormon elite corps work secretly and individually searching the town for their last Gentile victim, young Nancy Williams. In disguise as "that cussed boy" Billy Piper, Nancy tries to elude the Danites. The influence of Bret Harte (a member, with Miller, of the Bohemian Club, San Francisco) seems strongest in Miller's characterizations of frontier townsfolk. Rough miners; a sentimental and missionary-minded widow; kind Sandy McGee ("a king, this man," in spite of his illiteracy); the satirically named Parson who "could outswear any man in Camp"; the ineffectual Judge, "Chosen because he was fit for nothing else in this Glorious climate of Californy"; Captain Tommy, "a woman with a bad name but a good heart"; her friend Bunkerhill; and the town laundryman, "heathen Chinee" Washee-Washee—all are dramatized counterparts of the citizens of Harte's boomtowns, Poker Flat, Roaring Camp, and Red Gulch. Other suggestions of Miller's indebtedness to Harte appear on those occasions when "the poet of the Sierras," deliberately halting the action, romantically glorifies the grandeur of California's mountain peaks and her "glorious climate." In such scenes the ugly town and its mines seem mean and small against the poetized backdrop of "the mighty Sierras." Once the sensitive Billy Piper muses that the panorama of majestic mountains, towering over the town, seems a miracle and a symbol of "all the majesty and mystery of this calm, still world."[43]

Miller, encouraged by the instantaneous success of *The Danites*, composed three other local color plays. *Forty-Nine: an Idyl Drama of the Sierras*,[44] first produced at Haverly's Theatre, New York, on October 1, 1881, is a weak dramatization of the persistent efforts of an Argonaut who finally tunneled through to a "gold find." The melodramatic plot—a revision of a Miller story in the *Overland Monthly*—ending on a moralistic note about success, adds nothing new or memorable to the dramatization of the western small town. The gambling and mining scenes, the passages expressive of Miller's antagonism toward the Mormons and the Chinese, and the stereotyped regional characters explain why this western was a flop. Thereafter, Miller was unable to find a producer for *Tally Ho!* (based upon Horace Greeley's record of his crossing the Sierras by stagecoach) and *An Oregon Idyll*, a dramatized glorification of the natural grandeur of the Pacific Northwest.[45]

From the late fifties onward Mormonism was treated, pro and con, in other less notable plays, not all of which dealt with the frontier town. Fears felt by Californians that bands of Mormons, as well as of "heathen Chinee," would gain control of their state brought forth further dramatizations.[46] Pro-Mormons vigorously, if not too artistically, replied with rebuttals. In 1858 (the same year that Samuel French published *The Mormons*) Wallack's Theatre, New York, produced a venomous farce, *Deseret Deserted; or, The Last Days of Brigham Young*, a vilification of Young as scoundrel and drunkard written by the (Club.[47] From the Golden Era dates also lawyer William H. Rhodes's *The Mormon Prophet*, a play about Joseph Smith which, though unacted, was read to appreciative San Francisco audiences.[48] Although anti-Mormonism persisted, more favorable interpretations of the Mormons gradually began to appear, and by the 1910 era the dramatic efforts of the Mormon Mutual Improvement Association were creating a sense of respect for Mormon leadership and accomplishments. Faithful playwrights, by directing religious plays for the more than five hundred wards in Utah and by publishing their pro-Mormon dramas (first released in the *M.I.A. Book of Plays*, 1929), presented the theme of "the historic sense of a people who have suffered and sacrificed for the faith."[49] Most notable of such plays offsetting the bitter disparagement of *The Mormons* and *The Danites*, Annie D. Palmer's *The Rescue* (1927) dramatizes the plight of early Salt Lake settlers and their salvation by the "miracle" of the sea gulls. Such frontier dramas as Ruth Hudson Hale's *Handcart Trails* (1940) and *It Shall Keep Thee* (1941), by Nathan Hale and Ruth Hale, are more ardent expressions of the Mormon faith than they are realistic picturings of life in those lonely little settlements which Mormon pioneers planted in the deserts of Utah.

The High Sierras Again

The California which idealistic Frank Harte first saw during the years of his youth and journalistic apprenticeship was stimulating to his romantic imagination. Soon after his arrival in Oakland in 1854, he found exciting adventure crowding in on him during his constantly changing career as teacher, private tutor, druggist's clerk, typesetter in a rural newspaper office, and an eager witness of the free life in the mining camps. As a youthful contributor of satires, sketches, and poems to the *Golden Era*, the *Californian*, and other periodicals, Harte gradually realized the literary possibilities of California. His first significant literary use of the California frontier and its flush times dates, however, from the summer of 1868. On July 1 the first issue of a new magazine, the *Overland Monthly*, with Harte introduced as editor, was put on sale at San Francisco stands. In the August issue the inclusion of "The Luck of Roaring Camp" not only made history for the *Overland* but also gave Harte wide recognition as a local colorist. As succeeding issues gained wider circulation, readers far and wide saw in print seven other Harte stories picturing western boomtowns with strange and crude names and lusty citizens.[50] Poker Flat, Red Gulch, Rough and Ready, Roaring Camp, and other straggling towns, teeming with gentleman gamblers, rough miners, hetaerae, monte-hall operators, courageous expressmen like Yuba Bill, and daring highwaymen, as well as more stable folk, became familiar—and even sometimes shocking—to a reading public already aware of the mining camp scenes humorously portrayed in Sam Clemens' newly published *The Celebrated Jumping Frog of Calaveras County and Other Sketches* (1867).

From his youth until his departure from San Francisco in 1871, Harte, long interested in drama, witnessed the continued expansion of the city's theatrical activities. As early as 1849 San Francisco had become the center of an extraordinary ferment of dramatic activity. By the time the late sixties and seventies had marked Harte's triumphs as local colorist and editor, the "lively, colorful, and multifarious theatre" of the Gold Rush had changed, yielding to the form and pressures of civic expansion. The theatrical ventures of that born showman and entrepreneur Thomas Maguire had expanded to include his management of the Alhambra, Shiel's Opera House, and the Baldwin Academy of Music. As other "temples of art" and the smaller bijoux increased, likewise "those temples of the cancan—the melodeons and music halls—flourished and multiplied."[51] Female wrestlers, ribald burlesques of current dramas, beer gardens, hippodrome attractions such as chariot races and steeplechase events, minstrels, "sensation plays," and various extravaganzas furnished plenty of competition for the managers of a better type of theatrical entertainment. Fortunately such a rage for entertainment, in any form, did encourage experimentation in scenic innovations, lighting effects, and seating arrangements, as well as in dramatic genre and materials.

However mad this scramble of dramatic activity may have been, it was largely responsible, long after Delano's on-the-scene reporting, for the appearance of a different point of view about the stage presentation of western town life. This new attitude—marked by an odd mixture of Dickensian sentimentality, romantic glorification of California's scenery, and realism—stemmed from the stories of Bret Harte. By 1875 Harte, then in the East, was to make another type of optimistic fictional excursion into the Gold Rush towns through the medium of drama. Interested in plays from the time of his New York youth, Harte during the sixties and seventies gained wide acquaintance with California's theatrical progress by his regular attendance at San Francisco's theaters and his newspaper work as dramatic critic. Encouraged by actors Stuart Robson and Lawrence Barrett, he finally completed a dramatization of "Mr. Thompson's Prodigal," one of the least successful of his *Overland* stories. Ironically, although he had created widely imitated local color stories, Harte lacked the ability to turn successful playwright.

Although he strove through the use of local color to picture typical scenes in a teeming California shantytown of the fifties, Harte melodramatized the story's action. His best characterizations resulted from the inclusion of several effective portrayals from his earlier fiction, notably gentlemanly John Oakhurst (gambler in "The Outcasts of Poker Flat"), pretentious Colonel Culpepper Starbottle, supposedly of the southern "plantocracy," and a Chinese laundryman, Hop Sing. Hard-drinking Sandy Morton and citified Miss Mary (originally the lovers in "The Idyl of Red Gulch"), Concho, and other frontier townspeople from Harte's stories gave a semblance of reality to the dramatized rough and ready settlement of Sandy Bar. Notwithstanding these regional touches, *Two Men from Sandy Bar*, as the play was billed for its disappointing Chicago tryout and its New York premiere on August 28, 1876, proved theatrically unsuccessful. Contemporary critics directed their satire against the incoherence of its long and shallow plot, its effect of aimlessness, and its mushiness of tone.[52] Stuart Robson, in the star role of Colonel Starbottle, displeased some spectators with his unnatural enunciation, "which was not only not Western but not anything known to civilization—[so] killed it." His speech was condemned as "suitable only for the rankest burlesque."[53] Nevertheless, *Two Men from Sandy Bar*, although obviously "a confused melodrama," at least had some originality in theme. Harte was the first to dramatize the idea of loyalty among California mining partners, as he was first in portraying Spanish characters indigenous to the California locale.[54] Also, Sandy Bar, even if not depicted with complete historical accuracy, did bear some resemblance to those jerry-built mining towns which once dotted the great valley of Central California, the background of Harte's mining camp narratives. Certainly Sandy Bar, like nearby Red Gulch, was to offer a pattern of contrasts for other contemporary playwrights, such as Miller and Campbell, who also put the western town on the stage. On the one hand, there was the drab town itself, with its wooden hotel, an express office, several saloons and gambling halls, its low rickety houses along a dusty main street, scattered cabins along the hillside, freshly hewn stumps, and newly cleared lots. But Harte contrasted this primitive mining settlement, where typically life was hard and coarse, with highly romanticized scenes resembling vistas of the snowcapped Sierras, thus setting up another scenic pattern to be widely adapted to the stage.

It was not theatrical Colonel Starbottle, but the minor part of Hop Sing, cleverly interpreted by C. T. Parsloe, which gave Harte the inspiration for a humorous play about another Chinaman. "Harte's idea was to write a play especially for Parsloe in a Chinese character, and for this play to take as collaborator, his old friend Mark Twain."[55] As a theatergoer, Harte of course knew that American audiences delighted in highly comic and often rough caricatures by which skilful comedians mimicked recognizable American types. Among the favorite comedians of the seventies was F. S. Chanfrau, who popularized the role of Kit Redding, T. B. DeWalden's Arkansas Traveler, by stressing the "manly yet simple nature" of this pioneer character. Then there appeared at Rochester, New York, on September 23, 1872, a most adventurous stage pioneer, heroic Davy Crockett as dramatized by Frank Hitchcock (or Murdoch). Frank Mayo's robust acting of Crockett kept Hitchcock's frontier comedy alive for nearly two thousand performances throughout the country, including production in San Francisco.

Furthermore, as Harte must have known, the real Crockett as frontier politician may have inspired another mimic politician: "a gentleman of magnificent vistas," southwestern Colonel Mulberry Sellers. Harte, no doubt, was aware that Clemens'   success at playwriting originated in such native funmaking. At any rate, audience acclaim of this kind of foolery prompted an enterprising but unauthorized adapter, San Francisco journalist Gilbert S. Densmore, to dramatize *The Gilded Age* shortly after its publication. Using this first adaptation, actor John T. Raymond produced *The Gilded Age* on April 23, 1874, at the California Theatre. Later, by a contract with Raymond, Mark Twain wrote his version, which succeeded largely because Raymond's fine acting made out of the visionary Kentuckian "a harmonious whole" and a recognizable American character "single and strong behind all its eccentricities."[56] Raymond's sympathetic portrayal of the sanguine Sellers' unbounded faith in self was in tune with the times. Moreover, it overshadowed Mark Twain's weaknesses in dramatic construction—his introduction of forced incidents such as a steamboat explosion and his failure to achieve dramatic development of action or character.

Perhaps Harte was impressed by the long run of the Twain version at the Park Theatre—119 nights, beginning on September 16, 1874. Whether for that reason or another, Harte did appear in Hartford in the fall of 1876, with a proposal of his plan for collaboration with Mark Twain, suggesting that Scotty Briggs of *Roughing It* would have theatrical appeal if teamed with Ah Sin, already famous as the wily "heathen Chinee" of Harte's own poem.[57] In spite of their temperamental differences, the humorists, having agreed on collaboration, finally completed *Ah Sin* in time for its presentation, before a brilliant audience, at the National Theatre, Washington, on May 7, 1877.

Neither the Washington premiere, the opening at Daly's Fifth Avenue Theatre on July 31, nor the road productions saved the play. The reasons for failure are obvious. Plot synopses reveal weak, commonplace, and unoriginal action centering around vigilante activities.[58] "Tangled and unconsequential incidents" concerning both Ah Sin and some thinly sketched frontier Californians take place against the background of a primitive settlement "upon Stanislaus." On occasion, the broadly humorous language and Parsloe's acting as Ah Sin proved popular with the Washington and New York audiences, but they did not please the drama critics. Accordingly, the play, which remained unprinted, disappeared from the boards.

If Harte and Mark Twain failed to achieve substantial success as playwrights, the successful theatrical use of their California material by other playmakers at least signified its intrinsically dramatic quality. The staging of *The Gilded Age*, with its portrayal of a comparatively stabilized frontier near the Mississippi, popularized, in the character of Colonel Mulberry Sellers, an optimistic spellbinder whose outlook was in keeping with the promise of the West and the rosy dreams of pioneers. As for Harte, the keynotes of his western community portrayals—humor and sentimentality, impressionism and paradox, realism and romanticism— all helped Daly, Miller, Campbell, Wister, Hoyt, and other playwrights to make their contributions to the dramatizations of the western small town and of the lawlessness of a brief and crowded era.

Another sojourner briefly connected with San Francisco's literary frontier was Bartley Thomas Campbell, a Pittsburgh native of Irish descent. Campbell—journalist and writer of popular magazine tales, poems, and melodramas—seems to have begun his career as dramatist sometime early in 1871.[59] From 1872 until 1876, after a period of bohemian living, Campbell worked in Chicago as resident author and general assistant for the R. M. Hooley Theatre, advertised as "The Parlor Home of Comedy." During the summer of 1874, Campbell went with the Hooley Company of twenty-six to San Francisco, where he formed a lasting friendship with Mark Twain, became acquainted with Bret Harte, and was invited to membership in the Bohemian Club.[60] Of more importance, during his California stay Campbell discovered local color material for two of his most popular plays: *How Women Love* (later produced as *The Vigilantes*) and *My Partner*.

How Women Love; or, The Heart of the Sierras, in five sensational and poorly constructed acts, was staged first at Philadelphia's Arch Street Theatre on May 21-26, 1877, and in October was revived in Chicago. Retitled *The Vigilantes*, this "drama of sensation" opened July 1, 1878, at the Grand Opera House, New York.[61] Both versions, with obvious borrowings from "The Outcasts of Poker Flat" and *Gabriel Conroy*, but thinly reconstruct mining town scenes and typical characters, such as the honest miner Joe Comstock, belonging to the region of the Sierras. One contemporary reviewer, reporting in the *Philadelphia Inquirer* for May 22 concerning its initial performance, dismissed the play as "a very poor affair, so poor as to be beneath serious criticism," with melodramatic incidents "fearfully and wonderfully compounded." Nevertheless, other critics found "the story full of action," the western "personages introduced clearly drawn," and the fourth act "a splendidly effective piece of dramatic writing . . ."[62]

My Partner fared better.[63] While also revealing Campbell's strong reliance on Harte's stories and on Miller's plays and tales, *My Partner* was copyrighted in 1880 as an "Original American play in four acts." Although Campbell again responded to the popular demand for sentimentality and theatrical situations, he produced, through his realistic use of local color and less reliance on the idyllic, a dramatization of life in the

Sierras much better than that contained in *The Danites*. His realistic sets, complete with a gaudy Golden Gate Hotel and miners' cabins, help in transferring to the stage the minutiae of life in an 1879 mining town, situated in Siskiyou County near Mount Shasta.

In the development of his several rather bold themes, Campbell brings into play certain natively western elements: Sam Bowler's enthusiastic calling of the figures for the dancers at a hotel ball; miners happily "liquoring up" at the Golden Gate bar; unscrupulous "Major" Britt's spellbinding electioneering tricks to gain votes and to close "the sluice gates of vituperation"; and the loyalty of Wing Lee, Golden Gate handyman who aids the disgraced heroine, Mary Brandon. Campbell's basic theme, also borrowed from Harte, concerns the breaking of the close bond of friendship between two mining partners—loyal and gentle Joe Saunders and weak-willed Ned Singleton—because both love Mary. For some theatergoers and critics of the 1880's Campbell's treatment of seduction was quite bold. On the other hand, the theatrical scenes concerning Ned's betrayal of Mary under his promise of marriage, his murder by vengeful Josiah Scraggs, and other romantic episodes suggest that as late as 1879 life in the small towns within sight of Mount Shasta could parallel the excitement of an earlier frontier.

The last of the notable plays localized in mining towns in California's High Sierras was staged first almost contemporaneously with the final real gold rush at Tonopah, Nevada, and the building of the last transcontinental railroad, the Chicago, Milwaukee, and St. Paul's Puget Sound extension.[64] On October 3, 1905, at the new Belasco Theatre in Pittsburgh, David Belasco's "museum piece," *The Girl of the Golden West*, for all of its mixture of hokum, elementary theatricalism, and frontier romance, added to the literary map of early California still another tumultous "jumping-off place," the mining community of Cloudy Mountain during the gold fever of 1849–50. Perhaps because of its riproaring melodramatic plot concerning Minnie Falconer, the girl who operates the Polka Saloon, and her love for Dick Johnson (actually Ramerrez, the road agent), this "thoroughly Belascoized creation" has had great popularity.[65] Even the latest revival, on November 5, 1957, at the Phyllis Anderson Theatre, New York, was played as "straight Belasco," with Brooks Atkinson, in his *Times* review, conceding that "the Belasco melodrama cannot be laughed entirely away."[66]

Among the things which have not been laughed away entirely are various records of the acting largely responsible for the early stage success of *The Girl*. For example, the "Fond Memories" issue of *Stage* (August, 1937) and Craig Timberlake's *The Bishop of Broadway* pic-

Maxwell Anderson's *Night Over Taos* (1932), was to develop from a comparable and contemporary movement: the westward expansion in 1847 by forces of the United States into the Indian-Spanish domain of New Mexico. This romantic tragedy of manifest destiny concerns principally the ancient line of the Montoyas, at last overthrown by the invading forces of democracy.

Symbolically titled, this tragedy of the feudalistic *ricos*, their families, and faithful peons develops by vivid scenes, exciting domestic and military conflicts, and poetic philosophizing about the dying ideals of imperialistic Spain. People of various stations and nationalities are involved; yet Anderson achieves artistic unity in spite of many overlong passages about political theory and other ideas. Robert Edmond Jones's one set for the three acts shows the great adobe hall of Pablo Montoya's hacienda at Taos in the year 1847. From this hacienda in the picturesque town Pablo, attended by his sons Federico and Felipe, his mistresses, and his retainers, long has managed his eighteen-thousand-acre domain, exercised powerful influence over the neighboring aristocrats, and inspired loyalty in the simpler citizens of Taos. The plot is focalized further by the limitation of time to the fatal winter night following a battle, reported as having taken place in a mountain pass, with a superior force of gringos. Not only the better equipment of the Americans but also the treacheries, lusts, and hates of the Montoyas account for the night— the darkness of destruction—which falls upon Pablo, his household, and the town. Beset by foes from without and from within, Pablo is indeed a fallen giant and symbol of a crumbling civilization; yet, in the words of Martinez, priest of Taos, Pablo in his prime had greatness in him.

> Wherever he went
> He carried with him the center of an age,
> The center of a culture, the people's hearts
> Clung to him like vines to rock![70]

Anderson's skill in using "messenger speeches" and other exposition to portray the adobe village and its picturesque countryside shows the province of Taos as resembling "a little island empire." Yet this "arm of Spain" is in danger of being lopped off by those "tricksters from the north." A prisoner, a Yankee officer, who urges Pablo to concede some part of his region to American ownership lest he be conquered, sees the Catholic town and its wide valley as a military prize ready for the taking. ("It's a fertile valley,/And a handsome town, and it's rich.") On this night of tragedy the simple people of Taos, largely superstitious Mexican peons and Indians, begin escaping to the hills. With its people panic-stricken and fleeing, "The town's a caravan." Long before the American attack, however, Taos had been the dwelling place of "an old, proud race." Pablo Montoya, Don Hermano, Don Miguel, and even the kindly Catholic priest were masters over the lesser townspeople. And Pablo pridefully explains why.

> For this is our place,
> We wrought it out of a desert, built it up
> To beauty and use; we live here well, we have
> Customs and arts and wisdom handed down
> To us through centuries.[71]

To whatever degree the long speeches and the numerous minor characters caused the stage failure of *Night Over Taos*, Anderson succeeded beautifully—sometimes by means of near-great language—in evoking the spirit of place and of time made universal. In some respects the problems of the leaders of Taos correspond to the crises which arose to challenge the nation in the 1930's, when the play was written. Certainly, this dramatized portrayal of Taos not only is the most artistic among the stage pictures of western or southwestern towns, but also is cogently applicable to our contemporary struggle for survival.

Thoreau's chafing under the restraints of the older society of Concord motivated his bold declaration of freedom: "Eastward I go only by force, but westward I go free . . . there are no towns or cities of enough consequence to disturb me. . . . I must walk toward Oregon and not toward Europe." Akin to such wishing for freedom from the irritations and inhibitions of life in a long-established community is the questing temper of those pioneers who, unlike Thoreau, actually migrated westward. Some of these became town-makers and, like Delano, recorders of life in the newly built settlements. In turn, as western settlements of many types appealed to the imagination of our playwrights, frontier locales, characters, and speech—sometimes treated romantically, and again realistically—left their mark on popular drama.

V. "The Lonesome Lands": Range Towns and Others

The Cattle Kingdom

SINCE, as Mari Sandoz has written, "the rancher is the encompassing, the continuous symbol of modern man on the Great Plains," the cow towns and environing ranchlands have been the source of materials for varied dramatizations of community life in the almost limitless range country.

In most parts of the country during the busy post–Civil War years our older individual, isolated life gradually gave way to the demands of a more standardized society. The range country was in various respects an exception. In spite of the mad scramble for rail routes and subsidies, land and town sites, mineral rights and freight rates, much of this region, comparable to the isolated land pictured in *Horizon, A Texas Steer*, and *The Virginian*, remained for a while virtually untouched by the forces of a growing industrialism. Except for the larger towns in the mining zones, such as Denver and Leadville, and the cattle-shipping centers, such as Kansas City and Dodge City, generally the range country settlements were, even at the turn of the century, only small towns set down on the vast prairies.[1] Throughout the open range from the Dakotas, Nebraska, and Kansas to Montana, Wyoming, Colorado, New Mexico, and West Texas, the cowboy was king until the 1880's. In this widespread territory where cattle roamed the ranges, owners of large "spreads"—actual prototypes for Hoyt's Maverick Brander and Wister's Judge Henry— made fortunes from their thousands of Durhams, Herefords, Longhorns, and other stock. Of literary significance was the "legend bequeathed the nation of an exciting Wild West where bronzed, lean horsemen rode the range for lonely weeks, tore up the cattle towns, drank and gambled with carefree exuberance, and always shot straight from the hip."[2] Such cattle towns, although seemingly inconsequential places, have been diversely portrayed in novels by Hamlin Garland and Emerson Hough, as well as in the stories of Alfred Henry Lewis, Andy Adams, and others. In drama, from the early seventies to the opening of the new century, still others—Daly, Hoyt, Thomas, Wister, and Moody—were to offer their stage interpretations of the turbulent ranching frontier before "the edge was worn off . . . by the grind of the wheels of civilization."

On February 2, 1871, Harte, encouraged by an offer by some Chicagoans to become editor of the proposed *Lakeside Monthly,* left San

135

Francisco, looking hopefully to the East for further laurels. Ironically, just a few weeks later a New York man of the theater achieved a much better dramatization of frontier life than any theatrical pieces by Harte or Mark Twain. On the evening of March 21 when the second-act curtain rose at New York's Olympic Theatre its patrons, too often amused by melodramas, saw an unusually realistic picturing of a scene in "one of the wooden cities of the West." On stage was a westernized backdrop—a piazzaed "Hotel of primitive order at left, with portico, etc. Sign: 'Occidental Hotel, on the European plan.' " On the right, a two-storied building with painted signs denoting a printing office ("The Clarion of the West") and the Pacific Express office brought spectators face to face with the "town of Rogue's Rest—sixty miles from Fort Jackson" and located in the Far West somewhere "just this side of the Horizon."[3] Here, complete with motifs of local color, was the best of the several sets provided for an "original drama of contemporaneous society and of American frontier peril," the five-act *Horizon* (with seven tableaux) written, rehearsed, and produced by the versatile Augustin Daly. A. M. Palmer, who was among these early spectators, years later remembered *Horizon* for its dramatic qualities and its realistic portrayal of native characters and manners. In conversation with Francis Daly, he remarked enthusiastically that *Horizon* "was the best American play I have ever seen. More than that it was the best play your brother ever wrote; and it was the least appreciated by the public."[4]

Possibly Daly's bold departure from the then popular and sentimental glorification of the West in favor of a more realistic approach accounts for this lack of appreciation. Generally, Daly's realistic thinking, a bit reminiscent of Alonzo Delano's lusty reportorial method, takes the form of humorously satiric commentary on social problems connected with enterprising Rogue's Rest and the vast plains surrounding it. The currents of his thoughts about the Far West touch upon the typical frontiersman's independence of traditional legal authority and his tendency to rely on expediency rather than law. The citizens of Rogue's Rest, boisterous and freedom-loving, scoff at Congressional law and disregard local decree as they wish. Their mayor or "boss," one Rocks of Tennessee, recognizes the power of a newly formed Vigilance Committee, although he complains to a group of rough settlers: "You've tilted me out of my lawful authority as Mayor of this settlement and you've taken the law into your own hands." Rocks admits ruefully that the "civil authority wasn't able to control" all of the "blacklegs, horse-thieves and other alibis and aliases" which had overrun the settlement. He, therefore, is "much obliged" to the "hard-fisted, hard-working men" of the Vigilance

"There is a flock of yellow-birds around her head." Illustration of a Salem witchcraft trial, from Mary E. Wilkins (Freeman), *Giles Corey, Yeoman* (1893).

Playbill for a London performance (1851) of Samuel Woodworth's *The Forest Rose*, starring Joshua Silsbee. *Theatre Collection, New York Public Library*.

MR. JOSH SILSBEE AS JONATHAN PLOUGHBOY

IN SAMUEL WOODWORTH'S
COMIC DRAMA OF THE FOREST ROSE

BLANDFORD. "Are you a shop-keeper?
JONATHAN. Wal, yees; I guess maybe I
would come under that head; for I sells
everything in created nater, and a
darn'd sight more true."

Act I, Sc. 3.

Joshua Silsbee as Jonathan Ploughboy in *The Forest Rose* (engraving by J. Moore). *Theatre Collection, New York Public Library.*

British comedian Charles Mathews the Elder on stage at the Park Theatre, where he appeared on November 7, 1822, during his first American tour. *Eno Collection, New York Public Library.*

The "New" Theatre in New York, possibly the First Park Theatre, opened in 1798, destroyed by fire in 1820, rebuilt and reopened in 1821, destroyed by fire in 1848. *Eno Collection, New York Public Library.*

Above, an 1828 street scene in "Little Old New York" (Broadway from the Bowling Green) picturing fashionable strollers like Charlotte and Letitia in *The Contrast*, who delighted "to trip it on the Mall, or walk on the Battery." Below, etched view (1834) of New York's South Street waterfront, from Maiden Lane: possibly the prototype after which the mercantile activity in Mrs. Mowatt's *Fashion* was patterned. *Eno Collection, New York Public Library.*

Joseph Jefferson as Rip Van Winkle, with playbill for the October 15, 1870, performance of Dion Boucicault's *Rip Van Winkle; Or, The Sleep of Twenty Years*, at Booth's Theatre, New York. *Hill Collection, Dallas Public Library.*

Committee who unite to clean up the town themselves.[5] The spirit of frontier lawlessness is highlighted further by the admission by lobbyist Sundown Rowse, Esquire (freely satirized as "A distinguished member of the *Third House* at Washington") that he knew "one town where every inhabitant's got another name. They take ranks there according to the amount of debts they ran away from. The worst insolvent is elected Sheriff."[6]

Also, "out towards the Horizon," where the "names on the land" could be as crude as Dogs' Ears, All Gone, Hollo Bill, and Rogue's Rest, neither settlers, soldiers, nor Plains Indians lived "just as they do in romances." For skeptical Daly, savages in the vicinity of Rogue's Rest bore little resemblance to the noble warriors of the Leatherstocking Tales. For example, Chief Wannemucka, "civilized Indian and 'Untutored Savage,' " is so crafty that he learns the white men's secrets either under pretense of being in a drunken stupor or while playing poker. Even unscrupulous Sundown Rowse is taken aback. "Who'd have thought of this romantic injun sporting a deck and offering to play poker? . . . That knocks the romance . . ."[7] Cynical Loder, a John Oakhurst type of gentlemanly gambler, has a satiric retort: "That's civilization, my friend! When the noble savage was in his native state, he went for the hair of your head. Now he's in the midst of civilization, he carries the weapons of enlightenment [a greasy pack of cards], and goes for the money in your pocket."[8] As the poker game progresses, the idea of caste even among gamblers, a familiar motif derived from Harte, appears in Loder's self-classification as "an outpost of progress": "It's a damned disgrace to John Loder to be walked out of town with a greasy injun!"

Elsewhere, however, *Horizon* shows some of the taint of romanticism. In the love story of frail Med, "White Flower of the Plains", and aristocratic West Pointer Alleyn Van Dorf, Daly lapses into the use of the popular Harte devices of sentimentality and romantic contrasts. In using such contrasting characters, however, he foreshadowed Owen Wister's later dramatization of the conflict between his untutored Virginian and a "civilized" New Englander. Fortunately, the melodramatic Indian skirmishing is balanced by Daly's insistence on minority rights and frontier justice, notably in relation to Cephas (a hymnsinging Negro) and the Heathen Chinee. Through Rowse, the play's most satiric portrait, Daly ridicules Washington lobbyists, soon to be characterized at length in *The Gilded Age* and Henry Adams' *Democracy*. Another phase of political corruption then current is exposed in the character of Miss Columbia Rowse, "the Belle of *Both*

Houses and fascinator of the Lawmakers," prototype of Laura Hawkins, the clever and attractive female lobbyist of *The Gilded Age.* Obviously both Sundown and his daughter "Columby," antedating the appearance of Beriah Sellers and Laura by three years, satirically symbolize the fever of speculation and the political chicanery of the sixties and seventies. Rowse brags about western railroad building and the planting of "cities in the wilderness" bearing his name. Having prospected in every direction from Rogue's Rest, he envisions "the foundation of Rowseville, the future metropolis of the West."[9] In Alleyn's opinion, Rowse typifies the shrewd, and sometimes honest, politician of the time. In the guise of caretakers of the public interest, Rowse and his fellow politicians adhere to the adage: "What's everybody's business is nobody's business." But, says Alleyn: "Now the politicians do everybody's business and account to nobody for the way they do it. That's Rowse's way."[10]

In the history of our small-town drama Daly was the first playwright to set in motion a cycle of plays re-creating frontier life in the widely stretching range country. Others, like Delano and Miller, dramatized the excitements of mining settlements in different decades. Daly, in his turn, brought to the stage the traditions of a raw but rapidly growing border town on the plains, somewhat similar to the Wyoming towns so well known to young Theodore Roosevelt. Rogue's Rest, in short, appears in *Horizon* not so much in lonely isolation, but as a dramatized image of the burgeoning enterprise of frontier plainsmen. For all its violence and primitivism, Daly's town symbolizes a familiar American dream: mushroom settlements, even as primitive as Rogue's Rest, could flourish and grow into "the magic cities of the West."

It was not, however, until twenty years after *Horizon* that the cycle of range country plays begun by Daly was again to move forward. In 1890 Charles Hale Hoyt, who had already delighted thousands with numerous farce comedies, further revealed his spontaneous wit when his most popular social satire, *A Texas Steer*, opened on September 29 at Philadelphia's Chestnut Street Theatre and on November 10 at New York's Bijou Theatre. Hoyt's subtitle, *"Money Makes the Mare Go,"* wittily sums up the active principle—the triumph of a wealthy Texas cattleman over the machinery of politics, local and national—in this farcical "collection of saws and instances." Indeed, the day of the cattleman as imaged in the play's prologue, dawns politically when the neighborly constituents, white and Negro alike, in a Texas frontier town elect their richest cattle king, Maverick Brander, to Congress. Coupling his own experiences—both as a Colorado stock raiser and as a *Boston Post* reporter well versed in politics—with his faith in the "extraordinary [literary] possibility of American politics, and the development of statesmanship of the average type," Hoyt through a prologue and three acts dramatizes the Brander family's "march on Washington," their rebuffs, and their final attainment of both political and social education. (Hoyt's own practical political participation was to come a bit later, in 1893 and 1895, when he served actively as a member of the New Hampshire legislature.)[11]

As his two western dramas—*A Texas Steer* and *A Trip to Chinatown* (1891)—clearly reveal, Hoyt "may not have been important as a dramatist, but he was a popular playwright who dealt with the contemporary American Scene."[12] He is best remembered as a genial entertainer of the gaslight era who provoked laughter by his many farce comedies as readily as did Joseph Weber and Lew Fields with their German-Jewish dialect sketches and Edward Harrigan with his impersonations of Irish-American (in the Mulligan series) and Negro types. The scope of Hoyt's material was wide, depicting the East—New Hampshire especially—along with the West and the city as well as rural areas and small towns. His varied characters, more highly individualized than Harrigan's, "came from the everyday experience of ordinary people," such as his parents and fellow citizens in his birthplace, Concord, and in Charlestown, New Hampshire.[13] Among his small-town and rural characters are grass-roots politicians, farmers and ranchers, hotel proprietors and guests, brakemen, depot agents and telegraph operators, drummers, lightning-rod salesmen, clergymen, deacons, choir singers, bank officials, squires, merchants, doctors, schoolteachers, gossipy women, saloonkeepers, sheriffs, soldiers, bandmasters, and other folk who, if sometimes farcically introduced, generally indicate Hoyt's close familiarity with country and small-town life.

Limiting his cow-town scenes to the election excitement of the prologue, Hoyt freely uses the three acts of *A Texas Steer* for a fast-moving and comic interpretation of the frequently portrayed rise of the ordinary American by means of "a gospel of wealth." His small-town Texans, rich but socially unsophisticated, are transplanted suddenly, by the irony of a political circumstance, to supposedly civilized Washington, D.C., to them a strange world culturally as well as politically. In spite of their cowboy land speech and frontier ways, the Branders have enough native shrewdness, courage, and integrity to survive the complexities, as well as the corruptions, of their alien environment. In the end, Maverick, fully aware that "Washington is a rough town for a stranger," is jubilant that Washington lobbyists are going to Texas to persuade the voters of his district to re-elect him. In short, he has not "been a damn fool for coming."

The free society of the range towns, ranches, and plains settlements clustered around forts was further recorded in dramas by Augustus Thomas, Owen Wister, and William Vaughn Moody. Actual observers of the West, this trio became popular during the era of the strenuous life inaugurated by Theodore Roosevelt. Then, at the turn of the century, "All at once fiction began to be talked of in terms of 'red blood,' 'men with the bark on,' supermen, and their deeds in the wild areas of actual adventure." It was during this time of Rooseveltian intensity that these playwrights recognized the fictional possibilities of life on the range. "No more historical dreamings: the demand was for reality."[14] Of these three playwrights, versatile Thomas, a native of St. Louis, gained wide recognition throughout the eighties and nineties for the breadth of his interests in American life and for his patriotism, which influenced him in the creation of a series of regional, or state, dramas, originating in 1891 with the April 1 production of *Alabama* at the Madison Square Theatre in New York.

By June, 1899, with the Chicago production of *Arizona* at Hamlin's Grand Opera House, Thomas had extended his range of interest in the play of locality to materials which he had gathered through close observation of the West when he traveled to Arizona in March, 1897. Both in the autobiographical *The Print of My Remembrance* (1922) and in the play of locality to materials which he had gathered through close obser- is reality—here is the West painted in primary colors, with no exaggeration." In truth, *Arizona* (like *The Witching Hour* and *The Copperhead*) accounted, in part, for Winter's praise: "Thomas is a born dramatist."[15]

In reviewing New York's dramatic season of 1900-1901, William Dean Howells recalled seeing seven or eight plays which effectively refuted the critics' complaint that the American theater had then fallen into decay.[16] Howells' faith in native drama seems to have been bolstered by his evident pleasure in "hearing the pure American note in its variety, as we get it in Mr. Herne's 'Sag Harbor,' or Mr. Thomas' 'Arizona.' " (*Arizona* had opened in New York, at the Herald Square Theatre, on September 10.) After having seen a great deal of Civil War drama, Howells found "a refreshing novelty in Mr. Thomas' pictures of army-post life in Arizona." Thomas' "scrupulous aesthetic conscience" seemed to Howells best displayed in his achieving an American atmosphere, truly Arizonan. "In its intense distinctness the local color has a peculiar charm; the picturesqueness of the life is extraordinarily vivid, and there is no shadow of uncertainty in the action; it is sharp and rapid, as if it were the nervous response of human nature keyed to sympathy with the moistureless air of the region, . . . " Howells' empathic reaction applies not only to the raw little army settlement around adobe Fort Grant, but also to the mixed population—American, Mexican, Chinese, Indian, and German—of the mountain-encircled Aravaipa ranch where the action mostly occurs.

Thomas' realism of place was not determined by haphazard methods. Rather, the local color distinguishing *Arizona* from the ordinary melodrama of the time is historically accurate, the result of Thomas' keen and alert intelligence actively at work throughout what he remembered as "one of the most enjoyable sojourns of my life." The exciting weeks of March, 1897, which he spent alternately at Fort Grant and other Arizona posts, at the Sierra Bonita Ranch (the vast Aravaipa Valley holdings of cattle king Henry C. Hooker), and at Willcox, the primitive whistle-stop twenty miles distant, reaffirmed Thomas' belief that "a man's education may constantly go forward." Surely his own education moved forward as he acquainted himself with western scenes and regional types, some of whom were characterized later in *Arizona*. Thomas notes, for instance, that ". . . hundreds of the lines I finally gave to Henry Canby, the rancher in the play of 'Arizona,' were Hooker's own words, which I remembered and as soon as I was alone set down because of their picturesque quality and their great simplicity and directness."[17] Moreover, one of the most widely quoted passages from the play— Canby's explanation of how he judged men—came directly from rancher Hooker's own description of the way by which he hired his cowboys. Addressing Lieutenant Denton, a young cavalryman who is forced to resign from the Eleventh United States Cavalry, Canby explains the way of justice along "the wide horizon" of Arizona:

"We take a man on here, and ask no questions. We know when he throws his saddle on his horse, whether he understands his business or not. He may be a minister backslidin', or a banker savin' his last lung, or a train-robber on his vacation—we don't care. A good many of our most useful men have made their mistakes. All we care about now is, will they stand the gaff? Will they set sixty hours in the saddle, holdin' a herd that's trying to stampede all the time? Now, without makin' you any fine talk, you can give anyone of 'em the fifteen ball. I don't know whether it's somethin' you learned in the school [West Point], or whether you just happened to pick the right kind of a grandfather, or what. But your equal has never been in this territory in my time."[18]

As for Denton, one agrees with Howells that this impulsive West Pointer is portrayed as "a young romantic ass"—a *stage* hero rather

rather than a *real* one—willing to make too many unnecessary sacrifices. And the most disastrous of these is for Estrella Bonham. Estrella, rancher Canby's spoiled daughter, turns emotionally from her middle-aged husband, Colonel Bonham, simply because she finds social life at Fort Grant too dull. A fool and worse, Estrella enjoys little other amusement except flirting and dancing, a tendency which makes her an easy dupe when Captain Hodgman proposes their elopement to New Orleans, a daring plan to be financed by her jewels. Denton, rather than Hodgman, however, is victimized. In his chivalric efforts to save Estrella's reputation by refusing to explain his accidental presence in her company late one night when he discovers the lovers planning their elopement, Denton suffers multiple loss. He resigns his lieutenancy rather than tell Bonham, his benefactor, the truth. His own love for Bonita Canby, Estrella's younger sister, is challenged. Worst of all, he is unjustly charged with the theft of Estrella's jewels.

At this point, it is well to recall that Thomas possessed ingenuity in plot construction. As Moses has reported, Thomas had technique at his fingertips.[19] In the resolution of the action in *Arizona*, Thomas adheres closely to the central theme frequently dramatized in his several state plays: woman's love in different manifestations. If flippant Estrella, who eventually does repent, symbolizes the emotional and unfaithful wife, Bonita, the real heroine, although "frisky and harum-scarum," is sincere in her love for Denton. "The woman with a past" finds representation in Sergeant Kellar's daughter Lena, who, after having been seduced and deserted by Captain Hodgman, at last finds happiness with Canby's vaquero, mandolin-playing Tony Serrano. Untroubled by any distinction between the good and bad English words learned from the troopers, Tony finishes his lover's declaration, after singing "*Adios Amor*," with "and damn to hell my soul, I love you!" Finally, the bickerings of the older Canbys furnish a note of satiric humor as vain and bossy Mrs. Canby nags easy-going Henry mainly because of the dulness of her own life. ("I never been out, Colonel, in my [diamond] breast-pin but once in five years and that was to the opera in El Paso.") Matching the Canbys in humorously highlighted differences, Miss McCullogh, a prim schoolteacher, and Dr. Fenton, cigar-smoking and cardplaying post surgeon, are also developments from real people known to Thomas on his western tour.

Perhaps the strongest quality of *Arizona* is Thomas' realistic portrayal of life on a large Aravaipa ranch and in nearby settlements at the outbreak of the Spanish-American War. Willcox, unnamed but described in the dialogue, appeared "at that time [as] a little one-street row of one-story shops and barrooms." A twenty-mile jog from Fort Grant, this lonely way station was usually reached by a four-mule army "ambulance" or a little two-horse depot wagon. Of more importance to Thomas' melodrama is the realistic set of the second act showing Colonel Bonham's drawing room. A vista reveals it as the most select part of the officers' "doby" quarters, several two-story buildings adjacent to one-story bungalows with porches, all facing a dusty parade ground. (It is interesting to compare Thomas' scenic notes with the detailed description of another Arizona outpost of the period, Fort Delivery, as given in Paul Horgan's *A Distant Trumpet*, 1960, pp. 228 ff.)

In this compact community at Fort Grant, some ten or twelve miles from the Canby ranch, life centers around Colonel Bonham (a traditional disciplinarian) and Estrella, a circle of unattached young officers, a few married officers, and their ladies. In addition to the troopers, there are a few wives down at the barracks, and one or two daughters of the enlisted men. Lena is such a girl. Of the motley types among the citizenry of the fort, the best portrayed is Mexican Tony Serrano, the personable vaquero regularly used as messenger between the fort and the nearby ranches. As Thomas lengthily explains in *The Print of My Remembrance,* Tony was woven into the plot after Nan Sumner, daughter of the commanding officer at Fort Grant, had described for the playwright a real vaquero, one Vincent Serrano, on messenger detail in Aravaipa Valley.[20] Even earlier, in 1896, at his home in New Rochelle, New York, Thomas had been fascinated by a haunting melody played on his piano by Joseph D. Redding, a San Francisco guest. As Redding repeated the melody, Thomas "slowly hammered out" several stanzas concluding, "Who know all her perfidy, love her,/Then why call it madness in me?" Later when the words were translated into Spanish by Vincent's mother, Thomas had the unifying musical theme of "Adios Amor" (ending *"Sabiendo tu perfidio te adora,/Porque lo llama locura?"*), appropriately used to link the life of the singing vaquero with that of the German maid Lena. A final realistic touch gave timeliness to Denton's role. On the morning of February 16, 1898, Thomas and Frederic Remington, then his New Rochelle neighbor, heard the news about the sinking of the *Maine* in Havana's harbor. Thereafter, as Thomas explained, "It wasn't a difficult task to take out all the Indian stuff [a raid by San Carlos Apaches] in my manuscript and to make the motive the getting together of a troop of cowboys [with Denton as their captain]. My impulse was prophetic of the Rough Riders."[21]

In *Colorado* (1901) and *Rio Grande* (1916) Thomas continued his cycle of western plays by localizing his scenes in the Rocky Mountain

West and the lower reaches of the range country respectively.[22] Responding to Charles Frohman's request for "another one of those rough plays,"
Thomas gladly journeyed to Colorado in search of new local color
material. Unfortunately, his two weeks of roughing it in mining camps
and under the guidance of Phil Flynn, a tough and practical miner,
resulted in "a play that was heavy and overcumbered with material and
dramatic machinery." His experiences at Leadville, Little Cimarron
Camp, Cripple Creek, and other mining settlements gave Thomas such
excessive "stuff," including sectional character studies, that his play,
with its five scattered interests, failed to focus.[23] In short, *Colorado*
proved unsuccessful in Frohman's 1901 production at Wallack's Theatre, New York, with Wilton Lackaye in the key role of Frank Austin,
mining engineer. As a play, it adds nothing really new to earlier dramatizations of mining towns in the West, except a change in state locale
and detailed data about the growth of a rough settlement into Austin
City. In the Frohman-produced *Rio Grande*, at New York's Empire
Theatre in April, 1916, Thomas returned, but with less success, to the
same pattern of military community life featured in *Arizona*. (Daniel
Frohman considered *Arizona* "one of the great successes of the American stage.") The military scene, here localized on the border during
the war with Mexico, is suggestive of *Arizona*, as is the main theme of
illicit love between the colonel's wife and a youthful officer. This pair
of lovers, unlike Estrella and Hodgman, is so very guilty that the lieutenant commits suicide, offstage. Moses, charging in 1921 that Thomas'
whole game is to capture his audience as he can by strategy, regardless
of the tenability of the subject, suggests why the playwright erred in the
writing of *Rio Grande*. "Hence, when he fitted up 'Arizona' in clothes
to suit recent Mexican complications, and called his play 'Rio Grande,'
he found that he had lost the early sincerity of 'Alabama,' and his raci-
ness was swamped in an apparent sophistication which only added to
his artificial method of conceiving a plot."[24] *Colorado*, with its scenes
of shaft houses, hastily built railroads, a miners' boardinghouse, and
cabins, is more convincing than *Rio Grande* in its descriptions of
regional town life.

Thomas was more successful with the other plays in his lively territorial series. Of these, *Alabama, Colonel Carter of Cartersville*, and
The Witching Hour portray southern town and plantation life. On the
other hand, *In Mizzoura* (1893) and *The Copperhead* (1917) spotlight still another geographic sector on the map of imaginary western
towns: the provincial villages and farming communities immediately to
the west of the Mississippi, in Missouri and Illinois. *In Mizzoura*, rep-

resentative of Thomas' early period when his plays were most racy and native, reveals his democratic sympathies and his familiarity with Pike County folk customs, speech, and thinking. Thomas' preface (1916) to this early play of the soil suggests the variety of incentives which shaped his thought and stimulated his powers of invention as he crystallized his pictures of Bowling Green, Missouri. With dexterity, he suited the features, voice, and physique of his village hero, Jim Radburn, to the eccentricities of the actor Nat Goodwin. Using a mosaic of personal odds and ends—in Moses' opinion, "working more with chips than with whole planks from a virgin forest"—Thomas envisioned Jim as a Pike County sheriff, a "rough diamond" much older than Kate Vernon, who was of a finer strain than himself, but whom he long had loved and for whom he had secretly made sacrifices to pay for her college education.

According to his preface and autobiography, Thomas drew upon his early and varied employment in the express and railroad business, as well as upon his assignments as reporter for the *St. Louis Republican* and *Post-Dispatch,* for useful "chips" in finishing the portrait of Sheriff Radburn. Always careful in observing the "small psychologies of men," Thomas created a rival for Jim in the "glorified and beautiful matinee idol" Robert Travers, a "city chap" to the Bowling Green folks. From his *Post-Dispatch* reporting on the notorious "Jim Cummings" (or Whitlock) express robbery, Thomas found a model for gentlemanly Travers. His identity unknown to the simple villagers of Bowling Green, Travers, like the real Cummings, was the daring robber of $120,000 in greenbacks from the mail clerk on one of the Missouri Pacific trains. Thomas' clerk, Sam Fowler, mistakenly jailed as a suspected accomplice in the robbery, is connected with the sheriff both as a native of the town and as the lover of Em'ly, Radburn's sister. Political reporting provides another "chip" for the rounding out of the Radburn characterization. Local politics, whether concerning coroner-druggist Clark or the reelection of the sheriff, arouses excitement among Bowling Green's drugstore loungers and other citizens. Town gossip reaches fever pitch when Jo Vernon, Kate's father and the local blacksmith, announces his candidacy for the state legislature, in competition with Jim Radburn, his old friend. Thomas is skilful in creating minor scenes effectively contrasting the usual small-town dulness and narrowness with the occasional excitements which break community somnolence, such as train robberies, elections, trials, and, as in Sheriff Radburn's case, the discovery of a river clay or "gumbo" which when fired could be used commercially for railroad beds. In Bowling Green, as in the later Gopher Prairie, the "village virus" so affects most of its citizens that they prefer the gossip, the "lickerish," and the "sody water" at Clark's drugstore and stagecoach depot to what Kate Vernon called the "truest kinship . . . not a thing of blood, but of ideas."

Neither in *In Mizzoura* nor in other plays does Thomas show any inclination to be stirred by the large social problems of the day. On the other hand, his success in catching the native atmosphere of Pike County extends even to his minor characterizations. Among these, overworked Mrs. Jo Vernon, with her homely speech, suggests Thomas' command of the Pike dialect, as well as a sympathetic understanding of lowly types. Longing ever in vain for a hired girl, Mrs. Vernon makes her poverty more bearable by tired complaints about the Missouri heat, the unscreened windows admitting swarms of "skeeters," and the eternal household chores. ("It's all well enough for those Salvation women who ain't got a thing to do but pound tambourines, but if they had the washin', and ironin', an' cookin' to do for a fambly of six — an' three dogs—they'd need something [such as a quart bottle of the St. Louis beer which Mrs. Vernon gets by a prescription] to keep body an' soul together.")[25] Equally "small-townish," Dave, Jo Vernon's assistant, hopes to marry Lizbeth Vernon, who has simpler tastes than has her sister Kate. As a handyman, Dave has "almost made a set o' furniture myself. . . . I tell you—you can make anything that's made out of wood —with a draw-knife."[26] Colonel Bollinger, petty politician, knows all the tricks of small-town " 'lectioneering." Last, Esrom, a half-witted Negro, spends more time absently playing his Jew's-harp than working the bellows at the blacksmith's shop.

With *In Mizzoura* Thomas rescued the dramatized western town from what he scorned as "the hazy geography of the mining camps." Moreover, he fixed his trio of lovers—honest Jim Radburn, personable but corrupt Travers, and Kate Vernon—in that section of Missouri not many miles below Sam Clemens' Hannibal. A further motif helping to pinpoint the locale was Jo Vernon's folksy pronunciation of the state name, *Mizzoura*, "as it was spelt on many territorial charts." Furthermore, Thomas' skill in introducing trifles—the dog "fannell," the linen dusters and paper collars, Mrs. Vernon's saying "An' the milk's hangin' in the cistern," the housewives' reliance on an itinerant furniture repairman, and the faith in flaxseed and gumbo poultices—enriched the verisimilitude of his Missouri characterizations and scenes. Finally, it seemed to some of Thomas' friends that the key sequences in the love triangle of his comedy were manifestly reproduced, except for a change of locale, some thirteen years later in *The Girl of the Golden West.*

Thomas' generosity in regard to this charge of plagiarism against Belasco is clearly revealed in *The Print of My Remembrance*, Chapter XXIII.

Later evidence of Thomas' insight into midwestern community ways appears abundantly in *The Copperhead*, a homegrown Civil War play based on Frederic Landis' short story, *The Glory of His Country*.[27] Originally presented as a "one-acter" for members of the Lambs' Club, New York, this chronicle history presents the vital drama of a poor farmer, ordinary Milt Shanks, who patriotically undergoes painful self-sacrifices while serving as spy for Abraham Lincoln, his former neighbor. The first two acts (dated 1861-63) dramatize the dilemma of Shanks, a supposed Copperhead, as he, his family, and his neighbors in Millville, a rural settlement in southern Illinois, feel the impact of Lincoln's call for volunteers, the telegraphed news of the fall of Vicksburg, and the disturbing rise of local Copperheads. The patriotic stir of the opening years of the war motivates most of the initial community activity in Millville. A country band plays the martial songs of the time: "Johnny Comes Marching Home," "John Brown's Body" (played as a marching song), and "Rally Round the Flag." Millville volunteers parade in unmilitary fashion in homemade uniforms and drill with old rifles. Old and young women, working at home and church, busy themselves with making uniforms, picking cotton lint for bandages, and molding bullets. A church patriotic pageant, with booths, serves the ladies both as a social outlet and a moneymaking effort for the benefit of the boys. But pipe-smoking Grandma Perley, toughened by life, sturdy at seventy-five, and rich in folk wisdom, yearns to do more. While heroically molding minnie balls, she wishes, "Lord—if I'd only been a man!" As the irregularly uniformed volunteers come marching and singing down the road toward their point of embarkation for Vicksburg, Grandma waves her apron and shouts, "We're comin', Father Abraham, a hundred thousand strong!"[28]

And in her opinion, as in that of other neighbors, Milt Shanks, besmirched by his rumored association with the "Knights of the Golden Circle" and his refusal to join Captain Hardy and his company, is less than a man and his wife Martha is an object of pity. The intensity of the hatred for Shanks deepens as he resists the pleas of his wife and only son to support his country. In humiliation, Joey Shanks, barely sixteen, impulsively joins the ranks of marchers out of Millville. Thereafter, for more than two years, Joey engages in the siege at Vicksburg and in other fighting. At home Milt's dilemma becomes all the more difficult because of his public disgrace. In a sensational trial he and Copperhead Lem Tollard are accused of horse-stealing and of murdering two members of a posse. Grandma Perley, in a fine domestic scene, reassures Martha: "They didn't hang him—at any rate." Utterly disconsolate, Martha questions, "What comfort kin Joey git from that? The *verdict* was hangin', and they'd a hung him only the governor committed all o' their sentences to life in the penitentiary." Such bitter news was "a thunderbolt to Joey" at Vicksburg. Through the intervention of Grant, Milt is released, but his happiness is ruined. Joey, who denounces his father, is killed at Vicksburg. Martha dies of grief; and Milt, ever faithful to his role as pretended sympathizer with the Confederacy, is left in bitterness with Elsie, his small daughter.

The second epoch (Acts III and IV), forty years later, concerns another aspect of small-town life. The Civil War village has grown into a thriving town; yet it is still populated by "people who can carry on hatred for a lifetime." Old suspicions and animosities, while softened a bit by time, still prevail against Milt Shanks, now seventy-eight. "Once a copperhead—always a copperhead—" so say the old-timers. With his war role still unrevealed, old Milt now fears that his past reputation will ruin for Madeline King, his musically trained granddaughter, her chance to obtain a teaching position in Millville. Deeply troubled by this crisis and concerned, too, about the girl's love for respectable Philip Manning, a local lawyer, Milt at last boldly resolves to reveal the truth. The scene of revelation, in the modest Shanks cottage, is deeply moving. Apparently Lionel Barrymore's sympathetic enactment of Milt's confession of his devotion to country and of the risks he took to help the North during the Civil War made the community intolerance which ruined his happiness seem all the more meanspirited. The old man's fervent description of his command meeting long ago with President Lincoln is movingly expressive of how patriotism may exalt even the most commonplace of men. Lincoln's words, as old Milt recalls them, were:

"Milt, how much do you love your country? . . . Would you give up sumpin' more'n life? . . . It means to be odious in the eyes of men *and* women—ter eat yer heart out—alone—fur you can't tell yer wife—yer chile—ner friend . . . The Southern sympathizers are organizing in our State—really worse than the soldiers. I want you ter jine them Knights o' the Golden Circle—ter be one of them—their leader, if you kin. I need you, Milt. Yer country needs you."[29]

Among our playwrights interpreting the small-town West, Thomas, as the most prolific, made the largest number of bids for recognition with his many pictures of the American hinterland, mostly an outgrowth of his own far western and midwestern travel, railroading, journalism, and other experiences. Thomas once wrote that "incidents, character bits, and situations in . . . newspaper work . . . helped pack a mental record upon which I drew more or less for some sixty plays, big and little," including *In Mizzoura* and *The Copperhead*.[30] Today his experimentation with themes of social significance seems tenuous; yet his graphic pictures of Bowling Green, Fort Grant, the Little Cimarron and Rio Grande locales, and Millville in half-southern and half-western Illinois foreshadow, at least, a more modern and familiar literary approach to the small town. A recent evaluation of the western mind reiterates an often-expressed dictum: "The great tragedies of American life are not found in financial failures but are expressed by the oppressive hold of the community, whether it be Winesburg, Ohio, Boston, or the Gopher Prairie of Sinclair Lewis."[31] In his much earlier analysis of western settlements, Thomas, though a competent technician, did not probe deeply into mental attitudes. Actually, he did little more than suggest that these communities are not just symbols, but are states of mind and conditions of the soul. In his well made plays he entertainingly presented outward aspects of the conventional or artificial (such as military) standards which bred intolerance in Bowling Green and Millville, as well as in the narrowed limits of Fort Grant. The simple people of Millville, with none except Grandma Perley emerging as a memorable individual, collectively censured Milt Shanks. Thus the town itself created a pernicious, but not complete, domination over Milt Shanks's spirit. There is no heartfelt confession of regret for the victimizing of the most patriotic citizen in the community. Estrella, in *Arizona*, did not suffer deeply for her selfish lying against young Denton, nor did Sarber, in *In Mizzoura*, have even a twinge of conscience for his brutal crippling of a dog or for his vicious smashing of Esrom's mouth, simply because he disliked the half-wit's harp tunes.

Range towns of Wyoming, Montana, and Arizona came into view again as plays by Wister, Moody, and Fitch were produced in the early 1900's. The first and one of the most popular, *The Virginian*, had its inception as early as 1885 when Wister, on a trip to Wyoming for his health, discovered in the Great Plains frontier a new wonderland and a genuinely appealing frontier society. On fourteen successive trips the well-to-do Philadelphian, according to Fanny Kemble Wister, his daughter and biographer, "ranged throughout the North and Southwest, from Oregon to Texas; but he loved Wyoming best of all, and The Virginian is set in Wyoming."[32] Now that the fifteen notebooks comprising Wister's *Western Journals (1885-1902)* have been found, one may trace from their graphic diary-like jottings the fascinating genesis of the tale of the

Virginian. The next step beyond notebook entries is marked by a *Harper's Magazine* story, "Lin McLean Went East," in the issue of January, 1892. Beyond this, the most artistic development was in the form of "the prime romantic novel of the Wild West." *The Virginian* (1902). This was followed by a four-act comedy. Completed with the assistance of producer Kirke La Shelle, this rather melodramatic staging of the novel opened, after a Boston tryout, on January 5, 1904, at the Manhattan Theatre, New York. With Dustin Farnum in the title role, the comedy had a run of four months and then proved popular on the road for about ten years, with a New York revival as late as 1928. Among the four motion picture versions, that of 1929 starring Gary Cooper, with Mary Brian, has been widely recognized for Cooper's creation of a lasting image of the American cowboy. (Recent evidence of the international appeal of this role may be found in Paul O'Neil's highly illustrated article, "Despedida A Gary Cooper, Caballero De La Pradera," *Life en Espagnol*, XVII, 26 de Junio de 1961, 56 ff.) A London performance in five acts and Henry Fonda's playing the key role in summer stock indicate further public interest in the Wyoming material.

Thus, step by step, Wister, as self-styled historical novelist turned playwright, contrived, both independently and collaboratively, to preserve the color of a vanished world. These several versions furnished partial answers to pertinent questions which Wister and a friend had asked in 1891:

"Why wasn't some Kipling saving the sage-brush for American literature, before the sage-brush and all that it signified went the way of the California forty-niner, went the way of the Mississippi steam-boat, went the way of everything? Roosevelt had seen the sage-brush true, had felt its poetry; and also Remington, who illustrated his articles so well. But what was fiction doing, fiction, the only thing that has always outlived fact?"[33]

Wister's firsthand acquaintances with Wyoming and its "wild glories" enabled him to discern the fictional possibilities of what he termed "that epic which was being lived at a gallop out in the sage-brush." Moreover, his imagination deepened by virtue of his close association with Wyoming ranchers and their families during a momentous era of transition as the territory's oldest industry, stock growing, underwent a process of adjustment. The older and freer ways of cattle raising, dependent upon the use of the open range, were declining with the introduction of new methods of plant and animal husbandry. In the mid-1880's Wister learned much about the antagonisms between smaller ranchers, the "grangers" (frontier dry-land farmers), sheep owners, and the larger cattle outfits typified by Judge Henry's in *The Virginian*. In 1888 the Wyoming legislature attempted to regulate roundups, the sale of mavericks, and the control of inspections by creating a Board of Live Stock Commissioners. In reality and as suggested in Wister's comedy, the new commission was immediately in trouble. Cattle stealing and mavericking flourished as never before. Lacking both full power and adequate subsidy, the commission had serious difficulty in controlling "the anarchy that ruled the ranges."[34] No man's cattle were safe. Even the herds of the big outfits were fair game for all. As late as July 25, 1891, the *Cheyenne Daily Leader* editorialized that cattle stealing had become almost respectable. "There are," the editorial commented, "only two horns to the dilemma, either the thieves or the cattlemen must go."[35] In both novel and play, Owen Wister caught the exciting story of the intermittent struggles of these Wyoming groups, their partial successes, their failures, and the ranching and small-town milieus in which they lived.

Much of the cow-town background which Wister described graphically in the novel does not appear in the play. The paucity of descriptive details for the construction of the small-town set for Act IV—the only act laid in Medicine Bow, Wyoming—contrasts sharply with the novel's fuller picturing of the same town as a "wretched husk of squalor" blotting the endlessly rolling plains of a sparsely settled region. Somber, false-fronted houses, rearing their pitiful masquerade amid a fringe of old tin cans, a diminutive station, two eating houses, a billiard hall, and a stable all combine to place Medicine Bow in the same class with dozens of actual cattle towns which once "littered the frontier from the Columbia to the Rio Grande, from the Missouri to the Sierras." These settlements, like Wister's novelized picture of Medicine Bow,

. . . lay stark, dotted over a planet of treeless dust, like soiled packs of cards. Each was similar to the next, as one old five-spot of clubs resembles another. Houses, empty bottles, and garbage, they were forever of the same shapeless pattern. More forlorn they were than stale bones. They seemed to have been strewn there by the wind and to be waiting till the wind should come again and blow them away.[36]

Wister's indictment of the monotony of design on which the western cattle towns were usually patterned is justified.[37] On the other hand, their littleness and foulness were lessened, he felt, by the overshadowing immensity and strange beauty of the environing hills and plains. This openness of the Wyoming country appealed most to the romancer in Wister. Britisher Ogden, a visitor on Judge Henry's ranch in the play, thinks of "this vast country and its future. Of its cruelty and perhaps of its justice . . . it seems to me like a young giant awaking from sleep. Stretching its mighty limbs blindly and crushing—crushing, and I wonder . . ."[38]

With its vivid descriptions of the open range and its characterizations of assertive frontier types on the ranches within two or three hundred miles of Medicine Bow, *The Virginian*, novel and play, contributes only incidentally to the literature of the frontier town. The brief Medicine Bow scenes are sufficient, however, to paint the prevailing mode of life in a Wyoming cow town of the nineteenth century. Its primitive society was enlivened periodically by the visits of cowboys like the Virginian "fooling around jumping from job to job and helling all over town between whiles," by drummers, and more rarely, by an easterner (such as, in reality, young Theodore Roosevelt or Owen Wister) hardy enough to venture into remote, alien country. Boardinghouse hoaxes, gambling, drinking, and shooting were typical enough of the town to mark it as distinctly on the frontier. On the neighboring ranches lively dances, bringing together "all the folks from miles around," are also the occasions for the christening of the new babies and such hoaxing (as in Act I of the play) as the mixing up of the sleeping infants brought for christening. Medicine Bow itself, for all of its meanness and sordidness, typified the self-reliant West where, in the phrasing of the Virginian (Judge Henry's foreman), no one could be "middling," as in the East, and flourish.

You've got to deal cyards *well*; you've got to steal *well*; and if you claim to be quick with your gun you must be quick, for you're a public temptation, and some man will not resist trying to prove he is quicker. You must break all the Commandments *well* in the Western country.[39]

And in the play (Act II) the Virginian philosophizes to Molly Wood, prim New England teacher, about "Life's Poker," observing that "a middlin doctor is a poor thing and a middlin lawyer is a poor thing, but keep me from a middlin man of God."

In a large measure Wister, with La Shelle's assistance, tried to bring to the stage the true Wyoming of the 1880's through his ranch and town scenes, the outgrowth of his experiences. Certain range types—ranch owners and their wives, cowboys good and bad, rustlers such as Trampas, a bishop, a saloonkeeper, and others—and the two outsiders (the pretty but prudish Vermonter, Molly Wood, and Ogden, British tenderfoot) are presented with accuracy of detail, but no depth of characterization. Of all the characters, the twenty-nine-year-old cowpuncher called the Virginian is the most successfully portrayed. His integrity and dry humor, his conversational reflections about religion and literature, his love for Molly, his concern about the conflict between territorial law and lawlessness, democracy, and kindred topics, and his tendency to speak in the vernacular fitted well the histrionic talents of actors Dustin Farnum, Gary Cooper, and, more recently, Henry Fonda. Mrs. Stokes, Wister's daughter, has recently noted that "there is no account in the *Journals* of anyone truly resembling the Virginian, despite the fact that several chapters of the novel stem directly from the *Journals*."[40] Relying on the *Journals*, Mrs. Stokes describes in detail a Corporal Skirdin—Arizona cowpuncher, scout, and cavalryman—who seemed to Wister "a sort of incarnation of my imaginary Virginian." Another frontiersman who made Wister sure of his ground was Dean Duke, foreman of a ranch at Apache Tejo (New Mexico), who apparently "ratified my imagination," as Wister wrote, in creating his romantic hero, the first cowpuncher to be fictionalized as a gentleman and a hero rather than as a murderous thug.[41] Thus "ratified," the Virginian proved utterly different from the heroes of the day. Good-looking, humorous, and human, he "got drunk, played practical jokes, and through him Wister coined the phrase now part of our language, 'When you call me that, smile!' " The Virginian, in the novel as on stage and screen, was "the progenitor of the cowboy as a folk hero." Most of all, however, as Montrose J. Moses emphasized long ago, "The strength of our American life lies in a marked companionship of the American people. We like evidences of this fact in our books; we applaud it on our stage. This is why 'The Virginian,' poor as it was in its dramatized form, drew, for reason of its quiet dignity of conception, its quick decision, and its elemental passion."[42]

Also expressive of the impulse of life in the range country is Moody's once daring drama of frontier Arizona, produced originally in 1906 by Margaret Anglin in Chicago as *A Sabine Woman* and later in the same year in New York as *The Great Divide*. In trying to treat the conflict between puritanism and passion realistically, Moody developed, sometimes lustily, the theme that a genteel young woman (Ruth Jordan of Milford Corners, Massachusetts) could love a rough but proud stranger (Stephen Ghent, Arizona cowboy and "roustabout miner") who had thrown dice with two drunken companions for possession of her. Skilled in the portrayal of human individualities, Moody demonstrates through Ruth and Stephen the sharp differentiation between the frontier society of Arizona and the gentility of puritan Milford Corners, between cultured love and elemental love. The mountain range separating the two widely different regions symbolizes the "divide" on which the mutual love of a man and a woman is frequently shattered. Ruth and Stephen's difficulty in trying to understand each other's point of view almost wrecks their marriage. The conflict is complex and dramatic. Idealistic Ruth, while loving her husband deeply, must learn, through suffering and a six-months' separation, to accept his crude standards without loss of self-respect. In turn, the less inhibited Stephen must become a "new man," cleansed through his own pain of false pride and insensitivity, before Ruth will accept him completely, realizing that he has led her "out of a world of little codes and customs into a great new world." Begging Stephen to release her from the narrow limitations of caste in Milford Corners, Ruth finally urges him, somewhat sentimentally, to "Teach me to live as you do!" Now, she too belongs "out yonder— beyond the Rockies, beyond—the Great Divide!"

Moody was successful in portraying his westernized hero, Stephen Ghent, as the ideal of personal independence, as "a son of the soil" capable of growth. His realism is most effective in scenes on the Arizona desert, in the Cordillera mining camps, and in a puritan Massachusetts town. On the other hand, Moody occasionally used, possibly for popular appeal, stage machinery, sentimentalism (as when Ruth kisses her mother's photograph goodbye), and didacticism (as in certain preachments about "the wages of sin"). Production difficulties, according to Moses, were such that "we toned down its lustier portions." In later years the poet's widow, Harriet (Tilden) Monroe, bitterly protested against the liberties which the Metro studio took in filming the play. "From time to time," she wrote, "I was called to a [California] conference, and in these conferences I remonstrated with all my might and main against the worst liberties they were taking with 'The Great Divide.' "[43]

In August, 1901, "Moody fulfilled an agreement with Hamlin Garland to make an excursion into the West, the West of cattle ranches and horseback riding which was then new to him—the very West, in fact, of *The Great Divide*, although the idea of the play was not suggested to him until several years later."[44] (Harriet's telling him, in the summer of 1903, about a dramatic happening in Arizona—the violation of a girl by three men—actually gave Moody the nucleus for a prose play. Accordingly, before enjoying further desert travel in 1904, Moody had already fully planned and to a great extent written what was to become *The Great Divide*.) On the other hand, the poet's hunger for purely American themes and his imaginative energy were stimulated by this early trip to the Rocky Mountain West. Certainly the regional coloring of his finished play, accurately and richly detailed, must have gained in verisimilitude from Moody's desert experiences. It is this local color, presented in somewhat polished but, in 1906, refreshingly original language, which most effectively connects *The Great Divide* with the dramatic literature of the western town.

The earlier action takes place against ranch and mining backgrounds. Frequent references in the dialogue to isolated settlements suggest how closely the economic and social interests of southern Arizona ranchers and Cordillera miners were associated with frontier settlements: trading stations, camps, and even mountain resorts. In Act I, for example, Ruth and her brother Philip and their friends are not wholly ranch-bound. Their conversation affords glimpses of nearby way stations, such as Cottonwood Wash, San Jacinto, and Lone Tree, the scene of a shindig, a lively "Mexican blowout" which draws every "man-jack" away from the Jordan ranch. Other local color touches include a boy's excitement about frontier entertainment of a livelier sort: "They was doin' some Navajo stunts on horseback, pulling chickens out of the sand at a gallop on the upswing."[45] The second act, tracing Stephen's successful mining operations in a Cordillera settlement, suggests the free ways of later mining towns. Miners Burt and Lon gossip in colloquial speech about affairs at Stephen's mine as well as about his unusual marriage. Their earthy talk reveals the primitive conditions in such typical mining communities in the Cordilleras as Rio Verde and End-of-the-Rainbow. Relying on a familiar Harte technique, Moody, by means of his New England characters, dramatically contrasts the strange beauty of the Arizona desert—its arroyos, mesas, dazzling sunlight, and majestic silence—with the crudity of its lonely little towns—"the ones that weren't finished"—and their untutored folk. However much the impressive setting reveals Moody's fidelity to the spirit of the desert Southwest and its environing mountains, *The Great Divide*, as well as his later *The Faith Healer*, springs from his interest in a human love story more than from the influence of locality.

Clyde [William] Fitch (1865-1909), one of the most prolific among the popular playwrights at the turn of the century, felt the pull of the West somewhat differently from the quite personal way in which Thomas, Moody, Wister, and others were stirred by their travels in the region. All of these, as we have seen, shared a deep feeling for native atmosphere. Fitch's interpretations, on the other hand, while having notable audience appeal, offered no original thinking about the basic problems of life in the West. Secondhand, superficial, and melodramatic, his western plays were written largely in response to the tastes of the theatergoers of the era. Fitch's best character-problem plays—*The Girl with the Green Eyes, The Truth,* and *The Climbers*—contributed to the beginnings of contemporary realism in the theater; yet his several western plays had little vital influence in furthering creative efforts in regional drama, except to indicate continuing public interest in frontier materials. The first of these, *The Cowboy and the Lady,* a three-act melodrama written in collaboration with Willis Steell, was produced by Charles Frohman in New York at the Knickerbocker Theatre. Written especially for Nat C. Goodwin and Maxine Elliott, his beautiful wife, this melodrama had a run of forty-four performances, beginning on Christmas Day, 1899. On March 13, 1899, it was presented at the Broad Street Theatre, Philadelphia, and on June 5 at the Duke of York's Theatre, London. Bret Harte, witnessing the unsuccessful London performance, believed that Fitch was too closely following his own fiction, notably in the creation of Midge, one of the leading female characters, who reminded Harte of his portrayal of women in California mining towns. The play's insignificance, no doubt, was the result of Fitch's hasty turning to material with which he was unfamiliar.[46] At any rate, when *The Cowboy and the Lady* was given in Philadelphia, Fitch's *Nathan Hale* beat it in box office receipts, and the playwright wrote to a friend: "If any play is going to beat it, I'd rather it was one of mine, eh?"[47]

In spite of its superficialities, *The Cowboy and the Lady* illustrates several of Fitch's dominant interests: his love of color and his attention to details, based largely upon his keen observation of the people he met. Charles Frohman, incidentally, was one of the few American managers who grasped the artistic value of this "Fitchian touch"—as Fitch said, "the value of the little things."[48] In this comedy, as in his others, Fitch insisted "that rattling good comedy, standing on its own legs, could spring from the simple affairs of American life . . . "[49] The affairs of simple folk furnish the stuff out of which, in *The Cowboy and the Lady,* Fitch fashioned a series of action-filled scenes of ranch and mining life in the late nineteenth century. To the bar and dance hall in Silverville, Colorado, come local cowboys, clerks, and other citizens (even Miss Prissims, who "talks a stream of chatter all the time") for excited gossip about the discovery of Weston's body in the room of Molly Parkins, an attractive dance hall girl. Earlier, Teddy North, a cowboy, had overheard a quarrel between philandering Weston and his ladylike wife, who threatened to kill him if he ventured into Molly's room. Subsequently Teddy, who remains silent about Mrs. Weston's threat, is charged as the murderer, in a crowded courtroom scene. To the astonishment of Silverville folk, Teddy is freed when "Quickfoot" Jim, long in love with Molly, confesses that he killed Weston for "two-timing" with his girl.[50]

Another Frohman production, *The Girl and the Judge*, which opened at New York's Lyceum Theatre, December 4, 1901, proved more successful. The excellent acting of Annie Russell as the heroine, Winifred Stanton, and of veteran "dear old Mrs. Gilbert" contributed toward its run of 125 performances. While the scene is but vaguely suggested as a town in "a Western state," the play had its origin in a story of actual kleptomania reported to Fitch by Judge Galloway, an Ohio friend. Thus inspired, Fitch dramatized the plight of an unsuccessful provincial family, the Stantons, disturbed by the shame of the mother, who was a kleptomaniac. With his usual attention to details, Fitch realistically portrayed the several dilemmas of the four key townspeople: of nervous Mrs. Stanton and insistent Winifred, who forces her mother to reveal her vice; of Mr. Stanton, who, while concealing his wife's weakness, turns to drinking; and of George Buckingham Chartris, an aristocratic probate judge—"a grand swell who will be Governor someday"—forced to choose between his love for Winifred and his legal duty. (His duty is made all the more difficult when Mrs. Stanton is accused of taking a valuable pin belonging to Mrs. Chartris, his mother.) Here, as elsewhere, Fitch subordinates background to the business of realizing all of the human traits, and even the humor, in his given situation: youth's struggle to achieve happiness in the face of crippling circumstances.[51]

During the very busy year of 1905, Fitch had several plays in production, among them *The Woman in the Case*, regarded by Quinn as "one of the finest types of melodrama our stage has known." Such praise, unfortunately, cannot be extended to a second collaboration with Steell. This was another melodrama of frontier life, *Wolfville: A Drama of the South West*, a four-act dramatization of Alfred Henry Lewis' sketches and stories of the free, uncertain life of the Arizona cattle and mining country, first published in 1897 as *Wolfville*. This fast-moving play, though produced by Frohman at the Broad Street Theatre, Philadelphia, on November 27, 1905, starring Nat C. Goodwin as Cherokee Hall, "a obnoxious kyard-sharp," was not too successful, perhaps because it lacked the indigenous descriptions of Lewis' original narratives. Lewis— a Cleveland lawyer and journalist who became a hobo cowpuncher in frontier Arizona—knew at firsthand the hard-riding, hard-living cowboy of the early Southwest. Thus, as a truer interpretation of the eccentricities of the cowboy as he appeared in town and on the range, Lewis' authentic Wolfville series is superior to the Fitch-Steell adaptation, however lively the latter's action.[52] The reason is apparent. As Moses has shown, Fitch's "technique was sometimes skilful, at other times it was hasty and crude; at its best it was more polished than vigorous. In the matter of dramatization, one might well imagine why Mr. Fitch was unsuccessful in turning Alfred Henry Lewis' 'Wolfeville Stories' into a Western play."[53]

The humor, frontier idiom, tall tales, and free life depicted in Lewis' sketches and stories of Arizona furnished Fitch and Steell with easily adaptable matter. More difficult must have been the problem of characterization and even of focal situation, for the original Wolfeville tales are held together principally by stress on a small town and a range locality. Also, Lewis' narrator, the best keynoted Wolfville citizen, actually is not very deeply characterized, certainly not to the extent of such individualized portrayal as, for example, that of Wilder's Stage Manager of *Our Town*. Lewis' homely teller of tales, presented merely as the Old Cattleman, is a familiar type—a loquacious old range man, widely observant of the life around him in the small town of Wolfville, in the nearby mines, in Tucson (the nearest city), and on his ranch. His drawled remarks about activities in Wolfville picture, on the surface, a typical cow town of the late nineties, with its gaudy gambling parlors and dance halls, saloons, rickety hotel, and even an "op'ry house." (In the play, action takes place in a dance hall called "The Road to Ruin," along the main street satirically named Broadway, and at the local stage station.) The counterpart of actual cattle towns in the frontier Southwest, Wolfville had a mixed population of cowmen, Mexicans, and Indians whose interests were not wholly confined to the cattle industry. According to the Old Cattleman's recollections, "cows is what you might call the leadin' industry, with whiskey an' faro-bank on the side"; but with the unearthing of ore, "the mines is opened, an' Wolfville's swelled tremendous. We-all even wins a county-seat fight with Red Dog, wherein we puts it all over that ornery hamlet . . . "[54] In Act IV of the play, with the news that "the Golden Comet Mine is going to pay out huge chunks of yellow gold," Sam Enright, before "liquoring up" at the Ruin, joyfully declares that "As Alcalde I 'low that this here news is bound to swell Wolfville tremjous."[55]

As the yarns of Wolfville's idiomatic "philosopher" suggest, local amusements made life exciting, if sometimes uncertain. In the play much use is made of a noisy election, a Mexican fandango, the forming of a posse, and a lynching. At the post office, at the Red Light, where "we libates," at the O. K. Restaurant, and even at the dance halls, where "we mebby watches 'em ballance all,' or 'swing your partners,' " the Old Cattleman "upholds the hours tellin' tales an' gossipin' about cattle and killin's, an' other topics common to a cow country."[56] Any cowboy desiring a change of entertainment knew that he might rely on the stage and his pony "to pull freight with" when Wolfville life became too tame "an' we thirsts for the meetropolitan gayety of Tucson." As for cultural benefits, "Then thar's Huggins's Bird Cage Op'ry House, an' now an' then we-all floats over thar an' takes in the dramy." On the stage, Cherokee Hall is at last identified as Charles Bradon, who has a college background, whereas the camp laundress, Benson Annie, admits "I was to school six months in Missouri, that's the only trouble with me!" Descriptions of the rivalry between dance hall operators, a Thanksgiving celebration with cowmen from Red Dog, quarrels with rustlers, excitement and fights over gambling stakes, funeral services for a Wolfvillian Buck Fanshaw, and the cowboys' lively interest in elections—all, through the Old Cattleman's idiomatic reporting, mark Lewis as a pioneer interpreter of the strenuous life of the old Southwest. Names like Faro Nell, Piñon Bill, Texas Thompson, Crawfish Jim, and Tucson Jennie, some of which are used in the dramatization, give a further "wild West" tone to the Wolfville tales. Although a bit imitative of Harte and Mark Twain, Lewis —but not his adapters—preserved in the richly detailed Wolfville scenes much of the true spirit of southwestern cow towns.[57]

If Fitch failed to create memorable interpretations of life in western communities, at least, like other producers of popular entertainment in the nineties, he did not pretend that he was purveying frontier history. Apparently during the Mauve Decade "a playgoer wanted plenty for his money; dramas ran four, five and six acts, and frequently a production would be preceded by a one-acter, . . ."[58] Theatrical listings of that decade and later suggest that many theater patrons were more titillated by the violent and novel excitements offered by western dramatizations than by the "new drama of ideas." Melodrama and farce flourished, especially under the aegis of Charles Frohman, who sponsored playwrights in their creation of new versions of old materials, including frontier experience. Other producers—Belasco, Daly, Palmer, and lesser ones—filled their seasonal programs with melodramatic representations of the West. Consider these random listings: Hoyt's frequently revived San Francisco farce, *A Trip to Chinatown*, in its first New York production—at the Harlem Opera House—on December 8, 1890, and his *A Texas Steer* at the Madison Square Theatre on January 8, 1894; Frohman's presentation of *The Luck of Roaring Camp* at the Empire, May 14, 1894, and of the Harte-Edgar Pemberton dramatization of Harte's "The Judgment of Bolivas Plain" as *Sue*, for thirty-one performances at Hoyt's Theatre beginning September 15, 1896, and starring Annie Russell; and two productions by William T. Keogh and Thomas H. Davis: Gus Heege's farce comedy, *Rush City*, at the Columbus Theatre, November 26, 1894, and William Haworth's *On the Mississippi*, also in 1894. Also popular were the forty-eight performances of Frank Mayo's dramatization of Mark Twain's *Pudd'nhead Wilson*, with a prologue and four acts, at the Herald Square Theatre (from April 15, 1895), with Charles E. Evans as producer and Mayo, E. L. Davenport, and Lucille La Verne in the cast. Revivals of frontier plays—*Sue* (1897), Miller's *The Danites* (1897), Edward E. Rose's *The Westerner* (1898), and Campbell's *My Partner* (1899)—indicate the continued appeal of the drama of the West, however superficial its treatment. The season of 1905–6 was marked by a memorable theatrical event, the opening in October at Wallack's Theatre of Edwin Milton Royle's sensationally popular *The Squaw Man*. Later played around the world, *The Squaw Man* "was a typical success of the day when romantic melodramas were popular." William S. Hart's portrayal of the "bad man" was a popular forerunner of Porter Emerson Brown's *The Bad Man*, produced as late as the season of 1920–21.[59]

The New Regionalism

Such a welter of melodrama and farce, at best but a reflection of public taste, added neither newness nor further artistic significance to the dramatized world of the small town in the West. As life in America became more and more uniform, relatively few artistic and truly memorable plays re-creating trans-Mississippi communities were to appear, and not all of these dealt primarily with the little town as an entity. To be sure, the "new regionalism," burgeoning in the twenties and thirties, stimulated new creative approaches to environmental materials. In time, this multiregional pattern was given color and movement, partly by certain literary rediscoveries of the West. Within various areas of the West, newcomers—writers, artists, and others—mostly "native sons," found inspiration and support through many channels: regional magazines such as *Midland* (Iowa), *Frontier* (Montana), the *Western Review* (later the *Rocky Mountain Review*), and the *Southwest Review*; folklore societies and their publications; university courses in regional literature manned by enthusiastic professors: J. Frank Dobie at Texas, Jay B. Hubbell and John H. McGinnis at Southern Methodist, W. S. Campbell (Stanley Vestal) at Oklahoma, and others; college dramatic societies, notably the Dakota Playmakers and, later, the Carolina Playmakers, directed by Frederick Henry Koch; community little theaters mushrooming in Pasadena, Dallas, and elsewhere; the Drama League of America's encouragement of a literary drama of native origin, and the pioneering

Theatre Arts, founded in 1918; books like Kenneth Macgowan's *Footlights Across America* (1929); newspaper book pages with a regional slant; and the personal appeal of native environment.[60] All of these and more helped to assert new attitudes toward provincial life in the West. During the twenties and thirties, therefore, new names began to be associated with community regional matter in the form of essays, poems, stories, novels, folk collections (as B. A. Botkin's *Folk-Say*, 1929), and plays, mostly shorter localized ones adaptable to little-theater stages and audiences.

The dramatic record of the small-town West produced by these newer regional responses long after the pioneering days were over has certainly not been uniform either in achievement and success or in point of view. The trans-Mississippi West, lengthening itself from the lonely mountain towns of the Northwest to the farms of the Dakotas, Nebraska, and Oklahoma and to the ranches above the Rio Grande, is most impressive because of its space, bigness, and openness. Such overwhelming vastness has continued, from the Gold Rush until this more recent regional movement, to bring about various extremes of locale, theme, and other qualities distinguishing the dramatization of life in western towns. Robert Finch, Lynn Riggs, Ellsworth Prouty Conkle, Virgil Geddes, and John William Rogers, Jr. are representative ranking talents emerging from the new regionalism to dramatize the life of their respective sections. All have proved adept at making drama from the everyday problems and conditions of simple folk types peculiar to the wide West: ranchers and cowpunchers, traders and freighters, prospecting miners and mining engineers, homesteaders, sheepherders, and town settlers, including bartenders, storekeepers, proprietors of stagecoach stations, hotel owners, depot telegraphers and other railroaders, doctors, wives of different temperaments, and other ordinary men and women of mixed racial groups, including Mexicans and Negroes. Mostly these regionalists have written little plays, often one-acters, better adapted to community theater groups than to the commercial stage. Generally, too, the talents of these young regionalists were not for the creation of memorable "inward plays," but for realistic vignettes, sometimes comic, sometimes somber, of human conditions throughout the western region.

Robert Finch, one of the gifted young playwrights moved by regional self-awareness, has localized most of his short plays in the Northern Rockies, mainly in Montana. Apparently his most vivid memories are associated with that state, his home since boyhood, rather than with Iowa, where he was born. His studies at the Yale Drama School and his three years (1937-40) of association with Professor Koch and the Carolina Playmakers, climaxed by a Rockefeller Fellowship, assuredly deepened his knowledge of stagecraft. Such enriching experience, however, did not weaken his interest in the unpretentious way of life which he had known intimately in the Northwest. Accordingly, Finch has succeeded, through the medium of the short play, in imaginatively interpreting the genuine ruggedness of plain people native to the range and nearby small towns. His *Plays of the American West*, a first volume containing fifteen of his more than twenty plays published by the forties, graphically presents many "figures in a landscape" in Montana, Utah, and Nevada.[61]

Finch's literary explorations in the Northwest have resulted in a galaxy of lively portraits (mostly two-dimensional, however) which clearly suggest the adaptability of westerners, past and present, to frontier violence, the harshness of the land, the loneliness and sordidness of the towns, and other frontier conditions. Except for a few wanderers, such as a folk singer of Irish heritage and a hobo, his characters—some pioneers, some contemporary—belong to different types of isolated towns. From story to story, the stage directions picture "a little mountain cow-town called Dublin Gulch" with its Pastime Saloon, "the coolest place in town these hot August days"; Nick's Camp for Tourists, hardly a town but more of a way station on a highway in the Nevada desert; "Paradise, a tiny railroad stop, high in the Rocky Mountains"; Virginia City, Montana Territory, many years ago; Bonanza, a mountain ghost town, once swarming with miners, and Crystal, another deserted mining camp; and the teeming county fairgrounds during rodeo time, located in another "little cow-town in the mountains, the center of all creation to the ranchers for fifty miles around."

Finch's feeling for his own milieu, as well as for the validity of its picturesque surroundings, shows up, in part, in his emphasis on community externalities. Cogent ideas or myths about civilization in the Northwest are either missing or subordinated to background color and outward events. In subject, as in mood, his small-town plays vary widely. For example, "Miracle at Dublin Gulch" concerns the comic clash of a wayfaring and gambling musician, Michael J. McCarthy, and the "regulars" at the Pastime Saloon, who lose all of their cash to that Irishman "blessed with amazin' luck," with their resentful spouses, belligerent because "That bum's been here ten days an' he's ruined the whole town." The somber "Murder in the Snow," made all the more suspenseful by a station agent's dream of an ax murder done "past midnight on a blizzardly night in the year 1870," dramatizes the tensions of travelers marooned in an isolated station of the Yellowstone and Western Stage Coach Company in Montana Territory. The fearful premonitions of station proprietor Bill Veachy, of grizzled Haze Phillips, a prospector who has exchanged his gold dust for supplies before returning to his Virginia City claim, and of Frank Parrish, a young eastern overlander, are made manifest on the several levels of realism of scene, of fantasy (Veachy's nightmarish dream), and of theatricalism suggestive of the older western melodrama. Veachy's grave concern about road agents and the welfare of Lloyd Magrady, his partner, long overdue in bringing gold dust and nuggets across the snow-laden Divide, is intensified by the howling winds outside, a murderous face at the station window, and the unexpected entrance of Shoshone Bob, Magrady's murderer. A suspense-filled companion play, "Johnny," or "Montana Night" as it was titled by the Carolina Playmakers, uses a similar set: a Virginia City supply station, "a blind for a band of road agents." The time, "before midnight of New Year's Eve" many years ago, and a blizzard howling down from the mountains all evening have not prevented the miners from coming into town to celebrate. One of these, Johnny, is "packin' fourteen ounces of gold dust" when he is robbed and brutally murdered by Gallagher and Benson, the station operators who "protected by their alleged status as traders, . . . plunder and murder, unsuspected and unpunished by the Vigilantes." Kindly prospector Wash Beidler, "from way back in Pike County," faintly resembling Alonzo Delano's lusty Pike County Jess, is an imaginative portrayal of one of those unglamorized but real heroes of the west: "the *good* men whose records of achievement and true courage need no aura of outlawry to make them worth remembrance."[62]

A nostalgic mood prevails in both "Ghost Town" and "The Day They All Come Back," each play being developed by devices of reminiscence. In both plays aged folk, living lonely lives in deserted mining towns, relive vicariously the exciting boom days of the late 1880's when gold-mad adventurers crowded into Bonanza and Crystal. In "Rodeo" there is a contrasting stress on youth, much as in Phil Stong's *State Fair*, against the background of the county fairgrounds in a small cow town in the mountains. In all three of these plays Finch, working well within the limits of his one-act medium, achieves fine versimilitude in picturing crowds. In "Ghost Town," as in "The Day They All Come Back," a loquacious old-timer remembers the glorious past when the Gulch "was plumb full o' miners—the biggest stampede I ever did see," with "people comin' overland from 'way back east—road agents, gamblers, miners, greenhorns . . . , all after the gold." Old Bill remembers the "cheerin' and shoutin' and singin' and men rushin' out with their gold pans into the hills, shore they'd git rich overnight." Equally graphic is the achievement of the impression of teeming crowds by dialogue, a carnival set, and sound effects, in the "Rodeo" scenes along a small midway. ("The sound of the crowd is a buzz in the air, and on the breeze is the music from the merry-go-round.") Here and elsewhere, Finch displays a fine talent for evoking community scenes and characterizing genuinely American folk.

Nebraska's small towns and prairies have been celebrated unforgettably in novels and short stories, with notably high artistry in Willa Cather's *O Pioneers!* (1913), *My Ántonia* (1918), *One of Ours* (1923), and "The Sculptor's Funeral" (1920). Sharing with contemporary village controversialists an interest in insurgency, Miss Cather wrote memorably of the clash between provincial Nebraskans and their rural or village environments. Her youthful Thea Kronborg, Ántonia Shimerda, Harvey Merrick, and Claude Wheeler, their restlessness stirred by yearnings of the spirit and vague dissatisfactions, seem spiritually akin to the disturbed citizens of Spoon River, Gopher Prairie, and Winesburg. All yearn for richer, fuller experiences, for escape from the dulness and mediocrity of their prairie environments. Through Miss Cather's artistry, themes and problems of youth struggling with the Bright Medusa, her symbol of ambition, are related to highly individualized and vibrant midwesterners.

By contrast with the novelists and storytellers, midwestern playwrights during the twenties and thirties generally showed little awareness of the dramatic possibilities of Nebraska's prairies and little towns. An exception, however, is Ellsworth Prouty Conkle, now a professor in the College of Fine Arts at the University of Texas. Through his youthful years (until he was nineteen) in his native Peru, Nebraska, and through his training at the state universities of Nebraska and Iowa, Conkle gained an intimate knowledge of rural and small-town Mid-America. His graduate studies at Yale (1926-27) under George Pierce Baker, as well as his teaching in North Dakota, gave further impetus to Conkle's desire to re-create dramatically down-to-earth scenes and provincial folk belonging to a generation older than his own and native to the limited world of Nebraska's farms and villages. His exploitation of the provinces began modestly with one-act sketches, *Crick Bottom Plays* (1928), "based almost wholly on the life he knew; it was easy for him to write about people with whom he had put up hay, plowed corn, gone to charivaris, picnics and funerals."[63]

Sharing with Willa Cather and Ruth Suckow a keen insight into the manners and minds of country people, living on farms and in villages of the "Heartland," Conkle brought to these early one-acters a decidedly

idiomatic speech, folk humor, and subjects of conversation characteristic of simple, unworldly midwesterners. His Nebraska villages and
countryside comprise a background little affected by the changing society
of about 1905. Certainly the changes in the West at that time—the
increase of wealth, the establishment of more distinct social classes, and
a growing uniformity in social behavior—barely touched Conkle's
western scene. Rather, the implication in such sketches as " 'Lection,"
"Things *Is* That-A-Way," and "Warter-Wucks" is that the Crick Bottom
rustics had little to do with "the bristling march of events." There are
no sketches of cultivated people, such as Miss Cather included in her
Nebraska novels and stories; rather, the Crick Bottom Folk, often crude
and meanspirited, are mostly tillers of the soil. The community relationships in these sketches are of ordinary provincials, generally lacking
in imagination, generous impulses, and the finer strains in human nature.
Even the sentiment of love—in "Sparkin' "—concerns a clodhopper of a
hired man and an untutored farm girl. Village or rural discontents thwart
in different ways the desires of the few natives yearning to escape. Carping Granny Painsberry, in "Sparkin'," is a domineering "killjoy" when
Orry Sparks comes "a-courtin' " shy and pretty Essie Hanna, her granddaughter. Hayd Liggett and Hank Wagner—two village ne'er-do-wells,
"perty small punkins"—are stumbling blocks in the path of their children, Cynthie Liggett and Raff Wagner, young lovers "hankering" for
the world outside, "that fur land wherever et is." The five men sitting up
with the corpse of Minnie Field while away the night by gossip, which
reveals not only their crude selves but the dead woman's years of struggle
to find a bit of beauty. Most sharply drawn, however, is their portrait
of Tip Field, so unfeeling about the loss of his wife that he plans now to
cut up her parlor organ for "kindlin' wood"—the organ which cost
Minnie seven hard years of saving butter and egg money. Elsewhere,
meanness of spirit is expressed with a folksy humor, as in connection
with the cheating in a community election and the efforts to prevent the
town council from sanctioning plans for more modern water works.

In later plays Conkle has used his birthplace as the realistic backdrop
for a variety of midwesterners who are a part of the village from the
pioneering "day[s] of decision" in the 1840's until the mid-1920's and
later. Historically the best of these plays, *In The Shadow of a Rock*
(1936)[64] sketches violent scenes in frontier Nebraska Territory when the
village of Peru was a slave station along the Underground Railroad.
Conflicts, in both opinion and action, between abolitionists and slave
owners provide the crises. A courageous and compassionate widow, a
storekeeper, in protecting two Negro babies brought to the Peru station

along the "U.G." by John Brown, becomes the symbol of "the shadow of a rock in a weary land." The folk idea in Peru's community life appears also in *Loolie and Other Short Plays* (1935), wherein characterization is marked by quirks and peculiarities, as in the portrayal of a death scene, where a simple soul, a grandmother, naïvely views heaven as a facsimile of the village of Peru. In other plays village eccentrics and rebels are more humorously dramatized. For example, *Forty-nine Dogs in a Meat House* (undated) satirizes the crusading spirit of the "good ladies" of the local church bent upon a cleanup campaign. In the ensuing battle of the sexes the town males, organized in a group called "The Forty-nine Dogs," resort to deprivation of sex to outwit the crusading women.

In general, Conkle's plays, with abundant idiomatic dialogue and humor of character and situation, reveal that he early reached an understanding of human experience within a specific geographical milieu. Setting his stage with realistic scenes of mid-American villages, past and present, he has been primarily concerned with portraying rural and small-town folk with "obscure destinies." Moreover, his sometimes caustic satire offers a corrective for the easy optimism of earlier western playwrights—Delano and Belasco, for example—and such western heroes as Davy Crockett and Colonel Beriah Sellers.

As to southwestern drama of the thirties, the late John William Rogers, Jr., Dallas critic and playwright, declared in 1943:

Any creative expression in dramatic form sufficiently vigorous to merit more than passing local attention, however, is a recent manifestation. It came about under the same impulse that made our painters realize the land about them could be really exciting to paint and our storytellers perceive that the extraordinary variety of civilizations that have flowed together here, is of high human interest. Inadvertently, also, it happens to be a product of little theatre activity, which in the twenties spread like a rash over this region.[65]

In his own short plays Rogers has shown cogently how a variety of community materials of high human interest have "flowed together." Apparently his primary concern was not with the Texas small town per se, but largely with its close relationship with the problems and social attitudes of the people throughout the environing countryside. Also, his regional boundaries, loosely as much southern as western, or southwestern, are not so sharply limited or localized as those marking many western small-town dramas. To illustrate, his *Judge Lynch*, published in 1924 in the *Southwest Review*, was produced by the Dallas Little Theatre and won the David Belasco Cup in the 1923 community drama tournament. Such recognition may have come about because of the realistic technique and the timeliness of the play's subject: lynching, a problem then as much southwestern as southern. Antedating Faulkner's "Dry September" (1931), *Judge Lynch*, with its meticulously realistic evocation of scene and characters, brings to life the fear-haunted, prejudice-ridden people of a rural settlement rather than of an incorporated town.[66] The community, however, is a compact little world in itself, with the Joplins and other farming folk drawn together by the brutal and mysterious murder of Squire Tatum. Their mutual fear of other attacks by "that Jacks nigger," the Squire's falsely accused tenant, and their mob lynching of the innocent and terrified Negro offer a pattern of unleashed emotions which motivate tragedy in a crossroads hamlet.

A few other plays clearly indicate that from the study of his native region Rogers was creatively aware of its frontier history, its folk suspicions, biases, and social attitudes. Among these, "The Rescue of Cynthia Ann" (1929) and "Western People" (1934) show the truth of J. Frank Dobie's candid declaration: "Like historical fiction, drama of the Southwest has been less dramatic than actuality and less realistic than real characters."[67]

"The Rescue of Cynthia Ann" is an episodic dramatization based upon the experience of Cynthia Ann Parker, a white girl long held in captivity by Indians. Limited to certain events in the late afternoon of December 31, 1860, this little play is set in the Evans house at Fort Cooper, Texas, where the captain's wife, Mrs. Evans, allows a lively little girl and two neighbors, pioneer women intensely curious about the "Injun woman," to stare at her house-prisoner, the now tanned, weather-beaten, and altogether unromantic Cynthia Ann, the squaw of Chief Pete Nocona, and her papoose.[68] In writing "Westward People" Rogers, while developing "an incident which is not a literal historical fact," has succeeded in his purpose of "making it express a real historical truth," well summed up in his epigraph chosen from Archibald Mac-Leish: "And all the land lay waiting her westward people." In his characterization of Mrs. Mary Austin Holley, based upon her *Letters From Texas* (1833), Rogers has keynoted the truth that "the prospects of a new country" are inevitably coupled with "the retrospect of the old." The slight action of the plot takes place in December, 1831, against a background typifying a Texas log-cabin settlement, the "Kincheloe Neighborhood" of Stephen F. Austin's colony.

Rogers' gifts for facile and witty satire enabled him to create hilarious drawing-room comedies, first presented before society audiences at the Little Theatre of Dallas. Both *Roam Though I May* (1932) and *Where the Dear Antelope Play* (1941) center around amusing domestic and community situations affecting the lives of "uppercrust" Texans of Dallas and his mythical Indian City, Texas, during the 1930's.[69] In both comedies Rogers delightfully pokes fun at the power elite of Dallas and Indian City, who pride themselves on their family trees and reunions, antiques, memberships in "culture" clubs, their financial support of interior decorators, mural artists, and local symphony orchestras, and other marks of social prestige in this changing era.

Among other changes, the general stir of experimental activity in the arts during the twenties and later brought new and imaginatively conceived versions of dialogue sequences, characterizations, and stage design. In many cases the settings proved more revealing of theme and motivation than the characters themselves.[70] This applies, with certain reservations, to a few more plays of western locality whose authors first found audiences through the "tributary theatre." During the season of 1931, for example, theaters of town and gown groups found an increasing interest in new plays of the western scene. At Syracuse University Lynn Riggs's tragic *Big Lake*, produced under the direction of Sawyer Falk, and Witter Bynner's self-directed *A Night Wind*, presented by the Santa Fe Players, evidenced the depth and richness of indigenous materials. Albert Riebling, in pleading the case for a theater devoted to the native playwright, says that in their second season at the Detroit Playhouse he and his staff "decided to produce nothing but untried American plays."[71] Such an experimental policy led to the fruitful presentation in the Detroit Playhouse of new provincial dramas, including Conkle's cycle of Crick Bottom one-acters, Virgil Geddes' *Behind the Night* and *So Late Begins*, and Lynn Riggs's *A Lantern to See By*, which received wholehearted praise. Earlier, in the spring of 1925, another native interpreter of the West, Dan Totheroh, was introduced to the public by the University of California's production of *Wild Birds*, a poignant midwestern farm play and a moving tragedy of desire and hope, comparable in its treatment of the failure of aspiration to Thomas Hardy's somber *Jude the Obscure*.

The provincial Nebraska locale—largely farm settlements not too many miles distant from larger trading centers—reappears in several plays by Virgil Geddes. Effectively original in his treatment of regional matter, he has dramatized Nebraska settings and natives by simple realism rather than by the overused techniques of folksy speech and westernized dress. In fact, in his texts he uses dialect and local flavor sparingly, for, as he has written, it has been his "experience and feeling that peculiarities of talk and isolated manners do not provide the music and emotional tone of drama and detract from the body and reach of a play's thematic whole."[72] The starkness of his scenes is an appropriate backdrop for his naturally portrayed provincials, somewhat akin in their frustrations and sufferings to Sherwood Anderson's inhibited Winesburgians. His principal gift "is the ability to deal unselfconsciously with human beings, to reveal them dispassionately *being themselves,* and not the mouthpieces or pawns of the playwright."[73] His bold thematic use of incest in an early two-act tragedy, *The Earth Between,* stirred up heated controversy between British St. John Ervine and the New York critics when the Provincetown Players produced it in Greenwich Village on March 5, 1929. Barrett H. Clark upheld Geddes on the basis that his work showed "a sense of life, observed with the cold eye of a scientist, yet intensely alive." On the other hand, Ervine in his review for the *New York World* (March 7, 1929), while granting that "Mr. Geddes is not without talent," urged him to forget that he ever read *Desire Under the Elms.* The play is truly a tragedy of desire. "Old man" Nat Jennings, a fifty-year-old farmer whose wife has died, feels an unnatural attraction for his daughter Floy. Discovering that his young hired hand Jake is ready to fall in love with Floy, Jennings orders the youth to sleep in a dampened, moldy barn, where he contracts pneumonia and dies. After the funeral—a realistically presented community scene—Jennings, on his knees in a wheatfield, embraces Floy, telling her passionately that she is his woman. Floy, confused, feels that there is something between them. "Something heavy; so you can't push it away. Like it was the earth, itself."

Further representative of Geddes' inherent sense of the dramatic values to be found in isolated community life is a cycle of plays, *Native Ground*: "Native Ground," "The Plowshare's Gleam," and "As the Crow Flies." This trilogy, tragic in tone, portrays the cramped lives of Nebraska and North Dakota farmers and villagers early in the present century. "Native Ground," written in 1928, was produced the following season at the Experimental Theatre, Boston. "As the Crow Flies" was to have been produced in the spring of 1930 by the Provincetown Players at the Garrick Theatre, but no performance took place. *Native Ground* is a midwestern saga of desire and unfulfilment. The trilogy traces the demoralizing influence of an isolated existence, first in Nebraska and later in North Dakota, upon several generations of Bentleys. The central action has to do with pretty Myrtle Bentley, who feels drawn toward Milton Rogers, a roving farmhand many years her senior, who had been in love with her mother, Lora, the wife of farmer Lars Bentley. Neither Lars nor Myrtle knows that according to Lora's belief, Milton is the girl's own father. Folk destiny, as presented in this trilogy, is marked everywhere by dramatic irony. Lars, ignorant of the truth, insists that Milton and Myrtle escape to Milton's Dakota farm. This they do, living in the Dakota community as man and wife, though without carnal relations. Lars's own desire for grandchildren seems assured when at last Myrtle becomes pregnant, not, however, by Milton but by an itinerant farmhand; but the child dies. In these and similar happenings throughout the trilogy, Geddes' native ground—the isolated farms and the sordid agricultural villages—seems to foster tragedy.

The close ties among western farm folk, homesteaders, and agricultural villagers are again memorably portrayed in the tragedies of Oakland-born Dan Totheroh. Motivated by theatrical interests since youth, Totheroh wrote his first play in high school at San Rafael, California, and later acted in stock and vaudeville. From 1921 to 1923, following his war service, he was active in little theater work in Los Angeles and San Francisco, gaining further experience through assisting, as playwright and producer, California's pageant director, Garnet Holme. Before and after his 1924 position as producing director of drama at the University of California, he won some recognition for his short regional plays, several of which he submitted to *The Drama*.[74] Representative of this early work, "In the Darkness" reaffirms the tragedy of lonely, beauty-starved pioneer women, whose barrenness of existence on isolated prairie homesteads may become a torment. Even the occasional visitors—perhaps a messenger boy from the village of Hempton or Arth, a sympathetic sheepherder—do not relieve the homesteader's wife, Lessie, from her brooding. Only a more tragic darkness, her husband's loss of his eyesight, could cure Lessie of her disillusionment and make her forget her plans to flee the monotony of her prairie community by escaping with Arth.[75]

Equally somber in tone are "Good Vintage" (1930) and "The Great Dark" (1931). The opening of the first play, with its quick revelation of Joe Garcia's wealth from his rich vineyards in Sonoma County, California, keynotes a holiday mood among the Napa Valley winegrowers, the merchants, and other citizens of nearby Napa. The annual Grape Festival, enlivened by parades, bands, and dances, is about to open. All of the Garcias are jubilant because soon young Julia Garcia—"lithe and Latin—dusky as a purple grape herself"—is to be crowned "Queen of the Vineyards." The celebration of Joe's good vintage ends in bitter irony when the jealous Arbinis, rival vintners, in an attempt to assassinate Joe mistakenly kill "Queen" Julia. In "The Great Dark" a mine disaster in a western town brings together the harried women of the town, with conflict arising when the wife and the mistress of one of the miners wait together at the mine shaft for the latest reports from "the great dark." A third one-acter, "Seeing the Elephant," suggests the historical truth which marks Delano's frontier plays in its realistic tale of the Mannings, a typical pioneer family moving "somewhere along the trail to California in the long trek of '49." Especially relevant to the dramatic history of the provincial West are the visions of prosperity which Eben Manning, leader of the family caravan, associates with the newly settled communities beyond the Rockies. "Here we're headin' West, after all. . . . Fact is, I allus *did* wanta see that Californy country. They say land's rich as cream an' mighty easy to plow. You kin plant most anythin' an' up it comes, most over night, an' big as all outdoors."[76]

Without question, *Wild Birds* is Totheroh's most distinguished play, a revelation of his skill in using many of the resources of the American scene. A jury—Eugene O'Neill, Susan Glaspell, and George Jean Nathan—singled it out by awarding Totheroh the Hearst Prize for submitting the best manuscript for production in the Greek Theatre at the University of California. Following the initial production in the Greek Theatre, the play was performed for two weeks at San Francisco's Players Club and in the spring of 1925 at a Greenwich Village little theater, the Cherry Lane, where it lasted for five weeks.[77] The scene of this three-act tragedy is a typically midwestern landscape: the plains baked under the midday sun or transformed by the magic of the moon. All of the natural elements characterizing the prairie locale—more specifically, the Slag farm on the prairie—form a background poetically designed to heighten the effect of the tragedy played against it. The central situation of the poignant drama concerns the subjection of helpless and beauty-loving youth to malice and cruelty which produce death. Two "wild birds"—seventeen-year-old Maizie, "rescued" by farmer Slag from a small-town orphanage, and Adam Larson, youthful escapee from a reform school—are pitted against a formidable trio: sadistic John Slag ("That man of your'n air a devil," says George Marshall, a hired hand); lank Mrs. Slag, willing to let frail Maizie do all the heavy household work; and meanspirited Corie Slag, who resembles her mother with "the same straight-lipped mouth and pale blue eyes" and the same mistreatment of Maizie.

Maizie's yearning for beauty and happiness, expressed in the wistful, searching expression in her eyes, is but partially fulfilled by her daily discoveries of natural loveliness on the prairie. A little wild bird trapped as she is, the delicate coloring of the wreath of star-fires around her head, and the moonlight ("Everything air white an' silver")—all of these miracles momentarily release the girl from drudgery. Better still, she and Adam secretly "talk of the dreams they have dreamt and the dreams that may come true." But the freedom they dream about is never realized. John Slag unfeelingly beats young Adam to death; and Maizie, carrying Adam's child, commits suicide by drowning in the farm well. Such a bare outline of the central situation by no means suggests Totheroh's art in narration. His use of minutiae skilfully reveals the sharp contrast between the dreams of youth and the sordidness of their surroundings. The tale-bearing blacksmith at the village of Carston who informs Slag of Maizie and Adam's attempt to run away; an evangelical tent on the outskirts of a prairie settlement with the evening service going on and the preacher raising his voice "high and wrathfully" against "ye generation of vipers"; Milt Pollard's wanting "a wife that he can be proud of to show 'round and take to fairs, tent meetin's and places"; and John Slag's "irritation at having to fix up and go to town when a home wedding [for Corie and plain-faced Milt Pollard] would much more easily and cheaply have served all practical purposes"—all of these are typical of a crass community pattern which offers no solace for the "little wild things, runnin' away to love each other."[78]

In Lynn Riggs our American theater found a poet who brought to it an authenic note of ecstasy and passion, expressed in terms of drama. Gifted, like Geddes and Totheroh, with the ability to take the materials of ordinary life and mold them into forms of stirring beauty, Riggs often used a subtle poetic style to reproduce the rhythms of everyday Oklahoma speech. Born on a farm near Claremore, Indian Territory, in 1899, Riggs skilfully used the rich folk material and idiom of his native district in drama, songs, and serious poetry. Actually *Oklahoma!*, as well as Riggs's own dramatic career, had a modest beginning in 1925 when French issued *Knives from Syria*, his first published play. In this one-acter, as in so much regional fiction growing out of the revolt from the village during the era, the basic theme dramatizes the bitter clash between rebellious and aspiring youth and a harsh, unpromising environment. Rhodie, in her desire to escape the imprisoning farm by fleeing to Claremore and the beckoning world beyond, romantically sees in an ordinary peddler, selling "knives from Syria" and various "pretties" to farm and village women, her best chance for matrimony and opportunity to glimpse "the hills *he* told me about." Later in *Green Grow the Lilacs* the hawker reappears as a little, wiry, swarthy Syrian, acquisitive and cunning, berated by Aunt Eller as "Mister Pedler Man . . . that ud sell a pore old woman a eggbeater that wasn't no good." Subsequently in *Oklahoma!* this character assumes a more individualized role as Eli Hakim, Persian peddler.

Having spent most of his life in the great open spaces of Oklahoma, Texas, and New Mexico, Riggs, son of a part-Cherokee cowpuncher, had his best successes with plays of the range, the pioneer homestead, and the little prairie town. Moreover, "that lost West which is neither Far nor Middle nor South" strongly appealed to him.[79] Early playlets were mostly developed around frontier scenes and folk of what he termed "the lonesome West" of the era around 1900.[80] The tragic action of his two-part, poetically styled *Big Lake* (1927) takes place in the Indian Territory in 1906. Two teen-agers, Betty and Lloyd, from the crude settlement of Verdigree Switch, are so disturbed by a vague restlessness that they do not join their classmates at the chosen picnic site near the Big Lake. Their love of solitude, however, leads them astray to the lakeside cabin of a murderer. The murderer, in a frantic effort to save himself, persuades the pursuing officers that young Lloyd is the guilty one. His false and callous charge leads the overzealous "Shuruff" to shoot Lloyd, as he and Betty are rowing on the lake. Betty dies by drowning. This poignant tragedy of the star-crossed lovers is a genuinely moving re-creation of simple life in the Oklahoma backwoods. The narrowness of the social outlook of the "better class" in Verdigree is best symbolized by puritanic Miss Meredith, the prim Sunday-school teacher and uncheerful chaperone of the picnickers. By contrast, the ecstasy shared by Betty and Lloyd, an awakening born of the sheer joy of being alive and near the shining Big Lake, typifies release from their drab and restrictive village world of Verdigree and its equally sordid neighboring villages of Foyil, Claremont, Sageeyah, and "Pryor Crick." Alas, these youthful seekers discover that "They's no place fer us—nowhur—" except on the lake. Ironically, their refuge, the lake, brings death to both. Another frontier playlet, "Reckless" (1928), is also set in the Indian Territory "many years ago" and dramatizes the spirit of southwestern self-reliance and endurance as expressed in a once popular lyric:

> Wild and reckless
> Born in Texas
> Suckled by a bear,
> Steel backbone,
> Tail screwed on,
> Twelve feet long,
> Dare any son of a gun to step on it![81]

In several other plays Riggs further dramatized the exuberant and sometimes lawless energies of Indian Territory settlers, real and mythical. One of these, which lasted for two weeks on Broadway, was

Roadside, or *Borned in Texas* (1930). Seemingly an expansion of "Reckless," this comedy concerns an uninhibited braggart, "a latterday Davy Crockett," as Willard Thorp has described him, who, after wrecking a courtroom in the Indian Territory, in 1905 lights out for Texas with his equally wild mate Hannie and her Pap. Producer Arthur Hopkins, in his introduction to the published play, lavishly praised it as "the first American dramatic classic."[82] In a 1928 farm play, *A Lantern to See By,* Riggs experimented with a similar theme of wild energy and unrestrained ego in portraying a strong-willed farmer whose tyranny over his pregnant wife and weak-spirited son finally goads the youth to patricide. *Sump'n Like Wings,* also of 1928, reiterates the theme of revolt used in *Knives from Syria*: a neglected daughter, turned prostitute, determines to work out her destiny, however obscure, with her lover in town. But her stubborn efforts, like those of others among Riggs's characters, end in futility. While she does escape from a deadly hotel life, she enters into nothing more promising than the world of her own selfish desires.

Concerning his most popular play, Riggs once wrote, "I didn't have to invent anything for 'Green Grow the Lilacs' . . . . I was saturated in Oklahoma history and legend from the time I learned to walk!" Rich in local color, folk traditions, and humor, this bittersweet melodrama was produced by the Theatre Guild in 1931 by Theresa Helburn and Lawrence Langner, with Franchot Tone and June Walker successfully acting the roles of the cowboy lover, Curly McLain, and Laurey Williams, his girl. In fact, "the great native flavor, and dances," as well as "the gaiety and freshness, the poetry and humor of the people in Lynn Riggs's play" gave Miss Helburn the idea of having the Guild sponsor a musical rich in American pioneer history and lusty with pioneer grit and humor. When her "sizzling plans" had materialized, in the spring of 1943, *Oklahoma!* was on the boards for its sensational New York run of 2,248 performances.[83]

Certain undercurrents of seriousness in Riggs's comedy contrast with the folk interest in fun and frolic and young love. In the drama of the vanishing range, the inevitable conflict between the old free ways of the cattle kings and the new order of farmers fills Curly with feelings of nostalgia and uneasiness. Dispirited because he has no farmlands to offer Laurey, Curly berates himself as "a good-fur-nothing cowpuncher," afraid that "Now the cattle business'll soon be over with. The ranches are breakin' up fast. They're puttin' in barbed w'ar, and plowin' up the sod fer wheat and corn. Purty soon they won't be no more grazin' —thousands of acres—no place fer the cowbody to lay his head."[84]

The old differences between town and country reappear in Aunt Eller's acidulous outburst against "Them *town* fools!"—her uncomplimentary dismissal of all those male townsmen who took part in "the bawdy ministrations" of the "shivoreein' " which brought sorrow to Curly and Laurey and of the "lawmen" who have "Curly settin' in the cooler at Claremore." Then, there is the melodramatic circumstance, on Curly and Laurey's wedding night, of hired hand Jeeter Fry's frenzied knife-attack on Curly, their struggle, and Jeeter's accidental death by his falling on his own knife, bought from a Syrian peddler. A neighborhood justice of the peace then takes Curly into Claremore "to tell the *law*." From the early scenes Jeeter (the original of Jud in *Oklahoma!*), as the "dark and sullen" and vulgar hired man at Aunt Eller's place, is one of the symbols of evil in a changing frontier society. Eventually released, Curly acts in the spirit of western optimism. He wastes no time in idle regrets, for he knows that now there's something more for him to do than sing sentimental and plaintive ditties like "Green grow the lilacs, all sparkling with dew,/I'm lonely, my darling, since parting with you, . . ." As he says, "Country a-changin', got to change with it!"[85]

Like other contemporary regional dramas, *Green Grow the Lilacs* follows actuality in describing another phenomenal change concurrent with the breaking up of the big spreads: town building. Throughout the six scenes of the *Lilacs* Aunt Eller Williams, her niece Laurey, Curly, and other characters frequently refer, favorably and unfavorably, to certain towns which had sprung up in the Indian Territory by 1900. Laurey, reveling in the free life at Aunt Eller's homestead, passionately declares: "But I'd shore hate to leave here, though, and go some'eres else—like to a town or some place—."[86] Further moved by their sense of locality, these farm people identify their neighbors with country settlements or towns of the region. Curly talks about "Old man Parker's boy up here by Claremore," as well as about his riding broncs at the Claremore Fair. Once, when in open country, Curly "got onto which way I was headin' " by seeing the "lights 'way over towards Claremore." Community spirit further pervades conversations about trading and social centers, large and small: Tulsa, Pryor, Verdigree, Catoosie, and other settlements. Characteristic of folk speech and thinking are such small-town references as "up by Quapaw," "up here by Sweetwater," "tother side of Justus," "to Vinita to the crazy house," "way off in Joplin," "a dance at Bushyhead," and the "Dog Crick" community where "old man Peck" entertained neighbors at a spirited play-party.

Although *Green Grow the Lilacs* furnished the basis for *Oklahoma!*, the musical became in effect a new play, compounded of many things:

story, music, lyrics, dances, settings, and costumes, all welded together into a smooth unit. The directional abilities of the Helburn-Langner-Rouben Mamoulian team combined with the creative arts of Richard Rodgers for the music, the late Oscar Hammerstein, II, for the lyrics, Agnes de Mille for the choreography, Lemuel Ayers, "whose settings would seem to have been stolen out of an Oklahoma town one night when nobody was looking," Miles White for the costume designs, and a large cast to create and produce a truly spirited musical, American to the core.

David Belasco believed it inevitable that the American theater should "respond to the thought, movements, and proclivities of its own time." He compared the stage in general to "a mirror in which are reflected the manners and peculiarities of life of its contemporaneous day."[87] As such a mirror the theater in the United States, from the 1840's until recent decades, has been affected by thought about the far-reaching West, by the regional social, political, and economic customs from which it springs.

VI. "The Old Home Town in Days Gone By"

Oh, Home-Folks! you're the best of all
'At ranges this terestchul ball,—
But, north or south, or east or west,
It's home is where you're at your best.
        —JAMES WHITCOMB RILEY

DURING THE ERA of the New Humanism and *America's Coming-of-Age*, young Van Wyck Brooks and other insurgent critics began protesting vigorously against the long prevalence in this country of a false Americanism. The United States, they felt, had become "a realm of self-congratulation" and the picture of ease, contentment, and complacency. What it needed most was a strong dose of fundamental doubt. For too long, Brooks protested, "the writers of America [had] chanted a unanimous hymn to progress."[1] Also, everywhere the hopeful but blind public, unconverted to truthful criticism, had failed to question the happy thinking of those writers who gilded reality. Sentimental and cheerful, many people accepted, in spite of America's new confrontations, such superlative declarations as Meredith Nicholson's to the flattering effect that "if there is any manifestation on earth of a divine ordering of things, it is here [in 1918] in America," especially in the Middle West where there flourishes "an infinitely superior breed of humanity."[2] Deploring this "complacency to which our national optimism gave birth," Brooks questioned whether such optimism, coupled with philistinism, was ever a symptom of national health. As early as 1913, he himself had recognized the need in this country for "a clear sense of the true values of life" to offset "the malady of the ideal." Kindred thinkers, among them the poet Edwin Arlington Robinson, disturbed by "this barren age of ours" and the "lack of a beacon bright," shared Brooks's dismay. On the whole, however, the philistine majority, unaroused to a sense of the limitations of their bourgeois milieu, continued for a while longer "to manifest their divinity." Indeed, the "Age of Confidence, of naïveté, and pale-pink romanticism"[3]—Henry Seidel Canby's description of the period of his youth in Wilmington, Delaware—left its imprint upon the once popular plays of small-town life at the turn of the century and later.

Brooksian and other contemporary protests brought no rapid change in American thinking. The sway of complacency and of the genteel tradition continued even beyond the Mauve Decade. Nevertheless, with time moving forward toward the Jazz Age and the great changes in

American life—the automobile, new highways, market centers, consolidated schools, mail-order houses, the radio, and similar things—the cityward shift became even more widespread. In Sherwood Anderson's words, "Life in the towns [began] spreading out in a new way, the old tight close life broken up by the coming of the new big paved highways, the stream of cars always flowing through the towns, endless rush of cars, American restlessness."[4] With this movement of thousands into the growing cities, another angle of vision began to dominate popular thinking about the blessings to be found in the Valley of Democracy and other provincial areas. As small towns and their surrounding farms, abandoned by many of their inhabitants, began losing their economic and cultural significance, Americans transplanted to the cities needed some reassurance "that life was still wholesome among the plain people of the back country."[5] Their nostalgic attitudes toward our provincial experience in the United States led to a kind of mythmaking, which celebrated country virtues, smiling villages, and neighborly towns. Hence, fictional excursions into the provinces, into the idealized towns, continued to have wide appeal. Certainly, the idea that the small place— the old hometown—is the seed ground for everything that is basically democratic determined the demand during the nineties, and later, for "grass roots" plays. "Folks and their folksiness" (Nicholson's phrase) stirred the imagination of popular playwrights and players during this brief "golden day."

Among the most popular of these hometown or "old homestead" plays were certain later Down East presentations, which as we have noted were end-of-the-century continuations of the initial Yankee comedies. The creators of these new "sons of Jonathan," rather than portraying in each comedy only one key character, a bit refined though speaking in Yankee dialect, generally present Down East action in which all of the "home folks" are more or less humorous and sometimes grotesque imitations of actual country and small-town types. Using many idioms borrowed from real Yankee phraseology, these stage provincials speak a dialect approximating the folksy conversation actually heard around the stove in the general store of any small northeastern town in days gone by. (Indeed today this sense of "togetherness" marks the neighborhood folk in country or general stores in small communities everywhere, just as it marked their New England forerunners who played a part in the developing rural life of that region from the 1790's onward.)[6] Even while the then radical new realism was developing at the close of the Civil War, actor Denman Thompson, the first of the later Yankee dramatizers, began experimenting with skits of Yankee ruralism.

We have discussed in Chapter II his initial variety sketch of 1875, *Joshua Whitcomb*, and its expansion into a sentimental four-act comedy of 1886 called *The Old Homestead*. Belonging more to the stage and the genre poetry of Whittier than to the drama, *The Old Homestead* is intrinsically significant as an influence on the vogue for sentimental and humorous plays during "the twilight interval" of American writing until the 1900's.

Four years after Thompson first experimented with the Joshua role and more than a dozen years before "the final glory" of his own *Shore Acres* and *Sag Harbor*, James A. Herne began winning a comfortable fortune and a reputation as an actor of remarkable naturalness. This professional progress began when he adapted the Yankee formula to a Belasco play, *Chums*, which he refashioned, with Belasco's collaboration, into *Hearts of Oak*. With this six-act drama of simple workers of Marblehead, Massachusetts, as they lived during the 1850's, Herne became one of the popular hometown playwrights. In a period when much popular entertainment was artificial and meretricious, its very simplicity and strong heart appeal, dominant notes in all the Herne plays, gave *Hearts of Oak* immediate distinction.[7] For the 1870's the play was indeed experimental in its introduction of a live baby, a home-like supper on stage, and other realistic effects. In its first production at San Francisco's Baldwin Theatre, on September 9, 1879, Herne was featured successfully as Terry Dennison, the "sailor miller" and pro-tagonist, and Mrs. Herne as Chrystal, the "sweetheart." Thereafter, as performances were presented throughout the country, *Hearts of Oak* gave Herne repeated opportunities, in the miller's role, to develop those qualities which Julie A. Herne, his daughter and biographer, has said made his acting unique: "his love of home, of children, of simple, kindly people, his quaint humor and his deep vein of sentiment."[8]

At the first curtain rise the backdrop pictures a wild, picturesque beach near Marblehead during a torrential coastal storm of 1859. In this, Herne's earliest experiment with "art for truth's sake," all of the theatrical effects—the movement of the sea, the noise of the surf, the rain and storm sounds—are practical accompaniments to the anxiety of the assembled wreckers, men and women mill workers, and sundry vil-lagers. These Marblehead folk, wearing rubber coats and sou'westers and carrying lanterns, prayerfully watch the bark *Nantucket* being dashed against the rocky shore. While the vessel is completely wrecked, Ned Fairweather, a handsome though ironically named young sailor, is among the few on board to escape drowning.

His dramatic return to the village at once motivates action according to a triangular pattern of conflict. Act II, set in Terry Dennison's gristmill, brings on stage certain key folk of Marblehead. The first of these, the stalwart miller Terry, in his early forties, is simple and kindly, frank, honest, and generous. His generosity extends to the whole town. His mill hands singing their work songs; Uncle Davy, his father, "a spry, wiry old man of seventy, fussy and mildly irascible in manner"; Owen Garroway, "a gnarled heavy-set fisherman"; and two orphaned waifs taken into his home years before—all of these, and other villagers, have known Terry's liberality. The orphans, now grown, are the pretty girl Chrystal and Ned, long at sea. They love each other, but realize that their mutual passion must be concealed when they discover that Terry yearns to make Chrystal his wife. Such an emotional entanglement, complicated by a series of sacrifices, is resolved but temporarily by Chrystal's concealing her love for Ned and by the anguished young sailor's return to duty. Her marriage to Terry and the birth of their daughter, while symbolizing complete felicity before the townspeople, do not free Chrystal from her longing for Ned. Outwardly, these years of marriage—Acts III-V—are portrayed against a realistic background of Marblehead folk life. Delightful humor, as expressed in the Down East dialect of Uncle Davy, Terry's gawky maidservant Tawdrey, and his spinsterish Aunt Betsey, offsets the melodrama and sentimentality of these scenes.

From the time of Ned's reappearance in Marblehead, melodrama marks much of the action, except for the quiet dignity of the finale. Upon his realizing his wife's love for Ned, Terry disappears into the Klondike. Years pass without news of him. At last, as the two lovers are being married in Marblehead Church, a broken and blinded pauper, by coincidence, meets and talks with Chrystal's little girl. The stranger, of course, is Terry, so changed that he is unrecognized except by Owen and Ned. Chrystal does not recognize Terry until after his death. His dying, at the finale, frees Chrystal and Ned. Herne's natural acting gave credence and dignity to Terry's difficult self-sacrifices.

Regardless of its once popular heart appeal, *Hearts of Oak* seems fairly plausible today mainly by virtue of Herne's then radical experimenting with realistic characterization and Down East town scenes. Adept at creating natural portraits of older folk, such as crotchety Uncle Davy, pert Aunt Betsey, and sea-toughened Owen, Herne in this apprenticeship play also mastered various realistic aspects of coastal village life and seafaring folk. His effective stage use of popular chanteys and work songs (for the gristmillers), of real properties, authentic dress, and other practical effects introduced Herne as a popular actor turned playwright.

Discouraged by the failure of *The Minute Men,* his Revolutionary War melodrama, Herne and his wife revived *Hearts of Oak.* On tour during 1886-87 he composed the first version of another Down East play, *Mary, the Fisherman's Child,* later revised as *Drifting Apart.*[9] First produced on May 7, 1888, at the People's Theatre, New York, *Drifting Apart* deals thematically with the deleterious effects of drink upon the lives of Massachusetts villagers, principally a Gloucester fisherman, Jack Hepburne (acted by Herne), and his wife Mary (Mrs. Herne's role). Like *Hearts of Oak,* this second Down East play portrays realistic scenes of home life in a coastal town. Its scenes of tragic power and stark realism, as in the poignant episode of Jack's nightmarish dreaming about the deaths of Mary and their child through starvation, gave Herne a place among the realists. Although it proved a financial failure, *Drifting Apart* brought to both of the Hernes considerable recognition among players and critics as artistic, truthful performers. Managers, however, generally were so hostile to the play's realism that it could be booked nowhere except in popularly priced theaters for one-night stands. Encouragement came to the Hernes quite unexpectedly, when young Hamlin Garland, then beginning his crusade for "Veritism," chanced to see a performance of *Drifting Apart* in a cheap theater. His seeking out the Hernes led to a mutual friendship. As their enthusiastic champion, Garland introduced the players to Howells, *Arena* editor B. O. Flower, painter John J. Enneking, and other Boston intellectuals, sometimes regarded as "radicals" for their interest in touchy social issues of the time. Stimulated by their recognition of his and Katherine's talents, Herne responded more deeply than ever to the problems of modernism. His deepening awareness of the social and moral problems existing in the world about him motivated Herne's attempts to dramatize certain issues of social conduct.[10]

His first experimentation with the drama of ideas owed much to his stimulating friendship with Garland, his meeting with Henry George, and his avid reading of *Progress and Poverty* and other cogent writing.[11] In the early summer of 1888 Herne began writing *The Hawthornes,* a realistic domestic drama destined to undergo title and other changes. First produced at McVicker's Theatre, Chicago, on May 23, 1892, the play was then billed as *Shore Acres Subdivision* and a bit later as *Uncle Nat.* These Chicago performances met with fair success. By the time of its successful Boston and New York presentations, in 1893, the new comedy was called *Shore Acres.* Under this title, as we have noted in Chapter II, it eventually was to become the most successful and best loved of all his dramas and for the next five years was to provide Herne, cast as Uncle Nat Berry, with his most popular role.[12] In boldly adapting to this play such vital and then controversial issues as speculation in real estate, intolerance, and the rights of children to lead independent lives, Herne slowly overcame the opposition which managers and others usually showed to dramatists of advanced ideas.

Herne had thought through his plot before localizing the setting for *Shore Acres* in Lemoine, Maine. In response to his wife's urging, Herne, with his family, spent the summer of 1889 in Lemoine in order to acquaint himself with its local color. Like his wife, Herne was so delighted with this little town and its people that he decided to place the action of his play against this background. Also, Herne discovered in the local excitement of a land boom, in otherwise peaceful Lemoine, one of the key motifs for his plot of brother against brother. Beautifully knolled Shore Acres Farm—the site of a lighthouse—became the focal point for a deal in land speculation which creates a rift in the Berry household.

The minutely descriptive local color of the stage direction is authentic, an outgrowth of Herne's close observations of the Lemoine community and its picturesque farmlands between pine-covered hills and the bay. A regional tone appears also in the native titles of the four acts, describing "hayin' time," the boat *Liddy Ann* in "a Sou'wester," and Maine family life. Mostly the Down Easters in the play respect the traditional Yankee routine of hard work. Among them, however, there are sharp contrasts in temperaments, symbolizing the key conflict between village traditionalism and the spirit of change. Benevolent Uncle Nat Berry begs Martin not to listen to the get-rich-quick schemes of widower Josiah Blake, postmaster and storekeeper in Berry Village, who proposes an easy plan for converting Shore Acres farm into a new resort subdivision. Satirically symbolizing the current "go-aheadism," Blake insists that they are living in a practical age—"this bustlin', go-ahead, money-makin', devil-take-the-hindermost day of ours—." His glowing and patronizing sales talk at last convinces Martin that "the boom's a-comin' here jes' as sure as you're born." Together these two envision summer cottages built along "the sightliest shore front to be found on the coast." With the aplomb of a Beriah Sellers, Blake mentally blueprints Shore Acres Subdivision, complete with quarter-acre lots, "avenoos," driveways, and trees.[13]

Such easy money, however, has little appeal for weather-beaten Nat. Rather, his chief interest in his frank comradeship with his seventeen-year-old niece, Helen (enacted by Mrs. Herne). Nat's deep interest in her emotional problems and his tenderness for her contrast with Martin's resentment of his daughter's spirit of independence and youthful intolerance. With a stubbornness matching Helen's determination to lead her own life, Martin opposes her marriage to Dr. Sam Warren, largely because the young freethinker is always reading the newest books and "a-bringin' the books here, a-learnin' my daughter a pack of lies, about me and my parents a-comin' from monkeys——."[14] One of these damnable books was Howells' *A Hazard of New Fortunes*, an appropriate enough symbol of Sam's hope to find a new fortune for himself and Helen in the Far West, free from the taint of Down East intolerance.

Such conflict of wills is at odds with lovable Uncle Nat's belief that life is too short for unhappiness. That is why he aids the lovers to escape by boarding the *Liddy Ann*. In his third-act struggle with Martin, who is fighting to keep him from lighting the beacon and saving the storm-endangered boat, Nat, in an unusual burst of energy, ends his years of self-effacement by forcing Martin away from the stairway to the beacon; but his exhaustion keeps old Nat from reaching the light. At curtain fall, he calls out in anguish: "God help me! I hain't got the strength!" Happily, the next scene, on the decks of the *Liddy Ann*, reveals that the sudden shining of the light saved the boat from the rocks.

With its action fifteen months later, the fourth act shows Herne's realistic artistry in the picture of the cozy kitchen at Shore Acres, on a stormy Christmas Eve. The younger Berry children, excited about Christmas, are delighting in Uncle Nat's tales and teasing. The contrast between the brothers is striking. Jovial Nat feels that with the heavy snowstorm "It . . . seems kinder more Christmassier—somehow." Martin, meanwhile, pores dejectedly over a blueprint map of the farm, which has been surveyed and laid off in town lots. His wife Ann chides him with having "cut the farm all up inter griddle cakes." Martin, bitter with remorse from having driven Helen out of the home, is even more dispirited when Blake arrives with the news that the Land Company is "busted" and "You'll hev to begin all over agin—seed down the avenoos—cut down the shade trees—an' plow up the hotel site." At this point the happy "old hometown" formula prevails, as Helen and Sam, now prosperous, arrive from the West with their baby. Martin's forgiveness of the couple restores normal routine and happy living at Shore Acres.

In 1899 Herne ended his career as playwright, as he had begun it, by adapting the Down East formula to a Long Island community—this time in the comedy *Sag Harbor*, discussed earlier. Suitably subtitled "An Old Story," this four-acter is actually a reworking of *Hearts of Oak*. Replacing the earlier foster father-son motif with a similar relationship between brother and brother, Herne again created a drama around domestic entanglements. Moreover, he shifted his scene from Marblehead to a quiet fishing and former whaling center, Sag Harbor on Long Island, another village actually known to the Hernes. (The dialogue is filled with references to Greenport, faraway Marblehead, and other small towns.) Terry Dennison's gristmill is changed to Ben Turner's "little old country shipyard" as it appeared in May, 1895. Instead of Uncle Davy there is tanned, wrinkled, gray-haired Cap'n Dan Marble, "a hale, hearty man in his late fifties" who makes his living by using his sloop *Kacy* for winter fishing and summer vacationers. Humor is added in the character of Elizabeth Anne Turner, "a sweet wholesome-looking woman of the New England type, about forty-five," courted by Cap'n Dan for "way nigh on to fifteen years." As in *Hearts of Oak*, the plot is based on "a triangle of love," involving the Turner brothers, both in love with orphaned Martha Reese (Julie Herne's part). Young Martha, affectionate as Chrystal, marries the older Ben Turner out of gratitude and sentiment, though Frank, absent on naval duty for five years, is the one she loves. A new focal point differentiates this from the older comedy in that Cap'n Dan, rather than the husband, is the protagonist. Also, by deleting the Klondike episode and other melodramatic parts of *Hearts of Oak*, Herne produced a plot of greater realism and in the natural portrait of Dan Marble a most memorable hometown character.

Illustrative of his versatility in writing, as in acting, is the fact that Herne wrote his most artistic completed drama of ideas just at the time of his absorption with Down East folkways. Miss Herne recalls that before *Shore Acres* could be produced another plot idea "took possession of Herne, and clamored to be written."[15] This was the leitmotif of *Margaret Fleming*, to which we have referred earlier—a powerful play of marital infidelity in an upper-class family living in a spreading industrial town in Massachusetts. As a labor mart of the 1890's, Canton had a mixed population of long established familities like the mill-owning Flemings, middle-class shopkeepers, factory foremen, and the laboring class, mill workers and domestics many of whom were immigrants like Marie Bindley—nursemaid in the Fleming home—and her unfortunate sister, Lena Schmidt. Using a wealth of realistic detail, Herne seriously dramatized a controversial problem of social conduct. His background for this human question symbolizes a significant phase in New England's town development—the transformation of once peaceful villages, through industry and the influx of foreign workers, into thriving mill towns, as Howells had just shown in *Annie Kilburn* (1888). Herne's theatrical use of such a milieu is further suggestive of his growing interest in pressing problems of progress and poverty. The production problems of the superintendent of the Fleming Mill, the working conditions of the employees, the moral decline of old Joe Fletcher, once a trusted foreman, the efforts of Maria and her husband Joe at keeping a small shop, and the fate of immigrant girls like Lena contrast realistically with the elegant appointments of the Fleming home and the luxurious furnishings of Philip Fleming's office at the mill.

Herne's personal struggle to gain production and acceptance for this once daring social drama is now well known to students of Quinn's "James A. Herne and the Realism of Character."[16] The private subsidizing of the three tryout performances, opening on July 4, 1890, at Lynn, and of the two-week run in Boston, beginning on May 4, 1891, in rented Chickering Hall, signalizes one of the first attempts in the United States to establish an independent art theater. Even so, the Boston production, though greeted with enthusiasm by friendly intellectuals and arousing some critical approval, revealed that the ideas in *Margaret Fleming* were too advanced for Victorian-minded audiences. A Boston revival in October, 1891, and a December matinee at Palmer's Theatre, New York, were similarly received. The revivals of 1894, 1907, and 1915, while furnishing Chrystal and Julie Herne with fine roles, emphasized anew their father's courage and dramatic pioneering.

In this advanced drama Herne daringly and psychologically characterizes a genteel, protected young wife, happy in the apparent devotion of a loving husband and the love of their little girl. Herne's portrayal of Margaret Fleming, faced with a moral dilemma, is not unlike James's "portrait" of disillusioned Isabel Archer. Both young wives, in the beginning idealistic and romantic, are subjected eventually to much mental anguish and self-sacrifice. Their final decisions symbolize woman's capacity for growing in tragic consciousness. Margaret's first awareness of the complexities and dangers of life outside her charming home circle comes through painful shock. Accidentally learning that her handsome husband Philip is a moral weakling, Mrs. Fleming reacts to the truth with quiet courage. Without the heroics then popular in melodrama, she resolutely seeks the unpleasant facts about Philip's liaison with the German immigrant girl Lena.

With skilfully handled realism, Herne presents a scene, in Act II, between Margaret and Dr. Larkin (the *raisonneur*), which discloses that if the young wife is subjected to too much stress and strain she may lose her eyesight as a result of developing glaucoma. Nevertheless, in Act III, Margaret goes, at Maria's request, to Mrs. Burton's cottage, where in an offstage room Lena lies dead. The shocking experience of learning, through a letter written by Lena, that her baby boy is Philip's hastens Margaret's loss of sight. The tense moment in the Burton cottage, as

Margaret's vision is growing dimmer, is enacted through a calm and natural expression of words and gestures. As remorseful Philip dashes into the room, Margaret, moved by womanly pity, takes Lena's fretful child into her arms, gropes her way to the sofa, and vainly tries to comfort the "poor little thing." Just before curtain fall, "Then scarcely conscious of what she is doing, suddenly with an impatient swift movement she unbuttons her dress to give nourishment to the child, when the picture fades away into darkness."[17]

According to the original version of the fourth act, the action moves away from the Canton locale. During the passage of five years the scene shifts to Boston Common and a small shop at the North End, Lena's boy dies, and revengeful Maria kidnaps Lucy, Margaret and Philip's child. In the final scene, Margaret and Philip come to a police station in their search for Lucy. This scene is one of renunciation, for Margaret, standing alone as the stage curtains begin closing, refuses to forgive Philip, as she says goodbye.

The second conclusion, the one now used, pictures Margaret, now blind, as facing her future with dignity and calmness. When Philip eventually returns to their Canton home, after attempting suicide, Margaret receives him courteously, but with restraint. She forgives his infidelity, but intimates that she cannot be his wife. His consenting to resume his place at the mill, as Margaret advises, brings to her "a serene joy [which] illuminates her face." At last there is the barest suggestion of restored tranquillity and triumph of principles to compensate for Margaret's suffering and self-sacrifice.[18]

A sharp departure from Herne's popular hometown comedies, *Margaret Fleming*, as Garland wrote of the Boston premiere, was thought of in the 1890's as "one of the most radical plays from a native author ever performed in America."[19] The radicalism of the play for its time, aside from its frank treatment of marital infidelity, stemmed from its utter simplicity of presentation, "bare of all mechanical illusion, and shorn of all its scenic and atmospheric effects." Its seriousness of theme is relieved somewhat by the humor of characterization in old Joe Fletcher, Maria's husband and formerly a respected worker at the Fleming mill. Now reduced to street peddling, Joe is an earthy, likable fellow, admirably enacted by Herne. Mrs. Herne, in the role of Margaret, seemed to spectator Garland "to be all of the woman, and something of the seer, as she stands there as Margaret whose blindness has somehow given her inward light, and conviction, and strength. She seemed to be speaking for all womankind, ..."

For the time being Herne's experimentation with the drama of ideas brought no sweeping change in the dramatization of American materials, including small-town themes. Rather, at the century's end even his "delicately faithful pictures of rural life" (William Archer's description) found no equal. On the other hand, the Down East formula, or its equivalent, was repeated over and over again, generally without originality, as rural dramas continued to be used by touring companies performing in small-town "opera houses," tents, or IOOF lodge halls. Obviously, out of this welter of provincial plays only a few artistic ones emerged, and many of the playwrights are either forgotten or remembered just for a particular play or two. Among the more prolific and commercially successful of Herne's contemporaries, Charles Hale Hoyt of New Hampshire became widely known as "the father of American farce." Hoyt, like Herne, tried to go beyond the popular presentation of mere types to create more individualized, or living, persons whose conduct suggests the everyday experiences of the ordinary people whom he had known in New England, the Southwest, California, and elsewhere. In this regard his biographer and editor considers Hoyt the forerunner of George M. Cohan and of Kaufman, Connelly, and Hart.[20] Among his kindly and universalized satires (excluding the popular *A Texas Steer* and *A Trip to Chinatown*), several, mostly emotional in tone and set against his native New England background, belong to the category of popular hometown plays.

The first of these, *A Bunch of Keys*, is an early farce presumably based upon his own father's experiences in trying to run a hotel in Concord, New Hampshire, without any previous training in such an operation.[21] A hit play after its production in New York's San Francisco Opera House on March 26, 1883, *A Bunch of Keys; Or, The Hotel* humorously portrays life at the Grand View Hotel, near a railroad station, in a rustic village. At curtain rise, pretty Dolly Dobbs, bored with rusticity, complains to Jonas Grimes, a brakeman, about the miserable time she has had ever since the closing of the hotel: "There's been no drummers along and I've nobody to flirt with but brakemen." Jonas' cheerful singing only adds to her fit of blues and irritation. Soon, however, fast action and slapstick comedy get under way with the arrival of an unscrupulous lawyer, Littleton Snaggs, to read the strange will of Jotham Keys "of the town of Leominster, Massachusetts." Expressing by his last testament his belief that "a homely woman has a hard time in this world; a pretty one may be a fool, but she will get a husband," eccentric Uncle Jotham wills that his property, the Grand View Hotel, shall be reopened one month after the date of his death and that the first drummer who is a total stranger to arrive at the hotel shall be asked to decide which one of his nieces—the "Bunch of Keys"—is the homeliest. Great excitement stirs the villagers as Teddy, Rose, and May Keys, with their boyfriends, try various schemes to meet the terms of the will. At the end, when Snaggs is ousted as lawyer and berates the village as "the meanest town I ever saw," the three Keys, in accordance with a codicil attached to their uncle's will, decide that "we shall divide the property equally and no one shall know which of the Bunch of Keys was the homeliest."[22]

In *A Rag Baby* (1884) Hoyt again satirized aspects of small-town life by his pictures of the domestic troubles of a farcically described undertaker, Christian Berriel. Following his separation from his wife, the undertaker is in such ill health that he enrols his child in Miss Pratt's school. His scheming brother-in-law, Tony Jay, resorts to a ridiculous means of gaining control of his niece, in order to return the child to his sister. He buys a drugstore so that, without detection, he can keep Christian Berriel ill by supplying him with the wrong medicines. The two acts laid in the drugstore vividly portray small-town scenes connected with the hilarious efforts of Tony and Old Sport, his assistant, to take charge of his niece.

Other inconsequential, but popular, farces followed until 1888, when to some extent Hoyt turned aside from the hokum of farce to present, in a San Francisco engagement (April 4-22), the better plotted *A Midnight Bell.* Later it was played in a revised form at New York's Bijou Theatre, from March 5 until June 29, 1889.[23] In an amusing preface Hoyt had announced that "this is a legitimate comedy" with "a modern and unassuming plot." More than this, it is a New England village comedy, whose popular Gothic touch—in the mysterious ringing of the meetinghouse bell at midnight—does not overshadow the ordinary doings of a large variety of villagers and a few city visitors in an old-fashioned community of the 1880's. The realistic Yankeeisms of Deacon Lemuel Tidd, the village fiddler Ezekial Slover, old maid Lizzie Grout, Nellie Bowen, "The Soprano of the Choir," the mischief-making schoolboy Martin Tripp, and Hannah, "The Village Help," tally with the authentic minutiae on the property list. These properties in themselves—a haircloth sofa, several old-fashioned engravings, mantel ornaments, a large rocker by the fire, blue delftware on the dresser, a grandfather's clock, and other furnishings—authentically set the stage for the first scene: the dining room in the home of the bank president, Squire Olcott. The successive scenes, set respectively in the village school, in a Yankee old maid's "best room"—the parlor of gossipy Miss Lizzie's—and at the church, are all in keeping with the reality of a New England winter background of long ago. Often humor arises from the timeworn conflict between young and old, as when Olcott's nephew Ned sees those invincible gossips, Lizzie Grout and Nellie Bowen, as leaders of "that crowd of superannuated old fossils" making up the Sewing Society and pokes fun at the Deacon as "Old Practical" who has "got to tend to everything that happens in this town." Unfortunately, the plot projected against such recognizable village backgrounds concerns stereotyped motifs, including a bank robbery, a proposed elopement, a schoolroom episode of local intolerance toward the teacher and unjust criticism of the minister. More praiseworthy is young Maude Adams' portrayal of Dot Bradbury, the minister's teen-age sister, a role in which the actress made her stage debut at the Bijou.

Hastily composed and farcical though Hoyt's plays typically are, occasionally they are exposures of the sham, hypocrisy, and sanctimoniousness which the playwright had seen, and despised, in small-town folk. *A Temperance Town*, presented at Hoyt's Madison Square Theatre, September 17, 1893, is a scathing satire, explained in the printed preface as a protest against "the prohibitory laws of Vermont, where a man named Kibling is now serving a sentence of something like sixty years for selling about seven hundred glasses of liquor (less than most of our respectable city hotels sell in a day)." This play, ironically set in the Thanksgiving period of 1882, "is intended to be more or less truthful presentation of certain phases and incidents of life, relating to the sale and use of liquor, in a small village in a prohibition state."[24] Motivation of action starts with the not too admirable schemes of zealous "do-gooders" to carry on their moral warfare for "our glorious cause," namely a raid on the saloon operated by a disabled Union soldier, Fred Oakhurst. Overlooking the fact that "they stayed at home [during the Civil War] while he was doing the fighting," these "temperance cranks" show no compassion either for Oakhurst in his poverty or for his sick wife and ailing child. All appear as miserable hypocrites whose false piety binds them both to Deacon Kneeland Pray, the "boss ramrod" and owner of a drugstore where he himself, by Dr. Cadwell Sawyer's prescriptions, sells liquor on the sly, and to the Reverend Ernest Hardman, so intent on their crusade against "these wreckers of our homes" that he mistreats his wife and turns his daughter Ruth from his parsonage. (Ruth's role was played by Caroline Miskel, later the second Mrs. Hoyt. Actually the role was planned for Flora Walsh, Hoyt's first wife, who died after the play's first opening.)[25] Ruth's guilt was that of nursing the wife and child of "that rum-seller." Dr. Sawyer's meanness of spirit is satirized in his callous refusal to visit the Oakhurst child unless the saloonkeeper first pays the medical bill. These zealots further damn themselves by their supercilious attitude toward the three Joneses: Ming Jones, village handyman and one of the "rum crowd," Mrs. Jones, town washwoman and hired cook, and their undisciplined son. As the town's "little cusses," the Joneses lack respectability. Thus the "good people" of Temperance Town expose themselves as pious meddlers by their abortive efforts, including a court trial to send Oakhurst to prison for his alleged "illegal traffic" and, according to Hardman, the damnable "unholy traffic" of gambling in the form of a village raffle. In spite of its sentimentality, stilted dialogue, cardboard characters, and farcical elements, *A Temperance Town* anticipated the "revolt from the village" plays of the 1920's. Its satire was directed most pointedly against the then popular myth of the old hometown as a place of sweetness and light.

Hoyt's next village play, *A Milk White Flag*, was performed first at Wilkes-Barre, Pennsylvania, on December 23, 1893, before its successful run of October 8, 1894, to February 23, 1895, at Hoyt's Theatre.[26] Again a printed preface amusingly introduces the scene as a field of battle: "not necessarily St. Albans, Vt., or Harrisburg, Pa., but a town of that deliciously provincial character was in the author's thoughts as he wrote. Visitors from the West may imagine Zanesville, Ohio, or Oshkosh, Wis."[27] There is little native stuff of any value in this simon-pure farce; yet its continued appeal to the naïve and "credulous emotionals" (George Jean Nathan's term) of the time is proof of Hoyt's ability to capture audiences. Action mostly grows out of the comical battle of wits waged between rival town factions, involving a large number of provincial types, all satirically named. The showily uniformed Ransome Guards comically carry their pure white regimental flag "on the Field of Mars" and "in the court of Venus" in an effort to outshine a rival regiment called the Daly Blues. Like Longstreet's gawky, unmilitary Georgians in "The Militia Company Drill," these citizen-soldiers of Hoyt's town farcically illustrate the old theme of "My Double and How He Undid Me." In civilian life the 399 officers and one private belonging to the Ransome Guards are ordinary men: one a lawyer, another a coal merchant, then a doctor, a bandmaster, a dance master, an undertaker, a railway contractor, and others. The delight of small-town people in parades, marching bands, showy funeral processions, and hoaxes is coupled with local excitement over a railroad building boom, a life insurance swindle, and the war opera—"Hell with the Enemy"—being composed by the bandmaster. The simple humbug of the play is also enlivened by songs. While not so popular as "Reuben, Reuben, I've been thinking" (of *Chinatown*), "We Are Warriors Bold" and "A Milk White Flag" were spirited and lilting enough to appeal to spectators of the nineties.

On the whole, Herne's work illustrates again, so Moses felt, "the undoubted fact that American life—the true American life—lies between great cities; that there is more of native stamina in the small community . . ."[28] If Herne's impetus was more inward than external, Hoyt's was the reverse. Indeed, his comical presentations of New England village life of the eighties, while enormously popular, displayed little of its folk passion. For all of his cleverness and use of multifarious background details, Hoyt did not succeed in getting to the bone of local life and outlook. The real quality of New England implies more than stabs at depicting Yankee types, however individualized, and the scattering of "by goshes" through the dialogue.[29]

Unfortunately for the growth of native drama, the challenge implicit in the rich variety of our small-town life, as in the ferment of American society in general, produced all too few artistic plays about the village. All the while, however, superficial images of the small place proliferated as grass-roots comedies were booked repeatedly by the New York and other theaters, often with continuous performances and revivals advertised. These popular dramatic recordings of village life were folksy and sentimental enough to entertain, without shocking, on a commercial basis. To illustrate, in *Old Jed Prouty* William Gill and Richard Golden featured scenes in Buckport, Maine, starring a frank and kindly tavernkeeper, the counterpart of Joshua Whitcomb in his folk attitudes and scorn of "city swells." First performed in New York at the Union Square Theatre on March 13, 1889, the comedy proved successful enough to warrant a revival as late as 1894.[30] Also first produced in New York in March, 1889, Charles Barnard and Neil Burgess' *The County Fair* centered around a folk activity much treated in rural fiction. It was still being played in 1896, possibly because of the popularity of old maid Abigail Prue (Burgess' role), whose sentimentality and kindness, in spite of her tart manner, reminded spectators of the lovable Joshua Whitcomb and Uncle Nat characterizations. Throughout the nineties, and even later, pastoral images of the small town, glorifying its folkways, were kept before the public with the staging of such comedies as Edward E. Kiddi's *Peaceful Valley* (1894); Alice E. Ives and Jerome H. Eddy's *The Village Postmaster*, a four-acter performed until 1900; and Lottie Blair Parker's enormously popular melodrama, *Way Down East*. No doubt its conventional and familiar characterizations, such as the stern father and the farmer's daughter, with humor thrown in, accounted for its New York run, from its opening on February 7, 1898, of 361 performances.

For many weeks during 1901 the Fourteenth Street Theatre, New York, billed in quick succession a series of community plays. The first of these, *Up York State*, by David Higgins and Georgia Waldron, lasted for sixteen performances, beginning September 16, with a December revival of fifty-four performances. Opening on October 21, *New England Folks*, by Eugene W. Presbrey, who in 1900 had staged *The Village Postmaster* for this same theater, was performed sixty-four times. And in October of the next year patrons of the Savoy were seeing Edward E. Rose's popular dramatization and Charles Frohman's production of Irving Bacheller's *Eben Holden*, a novel about a genial rural philosopher in a Vermont village. By December Frohman was busy at the Garden Theatre diverting attention from the Down Easters by his production, for sixty-four performances, of *Alice of Old Vincennes,* the dramatized version by Rose of Maurice Thompson's immensely popular small-town novel.

"Native grounds" themes again found facile and repeated treatment in the once acclaimed comedies of an 1881 Harvard graduate, Charles Turney Dazey (1855-1938). Leaving his Illinois home to study at the College of Arts at Lexington, Dazey had opportunity to observe enough of the regional life of the state to write a skilfully plotted melodrama, *In Old Kentucky*. Contrasting the primitivism of mountain folk with the life of the Blue Grass patricians, the play appealed by virtue of its emotional scenes about horse racing, accusations of murder, and the love developing between aristocratic Frank Layson and Madge, from the "mountings." Sensationally popular from the summer of 1893, when a stock company produced it at the Grand Opera House in St. Paul, *In Old Kentucky* was the first of many provincial plays which Dazey wrote, the last in 1937. More akin to the Down East plays is his bucolic four-act *Home Folks*, New England in quality but midwestern in locale. With a cast including William S. Hart and Chrystal and Julie Herne, *Home Folks* won public favor from the first. It was given thirty-four performances, beginning December 26, 1904, at the New York Theatre, and later was produced at McVicker's in Chicago. Set in the Illinois farming town of Red Oak, the comedy has much of the sentimental quality of James Whitcomb Riley's lyric, "Home Folks," which prefaces the typed prompt copy in the Theatre Collection at the New York Public Library. Riley's vernacular verse glorifying "busyness" and common sense describes the sort of ruralism typical of the people living in Red Oak Township:

> Home-folks has crops to plant and plow
> Er lives in town and keeps a cow;
> But whether country-jakes or town,
> They know when eggs is up or down.

The pattern of characterization in *Home Folks* closely parallels the types of country townsfolk peopling the Down East villages. Small-town election excitement centers around John Selby, an Illinois farmer who is candidate for the legislature, and the rival candidate, Paul Niles, the nephew of old Mat Niles, richest man in the township. Provincial intolerance appears in the difference of social status between the village belle, a hired girl, a strange young woman from St. Louis, Joe Hawkins who is "fit only to fiddle and to fish," Sis Durkee ("Only a Bottomite"), and Walter Clayton "who has gone wrong." As in the Down East comedies, in *Home Folks* the justice of the peace is dignified as "squire" and Si Heckle is both postmaster and storekeeper at Red Oak. The villagers in general speak in provincial language. Their folk songs, such as "Marching through Georgia" and "Jordan," suggest that singing gives as much pleasure as diving into the swimming hole by the old sawmill. There was popular appeal also in the stress upon work, keynoted in "Jordan":

> So take off your coat, boys,
> And roll up your sleeves—
> For Jordan's a hard road to travel, . . .

In Dazey's four-act *The Suburban*[31] the town scene is far removed from the rural village of Red Oak. In an area called Suburban, near Sheepshead Bay, New York, are gaming rooms, a restaurant, paddocks, a grandstand and track, and cottages. The folk have no place here, for the action, like that of Sherwood Anderson's "I'm a Fool" (now dramatized), belongs to the racetrack and gambling world. The proprietor of the Transylvania Club, operators of the faro tables, guests, spectators at the races, bookmakers, policemen, servants, and others crowd the stage. Meanwhile, as the Dazey production continued, a new town play was to make theatrical history.

Public interest in the "Town Hall Tonight" sort of entertainment was stirred again when Charles Frohman celebrated the opening season of the new twentieth century by acquiring at the same time a new play, a new star, and a fortune. Such luck he owed largely to a chance sidewalk chat with Denman Thompson, who began chuckling about "a book I read last night, called 'David Harum.' " To Frohman's question, "Was it interesting?" the actor replied: "The Best American story I ever read." At once Frohman dashed off to buy a copy, which he read that very day.

As quickly he made a contract for its dramatization, from which venture he eventually cleared nearly half a million dollars. Thus, as his brother Daniel has recorded, "Again history repeated itself in a picturesque approach to a Frohman success."[32] The diverting novel which caused Frohman's excitement was, indeed, as American—as indigenous—as *Uncle Remus: His Songs and His Sayings* and *Huckleberry Finn*. Oddly it was the work of a nonliterary man, banker Edward Noyes Westcott (1847-1898) of Syracuse. In the 1890's when he was in Italy for his health, Westcott amused himself during days of invalidism by adapting his own experiences and observations in provincial New York to a novel of small-town life. The result was an amazing *coup d'essai, David Harum: A Story of American Life* (1898). Ironically, although at first rejected by several publishers, the novel became a best seller—a sort of American classic—after Westcott's death. In that very year, under contract to Frohman, Ripley and M. W. Hitchcock quickly recognized the dramatic possibilities in the original character of Harum, a genuine and rare provincial, a delightfully quaint country philanthropist and canny horse trader. Frohman, as producer, carefully considered four men for this role: Thompson, Herne, Sol Smith, and William Crane. Finally deciding that Thompson was too old, Herne had been too long associated with the *Shore Acres* type to adapt his talents to the Westcott hero, and Smith did not meet the requirements, Frohman chose Crane as the ideal interpreter. At once a sensation, the fresh comedy created by the Hitchcocks and carefully rehearsed by Frohman delighted Garrick Theatre patrons for 148 performances. In 1904 a revival, beginning on April 4 and again starring Crane, ran for thirty-two showings. As late as 1938 Charles Coburn, as both producer and star performer, supervised a revival of the comedy at the Mohawk Drama Festival.

At last some of Herne's principles of realism began to affect the form of community drama. True, the Hitchcocks had worked fast so that their prompt copy for Frohman might be ready in time for the opening (on October 1, 1900) of *David Harum, a Comedy in 3 Acts.*[33] Thus hastily following the Westcott novel, they did use a shopworn plot motif of young love; but, like the novelist, they applied it in a new way. Rejecting the then popular success theme of the country, or hometown, boy destined to become a metropolitan leader, these adapters faithfully followed the novel in plotting the progress of college-trained John Lenox, "a hero in reduced circumstances" who finds happiness in his love for Mary Blake, a local teacher, and business advancement as David Harum's assistant in the Homeville Bank. David, "a stocky, ruddy-faced man in his early fifties," is no romanticized do-gooder, although his kindness, dryly, humorously, and rather illiterately expressed, is felt throughout Homeville. His many aphoristic comments tend to suggest the Yankee shrewdness and hardfisted philosophy which have made him successful in banking and horse trading, rather than his softhearted feeling for the unfortunate. Offhand, then, his folk wisdom appears wholly pragmatic, as in his saying: " 'Bus'nis is bus'nis' ain't part of the Golden Rule, I allow, but the way it gen'ally runs, fur's I've found out, is 'Do unto the other feller the way he'd like to do unto you, an' do it fust.' "

Frohman's realistic sets, closely corresponding to Westcott's sometimes drab scenes, suggest that Homeville in the nineties, while not so ugly as Spoon River or Gopher Prairie, was by no means a New York Dreamthorp. All is not roseate. John Lenox's unpleasant experiences in a wooden shack of a hotel, a New York counterpart, or forerunner, of Gopher Prairie's Minniemashie House, introduced him at once to the crudities of life in Homeville. In the first two acts the exterior and interior views of Harum's bank (with his home attached) are no more impressive than the glimpses given of other village establishments. In Act III, a pleasanter village prospect is achieved by covering the veranda of "the old-fashioned white structure" with wisteria and climbing roses. White muslin curtains at the windows of the home part of the building suggest the work of Aunt Polly Bixbee, Harum's buxom older sister and housekeeper.

Finally, the Hitchcocks, again closely following the novel, still further pointed the way toward the more modern realism of Sherwood Anderson, Sinclair Lewis, and other new playwrights of the twenties.[34] This they accomplished, in part, by peopling Homeville with all sorts of folk. Symbolical of both the normal qualities and the peculiarities of Homeville's citizens and visitors are such realistically conceived characters as Bill Montag, "a Homeville tough"; Widow Cullom, "who has seen better days"; General Wolsey, New York lawyer and scheming guardian of Miss Blake; Zeke Swinney, usurer; Amos Elright, hotel landlord; and Deacon Perkins, sanctimonious "pillar of the church" and unscrupulous trader who tried to outwit David Harum in a "horse swap."

A Hoosier "settlement of corn-fed natives" and Other Indiana Towns

The naturalness of the role of David Harum, enhanced by Crane's easy treatment, added to the "home folks" album another portrait comparable to Herne's Uncle Nat and Terry Dennison. Such a realistic pattern of characterization was to reappear in 1903, when a young Hoosier townsman and journalist, already popularly recognized for his *Fables in Slang*, completed what the critics agreed was "the best of all rural dramas." This new playwright was genial George Ade, self-inscribed as a product of "the general environment of yokelism," and the play, *The County Chairman*, was his experimental "straight comedy-drama of village life and politics." Momentarily breaking away from "literary outlawry," as he designated his moneymaking but slangy *Fables* and popular musical comedies (*The Sultan of Sulu* and *Peggy from Paris*), Ade for the first time wrote a four-act comedy of midwestern country-town life "for talking actors instead of singing dancers." He thus moved forward a bit toward Herne's ideal of realism, largely by placing his folk scenes in Antioch, a one-horse town in Indiana, during the early eighties. Thus, in a way the Down Easter was moving to Hoosier Land, although in Ade's comedy there appeared little of such overused Down East elements as romantic mystery, as in Hoyt's *A Midnight Bell*, or triangular entanglements, as in *Drifting Apart*.

As the hero of Ade's plausible and amusing story of neighborhood factions and political feuds, bachelor Jim Hackler, ex-soldier now lawyer and political chairman of Jefferson County, is every bit as natively small-townish as David Harum. (Maclyn Arbuckle was a "natural" for the role.) In Ade's words, the comedy in which Jim is the key figure is "homely and . . . largely an attempt to go back to the queer eighties . . . and reproduce something of the temper and atmosphere and crudities as they cropped up in a settlement of corn-fed natives, far from the allurements and distracting influences of any big city."[35] Like some of Hoyt's caricatured townsfolk, occasionally the politically animated citizens of Antioch appear as little more than ridiculous spokesmen for Ade's genial satire. The most theatrically amusing of these, "Sassafras" Livingstone, a colored loafer forever begging or borrowing, became one of the hits of the show through the talents of an old-time minstrel performer and comedian, Willis Sweatman.[36]

The core of the play, however, is in the more serious characterization, an outgrowth of Ade's intense interest in the drama of daily life wherever he was. As Dorothy Ritter Russo suggests, it was, perhaps, Ade's avid interest in people, combined with a broadness of concern with places and events and personal integrity, that accounts for the vitality of his work.[37] Apparently the popular appeal of *The County Chairman* came largely from the role of the Honorable Jim Hackler, whose friendly personality and folk shrewdness entrenched him in a strong enough position to control the town politically. Difficulties arise, however, as opposing factions excitedly and unscrupulously campaign for Antioch's favorite sons, rival candidates for the place of prosecuting attorney for

Jefferson County. Out of this campaign comes the central conflict. Tilford Wheeler, Hackler's youthful assistant and political dark horse, is
nominated at the county convention to oppose the conservative incum-
bent, prosperous Judge Rigby, whose daughter, a young teacher, is in
love with Tilford.

"Politics is in the air" as the curtain goes up for Act I to reveal Vance
Jimmison's General Store, facing Main Street in the village of Antioch.
On this August afternoon "the store's wide porch is fairly littered with
an assortment of unpacked merchandise and various natives in country
dress." On this hot, lazy day the usual loungers and whittlers, most of
them coatless, have made themselves as comfortable as possible. While
one of them is lazily playing his harmonica, his companions gossip spas-
modically about what's happening at the Boggsville convention. Jefferson Briscoe, the most aggressive of the veranda orators except when his
shrewish wife is in sight, spurs on the guessing about the nominations.
As the five-thirty train from Boggsville whistles, others drift toward the
porch to hear the news. Just as Lucy Rigby and her lover, with a crowd
of picnicking children, have reached Main Street, Jim Hackler comes
from the depot. A large man, "full of good-natured bluster and bursting
in a dignified way with amiability," he strides toward Jimmison's store
to announce to the wildly questioning folk, the Judge included, the astonishing news that young Tilford has been nominated to run against
Rigby.

The entanglement that follows—Rigby's growing dislike for Tilford,
his forbidding Lucy to see him again, Hackler's revelation of his own
youthful love for Mrs. Rigby and of Rigby's trickery in marrying her,
and the charge that the Judge had misappropriated funds belonging to
a ward—are untwisted at last by Tilford's winning both the election, in
a tight race, and Lucy's love. More effectively handled than this rather
formularized plot are the realistic details by which Ade achieves on
stage the excitement of a hotly contested election in a Hoosier town.
The scene hums with life and creative observation. "The spread eagle
business"—Hackler's derisive reference to the Judge's campaign meeting
in the Courthouse Square—becomes quite lively. Flags and bunting dec-
orate the speakers' platform. Music is furnished by a fife and drum corps
and a glee club singing campaign songs. Scattered groups of voters are
asked to contribute to a collection for new uniforms for the band, while
Sassafras solicits funds for his private use. A sense of small-town intimacy marks the appearance of the several pairs of lovers: milliner Lo-
rena Watkins, who has brought drummer Whittaker, and Chick Elzey
and Jupiter Pettaway carrying a heavy lunch basket.

The names given both major and minor characters are most appropriate. Ade once related how he chose such names. While he was working out plot details, he visited in the Vicksburg, Mississippi, home of a southern yarnspinner, who showed Ade about the town. In the lobby of the courthouse Ade read a bulletin-board list of tax-delinquent citizens. Later securing a copy of this "grand roster of old Anglo-Saxon names," he was able to create for *The County Chairman* a cast of "undiluted American" folk names which actually were "authentic and home-grown."[38] Thus Antioch citizens bore real Mississippi names, such as those given the newspaper editors (Wilson Prewitt and Riley Cleaver), the drummer from "Saint Looee" (Joe Whittaker), Miss Watkins who "simply adores drummers," Mrs. Jefferson Briscoe whose "tone is firm and commanding," Sassafras Livingstone who flatteringly lies to each candidate, telling each one that his two-day old baby (actually a girl) is named for him. Another folk touch is that of Jim Hackler's attributing his frequent aphorisms, always misquoted, to "Bill" Shakespeare. Often the shrewdness which has made him a local political success is expressed in such sayings as "But if you don't git aboard at the right minute you're liable to be a dead card all the rest of your life," and "It's easier for a rich man to get into heaven than for a politician to go through the eye of a needle." But, as Jim says, elections give Prewitt and Cleaver something to put into their papers. "Politics—why, we couldn't get along without 'em." At the last, thinking about how he helped Tilford and Lucy renew their mutual faith, Jim exclaims: "Well, am I a County Chairman or a matrimonial agent!"[39]

In 1896 William Dean Howells, whose critical approval then meant much to young writers, highly praised Ade's newly published *Artie, a Story of the Streets and Town* as a superlative "study of American town life in the West." Somewhat later, in an optimistic account of the "Chicago School of Fiction" (in the *North American Review*, May, 1903), Howells paid further tribute to Ade's versatility: "But our life, our good, kind, droll ridiculous American life, is really inexhaustible, and Mr. Ade, who knows its breadths and depths as few others have known them, drops his net into it anywhere, and pulls it up full of queer fish which abound in it." Ade in the meantime had been busy dropping his net into another sea of midwestern town life, but, according to his biographer, he had not crystallized his thinking about certain small-town material which eventually was to be shaped into a Hoytian comedy, tremendously popular.

In 1902, with the assistance of his brother Will, Ade began building an impressive estate on a four-hundred-acre farm near the town of

Brook, Indiana. A grove of century-old oaks at one corner of the farm, near the Iroquois River, became the site of Hazelden, with its Elizabethan styled main house, just a little shack "about the size of a girls' school." Happily established here in isolation from the hubbub of Chicago, Ade set to work, during the summer of 1904, recasting into scenario form the ideas he had had for some six years for a novel to be called *The College Widow*. Later he added dialogue and stage directions, which were scarcely changed during rehearsals.[40] In this way Ade completed *The College Widow*, a farcically exaggerated comedy entertaining in its day because of its clever satire and its ridiculous portrayal of the excitement of college football rivalries.

The slight plot revolves around the intense rivalry between two freshwater colleges, presumably in neighboring towns of the Midwest. Selfmade Hiram Bolton, now a railroad president, has gratefully endowed Bingham (a Baptist college) with quadrangles, chapels, and other "furbelows" because his expulsion as a freshman freed him for becoming successful in business enterprises. As the action begins his son, Billy, a popular halfback, is en route to register at Bingham, when he stops off at Atwater (a Presbyterian stronghold) to join his father Hiram for a visit with an old-time friend, Dr. Witherspoon, Atwater's president. Laughable mixups occur with great rapidity when the town belle and "college widow," Jane Witherspoon (the "prexy's" beautiful daughter), charms Billy into saving Atwater's reputation in football by becoming its halfback. Defying his angry father, Billy remains to bring glory to the Atwater team, gain Jane's love, and hear Hiram's condemnation of him, "You're a hell of a Baptist!"

Ade's youthful admiration for the Hoyt farces, which he enjoyed in performance in Chicago, is reflected in his amusing but exaggerated characterizations. During the entire comedy Flora Wiggins (Gertrude Quinlan's role)—the sarcastic daughter of a local boardinghouse keeper—drifts in and out doggedly trying to collect $18.00 from "Stub" Tallmadge. ("I've met so many college comedians I ain't got a laugh left in my system," she tells Tallmadge.) Equally farcical is Hiram Bolton's insistence that a college education is worthless. "Oh," he grants, "colleges do some good—they keep a good many light-weights out of the railroad business." As for his own feeling, he protests that "there ain't any money in a college education," adding that he had always been "so grateful to Bingham College for savin' me from a professional career that I've put up three or four buildings for them."

As one of the "slang plays" and football "comics" so popular at the opening of the twentieth century, *The College Widow* fails to present a truly realistic picture of a small college town. Rather, the portrayal is superficial, with continual excitement created by the slangy comments of the athletes at their training tables, by the rival college yells at the big game, the fraternity singsongs, dances in the gymnasium, and other parties, and the groups of students at the Grand Central Hotel of Act IV. *The College Widow*, therefore, with its stage professors, presidents, and student types, gives no suggestion of the deeper aspects of homespun America and all too little of the real activities which Ade himself knew very well during his student days at Purdue.

At the turn of the century popular faith in the friendly village myth continued as another Hoosier—one of Ade's young contemporaries—turned playwright. Glibly termed a "James Whitcomb Riley with a college education, writing fiction instead of verse," Newton Booth Tarkington (1869-1946), after his college days at Purdue and Princeton, ended a seven-year literary apprenticeship in 1899 with the publication of his first novel, *The Gentleman from Indiana*. A year later, with the romantic "Monsieur Beaucaire," young Tarkington gained much popular success, which continued when in 1901 Richard Mansfield produced Tarkington's dramatization done in collaboration with Evelyn Greenleaf Sutherland. Then, working independently, Tarkington dramatized *The Gentleman from Indiana*. In its novel form Tarkington had cut for himself a village pattern which he was to use often in his later stories of the "dear good people" of Indiana towns. In this, as in other Tarkington novels, the rewards of material success and love are bestowed upon a worthy young hero, easterner John Harkless, sturdily self-reliant and eventually victorious in his efforts to bring about civic improvement as a newly arrived newspaper editor in Plattville, Illinois. The conventional plot, akin in theme to *The Hoosier Schoolmaster*, concerns the triumphs of this upright and college-bred young editor over the Whitecaps, troublemakers from a nearby shantytown. This excellent youth puts an end to the vice ring controlled by the rowdy Whitecaps, restores village peace of mind, escapes harm from his enemies, marries the girl of his choice (Helen Sherwood), and is rewarded by the admiring townspeople—"the beautiful people"—by being nominated for Congress.

According to biographer James Woodress, the hamlet of Plattville, with its folksy people, is a realistic fictionalization growing out of Tarkington's memories of his boyhood visits to relatives in Marshall, Illinois, during the early eighties. The easygoing little hometown, symbolizing, says Woodress, "the timeless perfecion of a boy's heaven," emerges in *The Gentleman from Indiana* as a Hoosier hamlet based upon the adult Tarkington's nostalgic impressions of the summertime happiness enjoyed long ago in company with his cousin, Fenton Booth of Marshall.[41] Moreover, an earlier biographer, Robert Cortes Holliday, has pointed out that the Indianapolis of Tarkington's youth was a town and "that B. T. is neither a city nor a country boy, but a town boy."[42] This circumstance, no doubt, accounts for the repeated use in his fiction of many aspects of small-town life, including the more sentimental and uncritical approach which characterizes *The Gentleman from Indiana*.

In 1908-9 Tarkington's collaboration with Harry Leon Wilson produced such popular plays as *The Man from Home*, concerning Hoosiers abroad, and *Your Humble Servant*. During the exciting years to follow, Tarkington's popularity as an amusing interpreter of small-town life grew as his *Penrod* and other stories were adapted to the stage. The first of these to be produced was the four-act dramatization of *Seventeen*, his nostalgic tale of adolescence written in 1916 as an outgrowth of *Penrod*.[43] This hilarious play, made by Hugh Stanilaus Stamge and Stannard Mears and staged by Stuart Walker at the Booth Theater, New York, from January 22, 1918, for 225 performances, not only gave key roles to Ruth Gordon and Gregory Kelly but furnished rollicking fun as "A Tale of Youth and Summer time." And that particular summer brought the anguish of puppy love to Willie Baxter (William Sylvanus Baxter, Jr.) when an insufferable baby-talking charmer, Lola Pratt, came to visit May Parcher and disturb the tranquillity of the old-fashioned town. Willie, as an awkward mooncalf trying clumsily to achieve man's estate, suffers from the yearnings of adolescent love, the humiliations seemingly heaped upon him by his unperceptive family, and the tough competition with Joe Bullitt and Johnny Watson, also smitten by Lola's charms. At last Lola departs, leaving a less irritable Mr. Parcher, a wiser Willie Baxter (now concerned about his freshman year at college), and a more peaceful community.

Some time before writing *Seventeen*, Tarkington, like his Indianapolis neighbor, James Whitcomb Riley, made further popular use of old hometown scenes and characters when in 1914 he published the first of the *Penrod* series. To the popular genre of village tales about the antics and scrapes of small boys Tarkington brought a great deal of insight largely developed through his own boyhood experiences in Indianapolis and Marshall and his mature observation of his three nephews. Augmenting the earlier gallery of portraits of small-town boys created by Mark Twain, Thomas Bailey Aldrich, Stephen Crane, William Allen White, and others, Tarkington amusingly presented, against the background of a pleasant midwestern town, rebellious Penrod Schofield (hampered in his adventures by his family's middle-class standards), his pal Sam Williams, the Negro brothers Herman and Verman, bullying Rupe Collins, and Georgie Bassett, the Little Gentleman whose perfect and saintly behavior is a constant torment to Penrod. Such were the familiar, but somewhat exaggerated, boyish types whose characteristic frays and rebellions against the tyranny of parents and teachers were adapted for the stage, as a four-act comedy, by Edward E. Rose. Produced by George C. Tyler, Klaw, and Erlanger at the Globe Theatre, New York, the comedy ran for forty-eight performances, the first on September 2, 1918. Moreover, during this run Tarkington's interest in Helen Hayes, then but seventeen and acting in her first adult role, was so stirred by her fine performance in the part of the older sister Margaret that he was to use her talents in later plays, notably *Clarence* and *The Wren*.

Tarkington, as an interpreter of the small town, illustrates what happened to various extollers of folksiness popular in the early twentieth century. As a young writer he used too freely what one critic has called nice pinks and yellows in his often uncritical and sentimental portrayals of late nineteenth-century town life. In his major phase, however, Tarkington, having observed the changes wrought by industry in Indianapolis and other Midland towns, turned to more realistic presentations of pressing social and economic problems of the industrialized town and small city. *The Magnificent Ambersons* (1918) and *Alice Adams* (1921), for example, reveal his powers in presenting the impact of a rapidly changing society upon family groups. Even so, in his later defenses of small-town ways and middle-class thinking, he retained certain earlier traits, such as the feeling that sex should not be featured too boldly in fiction.

Friendship Village

The myth of the friendly village, traceable to the flattery of the American countryside early appearing in romanticized village plays and poetry, long persisted, even while the rising force of naturalism began to reshape our fiction. The early fiction of E. W. Howe, Joseph Kirkland, and Hamlin Garland, revolutionary for its time in its naturalistic exposures of farm and town life in the Midlands, apparently had little effect upon certain idealistic temperaments of the early twentieth century. Among these was youthful Zona Gale, whose dreams of Beauty and Romance were shaped, during her sheltered girlhood, by her idealistic parents and the pleasant surroundings of her picturesque birthplace, the little river town of Portage, Wisconsin. The whole structure of a vanished society is recorded in her later autobiographical pictures of Portage. Her later memories brought to life the genuinely friendly folk, their pleasant though modest homes, and their round of neighborhood activities. The most vivid image, however, was that of her family home, a picket-fenced "brick cottage on maple-shaded Conant Street," with its "two heaven-kissing Lombardy poplars" by the front gate, the nine apple trees in the orchard, and a vegetable garden bordered by colorful four o'clocks, portulacas, and balsam.[44] Later, in lake-bordered Madison, where in 1899 she completed work for the M.A. at the University of Wisconsin, Zona Gale continued her romantic dreaming, as she extended her reading, worked for the university paper, and wrote romanticized poems and stories. After apprenticeship reporting in then socially conservative Milwaukee, Miss Gale went to New York, where she combined reporting for the *World* with short-story writing for the *Delineator, Everybody's,* the *Woman's Home Companion,* and other popular magazines. Still viewing life as a romantic idealist, she excluded from her stories "everything coarse, brutal, unpleasant as unfit to write about." Thus living in her personal ivory tower, she completed forty loosely connected stories about two old lovers, which, published in 1907 as *The Loves of Pelleas and Etarre,* had immediate popularity.

Sentimentally expressive of her youthful credo of sweetness and light, *The Loves* foreshadowed Miss Gale's creation of Friendship Village, a magic town which had its roots in Portage. By 1908 the stories of Friendship Village were being praised as picturing a new Utopia, "a typical midwestern small town, portrayed in all its intimate life 'with faithfulness, with loving tenderness, with appreciative understanding.' "[45] Such delight in community fellowship, then, gives the keynote to Miss Gale's early idealistic creed. The intimate associations of little hometowns provided motivation not only for *Friendship Village* but also for *Friendship Village Love Stories* (1909), *Neighborhood Stories* (1914), *Peace in Friendship Village* (1919), and other stories, as well as derivative plays. In Friendship Village people adventured together, "knowing the details of one another's lives, striving a little but companioning far more than striving, kindling to one another's interests instead of practicing the faint morality of mere civility."[46] In all of the Friendship series revelations of a democratic society are made through the medium of neighborhood intimacies (with gossip about all of the young people who are keeping company), church affairs, and civic matters. These are the commonplaces of narrow lives; yet the happy, grass-roots life of the Friendship villagers, however limited their environment, so caught the imagination of sentimental readers that Zona Gale responded later by dramatizing some of the material. Even before 1909 she gave encouragement to the newly organized Wisconsin Players (reorganized in 1926 as the Wisconsin Dramatic Guild) by writing for their use her best-known Friendship Village play, *Neighbours*, long a favorite with amateur groups. Miss Gale made no charges to such groups, requiring only that "any group who planted a tree in the community in which the play was to be given, could present it without a royalty payment."[47]

First printed in 1914 in *Wisconsin Plays*, this little play was again in Miss Gale's mind after her emancipation from Friendship Village, when in the twenties she began her more creative dramatic experimentation with the realistic and crowd-drawing *Miss Lulu Bett*. Stimulated by the success of *Miss Lulu Bett*, Miss Gale began adding now to *Neighbours* and several other previously written one-act plays.[48] Structured in short scenes, the play treats anew the theme of "togetherness" in the somnolent village at the conjunction of two rivers. Much of the action hinges upon the neighborly gossip which starts in a small-town kitchen. Mis' Diantha Abel, at her kitchen ironing board, talks—in folksy speech—to Grandma, who pertly airs her views about trivial domestic matters in such retorts as "I ain't no more interested in them carpet rags than I am in the dipthery." Showing no concern about the more significant issues of the time, these village women find satisfaction in borrowing starch, in ordering cord wood from Ezra Williams or groceries from Peter, in gossiping about babies and baby showers, in winning prizes for their home-canned fruit, and other such local matters. Talkative Diantha is typical of her neighbors and their intimacies when she declares, "My land a living! Carry Ellsworth with a boy on top of everything else!" and, "I hate di-plomacy in man or beast."

In another homey play, *Uncle Jimmy*, the revision of *Friendship Village* material revealed faint signs of Miss Gale's developing social consciousness, soon to be of deep significance in *Miss Lulu Bett* and other realistic plays. In a little midwestern town shabbily dressed Uncle Jimmy, a neighborhood hired hand nearing seventy, finds mental escape from the mean chores he is forced to do by dreaming of a trip which will take him away from Wisconsin. He not only confides his hopes to Grandma, herself seventy, but confesses to her also his opinions about the women for whom he works, including Mis' Amanda Toplady, Calliope Marsh, Mis' Postmaster Sykes, and others appearing in the original Friendship series. Although when his chance for a trip comes he is unable to go, Uncle Jimmy is not the victim of discontent, for, after all, "I got my funeral expenses saved up." Now, too, he realizes that "Hatin' the town you're in is like hatin' folks you see too much of."[49]

Perhaps by 1919 Zona Gale's idyllic village creed was responding enough to the demands of the new realism for her to be judged, in her own phrase, as "a daughter of tomorrow." At any rate, in that year she was apparently re-evaluating the provincial village of her stories. "The first editor to whom these Friendship Village stories were submitted declined them with the word that his acquaintance with small towns was wide but that he had never seen any such people as these. . . I am still not sure that he was not right."[50] Nevertheless, before wearying of her idyls of community friendliness and "the eternal saccharine," Miss Gale had succeeded, by book and stage, in fixing in the minds of countless impressionable readers and spectators treasured images of an ideal old hometown. Possibly such an appeal was widespread because Friendship Village, though lacking a definite location on the printed map of the United States, grew out of "a drowsy village on the banks of the Wisconsin" beloved by Zona Gale for "its memories, its tradition, and its settings . . ."[51]

The last of the provincials, however, was not a dweller in Friendship Village. Rather, the final popular figure among those stage provincials related to the Yankee and other folksy characters was a Californian: "Old Bill Jones, called Lightnin' because of his serene laziness" and first presented to the public at the Gaiety Theatre, New York, on August 26, 1918. The joint creation of playwright Winchell Smith and actor Frank Bacon, Bill is the "amiable, gentle liar, braggart and tippler" featured in *Lightnin'*, a sentimentalized character comedy which by the season of 1919-20 topped, with its eight hundred performances, the record for the longest continuous run in the history of the New York theaters to that time. Likable Frank Bacon, in the role of Lightnin', "started on the long, long run that brought him fame, a competence, and the worship of the multitude."[52] In this action-packed comedy the familiar image of the lovable but weak provincial is projected against the background of a resort town directly on the California-Nevada state line, a little community like the town in Hoyt's *A Bunch of Keys*. Although it had been Mrs. Jones's idea to turn their home into a summer hotel, the Calivada Hotel, Lightnin' takes the credit. Constantly envisioning himself as having distinction as lawyer, soldier, civil engineer, and promoter, Lightin' laments that he has always "been cheated out of my share." As a sort of latter-day Rip Van Winkle, this ne'er-do-well of Calivada is almost hoodwinked by promoters Thomas and Hammond, whose villainy includes schemes to defraud gullible Mrs. Jones and a young neighbor, John Marvin, of their rightfully owned properties. In a joyous finale, old Lightnin', by his native shrewdness, exposes the swindlers, reunites the lovers (John and the Joneses' adopted daughter, Mildred), and, in the manner of Rip Van Winkle, drinks to their happiness.

Well into the twentieth century, while American life was taking on a constantly accelerated pace, theater patrons were still finding amusement in a variety of sentimental village plays. Although the physical aspects of life in towns over the country kept changing and changing, the hometown play as a genre produced no memorable psychological studies of provincial Americans or the growing complexity of their milieu. Except for Herne's pioneering approach to social issues, playwrights of this type generally gave little or no serious treatment to small-town problems, such as labor struggles. As portrayed on the stage, the pattern of small-town life, in Homeville, Plattville, and Friendship Village, offered few complexities which were not readily simplified. Mostly such plays, ranging from the farcical to the sentimental, abound in scenes of the happy isolated existence of the era from the 1850's to the 1890's, with different regional types (often New Englanders and midwesterners) portrayed as living close to the land. Hometown, America, as thus dramatized, appealed widely as the focal point of a democratic, pleasant, uncomplicated, and, at times, amusing way of living. There seems to have been appeal, too, in what the late Sherwood Anderson once called "the old hunger for intimacy," often felt strongly by those uprooted provincials who though living for years in the city "remember vividly the intimacy of life in the towns" and "during all the years of their life as city men" remain "at heart small-towners." As Thomas Beer quipped, "This uncultivated hunger for pathetics was easily fed." But, with the movement toward naturalism, an opposition was being created. The time was ready for "astringent persons."

VII. Racial Prejudice and Economic Tension

AS THE Mauve Decade was nearing its close, small signs of uneasiness, quickened by the assertions and reassertions of village goodness, began to appear. Questioning persons like Van Wyck Brooks were moved to downright rejection of the still cherished images of the folksy, peaceful town. Those lovely small places described long ago by Andrew Jackson Downing as our "flourishing villages, with broad streets lined with maples and elms, behind which are goodly rows of neat and substantial buildings" were becoming but faint reminders of the past. Rejecting romantic notions about local customs, Edgar Lee Masters starkly portrayed unhappy townspeople broken by the tether of uniformity, as in this succinct case history from his annals of Spoon River:

> "Then I asked again
> Why Cato Braden died at fifty-one,
> And Will said: 'Winston Prairie, Illinois
> Killed Cato Braden.' "

By 1920 the nationwide tumult created by *Main Street* made "our comfortable tradition and sure faith" in the folksy virtues of our Hometowns, or Homevilles, more questionable than ever and, for the skeptical, well-nigh obsolete. In fiction, as in fact, the popular glorification of old-fashioned village America, safe in its quiet isolation, gradually dimmed before the new and satirically drawn pattern of Gopher Prairie, Minnesota, whose "Main Street," in Sinclair Lewis' oft-quoted words, "is the continuation of Main Streets everywhere." The once popular concept of Friendship Village could not for long withstand Lewis' astringent satire of Main Street as "the climax of civilization" and of American small towns generally as nothing but stagnant centers where "dullness is made God." Lewis' shouting, Lewis Gannett has observed, was about smugness. "Gopher Prairie was Any Town, USA, in 1919-20, and Any Town was smug."

Even before the twenties—the days of the Modern—changed the national outlook, the stage glorification of village ways was affected by a spirit of revolt slowly brewing in the world of the theater. Critics lamented the paucity of artistic and sincere plays, the power of the Klaw and Erlanger Syndicate with its commercial control over hundreds of theaters and bookings on the road, and the evils of the star system. But new forces were at work, and by degrees turned attention to the serious

207

need for intelligent support of the stage. Among the significant dramatic projects at the turn of the century, George Pierce Baker's course in playwriting at Harvard in 1905 and the establishment of the New Theatre in Chicago in 1906, followed by the New Theatre opening in New York in 1909, gave needed impetus to creativity. Especially notable was the presentation by New York's New Theatre, during its first season, of a strong native play, Edward Sheldon's *The Nigger*, first produced on December 4, 1909. In 1913 encouragement was given to new playwrights by the activity of director Winthrop Ames, who after the collapse of the New Theatre in New York offered a prize of $10,000 for the best play, to be submitted anonymously, by an American author. From the nearly 1,700 plays received, the judges—Augustus Thomas, Adolph Klauber, and Ames—awarded the prize in 1914 to Alice Brown's New England village play, *Children of Earth*, which Ames produced on January 12, 1915, at the Booth Theatre, New York. In time other portrayers of the small town seemingly realized that they could no longer continue to acquiesce in popular concepts of sweetness and light as the prevailing virtues in village America. For example, by 1918 changes in their perspectives made possible the emergence of Zona Gale and Booth Tarkington from the sentiment which for years had bound them to the celebration of folksiness. In that year both entered on more mature creative lives through their emancipation from the friendly village. Miss Gale's completion of *Birth*, a long novel later dramatized as *Mister Pitt*, and Tarkington's publication of *The Magnificent Ambersons*, a realistic forerunner to *Alice Adams*, signaled their changing attitudes toward the "dear people" each had known intimately.

Interest in a more modern theater was generated slowly, largely in urban centers and in colleges. The stirring of new thought, the change from a late-Victorian mercantile and agrarian society to an industrial one, ethnic problems, and the restless spirit of the times created the matrix for realistic plays about the little town. As such plays proliferated, audiences began to see a variety of modern scenes and action displaying the more unpleasant and even seamier phases of community life, from region to region. With the winds of change blowing fiercely, playwrights began to call attention to community social problems and ideas once taboo. Their experimentation with fresh themes, greater realism of characterization, unusual techniques, and other newer tools marked their dramas of town life as genuine efforts to confront the major issues of the young century. In short, the movement toward the Age of Enterprise could be seen, more or less realistically, from the perspective of a revitalized stage, which often took spectators imaginatively into the byways of the nation.

The growing complexity of our national life prompted dramatists to deal, often daringly, with controversial problems: ethnic dilemmas and racial prejudice, conflicts between factory owners and workers, the struggles of townsfolk for economic survival as the more ambitious villagers moved cityward, alarm about the spread of Marxian theory, political disagreements, agricultural problems, and a spreading standardization of living which meant the loss of the old individuality among the people of the little town. Some playwrights, perturbed by the conquest of the American town and the old-fashioned values of provincial life by the new industrial order, sought answers in history. All in all, the "Happy, Happy Days" were fast disappearing as the crowded Coketowns and Middletowns dotted the native scene. Even the new Spoon River became "a ganglion of Chicago."

Among the issues frequently facing citizens along both the main thoroughfares and the back streets of little towns, racial problems— miscegenation, economic discrimination, segregation, and even riots— have generally been dramatized in relation to the system of color-castes prevailing in southern localities. Over the years dramatic treatments of the relationship between the whites and the Negroes on plantations and farms and in towns of the Deep South have presented controversial themes, characters, and scenes with varying degrees of romanticism, realism, and stage success.

One popular motif has been the friendly relationship between master and slave in a glorified version of the antebellum order. First produced in the crucial period of 1859 and popular for years afterward, a plantation melodrama daring for its time, *The Octoroon, Or Life in Louisiana*, thrilled audiences in this country and in London because in it Dion Boucicault boldly and theatrically adapted to the stage the then inflammable material of slavery, miscegenation, and mistreatment of the Indian. In the early 1890's two of Augustus Thomas' "locality plays" somewhat indirectly touched upon the southern town and the caste system. The better of these, *Alabama,* which opened on April 1, 1891, at the Madison Square Theatre, starred Edmund Milton Holland in the key role of "a relic of the Confederacy," Colonel Moberly of Talladega, Alabama.[1] The complicated plot, beginning with happenings of May, 1880, concerns the conflicting reactions of landowners in and near Talladega when they are faced with the changes about to be wrought by a northern economic order, symbolized by a railroad to be built through their picturesque and peaceful bayou country. The more sluggish townspeople, "an indolent old bunch of swamp moss" deaf to outside opportunity, do not want their peace disturbed by the new threat posed by agents of the Gulf and Midland Railroad. Other citizens, susceptible to bribery, are willing to lobby for the railroad project at meetings of the town's Assembly Committee and to advertise the proposed route in the *Talladega Sentinel*. In this romantic and sentimental tale, in which probability is not scrupulously considered, most of the wrangling is between factions of the white citizens. The introduction of an "old-timey" Negro servant, Decatur or "Uncle 'Catur," does little more than add a stereotyped minor character to help identify Captain Davenport, the railroad builder, as Harry Preston, the long absent son-in-law of Colonel Moberly.

At the urging of Richard Watson Gilder, an entertaining southern storyteller, Francis Hopkinson Smith, wrote out some of his Negro stories for the *Century*.[2] Completed as *Colonel Carter of Cartersville*, these tales, within the current of local color, "had the charm of a chivalry that seemed a little remote."[3] "Frank, generous, tender-hearted" Colonel Carter, though proud of his ancestry and his state, is remote from his native Cartersville, living as an expatriate in New York. With the help of his faithful Negro servant Chad, Colonel Carter, his fortune gone, lives as a hanger-on in a Wall Street office and as a dreamer of better things in the future for the natives of Fairfax County, Virginia. The romantic glow of this novelette proved so appealing that Augustus Thomas successfully produced his dramatization of it in New York, at Palmer's Theatre, on March 22, 1892. Again Holland, cast as the Colonel, helped make a southern gentleman's world of dreams theatrically appealing. But the face of reality—the revelation of the real problems of a war-devastated South—is missing. Instead, in William Winter's opinion, Thomas created a pleasing "blend of sympathy, sweetness, and eccentric humor." Cartersville is lost in the mists of romanticism.

By 1910 the new strains entering into our literature of the small town had given momentum to the rise of the problem play begun by Herne. Mixed signs of America's "coming-of-age" are to be found, for example, in the thesis plays of Chicago-born Edward Brewster Sheldon (1886-1946), who as a graduate of the Harvard Workshop 47 "scented the new times" but still was bound by a lingering romanticism. In his second play, *The Nigger*, Sheldon, already an able craftsman at twenty-four, provided New York's New Theatre patrons with controversial matter: strong sociological problems concerning caste taboos, political corruption, and the employment of Negroes as policemen, as these issues eventually led to rioting in a southern community.

In the course of a somewhat melodramatic plot and romantic love story, the caste stigma becomes a vigorous and awful reality when a young southern governor, Philip Morrow, patrician planter and outspoken advocate of white supremacy, discovers shortly after his election that he is actually the grandson of Belle, a quadroon slave once his grandfather's mistress. His dilemma is made all the more difficult by his having declared before his election that "Things have changed some since the wah, an' if we want t' keep our blood clean, we've got to know that *white's white* and *black's black*—an mixin' 'em's damnation!"[4] Theatricalism and irony mark Morrow's unsuccessful attempts, as sheriff of Westbury County, to protect a young rapist from an angry mob led by Jake Willis, whose daughter Mamie dies as a result of the assault. The guilty youth is Joe, shiftless grandson of Morrow's faithful and aged Mammy Jinny, the secretive sister of Belle, long ago "sold down river" by grandfather Morrow. The news of Mamie's death, the angry white posse with their baying bloodhounds, the hesitancy of the cowardly jail wardens, and the lynching of the utterly terrified Joe all combine to create, in the first act, a scene of tremendous intensity. As Mammy Jinny pleads with her "Marse Phil" to let Joe hide in Morrow's Rest, the family mansion, the distraught old servant partially reveals her long-kept secret about Morrow's blood kinship with the ill-fated Joe. Jinny's agonized plea, "Listen, Marse Phil, yo *mus'* keep him heah—'kaze he's yo'—," is overheard by suspicious Clifton Noyes, Morrow's jealous cousin and a persistent schemer for the control of the family estate.

Sheldon makes use of ethnic, economic, and political forces to give insights into the complexities of human nature. In particular, Cliff shrewdly uses all three to satisfy his greed. As president of the Noyes Distillery Works, he has enriched himself through the sale of whiskey to Negroes. By chance he discovers, among the dusty records at Morrow's Rest, a confessional letter which Belle wrote to her lover, the elder Morrow, before she was sold in New Orleans. Now Cliff can gloat: "Yo' prope'ty, 'Morrow's Rest,' eve'thin' you inherited, belong by rights to me. Why, you ain't even got yo' name. Can you grasp it, ol' man?"[5] To insure his continued economic success, he threatens to use his newspaper to expose Philip as a "White Niggah" if, as governor, he signs a prohibition bill—sponsored by Senator Long, himself a "White Niggah"—already passed by the state legislature for the betterment of the condition of the Negro. ". . . what a nice big bust-up it'd be if people knew they had a niggah Gove'noh!"

The first "big bust-up" to occur, however, is of a personal and sentimental nature. It accents, with considerable theatricalism, the basic theme of the play: the magnetism of the romantic love between Philip and his fiancée, Georgiana Byrd, a pretty local belle. Although emotionally shaken by Cliff's ugly disclosure, Philip fearlessly tells Georgie the truth about himself. Horrified, she breaks away from his embraces with loathing, rejecting his plea that "love's the only thing to carry us across, . . ." This is but the first crisis which Philip must meet, following his decision not "to knuckle under" to Noyes and his demands for a veto to the prohibition bill. Although later a tearful Georgia returns to tell Phil that she still loves him, he stubbornly prepares to meet another crisis. With Georgie near him, Phil goes out on the balcony of the governor's mansion to disclose to a crowd of citizens the truth about his "tainted blood." Before he can say a word, and before we can learn the popular reaction to his story, a colonel greets him as "yo' Excellency, the Comin' Man!" and the curtain falls as a regimental band plays "America."

Thus the third act, a throwback to the sentimental dramas that were popular in Sheldon's youth, weakens the force of the first two acts, with their daring treatment of timely racial problems. Nevertheless, the play as a whole was bold in its treatment of the then forbidden stage subject of miscegenation—too bold, in fact, for any but the New Theatre to produce in repertory.

Through the realism of its scenes of southern community life of the 1909 era, *The Nigger* contributed to the progressive trend in the drama of the time. Sheldon is convincing in his pictures of the village community near Morrow's Rest, with its mixed population of landed whites, poor whites, and Negroes. Equally convincing are the activities in the capital: political lobbying, partisan journalism, the crass commercialism exhibited in connection with Noyes's distillery interests, the use of troops to quell a race riot, and the political rise of the "White Negro," coupled with open hostility toward the Negrophile. At least, if Sheldon, as an early enthusiastic student of George Pierce Baker, "might not have impressed an observer as a rippling wave of the future,"[6] *The Nigger* expressed his broad social sympathies and his sense of locality.

During the years following the production of *The Nigger*, plays about small towns down South held little echo of "dark laughter," uninhibited and earthy. Southern dramas of social protest, mostly by northerners, defined sharply, if not always artistically, community dilemmas produced by the efforts of white citizens to "keep the Negro in his place."[7] Such stage treatments of racial realities significantly revealed the indignation of liberal, or even radical, playwrights, aroused by newspaper and other reports of flagrant injustice toward the Negro. On occasion, these dramatic re-creations of a complicated society, however provincial and limited, appeared by way of a theatrical or sensational interpretation of a current *cause célèbre*, usually a court trial or a worker's strike throwing an entire community into confusion. The facts, sometimes distorted, were there but were rarely displayed with imaginative creativity. Condemnation, hampering the imagination, failed to bring to life the real provincial South, which, in Sherwood Anderson's memories, was "a rich place, rank with life, fairly rancid with life" with its "big slow river crawling down between the mud banks of an empire" and its "river-tough towns."[8]

In the twenties and the early thirties, strikes and trials—notably the controversial Scopes trial at Dayton, Tennessee, during the summer of 1925 and the Scottsboro trial in Alabama, opening in April, 1931—served to dramatize the suppression of freedom by what Mencken called the "booboisie" and the bitter struggles of minority groups, especially the Negroes, the Irish, and the Jews. Repercussions in the area of provincial drama stimulated the production of plays of social protest, whose satire and experimental techniques expressed not only a new theater but a chaotic age.

In drama, the ideal picture of southern towns, typified by Augustus Thomas' Cartersville, is one of wide, shady streets, with old colonial homes of white painted wood or of mellowed red brick with white pillars and façade. Another type of southern town, to be matched in other parts of the country, is the small industrial town where "men exist rather than live, where row after row of drab and practically uniform houses stretch into a monstrous eyesore, where, until recently, men labored for ten or twelve hours a day for meager wages, . . ."[9] The dramatization of such industrial towns was given momentum early in 1925 when the Theatre Guild experimented with a production of John Howard Lawson's *Processional*, a loosely plotted expression of the American scene in native idiom. As his preface to this play explains, Lawson in the early twenties rejected the older realism of "the facile mood of Expressionism," shown in his *Roger Bloomer* (1923). In *Processional*, which he called "a jazz symphony of American life," he experimented with "essentially vaudevillesque" technique, much to the irritation of some spectators. The excellent acting of June Walker and George Abbott, the mining town settings by Mordecai Gorelik, and the direction by Philip Moeller carried the experiment through ninety-six performances. There was questioning of the validity of Lawson's contention, in his preface, that in vaudeville he could find not only good theater, but a representation of reality as well. There was also critical reporting on "the misery of genius still inchoate and fumbling for its forms" and on the first-night audience sitting "in glum affront at the temerity of an American gone imaginative and rid of the four-square limits of the stage."[10] Apparently Lawson was trying to demonstrate that "the form of the theatre at a given time is determined by social and economic conditions and is a reflection of contemporary society."[11] In *Processional*, a "sardonic scramble," he tried to create by vaudevillian stereotypes, by the jazz tempo of workers' songs and bands, and by native idioms a feeling for "the syncopated chaos of American life."

The bare story is played through a rapid succession of expressionistic scenes picturing "the cheap, brassy, tragical, comical, cruel, persevering carnival of life in a West Virginia mining town." The theme—the processional of "man struggling in all his nakedness, wretchedness, and bravery" through crime and punishment toward redemption—develops by means of a small-town nightmare. Dynamite Jim, a mountain native involved in a coal mine strike, is jailed by "the law and order bunch" for his part in fomenting "industrial warfare" against the "Silk Hats." He escapes, but bayonets a shivering soldier who tries to arrest him and flees to a dilapidated barn—the makeshift home of his destitute mother and grandmother—with the sheriff in fast pursuit. Jim then hides "in the black mouth of a mine [where] he rapes the jingly-hearted young daughter of old Isaac Cohen, the town store keeper." As soldiers surround him again, Jim, badly injured, flees for the last time. For six months his mother, a prostitute calling herself Mrs. Euphemia Stewart Flimmins, and Sadie Cohen, now pregnant, mourn him as the victim of hanging. Saved by a farmer, Jim at last, though blind and dumbly frustrated, comes home to them. But "the black punishment of his blindness" and the "dawning womanhood" of pleasure-loving Sadie lead to their redemption and eventual union in a jazz wedding on a hilltop overlooking the shabby coal town. As a brassy finale, a jazz band plays while the whole noisy crowd— Klansmen "unmasked as a ballet-dancing lot of Jews, negroes and whatnots, to bawl competition with the laborers, the soldiery and the highhatters"—parades around the couple. "Then the Procession marches down through the audience," disappearing at the rear of the theater with increasing noise and rhythm.[12]

Lawson's expressionistic "rhapsody in red" antedated by almost a decade John Wexley's dramatic response in 1934 to the sensational Scottsboro affair. His spirited proletarian drama, *They Shall Not Die*, resembles *Processional* in its often melodramatic pictures of confusion in a small industrial town. Of course, the fictional mill town of Cookesville, where dormant prejudices mount to fever pitch as white citizens declare, "Them negroes must be kept in their place!" is a thinly disguised Scottsboro, the county seat and trade center of Jackson County in northeast Alabama. Wexley's exceedingly current problem of racial injustice and the mockery of court procedure had its real start in April, 1931, when nine Negro boys, aged thirteen to nineteen, were charged with having raped two white mill-town girls on a freight train in Alabama. The boys were brought to speedy trial in Scottsboro, convicted, and sentenced to death. Believing the case unproved and the verdict the result of southern racial prejudice, northern liberals and radicals came to the defense of the accused, thus changing the aspect of a small-town case into a *cause célèbre*. In 1932 the Supreme Court declared that the original verdict represented a mistrial because the defendants' right to counsel had been infringed upon. After a long period of widely publicized court action, the case was returned to the Supreme Court, which in 1935 handed down the momentous decision that the case must be retried on grounds that Negroes had been denied, by custom and practice, not by law, the right to serve on juries.

In trying to awaken the public to protest against such miscarriage of justice as the Scottsboro verdict implied, Wexley became "blazing mad" enough to produce what Brooks Atkinson's *Times* review described as "a tremendously powerful play"—"one of terrifying and courageous bluntness of statement." On the other hand, quite recently John Gassner has deplored Wexley's restricting "his moral imagination while giving vent to his indignation."[13] With considerable clarity and force Wexley makes vivid drama out of his Cookesville and other Alabama scenes: local drama revealing the popular excitement of the execution day after "a nice, speedy trial," the news that the Supreme Court had ordered a new trial, the unexpected decision of the younger girl in the case, Lucy Wells (in real life, Ruby Bates), to defy all the forces of the bigoted town by truthfully declaring that the rape charge was false, the new trial at nearby Dexter with a famous Jewish lawyer from New York, Nathan G. Rubin, as defense attorney, and Lucy's surprise entrance as a defense witness to expose the frame-up. When the jury files out, "from behind the door is heard their derisive laughter," in spite of the fact that Rubin, enacted by Claude Rains, had appealed to the jury's "reason as logical, intelligent human beings, determined to give this poor scrap of colored humanity a fair, square deal."[14] Indignant at the laughter, Rubin defiantly challenges the townsfolk: "This case isn't ended yet—We're only beginning— . . . These boys—they shall not die!" With these words, the Cookesville conflict between the forces of justice and sectional prejudice ends on a note of suspense. What is missing in the whole play, says Gassner, is a strong dramatic picture of "humanity in its multidimensional reality." (Among the Negro dramatists who were finding a hearing on Broadway during the thirties, Missouri-born Langston Hughes showed deep concern, in drama as in poetry, over the plight of the modern Negro in the South. His *Scottsboro Limited* of 1932 is a proletarian one-acter exposing the cruelties of the Negro's oppressors and the limitations imposed upon the race at Scottsboro.)

They Shall Not Die came to the stage during America's awakening from a kind of historic complacency and at a time of revolt when, in Alfred Kazin's phrase, "all the birds began to sing." On the stage this chorus was in tune with melancholy "songs" touching upon darker aspects in the lives of southern mill-town workers, white and black. Director Frederick H. Koch highlighted the fourteenth season of the Carolina Playmakers, 1931-32, with the Chapel Hill presentation of *Strike Song* by Loretto Carroll Bailey and J. O. Bailey. Their new play of southern mill people, programmed as "one of the most ambitious efforts of the Playmakers toward the creation of a native folkdrama," is based frankly upon their study of the conflicts involved in the industrialization of the Piedmont South. Mrs. Bailey has said that the idea of a strike in a mill village grew out of suggestions made by spectators of her first play, *Job's Kinfolks*, which dramatized mill-town life only incidentally, though it was produced at the time when the North Carolina textile mills were attracting wide attention. In *Strike Song* the Baileys offer no solution to the labor problem but do present realistically, from different points of view, material near at hand in the struggles at Gastonia, Marion, Elizabethton, and Danville. Two interesting features of the play are the realistic sets, notably that showing a tent city, erected to shelter the strikers who have been evicted from the company houses, and the use of old ballad tunes with words taken in part from the songs sung by southern textile workers in actual strike conditions.[15]

More than a dozen years before *Strike Song*, the confusions and tensions of an industrialized South were stirring the questioning intelligence of the first young man to enrol in Professor Koch's original class of Carolina Playmakers. In the fall semester of 1918 Thomas Wolfe of Asheville —and soon thereafter another native Carolinian, Paul Green—responded exuberantly to the stimulating enthusiasm of Koch by experimenting with "native stuff," in accordance with the professor's dicta about the dramatic possibilities of regional life. As a result, young Wolfe's *The Return of Buck Gavin, A Tragedy of the Mountain People* had a place on the Playmakers' first program, presented in the Chapel Hill High School Auditorium, March 14 and 15, 1919.[16] Thereafter many other folk characters and backgrounds native to North Carolina and the South came to life through the talents of various Playmakers: the tenant-farm woman as portrayed in Paul and Erma Green's *Fixin's* (1924), vagabonds as in Green's "The No 'Count Boy" (1924), and numerous townspeople. In later years Wolfe, describing his Chapel Hill experiments, recalled that he "scribbled constantly and at random," dashing off one-act plays. This experience as collegiate writer and sometime actor with the Playmakers turned his interests in the direction of a hoped-for career in playwriting, a dream which was to bring disillusionment. In September, 1920, after his graduation from the University of North Carolina, Tom Wolfe, with the encouragement of Frederick Koch, himself a former student of George Pierce Baker, entered the Graduate School of Arts and Sciences at Harvard.

Lonely in Cambridge, remote from "the old democratic atmosphere of Chapel Hill," he moved into a new and alien world where "his Southern provincialism was in conflict with the aesthetic and intellectually snobbish members" of Professor Baker's English 47 Workshop.[17] Refusing to conform to what he thought the sterile and imitative interests of his class-mates, Wolfe in November, 1920, fell to work "in a state of 'pure exaltation,'" revising a tragic one-acter, *The Mountains*, begun at Chapel Hill. Bitter with disappointment at "the complete and dismal failure" of the Workshop production of the play in October, 1921, Wolfe neverthe-less responded to Baker's technical and critical guidance by spending much of his second year at Harvard in expanding it into three acts.[18] Also, as early as his first year with the Workshop, Wolfe had thought of the main theme for a long regional tragedy, which he wrote and revised for the next four years. At first called *The Heirs* or *The Wasters* and finally published as *Mannerhouse* (1948), this family drama is an outgrowth of his thinking in dramatic terms about the landowning Pentlands, his mother's people from the Carolina mountains. Wolfe later incorporated into Chapter LXII in *Of Time and the River* a detailed evaluation of *Mannerhouse*, in which he explained that its regional subject

was the decline and fall and ultimate extinction of a proud old family of the Southern aristocracy in the years that followed the Civil War, the ultimate decay of all its fortunes and the final acquisition of its proud estate, the grand old columned house that gave the play its name, by a vulgar, coarse and mean, but immensely able member of the rising "lower class."

The basic interests in *Mannerhouse* were to reappear in a socially satiric play started in 1922, when Wolfe during a summer visit to Ashe-ville discovered in hometown activities a powerful theme that would en-dure: "Greed, greed, greed," as typified by the three best ways to gain community distinction: "(1) Money, (2) more Money, and (3) a great deal of Money." Thus in a September letter to Mrs. Margaret Roberts of Asheville, Wolfe reported, with passionate certainty, that his new dra-matic attack, first titled *Niggertown*, was against "the knave, the toady, and the hog rich" then flourishing in North Carolina.[19] Turning this "disgusting spectacle" into drama, Wolfe caustically satirized the mad scramble of certain North Carolinians for local and state distinction, as symbolized in his final choice of *Welcome to Our City* as title. An emotional dramatization of economic discrimination and a race riot in Altamont, this sprawling tragedy consists of ten scenes of uneven length, with elaborate sets and a cast of more than thirty small-town characters, white and black. Money-grabbing realtors, hypocritically posing as civic uplifters with their platitudes quoted from Doctor Frank Crane, Edgar A. Guest, and the *American Magazine,* crafty and vulgar politicians, sanctimonious ministers, lawyers stooping to make a deal in real estate sales at the expense of the shanty-owning Negro, the new class of professional Negroes, and other citizens typify the entire society of Altamont and all the local manifestations of the booster spirit.[20]

In *Welcome to Our City*, set within the tensions of southern segregation, Wolfe coldly created both white and Negro characters "who, when joined, would destroy each other and themselves in the Battle of Status Quo."[21] Curiously prophetic of future social disorders in the Deep South, this play is a young dramatist's harsh and strident protest against the boomtown interests which were destroying the older and more peaceful relationship between the races in Altamont. Vivid, original, and at times poetic descriptions of people and scenes, heightened by passages of philosophic comment about social inequity and the fate of man, abound in dramatic contrasts. Straggling throughout a little valley and along a hillside is "a ragged line of whitewashed shacks and cheap one- and two-story buildings of brick." Above, at the top of the hill, is "a fine old house in colonial style, somewhat worn and weatherbeaten," once the mansion of the aristocratic Rutledges but now owned and occupied by Johnson, a mulatto doctor, and his family. In contrast, booming Whitetown shows plentiful signs of material advancement in its modern office buildings, the new mansions of the Rutledge Park addition, and an imposing country club. Wolfe's satire is almost vitriolic in the scenes exposing the wide-scale expansion plans of the Altamont Development Company. According to Bailey, a Rotarian company man, ". . . steps are even now underway to do away with the Negro settlement," where rickety shacks, crooked red clay streets, and Dr. Johnson's home deface the beauty of Altamont, which is otherwise a perfect "little world of a tourist paradise"—"Nature's Wonderland." Gulled by "the Romance of Big Business," Bailey foolishly boasts that "we no longer allow anything to stand in the way of progress in Altamont . . . the remedy in a case of this sort is surgery."

But the realtors' commercial schemes for developing "Altamont—

Bigger, Better, Brighter," at the expense of the Negroes, do not end in "Progress, Progress, Progress," but in the disaster of a bloody riot. In scenes which are dramatically unwieldy, though exciting, Wolfe portrays in succession the efforts of the developers to cheat the Negroes by forcing them to undersell their homes, the courageous public protest made by Johnson, who refuses to sell his property even at the behest of Lawyer Rutledge, the former owner; the burning of Darktown, including the doctor's home, by an unidentified mob; the coming of northern agitators and state militia; and the deliberate shooting of Johnson by young Lee Rutledge. At the impressive finale, Lawyer Rutledge, looking at Johnson's body, compassionately exclaims, "Poor fool! So still! So still! Why did you choose to become a Man?"

Young Wolfe hopefully submitted *Welcome to Our City*, the first full play which he tried to market, to Lawrence Langner of the Theatre Guild.[22] After months of delay, the Guild agreed to take the play provided that Wolfe make revisions, reducing the length by thirty minutes, eliminating some of the characters, and generally tightening the entire script. Though he tried to comply with the Guild's stipulations, Wolfe found he could not effect the necessary changes. "I have written this play with thirty-odd named characters because it required it, not because I didn't know how to save paint. Some day I'm going to write a play with fifty, eighty, a hundred people—a whole town, a whole race, a whole epoch . . ."[23] Though discouragement caused Wolfe to file away *Welcome to Our City* among other unpublished pieces, in his maturity he was to make Altamont the memorable background, during "the great processional of the years" (1884 to 1920), for the peculiarly individualized Pentlands and Gants and for their countless relationships with all classes in the town.

Racial tensions affecting the North Carolina community again come into theatrical view through the artistry and sympathy of one of Wolfe's fellow Playmakers. From a Carolina farm background, Paul Green was destined to achieve high distinction as a professional playwright and a champion of the Negro. Keenly responsive to the new patterns of life wrought by social and industrial changes in modern North Carolina, Green began in 1924 to interpret realistically, by novel and drama, debatable questions related to southern culture, agrarianism, industry, and racial tensions. While many of his plays—*In Abraham's Bosom, The Field God*, and others—present neglected aspects of farm life in eastern North Carolina, on occasion Green has dramatized, with consummate artistry, the prejudices and tensions stirring the life of usually somnolent towns.

Among such community plays, *Roll Sweet Chariot* (1934) was de-

signed, according to Green, as "a symphonic play of the Negro people,"
which, however, failed on Broadway. Originally titled *In the Valley*
(1928) and later (1931) *Potter's Field*, this is a sympathetic study,
original and experimental, of another Darktown of the 1920's, a down-
trodden community variously termed Potter's Field and Johnson's Gully
at "the edge of a college town in North Carolina." (According to the
In the Valley version, "Of late years the more respecting inhabitants
have restyled the place Johnstown.") This large settlement of huddled
shacks houses many laborers, who, while herding together, "sleeping and
eating as best they can," spend their evenings "laughing, singing, and
sitting before their shacks with their girls, or walking out if the weather
is fine towards the hilly fields that lie west of the town."[24] Much of the
community activity centers around the boardinghouse of old Quiviene
Lockley and her youngish and feeble-minded husband, Willie. Effectively
using Negro speech, incidental music, and folk songs, Green dramatizes
times of gaiety and humor, of tribulation and terror, in the drab lives of
the Lockleys and their boarders. Frequenters of old Quiviene's table are
Zeb Lockley, her son by a white man; Bantam Wilson, fugitive from a
chain gang, and his estranged wife Milly, cook for the white-folks; brick-
layer Tom Sterling, who now claims Milly as mistress; the fake minister
John Henry, who prospers by playing on the superstitions of several
boarders; laborer Ed Uzzell and his fellow workers; convicts; and drifters.
At table and other times their down-to-earth talk reveals the hard lot of
the Carolina Negro.

Bantam's attempt to shoot Sterling, because of Milly, prepares the
way for the concluding scene, which powerfully dramatizes the exploitation of the Negro. As this tragic finale opens, sweating convicts in striped
prison clothes are digging on a blazing dust-covered road, rhythmically
"swinging their picks aloft and bringing them down." All the while their
two white guards, more comfortable in the roadside shade, threaten with
rifles. The convicts, however, "like so many soulless puppets," continue
their rhythmic digging, at intervals raising their voices "in a chant, level,
patient, as eternal and tough as the earth in which they dig." At last
Tom Sterling falls to the ground from sheer exhaustion. He is damned
by the First Guard as "a stall boy," while the Second Guard mercilessly
beats his inert body with a leather thong. "Put a firecoal on his tail and
rise him." In a last effort Sterling, goaded to madness, attacks the Second
Guard, but too late, for the terrified First Guard shoots the convict
through the back. Four of the convicts drop their shovels and hover in a
horrified group. The other six, impassive and beaten in spirit, stoically
sing on: "I called my Jesus." Green's passionate comment near the end—

"God sits high in heaven, his face from the Negro, his hand towards the white man"—typifies the compassion he has shown for the underdog throughout the play. The people of Johnson's Gully fare no better than their fellows in Cookesville and Altamont's Darktown.

Community tensions of a different sort add a strong vein of social significance to still another of Green's plays, *Johnny Johnson*, presented first by the Group Theatre, New York, on November 19, 1936. Primarily an experimental antiwar tragicomedy, the play is also an imaginative and ironical "biography of a common man," of a simple tombstone cutter in a small southern town. Once, before circumstances removed him from his native village to the strange world of Europe and World War I, young Johnny Johnson was honored momentarily by the mayor and his fellow citizens on "an occasion most auspicious," the unveiling of his peace monument climaxing a celebration of the town's bicentennial. The hometown phase of Johnny's biography, presented in the first two of multiple scenes with village sets by Donald Oenslager, opens on April 6, 1917, with the pompous mayor's slogan-filled oration extolling the long tradition of peace in the village. Suddenly His Honor's platitudes are cut short by a "lanky barefoot boy . . . riding slowly on a ramshackle bicycle" and bringing the startling news of President Wilson's declaration of war against the Imperial German government. In these two scenes —"a bitter comic strip of music"—Green's portrayal of one small town caught in a frenzy of quickly stirred war fear, of crass opportunism, and of community pressure gains much in verisimilitude and poignant appeal through his skilful use of lyrical lampoons, the music of expatriated Kurt Weill, and the earnestly drawn character of Johnny. The humorous caricatures of other ordinary townsfolk—the mayor, the editor, a photographer, Johnny's sweetheart Minny Belle, and cowardly Anguish Howington, his rival in love—add an element of extravaganza. Johnny's stubborn and naïve adherence to his "peace obsession," while his neighbors shout about this "war to end wars," ironically leads to his commitment to a mental hospital. Meanwhile Howington, a slacker who stayed at home to become a rich man and mayor, is insane with greed. At the end, so Green implies, Johnny, humane and courageous, is the only sane person. Thus, the simple-souled stonemason becomes a symbol of the good men lost in a vile world of "Idiot's Delight." Like Sherwood, Green concludes with an appealing note: "Yet even so, JOHNNY JOHNSON is not hushed by this strange voice booming through the world."[25]

In dramas of this troubled era, the small-town spirit, good and bad, often marks the life of racially united groups dwelling within urban neighborhoods. Even a community of Negro workers, housed adjacent to a plantation commissary and a crossroads church, may approximate the social organization of an agricultural village. The simple people belonging to such restricted units within larger units—Catfish Row, the Brick House Plantation, or other settlements—share in common with small-town citizens a remarkable intimacy of association and neighborly gossip, family rivalries, prejudices, brawls, religious fervor, and economic successes and frustrations. Some fun is there, too. Picnics, fishing, crap games on the sly, singsongs (spirituals and work songs especially), dancing, and other carefree activities offset the maladjustments, the superstition and terror, the ignorance and the tribulation which may make folk life seem somber and, at times, melodramatic. Although closely united by neighborhood bonds, these people, as sometimes dramatized, also form an inseparable part of the larger urban or plantation society which produced them. Often, too, the plays reveal outside forces and sometimes uncontrollable circumstances, such as the white man's law and nature's fierce storms, which come to overwhelm the individual, frequently leading him to inevitable defeat. Again the playwright, too often relying on the tawdry tricks of melodrama, may turn defeat into a semblance of salvation or promise.

During the late twenties and the troubled thirties, when the vogue for Negro literature was rising, special types of southern communities began to appear in novel, story, and drama. Among the best-informed of the fictionalists native to the South, Charlestonian DuBose Heyward, in collaboration with his wife Dorothy, created authentic Negro communities as realistic backgrounds for plays which became a sensation on the stage. Having gained fame with his exciting novel *Porgy* (1925), Heyward, with the assistance of his wife, created from it a four-act folk play, which from its brilliant opening on October 10, 1927, at the Republic Theatre, New York, under the auspices of the Theatre Guild, made theater history.[26] Rouben Mamoulian, after spending time absorbing the atmosphere of Charleston, staged the play authentically with practically an all-Negro cast, a bold venture for the period. Also realistic were the tenement and island settings by Cleon Throckmorton, the Jenkins Orphanage Band "led by a tiny mite . . . already a master of jazz rhythms," the unhackneyed group singing of simple Negro melodies and spirituals, a ballet of the mourners' shadows upon a wall, the hourly chimes of St. Michael's, and a series of vivid scenes portraying a picturesque cast in mass formation.

This "richly mounted colorful pageant of life among the Charleston Negroes" is brought to a focus by the exciting conflict involving the crippled beggar Porgy, Bess, "a typical, but debased, Negro beauty," and

Crown, "a huge Negro of magnificent physique, a stevedore on the cotton wharfs." The crowded tenement court of Catfish Row—as full of people as a country-town square on Saturday night—offers an unforgettable locale for a direct study of the Negroes, with but occasional skirmishes with "de law" from the white man's world beyond the tenement gates. The spacious flagstoned court, once the center of a fine building belonging to a Charleston aristocrat, now swarms with Negroes. Here the picturesque, humorous, and tragic elements of Negro life are manifest in the lives of Porgy and his neighbors. Maria, matriarch of the court and keeper of the cookshop; Jake, captain of the fishing fleet, and his wife Clara; the young stevedore Robbins and his wife Serena; trouble-making Sporting Life, "high-yellow" bootlegger and dope peddler; Lily, the court hoyden, and many others form "a part of Catfish Row as it really is—an alien scene, a people as little known to most Americans as the people of the Congo."[27] In short, the life of Porgy and his associates in Catfish Row, when staged, turned out to be, as Percy Hammond wrote, "a thrilling bit of mysterious actuality."

The genius of Mamoulian, says Langner, welded the varying elements of the play together. Serena's anguish when Crown, in a quarrel, kills Robbins integrates with Porgy's troubles with his wayward mistress, Bess. Porgy's efforts to save her from Crown's influence—from drink and narcotics—are parts of an expertly unified combination, including her return to the now fugitive Crown (wanted for the murder of Robbins), the cripple's use of the great power in his arms to choke gigantic Crown to death, and his disbelief later when neighbors inform him that Bess has run away with Sporting Life to her dream world, "Noo Yo'k." As Serena says, "She worse dan dead." But Bess's disappearance into the faraway North, a place quite mysterious to his neighbors, does not deter Porgy from following after his "'oman." While naïve Lily conjectures that New York is "Up Nort'—past de Custom House," Porgy determinedly "turns his goat and drives slowly with bowed head toward the gate."[28]

The novel and the play, both epochal, were the progenitors of the Guild-sponsored folk opera, *Porgy and Bess* (1925), praised by Langner as "a landmark in the American musical theatre" for the pattern it set for musical plays of the 1940's and later.[29] With the libretto drawn from *Porgy*, the lyrics by Ira Gershwin, and the score by George Gershwin, this haunting musical version of life in Catfish Row has become a favorite with playgoers around the world. The revivals on Broadway (the Cheryl Crawford production in 1942 and the Blevins Davis-Robert Breen one in 1953), the nationwide tour presentations in 1952, and from 1952 to 1955 the twelve hundred performances sponsored by ANTA and the

State Department, given throughout Europe—at Milan's La Scala, in London, Paris, Berlin, Athens, Barcelona, Naples, Venice, Zagreb, and other cities—and in Africa in Casablanca, Cairo, and elsewhere, all helped make "the story of a South Carolina neighborhood and the un- spoiled, often elemental inhabitants thereof" and the Gershwin songs and music—"I Got Plenty o' Nuttin' " and "Bess, You is My Woman Now," especially—a phenomenon of the American scene and an expres- sion of goodwill abroad.[30]

The Heywards' pictures of Negro communities in South Carolina lost none of their rich earthiness when the two adapted DuBose Heyward's novel *Mamba's Daughters* to the stage. First performed at the Empire Theatre, New York, on January 3, 1939, this vigorous and valid, though thoroughly melodramatic, folk play was movingly acted by a largely Negro cast. Director Guthrie McClintic enriched the Heywards' interpre- tation of the singular qualities of the Negro spirit by his presentation of gifted players: Georgette Harvey as Mamba, Anne Brown as Gardenia, José Ferrer as St. Julian de Chatiny Wentworth, plantation owner, Ethel Waters, brilliant as Hagar, Canada Lee as Drayton, and J. Rosemond Johnson as the Reverend Quintus Whaley. Their acting was commensu- rate with the verisimilitude of character and scene in the script, itself a sympathetic portrayal of the Negro race as it once lived in field and town in Carolina.

Covering a period of twenty years, the plot, in spite of its elements of melodrama, gives a colorful and animated representation of two Negro communities: a Charleston waterfront neighborhood suggestive of Catfish Row, where Mamba lives in a tenement room, and a loosely organized community centered around the Brick Plantation store and a country church on Ediwander Island. Even the melodramatic events—Hagar's court trial, her penitentiary service, her murder of Gilly Bluton, who had raped Elissa, and her own suicide—show a real understanding of the nature and habits of simple South Carolina Negroes. Chief among these are three different types of woman. Honest old Mamba, "an untradi- tional mammy" wise and wheedling among "white folks," is the individ- ualized matriarch of the family upon which the plot centers. Her illiterate daughter Hagar, a giant of a woman slow of wit and simple of heart, moves through her stormy amoral existence motivated by feeling. Her gift for song and her almost fanatical devotion to her child express her large nature. Richard Lockridge, *New York Sun* critic, wrote that "in the playing of Ethel Waters, Hagar becomes magnificently like a force of nature." Lissa, Hagar's sensitive and musically talented daughter, in her success as a featured folk singer on a New York radio broadcast, becomes a symbol of the new generation of her race, able to rise to recognition through artistic ability.

Whether the action takes place in the Charleston neighborhood or the Ediwander settlement, Mamba acts unselfishly according to her principle of wanting very little for herself. She simply desires a good life "fo' my daughtuh an' my daughtuh's daughtuh."[31] As for Hagar, her disorganized life takes on direction—the protection and education of Lissa—from the time a judge sentences her to labor at the Ediwander settlement for her assault on a cheating and "puny little [white] man." At Ediwander not only are various scenes at the church and the island store enlivened by the comings and goings of the plantation Negroes, their rivalries, jealousies, brawling, and simple enjoyments, but they also become the community background for Hagar's developing purpose of shielding Lissa from Gilly's blackmail schemes. Once at a church service her bursting forth into pure Gullah in her singing of the triumphant spiritual "Come Out de Wilderness" shows the strong impact of her emotional nature upon her fellow workers, in a scene preparatory to her later misunderstood announcement that she is going far away from Ediwander. Her friends then insist that they must sing a farewell song for her. Hagar's response, at the close of Lissa's broadcast of "That Hallelujah Song," her mother's favorite spiritual, is a spellbinding declaration that "Dis night I strangle Gilly Bluton to deat' with my two han'."[32] Then she steps outside the commissary door and the report of a revolver is heard. The group is shocked into profound silence, except for deaf old Vina's quavering voice singing on: "Oh, my daughter, /Goin' to leabe yo' in de han',/Ob de kin' Sab-yor." Representing the Negro's sacrifice as well as his chance to rise from racial and economic obscurity, Hagar and Elissa appear indeed as children of darkness and light.

Porgy and *Mamba's Daughters*, as direct studies of the Negro spirit, emphasize personal and racial tensions rather than conflicts with the white man and his society. As mirrors held up to little communities, these plays, like *Porgy and Bess*, reveal the deep relationship between each neighborhood and its inhabitants. Both are intensely creative in characters such as Porgy, Bess, Mamba, and Hagar, presenting sympathetically the highlights and the shadows of individual personality. Each offers, with melodramatic touches, colorful genre pictures of stirring folk scenes and racial ways authenticated by colloquial dialogue, at times in Gullah, and thematic music and folksong. By contrast, DuBose Heyward's *Brass Ankle* (1931) gives a sharp edge and social significance to its powerful portrayal of the discord and tension triggered in a southern river town by an instance of miscegenation and kindred racial problems. As Act I opens a young storekeeper, Larry Leamer, and other leaders of Rivertown are scheming for new community business expansion, so that their village "will be a town, and not a fever dump on the edge of a swamp." On the other hand, Larry's pregnant wife Ruth, of "dark, sombre beauty," fears the changes which so speedily seem to be creating boom conditions, "upsetting the old life, making the village into a town, bringing electricity, changing the public road to Trade Street."[33] Ruth cautions Larry against the folly of "cutting up our happiness into neat little squares and selling it off for so much a front foot." Nevertheless, Larry, as secretary of the school board, listens in his own living room to false arguments by the "Reverent" Latterby, "fundamentalist preacher, sententious and verbose," Constable Jake Darcy, moonshiner Pink Jones, "profane, cunning, and lascivious," and Lee Burton. The issue before the board concerns whether "Brass Ankle" Luke Jackson's children, who "look as white as you or me," should be "kicked out of the white school." Darcy's watchword for the community conduct is "Black's black an' white's white." His argument is, "We're goin' to have a real town here, like Larry says, and it's got to be one hundred percent American."[34] And Larry, momentarily forgetting that Ruth is in protracted labor in an adjoining bedroom, urges, "Keep 'em where they belong," little dreaming how soon his own secure position is to be threatened.

Such a "stirring up [of] the fires of race antipathy"[35] is momentarily stemmed, as Dr. Wainwright enters, ordering an immediate adjournment of the meeting. It is then the doctor's painful duty to explain privately to Larry that Ruth, ignorant of her "taint," is the granddaughter of a "Brass Ankle," a race with white, Indian, and Negro blood commingled. Proud of the beauty of their elder child June, herself perfectly white, Larry is horrified at Dr. Wainwright's disclosure that his wife has just given birth to a Negro boy. Later Dr. Wainwright's kindly efforts to protect Ruth from Larry's bitterness and the town's scandalmongers lead him to suggest resettlement elsewhere. Ruth, however, in a frenzy to shield June, tries to control her own tragic dilemma. Calling in her self-righteous neighbors, gentle Ruth deliberately assumes a coarse manner as she lies to them, saying that "I'm white—as white as anybody in this room," and adding that her boy is the son of Davey, a Negro once employed by Larry. Before the curtain, Larry "with a strangling cry lurches toward her," grabs his gun, and shoots both mother and child.

In three powerfully realized acts Heyward, with fine craftsmanship, projects against one small-town background the tragedy of simple southerners caught by forces they can neither escape nor control. Rivertown, like Gopher Prairie, has its share of smug, falsely pious, selfish, sententious, and even lascivious citizens, against whom Ruth is powerless, except for her last desperate effort to remove the Brass Ankle taint from June. In her final frantic speech, she condemns the inquisitive and unforgiving women as the worst offenders: "You women like this God-forsaken town, don't you? This rotten little dump with its moonshine licker, everlasting church services, and you like to go to bed every night at nine-o'clock while the men stay out sometimes all night and raise hell."[86] As Richard Wright once described a bitter personal experience, Ruth's tragedy came from her terror in learning the reality—a Negro's reality—of the cruelty of a white world. Assuredly, in the fresh approach to racial problems Heyward in *Brass Ankle*, as elsewhere, has portrayed provincial whites and blacks of the Deep South in recognizably human terms.

Other tensions in the small town had, as we have seen, been recognized and sporadically attacked by playwrights since the turn of the century. But the change from the Genteel Tradition to realistic drama was not easily made, and in notable instances the "dimity convictions," the prudery, and the squeamishness of the "Rigidly Righteous" so prevailed as to bring neglect and frustration to bolder realists. Among these Theodore Dreiser (1871-1946), for his daring disregard of the cherished "linen decencies" of the era (1900 to about 1925), incurred the hostility of the "Unco Guid" and paid the penalty of being neglected by reputable publishers. The paucity of critical reference to his frustration and neglect as a playwright indicates Dreiser's struggle against both the abuse of the critics and the indifference of commercial producers.

Although disillusioned, young Dreiser took refuge in his belief that "Deep below deep lie the mysteries" (from *Hey Rub-a-Dub-Dub*) and that the writer's art must find some means of revealing these mysteries to a nation "so bent . . . upon more money" that "all we care about is to be rich and powerful." For Dreiser one such means was social drama which pictured city and town. His interest in provincial life was deep-seated, for when he was sixteen he had come from the center of American village life—his birthplace, Terre Haute, and other Indiana towns in which he lived as a youth. In his later turning to dramatic composition (1914-16) he went back "into the depths of the Commonplace," trying to discover in midwestern mill towns and farming communities "the whole substructure of ordinary American life which above ground could be beautiful, and dramatic, but was for such far distances humdrum and banal."[37] As he revealed in *Plays of the Natural and the Supernatural* (1916) and *The Hand of the Potter* (1918), he found "the wide dark pools of tragedy in which the foundations stood." These plays further show that the moralism which he had been taught as a youth in Indiana seemed flatly contradicted by what he experienced and observed in maturity.

His most ambitious drama, *The Hand of the Potter*, written in 1916, is the tragic tale of young Isadore Berchansky, "so strangely composed mentally and physically that he is bizarre . . . so badly compounded chemically that he seems never to be of one mood, and has a restless, jerky, fidgety gait and manner."[38] His crime of raping and murdering a neighbor's eleven-year-old daughter and his own suicide are symbolic of "the great Commonplace" of misery and poverty in the crowded Jewish section of the Upper East Side of New York City. During this same period—the time of the making of *The Titan*—Dreiser was also dramatizing social problems of ordinary people in small towns. Among the best of the short plays included in *Plays of the Natural and the Supernatural* and written at the same time as "The Lost Phoebe," "Free," and other stories, "The Girl in the Coffin" and "The Blue Sphere," were both disregarded by commercial managers. In 1917 the Washington Square Players skilfully produced "The Girl in the Coffin," but the 1921 production of *The Hand of the Potter*, by the Provincetown Players, was ineptly acted for a run of only three weeks. Otherwise, Dreiser's plays have never reached the commercial footlights.[39]

"The Blue Sphere," centering around a motif of abnormality, is as much an oddity among native provincial plays as "The Idiot Boy" is among Wordsworth's poems of humble life. Near the railroad tracks in midwestern Marydale, the neat cottage with picket-fenced yard belonging to grocer Joseph Delavan and his wife becomes a scene of tragedy when their three-year-old child Eddie, a crawling victim of elephantiasis, is lured beyond the picket gate by a hovering and moving ball—a beautiful but wholly imaginary "pale blue sphere"—into the strange world of the adjacent tracks. The afflicted boy—known as "The Monstrosity" among the neighbors—is killed by an express train as it rounds a curve. The tissue of this psychological playlet is thin; yet throughout the plot Dreiser gives a semblance of reality to the daily tensions suffered by both parents. Mrs. Delavan's anguished outburst of mother love at the child's death is a penance and self-reproach for her uncontrollable shuddering at the sight of Eddie during the "years of misery and discomfort and distress" which the child represents.

A more actable play, "The Girl in the Coffin," ties together the world of domestic tension and sorrow with a strike in a "foe beset" mill town, a textile center. At curtain rise, on a spring evening a black coffin on trestles stands in the neat parlor of William Magnet, a respected foreman of the loom workers. "The pallid profile and thick dark hair of a dead woman [Mary, Magnet's only child] are barely visible." By detailed stage directions Dreiser at once transmits the current of American reality by noting the commonplace furnishings in the Magnet parlor: a large crayon portrait of deceased Mrs. Magnet, a cheap mahogany upright piano, section bookcases filled with "sets," and "a large framed lithograph portrait of JOHN FERGUSON, [professional] strike leader, standing in oratorical attitude."[40] Such is the dimly lighted scene of a wake, with Mrs. Mamie Shaefer and Mrs. Margaret Rickert, wives of strikers, on hand to gossip about the strikers' general meeting, which Magnet was supposed to conduct that very evening, and to conjecture about the sudden decline of pretty Mary Magnet's cheerful spirits and health. They learn little from Mrs. Littig, Magnet's taciturn old housekeeper, except that the foreman may be at the cemetery or at the depot to meet Ferguson's train.

The substance of this deeply felt play is native: the economic struggles of mill-town operatives, whose survival depends upon the success of a strike throughout all five mills in the community. The main theme, however, concerns only three characters—Magnet, his daughter Mary, and Ferguson—and pertains to a mill girl's love for a married man, who has induced her to become his mistress. Their secret relationship terminates tragically when the girl dies, apparently in childbirth. Dramatic irony marks the scene in Magnet's parlor where Ferguson, persuasively begging the foreman's assistance in organizing a general strike, turns the conversation to the news he had heard of the death of a woman he knew—"the only human being I've ever known that could stand between me and mortal loneliness." In turn, Magnet, so grief-stricken that he cannot recognize the truth, desperately and fiercely confesses that "some rotten coward, some beast, some low down scoundrel has ruined my girl." His vow to kill "the damn dog" is cut short by his sudden departure to conduct the strikers' meeting. Alone, Ferguson looks desperately at the girl in the coffin. Then Mrs. Littig, handing him a long ribbon attached to a gold ring, sadly and timidly tells him that Mary "said I was to give you this . . . and to say she died happy."

Edgar Lee Masters, in his autobiographical *Across Spoon River*, not only praised the power of Dreiser's mind for its strength and fertility of ideas but also regarded him as "much greater than his books." Masters was impressed, too, by "the vast understanding that he has of people, of cities, of the game of life." In his plays of social criticism Dreiser's understanding extends also to the troubles of small-town folk, whose portraits he draws with "a kind of pliant humanism." On the other hand, as Masters recognized, "money and lust figure in his psyche," as when he dramatizes ruthless millowners and woman-hunters such as Ferguson.[41]

Plainly "The Girl in the Coffin" early advanced the theory that the womenfolk suffer most from the tensions and disorders disrupting life in mill towns. By contrast, another strike play, Albert Bein's *Let Freedom Ring* (1936), concerns the dilemma of a male protagonist. Picturing the movement of the mills into southern villages, Bein describes the impact of a change in environment upon the individual worker: the effect of the new times of the thirties upon sturdy mountaineers who left their homes in the North Carolina highlands to begin a mechanized existence in the newly industrialized valley towns. Paul Green's authentic novel of 1935, *This Body the Earth*, sympathetically develops a similar theme: a North Carolina sharecropper's thirst for love and power and the evils of the economic system which defeats him.

A dramatization of Grace Lumpkin's *To Make My Bread*, Bein's play opened at the Broadhurst Theatre, New York, on November 6, 1935. His protagonist, John McClure of Scottish heritage, possesses that inbred quality of mountain men, the spirit of freedom and self-reliance which brings him in such conflict with the owners that his future success as a mill worker is endangered. A strike led by his brother Kirk creates a tense situation for John, who now must choose one of two loyalties: his love for the McClure clan, or his feeling of responsibility toward the mill-owners, who had promoted him in recognition of his skill. In this dilemma, the family ties prove stronger, especially after Kirk dies in the strife. Both local color and authenticity of character add to Bein's realistic interpretation of confusion in a North Carolina mill town. Such achievement is wrought when, instead of relying upon the arguments of labor propaganda, he pictures the tensions between capital and labor by means of realistically portrayed operatives (notably the McClure brothers), the device of an offstage mob, and the spirit of union developed within the ranks of the strikers by Kirk's death.

During the season of 1937-38 a satiric, "half-futuristic, half-communistic" production, as Joseph Wood Krutch called it, associated with the Federal Theatre Project as part of the then current movement toward a political theater, offered most unconventionally a stylized stage picture of a mill town amidst labor disturbance. This was *The Cradle Will Rock*, Marc Blitzstein's controversial musical play, originally written for the Federal Theatre but canceled by Washington authorities, apparently because of its strong partisan elements. Immediately John Houseman and Orson Welles hired a hall and gave the play, in impromptu fashion without costumes and scenery, as the first offering of the Mercury Theatre. Their improvised production proved a sensation, drawing patrons to the new theater for over a hundred performances. Briefly, Blitzstein used art as a weapon for leftist social criticism focused around a union drive in Steeltown, U.S.A. Expressionistic techniques, characteristic of the revolutionary spirit in drama during the thirties, included the use of a bare stage where the entire cast sat or stood during the performance, music played by Blitzstein, and his role as a sort of stage manager introducing characters, giving stage directions, and making pertinent remarks.

A sharply satiric tone characterizes the main action restricted to a night court, where a prostitute is being booked. On the same evening the police have mistakenly run in all the members of the Liberty Committee, appointed by Steeltown's industrialist (satirically named Mr. Mister) to stem the tide of unionism and other radical movements. These zealots—caricatured as the Reverend Salvation, Dr. Specialist, President Trixie, and Editor Daily—are represented as guilty of a worse prostitution than the girl's, that of forfeiting their souls for money. Steeltown, suggestive of actual mill towns in the South and other industrialized districts, is controlled by Mr. Mister through his power in church, university, newspaper, and other community circles. His ludicrous characterization, burlesquing the local power structure, is matched in caustic satire by the portraits of Mrs. Mister as a "prominent clubwoman" and of their children as morons. Further ridicule of the effete and idle rich ranges from a song hilariously poking fun at "Art for art's sake" to Mister's futile attempts to bribe the labor organizer, Larry Foreman. At the finale, with Foreman threatening that "the cradle will rock and fall," offstage music and shouts indicate that the drive for unionism is wholly successful.

In the whirl of modern dramatic activity interpreting the tensions and prejudices within American villagedom, some writers have used themes of religious debate, moral conflict, and hypocrisy having either personal or social significance, or both. As early as 1913 William Hurlbut, in *The Strange Woman*, satirically contrasted the moral outlook of the smug citizens of Delphin, Iowa, with the views of a freethinking expatriate, played by Elsie Ferguson, accustomed to Parisian life. This shocking "new woman" has traveled, in company with her young lover, to Delphin to persuade his mother to consent to their living together without benefit of clergy. The "strange" woman's eventual conformity to the demand for marriage does not soften her ridicule of small-town pseudo-piety and secret sinning. Other reflections of Hurlbut's interest in exposing religious extremism and sham are to be found in *The Bride of the Lamb* (1926), *Bless You, Sister* (1927), and *Salvation* (1928), the latter two characterizing female evangelists during the era of Aimée Semple McPherson's religiosity. *The Bride of the Lamb*, starring Alice Brady, offers a tragic picture of the degeneration of a confused, sexually frustrated woman married to a small-town dentist. Seeking release from her marital unhappiness, she turns emotionally to religious enthusiasm and a sexual relationship with "Brother" Albaugh, an itinerant tent evangelist and a persuasive "go'getter for the Lord." Her passionate experience with the evangelist, the poisoning of her husband, and the shock of her discovery that Albaugh is married combine to drive the woman to insanity. At the end her degeneration is complete when, in her unbalanced condition, she publically announces that "Mr. Christ" is her bridegroom. Also appearing in 1926, Patrick Kearney's dramatization of Dreiser's *An American Tragedy* re-created, before packed houses, a tragic case history of personal repression and frustration. Clyde Griffith's dilemma is shown as beginning in his poverty-marked childhood under the dominating influences of a bleak religion and the Salvation Army.

During the decade of the fifties a successful arena theater—the Margo Jones Theatre in Dallas—programmed new plays which further characterized the impact of religion on the small community. Opening on December 12, 1951, under the direction of Ramsey Burch, *One Foot in Heaven* by Irving Phillips entertained audiences for twenty-four performances. Four years later Miss Jones herself directed—also for twenty-four performances, dating from January 1, 1955—another previously unproduced play, a semidocumentary drama which had its genesis in a sensational trial in a small Tennessee town.[42] This was *Inherit the Wind*, by Jerome Lawrence and Robert E. Lee, then little known as playwrights. Although acknowledging some indebtedness to the transcripts of the famous and bitter John T. Scopes trial in Dayton during the scorching July of 1925, the collaborators, in their preface, give assurance of deeper interests than copying history in their dramatization of "the shame of Tennessee." Nevertheless, throughout the three acts there are semihistoric folk scenes, enlivened by Peter Larkin's suitable multiple-level stage sets, expressing the day-by-day excitement occasioned in Hillsboro—a thinly disguised Dayton—by "all this monkey business." Larkin's background details picturing the courthouse square and the buildings along Main Street, with the foreground reserved for the courtroom funishings, all clearly remind the spectator that "the town is visible always, looming there, as much on trial as the individual defendant."[43] Even with such verisimilitude in stage design, *Inherit the Wind*, the authors claim, "is not history." Nor is it journalism. Rather, their purpose goes beyond either historical recording or journalistic reporting of the stubborn stand of the entrenched forces of bigotry—the Daytonian fundamentalists—against the invading forces of modernism and liberalism, the equally vocal proponents of science and religious freedom.

In their main purpose of exposing bigotry and taking a stand for personal integrity and the right to think, playwrights Lawrence and Lee dramatize the old theme of the one against the many. In lawyer Drummond's energetic argument, the fight for truth is a battling against "one of the peculiar imbecilities of our time . . . the grid of morality we have placed on human behavior." More personally, this fight belongs to Hillsboro's young biology teacher, Bertram (Bert) Cates, in his attempt to convince his narrow-spirited neighbors that as "a thinking man" he has the right to teach the new science, including the theories of evolution. Thus Hillsboro itself is put on trial, as its citizens react in awe, shock, or humor to the furious courtroom debates between skeptical Henry Drummond (Paul Muni's role) and the aging politician Matthew Harrison Brady (Ed Begley). Through the device of a sensational trial timed simply as "not too long ago," the authors contend that notable principles of conduct during the actual "battle of the giants" (the ailing William Jennings Bryan and criminal lawyer Clarence Darrow) in the twenties have taken on new dimensions and meaning for the fifties. For them the legal debate in the Rhea County courthouse concerning a teacher's right to teach Darwinism served as a historic instrument to demonstrate "the great danger to freedom, particularly academic freedom." In fact, "what happened to Dayton in 1925 was not in the remote past and could have happened yesterday."

The New York producer of the play, Herbert Shumlin, after seeing the Margo Jones production in Dallas, described Hillsboro as typical of those small towns hostile to disturbing new ideas. Such community stagnation may be thought of in relation to Matthew Brady's ironic use of Solomon's warning in the Book of Proverbs: "He that troubleth his own house . . . shall inherit the wind." And Hillsboro was destined to inherit the wind of notoriety and widespread ridicule. While Bert Cates was confined in a jail cell[44] and his sweetheart, Rachel Brown, was torn between loyalty to her fundamentalist father, the Reverend Jeremiah Brown, and support of Bert's Darwinian beliefs, most of the citizens at first engaged in festivities reminiscent of a Fourth of July picnic or a brush arbor revival, all in spite of the heat. As E. K. Hornbeck, satiric Baltimore reporter, quipped with Menckenian sting: "The boob has been de-boobed. Colonel Brady's virginal small-towner has been *had*—by Marconi and Montgomery Ward."

Throughout the action the authentic local color, much better than the characterization, gives the effect of folk drama. Special trains bring sightseers and reporters, as a result of the sensational publicity spread over the country by the tabloids. A lurid press and accompanying photographs reflect the demands of a reading public interested in entertainment and the tremendous appeal of ballyhoo. Throughout the town the holiday air is manifested by the uniformed bands, paraders carrying banners ("Are You a Man or a Monkey?"), hawkers of hot dogs and cold drinks, psalm-singing "Brother" Jeremiah Brown spellbinding the faithful sheltered under a huge tent, bailiff Meeker turning Bert and his cell into an exhibit, and other symbols of small-town "monkeyshines."

From area to area the old order's inability, or unwillingness, to cope with the rise of perplexing science and "newfangled" industry, with its influx of new, and often foreign, workers into strategically located towns, was bound to create community upheaval and even violence. In the South particularly, the stubborn resistance of native whites toward changes in the caste system led to extremes in racial discrimination, as evidenced in the Scottsboro case and in the humiliations and deprivations suffered by the Brass Ankles and other racial minorities. As big business flourished, clashes between the wealthy millowners, cotton factors, and other moneyed investors and the underprivileged operatives, chain gangs, tenant farmers—white and black—and mountaineers transplanted to the factories came under the observation of certain playwrights. Soon the drama of ideas reflected the discontent and injustice, rather than the progress, in factory towns. Along with political dissension, community-wide squabbles and debates about the choice to be made between a cherished fundamentalism ("Gimme that old time religion,/It's good enough for me!") and the "blasphemies of Science"—that "monkey business"—but added to the acrid spirit of the thirties. Their studious approach to such economic, spiritual, and other changes alerted numbers of play-wrights—among them, avant-garde experimenters like Lawson and Blitz-stein—to the increasing complexity even of small-town society. With their boldly realistic or expressionistic plays, they responded to the challenge offered by the new group theaters in New York and other cities and by the regional arena sponsoring new styles in writing, design, and acting. Too long, as their dramas of the town imply, the tinsel wrappings of romanticism had hidden from public view the sordid truths about Main Street. On the stage, the disorientations, the social disturbances, and the character problems of twentieth-century townsmen were nearer to reality.

VIII. Flight from Main Street

"THE EXPERIENCE of each age requires a new confession," so Emerson once wrote, "and the world always seems waiting for its poet." So it seemed as Robinson, Sandburg, Frost, and other new voices of the first decades of the twentieth century poetically quickened the emergence of a modern American spirit. Concurrently outspoken critics, writers of fiction, and other moderns attacked the conventions of the immediate past, tested new literary programs, and insisted upon a more realistic appraisal of American values. Drawing a variety of images and symbols from the American past, such modern mythologists, scornful of the narrow attitudes of the genteel generation, debunked a succession of cherished dreams which for generations had brightened the mass migrations of our developing civilization. Adopting reality as their basic standard, Van Wyck Brooks, Mencken, and other insurgent critics sought to understand the meaning of America. In an attempt to bridge the distance between nineteenth-century conventionality and the experimental conditions of the new century, they tried to vitalize the intellectual climate of the country. They discarded the prevailing image of somberly garbed Puritans, hoping to turn the wilderness shores of New England into a "New Jerusalem," offering instead unflattering criticism of American Puritanism as a force restricting the creative artist. Also, they dismissed as specious those once widely accepted promises which glorified our broad continental space, diversified soil, and human integrity and thus lured questing wayfarers westward. For these new thinkers the American pioneers' roseate dreams of a fruitful paradise in an unending new land seemed the dry rot of the genteel tradition.

"The moment was alive with creative energy and rebellion, with the hope of casting out the venerable American superstition," Morton Zabel has said of these prewar years. Searches for what Brooks termed "our usable past" led energetic writers to the discovery that one cause of the unrest and dislocation of their own time stemmed from the shifting of the center of American life, by the close of the Civil War, to the Mississippi Valley. Even then thousands were leaving the farms and small towns settled by their grandparents and parents. By the early twentieth century the bloating of cities and the expansion of population, with attendant shifts in power, were turning the thoughts not only of writers but of Americans in general toward new frontiers as exciting as those of the wilderness. These latter-day "back-trailers," as Hamlin Garland called them, began moving from the great Midwest and other regions to the new urban frontier: to Chicago, New York, Boston, San Francisco, and other cities. Many were simply responding to their dreams of that fascinating "Bitch Goddess Success" enshrined in the beckoning and golden cities, in much the same way in which Vachel Lindsay envisioned migration from his native Illinois town in *The Golden Book of Springfield* (1920). By the twenties such dreams of success were still stimulating restlessness in many townspeople and farm dwellers.

The spirit of enterprise, astir with new vigor, then offered a compelling American reality to the literary imagination. One dream of escapism frequently reflected in native drama tallies with the incessantly growing shift in population to the increasingly congested cities. In actuality the acceleration of life, as symbolized by urban multiplicity and giantism, continued to fascinate ambitious, restless youths on farms and in towns far and wide. Conversely, there were signs in dramas about the small town of the pitfalls that escapism had for the unwary. In 1920 Willa Cather, herself an uprooted villager, pessimistically symbolized the allurement of the city in the striking title of a collection of stories about the failures of restless young men and women: *Youth and the Bright Medusa*. Similarly, in certain contemporary plays dramatizing the clash between village characters and local environment, the city, its deadly power comparable to the stare of the fearsome Medusa, petrifies inexperienced farm and town youths, confronted with the harsh truth of urban competition and economic struggle. Desolated and despondent protagonists, like F. Scott Fitzgerald's "sad young men," even turn to suicide when they find neither welcome nor security in urban wastelands. For instance, in *Roger Bloomer* the solution chosen by Louise, Roger's sweetheart, and in Willa Cather's story "Paul's Case" Paul, both struggling to understand the city's legend of jazz and to achieve self-fulfilment amidst bigness, is finally to seek peace through suicide. But the fictional mastery of the way things are appears also in happier dramatizations of the urban experience of younger Americans. Tougher, better disciplined, or better trained escapists from rural and village life accept their ignorance and doubt, endure hardships, develop their skills, and do well for themselves in Megalopolis.

Reshaping village materials to the demands of realism, Booth Tarkington, Zona Gale, Edith Wharton, and other interpreters have emphasized the darkness of spirit enshrouding both youthful and older victims of narrow environments. The imbalance between the romantic ideals of the protagonists and the lack of charity, the spiritual bleakness, selfishness, and dulness of their neighbors has been thematically explored. Individual characterizations have included unhappily situated single women who dream of social success, romantic love, and domestic bliss. Often, however, their rebellion against domestic pressures and other environmental and personal limitations brings such heroines as Alice, in *Alice Adams*, Lulu in *Miss Lulu Bett*, and Alma Winemiller in *Summer and Smoke*, face to face with new and unpleasant dilemmas. Sometimes frustrated older men—embittered Ethan Frome and lonely Mister Pitt, for example—seek unsuccessfully to escape their harsh and drab environments. Other times, as in *Our Town*, a semiphilosophic approach is used to explain why certain townsmen, such as Editor Webb and Dr. Gibbs of Grover's Corners, New Hampshire, resisted the desire to escape to a larger professional center beyond their small-town world.

Various motivations prompt this search for a more satisfactory way of life outside the limits of the small community. Primarily, the greater stimulus of urban living leads inhibited characters to regard their provincial environments with distaste. Personality clashes with nagging or even hateful relatives, with intrusive neighbors, or perhaps with a whole community have been dramatized as factors creating resentment and hastening departures. Lulu Bett, a drudge, a nonentity in the household of her insufferable brother-in-law, Dwight Herbert Deacon, and her selfish sister Ina, dares to free herself from her drab routine as family chore girl. In some plays, attempts to escape an unsavory past have been connected with sexual frustration and economic struggle, as in the case of Ethan Frome, or with crime, as in that of Marcus Hubbard's contraband trading during the Civil War, in *Another Part of the Forest*.

In war plays, returned heroes are not always heroic after all. Supercilious Oswald Lane, a glorified veteran in Gilbert Emery's *The Hero*, must attempt flight from his worshipful fellow townsmen to escape detection as a thief and a seducer. Then there are those simple people who, lacking education and training to confront the demands of society openly, must resort to illegal action. Thus Ned McCobb's daughter, in the play of the same name, lucklessly involved in a Maine bootlegging racket, spends anxious days and nights trying to escape the notice of federal prohibition agents.

Also dramatized are the lower elements of society whose energetic and often ruthless action creates social reversals and enables them to rise to positions of dictatorial power. In *It Can't Happen Here* (1936) the problem of endurance or escapism by the town's unwary ruling class becomes increasingly complex, as the Corpos, a newly regimented Fascist organization, develops into a locally and nationally powerful political and military force. In this cogent play Sinclair Lewis and John C. Moffitt present the dilemmas facing a self-reliant country-style editor, Doremus Jessup, when disciplined Fascists shatter his easygoing and democratic world in Fort Beulah, Vermont. Another ruthless protagonist—the creation of Sinclair Lewis and Lloyd Lewis—is Ace Burdette, in *The Jayhawker,* a shrewd old fire-eater and blabbermouth reformer who talked and prayed his way from Kansas camp meetings to the United States Senate.

Finally, the variations in themes related to youth's response to the lure of the city have brought to the stage memorable characters such as George Willard in *Winesburg, Ohio*, Regina Hubbard in *Another Part of the Forest*, and Eugene Gant in *Look Homeward, Angel*. Intellectual curiosity, restlessness, longing for the social whirl, and hope for economic or professional betterment have quickened youth's desire to leave the familiar town for the glittering and exciting strangeness of the city. And some, like Roger Bloomer, were "dreamy kids" who came from the wide prairies "looking for golden women." Too, Europe and "All the wonderful far places I used to dream about!" may beckon a middle-aged Dodsworth as strongly, as in *Beyond the Horizon*, a youthful Rob Mayo. To both young and middle-aged rebels, then, the small community became, in Rob's words, "like the walls of a narrow prison yard shutting me in from all the freedom and wonder of life." Thus, "chucking" the hometown or farm meant "a free beginning . . . the right of release" for one's trip "beyond the horizon."

In early twentieth-century drama a composite image of the more modern small town began to emerge, interpreting the revolt from the village. The village malcontents in representative plays rarely appreciate a town's attractions, such as its quiet, neighborly, and inexpensive ways of living. Rather, moved to discontent by the appeal of the city as something grander and excitingly strange, these citizens, both youthful and mature, complain about the drab or ugly physical aspects of their limited communities. Often the human element is damned as unsympathetic and narrow-minded; in the minds and public expressions of stage townspeople, the small town usually appears as a hotbed of bigotry, gossip, and hypocrisy. In some plays nagging relatives and carping neighbors add to the misery of a protagonist. Other provincial plays picture the small place as matching the large community in its problems of caste and social discrimination. Where a town's socialites control the new country club set, much as Tarkington's "magnificent Ambersons" ruled the social circle of an earlier generation, the less affluent though respectable townspeople become rank outsiders. To young Alice Adams, defeated by her middle-class environment, her midwestern town seemed as unpromising a place as Winesburg, Ohio, appeared to ambitious George Willard or Altamont, North Carolina, to Eugene Gant, the dreamer. In other plays endless seasonal rounds of revival meetings or political rallies (as in *The Jayhawker*), all occasions for more emotionalism than spirituality or sincere patriotism, add their own unattractive touches to the drab image of the town. Even the traditional public rite of "blessing the [apple] trees," as so realistically described in Alice Brown's *Children of Earth*, shows that New England's farming villagers enjoy the "art" of carping gossip. Village newcomers, especially the "Portygee" wife of Peter Hale, member of an established family, become the butt of snobbish and malicious small talk. In general, these mythical towns, like Ethan Frome's Starkfield, are represented, from the point of view of disgruntled characters, as narrow communities from which "the smart ones get away."

In June, 1914, as we have noted, the Winthrop Ames drama prize of $10,000 was awarded to Alice Brown for her New England community play, *Children of Earth*. Ames's production of the play on January 12, 1915, while not a stage hit, brought before patrons of the Booth Theatre, New York, a memorable and poignant story of village spinsterhood. With action centered around old maid Mary Ellen Barstow, sensitively played by Effie Shannon, the plot moves forward on the note of an unmated woman's repressed and insurgent desire to reveal openly that she is warmly in love with life. At forty-six, Mary Ellen has a delicate loveliness "overlaid by a look of pathetic endurance." For years she "has dumbly fought down in herself every emotion that rebels against the recognized system of things." And in her village the traditional system of conduct implies that a single daughter must faithfully serve her aging parents.

The first act opens on a scene repeated in other provincial dramas: the breaking up of an old-fashioned household after a funeral. In this instance the death of niggardly, mean-hearted old Mr. Barstow reminds the neighbors of his domineering ways with his dutiful daughter and nurse, Mary Ellen. Years before, her older brother Aaron, chafing under Father Barstow's rigid household laws, had escaped from the village, eventually prospering as a New York manufacturer. Aaron's leaving had imposed upon his sister a bleak existence as housekeeper to a widowed father whose stern code excluded the joys of living. Having denied Mary Ellen, during her youth, permission to marry Nathan Buell, old Barstow for years thereafter demanded of her domestic servitude. When the crabbed old man dies, Aaron, equally domineering, suddenly reappears from Europe to reorder Mary Ellen's life. Against her wishes he proposes to close the homestead and uproot Mary Ellen by taking her to New York, in her eyes a place of terrifying strangeness.

In despair over Aaron's stubbornness, Mary Ellen revolts by inviting Nathan, now middle-aged and residing elsewhere, to return to the village. When Nathan appears as a crusty-souled, land-grabbing suitor, she is shocked by his ugliness and cupidity. Unnerved, she desperately accepts the offer of her longtime friend Peter Hale, whose Portuguese wife Jane is an alcoholic, to run away with him. Circumstances quickly turn Mary Ellen's revolt into resignation. Early on the morning of their elopement she and Peter, chancing to see Jane, brokenhearted, going through the woods toward the Barstow place to help out with the kitchen chores, are moved to remorse. After their return, the runaways must remain in the village as "children of earth," doing what they can to save their reputations. By the village code, they couldn't "go kickin' over the traces like that 'thout causin' talk." Nevertheless, Mary Ellen remains unrepentant, confessing to Jane: "An' I shall be glad all the days o' my life— glad I went an' glad I came back."[1]

The Barstow home place—a New England colonial house furnished with plain, old-fashioned furniture—reflects the tastes of simple householders in a farming village. The wainscoted sitting room, with a large fireplace, a nearby secretary-desk with a few books, a grandfather clock, braided rugs, and neatly designed china and pewter, at once gives the key to Mary Ellen's unexciting days. In its absence of rich adornment the house contrasts sharply with another provincial home, also associated with momentous family change necessitating the sale of a homestead. In Susan Glaspell's *Alison's House*, the Pulitzer Prize play for 1930, the old Stanhope homestead, unlike the plainer Barstow place, is pictured as a spacious two-storied mansion at the edge of an Iowa village on the Mississippi. Here several generations have lived in comfortable circumstances, until the eventful last day of the nineteenth century, December 31, 1899. On this day action begins in the richly carpeted and velvet-curtained library, where many family portraits and hundreds of books signify "a family of traditions and cultivation." At present this lovely room is a scene of confusion, as various Stanhopes come and go. They are the survivors of gifted Alison Stanhope (a character suggesting Emily Dickinson), a belatedly recognized American poet who had died eighteen years before.

Rich in tradition and filled with memories, Alison's house is the place where the family now gathers to take its last farewell and to share in the distribution of her books and other precious belongings which have been preserved by her old sister, Agatha. Miss Agatha's physical debility is the chief reason why her lawyer brother proposes to sell the house, for the devoted old lady refuses to leave. She prefers her solitude, her memories, and the company of a faithful servant to living with her brother in a distant city. Agatha knows that "our little town is our lives"—a symbol, as Amherst was for the Dickinsons, of the old life.

As the village bells are tolling the passage of the old century, Agatha, too, passes on, leaving in a little bag a secret which she has guarded carefully all the years since Alison's death. This secret, a sheaf of lyrics about Alison's problem of accepting the love of a man already married, comes as a shocking revelation to the younger members of the family; but to Alison's brother and a niece, who has sacrificed her reputation for love, the poet's self-revealing poems in celebration of her own love are merely confirmation of what they have suspected. In spite of Agatha's attempts to protect the Stanhope name, "Alison's words pass on—as a gife to all love . . . ," throwing new light on the life of the poet and revealing her as a truly great soul.[2]

Actually another notable characterization of bullied spinsterhood had been presented on stage a full decade before *Alison's House*. In 1920, with the publication of a realistic novelette, *Miss Lulu Bett*, it was apparent to discerning critics that Zona Gale again had chosen the way of credible realism first manifested in 1918 in her very carefully constructed novel *Birth*, "her truest portrait of village life." In these two village stories, which she later dramatized, Miss Gale utilized to the best advantage such an unusually direct method that she seemed to be saying, "Here are true things." Free from the sentimentality of the Friendship Village formula, *Miss Lulu Bett*, in its two forms, presents everyday family situations which mark the irony and inherent tragedy in the menial position of an inhibited unmarried sister. Beyond the almost bitter theme of Lulu Bett's poverty and domestic slavery, there is the recognizably true chronicle, woven with "many mingled threads of good and evil," describing the dull and petty town of Warbleton against whose background is clearly silhouetted the thoroughly commonplace and uninspired Deacon family. Though Miss Gale calls her play "an American Comedy of Manners," we do not laugh at Lulu Bett's predicament.

Brock Pemberton's successful initial staging of the comedy at the Belmont Theatre, New York, on December 27, 1920 brought to life the simple story of a village type: "a family beast of burden," who eventually rebels to the point of running away. As Pemberton wrote to Miss Gale, "the play has the same direct, incisive quality the book had; it cuts to the quick, and lays bare the lines of character . . ." With its simplicity, sincerity, and reality, the comedy not only brought a new note of truth to the theater, but also marked Miss Gale's own revolt against the popular "Belascoism" of the period. The play continued to attract capacity crowds to the Belmont, and in May, 1921, its excellence brought Miss Gale the $1,000 Pulitzer award.

The plot, terse and dramatic in every respect, moves toward Lulu's triumphant revolt. No longer will she be the family scapegoat and slavey. According to the novel, into her dull life comes an invalid marriage with a trifler, Ninian Deacon, Dwight's long-absent brother, who subsequently abandons her. She then marries another man. As the success of the play grew, controversy was occasioned by the third act as originally produced on December 27, 1920. In this version Lulu's unconventional marriage to Ninian, though outwardly an escape from her cheerless surroundings, develops her tragedy, until finally her release is implied by her warm friendship with Cornish, Warbleton's piano dealer. First, however, she must leave town for a while, for "I want to see out of my own eyes. For the first time in my life." In response to such an uncharacteristic declaration Mrs. Bett querulously asks "Lulie," before the curtain falls, "Who's going to do your work now, I'd like to know?" A later and sharply criticized solution, though technically known as "happy," signalizes Lulu's courageous revolt when she flatly exposes Dwight: "You've pretended so long you can't be honest with yourself, any of the time. Your whole life is a lie." At this point and to the astonishment of the family, Ninian unexpectedly reappears with the news that Cora Waters, his first wife, is dead. Lulu's happiness is assured as Ninian says, "I haven't any other wife—just Lulu." In response to her critics, Miss Gale defended her use of this happier solution by saying, "But—if a play is to present life—it must not always end an episode unhappily, because life does not always do so. It is true that the ironic, the satiric, the tragic, the casual, must close many and many a volume, must constitute many and many a curtain. But not all."[3]

Terseness of style marks the depictions both of Warbleton, a mean, humdrum place where small-minded hypocrisy flourishes, and of the commonplace Deacon family. By daring to write genuinely dull dialogue, Miss Gale not only departs from the artificial conversation traditional in American domestic plays, but ridicules, almost without a word of comment, the everyday talk of this ordinary household. She "has an ear, not merely for the vocabulary of the average man, but for the rhythms of his speech."[4] Small-town family conversation serves as the medium for presenting Dwight Herbert Deacon, "the high priest of this elaborate banality," and Monona, "the first normal stage child."[5] Miss Gale's adherence to uninspiring reality violates the traditional rules of drama. Above all, she creates ordinary, unexciting people. Disillusioned Grandma Bett is an old woman who is not sweet, and disagreeable Monona is a stage-child who is not cute. Dwight Herbert and Ina Deacon are dull, middle-class villagers, while Lulu belongs to the sisterhood of "lonely hearts." The same uninspired dialogue throughout intensifies a stultifying atmosphere of monotony and domestic routine. Note the character revelation in Mrs. Bett's whiny remarks:

MRS. BETT. I don't complain. But it wouldn't turn my head if some of you
          spoke to me once in a while . . .
DWIGHT.   *Ice* cream—it's *ice* cream. Who is it sits home and has *ice*
          cream put in her lap like a ku-ween?
MRS. BETT. Vanilly or chocolate?
DWIGHT.   Chocolate, Mama Bett.
MRS. BETT. Vanilly sets better . . . I'll put it in the ice chest—I *may* eat it.
          [Takes spoon from sideboard.][6]

While more emphasis is placed upon the Deacon household and the pathos of Lulu's position, the picture of Warbleton is not dimmed. The Chautauqua Circle, the popularity of croquet, and a picnic all furnish details indicating that "if the Friendships are sweet and dainty, so are they—whether called Warbleton or something less satiric—dull and petty, and they fashion their Deacons no less than their Pelleases and Etarres."[7]

During the twenties and thirties Miss Gale's growing disaffection for the Friendship Village formula was further expressed in two other mature and artistic plays, which, in Kazin's view, "were almost intolerably intense parodies of everyday American existence." Disillusionment, cynicism, a yearning for happiness, and resigned despair mark the temper of the provincial misfits and escapists portrayed in *Mister Pitt* (1925) and *Faint Perfume* (1934). Weariness with her own idyllic creed had appeared as early as 1918 in Miss Gale's mordant village criticism characterizing *Birth*, a realistic novel of a small Wisconsin town. In this novel Miss Gale declared for the first time her private revolt from the village. The portrait of Marshall Pitt—a timid little man pitied by his son and neighbors—gave promise of what the novelist was to achieve in *Miss Lulu Bett*. Flighty Barbara Pitt's desertion of her husband and her native town in the hope of finding beauty and pleasure in the city foreshadowed *Main Street*. In 1923, motivated by the stage success of *Miss Lulu Bett*, Miss Gale began dramatizing *Birth*. Ably assisted by folk playwright Lula Vollmer, she revised her material as *Mister Pitt*, successfully keeping her village gossips for choral effect throughout three interludes and adding a masked ballet to symbolize the passing years. Produced by Pemberton at the 39th Street Theatre, New York, the play opened successfully on January 22, 1924, with Walter Huston as Mr. Pitt, supported by Minna Gombell as Barbara, but lasted only six weeks on Broadway.

A drama of futility, *Mister Pitt* presents the long-lasting haplessness of a village paperhanger and door-to-door salesman of apple butter, tomato soup, pickles, and other such products. In spite of innate goodness he is always inept and unlucky. No miracle comes to reward him for his genuine merits. One person alone understands his true nature. The business card which he diffidently hands to genteel Mrs. Rachel Arrowsmith identifies him as "Mister Pitt, of Glidden's Gold Strap and Diamond Buckle. Extra Fine Products." At once recognizing his inherent worth, Mrs. Arrowsmith is sympathetic, whereas Barbara Pitt, mean-spirited and selfishly bent on escaping from both husband and town, never understands his gentleness and his yearning for better things. At the climax of Act II Pitt, determined to break through the entangling circumstances of his life, disappears from the town. As twenty years pass his son Jeffrey, who has grown up with a weakness for gambling, receives quarterly remittances of $50 for his university expenses, presumably from his father; actually the money comes from Rachel Arrowsmith.

On his eventual return Pitt, now "shrunken and aged greatly," reveals that escapism led to nothing except financial failure, even in gold-rich Alaska. The pathos of his situation is dramatized in his confession to his son: "I use' to lay awake nights figuring how I'd come back and buy a big house for you, Jeff. I didn't make it—I didn't make it. But if I could live awhile in that old house with my boy—say!"[8] All he has to show for twenty years of labor is a little chain of gold nuggets. ("I never seemed to catch the hang of getting along . . . . Ain't life the funniest thing?") Effective in her use of everyday experience, Miss Gale in dramatizing Pitt's story successfully pinpointed the irony implicit in a small town's failure to recognize generosity and charity when these are shown by a colorless, unassuming little salesman.

Faint Perfume, slightly autobiographical though objective in tone, is a domestic chronicle about entangling circumstances affecting the Perrin, Crumb, and Powers families living in a small town. It was first published in 1923 as a novel, became an immediate best seller, and was rewritten as a play in 1932. Following the original novel closely, the smoothly flowing dramatization involves another village escapist, Leda Perrin, daughter of a minister, John Perrin. Once Leda had been so attracted by the "bright Medusa" that she left her hometown to become a magazine writer in New York City. Now, returning to her father's home, with the prospect of reorientation, she falls in love with married Barnaby Powers. Family bitterness is quickened when Grandfather Ralph Crumb bequeaths $10,000 to his selfish grandniece, Richmiel (Crumb) Powers, provided that "she lets her son Oliver spend half his time with his father unconditionally." Otherwise Leda Perrin is to become the inheritor. Mama Crumb weepingly protests: "The idea of that strange girl stepping in here and carrying off all that Grandfather had! It's disgraceful."[9] In spite of all the acrimony, Leda does not again flee from the town, but stays because she feels that her father gives her "a sense of life" and because she loves Barnaby. Finally, in a denouement that is not too effective, Richmiel gives up both the money and her little son to Barnaby and Leda.

A further probing beneath the surface of middle-class life in a small town involves another youthful heroine who made a first appearance on the literary scene in 1921 in Booth Tarkington's family novel, *Alice Adams*. Intended as the third volume in a trilogy of midwestern town growth (earlier begun in *The Turmoil* and *The Magnificent Ambersons*), this domestic chronicle foreshadows Mencken's and Lewis' attacks on the "booboisie" in its exposures of the "corroding mania for riches" in the early twentieth century. A prospering small town in Indiana during the twenties is the setting for the pathetic social struggles of clever, pretty twenty-two-year-old Alice Adams, a daydreaming romantic who is almost defeated by her middle-class environment. Eager to continue acquaintance with the town's socially elite—those of "the frozen faces," as her brother Walter bitterly calls them—Alice enters foolishly into petty deceits to keep up appearances. In the embarrassing wallflower scene at the Palmers' fashionable dance, at the tragicomic dinner in the Adams cottage, and everywhere, the poor girl seems doomed to failure, for as their old-time acquaintances of village days prosper the Adamses sink lower in the social scale.

Finally, however, Alice bravely demonstrates that the way a person sees a town depends upon who she is. Her escape from her personal dilemma exemplifies what Cooper long ago called American "go-aheadism." While her embittered and dingdonging mother takes in roomers, Alice's self-pity gradually vanishes. Earlier as she had passed the entrance to the local business college she had ominously imagined "pretty girls turning into old maids 'taking dictation'—old maids of a dozen different types, yet all looking a little like herself." In the end, as she courageously mounts "the wooden stairway leading up to Frincke's Business College—the very doorway she had always looked upon as the end of youth and the end of hope"—she discovers that "half-way up the shadows were the heaviest, but after that the place began to seem brighter. There was an open window overhead somewhere, she found and the steps at the top were gay with sunshine."[10] By self-reliant action Alice manages not to be totally submerged by the town's new economic order. True, her social aspirations are gone, but she closes the door upon the dream world into which she had escaped for so long. Having learned that she must accept life as it is, she begins to adjust herself to the demands of reality. Although she loses Arthur Russell and the chance to marry into the Palmers' circle, she gains a comforting peace of mind.

In 1925 Tarkington began using the secretarial services of a talented young friend, Elizabeth Trotter, a Kennebunkport, Maine, summer resident from Philadelphia who worked for him devotedly until his death in 1946. In 1921 she created a realistic dramatization of *Alice Adams*, which, however, was not produced until later. A copy of the program for its first performance notes the production by the Gloucester School of the Theatre, East Gloucester, Massachusetts, on August 17 and 18, 1945.[11] On March 7, 1946, Tarkington made his last public appearance when the Indianapolis Civic Theatre produced Miss Trotter's version.[12] According to the introduction, "The play is not a tragedy; it is not a comedy . . . If the play . . . can also be 'a mirror held up to life,' then the dramatist need not apologize to the author." And midwestern town life is mirrored truthfully.

With her introduction of a large cast of recognizable provincial characters, Miss Trotter supplied detailed notes describing the appearance and nature of key figures, with special emphasis upon pretty Alice. Although "on exhibition she leads a life of gestures" and receives more championship than she needs from her silly mother, Alice emerges as a believable charmer. Nineteen-year-old Walter is misled by a code as false as Alice's. A "thin and shallow boy" and a scapegrace, he tactlessly reveals his scorn for the "berries," fatuous local socialites, by relying "heavily upon a lopsided jeering bark of a laugh."

The most tragic figure is simplehearted Virgil Adams, whose unimaginative mind offers him no escape from the domestic, business, and social problems which bring on a moral and physical breakdown. At fifty-five he is constantly harassed by the silliness and everlasting reproaches of his wife, who goads him into appropriating an unpatented formula belonging to his old-time employer. On the occasion of the painful dinner given for genteel Arthur Russell, Alice's summertime suitor, poor Adams is made acutely miserable by his wife's demands that he wear a dinner jacket and observe unaccustomed amenities.

Here indeed is an admirably controlled scene, in both novel and play, revealing with humor and pathos the appalling mediocrity of an ordinary family pretending to be fashionable. In Tarkington's own words, *Alice Adams* is a tragicomic "study of an American family never quite above the surface and becoming more deeply submerged." But Alice does not drown. To Mrs. Adams' complaint that "life is nothing but tragedy, tragedy, tragedy!" Alice replies, "I do think I'm beginning to have a *little* sense. At least I'm beginning—beginning!"

Other plays of the time turned popular attention to isolated agricultural communities in New York, Maine, and Massachusetts and to other harassed men and women seeking some form of escape from narrow environments. These dissatisfied souls include a few beauty-starved women who, like Alice Adams, are motivated by their unquenchable determination to outwit environment and to rise higher than circumstance. Such a determination appears in *The Detour* (1921), Owen Davis' realistic native drama about a Long Island farm and village woman who sacrifices a career for marriage. Though between 1898 and 1921 he had written more than 150 melodramas, Davis was deeply enough influenced by Ibsen and the early O'Neill plays to present in *The Detour*, which he called "the best play I have ever written," realistically drawn characters rather than the mere types of his western thrillers and "sexy" plays (*Nellie, the Beautiful Cloak Model* and others). Throughout *The Detour* he "sensed fully—noting the myriad facets shaped from the materials of the humblest life—shades of character and various motives inherent in locality and tradition."[13]

A family play, *The Detour* has the tang of the soil about it, "exuding a flavor born of struggle against environment." Unencumbered by the machinery of theatricalism then popular, the plot is starkly simple. It grows naturally out of provincial character and problems common to all who yearn for beauty, and it is enlivened by racy humor. Such realism of presentation no doubt resulted from the playwright's personal experience with humble life. A native of Maine and a Harvard graduate (1893), Davis was descended from "staid New England farmers and lawyers whose lives had been devoted to the stern necessity of grubbing an existence out of the rather stubborn soil of Maine and Vermont."[14] Once he viewed from his car a large farm near the village of Northport, Long Island, with its isolated house in the distance. There were evidences around the place, even in its isolation, of a woman's supervision. The detour which Davis' chauffeur had to make around the farm appealed to the playwright's creative mind, producing a faint glimmer of the idea that developed into *The Detour*.

The play evolved into a truthful study of a narrow, close life in a farming settlement near Northport and its effect upon the characters of the Hardys: the stubborn father, property-hungry Stephen, similar in his land-greed to Kirkland's Zury; his imaginative wife Helen, moved by mother love and wifely rebellion; and their daughter Kate, doomed to a drab life unless she understands that the word "detour" may mean "a turning" or "another way around, to get to the same place." The theme—the eternal quality of hope—largely concerns Mrs. Hardy and her womanly yearning for self-expression through her daughter. Unfortunately, Kate's talent for painting, as evaluated by a critic, proves far less adequate than the glorification of it in Helen's dreams. The latter's personal detour is succinctly stated. "The hope that was in me, the wanting to see something different, to do something bigger" is almost atrophied by "just drudgery, just work, nothing else; every other part of me just shriveled up."[15] Ironically, for all of Helen's sacrifices and struggles to hoard egg money for Kate's art study in New York, the girl prefers "tendin' store" and teaching in the nearby town of Northport. The confining claim of the soil is upon her. Her final choice is eventual marriage to Tom Lane, a neighboring farmer as stodgy and land-hungry as her father. As for Helen, her disappointment is not embittering, in the light of the future and that everlasting quality of hope "for the baby that ain't even born yet." As she admits, "Life sort of keeps goin' on forever, don't it?"

A representative of native genre work, *The Detour*, first produced at the Astor Theatre, New York, on August 23, 1921, with its lavish use of authentic details, penetrates deeply into American farm and village life. The conflict about escapism is largely between what Holmes' Autocrat called "arithmetical and algebraical minds." Helen's declaration of rebellion sums up the irritating differences which set her apart from Stephen: "I get so tired of sayin' nothin' but just exactly what's so, and listen to folks that don't ever mean the least mite more'n they say, or the least mite less! What's the use of your imagination!"[16] Under the sponsorship of Lee Shubert and with the "absolute perfection" of Augustin Duncan's direction, the play benefited by the excellent acting of Effie Shannon and Duncan in the key roles of Helen and Steve.

In 1923 Davis received the Pulitzer award for *Icebound*, a second genre play which brought him a long step forward from the days of *Nellie, the Beautiful Cloak Model*.[17] If Helen Hardy, as she says, needed "a key to the door that was shuttin' me out from life," the several Jordans, in tribal conclave at the old homestead in Veazie, Maine, know about a similar key but are hampered momentarily in getting possession of it. That magic key, which each one greedily desires, is the legacy expected from aged Mrs. Jordan, their matriarch who is dying in an upstairs chamber. In this opening scene, as elsewhere in *Icebound*, Davis' keen insight into New England character, into the souls of straitlaced folk like the Calvinistic Jordans—hard survivors of years of struggle with the land—reflects his own descent from "generations of Northern Maine small-town folk." Here in the cheerless homestead parlor, which "for a hundred years has been the rallying point of the Jordan family," relatives are gathered late one cold afternoon in October, 1922, to await the death of the stubborn head of the clan. "The room in which they wait is as dull and as drab as the lives of those who have lived within its walls. Here we have the cleanliness that is next to godliness, but no sign of either comfort or beauty, both of which are looked upon with suspicion as being signposts on the road to perdition."[18]

Gathered here, "the true Jordans by birth"—Henry, dully resigned because of business cares; widowed Sadie, forty, "thin and tight-lipped"; and dissatisfied Ella, a restless maiden lady of thirty-six—together with Henry's Emma, a stout and "rather formidable woman of forty, with a look of chronic displeasure," and Nettie, her vain and shallow daughter by a previous marriage, resentfully gossip about young Jane Crosby, a penniless second cousin who, as a charity domestic for eight years, has earned the respect of Mrs. Jordan. Their spiteful wrangling puzzles bespectacled Orin, Sadie's "pasty-faced boy of ten," and extends to the youngest Jordan, absent Ben, now under grand jury indictment for arson and "drunken devilment." Though the black sheep of the family, years younger than any of the others, "a wild, selfish, arrogant fellow, handsome but sulky and defiant," Ben always has been his mother's favorite. Now he is under family censure. As pious storekeeper Henry sanctimoniously complains, with a sense of family pride, "There hasn't been a Jordan before Ben, who disgraced the name in more'n a hundred years." And sharp-tongued Emma goads her husband about Jane, saying, "As soon as your mother's dead, you'll send her packing."

The authentic representation of family expectations in Act I, somewhat paralleling Mark Twain's portrayal of avarice among the Hadleyburgians, typifies collective escapism through greedy desire. Later, Ben contemptuously derides the family: " 'Crow buzzards' mother called us—the last of the Jordans—crow buzzards—and that's what we are." In anticipation of their inheritance, each Jordan, except Ben, daydreams about ways to spend the family holdings. Such indulgence in wish fulfilment, expressed through dialectal pronunciations, local sayings, and folk psychology,

marks *Icebound* as "an extract from reality." But as selfish dreams sometimes turn nightmarish, the Jordans' hopes for wealth are thwarted most
unexpectedly. To their boundless disappointment, grim Mother Jordan
has outwitted them all by leaving her property to Jane, declaring in a
letter that there is but one way to save Ben—"through a woman who
will hold out her heart to him and let him trample on it as he has on
mine." With the others fawning on her now that she has the Jordan
money, Jane marries Ben with no illusions about having everlasting
happiness, but simply because she loves him. Like Ben, Jane is
well aware of

"what nature's done for us Jordans,—brought us into the world half froze
before we was born. Brought us into the world mean, and hard, so's we
could live the hard, mean life we have to live . . . Sometimes somebody
sort of laughs, and it scares you; seems like laughter needs the sun, same as
flowers do. Icebound, that's what we are, all of us, inside and out."[19]

Nor does the bleak Puritanism of Henry add any cheer to the picture.
("A parlor's where a person's supposed to sit and think of God, and you
couldn't expect it to be cheerful!") Perhaps for Jane, with her shy
attempts to find a bit of beauty and her love for Ben, there is a chance
to escape from the bleak atmosphere of tradition-bound Veazie. With
the exception of Ben, and perhaps Nettie, the others exemplify the spirit
of Edwin Arlington Robinson's "New England," a region where

Joy shivers in the corner where she knits
And Conscience always has the rocking chair,
Cheerful as when he tortured into fits
The first cat that ever was killed by care.[20]

Sometime escapism is only the exchange of one trap for a worse one.
This is the case in another dramatization of the New England region
"where the wind is always north-north-east" and "passion is . . . a soilure
of the wits." The dramatic possibilities of Edith Wharton's *Ethan Frome*
(1911), a masterly interpretation of the strict New England code, had
long been recognized; though Lowell Barrington had made a dramatization, it remained for Owen Davis, working in collaboration with his son
Donald, to bring this tragedy of circumstances to the stage in an unforgettable version holding all the power and simplicity of the novel. First
presented on January 6, 1936, in Philadelphia, this "best dramatization
of a novel which I have even seen in a theatre," as John Anderson called
it in *The New York Evening Journal*, began its long career as a New

York success at the National Theatre on January 21. Critics at once acclaimed it highly, praising it as "a tragedy which is deeply stirring and rather grimly beautiful" (Richard Lockridge in the *New York Sun*) and as "one of the finest American plays" (Robert Garland in the *New York World Telegram*).

Such superlatives are all the more understandable if considered in the light of Davis' own account of the composition and casting of the play. In part 6 of *My First Fifty Years in the Theatre*, he recounts his experiences with Jed Harris and Max Gordon in connection with production contracts; the task of collaboration with Donald, lasting more than a year; and Gordon's casting of Raymond Massey, Pauline Lord, and Ruth Gordon in the key roles. Gordon called in Guthrie McClintic to do the staging and Jo Mielziner to design the scenery. (Five vivid sketches of the Mielziner stage sets embellish the published play.) The Davises' sensitive appreciation of Mrs. Wharton's grim but beautiful story soon brought them to the realization that "Good dramatizations are not made by cutting pages out of a novel and sticking them into a play manuscript." Owen Davis describes their chief task: "Ethan Frome, his wife Zenobia, and little Mattie Silver were glowing with life upon Mrs. Wharton's canvas, but she had given them no voices at all. It was a story of a very tender love, and of a hate so bitter that it could end only in a dreadful tragedy, but nowhere in the book was there a record of one single angry word." Mostly what Zenobia and Ethan had said was repeated in the words of some neighbor, and Mattie was only told about. Patiently the adapters had to put into the mouths of these three characters almost every word they had to say. Retaining the essential simplicity and almost overpowering poignancy of the novel, they fashioned a tragedy which, in the course of a prologue, three acts (totaling ten scenes), and an epilogue, covered the passing of twenty years.

By means of this excellent format they approximated what Edith Wharton had tried to do years earlier. In the autobiographical *A Backward Glance* (1934) she confessed that for years before her writing of *Ethan Frome* she "had wanted to draw life as it really was in the derelict mountain villages of New England, a life even in my time, and a thousandfold more a generation earlier, utterly unlike that seen through the rose-colored spectacles of my predecessors, . . ." Throughout her ten years of residence in Massachusetts, Mrs. Wharton had been deeply impressed by the cramped lives of the natives. As she saw it, provincial New England, a community no less compact than her fashionable New York, was bound by the forces of poverty, which repressed its victims more than did a social code. In her sight the snow-bound villages of Western Massachusetts were still grim places, morally and physically: insanity, incest and slow mental and moral starvation were hidden away behind the paintless wooden housefronts of the long village street, or in the isolated farm-houses on the neighboring hills; and Emily Bronte would have found as savage tragedies in our remoter valleys as on her Yorkshire moors.[21]

In refashioning Mrs. Wharton's "undiluted American materials," the Davises have constructed a tragedy which gradually, piece by piece, reveals details that hint at the nature of a long-drawn-out catastrophe—a "tragedy without finality." To the code of simple manners existing in the Starkfield and Bettsbridge communities they add the compulsion of poverty. Even at twenty-eight Ethan Frome, "a slim powerfully built New Englander . . . severe and hard and cold," has been cheated by straitened circumstances out of every opportunity for normal joy and happiness. Motivated by sheer loneliness and propinquity, Ethan has married Zenobia, four years his senior, the former nurse of his dying mother. Now, seven years later, Ethan finds himself inextricably bound to a chronic invalid and fretter who delights in whining to Jotham, the hired hand, and to stray visitors that "I ain't any better" or "I ain't up to moving a muscle." A hypochondriac habitually sipping from patent medicine bottles, Zeena enjoys "whinin' and moanin' for doctorin' and Energex Vibrators and hired girls," while Ethan's cattle are starving to death because he lacks money for feedstuff.[22] Embittered by his sordid circumstances, Ethan finds temporary happiness after the arrival of Zeena's impoverished young cousin, who comes to help out as a hired girl, without pay. In gay Mattie Silver he discovers an exquisite and tender love blooming on his bleak hillside. For a time Ethan forgets his hard fate. Poverty, however, binds him fast, refusing him escape from his deadly existence with Zeena, "tired, sickly, and seemingly ageless."

In time Zeena, suspecting her husband's growing love for "Matt," vindictively springs a trap. In Bettsbridge she secretly hires another girl and then orders homeless Mattie to go away at once—Zeena cares not where—maybe to return to the mills in Willimantis. This new expression of Zeena's meanness, her perpetual goading, and his poverty drive Ethan, in a mad outburst of rebellion, to try to escape his despair by a suicide pact. As the aftermath of this crucial scene of Mattie's dismissal, Ethan and Mattie decide to find release by guiding their bobsled down a snowy, icy slope into the huge black elm at its base.

The outcome, as portrayed in the Epilogue, is not death as planned. As though the Eumenides were forever to pursue the lovers, the three victims at the Frome place are doomed to a seemingly endless life together, more imprisoning than the condition against which Ethan had rebelled. Badly lamed in the suicide attempt, Ethan has been fated to bear for twenty years with apparent impassivity the presence in his house not only of the slatternly Zeena, now fifty-five and the unsightly object of his hate, but of the girl he once loved, now a hopelessly crippled and petulant wreck.

What is Ethan Frome's tragic flaw? Repression? Inaction? A more energetic young man, no doubt, would have found some way to escape, despite his poverty. Ethan's character, however, had been shaped by a harsh and binding environment. The only art known to this inarticulate, awkward villager is that of enduring his unresolvable maladjustment in as tight-lipped a way as possible. Circumstances—his marriage of convenience to Zenobia and the tragic turn of his love for Mattie—trapped him, making his burden infinitely heavy and placing upon him such a responsibility that he can do nothing to extricate himself or to save his fellow victims. Though he is far more icebound than any of the Jordans, the greater consequence of his failure may have been the deepening of his stature, as suggested in the Epilogue. Regarding Ethan's failure to escape as a mark of spiritual victory, one critic has noted that Edith Wharton's "sense of tragedy" was that "doom waited for the pure in heart; and it was better so."[23] The theme of the Frome tragedy is perhaps related to the fact that "Ethan fails because he is spiritually superior and materially useless." Some read into his defeat another proud affirmation of the enduring quality of sturdy New England provincials.

In 1936 Mrs. Wharton, whose living in France prevented her from ever seeing a performance of *Ethan Frome*, expressed the delight she felt, as she read the play, over the fact that "here at least is a new lease of life for 'Ethan.' " Her praise of the Davises included appreciation for their memorable re-creation of her ill-fated trio, and of the minor Starkfield figures as well. Jotham Powell, Harmon Gow, young Denis Eady who liked Mattie, the Varnums, the Hales, and other villagers attending the Starkfield church socials and the bobsled parties, as well as one newcomer—the young engineer whose inquiry in the Prologue about Ethan's bitter history accounts for the three acts as flashbacks—all add to the verisimilitude of "my poor little group of hungry lonely New England villagers," as Mrs. Wharton described them.[24] Jo Mielziner's realistic exterior and interior sets for the Frome place—its front view, the kitchen, and the bedroom—for the snowy hill, the outside of the vestry of the Starkfield Congregational Church on a winter evening, and other scenes were made all the more effective by skilful lighting, appropriate properties, and provincial costumes. Scenes of lyric beauty, as when Mattie on the hilltop one evening is awed by the faraway stars as Ethan explains their names, are balanced by those revealing the meanness of the human spirit. For example, dramatic tension is created by Mattie's accidental breaking of such a trivial thing as Zeena's red glass pickle jar, cherished as "Aunt Philura Maple's best pickle dish." All of these diverse elements, and many more, make the Davis dramatization a memorable representation of a narrow farming village in northern New England. More recently, on February 18, 1960, the Frome story was given still another new lease on life through a televised version as the "Dupont Show of the Month," written by Jacqueline Babbin and Audrey Gellen. This "Special," produced by David Susskind and directed by Alex Segal, featured an excellent cast including, among others, Julie Harris as Mattie, Sterling Hayden as Ethan, Clarice Blackburn as Zeena, and Arthur Hill as the Narrator.[25]

The importance of the emotional relationship of young people to their respective communities is a dominant theme in various plays of the 1920's and on into the 1930's. In America's heartland, for instance, two fictionalized small towns on the gently rolling midwestern plain bore the names of Excelsior, Iowa, and Winesburg, Ohio. Among their dissatisfied, vaguely searching youths were Roger Bloomer and George Willard, typical of those actual young men who used to "light out for the Territory" or the nearest city. While some of their fellow citizens were absorbed in the quest for money, these idealists, still uncertain of themselves and their relationships, were yearning for something better than their ordinary milieux.

John Howard Lawson's play, *Roger Bloomer*, deals with a young man's quest, at times frenetic, for the true mystery of life, for the fulfillment of the self through the discovery of beauty, love, and peace. His mind filled with the traditional uneasy attitudes of searching youth, Roger revolts against the humdrum complacency and stultifying pragmatism of his hometown. His escape from Excelsior to the complex urban jungle of New York City at first brings a terrifying aloneness. Isolated by his continued introspection and self-consciousness, he wanders the streets horrified by the distortions of values created by the money-mania. Everywhere he is appalled by man's loss of morality and individualism at a time when a mechanical conformity, shaped largely by Big Business, rules society. In the city, the conflict between a youth's high aspirations and his social environment is waged anew. Parallel case histories present the stories of two other Excelsior escapees, Louise, Roger's sweetheart and a former salesgirl in his father's store, and Eugene Poppin, whose philosophy is based upon competition. "A man's got to make good," says Eugene, "keep in right, learn when to keep his mouth shut, dress well, make useful friends . . ."[26] A "wise guy," Eugene uses the key to worldly success, whereas Louise, disillusioned by her contacts with "the guys with money," commits suicide. Although in the city Roger fails to find his "true picture," he gains freedom. The play ends on a hopeful note, as at the conclusion of a nightmare Louise's spirit visits Roger in prison, urging him to "face the music" and thus gain "a man's luck, . . ." Before the curtain falls, an attendant gruffly opens Roger's cell, saying, "Come on, you're free, there's the world out there." Thus Roger escapes the doom of the "hungry City," presumably by learning how to fight alone.

Roger Bloomer, Lawson's first play to reach Broadway, was produced originally by the Equity Players, at the Equity Theatre on March 1, 1923, and after March 15 at the Greenwich Village Theatre. The first production, incorporating many expressionistic techniques, was planned by Augustin Duncan, with Henry Hull in the role of young Roger. The script called for "an actor of sturdy virile appearance, giving [the] impression of an average American boy"—in short, a personator capable of presenting Roger's problem as that of a normal young man rather than of a neurasthenic. The scenic plan, though involving "the simplest use of setting conveying impression of single articles of furniture, and portable setting, spotted against curtains, with occasional use of painted drops," gives multiple suggestions of the feverish twenties. With the stage divided into sections, each spotlighted as change of scene demands, and with outer and inner curtains, a production may give the effect of quick and often simultaneous action. For example, in the Excelsior scenes of Act I the symbolic yellow outer curtain resembles fields of Iowa wheat and young trees. When these curtains part, a spotlight reveals the well-to-do Bloomer family at the dinner table, while the right side of the stage is in darkness. At the end of the meal Mr. and Mrs. Bloomer move into the shadowed area as lights dim in the dining room. Mr. Bloomer turns on a lamp to the extreme right, thus revealing the living room. Other techniques of expressionism, such as soliloquies, telegraphic dialogue, telescopic characterization, type characters (a College Examiner and others), lyrical dialogue, kaleidoscopic sequence, a nightmare with music, and drops, enable Lawson to portray two worlds in rapid succession: the small town ironically named Excelsior and the "City of stone and steel."

As the most completely expressionistic among the experimental plays of the twenties, *Roger Bloomer* is akin to Eugene O'Neill's *The Emperor Jones* (first produced in 1920), Elmer Rice's *The Adding Machine* (which opened at the Garrick on March 19, 1923), and *Beggar on Horseback* (1925), George S. Kaufman and Marc Connelly's hilarious fantasy. All of these "new" playwrights are caustic in their satire of modern society, notably in its economic aspects. Their protagonists— Roger, Brutus Jones, Mr. Zero, and pianist Neil McRae, another small town escapee—are victimized in one way or another by the stultifying effects of corporate business. Giantism, multiplicity, machine control, and other symbols of the age of enterprise are satirized by expressionistic methods as powerful means of thwarting, and sometimes crushing, the growth of the individual. Lawson's own penetrating satire, which becomes increasingly shrill, at first unmasks the dulness of the middle class in a "progressive" town resembling Lewis' Zenith. In the opening scene, the Bloomers' utterly commonplace table talk shifts attention from middle-aged Everett Bloomer, "swelling a little with prosperity" as owner of the biggest store in Excelsior, toward Roger "eighteen, an average American boy of Middle Western type, solidly built, keen face, vigorous character," and then to fatuous Mrs. Bloomer, echoer of her husband's platitudes. (There is a strong resemblance between those former townspeople, boastful manufacturer Cady and dull-minded Mrs. Cady, of *Beggar on Horseback*, and Mr. and Mrs. Bloomer.) Boasting about the "boomer spirit" in "little old Iowa," Everett magnifies his status as a small-town merchant into that of a chain store tycoon, saying, "I'm thinking of spreading, spreading . . . opening stores in other cities . . . there's America for you, Washington to Woolworth, business . . . spread . . . spread!"

As the imaginary Bloomers and Cadys were "buying small and selling big," popular writers for the *Saturday Evening Post* and other widely circulated magazines were glorifying the values of business competition, mass consumption, personal success, comfort, and prosperity. In contrast, more discerning and astringent writers, such as Ellen Glasgow, Eugene O'Neill, and Sherwood Anderson were matching the satiric protests of Lawson with their own truthful presentations of what they regarded as the blighting effects of the overemphasis on prosperity. In particular, Sherwood Anderson, "the last of the townsmen," as Maxwell Geismar once called him, began as early as 1916 and 1917, with *Windy McPherson's Son* and *Marching Men*, to examine searchingly what he considered the harmful effects of the cult of prosperity which was then transforming peaceful agricultural villages into bustling, business-bent towns, and even into ugly manufacturing cities. In 1919 the homely and finely developed vignettes of *Winesburg, Ohio: A Group of Tales of Ohio Small Town Life* demonstrated Anderson's power to probe beneath the flat, starved surfaces of small-town living. In this psychological study of small-town citizens Anderson, in the words of Lionel Trilling, created "not just a book" but "a personal souvenir" of a new and burgeoning America. Admittedly "an inveterate hunter of tales," Anderson, in characterizing people of Mid-America, abundantly proves that "odd things happen to people behind the walls of houses." The timeless inhabitants of Winesburg "are one thing inside their houses and another on the street. Sometimes the secrets, hidden away behind the walls of the houses, are merely sad, but sometimes they are exciting too."[27]

In a Chicago lately become self-conscious Anderson awakened to the realization that "life itself is a loose, flowing thing" and that "we are all controlled, constantly and deeply influenced by passing people, passing adventures . . ."[28] Surrounded by the hectic business atmosphere of Chicago, the struggling native of Camden, Ohio, received stimulation from creative friends and clarified his aims by viewing the work of Expressionist artists, Van Gogh in particular. In the confusion of the Chicago streets he recognized that there was unity in multiplicity, the unity of the city itself. As he pondered the relationship of the hurrying Chicagoans to the pattern of their city, Anderson questioned, "Why wouldn't it be possible to take as a subject the life of an American town and to create this subject by portraying in turn, with bold, simple colors, the lives of the inhabitants of the town?"[29] In 1915 a fellow boarder gave Anderson a copy of Edgar Lee Masters' *Spoon River Anthology*, which he stayed up all night to read. Six months later, as he began writing a few tales, he centered his interest on the small towns of his Ohio boyhood. In his *Memoirs* (1942) he has written that while he strove to create tales about provincial individuals, they belonged so much together that "they made something like a novel, a complete story . . ." In effect, "the characters of *Spoon River*, isolated with their own problems and yet connected by their small town background, had given him the clue" to *Winesburg, Ohio*.[30] This was the origin of the manuscript which, when it was finally accepted by Ben Huebsch, received little notice and sold only a few copies.

After several years this collection of tales began to attract wide attention. Its later history includes numerous critical notices, reprints, twenty-three foreign translations, and several dramatizations made for stage and dance performance.[31] In the fall of 1933 Anderson began reworking his plays. During 1934 he had some difficulty in the preparation of a stage version of the Winesburg tales. Casting aside the several versions unsuccessfully written with the assistance of collaborators, he himself made an entirely new play, retaining the spirit of the stories rather than following their exact pattern. Even so, the advice of Roger Sergel, Jasper Deeter—to whom he dedicated *Plays: Winesburg and Others* in 1937—and others helped in the completion of the script used in the first production in Deeter's Hedgerow Theatre in Moylan-Rose Valley, Pennsylvania. More recently, during the 1957-58 season, renewed interest in the Winesburg material was stirred by an unpublished dramatization made by Christopher Sergel, Roger Sergel's son, who did a thorough research job by rereading Anderson's works and visiting Clyde, Ohio, where he grew up. This version, premiered in New York on February 5, 1958, was made all the more effective by the acting of Dorothy McGuire.[32] During the week of July 17, 1958, at the Jacob's Pillow (Massachusetts) Dance Festival, choreographer Donald Saddler presented part one of his dance drama based on *Winesburg*. Skilfully welding Genevieve Pitot's music with the dance and the spoken word, he focused on four of Anderson's grotesques: Elizabeth Willard, whose uncontrollable love for her son George feeds "the feeble blaze of life that remained in her"; the Reverend Curtis Hartman, the Peeping-Tom minister who sees God in a naked woman; a love-starved spinster, Alice Hindman; and the Winesburg doxy, Louise Trunnion.[33]

Anderson had difficulty working within the limitations of theatrical form. Hence, his adaptation suffers by comparison with his original stories. These often present, in lyrical mood, rich pictures of a lovely Ohio countryside and a farm village such as Clyde, Ohio, was years ago; however, in the play *Winesburg* the small town and its environs seem cramped. The deliberately simple stage settings for the eight scenes and an epilogue, while giving the action a rapid flow, fail to provide a memorable background for the thirteen selected characters. Anderson's production notes, however, specify that *Winesburg* is "a play of character" with each individual given full development. "By extreme simplification of the settings emphasis is all on the people."[34] Such minimizing of the scenic effects tallies with Anderson's efforts in the tales to penetrate "the buried life, the unconscious psyche—that seat of touch, source of energies, desires, sentience, and the power of love and unity."[35] Thus throughout the eight scenes and epilogue the hidden realm of the key characters is illuminated at the expense of the physical presence of Winesburg. Tom, Elizabeth, and George Willard—a hotel-keeping family—Dr. Reefy, Dr. Parcival, Belle Carpenter, Banker White, all are disturbed by erotic and other personal longings. Each is seeking escape from a personal dilemma and is groping for a happier way of life. And in the struggles of these particular Winesburgians is suggested a vision of life astutely summarized by Paul Rosenfeld, Anderson's admiring critic:

"Almost, it seems, we touch an absolute existence, a curious semidivine life. Its chronic state is banality, prostration, dismemberment, unconsciousness; tensity with indefinite yearning and infinitely stretching desire. Its manifestation: the non-community of cranky or otherwise asocial solitaries, dispersed, impotent and imprisoned."[36] These are the fugitives for whom "the moment of realization is tragically brief." Sometimes such realization is accompanied by understanding and sincerity; sometimes by death, as in the case of Elizabeth Willard; sometimes by cynical escapism through alcoholism, as with Dr. Parcival, whose inebriated mind plays on such rationalizations as "My thoughts crucify me" and an alter-ego counseling: "Let life alone, Doctor Parcival. Don't salt it."

All of these Winesburgians are struggling against reality, each trying to save himself by a feeling of independence from an imprisoning milieu. A few—notably Belle Carpenter and George Willard—finally discover a new exit by withdrawing from Winesburg. The impulse to escape imaginatively from time present into time past or time imagined is especially hurtful to sickly Elizabeth Willard; but as for that self-styled "man of distinction," Dr. Parcival, his keen awareness of his dilemma, coupled with a comic spirit, enables him to rise above mawkish sentimentality. Even his self-praise is satiric and quizzical, as in this typical banter with saloonkeeper Ed Hanby about the "river of drunkenness": "Drunkenness, Ed, is one of life's privileges. It's a boat to ride in. Sometimes the boat rocks a little, but on you go, down, down the river of life. With me, Ed, it's different. Drunkenness has saved me. I'm too wise, Ed. I know too much to live among men without drunkenness."[37] With the years, Elizabeth's world has shrunk to the minuscule proportions of her room at the run-down Willard House and the shabby office of Dr. Reefy, her cherished friend and lover. Almost outside the stream of present time, Mrs. Willard, not long before her death, seeks escape from the bitter present by recalling a few happy days early in her marriage to ne'er-do-well Tom, to whom she entrusted the management of the hotel, the greater part of her patrimony. Mostly, however, her psychic world reveals that the bent of her temperament, as well as her motives, is now shaped by fixation concerning George's future, away from Winesburg. Her secret weapon against the husband she despises—inherited money hidden in a bedroom cranny—is given secretly to Dr. Reefy for eventual delivery to George.

For years two human temperaments and their reactions have existed side by side in the shabby Willard House. Tom Willard, still unsuccessful at middle age, loses himself in foolish dreaming about the money he will make some day, somehow. Irritated by his own failures and Elizabeth's nagging, Tom desperately tries to shape George's interests. "George, I want you to be what you can be . . . a Willard . . . a big man—a rich man—I want you to be rich—rich—the biggest, richest man in the state."[38] In a scene of great tension, Elizabeth, goaded by Tom's cheap pretense of bigness, angrily tells him about the money and confesses bluntly that he is not George's father. As he damns her as a slut, Elizabeth, infuriated and using her scissors as a dagger, raises her arm against him, when suddenly she is stricken by heart failure and dies.

From scene to scene youth appears in various and recognizable small-town personations. Helen White, sheltered and pampered daughter of the banker, is outwardly a model of respectability unsullied by association with Winesburg's undesirable element. Inwardly, Helen recognizes that college has given her only a temporary escape from her unexciting environment. Her boredom with her prim mother and with domestic restraints is offset by her secret disturbance as recurring thoughts of sex touch upon her proper friendship with George. In George's presence she is inhibited by the social standards of her class. At another extreme, a laborer's daughter and gossiped-about trollop, Louise Trunnion, freely offers herself to any man, even to George. Marriage to Ed Hanby, however, somewhat tames her spirit. The most amusingly satiric portrait is that of Seth Richmond, hypocritically proper but secretly lascivious bank teller, whose insidious remarks to Helen White against George's reputation seem to be a boomerang. Even temptress Louise spurns his begging for her favors.

George Willard, "mopey and dreamy," is not only the key figure among Winesburg's young people, but the unifying character in the plot. As reporter for the *Eagle*, George wanders through town and countryside, gradually forming new concepts of his fellow citizens. Primarily seeking "an order between intention and act, thought and deed, dream and reality," George enjoys indulging in mental exercises as the varied life of the town and his ambitions and experiences excite his fancy.[39] Throughout several years he becomes aware of the drama stirring beneath the surface of the outwardly humdrum lives of his townsmen. It is as if he awakened day by day to the realization that these people he has known all his life are dead spiritually and morally, even while living in Winesburg. Vaguely young George senses that they lead lives of sleepwalkers and daydreamers in the midst of daily routine. What he does not understand very deeply is that some persons, including his mother, are crushed by inhibitions. For instance, though George's friendly association with milliner Belle Carpenter, who is older than he, causes gossip, he is unaware of the ironic fact that respectable banker White is the father of Belle's unborn child and the main cause of her leaving Winesburg.

His own growth through self-criticism appears in his declaring to Elizabeth, "Mother—I guess I've got to get out of here." After her death he does leave, for Cleveland and eventual success. Before departing from the little town of his boyhood, George resembles hundreds of young people who go out from their hometowns into the cities. Stirred perhaps by his reluctance to leave the familiar haunts of the town and surrounding farms, he views his neighbors—even Joe Welling with his preposterous dreams—with unusual tenderness. His going, however, gives him a peculiar sense of detachment, causing him to see his associates as cramped souls, repressed and distorted by the stern customs which have increased their solitariness and refused them any outlet for the forces working within them. As a reporter George had learned much, as did Anderson himself, about the unusual amidst the commonplace. He had discovered, through his contacts with both average and odd types, that the very monotony of life in Winesburg warped the souls of otherwise normal individuals. Having learned some secrets about men and women who were only outwardly decorous, George developed a growing awareness that the pressure of outward conformity often distorted human spirits into grotesque forms. According to the epilogue, George, successful as a creative writer in Cleveland, has come to feel that his Winesburg life was a proper background for his great adventure. But the sensational finale presents a last picture of Tom Willard. Recently married to a prosperous widow, Tom is boasting before "the boys" in Hanby's saloon. His bragging moves from *his* son George's literary successes to the anticipated opening of the new Willard House, "the smartest little hotel in the state." In the ironic finale, wild shouts from the street announce that the Willard House is on fire. And the building is uninsured.

Other unhappy aspects of the Ohio scene come to life in a series of one-acters published in the *Winesburg* volume: "The Triumph of the Egg," "Mother," and "They Married Later." In each of these vignettes both Anderson and Raymond O'Neil, dramatizer of "The Egg," reveal with rare sympathy the plight and the hidden yearnings of ordinary small-towners. From "The Triumph of the Egg" there are the poor befuddled restaurant keeper and his frustrated wife, both scorned by their world, the laughing Bidwell, Ohio, folk who pass by their shabby place. (This playlet, which had its New York production by the Provincetown Players, was put on as curtain raiser for Eugene O'Neill's two-acter, "Diff'rent.") In "Mother," Mary Horton's quarrel with her unfeeling husband George, proprietor of a shabby little hotel in a midwestern town, recalls Elizabeth Willard's agitation and Tom's annoyance over George's supposed infatuation with "that whore" Belle Carpenter. The story of "They Married Later" touches upon the inhibitions of Bidwell, Ohio, newlyweds. Finally, in *I'm a Fool*, dramatized by Christopher Sergel, the racetrack scenes in Sandusky about 1900 populate the stage with "horsy" people. George, a boastful and lying stable hand, retells what happened when he pretended to three "swells"—one a lovely girl —to be the son of rich Walter Mathers of Marietta. When his friend Burt calls him "a pretty smart guy!" all that George can say is "Me? Smart? I'm a . . ." Too late, he realizes that deception has brought him nothing except exclusion from the company of the one girl he has ever really liked—a hard jolt, "one of the most bitterest I have ever had to face. And all come about through my own foolishness too."[40]

The Winesburgians and the people from Bidwell, whether moved by their hatred of village philistinism, "passion without body, sexuality without gaiety and joy," or by youthful ambition, might in their revolt have spoken the lines from Floyd Dell's *Moon-Calf* (1920):

> "Oh, the briary bush
> That pricks my heart so sore!
> If ever I get out of the briary bush
> I'll never get in any more!"

Dwellers along many imaginary Main Streets, beset by personal dissatisfactions, frustrations, fears, and moral weakness, have been caught in the "briary bush." War, politics, fear of the law, and revivalism have made them uneasy. For example, in the play ironically entitled *The Hero* the impact of overseas service during the 1919 era touches men, women, and children in an imaginary suburban village near New York City. In particular, the aftermath of World War I seriously affects all who live in the Lane home—a small, rented, jerry-built house painted "a cold, shabby white." This first successful play by Gilbert Emery (Emery Pottle) premiered at the Longacre Theatre in New York on March 14, 1921. A comparative study of two brothers who typify moral and physical heroism, the play presents the involvements of Andrew Lane and Oswald, his younger brother; Hester, Andrew's wife; Martha Roche, a Belgian refugee attached to the household; and psalm-singing old Mrs. Lane.

Always irresponsible, Oswald has embezzled some money and escaped from the town, as he had done before, this time to join the Foreign Legion, leaving behind a burden of debt, which uncomplaining Andrew quietly assumes. Returning in 1919, Oswald, though bemedalled as a war hero, shows that his moral nature is wholly unchanged. Now living in Andrew's home, he proves himself a rotter, taking whatever he can, with no feeling of moral obligation. Nevertheless, he charms Hester and seduces Marthe. Worse still, in order to escape again to France to "his own kind of a girl," he steals church money, for which Andrew as treasurer is responsible.

In a sensational last act, however, his escape plan is thwarted most unexpectedly. In rescuing his little nephew from a blazing kindergarten building, Oswald shows a burst of physical courage but suffers a double loss: the church funds and his own life. The others are deeply affected. Mother Lane resignedly sings in a cracked voice, "There is a fountain filled with blood." As Andrew sits with little Andy in his lap, he prepares himself to assume another debt which Oswald has put upon him. Hester, in deep remorse for the infidelity that was in her heart, belatedly sobs out her appreciation of Andrew as a man but lies to him about the theft, saying that Oswald was carrying the funds to the bank when the fire broke out. Thus Andrew retains his illusions about the nature of Oswald's "heroism." "Me? I'm just old Andy, I am—but Os—Os was a hero!"[41] A suspenseful family drama, *The Hero* puts on stage an ironic picture of the unchanging nature of man, against the shabby background of a New York small town. Oswald's youthful flight from the town did little to improve his moral nature, as his confession reveals:

"I'm a poor lot, Hester, I guess. I've hoboed it, and deadbeat it all over the darned place. Ever since I was a kid of sixteen I've seen the worst of everything—women and men—and God's made some birds, I'll say. I've gone down the line with 'em. Greasers in Mexico, chinks in Shanghai, wops in Naples, niggers in Port Said . . ."[42]

Another "briary bush" victim, of tougher fighting spirit than Andrew Lane, is Yankee Carrie Callahan, at thirty "spare, handsome, humorous," whose hard life, with "few ups and many, many downs" and various disasters, has left her unscarred and blessed with the shrewdness of sturdy Maine working folk. She is the spirited protagonist of Sidney Howard's Theatre Guild success *Ned McCobb's Daughter*, which opened successfully at the John Golden Theatre on November 22, 1926, directed by Philip Moeller and enhanced by Aline Bernstein's settings. As the indomitable daughter of ferryboat "Captain" Ned McCobb, Carrie wants all that she can possibly get materially while still maintaining her respectability. Through her operation of Carrie's Spa, which advertises, "Shore Dinners. Fresh Crab Meat Sandwiches. Antiques" at the terminus of the Kennebec Ferry, Mayberry, Maine, she has made friends among her fellow Down Easters because of her honest, straight-forward, and capable ways. Many troubles and bitter disappointments come her way, but Carrie never loses her perspective by idly dreaming of running away from Mayberry. Her worthless husband George, from New York's East Side, has done enough escaping for the two of them, though for a while he has been collecting fares on the boat piloted by honest Ned McCobb, former sea captain now reduced to operating a Kennebec ferry.

Carrie's newest misfortunes make her afraid of the "Federal Men." Her present ill luck comes from George, a moral weakling who has stolen ferry funds, has borrowed endlessly from her father, and has indulged in a sordid affair, involving abortion, with a cheap waitress. Over-excited by such family disgrace, Ned McCobb dies from a stroke. Carrie, then, is forced into an unwanted business association with her unscrupulous brother-in-law, bootlegger Babe Callahan, who attempts to convert her spa into a center of operations for his gang. George, when needed most, decamps again. Using her Yankee ingenuity, Carrie outwits Babe, who is adamant about using the Spa for his racket, by having her neighbors impersonate the "Federals" and by convincing Babe that the price of his escape must be the building costs for her new kitchen. The bootleggers do make their getaway, while Carrie, speedily restoring order, happily remains in Mayberry to make a Yankee bargain with Nat Glidden, a carpenter, to "build my kitchen for twelve hundred dollars, or, sure as hell's a man-trap, I'll build it myself."

Truth of characterization and situation is made all the more credible by Howard's careful selection of Down East scenic details and authentic properties to suggest the Yankee nature of generations of McCobbs who have lived in the Mayberry homestead, now partially used as Carrie's Spa. All the details of interior and exterior views are organically one with both the action and the main ideas of the play. Also, Howard has deepened the tone of his comedy by his command of two dialects, the everyday talk of the Maine Yankee and the New Yorkese of the Callahan gang. All of these elements—characterization, situation, scene, and speech—were skilfully brought into proper focus by the Theatre Guild's star cast: Clare Eames as Carrie, Margalo Gillmore as Jenny, the barmaid, Alfred Lunt as Baba, Earle Larimore as George, Alfred Perry as Ned McCobb, and Edward G. Robinson as Lawyer Grover.[43]

Expertly drawn bourgeois portraits of the strenuous thirties picture other village malcontents, some as tough-minded as Carrie Callahan, but far more scheming and even rapacious and ruthless. As a part of the widening range of social drama, these portraits testify that certain playwrights—Lillian Hellman, Sinclair Lewis, and others—were often sharply critical of their disagreeable and sometimes dangerous charac-

Playbills for February 11, 1864, and January 4, 1866, performances at the Great Salt Lake City Theatre. From George D. Pyper, *The Romance of an Old Playhouse* (1928).

THEATRE!

GREAT SALT LAKE CITY.

MANAGER, ... H. B. CLAWSON.
STAGE MANAGER, ... JOHN T. CAINE.

MR. G. B. WALDRON

Nick of the Woods

Thursday, Jan. 4, '66.

Will be presented, the celebrated Indian Drama, in 3 Acts, entitled,

NICK

OF THE

WOODS!

Reginald, Nathan,
the Woods,
nger,
Ashburne,
ho Waters

MR. G. B. WALDRON

ing Ralph Stackpole,
ruce,
ce,
Bruce,
uce,   Master BRADLEY CLAWSON.

Black Vulture,)
n,)

ers, by numerous Auxilliaries.

Mr J. S. LINDSAY.
Mr. J. R. CLAWSON.
Mr. D. McKENZIE.
Mr. J. A. THOMPSON.
Mr. D. J. McINTOSH.
Master BRADLEY CLAWSON.
Mr. J. C. GRAHAM.
Mr. N. S. LESLIE.
Mr. C. ATTWOOD.

Mr. E. G. WOOLLEY.
Mr. J. B. KELLY.
Mr. R. MATTHEWS.

Mrs. N. S. LESLIE.
Miss ADAMS.
Mrs. M. G. CLAWSON.
Miss ZINA.
Miss LOUISA.

THEATRE!!!

GREAT SALT LAKE CITY.

Manager, ... H. B. CLAWSON.
Stage Manager, ... JOHN T. CAINE.

PROFESSOR

SIMMONS

FOR

THIS NIGHT ONLY.

THURSDAY, FEB. 11, 1864.

In the Great, Weird, Wondrous and Invincibly Incomprehensible Programme prepared for this occasion;

Prof. SIMMONS

Will Perform the great FORSTER Feat of writing on the Arm in

LETTERS OF BLOOD;

OR THE

INCARNADINED CHIROGRAPHY.

The THEATRE ORCHESTRA will give an

ENHARMONIC PROLEGOMENA.

DOORS open at 7 o'clock.   OVERTURE at half-past 7.

Prices of Admission same as usual.

Babies in arms $10 Extra.

CASH or GRAIN only can be received in payment for TICKETS on this occasion.

Above, lithographed view (1849) of Sacramento, similar to the first-act setting of Alonzo Delano's *A Live Woman in the Mines* (1857). Below, scene (1849) at the San Francisco post office, which had its dramatic counterpart in *A Live Woman in the Mines*, Act I, scenes 2 and 3. *Stokes Collection, New York Public Library.*

C. C. Kuchel's lithograph of Virginia City, Nevada Territory (1861), typifying early mining town layouts and frontier architecture as featured in western plays. *Stokes Collection, New York Public Library.*

Chrystal Herne, actress daughter of James A. Herne and star of the revival of his *Margaret Fleming* (New Theatre, Chicago, 1907). *Theatre Collection, New York Public Library.*

Blanche Bates as Minnie Falconer in Belasco's *The Girl of the Golden West* (Belasco Theatre, New York, 1905). *Hill Collection, Dallas Public Library*.

Left, Frank Mayo in Murdoch's *Davy Crockett* (Rochester Theater, 1872). Right, F. S. Chanfrau as Kit Redding in Spencer's *Kit the Arkansas Traveler* (1870). Illustrations for "The American on the Stage," *Scribner's Monthly* (July, 1879).

ters. Among the most unforgettable of these imaginary townspeople, the acquisitive and villainous Hubbards, created by Miss Hellman (herself a southerner), move ruthlessly through a grim two-part family chronicle of the Deep South during a period of great social change, the 1880's to the 1900's. *Another Part of the Forest* (1946) and *The Little Foxes* (1939) dramatize with relentless realism the impact of a rising industrialism upon caste and class in Bowden, Alabama, beginning with the summer of 1880. The history of the Hubbards typifies the unimpeded enterprise of a new bourgeois way of life superimposed upon an older and more aristocratic way, or perhaps emerging from it: "a ruthless, crude certainty out of a sensitive, romantic uncertainty."[44]

As it is described in *Another Part of the Forest*, the economic rise of the Hubbards began in the risky business plied by unprincipled Marcus Hubbard, when the Civil War made possible an outlet for his profitable black marketeering. A traitor to his own South, Marcus was a shrewd opportunist. Outwardly and cautiously working within the law, he made his first big money by supplying Union troops with quantities of salt and other necessities. By 1880 his war profits have made Marcus an affluent merchant, banker, and householder. He is now comfortably established in Bowden, living with his timid and bullied wife Lavinia, his detestable sons Ben and Oscar, and his wilful twenty-year-old daughter Regina in a porticoed house on Main Street, "a good house built by a man of taste from whom Marcus Hubbard bought it after the Civil War." At the other extreme of Bowden's economic scale, the saddened Bagtrys and other members of the antebellum "landocracy," whose men served honorably during the war, are "dying on the vine" but are still struggling to exist in shabby gentility.

Flourishing parvenus like the Hubbards, symbols of the spirit of acquisitiveness during Reconstruction days, are indeed the greedy human counterparts of "the little foxes that spoil our vines: for our vines have tender grapes." With cunning animal instinct, Marcus and his clan—all except Lavinia—have come out of the forest to spoil the tenderest of grapes, the unkept but still beautiful Lionnet Plantation, for decades the cherished property of the now ruined Bagtrys. (Taking her odd title of *Another Part of the Forest* from *As You Like It*, Act III, scene 5, Miss Hellman wrote this play as a corrective to critical views of *The Little Foxes*, in order to dwell on the thesis that readers and audiences should not feel superior to the Hubbards, for greed and avarice are elements rampant in modern American society.) Like the rudest of the picnickers in V. L. Parrington's symbolic "Great Barbecue," Marcus grabs for the biggest hunk of meat, Lionnet Plantation. Ben, Oscar, and Regina, dis-

regarding the ineffectual protests of their more sensitive mother, quickly
develop individual techniques in the art of connivance and selfish acquisition. Each becomes familiar with the principles of "go-aheadism,"
speedily learning from their father's tough pragmatism that, as he dis-
approvingly tells John Bagtry, "Your people deserved to lose the war
and their world. It was a backward world, getting in the way of history."[45] Here, indeed, is free enterprise for the few through the exploitation of the many. As Miss Hellman implies in both of these plays,
ruthless exploitation in the economic world—even so small a world as
Bowden—brings exploitation into the family circle. Both Lavinia Hubbard and Birdie Bagtry, later Oscar's bullied wife, are pathetic women
who lose their identities among the more strident, greedy, industry-
minded Hubbards, who are almost "white trash." Nor does genteel
Horace Giddens, who becomes Regina's husband, fare any better. Just
before he has a heart attack, Regina callously tells Horace that she married him in her youth simply because she was "lonely for all the things
I wasn't going to get . . . I wanted the world." Now, after twenty years
of marriage, she deliberately causes his death by a cold refusal to get
him the medicine which might have prolonged his life and given him
opportunity to change his will, thus reducing her inheritance.

Though clannish ties exist, the Hubbards and their in-laws react to
their Alabama locale according to their individual natures and desires.
Most of them want more out of life than Bowden can offer. In *Another
Part of the Forest*, Marcus tries to escape his low origin by accumulating
"big money," acting on the principle that his wealth allows him to crush
the weak and attract the strong. Pathetic Lavinia, her wishes constantly
ignored, escapes her intolerable home situation by reading the Bible
and singing hymns in a nearby Negro church. As the cupidity of Marcus'
children is exposed in *The Little Foxes*, the town of Bowden, now a
symbol of the New South of the cotton mills, serves as a miniature theater for the exploitation and the swindling which the Hubbards impose
upon each other. Ben, Oscar, and young Leo, Oscar's son, form a
morally rotten trio bent upon appropriating Horace Giddens' bonds for
their own profit. Meanwhile Birdie, sympathetically portrayed by Pa-
tricia Collinge, has suffered so much intimidation at the hands of the
Hubbards that she desperately seeks an escape through her piano playing, an interest which draws her closer to Horace and his young daughter Alexandra. When music is not solace enough, Birdie drinks elder-
berry wine.

More than the others, Regina—a star role for Tallulah Bankhead—
has long been moved by an unquenchable desire to leave the dull town

forever. To that end, she began scheming early, in the summer of 1880, when by flattery she wheedled money from Marcus for boxes of dresses "imported" from Chicago. Through the years she has more than held her own against her brothers. Her marriage of convenience to Horace— "good society that family, and rich. Solid, quiet, rich"—was made solely to hasten her departure from Bowden and to assure her entry, according to her daydreaming, into the grandly brilliant social whirl of Chicago and, perhaps, of Europe. At the end, Regina, still imprisoned in Bowden, remains a lonely symbol of a despicable, strong-willed escapist undefeated—that is, almost so. Before the final curtain, usually docile Alexandra, suddenly revealing a strong strain of courage and mature insight, proves that her selfish elders had mistaken her docility for weakness. Announcing that she is leaving her mother and Bowden, Zan shows that the Hubbards can no more manage her than they can change themselves. Now she understands what Horace had tried to tell her. Quoting the faithful Negro servant Addie, she informs Regina that she understands about the existence of "people who ate the earth and other people who stood around and watched them do it. . . . Well, . . . Mama. I'm not going to stand around and watch you do it."[46]

As the curtain falls, the question of Regina's future remains undetermined. Thus put at bay, will she, an unrepentant murderess, destroy herself? Or will she manage, with Horace's money, an escape from her despised Main Street? Or, with bitter and hard spirit, will she reconcile her rebellious self to a lonely life in Bowden? Beyond Regina's unsolved personal dilemma, Miss Hellman, as a defender of the underdog, leaves unfavorable impressions of a man-made environment—an Alabama cotton-mill town where labor is cheap and no strikes are permitted, at its worst a symbol of the vices and inhumanity of American capitalism.

On informal occasions Sinclair Lewis delighted in displaying, for the entertainment of friends, his considerable skill in the art of mimicry.[47] He liked to exhibit his histrionic talents by acting out impromptu vignettes satirizing the eccentricities and stupidities of various types of people. His longtime fascination with the stage extended to his careful selection and rehearsing of the entire cast for the New York premiere of the Lewis-Moffitt dramatization of It Can't Happen Here, at the Adelphi Theatre. Also, his theatrical interests included a liking for amateur acting, as evidenced by his few roles in summer stock. On the gala evening of August 22, 1938, when the South Shore Players in Cohasset, Massachusetts, gave their opening performance of It Can't Happen Here before a capacity crowd, Lewis himself successfully enacted the role of Doremus Jessup. Acclaim came to him for his natural acting, made possible, says

Mark Schorer, because Lewis actually "was a small-town editor by nature."

In 1933, several years before the Cohasset excitement, Lewis had written, by invitation, a commemorative essay in celebration of the fiftieth anniversary of his Sauk Center, Minnesota, high-school annual. Paying tribute to his birthplace and his old school, he wrote: "It was a good time, a good place, and a good preparation for life." Moreover, he confessed, during the years of his varied career he had constantly felt "the long arm of the small town" as his thoughts turned to the prairie village of his youth.[48] During this same year this very motif—"the long arm of the small town"—appeared in connection with several of Lewis' characterizations, in two plays, representative of Americans who leave their native towns for wider worlds outside.

The first of these plays had its beginning when Lewis' interests turned toward Civil War history and those antislavery Kansans nicknamed Jayhawkers. A Chicago meeting with Lloyd Lewis, drama critic for that city's *News* and author of *Myths after Lincoln* and *General Sherman*, led the novelist to insist that they collaborate on a play about the time "when the Kansas-Missouri border was bright with the blood of 'hempen homespuns,' " whose differences over slavery and secession lasted from 1855 to 1864.[49] The result of this collaboration, after weeks of trouble in the fusing of the two talents, was a three-act play successively titled *The Skedaddler*, then *Brother Burdette*, and at last *The Jayhawker*, as it was billed for its first performance, at the National Theatre, Washington, D.C., on October 14, 1934. On November 5 its New York opening, at the Cort Theatre, starred Fred Stone in the role of Asa or "Ace" Burdette, that magnificent old fire-eater and fictional senator from "Bleeding Kansas." Stone's daughter Carol was cast as Nettie Burdette, a simple small-town girl whose love for Will Starling, a divinity student, offers romantic relief in contrast to the doubtful political schemes of the wily senator.

The Jayhawker is relatively significant in connection with village escapism mainly because its first scene realistically presents the home locale of a booming Kansas freesoiler and adventurous provincial who prayed his way from his midwestern community to the United States Senate in order that the slaves might be freed and the union preserved forever. While not primarily a play of small-town life, *The Jayhawker* dramatizes what happened to a "guerrilla fighter against the slavery advocates" after he left his hometown for Washington. Our special interest, then, is in the true-to-life first scene of Act I, describing an entertainment which frequently enlivened drab lives in frontier settlements: an outdoor camp meeting near a Kansas settlement. On this occasion, in March, 1861, a Methodist revival is being conducted under the direction of the Reverend Joseph Peavie, "a large, strapping rustic, with a mass of black hair, and the face of a corn-fed Henry Ward Beecher." Assisting him is earnest Will Starling, who has been studying theology at McKendree College but is now back home, shyly courting Nettie Burdette. While the gospel singing and preaching are in progress, the dramatic entrance of Asa Burdette, recently unchurched for various sins, brings "that old time religion" and politics together under the brush arbor. Burdette, with brazen hypocrisy, comes to the mourners' bench to profess repentance for his sins against the slavery advocates. Boldly pushing aside Preacher Peavie, Ace demonstrates that his windbag type of oratory has the power to sway crowds. Holding the "good folks" spellbound, he subtly shifts the interest of the congregation from his bogus confession to his qualifications as the first senator from Kansas. His success is assured as after the benediction Peavie says: "Yes, never knew a meeting so full of the Spirit as tonight, Senator." But it is the political spirit which then takes Asa Burdette, master of pettifoggery and mendacity, far away from his Kansas community. All in all, he is a robustly conceived character and, in the words of Robert Benchley, "as colorful an old son-of-a-gun as we have seen on the stage for many moons."

In 1933, in "The Art of Dramatization," Lewis unreservedly praised Sidney Howard's achievements of creation and adaptation when he undertook the dramatization of *Dodsworth*. Refashioning the long, loosely organized, but vigorous narrative of Lewis' novel, Howard created a new work of art with incidents that move swiftly and visually. The two opening scenes briefly but effectively dramatize again the idea of community escapism, this time through manufacturer Samuel Dodsworth's retirement from the presidency of the Revelation Motor Company and the preparations which he and his frivolous wife Fran are completing for a long European sojourn. These scenes offer a modification of "the long arm of the small town" motif, altered to apply to the larger but still stultifying background of Zenith, "an imaginary city not too far from either Cleveland or Detroit." Before the Dodsworths begin their expatriation, which eventually leads to their separation, these initial scenes not only place another "deadly, half-baked Middle Western town" on Lewis' literary landscape, but introduce two middle-aged provincials trying, in silly Fran's words, "to get us some new selves now!" and to discover "a new life all over from the beginning! A perfectly glorious, free, adventurous life!"[50]

During 1935 Lewis, responding to the public mood of fear generated by the rise of Nazi Germany, produced a best seller in a controversial novel tracing the imaginary rise of fascism in the United States— "very soon—or never." This topical novel, entitled *It Can't Happen Here*, described only the surface violence and terror of an imagined nightmarish spread of fascism. Its plot moves forward by a geographic plan, tracing Fascist growth from faint disaffection in a small town—Fort Beulah, Vermont—to a wider range in small cities like Lewis' Zenith, then to Washington, D.C., and the entire nation. In particular, the Fort Beulah scenes gain depth by the full-length characterization of a country editor,

a mild, rather indolent and somewhat sentimental Liberal, who disliked pomposity, the heavy humor of public men, and the itch for notoriety which made popular preachers and eloquent educators and amateur play-producers and rich lady reformers and rich lady sportswomen and almost every brand of rich lady come preeningly in to see newspaper editors, with photographs under their arms, and on their faces the simper of fake humility.[51]

Such was Doremus Jessup, amiable yet mildly cynical owner and editor of the Fort Beulah *Daily Informer*. A good deal of the action concerns the stubborn resistance to revolutionary change by which freedom-loving Doremus, his family, and his friends try to block the movement toward an American dictatorship being forced upon citizens by a militarized Corpos. Though his people, patriotic Vermonters for generations, believed in independent thinking and he himself is a sincere upholder of democratic principles, Doremus, more than his neighbors, is afraid that the United States, if caught unawares by the forces of bigotry, meanness, and terror, could be transformed into a dictatorship. As an editor, he is much disturbed by the quick growth of Huey Long's Louisiana empire and by Father Coughlin's ability to sway millions over the air.

These danger signals prompt Doremus to watch fearfully the swift rise to power of the noisiest of demagogues, Senator Berzelius Windrip, and his League of Forgotten Men. Aware of the speedy change which could topple a democratic government, Jessup nevertheless does not forsee how his own tall and hulking handyman, Shad Ledue, and other crude, sadistic zealots can help bring destruction to lovely Beulah Valley, as to the nation at large. Under Corpoism terrifying change does occur. Imprisoned in a concentration camp, Doremus "yearned for escape with a desire that was near to insanity; awake and asleep it was his obsession . . ." His eventual flight to Canada, to carry on in exile the fight for the preservation of "the free, inquiring, critical spirit," is the only way to save all that he holds dear. But he knows that "the men of ritual and the men of barbarism are capable of shutting up the men of science and silencing them forever."[52]

This is the gist of the controversial story for which Metro-Goldwyn-Mayer bought the film rights and had Sidney Howard do the script. Later it was rumored that the Film Production Code Administration had banned the film for fear of international complications. As Schorer's full account explains, in spite of certain pressure brought on the studio the film was not made, possibly for economic rather than political reasons. By October, 1936, however, another dramatization of the novel began to arouse interest. During the summer the directors of the Federal Theatre of the Works Progress Administration in Washington thought of a plan to produce *It Can't Happen Here*: a simultaneous opening of a new dramatization on October 20 in fifteen American cities. Although difficulties arose, the hastily written play form prepared by Lewis in collaboration with a Paramount screenwriter, John C. Moffitt, was ready for simultaneous production in eighteen cities on October 27. The play proved an immediate sensation, attracting large crowds everywhere, more for its political satire than for any great skill in dramaturgy.[53]

In its play form, as in the novel, *It Can't Happen Here* dramatizes the terrible intensity of a human dilemma occasioned by an almost overpowering political militarism. Generally in American small-town plays characters yearning for escape have been motivated by such causes as homelessness or an unhappy home life, the compulsive urge to be a hero, or ambition. For Doremus Jessup and his endangered group, leaving Fort Beulah and the country is a matter of saving their lives. To remain means imprisonment or death. With the increased spread of crimes of violence, such as the brutal killing of Dr. Greenhill, Jessup's son-in-law, of sadism, and of political imprisonment, Fort Beulah and Zenith citizens, like those elsewhere, must choose either active participation in the promotion of the new order, passive conformity, or a risky independence of thought and action. For the Jessups and other freedom-lovers a town, or a nation, dominated by agents of Corpoism becomes an intolerable hell. To escape certain doom they must exile themselves. Thus, escaping to Canada, Doremus joins an underground movement which has begun initiating counterattacks by propaganda and guerrilla warfare against the fascist "Big Brass." And he sadly realizes, too late, that "thus tyranny isn't primarily the fault of Big Business or of the demagogues. It's the fault of all the respectable Doremus Jessups that let the crooks come in without protest. I can't blame Buzz Windrip. It's us—the 'good' citizens." Awakening to his private duty, Doremus acknowledges that he must risk returning to the United States to do all within his power to preserve the spirit of inquiry, which "is more important than any pride, any party, any flag, red or white or striped."[54]

These various stage citizens in plays of the twenties and thirties, looking upon the "narrow but fascinating panorama" of small-town life with disfavor and for the most part eager to escape, resemble the real people described by Sherwood Anderson in *A Story Teller's Story* (1924). After much wandering, Anderson recalls, he had become "at last a writer, a writer whose sympathy went out to the little frame houses, on often mean streets in American towns, to defeated people, often with thwarted lives." Mostly the village escapists seen on our stages come from towns not unlike Winesburg, Ohio, which, as Anderson writes in his *Memoirs*, was no particular town. "It was a mythical town. It was people. I had got the characters everywhere about me, in towns in which I had lived, in the army, in factories, and offices."[55] So it was with other playwrights, most of them natives of small towns.

Anderson also describes the hegira from the small town to the city, which we have seen reflected in the plays we have discussed. "It has long been a legend," he wrote, "that every American small-town boy dreams of some day going away to live in the city. . . . He hungers to see the wonders in the world, to be an important figure out there."[56] In some plays "new things, new dreams in the heads of the boys in the towns" satisfy this hunger; in others, there is nothing but failure and despair. The neighborliness of the small town can be deceptive; Sinclair Lewis remembered from his Minnesota youth that "villages could be as inquisitorial as an army barracks," and that bitter memory found expression in his satires. The ultimate development of this dangerous quality of the small town is seen in *It Can't Happen Here*, which shows how, under certain circumstances, peaceful farming communities may be transformed into miniature arenas for the cruelest of political inquisitions.

IX. O'Neill's Lost Townsmen

"I know that life too darn well."

IN EUGENE O'NEILL'S autobiographical *The Straw* tubercular Stephen Murray, the young reporter hero, shares with Eileen Carmody, a fellow sanatorium patient, his dreams about a writing career. "I've had ideas for a series of short stories for the last couple of years—small town experiences, some of them actual. I know that life too darn well."[1] Actually there were periods when city-born O'Neill, whose birthplace was the Barrett House on Broadway at Forty-third Street in New York, did come to know certain aspects of American small-town life "darn well" from firsthand experience. When he was working on *The Straw* during the winter of 1918-19, he was living in a smaller place, West Point Pleasant, New Jersey, in the Old House belonging to Agnes Boulton, his second wife. At this time, too, he was not very far removed in years from his youthful experiences in several rural and small-town communities.

Numerous clues, both analyzed in such biographical studies as those by Doris M. Alexander, Arthur and Barbara Gelb, and Agnes Boulton, and utilized in about a dozen of the O'Neill plays, tell of the family's association with small-town life in Connecticut and elsewhere during the playwright's childhood and restless youth. The earliest such connection concerns New Haven, Connecticut, where O'Neill's beautiful and artistic mother, Ellen (Ella) Quinlan, was born in 1857. In his youth Eugene had some association with his mother's Connecticut relatives, the Brennans and the Sheridans, who later may have inspired some of his satiric provincial characterizations. During the years from 1895 to 1906, when handsome James O'Neill, Sr., his remarkable "road" actor father, and Mrs. O'Neill were constantly on tour to theatrical centers throughout the country, the lonely boy Eugene was placed in a succession of schools located in smaller communities. For a while, from 1896 to 1900, he was a boarding student at Catholic St. Aloysius Academy for Boys, an adjunct to Mount St. Vincent-on-Hudson, at Riverdale, New York. Here, as the Gelbs note, in the beautiful pastoral surroundings of the Bronx, Eugene developed an interest in nature, which was to be reflected in some of his provincial plays. Later, from September, 1902 to June, 1906, he attended and was graduated from Betts Academy in Stamford, Connecticut, spending his vacations with his parents and his elder brother Jamie at the family summer home at 325 Pequot Avenue, New London.

George Jean Nathan, who knew him as a friend for many years, once recalled that O'Neill was "essentially a man of the cities." Nevertheless, the small town appears repeatedly in his plays, most frequently reflecting his memories of local manners in New London and nearby Connecticut towns as he observed them during the period between 1912 and 1914. During August, 1912, two months before his ill-starred marriage to Kathleen Jenkins ended in divorce, Eugene was without income and so enervated by his illnesses on a gold expedition in Spanish Honduras that he came back to the New London cottage, "the closest the road-touring O'Neills ever came to a real home." For the next five months he worked as a cub reporter and a rewrite man for a friend of the family, Frederick P. Latimer, publisher and owner of the *New London Telegraph*. (Although Eugene's ill health made his resignation, on November 1, a necessity, he did not submit his last contribution—a poem, "To Winter"—until December 9.) Sympathizing with Eugene's intellectual delight in reading books and his religious unrest, Latimer generously gave his sardonic cub opportunities to cover the New London waterfront where he met various seafarers, to attend local meetings, to interview the town's leading citizens, and to write the "Laconics," a biweekly column of assorted prose and verse on the editorial page. Most of the verses were written by O'Neill himself, often in a satiric vein which reflected his rebellious and socialistic attitude toward society.

In late summer Eugene courted several local girls, the first being brunette Mabel Ramage, a pretty waitress in Stavros Peterson's elegant confectionary on State Street. As September was ending, Eugene, assigned to cover Bessie Young's wedding, met Maibelle Scott, a sheltered girl from one of the respectable New London families. His month-long love affair, largely "on an intellectual plane," with Maibelle was dramatically adapted, twenty years later, to Richard Miller and Muriel McComber's teen-age love situation in *Ah, Wilderness!* "While I in a dream abide," the title of one of the sentimental poems which Eugene addressed to Maibelle, described a happier aspect of his youthful experience with small-town living. Meantime there was his reporter's job to be done, and there were new acquaintances to deal with. Among these, Latimer—"the first one who really thought I had something to say, and believed I could do it"—used to enjoy arguing with Eugene about different philosophies, including socialism.[2] In their friendly chats the editor discovered "the most stubborn and irreconcilable social rebel I had ever met." Indeed, Latimer thought, this "was no ordinary boy," but a gifted youth "emphatically . . . different," whose "flashes in the quality of the stuff he gave the paper" moved Latimer to feel that Eugene possessed more than mere talent—"a very high order of genius."

Latimer's recognition of Eugene's imagination and keen wit, iconoclasm, and humanitarian sympathy for the underprivileged is balanced somewhat by the more astringent criticism of Malcolm Mollan. As city editor of the *Telegraph*, Mollan had difficulty in keeping Eugene's writing in line with ordinary newspaper standards. Readers of the *Telegraph* did not want literary accounts of local stabbings and similar disturbances which omitted the names of the participants. Nevertheless, Mollan recalled afterward—in an article for the Philadelphia *Public Ledger* on January 22, 1922—that his cub reporter, who once dashed about New London on assignments, even then gave promise of being "father to the man." In 1922 Mollan said he was not surprised that by then O'Neill had so developed his finely spun nature that he had become "as sensitive as a seismograph," bent on detecting the discords and maladjustments of human affairs.[3] Rather than dwelling on "happily placed characters," the young playwright was reaching out, far beyond the limits accorded the cub reporter, to discover submerged and victimized groups.

In 1913, when his tuberculosis case was considered arrested, Eugene left Gaylord Sanatorium to return to New London, where he spent the late spring and summer with his family at the Pequot Avenue cottage. During the autumn and winter of 1913-14, some nine or ten months of "reading, resting, exercising—and writing," he lived contentedly with the Rippins, an English family, in their Pequot Avenue boardinghouse— the Packard—overlooking the Thames River and Long Island Sound. Here in friendly association with three high-spirited daughters and motherly Mrs. Rippin, Eugene, in spite of the unfriendly manner of Mr. Rippin, found a pleasant environment conducive to relaxation, some casual lovemaking, and serious experimentation with playwriting.

By March, 1914, when he left the Packard, Eugene presumably had finished at least six one-acters and a full-length play. (His habit of destroying some of his early scripts and his later conflicting reports regarding the output of this apprenticeship period make an exact determination of the number of plays attempted and completed difficult.)[4] At any rate, among the plays written during his stay with the Rippins one at least gave a faint indication of his later interest in using small-town locales. This was *Abortion*, an unproduced one-acter reflective of his year at Princeton (1906-7) and of his guilty feelings about his unhappy marriage to Kathleen Jenkins and his disregard for their son, Eugene, Jr. Other New London experiences directed O'Neill, now twenty-five, toward further mental stocktaking. Continuing his wide reading already begun at Gaylord, he deepened and crystallized his mental patterns as he learned more about dramaturgic principles. His earlier reading of Shaw's *Quintessence of Ibsenism* influenced his scornful rejection of the happy endings then being demanded by admirers of Clyde Fitch and other contemporary playwrights. Also, the theories of Zola and Marx helped heighten his feeling that all too often economic pressures were used to exploit unfortunate "little people." During this exciting and burgeoning period Eugene discovered, from reading Dostoevsky's *The Idiot* and a recent translation of Strindberg's *The Dance of Death,* serious social attitudes which helped to shape his own developing artistic credo.[5] Strindberg's *Miss Julie*, with its suicide by hanging motif, and other plays guided O'Neill in his discovering beneath the surface of life the tensions motivating human behavior. In particular, he learned from Strindberg "how to discard realistic means altogether in order to project the mysterious forces that determine human life."[6]

Responsive chords also were struck as O'Neill gained further insight into the techniques of expressionism and dramatic symbolism from reading Wedekind's work. Nietzsche was still another literary guide who was to influence O'Neill's vision of life. But it was August Strindberg, as O'Neill acknowledged in his Nobel Prize speech of 1936, who "first gave me the vision of what modern drama could be, and first inspired me [during the winter of 1913-14] with the urge to write for the theatre itself."[7]

In his New London days, as his romance with Maibelle cooled, Eugene experienced another emotional involvement. In 1914 he fell in love again, this time with gray-eyed Beatrice Ash(e), the somewhat conventional daughter of Peter Ash(e), superintendent of New London's street trolleys. Her singing voice, high spirits, and charm delighted Eugene. Most of all, however, her willingness to listen sympathetically to his recitals of his private affairs—to his aspirations, his love poems addressed to her, his antagonism toward his father, and his radical political and religious views—gave him new confidence and inspiration to continue his writing experiments. His friendship with Beatrice, in spite of her father's displeasure, lasted well past September, 1914, when Eugene left New London for Cambridge to begin another phase of his development as a prospective playwright.

In this connection, New London was to give him still another friend in the drama critic Clayton Hamilton, who with his wife Gladys had a summer cottage there and enjoyed friendly chats with James O'Neill. In January, 1914, at Mrs. Rippin's boardinghouse, the Hamiltons had been attracted to shy, gifted, and restless Eugene. A bit later Eugene shyly came to the Hamilton cottage to ask Hamilton to criticize some of his apprenticeship plays and to offer hints about the proper construction of one-acters. Thus discovering Eugene's embryonic talent, Hamilton urged him to learn more about his "torturing trade" by studying with George Pierce Baker, director of the English 47 Workshop at Harvard.[8] At last, on July 16, Eugene, having with Hamilton's influence gained assurance of his father's financial support, wrote an application letter to Professor Baker, explaining his "ambition of becoming a playwright." Candidly reviewing his exact position, he referred to his experimentations with dramatic composition, noted a forthcoming collection of five plays (*Thirst and Other One Act Plays*, published in 1915 by the Gorham Press, Boston, on payment of $100 by James O'Neill), and mentioned not only his experiences as a seaman on merchant vessels but his wide reading in the field of drama.[9] Expressing dissatisfaction with his present training, which perhaps would make of him "a mediocre journey-man playwright," Eugene summed up his ideal: "I want to be an artist or nothing." As a prospective playwright, he felt that Professor Baker's seminar could offer him urgently needed professional training.

With Baker's approval, Eugene entered the Workshop class in September, remaining until May, 1915. As the Harvard experience progressed, New London gradually faded into the past, except for contacts by way of letters and occasional visits; nevertheless, the town left a deep imprint upon O'Neill's mind, for small-town motifs appearing in later plays are traceable to his memories of his youth in this Connecticut community.

In some of his small-town dramas, from *The First Man* to *Long Day's Journey into Night*, O'Neill utilized variations of the caste versus class motif reflecting his own family's lack of status in New London. Obviously, the four O'Neills were all different. As virtual newcomers to an old community, the O'Neills, in spite of Mrs. O'Neill's family connection with Connecticut, felt the sting of Yankee disapproval of stage people. The timeworn conflict between the established "nice people," proud of their cherished "respectabilities" (Ella O'Neill's term), and an actor's unconventional family set the O'Neills apart socially. Of course, they were not pariahs, as James's association with John McGinley and other friends proves. In fact, the narrowmindedness of New London society was not so apparent when the O'Neills first arrived in 1883. As the Gelbs have shown, in the beginning James and Ella seem to have been warmly received. "The snobbery that was to bedevil them developed later, with the influx of aristocratic summer residents."[10] It is true, however, that snobbish resort people, as well as the Yankee natives, Puritan and Anglo-American in their attitudes, looked with suspicion upon Irish-Americans, Portuguese, and other outsiders. Jamie often tauntingly called his father "an Irish bogtrotter" and, thoroughly bored by the "nice people," cynically declared that "whores were infinitely superior to 'nice girls.' "[11]

Puritan intolerance was again evidenced in the town gossip about Mrs. O'Neill's mysterious queerness, her unfortunate addiction to drugs which her husband and sons tried to ignore. Although Eugene enjoyed various social connections (some as a reporter) and several love affairs with respectable girls, New London leaders came to regard Jamie (by 1912 already turning hopelessly toward alcoholism and cheap women) and Eugene as "wild boys." Moreover, James, by candidly warning the Rippin girls against his sons' wildness, added to the unfavorable public picture. Also, while James O'Neill was reputedly quite affluent, he purchased for his family only a modest cottage at 325 Pequot Avenue, on the fringe of the better residential district. Such apparent parsimony did not endear him to the local theatrical colony, presided over by arrogant Richard Mansfield, who had purchased two fine estates where, in the assumed role of country gentleman, he gave lavish parties to which the O'Neills were never invited. James fared better otherwise by being admitted to the exclusive Thames Club and cordially accepted at the Crocker House, a large hotel on State Street. Among his hotel cronies, weathered Captain Nat Keeney, a yarner with uninhibited language, was the prototype for the whaling captain in *Ile* and Captain Turner in *Long Day's Journey into Night*.

Well-versed in maritime customs and lore through his own seafaring (1909, 1910-11, 1912), Eugene was fascinated by the tradition of sea history associated with this beautiful harbor town. As one of the busiest whaling ports in the world during the 1840's, it was topped only by New Bedford. During his days as reporter Eugene liked to listen to the yarns of old seamen he met along the wharves. The town's whaling history was later to be adapted to the action in *Ile* and *Diff'rent*. In addition, the town's economic activity growing out of shipping is pictured in connection with "the small New England seaport" where the Mannons "made a pile more in shippin' " and "started one of the fust Western Ocean packet lines." (*Homecoming*, Act I). And the columned mansion built by Abe Mannon—a monstrosity resembling a "pagan temple front stuck like a mask on Puritan gray ugliness"—resembles the places built in New England's seaports during the era of whaling prosperity.

O'Neill's provincial characters are rooted as to both time and place. They are given local habitations, generally in New England communities of limited range: seaport towns, college towns, and, less importantly, farm centers. Nevertheless, even the most highly individualized of his townsmen are "only secondarily, and for the sake of convenience, men and women specifically of a yesterday or a today and dressed in the mental or physical costumes of their period." Primarily, and often symbolically, they appear as "naked souls; forked radishes trying to be gods; helpless Lears exposed to the thunder of high heaven and the pitiless rain of God." Their very houses, their clothes, and their words, with which they vainly try "to conceal from themselves and others the real nature of their predicament," seem less real and substantial than the "sky of eternity . . . the only roof above them."[12] Generally his small-town characterizations reveal O'Neill's intensive explorations of provincial American experience and his deep concern for profound personal agitations and pressures. In these community plays as in others, his restless experimentation has put on stage bold new ideas, his versions of new techniques, and, when he is at his best, individualized but disenchanted townsmen, who on occasion try vainly to communicate not only with themselves but with God. Adapting expressionistic and other new techniques to his needs, he has taken various rebellious stands, satirizing a decaying Puritanism, ridiculing the complacencies of middle-class townsmen, and damning their "machine-worship, dollar-idolatry, and the entire cult of go-getting opportunism."[13] His many indictments against American materialism and other modern ills include exposures of circumscribed worlds wherein disturbed provincials are beset by tensions which make life well-nigh unendurable.

". . . a beginner—with prospects"[14]

In 1922 O'Neill declared in an interview, "Sure, I'll write about happiness, if I can happen to meet up with that luxury."[15] In dramatic composition that luxury largely escaped him, mainly because he felt keenly that "life is struggle, often, if not usually, unsuccessful struggle."[16] From the first, in his small-town plays as in others, his dramatic conceptions confirmed his tragic sense of life. Calamity, in one form or another, overtakes a number of the townspeople in these early plays. Always involved in dilemmas, they seem to suffer from the misery of existence. In particular, personal losses—of social reputation, love, religious faith, freedom, family happiness, and harmony—provide tragic symbols with which O'Neill experimented as early as 1913-14. The loss of hope furnished the theme for an unpublished four-act play, *Bread and Butter*.

A lost townsman, artistic John Brown of Bridgetown, Connecticut, by force of circumstance commits himself to domestic slavery when he marries a selfish philistine and begins working in her father's store. Thus losing his highest hope of becoming an artist, Brown shoots himself. In *Abortion,* another small-town play, O'Neill's theatrical imagination, toying with the shame of illegitimacy (a recalling of James O'Neill's youthful entanglement with Nettie Walsh) and of desertion (a reflection of his own desertion of Kathleen) focused upon what was to become a favorite theme, the motif of "servitude in love."

One of five experimental plays published in the unauthorized *Lost Plays of Eugene O'Neill* (1950), *Abortion* is a realistic one-acter, which in 1913-14 foreshadowed the ambivalences and tensions treated in later plays. It antedated *An American Tragedy* by a dozen years. Suggestive of the vaudeville sketch type of entertainment which flourished at the turn of the century, *Abortion* is a study of uneasy relationships and their inherent basic conflicts, as these develop in "a large eastern university in the United States" just before a championship baseball game. The young playwright, recalling his Princeton days, shows here a keen perception of college life during a time of exciting campus and town activities: a downtown parade, the championship game, quartet singing, "a canoe carnival, and bonfires, and dancing, and everything." This is the time, too, of conflict between students and "townies," the latter despising the Princetonians as a "lot of lazy no-good dudes spongin' on your old men." It is also the time of on-campus family reunions, such as the coming together of prosperous John Townsend, Mrs. Townsend, their vivacious teen-aged daughter Lucy, and their son's fiancée, socially proper Evelyn Sands. All have come to honor Jack Townsend, a campus hero at twenty-two. Evelyn's words of praise for his ballplaying are ironic: "It struck me," she sentimentalizes, "as symbolical of the way you would always play, in the game of life—fairly, squarely, strengthening those around you, refusing to weaken at critical moments, advancing others by sacrifices, . . ."[17]

What Evelyn does not know is that Jack is faced with the imminent loss of respectability and possibly of her love. Jack and his father, a kindly character resembling James O'Neill, alone know about the abortion performed a few days earlier on Nellie (a variant of "Nettie") Murray, a young secretary who had been seduced by Jack. Actually the paternity of the unborn child is uncertain, except to Jack, who is certain it would have been his. Mr. Townsend, in his own college youth "no St. Anthony," reminds his son that "we've retained a large portion of the original mud in our make-up." Jack's retort about his own dualism prefigures O'Neill's mature employment of the double, or divided, character—the *doppelgänger*—in *Days Without End* and *Strange Interlude*. The finer man in love with Evelyn and the grosser one—"the male beast who ran gibbering through the forest after its female"—symbolize a Jekyll-Hyde dualism in regard to sexual restraint, which, Jack quips, "everybody preaches but who practices it?"

Obviously *Abortion* is the work of a novice. A few elements, however, presage O'Neill's later position, far above that of "a mediocre journeyman playwright." For instance, the motif of dualism appears again in the satirically presented contrasts between two roommates: sensitive Jack Townsend and "Bull" Herron, "a huge, swarthy six-footer with a bull neck and an omnipresent grin, slow to anger and to understanding but—an All American tackle." The wide differences between college youths and "townies" of the 1913 era appear in the contrast between hero-worshipped Jack Townsend, in white flannels, and Nellie's tubercular brother, machinist Joe Murray. At the finale O'Neill creates a moving scene where the distraught brother, charging Jack with being a "dirty murderer," brings the news that Nellie has just died. Joe wildly threatens to tell the police about the abortion and tries to shoot Jack. Before the curtain falls, Jack gains possession of the pistol and kills himself. Outside the dormitory, crowds of students cheer him as their hero: "For he's a jolly good fellow!" Marked thus by violence in the last scene, this unproduced playlet remains as one of young O'Neill's dramatic rebuttals to the "all-pervading sunshine philosophy and childish evasion of grim reality" during the Mauve Decade.

Among the early one-acters foreshadowing O'Neill as a dramatist of failure, *The Rope* (1918) reveals the close relationship often existing between a small town—here a farming center and seaport—and its environing countryside, a relationship developed more artistically in *Beyond the Horizon* and *Desire under the Elms*. Primarily an ironic farm playlet, *The Rope* contains the germ of the tragic family complications which five years later frustrate the Cabots in *Desire under the Elms*. Old Abraham Bentley, a hard-bitten religious zealot, is kept alive by the unfatherly desire for a bitter revenge upon his prodigal and thieving son Luke. In the event of his return to the homestead, Luke is to inherit the farm, provided he atones for his sins by hanging himself with the rope which Abe has fastened to the barn rafters. Luke does return, not to claim the farm, but to torture Abe—"the damned son-of-a-gun"—into telling where he has concealed a bag of twenty-dollar gold pieces, a part of which Luke has stolen earlier. By an ironic turn of events, Luke's simpleminded niece, Mary Sweeney, accidentally discovers the bag, hidden on a rafter above the dangling rope. Skipping lightheartedly to the edge of a high cliff on the farm, the child gleefully tosses the shining hoard, coin by coin, into the ocean. This somber story of hate and greed, while restricted to a high headland, contains allusions enough to a nearby seaport to illustrate O'Neill's early preoccupation with small-town life, especially in its more unpleasant aspects. For instance, Annie Sweeney, old Abe's daughter, puritanically scorns her youthful stepmother, now dead, as "that harlot that was the talk o' the whole town!" with her "child [Luke] she *claimed* was your'n, and her goin' with this farmer and that, and even men off the ships in the port."[18] Thus servitude in love manifests itself in the inevitable conflict between cranky but lusty old Abe and his promiscuous young wife. Appropriately placed allusions to the taverns, the bank, the poorhouse, a lawyer's office, and the "country jays" in town for "Sunday meetin' " all suggest the reality of the seaport below the headland farm of the Bentleys.

If *The Rope* is a play of futility, *The Straw* (written also in 1918-19) once impressed Alexander Woollcott, reviewer of its premiere at the Greenwich Village Theatre on November 10, 1921, as being a "study of hope—hope in its most extraordinary and ironic manifestation." It is the hope of the tubercular—"the hope which is strongest and brightest on the very eve of death."[19] Based on young O'Neill's experiences as a reporter and a tubercular patient at Gaylord Sanatorium, *The Straw* presents a poignant romance of two youthful consumptives, Stephen Murray and Eileen Carmody, the roles originally enacted by Otto Kruger and Margalo Gillmore. While four of its five scenes have a crowded sanatorium as their background, the first act opens in "the kitchen of the Carmody home on the outskirts of a manufacturing town in Connecticut." As in so many of O'Neill's plays, action centers around a troubled family and the way it faces an unexpected dilemma. Bill Carmody, a drunken laborer whose overworked wife has been dead a year, with selfish cunning has turned over all household responsibilities to Eileen, the eldest of his "raft of children." Since her mother's death, Eileen by the very sweetness and unselfishness of her nature has held the family together as a unit. When tuberculosis forces her to enter a sanatorium, Eileen is in despair over the drunkenness of her father and the cowardice of her lover, Fred Nicholls. At the sanatorium she finds a fleeting happiness in her growing love for Stephen.

The theatrical appeal of the opening scene lies in the realistic portraits of an Irish workingman's large family, struggling to maintain itself economically in a small-town neighborhood. Divided characterization appears strongest in the two family strains: the coarser, fighting Carmody spirit, "Irish as Paddy's pig," and the bookish, sensitive Cullen nature of the dead mother manifested anew in Eileen and the delicate child Mary. There is appeal, too, in the humorous satire which unmasks Bill Carmody, with his self-pity, his whining tone of injury, and his pious unction when speaking to Dr. Stanton (a well-drawn portrait of a kindly small-town practitioner). Even the mésalliance between a laborer's daughter and the son of a manufacturer is shown with amusing satire, most of all in the picture of Fred, with his attitude of "man-about-small-town complacency," his fear of what people would say about him, and, in Bill's opinion, "no guts of a man in you." Most amusing, however, is the later full-blown portrait of Mrs. Brennan, the housekeeper replacing Eileen and later marrying Carmody. This masterpiece of satiric portrait painting angered O'Neill's New London relatives, the Brennans, though he claimed that the choice of name was accidental. And no wonder they were angry, for the domineering housekeeper is pictured as "a tall, stout woman, lusty and loud-voiced, with a broad, snub-nosed, florid face, a large mouth, the upper lip darkened by a suggestion of mustache, and little round blue eyes, hard and restless with a continued fuming irritation."[20] An equally satiric note marks Stephen Murray's devastating comments on the small town per se. Cynically describing his duties as reporter on "a small town rag," he confesses his boredom with a Gopher Prairie type of society:

"Getting the dope on the Social of the Queen Esther Circle in the basement of the Methodist Episcopal Church, unable to sleep through a meeting of the Common Council on account of the noisy oratory caused by John Smith's application for a permit to build a house; making a note that a tugboat towed two barges loaded with coal up the river, that Mrs. Perkins spent a week-end with relatives in Hicksville, that John Jones—Oh help! Why go on?"[21]

That's how Stephen, like reporter O'Neill, "knew everyone and everything in town by heart years ago." And such an indictment of "the village virus" antedated *Main Street* by a few years.

The year of 1920-21 was a season of triumphs for apprentice O'Neill. Contemporaneous with *Main Street,* two other community plays, *Diff'rent* and *The First Man,* with their stage pictures of village narrow-mindedness, intolerance, and false idealism, penetratingly interpreted the provincial New England mind and suggested what direction his creative mind was to follow. The Provincetown Players in their opening performance of *The Emperor Jones,* on November 3, 1920, at the Playwrights' Theatre and under the enthusiastic guidance of George Cram Cook, inspired Heywood Broun, in his *Tribune* review the next day, to praise O'Neill as "the most promising playwright in America." Shortly thereafter, on December 27, the Provincetowners, playing at the same theater, performed *Diff'rent,* a tragic two-acter laid in a New England whaling town in the 1890's and thirty years later. Of less artistic significance than *The Emperor Jones,* this naturalistically styled play (first titled *Thirty Years*) is memorable for O'Neill's further experimentation with maritime material and for his adaptation of the Strindbergian motif of sexual starvation to simple people in an American seacoast town. Not so successful was *The First Man,* written in 1921 but not produced until March 4, 1922, at the Neighborhood Playhouse by Augustin Duncan. But this was the period, too, of the production of *Gold* with its slight picturing of a California coastal community, of *The Straw,* and of *Anna Christie* in the summer and fall of 1921.

Diff'rent presents the tragedy of a sea captain's daughter, Emma Crosby, whose actual model was unmarried Lil Brennan, a relative of Ella O'Neill. Emma's story of self-imposed denial stems from her girlish idealization of the "high-fangled heroes in cheap novels" which she delighted in reading, as well as from something Puritan—a sort of Hawthornesque pride—in her temperament. From such influences she has a neurotic notion—springing from an idealistic view of sexual purity—that she and her fiancé, vigorous Captain Caleb Williams, are "different." When she insists that "You just got to be diff'rent from the rest" (the whalers of the village), Caleb uneasily answers, "Sailors ain't plaster saints, Emmer, . . ." Unfortunately, Emma's romantic dreaminess is coupled with a self-willed stubbornness. Two days before Emma and Caleb are to be married, after a three-year courtship, she chances to hear the rumor that on his "two-year whalin' vige" just ended he was seduced by a native girl of the South Sea Islands. Her pride in her ideal—her strange storybook notion about chastity—moves Emma to declare "I don't love—what he is now" and stubbornly refuse to take the marriage vows. Obsessed with the idea that Caleb must conform to a peculiar ideal of absolute purity, Emma shocks her family and the villagers by her intention to conform to the same extreme ideal. As Caleb, mystified by "Emmer's" queerness, starts a new voyage, this eccentric girl begins her inexplicable pursuit of the absolute. Like Miss Cather's Marian Forrester, she becomes "a lost lady." With the passing of thirty years, a self-imposed loneliness and spinsterhood become Emma Crosby's lot.

In her later anguish and increasing flightiness, Emma becomes more and more inarticulate in explaining her position to Caleb and his unromantic sister Harriet. Perhaps she was haunted by her mother's insistence in 1890 that "it'd be just like goin' agen an act of Nature for you not to marry him [Caleb]." After thirty years Emma's compulsive aberration has changed her into a sex-starved old maid, an easy dupe for scheming Benny Rogers, Caleb's glib young nephew. Benny's false proposals of love and marriage and his eventual cruel ridicule of her pitiful efforts to rejuvenate herself by wearing "new duds" finally lead Emma to realize the utter emptiness of her life. Her feeling of hopelessness becomes all the more poignant with faithful Caleb's final rejection of her and her differences. O'Neill's skill in dramatizing the final scene between Emma and Caleb, when she stuns him by blurting out her intention of marrying Benny, pictures a ridiculous older woman as becoming almost a tragic figure. ("Just because I'm a mite older'n him—can't them things happen just as well as any other—what d'you suppose?— can't I care for him same as any woman cares for a man?") Emma's cruel disillusion comes swiftly. Caleb, at last moved to the point of disgust, savagely declares that neither Emma nor Benny is worth any sacrifice which he could make. ("You ain't worth it—and he ain't—and no one ain't, nor nothin'. Folks be all crazy and rotten to the core and I'm done with the whole kit and caboodle of 'em. I kin only see one course out for me and I'm goin' to take it. 'A dead whale or a stove boat!' we says in whalin'—and my boat is stove!")[22] He rushes out to his barn and hangs himself. And Emma, taunted by Benny as "an old hen . . . that oughta been planted in the cemetery long ago!" moves like a sleepwalker, strangely whispering, "Wait, Caleb, I'm going down to the barn."

In dramatizing the tragic consequences of Emma Crosby's irrational flight from love, O'Neill, philosophical in his approach, is more preoccupied with her inner tensions than with any village, or regional, influence upon the shaping of her self-centered personality. The New England locale is merely coincidental, used as a dressing for his primary interest in emphasizing the differences between the real and the ideal— between reality and illusion—in human love. Nevertheless, the outward facts of the small town and its nautical inhabitants are there. Initially the village atmosphere is achieved in the realistic description of the properties for the first set: the scrupulously neat Crosby parlor on a Sunday in 1890. An old-fashioned piano, a clumsy marble-topped table, a bulky Bible with a brass clasp, and enlarged photographs of strained, stern-looking New Englanders all suggest the respectability of the Crosbys, whaling folk of long experience. The plain and sometimes humorous dialect of the Crosbys, Caleb, and other villagers contrasts sharply with the solemn family photographs. Actually these people are not sanctimonious and joyless Puritans. Captain Crosby, a Falstaffian seaman, and his son Jack are lusty whalers, akin to other "cussin' sailors" in their share of wickedness. Even the dialect spoken by Mrs. Crosby and Harriet is often earthy and filled with folk psychology.

While some critics have regarded *Diff'rent* as a mildly melodramatic "fable for Freudians," a study in perfectionism, and a warning against suppression, the fact remains that in this short tragedy O'Neill has skilfully created a seafaring family naturally adapted to its home environment, a recognizable elm-shaded whaling town, in the years between 1890 and 1920. Furthermore *Diff'rent* is a thematic link between past and future conceptions of sexual repression in connection with small-town people. Turning to the past, one may recognize in Emma's youthful refusal to submit to the life force a resemblance to Louisa Ellis, Mary E. Wilkins Freeman's New England "nun," who sacrificed love for a life of isolation. As for the future, this portrayal of a prudish, lonely, and sex-starved spinster is a forerunner not only of Lavinia Mannon and her strange fulfilment of the Mannon destiny but of Tennessee Williams' unhappy Alma Winemiller. As Doris V. Falk has shown, "In O'Neill's subsequent work the vengeance of nature upon Puritanic arrogance becomes a dominant motif."[23]

Another psychoanalytic and domestic play, *The First Man* (1921), is for the most part a satire on several types of lost or unhappy townspeople belonging to the "upper crust" in Bridgetown, Connecticut. The intellectually creative hero, Curtis Jayson, a recognized anthropologist governed by romantic idealism, loses his chance for marital happiness through his own egotistical illusions. In Act I he faces the greatest opportunity of his varied career when an invitation comes for him to participate in an Asian expedition to excavate what possibly may be the remains of "the first man." Since the tragic deaths of their two small girls, Curtis and his wife Martha, his unselfish and expert assistant, have been wandering so often on scientific trips that they have become "slave[s] to the Romance of the Rocks." Now driven by his work, which has taken the place of the children, Curtis selfishly expects Martha to accompany him to the Himalayas. For her part, Martha, though deeply in love with her husband, is gravely upset when he becomes furious at her confession of her pregnancy. Consumed by his possessive love and need for her, Curtis cannot bear the thought of sharing her affection with a child. In her final conflict between her desire for motherhood and Curtis' expectation that she will accompany him, Martha rejects his proposal for an abortion and at last dies in labor.

Among the lost townspeople are all the "high and mighty" Jaysons—

"a swarm of poisonous flies." According to their personal inclinations, they are lost to the forces of philistinism, envy, malice, vanity, snobbery, boredom, pride, and other evils attributed to "this rotten town." A faint light breaks into the general sunlessness of the play when Curtis' Cornell friend, Edward Bigelow, after his wife's death and under the influence of Martha's friendship, gives up his philandering, which shocked the town's prudes, and begins to enjoy the companionship of his children. Similarly, momentary happiness comes to Martha, whose discovery that a career in anthropology is not enough to offset the loss of her little girls intensifies her yearning for the happiness to come in loving her unborn child. At the finale, childless old Aunt Davidson "still remains [the] Jayson with unmuddled integrity." She alone happily consents to rear the baby boy for whom Martha died and to keep him free from "this obscene world" of the self-centered Jaysons. Immediately thereafter escapist Curtis, assured through his own usual egotism and possessive love that Martha as she lay dying has forgiven him, departs at last for "a big, free life" in Asia to search for "the first man." The question of whether his search will ever turn inward is not resolved.

On stage *The First Man*—one of his plays which O'Neill did not like —had no chance for success because unfair criticism of the childbirth scene gave the public the impression that the play was an obscene drama of gestation. Actually Martha Jayson's moaning during the agony of labor, as described in the script, was, in O'Neill's words, "painfully bungled" in production. Certain weaknesses, including mechanical flaws and Curt's unrealistic attitude toward parenthood—a reflection of young O'Neill's unconcern about his firstborn son—do detract from the play. But it has merits as well, quickly discernible to any reader familiar with the "first families" of a small town. Like Lewis, Anderson, and other contemporary interpreters of little worlds, O'Neill reveals here a keen understanding of the provincial mind. His Bridgetown, Connecticut, however, is no prairie village, but a larger place like New London, whose ruling families, such as the snobbish banking family of Jaysons, make fetishes of outward respectability and straitlaced standards in keeping with their social pretensions. The decadent "aristocracy" of this sizable New England town resembles somewhat the social decadence in Sarah Orne Jewett's Deephaven and the Massachusetts towns of Mrs. Freeman's stories. More significantly, the Jayson nature is as narrow-minded and as suspicious as the meanspirited temperament of the icebound Jordans of Veazie, Maine.

The satirical comedy throughout the opening act is as delightfully humorous as it is rare in O'Neill's plays. The family gathering for tea at Curt and Martha's home matches in realism and amusing, yet grim, humor the Jordan conclave which opens *Icebound*. As male head of the clan, John Jayson, stout and baldheaded at sixty, appears as a "typical, small-town, New England best-family banker, reserved in pose, unobtrusively important—a placid exterior hiding querulousness and a fussy temper." He shows the booster spirit by declaring that "Bridgetown isn't so bad, Martha, once you get used to us. . . . It's one of the most prosperous and wealthy towns in the U.S.—and that means the world, nowadays." John Junior looks like his father, but is "pompous, obtrusive, purse-and-family-proud." His "self-complacent air of authority, emptily assertive and loud," is most irritating especially to his younger sister Lily, a recent college graduate "full of nervous, thwarted energy" and rebellious against the petty pride and stultifying conventionalities of her family. Richard, who cannot forget his officer status during the war, is "a typical young Casino and country club member." Esther, Mark Sheffield's wife, middle-aged and stout, has "the round, unmarked, sentimentally contented face of one who lives unthinkingly from day to day, sheltered in an assured position in her little world." Mark possesses "the superficial craftiness of the lawyer mind." Among the other women of the conclave is Mrs. Davidson, at seventy-five looking "like some old lady in a daguerreotype," old-fashioned, unbending, and rigorous in manner. Quite a contrast to sweet-tempered and intellectual Martha, mouselike Emily, John Junior's wife, conceals beneath "an outward aspect of gentle, unprotected innocence a very active envy, a silly pride, and a mean malice." According to Lily's barb, these form the Grand Fleet, now moving in for "the first wave of attack."

And the butt of their tribal attack is the stranger in their midst, Martha, the daughter of a gold-mining engineer. Aunt Davidson constantly identifies Martha's father as a coal miner, beneath the notice of the lordly Jaysons. Martha's refusal to conform to the conventions of the family—and the town—makes her an open target. When Curt calls his wife from the drawing room Lily "spills the beans" about Martha's pregnancy. Then as John hints that Bigelow may be the father, the family circle becomes uneasy about the possibility of a scandal which would taint the Jayson name. (Later Bigelow derisively terms the Jaysons "the aboriginal natives of Bridgetown"—of "this stagnant hole"—who with others in this, "my native town, did me the honor of devoting its entire leisure for years to stinging me [like a swarm of mosquitoes] to death!") Persecuted by the family backbiting, Martha, with a sudden burst of courage, acidly questions their innuendoes about the low moral standards of her native town of Goldfield, Nevada: "Then you believe broadmindedness and clean thinking are a question of locality?" Thus the outsider, much like O'Neill in New London, triumphs over the "big frogs in tiny puddles." Such satire throughout the first act scores a triumph for O'Neill, too, largely for its astringent appraisal of a "Philistine small town," whose "very dull and deadly" first family, individually hypocritical and smug, looks "like a League of Nations" in judgment against Martha, the nonconformist within their circle.

By June, 1920, when *Beyond the Horizon* was named the Pulitzer Prize play, O'Neill was moving, sometimes to the tune of critical disparagement, beyond the limits of his self-styled status of "a beginner—with prospects." As early as 1918 theatrical historian Arthur Hornblow had granted that O'Neill was "a young playwright to be reckoned with." Some of the reviews of *Diff'rent* and other early small-town dramas credited him with having achieved a qualified dramatic effectiveness and having shown ample signs of ability and inventiveness. Reviewers acknowledged, too, his daring exploration of raw materials, including certain aspects of provincial life, the reality manifest in his character drawing, and his approach to craftsmanship, though this was often criticized as rugged and uneven. Some critics found the moods of these plays poignant and dramatically appealing; others thought them lifeless and monotonous. Signs of critical disfavor were relatively frequent, from play to play, with critic-spectators complaining about O'Neill's overemphasis on morbidity, human frailties, and violence, as in *Abortion*, *Diff'rent*, and *The First Man*. Maida Castellun, reviewing *Diff'rent* for the New York *Call* on January 14, 1921, granted that it was "an interesting sex psychology study," but objected to the hero's dying from " 'O'Neillitis' which is instinct for violent death rather than one from character or situation." Even as late as February, 1925, on the occasion of the Provincetowners' revival of *Diff'rent,* the critic for the *New York Telegram & Mail*, protesting against O'Neill's unhappy mood, felt that "Emma Crosby is probably the most enraging feminine creature a playwright ever conceived."

Though such critical "fouls along with the hits" tended to minimize his achievements, O'Neill's youthful handling of small-town materials, as of other subject matter, actually showed some promising treatments of a variety of social concepts, themes, provincial types and their tensions, and town locales. His dramatization of several phases of personal experience, such as his life in New London, foreshadows the "tragic dreams" of *Long Day's Journey into Night* and other mature plays. With each successive season O'Neill seemed to be achieving a certain importance, and often notoriety as well, as *The Emperor Jones* (1920),

The Hairy Ape (1922), *Anna Christie* (Pulitzer Prize, 1922), *All God's Chillun* (1924), and *Desire under the Elms* (1925) went into production. By 1925, when the innovational *Strange Interlude* was staged, O'Neill had made the transition from his beginning stage, with its experimentation with short plays and mostly conventional techniques (though some reference to masks and other new motifs appear), to the period of more philosophical ideas and new and often strange dramaturgy. In Heywood Broun's words, "a new Puritan of the theatre, finding man basically evil," had arrived.

"An artist or nothing"

One of the young critical insurgents of the 1915 era and later, Van Wyck Brooks, in *America's Coming-of-Age*, disparaged the "culture of industrialism" and its "crude, chaotic manifestations of the present day." Earlier an age of pioneering, unleashing the acquisitive instincts of men, had failed, he said, to promote the spirit of a living culture. And the spirit of the fifty years before 1915 had failed to produce "a living, active culture, releasing the creative energies of men." Rather, the push of material enterprise had so diverted these energies as "to prevent the anarchical, sceptical, extravagant, dynamic forces of the spirit from taking the wind out of the myth of 'progress' . . ." Our general cleverness, "gilding and idealizing everything it has touched," cannot be "the index of a really civilized society." We cannot, Brooks argued, "motivate the American scene and impregnate it with meaning" under the prevailing repressions of acquisitive enterprise. "For the creative impulses of men are always at war with their possessive impulses, and poetry . . . springs from brooding on just those aspects of experience that most retard the swift advance of the acquisitive mind." Americans, he warned in 1915, must remember that "literature is the vehicle of ideals and attitudes that have sprung from experience . . . that release the creative impulses of the individual and stimulate a reaction in the individual against his environment."[24] Under the pressures of an industrial society, such an objective is difficult to achieve.

Also in protest against the stultification of the spirit, H. L. Mencken joined with Brooks and other critics of the twenties in destroying the myth of democratic man as the complete citizen of the Kingdom of Dollarica. In his *Notes on Democracy* (1926), Mencken, while adding nothing new to his political philosophy, further aired his acidulous though amusing "prejudices" about the genus *American boob*. His fabulous dunce—the reverse of Whitman's optimistic portrait of democratic man —is "more ignorant of elementary anatomy and physiology than the

Egyptian quacks of 4000 B.C." Worst of all, "the fine arts are complete blanks" to the Menckenian boob. In short, "this character is an ideal monster, exactly like the Yahoo of Swift, and it has almost the same dreadful reality."[25] Some months earlier another critical gadfly, Upton Sinclair, in *Mammonart* arraigned the lack of personal integrity among artists who, he charged, have always been willing to sell their talents to Mammon. In 1924, in *Sticks and Stones*, Lewis Mumford had interpreted American civilization and art in terms of the monotony of native architecture.

But, as Brooks emphasized, "Only the creative mind can really apprehend the expressions of the creative mind." Much later Alfred Kazin was to describe this maligned "Dreadful Decade" as a challenge to those youthful creators with the courage to act: "In a country infested with Comstockery and Prohibition snoopers, monkey trials, and women's clubs prejudices, it was for the new generation to battle for freedom and the rights of personality."[26] Among the vigorous creative minds who dared resist the stranglehold upon the popular mind of the new Puritanism of the Menckenian "booboisie" and the ballyhooed doctrine of "Pragmatic Acquiescence," O'Neill repeatedly proved himself, during the twenties, a gifted rebel against the demands of a materialistic society. Accordingly, in his small-town plays of this decade his artistic energies were displayed in repeated denunciation of mass materialism. If in *The First Man* he had exposed most satirically the philistinism rampant in Bridgetown, Connecticut, by 1923-24 O'Neill had intensified his brooding about his own struggles as an artist in Philistia and his bitterly regretted acceptance of money and fame.

Such an inward searching goaded him into the composition of two complex plays—*Marco Millions* and *The Great God Brown*—which dramatized the dilemmas facing the sensitive philosophic man or the artist under mechanism and its attendant ills. As Matthew Josephson wrote in 1930, "The eternal drama for the artist becomes *resistance to the milieu*, as if the highest prerogative were the preservation of the individual type, the defense of the human self from dissolution in the horde."[27] In O'Neill's small-town characterizations of this prolific period, Dion Anthony and other O'Neill-like protagonists often take flight from the "Practical Realities" favored by the many. Pragmatic young "Marco of the Millions" is ridiculed as boasting to his ladylove that in the future he hopes to "have a million to his credit" and to be able to afford "a big wedding that will do us credit." Later in Cathay the great Kublai comes to regard him as a clown, who "has not even an immortal soul, he has only an acquisitive instinct." Threatening to send him back to Venice ("his native wallow"), the Kaan scorns Marco as a westerner who "has memorized everything and learned nothing," who "has looked at everything and seen nothing," who "has lusted for everything and loved nothing. He is only a shrewd and crafty greed." Dion Anthony, on the other hand, alive to emotional experiences, confesses to his youthful love for "music and rhythm and grace and song and laughter . . . [and] life and the beauty of flesh and the living colors of earth and sky and sea."

While the phenomena of America's industrial wealth and its spiritual poverty were being debunked during the twenties, O'Neill himself came to know the financier Otto Kahn, a donor to the Provincetown Players. Developing a dislike for Kahn, O'Neill came to regard the man as typifying one of the corroding influences of a mechanized civilization: the contemptible Great American Businessman. Perhaps he may have been irritated by Kahn because moneygrubbing James O'Neill, enriching himself through real estate and other transactions, annoyed his sons by his bent toward material wealth. At any rate, George Jean Nathan once wrote that O'Neill's dislike deepened when Kahn turned his "haughty critical shoulder" upon *The Great God Brown*. Asking why O'Neill did not use his talents more effectively in writing a play "apotheosizing American big business and the American business man," Kahn eventually was to receive a scoffing answer in *Marco Millions,* whose sardonic humor and tragic undertone gave "the most magnificent poke in the jaw that American big business and the American business man ever got."[28] This incident led O'Neill to develop a Babbitt-like theme which he had been mulling over for some years, pursuing from another angle the idea of the degenerative effects of materialism which he had adapted to *The Emperor Jones* and was to use again in *The Great God Brown*. Of these several plays, closely linked by subject matter, *The Great God Brown* alone portrays a town background as an environmental factor shaping the characters of the key trio involved.

Here, as elsewhere in O'Neill's dramas, the barriers which sensitive and frustrated characters have to throw up against the overwhelming material forces that have beleaguered them are of more dramatic moment than the evocation of community scene. And in this play, for the first time, O'Neill made full-scale use of masks to suggest the defenses which an individual must put up for protection against a crass world. On the other hand, the masking and unmasking of the characters, as changes and conflicts come into their lives, have enough relation to their outward environment to warrant an examination of the town itself.

Stage directions and other evidence reveal that Dion Anthony, Margaret his wife, and William (Billy) Brown are natives of a now sizable town, somewhat resembling Lewis' Zenith, which has increased in size since the childhood of these principal characters. With the material progress of the years, the town has become a place of sufficient outward prosperity to boast of a new municipal building, imposing office buildings, expensive churches, schools, banks, a casino, and other structures suggestive of New London. There are resident architects and contractors, designers and builders of solid residences, the symbols of a prosperous, bourgeois culture, as are their stereotyped furnishings—heavy leather armchairs, expensive tables, and "bookcases filled with sets, etc." Like the New London of 1912 and earlier, this imaginary town also has its brothels, as shown by the tawdrily furnished "parlor" of Cybel, a prostitute.

An automatic, nickel-in-the-slot player-piano is at center, rear. On its right is a dirty gilt secondhand sofa. At the left is a bald-spotted crimson plush chair. The backdrop for the rear wall is cheap wall-paper of a dull yellow-brown, resembling a blurred impression of a fallow field in early spring. There is a cheap alarm clock on top of the piano.[29]

This set, thus equipped to create an effect of cheapness, is a reminder of Jamie O'Neill's initiating youthful Eugene into the worldly ways of the often-raided brothels once located on Bradley Street, in New London's redlight district.[30] (Later in *Ah, Wilderness!* O'Neill was to use a similar set simulating the bar in a cheap hotel for teen-aged Richard Miller's fiasco with an older prostitute.)

Throughout the town various marks of progress abound, such as signs, in the spirit of Babbittry, suggesting local interest in "uplift, sunshine, popular pragamatism, [and] the gospel of advertising, or plain business." In the Prologue, as the two sets of parents, the Anthonys and the Browns, stroll away from the high-school commencement dance and converse about the future of Dion and Billy, American popular worship of "Practical Realities" is reflected in what they say about a college education as a sure key to worldly success. Their individual plans for each boy's future illustrate their easy surrender of humanistic values at the demand of pragmatic circumstance. Each couple seems to be groping for measurements to establish a scale of values in the material territory that surrounds them. Father Brown sets the pattern for his son's success as an architect by his jubilant prognostication: "Billy's got the stuff in him to win." On the other hand, Father Anthony, another reminder of James O'Neill, scorns colleges as the spawning grounds of

"lazy loafers to sponge on their poor old fathers! Let him [the poetic and imaginative Dion] slave like I had to! That'll teach him the value of a dollar! College'll only make him a bigger fool than he is already! I never got above grammar school but I've made money and established a sound business. Let him make a man out of himself like I made of myself!"[31]

The two parental views, obviously, are simply different patterns of the American dream of success.

Amid shifting scenes in this materially prosperous and progressive town there is played out a baffling, complex tragedy of the profundities and mysteries of modern life. A partially autobiographical dramatization, *The Great God Brown* is also a "study in masks" and "an exercise in unmasking" presenting the concept of the multiple self as it concerns the lives of two diametrically different friends: sardonic Dion Anthony, whose face when unmasked is "dark, spiritual, poetic, passionately super-sensitive, helplessly unprotected in its childlike, religious faith in life," and Billy Brown, in youth "handsome, tall, and athletic . . . with the easy self-assurance of a normal intelligence." Together these two exemplify the themes of character division and dissociation which fascinated O'Neill. Here in a small world of practicalities the artist-hero, Dion, appears as a divided man—a schizoid—caught in the grip of the material-istic forces which have a devastating effect upon his creative spirit. Through the years of his marriage to Margaret, his fatherhood, his paint-ing, and later his architectural designing, Dion's tragedy becomes a soul-stifling daily struggle to exist in Philistia.

The fourteen-year-long struggle endured by artistic, erratic Dion begins on the evening of his high-school commencement dance, when he declares his love for Margaret, who is also loved by his classmate, Billy Brown. Introduced thus in a prologue, which also furnishes the parental and boy-hood backgrounds of the two friends, Dion dominates the action until the finish of the second act, when he dies unmasked in Brown's library, but not until he has defiantly willed his mask to his astonished friend. For the past seven years Dion, whose maladjusted life has been darkened by his gambling and drinking, has found understanding and comfort only in the presence of Cybel, a sympathetic prostitute who, unlike Margaret, prefers seeing him without his usual mocking mask of Pan. Through the years, as Dion's pain and self-torture have increased, the Pan quality of his mask has become Mephistophelean. In the struggle between faith and dissipation—between Saint and Satan, according to Edwin A. Engel—for the possession of his soul, Dion tries to endure the offensive bourgeois ways prevailing in the world of "the Great God Mr. Brown." Comfortable in Cybel's presence without his mask, Dion calms his fears of death and transfers his "fixation on Mama Christianity" to Mama Earth, or Cybel.

Throughout the third and fourth acts, Brown, who though a successful builder and architect has needed the aid of Dion's artistic genius, assumes

Dion's mask, and hence his personality. Afterward, he poses sometimes as Dion and Margaret's husband, and again appears as himself, until his own death, five weeks later, in the arms of Cybel, who muses with "profound pain" about the everlasting cycle through which Everyman must pass: "Always spring comes again bearing life! Always again! Always, always, love and conception and birth and pain again—spring bringing the intolerable chalice of life again."[32] Thus a modern cycle of life, molded to a community pattern and portraying "the conflicting tides in the soul of Man," comes to a close, except for a brief epilogue bringing attention once more to Margaret, with her memories. Appearing again on the same pier beside the Casino where long ago she and Dion pledged their troth, Margaret, sweetly sentimental in the presence of her three sons, wears her mask of "the proud, indulgent Mother" who "knows her life-purpose well accomplished."

Keys to the individual natures of these masked overlapping characters may be found in O'Neill's "Memoranda on Masks" and his frequently cited notes interpreting the symbolical pattern of the play. In the "Memoranda" he notes that the technique of masks enables a playwright to express "those profound hidden conflicts of the mind which the probings of psychology continue to disclose to us." He asks, too, "For what, at bottom, is the new psychological insight into human cause and effect but a study in masks, an exercise in unmasking?" Explaining his provocative theme of man's potential and actual multiple self, O'Neill calls attention to the connotative names which he chose for his people:

Dion Anthony—Dionysus and St. Anthony—the creative pagan acceptance of life, fighting eternal war with the masochistic, life-denying spirit of Christianity as represented by St. Anthony—the whole struggle resulting in this modern day in mutual exhaustion—creative joy in life for life's sake frustrated, rendered abortive, distorted by morality from Pan into Satan, into a Mephistopheles mocking himself in order to feel alive; . . .

Margaret becomes O'Neill's "image of the modern direct descendant of the Marguerite of *Faust*—the eternal girl-woman with a virtuous simplicity of instinct, properly oblivious to everything but the means of maintaining the race." By contrast, Cybel is to be regarded as "an incarnation of Cybele, the Earth Mother doomed to segregation as a pariah in a world of unnatural laws . . ." The most satiric portrait of Brown appears as that of "the visionless demi-god of our new materialistic myth—a Success—building his life of exterior things, inwardly empty and resourceless, an uncreative creature of superficial preordained social grooves, a by-product forced aside into slack waters by the deep main current of life-desire."[33] Except for Margaret, these characters seem doomed to utter and irrevocable frustration in their individual striving for worldly success, for love, for achievement in artistic enterprise and creation, for the attainment of poetic and spiritual fulfilment, and for life-desire, "in the subtlest and deepest reaches of man's soul."

In this most penetrating and poetic play O'Neill goes back to the secret springs of psychoanalysis—to the parental backgrounds, the childhood, the inadequacies, and the stifled yearnings of his characters. A refrain of phrases, such as "The nights are so much colder than they used to be," helps turn the action back into a complete cycle and ties the epilogue to "that same sense of aching inevitability, youth without wisdom and world without end, as in the prologue." But O'Neill's dependence upon Freudian psychology and the mechanical techniques of asides, masks, soliloquies, and refrains extended far beyond the *The Great God Brown* of 1926.

Two years later, in the Theatre Guild production of *Strange Interlude* at the John Golden Theatre, spectators were again affected variously by another O'Neill innovation in dramatizing the intricate, relentless discord of personalities—his method of "double talk" or "double voice" revealing the inner selves behind the masks. As Joseph Wood Krutch reported in the *Nation* for February 15, 1928, no play of recent years had aroused so much preliminary speculation as had *Strange Interlude*. When its year and a half production first began, the play's odd triple method of dialogue, its extraordinary five-hour playing time, and its frank dramatization of the sexual compulsions of "Eternal Woman" really "split the critics." Some scorned it as "a theatrical monstrosity" and "an elaborate clinical psychological study," while others reviewed its nine-act probing of the neurotic mind of a nymphomaniac as "an interesting stunt." Critic John Anderson saw the play as "a profound drama of the subconscious," as did Richard Dana Skinner, who, impressed by its probing "deeply and terribly into the recesses of a neurotic mind," thought it "a dramatic novel." As both favorable and unfavorable criticism continued, *Strange Interlude*, enhanced by the superb acting of Lynn Fontanne, Earle Larimore, Glenn Anders, and Tom Powers, as well as by the artistry of set designer Jo Mielziner, proved a great popular success. Its 432 performances in New York were topped by a successful tour and the winning of the Pulitzer Prize.

Brooks Atkinson, in his opening night review for the *New York Times*, on January 31, 1928, spoke of the unoriginal story as lacking the importance of the experimental technique. Krutch, in his review for the *Nation*, queried: "Does O'Neill say anything worth saying in such unusual technique?" He believed so. Actually, however, the people dealt with are ordinary enough, though fortune or misfortune leads some of them far away from their small-town origins to cosmopolitan, and even foreign places. The story, divested of O'Neill's verbal power and stream-of-consciousness techniques, is basically a frank psychological study of a passionately possessive woman, for whom promiscuity becomes the normal thing. Its nine acts analyze contemporary American life in the light of "the anguish of Everywoman," as exemplified in the intimate relations of Nina Leeds, from youth to middle age, with the several men who influence her life.

The first of these relationships establishes the domination of Nina's father, a professor of Greek and Latin in a small university town in New England. Stern and protective toward Nina throughout her childhood, Professor Leeds, governed by his natural tendency toward a prim provincialism and a sense of possessiveness, continues his domination well past her twentieth birthday. Determinedly, he meddles with her plans to marry her aviator lover, Gordon Shaw, who then is killed in France. Embittered and anguished, Nina blames herself for having refused to give herself to Gordon. She does, however, reluctantly forgive her father, for he is still the symbol of reality of her life, as he continues to be for years afterward. But she cannot forget that Gordon was for her a symbol both of love and of escape from her meddling father.

Her deep emotional disturbance prompts Nina to choose another way of escape. In Act II she leaves the town to become a nurse, returning only after her father's death. During her year of service in a sanatorium, Nina tries to rid herself of an agonized feeling of "cowardly treachery toward Gordon" by a compulsive sexual promiscuity. Believing that "I must learn to give myself, . . . give and give until I can make that gift for a man's happiness without scruple, without fear, without joy except in his joy!" she "sacrifices" her body to wounded and crippled veterans.

When she returns to the town and her dead father's comfortable home, Nina has become disillusioned and cynical, disturbed by her futile search for God and happiness. "I tried hard," she says, "to play to the modern science God." To Charles Marsden, a neighbor and one of Professor Leeds's former students, Nina's "eyes seemed cynical . . . sick with men . . . as though I'd looked into the eyes of a prostitute . . ." Wounded in spirit, Nina has come to cynical disbelief in a God who cares nothing "about our trifling misery of death-born-of-birth." She shocks Marsden, a mother-dominated bachelor, by declaring that "the mistake began when God was created in a male image." Life, thus perverted, might have been happier, she argues, if mankind had "imagined life as created in the birthpain of God the Mother." (Here is a reminder of the image of Cybel,

in *The Great God Brown,* as the Earth Mother.) Disturbed by her outburst, "dear old Charlie" Marsden thinks of his own secret love for Nina,
ironically envisioning her, not as a whore, but as "my girl . . . not woman
. . . my little girl . . . and I am brave because of her little girl's pure love."
He is horrified, therefore, when she confesses "the stupid, morbid business" of her wartime sluttishness. Charlie's answer, delivered in profes-
sorial tones resembling her father's voice, is to advise her to marry diffi-
dent, good-natured young Sam Evans, whom she does not love, with the
reminder that Sam needs a helpmate to inspire him in making a career
for himself and that "when children come, love comes, you know."

Though Nina has asked cynically, "What's the use of bearing children?" after marrying Sam she enjoys a measure of happiness in discovering her pregnancy, until she learns from Sam's mother than the Evans
family has a secret curse of hereditary insanity. In her frantic fear she
resorts to abortion, but still is unhappily maladjusted until she enters into
a scientific liaison with young Dr. Ned Darrell, a neurologist, so that he
may father the child she now wants desperately. But this dispassionate
and scientific arrangement does not last, for Ned and Nina fall in love.
When their son Gordon is born, Sam is led to think that the child is his.
Passionately acquisitive, Nina at first desires to keep both lover and
child for herself. Ned, disturbed by her possessiveness and irritated by his
guilt, thwarts her plan to divorce Sam by announcing his intention of
going abroad at once for a lengthy sojourn.

During the twenty-five years of the action, young Gordon, regarding
Sam as his real father, loves him, but, quite ironically, has a strong dislike for Ned. During these years Nina fills her need for love through her
son, but characteristically exploits him also and, in the manner of her
own father, dominates young Gordon to the point of trying to stop his
marriage to Madeline. In the climax scene at the close of Act VI, Nina
contemplates her happiness in the light of her three men, whose "desires
converge in me! . . . to form one complete beautiful male desire which
I absorb . . . and am whole . . . they dissolve in me, their life is my life
. . . and the fourth man! . . . little man . . . little Gordon! . . . he is mine
too." Her pride of possession is soon cut short. Dr. Darrell, returned
after travel and research, discovers that he no longer loves Nina with the
old passion. Gordon defies her by marrying Madeline and leaving. Her
father is long since dead. Only the novelist—"dear old Charlie" with his
sexlessness—is left, after Sam dies. By Act IX Nina, connecting him
psychologically with her father, has at last decided to marry Marsden.
Then it is he, forgiving and paternal, who suggests that his "dear Nina
Cara Nina," now well into middle age, forget the Gordons. "So let's

you and me forget the whole distressing episode, regard it as an interlude,
of trial and preparation, say, in which our souls have been scraped clean
of impure flesh and made worthy to bleach in peace." And Nina, now no
longer able to struggle with herself or the images of the Father and the
Mother which have baffled her, muses thoughtfully: "Strange interlude!
Yes, our lives are merely dark interludes in the electrical display of God
the Father."[34]

As in *The Great God Brown*, the cycle now returns to its beginning.
Nina, long resident on the Evans estate on Long Island, yearns to return
to the university town of her childhood and youth "to rot in peace." Sick
of "the fight for happiness" and "those interludes of passion," she feels
now that "it will be a comfort to get home—to be old and to be at home
again at last—to be in love with peace together—to die in peace!" All of
this, of course, with "dear old Charlie," who—so his thoughts run—
"passed beyond desire, has all the luck at last."

Once, in commenting on dramatic technique, O'Neill remarked, "If I
thought there was only one way, I should be following the mechanistic
creed—which is the very thing I condemn." So it was that in writing the
innovational *Strange Interlude* O'Neill strove "to be an artist or nothing," experimenting freely in the process with ways of dramatizing both
the outer lives and the mental processes of a particular group of lost
townsmen. His continual quest for newness led him to use unusual forms
and to revamp the familiar asides and soliloquies. Searching for a deeper
way to communicate the thoughts of each character, he adopted a triple
method of speaking, so untried that seven weeks of rehearsal were required of the Theatre Guild players. First, each character, using ordinary dialogue, presented to his associates the outward "persona." Then
from scene to scene, in moments of lonely introspection, the hidden or
masked self found expression through a variant of the more conventional soliloquy. A third means of revealing individual hidden motives
and tensions was a sort of interior monologue—a personal criticism and
analysis by which each person reveals himself as being either in accord
with or at variance with the comments just spoken aloud. Thus the spectator immediately learns what each character secretly thinks and feels.

This triple technique posed production problems for director Philip
Moeller. Rejecting other schemes, he finally adopted the method of "arrested motion," a "sound-without-activity" procedure, which called for
the momentary cessation of all actual physical action and ordinary dialogue.[35] For the actors there was the added burden of learning to assume
a stiff and unnatural stance and to control facial muscles and voice during the recital of these interior monologues. But O'Neill insisted on the

best effect to show that "my people speak aloud what they think and what others aren't supposed to hear. They talk in prose—realistic or otherwise—blank verse or hexameter or rhymed couplets."

However novel the triple approach may have been, this unconventional method was not solely responsible for the play's success. As Barrett H. Clark observed, ". . . it is no more nor less than the triumph of O'Neill's art, his amazing gift for understanding and laying bare some of the complexities of the human mind and heart" which caused various critics witnessing the Guild production to recognize *Strange Interlude* as the greatest American play up to that time. Nevertheless, the length and the number of the interior monologues, while useful in fully analyzing the human mind, grow repetitious and tedious, notably after the sixth-act climax. The last three acts, with personalities recurring, as in the Gordon myth, have impressed spectators as unnecessarily burdensome and unwieldy. Sometimes the action is lost in a maze of rhetoric. It would seem that the histrionic talent of the original cast of seasoned players could have suggested by gestures or other means the gist of some of the lengthy stream-of-consciousness matter. Nina Leeds's neuroses and obsessions, like the disturbances of the other characters—notably Marsden's Oedipus complex and Darrell's cynicism arising from the sacrifice of his fatherhood—seem overly introduced and reintroduced. Some have objected to the portrait of the simpleminded businessman Sam Evans as resembling too much the picture of William Brown. Beyond these objections, however, there is the genuine achievement in *Strange Interlude* of a twentieth-century allegory exploring with deep insight the yearnings and temptation of the modern American woman. Even more, the play is a penetrating community history exposing the unfulfilment and predicament of a whole generation of New England townspeople, all questing, according to their individual needs, for personal happiness in times of social crisis.

In 1928-29, as the booming twenties neared the stock market debacle which ushered in the "bitter thirties," O'Neill was beginning his three-year exile in Europe and the Far East. During this period he became increasingly disturbed by his domestic broil with Agnes—a conflict ending in divorce on July 2, 1929—by his love affair with Carlotta Monterey, whom he married on July 22 of that year, and by the widespread feeling in the United States that "this is the best of times." Though social satirists in America were exposing the scandals of the bootlegging and racketeering element and ridiculing the recklessness of "flaming youth" —jazzy flappers and fur-coated, irresponsible rich boys—people at large appeared thoughtlessly cheerful and optimistic about the prospects for a continuing prosperity. As the national income mounted, so did the good feeling that boom days were here to stay. Under conditions such as these O'Neill, as an angry artist and upset person, looked at life steadily and found it tragic. It is no wonder then that *Dynamo*, completed in 1928, meant to him later something "written at a time when I shouldn't have written anything."

Perhaps he was right, for the play, when first produced by the Guild at the Martin Beck Theatre on February 11, 1929 generally received unfavorable press notices. At any rate, in *Dynamo* O'Neill gloomily extended his diagnosis of "the sickness of today as I feel it" along some of the lines of innovation heralded in *The Great God Brown* and *Strange Interlude*. Intended as the first part of a projected but never completed trilogy, *Dynamo* portrays a provincial youth's religious, scientific, and sexual conflicts, in conjunction with his growing distaste for the restrictions of his home and small-town environment in general. Here O'Neill's dramatization of the terrible intensity of the human dilemma, with its autobiographical undertones, traces Ruben Light's quest, often with misdirection of aim, for the meaning of existence. In this respect, *Dynamo* is reminiscent of Henry Adams' researches into the conflicts between religion and science. It reflects certain lines of theorizing in the chapter of *The Education of Henry Adams* called "The Dynamo and the Virgin" and in *Mont-Saint-Michel and Chartres* which postulate a "dynamic theory of history" and describe their searching author as a "runaway star." Like Adams and O'Neill himself, Reuben Light, struggling to attain peace and fulfilment, was a dreamer, a "runaway star."

More directly, O'Neill's so-called "Dynamolatry"—his fascination with the dynamo as a symbol of the Machine God—originated in his chance visit to a hydroelectric plant in Stevenson, Connecticut, near his Ridgefield home. At the end of the second act of the play the image of the dynamo is vividly described as "huge and black, with something of a massive female idol about it, ..." To Reuben, "It's like a great dark idol . . . like the old stone statues of gods people prayed to . . . only it's living and they were dead."

Equally impressed with the Stevenson dynamos was Lee Simonson, set designer for the Guild production, who has written at length about the impressions made upon him by the river, the dam, and the plant itself when he went, at O'Neill's suggestion, on an inspection tour. In doing this research, Simonson was following the directions given in a detailed memorandum which O'Neill sent from Europe, specifying how he wanted all sounds and offstage effects naturally related to the sets themselves. The thunder and lightning in Part One and the sound of the

water flowing over the nearby dam and the hum of the generator in Part
Three were not to be treated incidentally, but as "significant dramatic
overtones that are an integral part of the whole play." Complaining that
"I've never got what the script calls for" in effective sound and other
stage effects, O'Neill stressed the necessity of having a designer with "the
right mechanical flair," who could reproduce "the dramatic effect of the
lightning on people's faces" and the "thunder with a menacing, brooding
quality as if some Electrical God were on the hills impelling all these
people, effecting their thoughts and actions." His scenic scheme in Part
Three, a concentration of the features of the plant at Stevenson, could be
better executed, O'Neill claimed, if the designer would get expert information from General Electric and visit the Stevenson powerhouse.[36]
Simonson did try to follow "the trail of O'Neill's mind" by making that
visit and listening to "the swish of water in the sluice below, a rushing
accompaniment to the one dynamo that happened to be running at so
many hundred revolutions per minute." Accordingly, as Simonson left
that commonplace brick and steel powerhouse, he "was touched with a
terror and a veneration for the invisible forces controlling modern life
that are potentially its salvation and its destruction, its heaven and its
hell." In creating the sets for *Dynamo* Simonson shared, as he wrote in
The Stage Is Set, the poet's intuition, accepted his symbols, and tried "to
make the commonplace mechanical shapes of our industrial environment
significant of the forces for good and evil that they released."[37] Less successful, perhaps, were the sets for the first and second acts: two con-
structivist, or cut-away, houses occupied by the Light and Fife families
and suggesting the simple type of domestic architecture—stuccoed bungalows and white frame cottages—usually found in small towns of the
twenties. In spite of this, critic Gilbert Gabriel considered the settings
more eloquent than the play itself.

In an often reprinted letter to George Jean Nathan, O'Neill classified
the narrative form of *Dynamo* as "a symbolical and factual biography of
what is happening in a large section of the American (and not only
American) soul right now." His desire in writing this first unit of a proposed trilogy was to dig at the roots of a sick society, using a small-town
youth's case history to demonstrate "the death of an old God and the
failure of science and materialism to give any satisfying new one for the
surviving primitive religious instinct to find a meaning for life in, and to
comfort its fears of death with."[38] O'Neill, writing to the Guild's Board
of Managers, described the dialogue method in the play—an echo of
Strange Interlude—as "Interludism," whereby "thought will be as prominent as actual speech, but there will be less cutting-in of brief asides,"

mainly because this play deals with "less cerebral people" than does *Strange Interlude*.[39] Unfortunately his ambitious plan did not result in an artistically organized scrutiny of the modern soul.

Central among the play's wooden and relatively simple townspeople is Reuben Light, who, like many youths in modern community plays, graduates from high school without any definite purpose for the future. An oversensitive teen-ager with a poor economic background, he is so puzzled by the world about him and the mysteries of God and nature that, as conflicts arise, he becomes psychopathic in thought and action. Suffering from an Oedipus complex resembling Marsden's in *Strange Interlude*, eventually Reuben must battle neurotically with a a religious mania. First, he rebels against the cheerless fundamentalist faith of his father, the Reverend Hutchins Light, and the poverty of the family. Then he suffers emotionally from a practical joke by an atheistic and scoffing neighbor, Ramsay Fife, superintendent of the town's hydroelectric plant. Like earlier O'Neill heroes and young O'Neill himself, Reuben, in great confusion of spirit, leaves the shabby parsonage and gossipy town for months of hoboing. At last, finding nothing except irritation in the harsh Puritanism of his father, he recognizes no God except electricity, an echo of Nina Leeds's reference to "the electrical display of God the Father."

When he returns, the shrinking boy in him is gone. Two years of wandering have made Reuben "consciously hardboiled" and able to jeer at Preacher Light's fundamentalism and at blaspheming Fife's "foul ranting" against "the Bible-pounding breed." Nevertheless, he is deeply disturbed to learn from his grief-stricken father that during his absence his mother, always yearning for her son's return and forgiveness, has died. Getting a job in the powerhouse, Reuben gradually transfers his mother-complex to a mystical, passionate love for the dynamo.

Meanwhile, though he is tempted to resume an earlier lustful relationship with Ada, the Fifes's somewhat sluttish daughter, Reuben cannot forget her part in her father's scheme to humiliate him. Viewing her now as nothing except an object of physical desire, he turns away from Ada and romantic love. May Fife—Ada's mother and, with her amoral sexuality, a Cybel character—has an untroubled faith in the cycle of love, marriage, and birth. Attracted to Reuben, Mrs. Fife tries in vain to bring about a reconciliation with Ada. For his part, Reuben feels so much degraded by his earlier sexual intercourse with Ada that at the finale he lures her one evening into the powerhouse, where, in a melodramatic scene revealing his insane frenzy, he shoots her and then expiates his sins by electrocuting himself on his beloved dynamo. Ironically, though Reuben had youthfully rebelled against his father's sermons about an angry

God who speaks to him through lightning, at last it was God the Father's lightning, flowing through the dynamo, which destroyed him. And that humming dynamo, which "gives life to things," gave no heed to Reuben's prayer, though he had come to believe that the center of things "must be the Great Mother of Eternal Life, Electricity, and Dynamo is Her Divine Image on earth! Her power houses are the new churches!"[40]

During these years of considerable technical experimentation, O'Neill again featured, with scenic effectiveness, the New England small town of past eras, in both unconventionally and conventionally designed plays. With the first of these, *Mourning Becomes Electra*, he achieved his ambition to construct "with infinite pains and a hell of a lot of work," a trilogy —something he had failed to accomplish with *Dynamo* and *Days Without End*. In preparation for the big task of composing a Greek-style trilogy, O'Neill did some studying of the ancient Greek language and history. A lesser factor which stimulated O'Neill's intellectual interest in classical tragedy in the years after 1928 was the distinction which his son, Eugene Jr., a Yale student, was gaining for his Greek scholarship.

In the spring of 1926, while the elder O'Neill and Agnes were living on a thirteen-acre estate at Spithead, Bermuda, he set down the first of his copious notes on the making of a play, "A Fragmentary Work Diary." This was a brief note about his toying with the idea of creating a "Modern psychological drama using one of the old legends of Greek tragedy for its basic theme—the Electra story? the Medea?" He seemed beset, however, by doubts about whether an intelligent modern audience, "possessed of no belief in gods or supernatural retribution, could accept and be moved by" a "modern psychological approximation of the Greek sense of fate."[41]

Apparently his mourning over his mother's death in 1922 and Jamie's in 1923 and his estrangement from Agnes and his children, together with the work on *Strange Interlude* and *Marco Millions,* hindered his progress with the Greek idea until October and November of 1928, when he and Carlotta Monterey were on shipboard in the Arabian and China seas, en route to China. Work notes for these travel months record his absorption with a "Greek tragedy idea—story of Electra and family." Finding fault with the Greek story because Electra "peters out into undramatic married banality," O'Neill considered the possibilities of giving a "modern Electra figure in play tragic ending worthy of character." He questioned why the Furies in the Aeschylean *Eumenides* let Electra escape unpunished for her part in plotting the murders of Clytemnestra and her lover Aegisthus. A play of retribution about Electra's life after these murders possesses, he noted, as many imaginative possibilities as any of the plots in *Oresteia*. The fascinating monthly entries of the "Work Diary," concluded in September, 1931, reveal that O'Neill's interest in interpreting a classic plot, "trying to create around it, using techniques and discarding them, scorning the limitations of time in the modern theatre," increased mightily as he began outlining and composing his own trilogy—"Carlotta's play," as he chose to describe it.

Aeschylus opened his dynastic trilogy about the fate of the House of Atreus with the domestic tragedy *Agamemnon*, using a choral prelude and a watchman's speech to describe the royal capital of Argos, after the fall of Troy. Excitedly expectant, citizens await the return of "the great contestants," the brothers Menelaus and Agamemnon, co-rulers of Argos. The violence and civil discord which will divide the Greeks into factions and all but decimate the Atreidae are soon to come, extending the tragic action into *The Libation Bearers* and *The Eumenides*. Throughout the *Oresteia* the political tragedy of both foreign and civil war lies behind the domestic tragedy of Agamemnon's murder by his wife Clytemnestra and her paramour Aegisthus.

O'Neill, trying to resolve his problems of adaptation, decided that for a historical setting the American Civil War was the only possibility "as background for a drama of a murderous family love and hate" comparable to the dissension in the House of Atreus. The scene he chose was an Argos-like place: a small New England seaport and shipbuilding center much like New London with its small shipbuilding interests during earlier times. Living at this time in "a grim, savage, gloomy country of my own [imagination]," O'Neill thought of using one of his favorite motifs, the divided family group. As a New England counterpart to the Atreidae, his imaginary family of Mannons had to be the "town's best—shipbuilders and owners—wealthy for [the] period." His Agamemnon-character he envisioned as Ezra Mannon, the "town's leading citizen, Mayor before the war, now Brigadier General Grant's Army." Also in harmony with the opening scene of the *Agamemnon* immediately after the fall of Troy is O'Neill's selection of the day of General Lee's surrender, April 9, 1865, as the time for Ezra Mannon's return to town and home. Agamemnon's imposing palace in the initial scene of the *Oresteia* becomes in O'Neill's scheme a two-story New England mansion of the "Greek temple front type that was the rage in 1st half of the 19th century." Just as the palace in Argos is linked with Atreus, founder of a dynasty, so is the substantial Mannon house—"a New England house of Atreus"—a sturdy, old home built in 1830 by "Atreus-character, Agamemnon's father," Abe Mannon.

O'Neill's expertness in social satire is evident in his work note about the falsity of architectural styles found in some of early New England's more pretentious homes. The Mannon house, as he first sketched it, was to appear as a "grotesque perversion of everything [the] Greek temple expressed of [the] meaning of life." With all its faults, the New England provincial background was, however, the "best possible dramatically for Greek plot of crime and retribution, chain of fate." Also, the Puritan conviction that man was born to sin and punishment suited O'Neill's plan for portraying his Orestes-character by the furies within him, his Puritan conscience destroying his peace of mind. A highly creative adapter, O'Neill from the beginning outlined original departures from the Greek story, including Electra's love for her mother's lover, Aegisthus. Thus fated to be her own mother's rival in love, Electra was envisioned as suffering constant defeat—"first for father's love, then for brother's, finally for Aegisthus." Another departure he liked was the attributing of Clytemnestra's hatred for Agamemnon to his "sexual frustration in his puritan sense of guilt turning love into lust," though before marriage she had loved him romantically.

Still drawing heavily upon the Greek legend, O'Neill wove into the texture of his outline the "rivalry, hatred, love, lust, revenge in the past between Agamemnon's father, Atreus, and Aegisthus' father, Thyestes . . . hatred of Atreus for brother—revenge—banishment." He thought, too, about the strong facial resemblance between Aegisthus, first cousin to Agamemnon and Orestes, noting that "his resemblance to Orestes attracts Clytemnestra—his resemblance to her father attracts Electra." O'Neill's version was to include Electra's adoration for her father, her devotion to Orestes, and her hatred for her mother. Also, he tried to work out the complexities of Agamemnon's tensions: his frustration in love for Clytemnestra, his adoration for the daughter Electra who resembles her, and his jealousy of his son, his wife's favorite.

As may be seen in the work notes, O'Neill repeatedly experimented with mechanical means to enhance the presentation of his Yankee Greeks. In his laborious rewriting of the first draft of the plays he finally rejected the half-mask, substituting makeup for masks when each character delivered a stylized soliloquy. Whereas the main characters were to reveal their inner lives, the simple townspeople, as foils to the "uppish" and "top dog" Mannons, were to be restricted to exterior characterization. At the opening of each play, the townsfolk, outside the house, were to form a fixed chorus pattern, typifying the "prying, commenting, curious town as an ever-present background for the drama of the Mannon family." Further dramatic and symbolic contrast was to be achieved in another brother-sister combination—Peter and Hazel Niles, romantically linked with the House of Mannon—conceived of as almost characterless and representing "the untroubled, contented 'good,' a sweet, constant unselfconscious, untempted virtue amid which evil passion works, unrecognized by them—(until the end)—but emphasized by their contrast." O'Neill conjectured also that the motivating hate out of the Mannon past could be handled by the use of family portraits, the recurrent motif of the women's hair (the peculiar gold-brown hair alike in Electra-Lavinia and her mother, the same as the hair of the dead mother of Adam Brant), and the emphasis on sea motifs, which signify both the maritime activities of the Mannons and the symbolic idea of escape and release in "the Blessed Isles." Then in the work notes there is consideration of the family hate attached to old Abe Mannon's house, but this is not a new motif for O'Neill. In *Dynamo*, for example, both Reuben and his mother hate the damp, poorly equipped parsonage in which the Light family has been economically imprisoned for twenty-three years. In *Strange Interlude* Sam Evans' widowed mother lives in a house that has "lost its soul."

O'Neill's preliminary drafting of "this damn trilogy," as he once called it, included his mulling over various names for his characters which would be similar to the Greek ones. What he called his "touch job of picking the right names" included drawing up the following trial list:

> Agamemnon—(Asa), (Ezra) Mannon
> Clytemnestra—Christine (?)
> Orestes—Orin
> (Electra—Eleanor (?) Ellen (?) Elsa (?)
> (Laodicea—Lavinia (this sounds more like it) Vinnie
> (Called in the family)
> Aegisthus—Augustus (?) Alan Adam (?)
> Pylades—Paul (?) Peter (?)
> Hermione—Hazel—Hesther

Bothersome also was the selection of a title appropriate to the Greek idea of fate. O'Neill explained the unusual title finally selected, *Mourning Becomes Electra*: "in the old sense of [the] word—it befits—it becomes Electra to mourn—it is her fate,—also, in usual sense (made ironical here), mourning (black) is becoming to her—it is the only color that becomes her destiny—."[42] With this as the title of the trilogy, he finally decided upon *Homecoming*, *The Hunted* (the last title selected), and *The Haunted* to designate the three constituent plays.

By September, 1931, when O'Neill was correcting the second galleys sent by Liveright, his often redrafted "M.B.E." was a new and complex creation, though it followed broadly the Aeschylean version of the Electra story, with some possible influence from Euripides and Sophocles.

Within the framework of classic tragedy, the three plays progressively portray, with increasing tragic intensity, a family of lost townspeople, who, like their counterparts in other O'Neill plays, are destined for disillusionment, destruction, and bitter punishment by self-imposed penance in their "House of Death." All of the passion-charged but ill-fated Mannons, then, represent a moribund tradition symbolized, in the expert exposition of *Homecoming*, by the isolation and general "somber gray ugliness" of the ancestral mansion itself. As shown by a special curtain, the house, built within a thirty-acre estate, is located on a slightly elevated site, about three hundred feet from the locust- and elm-bordered street. Enclosed by a white picket fence and a tall hedge, the extensive grounds are beautified by scattered maples, a grove of pine trees, lilac and syringa bushes, gardens, and greenhouses. The white wooden portico, with its six temple-like columns, appears as an "incongruous mask fixed on the house" to hide its somberness. Thus imposing in its ugliness, the isolated Mannon house offers to the humbler townspeople a showplace and a symbol of the social and economic superiority of the family. " 'Tain't everyone can git to see the Mannon place close to. They're strict about trespassin,' " old Seth Beckwith, the family gardener and the unifying character of the trilogy, warns his sightseeing guests, Amos Ames, his wife Louisa, and her cousin Minnie. Oblivious of the warning, Minnie, a simple and awed villager, can only exclaim, "My sakes! What a purty house!" More symbolically, the masklike portico screens from a gossipy, small-town world the rottenness of the Mannon family annals.

Secure in their prosperous shipping interests, the "durned old Mannons" have for years ruled the community at large from this secluded estate. As Seth boasts, they have "been top dog here for near on two hundred years and don't let folks forget it." For all of their wealth, however, throughout several generations the Mannons in their tragic relationships have typified thematically, in Edwin A. Engel's phrasing, "man's yearning throughout his 'death-in-life' . . . for 'death-birth-peace'!" The present head of the family, Brigadier General Ezra Mannon, blessed with wealth, a beautiful wife, a daughter (Lavinia), a son (Orin), and both civil and military titles, nevertheless is the victim of a rigid Puritanical force which dooms him to marital unhappiness, a "death-in-life" existence for a proud Mannon. Also trapped, his wife Christine, strangely lovely with gold-brown hair, passionately scorns the mansion as a sepulchre—"pagan temple front stuck like a mask on Puritan ugliness." She despises old Abe Mannon for building such a monstrosity—"a temple for his hatred" for his brother David, whom he exiled, with his French-Canadian wife, Marie Brantôme, and cheated out of his patrimony. The

Mannon house, whose spaciousness awes the simple townsmen, is an ironic symbol, a prison for the members of Ezra's family, all trapped in their searches for love and understanding. As Lavinia says in sealing her doom, at the conclusion of *The Haunted*, "It takes the Mannons to punish themselves for being born!" That is the Mannon destiny. The gloom and foreboding associated with the house are made all the more realistic by Seth's repeated singing of the melancholy chanty "Shenandoah" and the chantyman's sentimental dirge, "Hanging Johnny," illustrations of O'Neill's fondness for creating atmosphere by sound devices.

Finally, Seth's friends, types of townspeople rather than individuals, form "a chorus representing the town come to look and listen and spy on the rich and exclusive Mannons." Comic relief comes from their folksy disparagement of the Mannons as well as from O'Neill's satiric portraits of Ames as a garrulous gossip-monger . . . devoid of evil intent," of Louisa as "a similar scandal-bearing type, her tongue . . . sharpened by malice," and of Minnie, "the meek, eager-listener type, with a small round face, round stupid eyes, and a round mouth pursed out to drink in gossip."[43] Socially higher citizens, professional people and businessmen, are equally amusing in their views about the Mannons. Josiah Borden, manager of the Mannon shipping company, is shrewd and competent, while his wife is "a typical New England woman of pure English ancestry, with a horse face, buck teeth and big feet . . ." Fiftyish Everett Hill typifies the "well-fed minister of a prosperous smalltown [Congregational] church." He is described as "stout and unctuous, snobbish and ingratiating, conscious of godliness, but timid and always feeling his way," especially in matters concerning the powerful Mannons. Mrs. Hill appears as "a sallow, flabby, self-effacing minister's wife." Doctor Blake, who has long served the Mannons, is also a familiar type: "the old kindly best-family physician—a stout, self-important old man with a stubborn opinionated expression." Other minor characters offer another cross-section view of the local citizenry. Wiry old Abner Small, a hardware store clerk with "a wispy goat's beard," Joe Silva, a middle-aged Portuguese fishing captain, fat and boisterous, and Ira Mackel, a sly farmer with "a drawling wheezy cackle" all pass caustic judgment on the Mannons, who have "the town lickin' their boots."

The Mannons are doubly trapped by the sense of family guilt stemming from the early mistreatment of Marie Brantôme and by individual drives. The calamitous family history, which haunts the later generations, began when Abe Mannon, driven by greed and sexual desire, cheated Dave out of his share of the shipping business and drove him, with Marie, away from the Mannon homestead. This "act of guile" enabled Abe to leave his son Ezra a fortune, which had been increased through his operation of one of the first Western Ocean packet lines. Hypocritically respectable, Abe memorialized his name by building the mansion on the hill, while exiled Dave and Marie almost starved. Dave, however, was guilty of offenses against Marie, who nevertheless loved him. In the Far West, where his misfortunes multiplied, Dave was no longer a proud Mannon, but a drunken bum who cravenly neglected and mistreated his wife and young son. Broken by adversity and the growing hate of his son Adam Brant, Dave at last accomplished, as Adam bitterly declares, the "only decent thing he ever did": he went to the barn and hanged himself. Years later even Ezra is guilty of ignoring Marie's letter requesting a loan. In his turn, Adam Brant, when in 1865 he is established as captain of the *Flying Trades*, brands Ezra as a murderer when he tells Lavinia, with vindictive passion, that his poverty-stricken mother, weakened by sickness and starvation, "died in my arms."

Ezra himself seems to have been driven by the force of "the Great God Success," topping off a long list of community achievements by his military distinction. As a symbol of American activism, he stirs Amos Ames, the carpenter, to the admiring words, "This town's real proud of Ezra." Nevertheless, the portrait in his study shows Ezra's face as "handsome in a stern, aloof fashion . . . cold and emotionless." In actuality and largely because of his judgeship and military rank, his air is brusque and authoritative, giving the impression that he is continually withholding emotion from his voice. Most of all, he is tragically plagued with the family ineptitude in lovemaking. On returning from his Civil War service, Ezra, frustrated by the inescapable fact of the failure of their marriage, forgets his pride to plead with Christine, who is dissatisfied and unhappy, for a marital reconciliation. There has "always been some barrier between us—a wall hiding us from each other." Bitterly he regrets that "folks in town look on me as so able! Ha! Able for what? Not for what I wanted most in life!" So, now "thinking of what I'd lost," he begs Christine to love him.

But, by implication, the wall which destroyed their love was built on their wedding night, when Ezra's passionate sexuality is supposed to have repelled Christine. Quinn suggests that this implication is a flaw in the plot, for Ezra's nature, as portrayed in *Homecoming*, does not appear brutal and coarse. Moreover, Christine is characterized as a sensuous woman with no instinctive horror of passion. As the years pass, however, her repulsion has deepened into hatred and marital estrangement, even to the point of creating within her an intense dislike for Vinnie, her firstborn child. By happy contrast, Orin, born when Ezra was away in service during the Mexican War, from the first seemed wholly her child and was thus the object of her deep love. Lavinia, now grown into young woman-hood, hates her mother but adores her father. With easy transference of affection, she becomes Christine's jealous rival for the love not only of Orin but secretly of Adam Brant. "You've tried to become the wife of your father and the mother of Orin! You've always schemed to steal my place!" Christine accuses her. The reverse is true of Orin, whose mother fixation is greater than any love he has for his father. Adam Brant, in love with his cousin's wife, is also the victim of fixations: first, his con-stant love for his mother, and then his desire for revenge on the full-blooded Mannons. Such are the principal drives back of the violent action which begins anew in April, 1865, when the homecoming of the town's "conquering hero" is celebrated by a parade, band playing, patriotic singing, free drinks, and general hilarity.

But in this house of hidden hatred, old antagonisms, still smoldering, flare into violence. In *Homecoming*, the embittered Lavinia tries to break up Christine's illicit romance by demanding that she send Adam away. Affecting acquiescence, Christine in private shrewdly urges Adam to send her a box of poison. Strong-willed, she is determined to free herself from the husband who has held her in bondage by administering poison, rather than a prescribed stimulant, when he suffers from his heart ailment. The opportunity comes when Ezra, as a result of his wife's goading and her shocking revelation that Marie Brantôme's son is her lover, does have a heart attack. Quickly Christine gives him a poisoned pellet instead of the stimulant. As if awakened from a nightmare, Lavinia comes into the bedroom just in time to hear her father incoherently gasp, "She's guilty —not medicine!" A few minutes later he dies in Lavinia's arms. It is only when she accidentally discovers the box of poison, which had fallen to the floor, that Lavinia is moved by "a dreadful, horrified certainty" of her mother's guilt. After this tragic scene Lavinia, rather than Christine, dominates the action.

Thereafter Lavinia's constant spying and her scornful, accusing gaze unnerve Christine, who tries hard to allay the suspicion which Vinnie has created against her. When Orin returns after recuperating from a battle wound, she temporarily regains his close affection. All the while Lavinia moves about like a black-garbed and vengeful specter of gloom and calamity. Claiming that Lavinia is "out of her head with grief," Christine quiets Orin's suspicions for a while. Nevertheless, he swears that if he ever learns that Captain Brant is guilty of an illicit relationship with Christine, he will kill him. Lavinia slyly plays upon this idea, to the point of persuading Orin, two days after their father's funeral, to accompany her to the *Flying Trades* in Boston harbor to eavesdrop on the lovers.

In their cabin rendezvous Captain Brant calms Christine's fears by promising to escape with her to "the Blessed Isles," where "there's peace, and forgetfulness." (Orin had previously spoken to his mother of such an island haven as an escape from the cheerlessness of the Mannons.) After Christine leaves, Orin, motivated by "a savage, revengeful rage" because his mother has transferred her love from him to a stranger, shoots Brant when he returns to the cabin. Then, goaded by Lavinia, he rifles the place to "make it look as if thieves killed him." Having completed this, Orin, with a strange fascinated expression in his eyes, stares into Brant's face, startled by the close resemblance between Brant, his father, and himself, and says, "Maybe I've committed suicide!" Here the Oedipus complex takes a new turn. Orin, in his jealous desire to get rid of his father so that he might have his mother to himself, had not counted upon a new rival for her affection. Now, as he gazes horrified, he recognizes his own image in his rival's still face.

Upon their return to the Mannon house, Vinnie and Orin stun Christine by their report of what they have done. Orin, in a state of morbid excitement, is bewildered by his mother's stricken anguish. He strives vainly to regain her affection, desperately begging her to remember "our island" and proposing a voyage together to the South Seas. But Christine's face has become a tragic death mask. She rushes into Ezra's study and shoots herself. During this tense finale of *The Hunted*, Vinnie, shaken but implacable, excuses the murder of Brant as an act of justice prompted by a sense of duty to avenge her father. Her expression of love for Orin and her determined promise to make him forget the violence of the past inaugurate the action of *The Haunted*. Orin, however, is so "haunted by death" and a guilt complex—the Furies or Eumenides— that he cries out in tortured self-accusation, "I murdered her."

In *The Haunted* Lavinia, who has Orin under her control, resists the evil destiny of the Mannons by taking him on a long voyage to the South Seas. After a year of attempted expiation, both, when they return to face their ghosts, are still involved in "the crime and retribution, chain of fate" which has haunted the Mannons for years. At first Lavinia seems affected less than her brother. Having rationalized about her filial duty, she seems happier. During the trip she has blossomed out and now, by the rearrangement of her hair and an imitation in dress and manner, she so strikingly resembles her mother that the chorus of townspeople have cause for gossip. By contrast, Orin is still pursued by his private furies. He transfers his incestuous love for his mother to Vinnie, at the same time showing intense jealousy of her attentions to other men, including

Peter Niles, her fiancé. "Can't you see," he cries, "I'm now in Father's place and you're Mother? That's the evil destiny out of the past I haven't dared predict! I'm the Mannon you're chained to!" Orin even hints to Peter that on the Blessed Isles Vinnie was promiscuous: "I guess I'm too much of a Mannon after all to turn into a pagan. But you should have seen Vinnie with the men—!" In short, for guilt-beset Orin, life has become "darkness without a star to guide us!"

Seeking another way of expiation, Orin in remorse begins writing a frank history—a chronicle of the outraged pride, the debased Puritanism, the vindictive justice, and other fatal traits of the Mannon line. Vinnie's fear that he will make a public disclosure of the Mannons' dishonor emphasizes a familiar small-town obsession, especially strong during this period: provincial worship of outward respectability and gentility as a way to success. Now able, with her new sexuality, to return his love, Lavinia begs guileless Peter, her childhood sweetheart, to marry her. At the same time she fears that Orin's history will reveal too much about the secrets of the past. In turn, Orin's introversion moves him to hate his sister as much as he desires her, for she has become a constant reminder of his guilt. Crazed by her love for Peter, he threatens to expose her real nature if she consents to marriage. At last, distracted and repelled by Orin's morbid possessiveness, another symbol of the family incest pattern, Lavinia angrily shouts, "You'd kill yourself if you weren't a coward!" When Peter's arrival interrupts their quarreling, Orin goes into the haunted study on the excuse of cleaning his pistol. Now driven to madness, he can no longer face the "darkness of death in life"; so, he shoots himself. Though his death is referred to as accidental, Lavinia now feels the sharp pricks of her Puritan conscience. Hazel, however, suspects that her lover's supposed accident was like "so many strange hidden things out of the Mannon past"—something vile and sinister. Fearful for Peter's safety, Hazel pleads with Lavinia to release him from his pledge of marriage. In response, Lavinia faces the bitter truth of her own lost innocence. She knows too well that the Mannons would forever block her happiness. The others, by dying, had shown themselves cowards. She would live. Moved by an impulse toward masochism, she yields to fate. In a scene of hysterical lying she sends Peter away and, instructing Seth to board up the shutters of the windows, retreats through the porticoed door, declaring, "I'm bound here—to the Mannon dead!" As the last Mannon, she must punish herself. "Living here alone with the dead is a worse act of justice than death or prison!"

O'Neill's "grand opus," as Lawrence Langner later recalled, was received enthusiastically by the Board of the Theatre Guild. The success of

its production seemed assured when Alice Brady, "the finest actress available for the part of Lavinia," signed her contract. Other assignments
proved most fortunate. As Langner remembers, in connection with the
brilliant opening on October 26, 1931,

Alla Nazimova gave an unforgettable performance in the role of Christine
while Earle Larimore's Orin was so flawless that you felt Orin in person was
appearing on the stage. With their acting, the magnificent direction by Philip
Moeller, the inspired support of the cast, and the stark Grecian columns and
Victorian interiors of Robert Edmond Jones, *Mourning Becomes Electra* was
a high watermark in the American theatre."[44]

Although there were detractors, "the day after the opening the New
York drama critics saluted its advent with an accolade of praise which
has never been surpassed or even equalled." Langner's personal reaction
as he watched the five-hour-long play progress was that he passed "from
ever-increasing climax to climax with a crescendo which leaves you stag-
gering at the end of the play." Brooks Atkinson, in his *New York Times*
review, praised O'Neill's creation of "a universal tragedy of tremendous
stature—deep, dark, solid, uncompromising and grim." He liked its
heroic and magnificently wrought style and structure, as well as the consummate artistry and passion shown in the acting of Alice Brady and
Mme. Nazimova—although in a November 1 reappraisal he felt that its
lack of nobility of character and appropriate language prevented the play
from being a great drama. Gilbert Gabriel in the *New York American*
noted O'Neill's achievement of new stature with his "grand scheme
grandly fulfilled," a recognition matched by Richard Lockridge's praise
in the *New York Sun* to the effect that this "implacable and unrelenting
tragedy" marked O'Neill's emergence as an artist in the theater.
      Combined with his ambitious adaptation of a tragic Greek legend to
the American Civil War era, O'Neill's masterly creation of an unnamed
yet realistically conceived New England seaport offers still further proof
of his dramaturgical artistry. Ancillary though it is to his moving tragedy
of family guilt, the town, nevertheless, is quite as necessary to his grand
scheme as the ocean is to the plotting of *Moby Dick*, or the Mississippi
to *Huckleberry Finn*. "Mannonport," as it might quite fittingly have been
called, is an old enough community to provide a proper setting for an
established maritime family, whose fate testifies to the power of the past
over the present. As stressed at intervals by the choral gossips from different levels of society, the spiritual malaise of the Mannons is co-ordi-
nated dramatically with the decadence of the town itself. In the town, as
in the nation, the merging of a romantic "Golden Day" with a newer,

tough era of enterprise left in its wake a great deal of traditional narrow-mindedness and prudery, as unpleasant as the greed and crassness of materialism. The town's respectable citizens—the Reverend Everett Hill, his wife, and their associates—appear as very proper New Englanders, straitlaced and suspicious yet cautiously restrained in their criticism of the rich Mannons. The lower ranks, with Seth Beckwith as their expositor, are more outspoken and earthy, though on occasion their uncensored comments reveal that they have inherited taints from Puritanism. Town gossip, whether by polite innuendo, malicious backbiting, or ribald joking, becomes an effective dramatic force, serving at times as a strong antagonist. When Christine suggests that she and Adam could escape by shipping as passengers on another ship bound for the Far East, he gloomily demurs, saying, "But everyone in the town would know you were gone. It would start suspicion—." Again, the town chorus, by manifold references, relates the tragedy destroying the House of Mannon to actual events: the widespread community rejoicing in celebration of the end of the war, the assassination of President Lincoln, and the collapsing of a rotten society. Nor is this town singular, for frequent references to a cluster of towns, including New Bedford, suggest not only the maritime activities of the region, but a nationwide acquiescence in practical pursuits. Even the comments of the lugubrious chantyman have the force of a prophecy about community change and the fate of the Mannons: ". . . the old days is dyin' . . . Everything is dyin'! Abe Lincoln is dead . . . an' I seed in the paper where Ezra Mannon was dead!" Against such a changing and now leaderless community background, the tragic history of family downfall plays itself out to the last survivor. The Mannons' bigoted Puritan attitude toward love, their reaction to the power of heredity—to "the Oedipus and Electra complexes handed down through parents to children in a vicious, never-ending circle"—their sexual conflicts, and even their fear of the gossipy town tragically brand each one, generation by generation. In many ways, *Mourning Becomes Electra,* with all its flaws in presenting the stained souls of the Mannons, remains the most powerful and pessimistic presentation of decadents in the dramatic history of the American small town.

"The Real America"

From 1931 to 1934 O'Neill struggled with his personal despair and hope as he continued his search for certainty in a world of increasing multiplicity and chaos. Lionel Trilling, in a contemporary revaluation of O'Neill's quest for a satisfactory answer to life's problems—for the "somehow" or solution—commented upon his always moving, by means of experimental symbolism and myth, toward some kind of finality promised by religion and philosophy.[45] During 1932 his exploring mind again turned toward the predicament of modern man, as he sought to dramatize a love which transcended mortal life and could last forever. Slowly there came into being a new play—a sort of "Christian idyl"— in which he tried to give theatrical form to the disassociated personality of his hero through the *doppelgänger* motif. First titled *An End of Days*, then *Days Without End*, this painful play, when finished, became, he thought, "a damned interesting piece of work" in its complex portrayal of the questioning rebellion of successful John Loving, its central character at war with his own nature. As Lawrence Langner records, from a letter written to him by O'Neill,

While he was struggling with *Days Without End* and under the usual strain which his writing imposed upon him, he awoke one morning supremely happy, having dreamed an entire play which reminded him of his childhood. He literally rushed to his study, poured out the play on paper and finished it in less than four weeks. "It was," he told me, "like a holiday from the other play."[46]

This was *Ah, Wilderness!*, his one comedy, which, after its opening at the Guild Theatre on October 2, 1933, was to become his most popular play. And no wonder, for, as Langner has noted, "the play's quality of nostalgic sentiment made it overnight a piece of Americana as indigenous to our soil as a folk song. And with the passage of time, this play has proved the most endearing, if not the most enduring, of his works."

Apparently, then, while he and Carlotta were quietly settled at their "castle," Casa Genotta, on Sea Island, Georgia, conditions were conducive to the nostalgic recalling of his youthful associations, notably those with the family of newspaper editor John McGinley, in New London. A bit later O'Neill gave expression to his serious thoughts, during that summer of 1932, about creating "a play true to the spirit of the American large small-town at the turn of the century," in which he hoped to recapture the right "atmosphere, sentiment, an exact evocation of the mood of the dead past." This was to be done in pleasant remembrance of a simple way of family living in which people were not tragically tormented to the extremity of hiding their real selves behind masks. A gleam of hope appears in his sentimental feeling that "to me, the America which was (and is) the real America found its unique expression in such middle class families as the Millers, among whom so many of my own generation passed from adolescence to manhood."[47] Such was the sentiment that motivated the writing of what

O'Neill called "a comedy of recollection" and "a dream walking." Gilbert Gabriel interpreted his four acts of unphilosophic, uncomplicated sketches of "togetherness" in a Connecticut coastal town of the Mauve Decade (1906) as "a comedy of recantation," and Richard Lockridge saw it as a humorous portrayal of "just plain folks." Moreover, Gabriel's prediction in the New York *American*, for October 3, 1933, that "this morning all the dolts in creation and criticism will be remarking that O'Neill has turned Tarkington" proved partially true, for some did draw comparisons. At any rate, this native folk comedy was a quiet interlude and a human, tender play of remembrance and wish fulfilment whose antithesis was *Long Day's Journey into Night* with its painful family scenes.

Actually the protagonist of *Ah, Wilderness!* seems to be an entire upper-middle-class family, the Millers, all portrayed with the realism of portraits in an old-fashioned family album. Nat Miller, paterfamilias and editor of the local *Globe*, is "in his late fifties, a tall, dark, spare man, a little stoop-shouldered, more than a little bald, dressed with an awkward attempt at sober respectability . . ." Essie Miller, a short, stout woman of around fifty who must have been decidedly pretty as a girl, now has "a bustling, mother-of-a-family manner." Her sister-in-law, Lily Miller, is at forty-two tall, dark, and thin, and outwardly conforms to "the conventional type of old-maid school teacher, even to wearing glasses." Sid Davis, her longtime suitor and Mrs. Miller's brother, is a rolling stone type of reporter and at forty-five is "short and fat, bald-headed, with the Puckish face of a Peck's Bad Boy who has never grown up."

Of the four children still at home the eldest, nineteen-year-old Arthur, typifies the muscular Yale football lineman of the period. Vivacious Mildred, just fifteen, is popularly thought of as attractive. Tommy, "a chubby, sun-burnt boy of eleven," bursting with bottled-up energy, is determined to celebrate the Fourth of July as noisily as possible.

Central in the simple plot is Richard (or Dick), whose extreme sensitiveness and "restless, apprehensive, defiant, shy, dreamy, and self-conscious intelligence" make him at seventeen a "ringer" for young O'Neill during his New London days. He appears alternately as a simple small-town boy and as a poseur, solemnly playing the role of rebel against community conventions. As the Millers' "problem boy," Richard, with all the rebelliousness of adolescence, imagines himself a social radical. He enjoys reading "awful books" by Carlyle, such as *The French Revolution*, and by Swinburne, Ibsen, Shaw, Wilde, and other "shocking" authors. He jolts his elders by his railing against what he considers the stupid restraints of local society, Victorian in its taboos. He sneers at the Fourth of July celebration as "a stupid farce." What, then, suits his adolescent fancy? As Nat Miller says, "Poetry's his meat nowadays, I think—love poetry—and socialism, too, I suspect from some dire declarations he's made." Dick particularly enjoys spouting, usually at the wrong moment, snatches from *The Rubaiyat of Omar Khayyam*—"that's the best of all!" Unfortunately he goes too far when he sends fervid quotations from erotic poetry to his naïve high-school sweetheart, Muriel McComber, who is "fifteen going on sixteen." In fatherly wrath storekeeper David McComber charges Dick with being "dissolute and blasphemous" and bent upon corrupting his daughter's morals.

Called on the carpet by the family, Dick feels that he is doomed to lose Muriel's true love. Assuming a hard-boiled attitude, he exclaims, "Ah, what the hell do I care! I'll show them!" An unexpected opportunity to prove his manhood comes when one of Arthur's Yale classmates persuades him to meet "a couple of swift babies from New Haven" at the Pleasant Beach House, a sordid hotel ironically named. In the place of assignation—a small, dingy back room to the rear of the bar— Dick is ill at ease, though he assumes a false sophistication and is determined "to go the pace that kills." Nervous in the presence of his assigned "baby doll," Belle, a cheap collegiate tart, he responds to her goading by reciting poetry, becoming thoroughly intoxicated, and parting with most of his savings. This most humiliating and ludicrous experience ends with his being thrown out of the barroom for being under age and for being editor Miller's son. At long last, "he comes home at awful midnight to give an exhibition of first souse before the entire outraged family, and to be swished off ingloriously to bed." Afterward, displaying uncommon horse sense, Richard soberly admits that he made "a darned slob" of himself.

But the aftermath of his spree is not too unhappy. The next day Dick momentarily forgets to assume his usual "double-dyed sardonicism" as he listens with respect, and some embarrassment, to Nat Miller's "gentle but abysmal lecture" on morality and social hygiene. The boy's severest punishment comes when he confesses that he intends to get a job and marry Muriel. His father promptly decides that Dick must prepare to enter Yale. And Richard's happiness is complete when he and Muriel, in a tender love scene on a moonlit beach, reconcile their differences. Before curtainfall other love elements assure a happy and sentimental existence for certain grown-ups in Smalltown, Connecticut. As for "poor Lily," Mrs. Miller tells Nat that Sid will never give up his drinking habits, "and she'll never marry him. But she seems to get some queer satisfaction out of fussing over him like a hen that's hatched a duck . . ." At the end, Mrs. Miller, happy over Richard and "love's young dream," sentimentally echoes the expressions of the two mothers in the Prologue of *The Great God Brown*: "Yes, I don't believe I've hardly ever seen such a beautiful night—with such a wonderful moon." And Nat recalls the moonlight nights when he and Essie were courting. With gentle nostalgic melancholy he recites the lament from the *Rubaiyat*: "Yet! Ah, that Spring should vanish with the Rose! That Youth's sweet-scented manuscript should close!" On second thought, he remembers the love of middle age. "Well, Spring isn't everything, is it, Essie? There's a lot to be said for Autumn. That's got beauty, too. And Winter —if you're together."[48]

When at last *Days Without End* was ready to be submitted to the Theatre Guild, O'Neill chanced to examine the quickly written first draft of *Ah, Wilderness!* which, to his surprise, seemed about as good as if he had reworked it. Accordingly, he delivered the draft unrevised to the Guild directors, who bought the comedy immediately and started rehearsals within a week. On October 2, 1933, when the play opened, the Guild paid George M. Cohan the rare honor of putting his name up in large lights on the marquee alongside O'Neill's. His successive performances in the role of Nat Miller were highly praised. Gilbert Gabriel, for instance, thought that Cohan's empathic interpretation was "heart-deep in fatherly wisdom and humanity, as honest as natural, and thoroughly understanding, masterly spoken throughout." (Will Rogers' stage impersonation in San Francisco was as successful as was Walter Huston's on the screen.) High commendation was accorded the acting in the unforgettably touching scenes where Cohan appeared with Elisha Cook, Jr., excellent in young Richard's role. Some first-night spectators felt that in such intimate scenes Cohan became not merely the American father but almost the "universal" father.[49] In fact, the entire cast, under Philip Moeller's brilliant direction, was admirable, with Marjorie Marquis as Essie, Eda Heinemann as Lily, Gene Lockhart in Sid Davis' role, and Ruth Gilbert as young Muriel. Robert Edmond Jones's settings—realistic scenes of the Miller parlor and dining room, the shabby Pleasant Beach House, and the moonlit beach—all helped to re-create a small-town environment in Connecticut as it might have existed in July, 1906. The 289 performances of this original production emphasized the perennial theatrical popularity of pictures of the decencies of American family life. And O'Neill was pleased with his comedy's phenomenal success in what he satirically described, in a letter to Langner, as "the

Amusement Racket which New York vaingloriously calls The Theatre."

Unlike many of O'Neill's provincial Americans, the respectable Connecticut Millers, their in-laws, and their neighbors are neither tragically trapped nor lost townsmen, although they were created during his extended composition of *Days Without End*, when he was experimenting anew with the painful problem of a personality torn between belief and unbelief. But his interest in the conflicts of divided personalities was not wholly lost as he composed this genial genre comedy. Actually here he merely readjusted a number of his well-tested tragic situations to a story in a lighter mood. For the most part reconciliation takes the place of the tragic trauma of division in *Days Without End* and earlier plays. A misunderstood youth, at odds with his family, is at last reconciled with them most happily. Moreover, his pose of manly sophistication and superiority over women fades before his adolescent thoughts about his lovely Muriel, her irritating naïveté and irresolution notwithstanding. In Smalltown respectable citizens come in contact with a shameless chippie, but no tragic aftermath mars their lives. A drunkard and a failure, unlike the pitiable drifters and dreamers in *The Iceman Cometh*, is finally, though conditionally, tolerated by a spinsterish schoolteacher. Purposely, O'Neill's tragically and widely used images of the Father and the Mother are here toned down to suit the demands of nostalgic comedy. Unlike the unhappy and repressed Mrs. Light or the sexy Mrs. Fife, Essie Miller is an ordinary homebody, constantly alert to the moral and physical needs of her large household. Further, in contrast with the situations involving the father images in *The Great God Brown*, *Dynamo*, and other dramas, the conflict between the tyrannical father, David McComber, and the tolerant father, Nat Miller, resolves itself peaceably. Here, as in *Mourning Becomes Electra*, there reappears the sharp difference between small-town haves and have-nots —between a proper Victorian citizenry and the baser elements of the town—but no permanent social complication results. All of these divisions featured throughout *Ah, Wilderness!* lack the tensions and tragic strains of O'Neill's more somber and typical dramas of failure and alienation. Was he, then, in this delightful comedy momentarily out of character, or was he merely presenting the other side of the coin?

Perhaps an answer may be found in his writing to Langner on October 29, 1933, concerning his difficulties with *Days Without End*:

For, after all, this play, like *Ah, Wilderness!* but in a deeper sense, is the paying of an old debt on my part—a gesture toward more comprehensive unembittered understanding and inner freedom—the breaking away from an old formula that I had enslaved myself with, and the appreciation that there is their own truth in other formulas, too, and that any life-giving formula is as fit a subject for drama as any other.[50]

Still another answer may be hidden in O'Neill's acknowledgment that there is "a background of real life behind my work." In fact, some of his close friends had acquaintance with the atmosphere of the happy, uncomplicated era around 1906, as is implied in the dedication of the comedy to George Jean Nathan, "Who also, once upon a time, in peg-top trousers went the pace that kills along the road to ruin." The recent research of the Gelbs and other O'Neill specialists shows how certain elements in *Ah, Wilderness!* and other autobiographical plays remind one that Gene O'Neill, like Richard Miller, was seventeen in 1906. Certainly the comedy reflects phases of the New London experiences of his lost youth, although in an interview with Brooks Atkinson O'Neill "disclaimed anything but a superficial kinship with Richard Miller or his family."[51]

His memories of his own pleasurable participation in New London's annual Fourth of July celebrations, of the popular player-piano tunes of the era, as featured in the barroom scenes along with an Irish bartender, of early slang and colloquial speech, of small-town architecture, and of certain general types of citizens found in any large-small town helped him give an air of verisimilitude to his nostalgic comedy. As the Gelbs show in great detail, New Londoners, including his own family and the McGinleys, appear to have served as models for some of the characters. Like Nat Miller, John McGinley was editor, part owner, and cofounder of a New London paper, the *Day*, in the early 1880's, about the time when James and Ella O'Neill bought their Pequot Avenue house. Furthermore, the McGinley household, with its friendly ways and pleasant domesticity, quite unlike the O'Neills' way of living, suggests the closely knit Miller family. The Millers' Irish maid Norah is a reminder of a similar type of hired girl who once worked for the O'Neills. Also, Tim Sullivan, a New London policeman, poetry-spouting Hutch Collins, Lil Brennan, Ella O'Neill's cousin who served as the model for Lily Miller, good-natured Evelyn McGinley who, rather than Ella O'Neill, was the prototype for Essie Miller, all seem to have given a pull to O'Neill's imagination as he was composing *Ah, Wilderness!*[52] These and other fragments of autobiography not only account for O'Neill's deep personal affection for *Ah, Wilderness!* but also help explain why, in a nostalgic mood, he once thought of the American small town, as it existed at the turn of the century, as "the real America."

"A Raft of Dreams"

By November, 1936, the O'Neills, having decided to sell Casa Genotta, departed from their "Blessed Isle" for Seattle, Washington. In the Northwest O'Neill hoped to get material from various areas for a multi-play cycle, *A Tale of Possessors Self-Dispossessed*, a saga whose length, in the planning stages, changed from time to time. By 1935, says Jordan Y. Miller, the number of plays projected had reached seven.[53] Annoyed by the inevitable publicity brought upon them by the awarding of the Nobel Prize on November 12, the O'Neills sought privacy in December by moving to a 158-acre estate in Contra Costa County, California, the site of Tao House, a Chinese-styled mansion built according to their specifications. In these picturesque surroundings O'Neill was to live and write from December, 1937, until December, 1943, when difficulties caused another move. These were most productive years, for in spite of an increasing chronic illness, he finished *A Touch of the Poet* (1935-42), *The Iceman Cometh* (1939), and *A Moon for the Misbegotten* (1943). In addition to *A Touch of the Poet*, he began other parts of *A Tale of Possessors*.

As he pondered about the projected cycle—"a scheme quite on a grand scale"—his pleasant memories which had given him so much delight during the composing of *Ah, Wilderness!* gradually faded. The "old vein of ironic tragedy" began to return. Now, as his cycle—a "stupendous thing"—was gradually taking shape, his imagination played upon phases of American possessiveness and materialism which had burgeoned during the eighteenth and nineteenth centuries. Such stages of native development were projected as parts of the spiritual and psychological history of a migrating American family, who for a period of 150 years moved back and forth through the East, the Midwest, and the West. (Here O'Neill was making still another dramatic correlation with the tension-filled story of his own wandering family.) In fact, O'Neill became so deeply involved with his writing and his imaginative excursions into the past that "he now excluded almost everything and everyone in the contemporary world—except his wife."[54]

By such unstinting labor he was able to complete in 1942 *A Touch of the Poet*, originally titled *(The) Hair of the Dog*, once thought of as the title for the entire cycle. As the first of the cycle to be completed, although it was not published until 1957, the *Poet*, in spite of its historical setting in the Jacksonian era, is marked by various autobiographical fragments describing the settlement of the Irish in the Boston area.[55] In this play of alienation and failure O'Neill, as he wrote to Barrett H. Clark in 1937, dramatized "the way the world wags" in a small New England town populated by the older Yankee families and the later immigrants from Ireland, Portugal, and other countries. Throughout the action he demonstrates his sure feeling "that Man has definitely decided to destroy himself, and this seems to me the only truly wise decision he has ever made."[56] And the *Poet*, as much as the *Iceman*, is a tale of dreamers, notably of an Irish dreamer and poseur who destroys himself when his ambitions fail. Here again the tragic sense of social isolation and the struggle to belong are set imaginatively against a village background.

As he was completing the scenarios of three of the cycle plays, the playwright's interest in the Irish Melody family and the Yankee Harfords had already taken his thoughts back to July, 1828, to a village world outside Boston before Sara Melody's marriage to Simon Harford, dreamer and heir to a shipping fortune. Sequentially another drama, entitled *More Stately Mansions*, was to portray the different mansions near Boston occupied by Simon and Sara Harford, from 1837 to 1842, or later. Exactly what further treatment of eighteenth- and nineteenth-century community life O'Neill may have planned cannot be known. Unfortunately his ambition to complete his cyclic family history was thwarted by his worsening health and concomitant tragic blows. On February 21, 1944, in order to prevent others from tampering with his "elephant opus," he destroyed two plays—(*The*) *Greed of the Meek* and *And Give Me* (*Us*) *Death*. But he kept intact the lengthy manuscript of *More Stately Mansions*, which Mrs. O'Neill later sent to Yale. Since he still wanted to complete the cycle, though in revised form, he did keep most of his notes. Nevertheless, Mrs. O'Neill reports, as his physical and mental health declined, her husband finally in 1953, with her help, tore to pieces and burned the manuscripts of his cycle. By November 27 of that year, O'Neill was dead. Somehow an unedited typescript of *More Stately Mansions* was not destroyed; and a shortened acting version, made by director Karl Ragnar Gierow, was finally produced in Stockholm's Royal Dramatic Theatre on November 9, 1962.[57]

Similar to Harry Hope's cheap ginmill in *The Iceman Cometh*, the unchanging scene for *A Touch of the Poet* is a run-down tavern—Melody's Tavern, "in a village a few miles from Boston," as it appeared on July 27, 1828. Formerly prosperous as a stagecoach stop, this century-old tavern "has fallen upon neglected days" with the discontinuance of the stage line. The once spacious dining room–taproom, beamed and paneled in oak, is now a cheap saloon, turned into an eyesore by a flimsily built partition "painted in imitation of the old

paneled walls" and by other changes. Such is the single set which symbolizes the failure of the Melody family, Irish immigrants, to achieve
status and amass wealth in Massachusetts. The effects of Yankee civilization upon the soul and character of the protagonist, Cornelius
("Con") Melody, have been devastating. In self-pity he rationalizes
over the fact that he has been "a credulous gull and let the thieving
Yankees swindle me of all I had when we came here, . . ." By late July,
1828, his predicament, as an Irish outsider in a puritan-philistine world,
is evidenced by the look of "wrecked distinction" about his face, "of
brooding, humiliated pride." Con makes the most of every opportunity
to display his bleeding heart to his sycophantic cronies, mostly Irish,
who frequent his barroom for free drinks. Men of obscure destinies,
they submit, for the price of a drink, to listening to Con's oft-repeated
and windy recital of his brave action as a major during the bloody battle
of Talavera, along Spain's Tagus River, long ago in 1809. He can never
forget July 27, the anniversary of Talavera, when, during his annual
free dinner and drinking bout for the barflies, he struts about in his
carefully kept scarlet uniform, for him a symbol of his former status
as an officer and a gentleman.

But Major Cornelius indulges in his memories of past glory at the
expense of Nora, his overworked, slovenly wife, and his daughter Sara,
unwillingly pressed into service as the waitress and chambermaid, who
prefers all her own "crazy dreams of riches and a grand estate and me
a haughty lady riding around in a carriage with coachman and footman."[58] During his periods of arrogant posturing as a pseudo-gentleman,
Cornelius cannot let peasant-born Nora, whom he seduced before marriage, forget that though he is the son of an Irish shebeen keeper, he
fought his way up the Irish social scale and, as a British officer, played
"at the game of gentleman's honor, too!" What he does not boast about
is the truth that, as an officer under Wellington during the Napoleonic
Wars, he disgraced himself. With the loss of his commission, he sought
to regain status by emigrating with his wife and child to New England.
Even here, as Sara's bitter scorn suggests, he proved "the easiest fool
ever came to America!" While he has done no "rampagin' wid women
here," as he did as an officer, the "damned Yankee gentry won't let
him come near them." And Con intensifies his aloneness by considering
"the few Irish around here to be scum beneath his notice." The irony
of such snobbishness is that Con's "father wasn't of the quality in
Galway like he makes out, but a thievin' shebeen keeper who got rich
by moneylendin' and squeezin' tenants and every manner of trick."[59]

There is sardonic personal history, thinly disguised, in Major

Melody's lording over his impoverished barroom habitués in much the same way that James O'Neill, in the roles of Monte Cristo and other romantic characters, towered over stage underlings. They are brothers under the skin in their humble origins and their dreams of becoming someday, somehow, accepted as New World gentlemen. O'Neill's description of "our great gentleman," as Sara scornfully calls her father, tallies somewhat with portraits of James O'Neill when he was a handsome matinee idol. Melody, at forty-five, is tall, broad-shouldered, with a soldierly bearing. His now ruined face, which most shows the ravages of dissipation, "was once extraordinarily handsome in a reckless, arrogant fashion. It is still handsome—the face of an embittered Byronic hero . . ." His thick, curly iron-gray hair, his charm as a ladies' man, his self-delusion and Byronic theatricalism, his yearning for social acceptance in the town, his love for romantic poetry—Byron's especially —his love-hate attitude toward Sara, and his weakness for drink, offset by his ability to hold his liquor, all are reminders of the histrionic James O'Neill. Another suggestion of his father is O'Neill's conviction that the loneliest persons are the proudest, expressed in the Major's flamboyant recital of Byron's defiant lines, "I have not loved the World, nor the World me;/ I have not flattered its rank breath, not bowed/ To its idolatries a patient knee . . ." and in his bitter denunciation of the neighboring Yankees as "clumsy, fish-blooded louts" in their lovemaking. In such histrionic defiance, as in other ways, Melody is as much the actor as James O'Neill. But, as Gassner has said, Melody's pretense "is not just a matter of common histrionics, but of men's rising 'on the stepping stones/ Of their dead selves to higher things' by some charisma of personality, by some will to believe, and by some power of the imagination."[60]

Con's pretensions to refinement victimize his family and isolate him from the Yankee aristocrats, whose "damned Puritan background" and habit of "seeing sin hiding under every bush" evoke his bitter scorn. His "mad dreams" also antagonize the town's Irish "scum," putting them in a rage when, ironically, he sides with the high-toned Yankees by coming out against Andrew Jackson, that "contemptible, drunken scoundrel!" and by lambasting the Democrats. Con's scathing denunciation of "that idol of the riffraff" and "the cursed destiny in these decadent times," while amusing, is significantly typical of O'Neill's practice of linking family relationships—notably those of the Mannons—with social history. The Major's dictum that "everywhere the scum rises to the top" typifies O'Neill's use of the past to expose modern social problems, a technique which links his work with Faulkner's more recent exposure of small-town "Snopesism." While Nora and Sara secretly enjoy Con's pretensions, they also spoil to some degree the intended effects of his posing, as when they intrude during his boastful conversation with that "grand Yankee lady," Mrs. Henry Harford. Nora, with her dumpy body, her sagging breasts, and her old clothes "like a bag covering it, tied around the middle," has aged herself beyond her forty years by toiling at menial tasks to support his pretentious ways. While she satisfies his need for a woman who understands, Nora is an ever-present reminder of his marriage to an Irish bogtrotter. Sara, dreaming of rising in the community, irritates her father by her taunting remarks about his self-indulgence which stands in her way to success. Although she possesses a sort of unadorned beauty, Sara also has a touch of coarseness and sensuality about her mouth, showing a kinship with Con's "tough peasant vitality." Her large feet and broad, ugly hands with stubby fingers, together with her tendency to lapse into brogue, remind Con of his own family's peasant origins in Galway.

This family situation becomes all the more complicated when the town's old Puritan line is joined, quite fortuitously, with its Irish-American stock. Young Simon Harford, in quiet rebellion against his father's pragmatism, is a dreamer of romantic dreams who, as Con confirms later, is "a young fool, full av dacency and dreams, and looney, too, wid a touch av the poet in him."[61] Experimenting with a kind of Thoreauvian living, Simon, an offstage character, occupies a cabin on Con's property, spending his time thinking "great thoughts about what life means" and planning a book about the joys of independent living. When Sara breaks into this solitude, however, his writing consists of nothing more than secret love lyrics. At the time when she finds him ill and removes him to a room in the tavern, Sara sets her cap for the shy aristocrat, even to the point of deliberately turning seductress to insure their marriage. Domestic troubles begin when beautiful Deborah Harford, Simon's fragile, ladylike mother, ventures from her fine mansion to enter the shabby inn. In an interview with the Major, who puts on airs and tries to flirt with her, Deborah cautions him against furthering a marriage between her son and his daughter. (The word portrait of Deborah suggests that Ella O'Neill was the actual prototype.)

Her warning addressed to Sara—in one of the longest speeches in the play—is a discourse upon the history of the Harford family, whose motivating spirit of enterprise parallels a dominant trait among the Mannons. As she says, Simon, "an inveterate dreamer" moved by a dream of "self-emancipation at the breast of Nature," is simply following the family bent toward dreaming. She warns Sara that "the Harfords have been great dreamers," but their dreams have been material ones. Even wars—the Revolutionary War and the War of 1812—have been to the Harfords merely opportunities to fulfil the family dream of amassing wealth. Privateering, the Northwest trade, and other enterprises typify "their long battle to escape the enslavement of freedom by enslaving it." Most of all, she emphasizes, "the Harford pursuit of freedom imposed upon the women who shared their lives."

Always the Harford men have refused to be deterred in their drive toward status and wealth. So it happens that Henry Harford sends his unctuous advocate to buy Con off. Insulted, Con, still wearing his Talavera uniform, rushes out of the inn furiously to avenge his honor by challenging Harford to a duel, quite forgetting that duels have been outlawed. The fiasco which follows ends with the complete routing of Con and Jamie Cregan, a member of his Talavera company, by the police and the Harford servants. This disaster so disillusions him that he returns to the inn, a bedraggled and unmasked man, stripped of all his pretended glory, and lapses into the coarse brogue and other loutish ways of his Galway boyhood.

Beyond his concern with social history O'Neill again explores the crises confronting the divided character, or *doppelgänger*. At the close of this eventful Talavera day, Melody resolves the conflict between his warring selves by, first of all, impulsively shooting his cherished thoroughbred mare, like his beautiful uniform a symbol of his predilection for gentility. Then, quite chastened, he objectively exposes the game of "play-actin' " so long indulged in by "the late lamented auld liar and lunatic, Major Cornelius Melody, av His Majesty's Seventh Dragoons." Now relieved that the Major's "last bit av lyin' pride is murthered and stinkin'," Con vulgarly advises Sara that her first step toward uniting "earthy immigrants with the cold-blooded Yankees" is to "make the young Yankee gintleman have you in his bed."[62] After this catharsis, Con Melody rejoins his class—the barroom cronies.

As for the Melody women, O'Neill at the last probes into the old problem of the triumph of love over false pride. Sara, taking the initiative in lovemaking, becomes happily engaged to her Yankee gentleman, after discovering that "it was through him she found the love in herself." As she tells Nora, in one way Simon "doesn't count at all, because it's your own love you love in him and to keep that your pride will do anything." Earlier Nora had emotionally revealed to her daughter how long ago she, a peasant colleen, realized her own dream through deep pride in her love for Con. Love comes, she says, "when, if all the fires of hell was between you, you'd walk in them gladly to be with him, and sing with joy at your own burnin', if only his kiss was on your mouth! That's love, and I'm proud I've known the great sorrow and joy of it!"[63] This is why, at the finale, Nora can turn to Sara and say teasingly, "Shame on you to cry when you have love. What would the young lad think of you?" Moreover, because of the depth of her own love she can forgive Con for his abuse of her. With keen insight, she understands why he spouted Byron "to pretend himself was a lord wid the touch av the poet." And if now he wants to keep on "makin' game of everyone, puttin on the brogue and actin' like one av thim" in the bar, may it bring him "peace and company in his loneliness," for "God pity him, he's had to live all his life alone in the hell av pride." Of course, beyond Con's pride and his vainglorious dreams of escaping the commonplace, there is an exposure of a young and materialistic America and scorn for "the rule of the *canaille* in a leveling democracy." Con's pride and his soaring imagination were simply means by which he tried to escape being trapped in an early nineteenth-century Massachusetts town.

This complicated emotional web linking the three Melodys to each other, as well as to their Yankee contemporaries and Irish compatriots, forms the basis for a compelling, but unfinished, family drama which has been compared to Ibsen's *The Wild Duck.* As Karl Ragnar Gierow has shown, in *More Stately Mansions*[64] (published in 1964), the story of Simon and Sara has the same small-town setting as in *A Touch of the Poet.* Its first scene is near Melody's tavern, to which Sara, for some years now Mrs. Harford, has returned to attend her father's funeral. As the title suggests, this cycle play, describing the Harford dynasty, fulfils Melody's last-act prophecy in the *Poet* about Sara's future: ". . . and she'll live in a Yankee mansion, as big as a castle, on a grand estate of stately woodland." And here is still another example of O'Neill's interest in self-determination, rather than economic determinism. *A Touch of the Poet* reached New York in a roundabout way, having been first performed at the Royal Dramatic Theatre in Stockholm in March, 1958. On October 2, under Harold Clurman's direction, it opened at the Helen Hayes Theatre for a run of 284 performances. The acting of Helen Hayes as Nora, Kim Stanley as Sara, Eric Portman as Con, and Betty Field as Deborah Harford, together with Ben Edwards' set design, aroused a degree of enthusiasm among critics, though some, such as Brooks Atkinson and Joseph Wood Krutch, commented upon O'Neill's lack of a facile style and remarked on his continued notes of hatred and bitterness.

The interlinking, from 1832 to 1941, of the fortunes of the Yankee Harfords with the rise of the beautiful daughter of an Irish tavern-keeper dramatizes, in *More Stately Mansions*, the devastating effect upon a proud family of too much greed for business success and power. Such was the gist of the shortened Swedish version, by Karl Ragnar Gierow, which was produced for the first time, in Stockholm on November 9, 1962. Now, thanks to the 1964 release by the Yale Press of the Gierow version, meticulously edited by Donald Gallup, this play is readily available to the student who wishes to trace the corruption of the Harfords, including Sara Melody Harford, to its bitter end.

Less limited in its locale than *A Touch of the Poet*, this sequel, beginning with a scene in the woods near Con Melody's village tavern, where Sara first met Simon Harford, provides a tracing of Simon and Sara's married life. At first happily established in a comfortable home in a textile-mill town about forty miles from the city, Simon and Sara, with their four sons, live a peaceful and moderately prosperous life. Simon, once something of a moon calf with "a touch of the poet," has become a prospering mill president. Even so, at thirty-one he is beginning to show nervous tension, "the mental strain of a man who has been working too hard and puts unrelieved pressure on himself." The tension increases when, at his father's death, Simon rather than his inefficient brother Joel is selected to direct the affairs of his father's shipping interests in the city. After that, his preoccupation with business becomes such an obsession that his marital happiness is threatened. Complex difficulties multiply as Simon and Sara move into his mother's mansion. Thereafter the action centers around the bitter struggle between Sara, beautiful but coarse, and aristocratic Deborah Harford for dominance over Simon, body and soul. In the tragic end all of the possessors are dispossessed.

"From a Black Abyss"

Until the end of his creative activity in the early forties, O'Neill's personal situation persistently obtruded itself into his dramas, especially the small-town ones. Isolated at Tao House, he labored under painful emotional and physical strain on the undisguisedly autobiographical *Long Day's Journey into Night*. At the opening of these years of toil O'Neill had felt compelled to return creatively to one of the black abysses of memory: to August, 1912, when all four of the O'Neills, while summering at their New London cottage, were facing heartbreaking family and personal crises. As Carlotta has reported, "he had to write the play . . . because it was a thing that haunted him." Moreover, now that his parents and Jamie were long since dead and his own health was failing, he wanted "to forgive his family and himself."[65] In 1939 O'Neill began to draw heavily, just as he had done in some of his earlier plays, upon his memories of his own youthful ideals, anxieties, resentments, and bitterness in order to refashion them, with remorse and compassion, into a tense family situation played out against a small-town background of 1912. The tragic problems for the play's Tyrones, as among his small-town characters generally, were those problems of his own family that once were most urgent for him. Hence, when he had finished the *Journey* O'Neill, in presenting the original script to Carlotta as a twelfth anniversary gift, wrote a deeply emotional letter to her about "this play of old sorrow, written in tears and blood." Through her loving assistance he had at last been able to face his dead and to write "with deep pity and understanding and forgiveness for all the four haunted Tyrones."[66]

This dark day experienced by the Irish Tyrones so thinly disguised the painful and sordid past of the O'Neills that only a few friends were allowed to see the *Journey* manuscript. Moreover, O'Neill's declaration, "There is one person [i.e., himself as Edmund Tyrone] in it still alive," in part explains his stipulation that the play be neither performed nor published until twenty-five years after his death. As a precautionary measure, copies were locked in the vault of his publisher, Random House, and other copies, along with early drafts and working notes, were placed in the Yale University Library. Nevertheless, in February, 1956—three years after O'Neill's death and after Random House can-celed its contract rather than violate the original twenty-five year limit—the Yale University Press, with Mrs. O'Neill's permission, published the play. Before this volume was marketed, however, *Long Day's Journey*, again by Mrs. O'Neill's consent and in accordance with O'Neill's hopes, was performed successfully in Stockholm. In spite of the play's four and one-half hours of playing length, its theatrical viability enthralled the Swedes and helped bring about a remarkably rapid change in critical opinion and audience appreciation of O'Neill's work. On the American scene, in November of that year, Mrs. O'Neill herself was to say that the remarkable resurgence of interest in her husband's work stemmed from this Stockholm premiere. "Sweden did this for O'Neill, not Amer-ica. America was not a damn bit interested."[67] Furthermore, it was José Quintero's brilliant and subtle directing for the Circle-in-the-Square revival of *The Iceman Cometh*, in May, 1956, that prompted Mrs. O'Neill to invite him to direct *Long Day's Journey* in an American pre-miere. His acceptance made theatrical history and provided an impres-sive climax for O'Neill's posthumous career.

While not social history, *Long Day's Journey* gives the reader, or spectator, a remarkable sense of the decade around 1912 and of Connecticut's port town life. Throughout its four tense acts the town of New London, as it appeared in August, 1912—six years later than the July scenes of *Ah, Wilderness!*—is of no importance per se but functions only as an environmental backdrop to the social alienation of the Tyrones. At the opposite extreme from the settled and respectable Nat Miller family, the Tyrones are stigmatized as "queer acting folk," on the fringe, but not beyond the fringe, of the town's social circles. These two New London plays have been looked upon "as two sides of the same coin—one a benign glimpse of what the O'Neill family, at its best, aspired to be and the other a balefully heightened picture of what it was at its worst."[68]

In the *Journey*, fleeting glimpses of several phases of the town's life emerge from scene to scene in relation to each character's interests or desires. The self-pitying mother, Mary Cavan Tyrone, suffers from loneliness as a result not only of the town's caste system but also of her drug addiction. Mary's nervous talking about wanting a real home is nothing but wish fulfilment, an agonized longing born of long dissociation as a touring actor's wife. Though she acknowledges that some of their fellow citizens are only "big frogs in a little puddle," still there is an undercurrent of lonely yearning when, imprisoned in her fogbound cottage, she wishes to be like the Chatfields and other first families who "stand for something" and own "decent presentable homes they don't have to be ashamed of." Even while she tells Edmund, her younger son, of her hate for the town and for everyone in it, Mary envies those fortunate enough to have "friends who entertain them and whom they entertain."

Edmund reminds his mother that he, too, scorns "this hick burg," even while admitting that, on second thought, the "town's not so bad . . . it's the only home we've had." Nevertheless, he says that he and Jamie, ten years his elder, are "bored stiff" by the town's "respectable parents" and their "nice girls" who worship decorum. Edmund prefers reading and an occasional drinking spree with Jamie, now at thirty-three a "beguiling ne'er-do-well, with a strain of the sentimentally poetic, attractive to women and popular with men." Always exerting a strong influence upon Edmund, the "Kid," Jamie has an easy familiarity with New London's "booze joints" and houses of prostitution.

Their matinee idol father, James Tyrone, now sixty-five, has never lacked certain types of friendly and even convivial associates in the town. As Mary laments to Edmund, "All he likes is to hobnob with men at the Club or in a barroom. Jamie and you are the same way, but you're not to blame. You've never had a chance to meet decent people here."[69] On occasion James's business interests bring him into contact with other townsmen such as Doctor Hardy, a quack whom he engages to examine Edmund, and McGuire, a realtor who beguiles him into believing that New London is soon to experience a real estate boom. Behind his weakness for drink and his improbable speculation in real estate there is a penchant for penny-wise bargains which arouses the animosity of his sons. His temporizing in matters that count also affects his own career, in which he might have triumphed as a Shakespearean actor had he not succumbed to the easy lure of popular roles. James's stinginess extends even to his hiring of cheap Irish domestic help, Bridget the cook and Cathleen the second girl, both generally unskilled. Also, while neighboring householders employ yardmen, James demands that his sons aid him in mowing their grass and clipping the hedges, a task they always perform with deep resentment.

Though the *Journey* is one of O'Neill's leviathans, with long acting hours "of turbulence and fatefulness," a remarkable feature is its lack of action in the conventional sense of plot. Activity is restricted largely to many-faceted portrayals of each of the haunted Tyrones in a complex relationship of vengeful hatred or deep affection, or both at the same time, to each of the others. As Gilbert Seldes has said, "The play is a search for causes, as near to the primal cause as O'Neill can get."[70] The "primal cause" for the Tyrones, being what they are—a collective failure —is that all suffer from a primal curse, the "curse of the misbegotten." Their individual lives have been guilt-ridden. Since their mental agonizing must be considered along with their outer lives, frequently complicated by pretenses, it may be said that there are eight main characters, for each Tyrone has a *doppelgänger*. In addition, O'Neill's dramatic accomplishment in the development of the doubly characterized Tyrones is complexly achieved, by sheer power and compassion, along several planes.

First, on the plane of impulse, the Tyrones respond spontaneously and without reflection, as humorously illustrated in the family joke about a Tyrone farm tenant, wily Shaughnessy, whose pigs bathed in the ice pond belonging to Harker, the Standard Oil millionaire. Then, there is the plane of relation to society—in this instance, to small-town social circles which, as noted earlier, largely exclude the Tyrones. Such exclusion leads to pretenses, as when pathetic Mary Tyrone, sometimes accompanied by the maid Cathleen, tries to impress local socialites by directing the chauffeur to drive James's secondhand Packard past the town's mansions. On the plane of compromise James and his sons forget their bickering long enough to tolerate Mary's disturbing drug habit and mental withdrawal rather than risk a disastrous correction. Once in bitter anguish Edmund momentarily forgets to restrain himself as he condemns his mother: "It's pretty hard to take at times, having a dope fiend for a mother!" Along the plane of contemplation Edmund, given to shaking revelations of self-truth, searches hopefully for the truth of what the Tyrones were. As improvident as Jamie, but of a much more sensitive and intellectual bent and now feverish from a developing consumption, Edmund bitterly meditates about his own identity: ". . . a stranger who never feels at home, who does not really want and is not really wanted, who can never belong, who must always be a little in love with death!"[71]

Finally, there is the plane of escape and dreams, along which all of these misbegotten Tyrones move, just as from act to act "they slip back and forth from one plane to another in a grim dance of life."[72] Mary, who takes to narcotics to forget the terrors of life, escapes by way of pleasant memories of her convent schooling and her dreams of someday having a real home. James, haunted by his poverty-stricken Irish childhood, dreams of becoming a local man of property. And Edmund, cynically regarding himself as a misunderstood stranger in "this hick burg," has never felt "the joy of belonging to a fulfilment beyond men's lousy, pitiful, greedy fears and hopes and dreams." Jamie, who has a real love for his mother but hates his father, admits in a fit of drunkenness that, though he loves Edmund, he also has the subconscious desire to destroy him.

This multi-faceted tragedy, merciless as autobiography, becomes a continuously absorbing exposition of Mary Tyrone's bitter confession to James: "The past is the present, isn't it? It's the future, too. We all try to lie out of that, but life won't let us."[73] She cannot forget the past. Confronted with their individual dilemmas, each of the four Tyrones moves from the early morning's surface gaiety and light teasing into the evening's harsh recriminations. Each tries to blame someone else for his own mistakes. Mary's sense of guilt dates from the early days of her marriage when another son, Eugene, died of neglect while still a baby. Through the years Mary has indulged in self-blame because at that time she had yielded to James's insistence that she accompany him on a theatrical tour. In her absence Jamie, ill with measles, slipped into the nursery, exposing the baby to the disease. As the years pass, Mary continues to blame James for his insistence that she have another child to take the place of the lost baby. Now, as her neuroticism has grown worse, she recalls that during her last pregnancy, with Edmund, she was afraid that "something terrible would happen." As a devout Catholic, she had then felt that she was unworthy to have another child. "God would punish me if I did."

James's guilt stems from his stinginess. When Edmund was born he was too niggardly to employ a reputable doctor. The quack who attended the birth gave Mary morphine, thus initiating the addiction which for years thereafter was to cause her mental and physical suffering. Because of James's parsimony in refusing to pay for an effective cure, Mary constantly falls back into the habit of using drugs. As the play opens and the long day begins, she has just returned once again to the New London cottage following another period of hospitalization.

Jamie, though now thirty-three, is still haunted by a feeling of guilt when he recalls his part in the death of the baby Eugene. His remorse deepens as Mary charges that he had entered the baby's room on purpose. "He was jealous of the baby. He'd been warned that it might kill the baby." Sensitive and introverted Edmund, O'Neill's counterpart, feels guilty for ever having been born, thus sharing with his "Old Man" the feeling of having helped turn his mother into a dope addict. Moreover, the jealousy and affection between the brothers add as strongly to the day's distress as do the hatred and love between James and his sons. The three men, however, are united by their common rejection of the actuality of Mary's condition. On occasion they pretend that she is not under the influence of dope, and again they denounce her for her weakness, though each strikes at the other to defend her.

For the Circle in the Square premiere of this tragedy of human error and misery, O'Neill's meticulous description of the Tyrone summer house, as it appeared throughout one day in August, 1912, was adapted most expertly to a period set designed by David Hays, then at twenty-six the youngest designer on Broadway. Hays added to the production's total truthfulness by creating a set wholly in keeping with the informal kind of life lived in an actor's summer place. Enhanced by Tharon Musser's sensitive lighting, the Hays set changed character as the day lengthened into night, thus heightening the most dramatic moments. By around half past six in the evening the gathering fog, with its accompanying foghorn, had brought on a darkness, real and symbolic, which quite overshadowed the bright sunshine of the morning hours. Throughout these hours of light and darkness Hays's realistic design had the look of a much-used family room of the period. Double doorways with portieres, a wicker couch with matching chairs and a table, an ordinary oak desk and rocker, a reading lamp, and an inoffensive rug helped give a family air to the room. A small bookcase, with a picture of Shakespeare above it, held a motley collection of novels by Balzac, Zola, and Stendhal, philosophical and sociological works by Nietzsche, Marx, and others, plays by Ibsen, Strindberg, and Shaw, and poems by Swinburne, Wilde, Ernest Dowson, and Kipling. A large, glassed-in case was filled with sets of Shakespeare, Dumas, Hugo, old plays, poetry, and histories, including several of Ireland. "The astonishing thing about these sets," as O'Neill noted, "is that all the volumes have the look of having been read and reread." During the daylight hours the entire room was lighted by a series of three windows which also provided views of the lawn, the waterfront avenue, and the harbor beyond, thereby bringing the Tyrones into contact with the town.

Quintero's directing, with its fidelity to O'Neill's stage directions, slowly and naturally developed the broken world of the Tyrones. Beginning on a relaxed and almost jovial note, he allowed the various loyalties and tensions of a family relationship to proceed as though they were a part of life, rather than scenes from a play. As the night moved nearer, he gradually intensified the play's elements of tension and mental torture. In this achievement he had the support of a dedicated cast, whose empathy led to their triumphs over the difficulties of the script. While, by the end of the play, nothing really is resolved for the Tyrones, a great deal was done in production by five skilful and sympathetic players. Frederic March, as the skinflint father, and Jason Robards, Jr., as the dissolute elder son, with the most demanding roles to play, performed with remarkable skill and range. March's aging James Tyrone was a steadily sustained personation, portraying from the first scene his resignation to Jamie's and Edmund's waywardness and his cheerful hope that at last Mary had been cured of her addiction to narcotics. When however she did return to using dope, James, as interpreted by March, resigned himself to spending the rest of his life without faith. In portraying James's efforts to forget by drinking whiskey, March pictured him as always governed by self-discipline. No stunt performance of inebriation marred his excellent interpretation. In sharp contrast, Robards' alcoholic Jamie was loud, with wild and wilful expressions of his ambivalent feelings of love and hate toward Edmund. Bradford Dillman, as Edmund, and Florence Eldridge, as Mary, made these roles coherent and quite moving.

Miss Eldridge gave her most affecting performances in those scenes in which Mary Tyrone nervously tries to defend her addiction before what she imagines to be the accusations of her men. Particularly moving was her interpretation of the painful scene at the finale when Mary, with a mad look in her eyes and "a marble mask of girlish innocence," returns to the living room carelessly trailing along the floor her "old-fashioned white satin wedding gown." Miss Eldridge, by appropriately vague looks, gestures, and words, skilfully revealed how Mary, strangely preoccupied, had retreated within herself. Seemingly unaware of the presence of her shocked husband and sons, Mary dreamily re-enacts some of the happy experiences of her convent days, before she fell in love with James Tyrone and entered a strange world for which she had no preparation. Finally, to use Edmund's phrase, the curtain fell upon "us fog people."

Dillman, as sensitive, poetic Edmund, interpreted genuinely the lyric passages which express a young dreamer's need for freedom, notably for that ecstatic freedom which once he had found at sea. In that moment, Edmund recalls, ". . . I lost myself—actually lost my life. I was set free! I dissolved in the sea, became white sails and flying spray, became beauty and rhythm, became moonlight and the ship and the high dim-starred sky!" Alone on deck he had found momentary "peace and unity and a wild joy" and had discovered something greater than his own life, or the life of Man: ". . . God, if you want to put it that way."[74] Now, at the end of this long day's journey, his remembrance of such lost beauty gives Edmund one means of escaping from his present bitter discoveries about his mother's drug habit, his father's egotism and miserliness, his brother's failures and enmity toward him, and his own tubercular condition which will exile him indefinitely to a sanatorium. Feeling that he has come to the end of his quest for life's meaning, Edmund deliberately gives way to drunkenness and becomes lost in the fog again, stumbling on toward nowhere. If, as Henry Hewes felt, Dillman made Edmund seem "more a young Keats than a young O'Neill," nevertheless his portrayal was effective and moving.

Katherine Ross, in the minor part of the slow-witted and clumsy Irish servant, the second girl Cathleen, performed on such a high level that she drew critical praise for her playing with "freshness and taste . . . exactly right . . . excellent." And the appropriate period costume designs by Motley—*nom de théâtre* for Elizabeth Montgomery—and the work of Quintero's co-producers, young Leigh Connell and Theodore Mann, helped make *Long Day's Journey into Night* "a stunning theatrical experience" and a sensation of the 1956-57 season. All theatrical values combined to win for this play "of blood and tears" the first posthumous Pulitzer Prize ever awarded.

The *Journey* was written as O'Neill's personal testament, releasing the ghosts of old sorrows from his heart and mind. As the most memorable of his autobiographical plays, it calls to mind that, in general, the varied people in his small-town world frequently behave in the ways he himself felt. Mostly, they are a disenchanted lot, as unhappy as alcoholic James

Tyrone, Jr., and oversized Josie Hogan in *A Moon for the Misbegotten*, a farm tragedy, again featuring Jamie O'Neill, which was written in 1943, just two years after the completion of the *Journey*. (The great success of the *Journey* led to a not too successful posthumous production of the *Moon* in May, 1957.)

By and large, in O'Neill's varied plays set in American small towns there is relatively little realization of an external nature, particularly in regard to the towns themselves. Rather, O'Neill often chose to go back to the secret springs of psychoanalysis: to the parental backgrounds, the youthful deprivations, the stifled yearnings, and the questing spirit of his protagonists. And in such a "return to the fountains" there is much reconstruction, within the range of O'Neill's own emotions, of the intricate, relentless discord of personalities, frequently behind symbols that are only skin-deep. In projecting his peopled cosmos, or microcosm, he was not always successful in his efforts to reach the impersonal through dramatic camouflage.

While he was a bold experimenter with considerable verbal dexterity, critics have felt that he failed to achieve greatness in the handling of poetic language. Nevertheless, the scope of his efforts in the use of historic time, geographic backgrounds, and technical innovation and his range of provincial types of both low and high status is the widest in the entire dramatic history of the American small town. No other native playwright has equaled his preoccupation with haunted provincials whose mental and physical suffering and frustration drive them to tragedy.

Although *Ah, Wilderness!* was a lightheartedly nostalgic wish fulfilment, O'Neill characteristically dramatized the human dilemmas of a varied philistine world, from the Civil War to the modern years of crisis. Many of the townspeople in his versions of Philistia, whether Irish-Americans, Yankee aristocrats, or humbler seagoing men, must endure soul-stifling daily struggles merely to exist. In a number of plays whole families suffer from such afflictions as sexual frustrations, unsuccessful religious and other questing, greed for land, social ambitions, snobbery, and comparable ills. Some resolve these inner conflicts; others fail in their search for happiness or for a philosophy which can give meaning to the inevitable conflicts of their lives. Beginning with small discoveries of the tensions beneath the surface of life which motivate human behavior, O'Neill progressed through the years toward some of his best achievements in the unmasking of American provincials. His diversified portraits of lost townsmen, realized through experimental techniques, suggest the success, within limits, of his long-continued striving to become "an artist or nothing."

X. More Southern Exposures

THE CHANGE from the brilliantly creative twenties to the depressed and bitter thirties was marked by widespread confusion regarding the underlying natures of the rural and the metropolitan worlds in the United States. These worlds, these environments poles apart, represented "in their essence the antipodes of human experience: one is inherent, the other is intrusive; one is natural, the other mechanized; . . ."[1] The realm of the cacophonous city, the domain of standardized existence peopled by the power elite, organization men, and the masses, has been pictured as a transient, ever-changing environment. With the years, urban complexity grew until by the late fifties, as one city planner recognized, "into the American landscape go explosives of the expanding community, and havoc rules."[2] Decade by decade the bulging city, with its satellite towns, has remained the symbol of change and progress. In contrast, there is the view that rural environments, from region to region, have provided man with what stays: a more elemental setting providing closer contact between man and nature, and between man and man, in the sense of a communal or neighborhood association. Here, indeed, in spite of a spreading standardization, existed—and still exists—another world: the farms, agricultural villages, and towns of rural America. Here in the hinterlands have dwelt many types of Americans whose fictional counterparts have continued, season after season, to enrich the drama of the small town.

As we have noted earlier, the indigenous life of the South, in its manifold aspects, has long been interpreted dramatically by both native and non-southern playwrights. Some of these, reacting against the evils and complexities of urbanism, have shared "the poet's conspiracy against the city," and offered instead dramatized illusions of the solace of the country and the small town. While some have felt that the city is a symbol of all that is civilized, polite, urbane, still others have held to the notion that "a rural environment is more congenial to human happiness than the environments of a city."[3] On the other hand, one of the prevailing convictions of the twenties was that "a pre-institutional life, a simple, primitive life, which antedated the destructive growth of industrial America, was a lost and irrecoverable ideal."[4] The sensitivity of writers to the complications and the persuasions of the present influenced their belief that the modern world had modified or even destroyed American innocence.

For some of our retrospective playwrights, seeking clues to the loss of innocence, life in southern small towns seemed rich in materials for dramatic expansion. On occasion southern dramatists such as Thomas Wolfe, uprooted from their native grounds and motivated by loneliness, wrote all the more dramatically because of their dissociation from their home places. Others, like William Faulkner, have written in close association with their local communities. Outsiders, such as Marc Connelly, have been skilful adapters, closely studying earlier records of the milieu and the mores of the folk they sought to portray. Moreover, in our changing theater since the early thirties, playgoers have been made aware of the customs and beliefs of imaginary townspeople, both white and black, scattered over a relatively wide southern area, including lower Louisiana, Mississippi, Georgia, Tennessee, and North Carolina.

In 1930, the same year when southern critics published *I'll Take My Stand* and Irving S. Babbitt and other New Humanists were lamenting that life in the United States was tawdry, cheap, dull, and slavishly worshipful of wealth and machinery, a young Pennsylvanian, Marc Connelly, drew a torrent of emotional praise from the critical press for his folk fable which opened on February 26 at the Mansfield Theatre, New York City. His *The Green Pastures* was simply a theatrical adaptation of *Ol' Man Adam an' His Chillun* (1928), Negro sketches by Roark Bradford. On stage it succeeded, as what Joseph Wood Krutch called "one of the most moving creations I have ever seen in the theatre," for its remarkable representation of a supposedly true Negro version of Christian mythology. Using multiple images of faith, Connelly portrayed the Louisiana Negro's naïve idea of heaven and of the world in those halcyon days when, according to belief, "God walked the earth in the likeness of man."

In a prefatory note, Connelly interpreted his folk play as an attempt "to present certain aspects of a living religion in terms of its believers." Such fervent religion, he wrote, once was part of the experience of thousands of untutored Negroes in the Deep South, who, moved by "terrific spiritual hunger and the greatest humility . . . have adapted the contents of the Bible to the consistencies of their everyday lives."[5] Accepting the Old Testament as "a chronicle of wonders which happened to people like themselves in vague but actual places," these simple Christians are characterized as believing in rules of conduct which, if faithfully followed, will lead them to "a tangible, three-dimensional Heaven." Since they belong to a district where fish fries are popular, these Louisiana villagers envision the angels as having "magnificent fish fries through an eternity somewhat resembling a series of earthly holidays." The Lord Jehovah, in their eyes an anthropomorphic deity, will walk the earth as a virtuous and compassionate patriarch, an ever present comforter to his followers. In fact, so familiar a figure is the Lord that in the opening scene a Negro Sunday School teacher, elderly Mr. Deshee, describes Him to a class of children as resembling the locally famous Reverend Mr. Dubois.

This opening scene, a framework for the sixteen scenes to follow, pictures, in realistic dialogue, one corner in a Negro church in a lower Louisiana town at Sunday School time. As ten squirming children listen, "with varied degrees of interest," the kindly old preacher, Mr. Deshee, is reading from the Bible, pausing now and then to interrogate the children and to dramatize narratives from Genesis in supposedly Negro images. Mr. Deshee's homely images suggest the pattern of the play's whole structure: a basic regional scene which quickly shifts into a two-part fantasy, all delightfully expressing the simplehearted preacher's powers of imagination as applied to the answering of a child's question: "What did God look like, Mr. Deshee?" Thereafter the Lord is pictured imaginatively as moving about Heaven and Earth in dignified semblance of old Mr. Dubois in a frock coat. As the dimming lights close scene 1, Mr. Deshee's biblical dramatizations open on the first of ten scenes of Part I: a heavenly fish fry held under a huge live oak near a riverbank. With an authentic regional set created by Robert Edmond Jones, with brightly colored robes and wings appropriate for the Mammy Angels, the Men Angels, and even the Cherubs, and "wid b'iled custard and ten cent seegars for de adults," this scene happily initiates Mr. Deshee's presentation of the Negro's anthropomorphic concept of God and Heaven, with his narrative brought forward to the time of the disembarking from the Ark. We follow here in rapid succession the scenes of the Creation, of the Fall of Man, of the Deluge, and of the Ark. Part II, in seven scenes, chiefly dramatizes the wrath of God against sinful Man. The narrative is here focused upon the treadmill march of the children of Israel, on Moses and Aaron and the Egyptian plagues, on the prophet Hosea, on Jacob and Joshua, and finally on "de Lawd," who at last shows mercy through his own suffering and faith in Man's potentialities for triumphing over evil. If the God of Moses be one of wrath, "de Lawd God of Hosea" is the symbol of mercy.

As Carl Carmer once wrote of the initial production, "Much that makes *The Green Pastures* an enchanted performance cannot be transplanted on the written page."[6] Connelly's directing his players to "imagine themselves small-town folk giving a performance for their local church" produced an illusion of verisimilitude. The large and gifted cast of Negro actors; the stage groupings arranged by Connelly himself; the full richness of the dialect with its earthy idiom; the power and poignancy of the spirituals or choral commentary sung by the Hall Johnson choir; Robert Edmond Jones's detailed stage sets, notably for the fish fry and the Ark scenes, complete with billowing waves and treadmill; and the atmospheric lighting effects—all of these are difficult to imagine from the mere reading about them. The supreme difficulty of the portrayal of "De Lawd" was solved most admirably by the empathic acting of Richard B. Harrison, whose sensitive interpretation was deepened by a touching dignity and benevolence as well as humor, qualities which made him popular in New York and on the road over a period of five years.

The imagination which conceived God in the guise of a Negro preacher, and Gabriel [Wesley Hill's superbly enacted role] in the guise of an amiable giant fingering his trumpet with nervous eagerness . . . was an imagination so richly concrete as to leave no room for question, and hence capable of creating a world in which everything seems both inevitable and right.[7]

Photographically clear stage directions, folk psychology, and colloquial dialogue evoke many aspects of Negro life in a Louisiana community, where much activity centers around the modest church. Innumerable reflections of Connelly's trips to Louisiana in search of authentic localisms suggest the tenor of life for a simple folk, to whom faith and sin were absolutes. Representative images of community ways include Noah's house resembling a neatly kept Negro cabin, God's office with the furnishings of a small-town lawyer's office, Gabriel's trumpet and the Babylonian Band calling to mind the Negro bands which once flourished in the South, a lodge ritual, vignettes of Zeba and the gaudily dressed chippies at a New Orleans gambling dive, the operation of the southern penal code, the Ark with the semblance of a Texas, the gusto for food ("Let it be a whole mess of firmament!"), and the delight in Sunday finery. All these suggest Connelly's deep insight into the simple, unsophisticated faith and the economic condition of Louisiana's Negro provincials. They suggest, too, the reasons why *The Green Pastures*, the Pulitzer Prize play for 1929-30, was called by Brooks Atkinson "the best-loved play of the century." At the same time, Dana Skinner, typifying the voices of vigorous dissent, condemned it, in the *Commonweal*, for its "spurious simplicity" or "forced naïveté," its "distinctly satiric twist," its "mixture of images," and its "lack of solemn grandeur."

Perhaps the rare excellence of *The Green Pastures* was its power to persuade audiences to accept the Bible spirit in terms of earthly familiarity. Connelly, himself, trying to give folksy expression to the truth of the spirit, learned, as he has said, that "simple people, no matter of what race, always seem to be near the center of things." Stage revivals, in the United States and Europe, and a movie version have kept alive in modern audiences both enthusiasm and the spirit of dissent. It is undeniably true, for example, that a 1951 New York production of *The Green Pastures*, with William Marshall as De Lawd and James Fuller as Gabriel, could not match the successful scoring of the season's hit, Rodgers and Hammerstein's *The King and I*, starring Gertrude Lawrence and Yul Brynner.

As the twenties lengthened into the thirties, the pervasive disenchantment of our world helped to hasten further shaping and reshaping of the dramatized images of the small town. Out of this new surge of exploration came some community plays at variance with the myth that rural environments generally provide man "with what stays." At the time when Connelly was reworking Bradford's Negro sketches, other playwrights were rejecting "our comfortable tradition and sure faith" and were releasing their energies in dramas of social protest. In this regard the South was not spared, as we have noted in Chapter VIII.

By the mid-forties and early fifties the imaginative literature about small towns in the South was to dominate the scene and to reach full expression in the writing of such talented newcomers as Lillian Hellman, Tennessee Williams, Carson McCullers, and William Faulkner, whose first novel, *Soldiers' Pay*, had appeared as early as 1926. Their best plays are largely the story of southerners as understood by southerners. In their imaginative exploration of southern towns these playwrights were involved in the significant experience of a national self-discovery during years of crisis. Their obsession with certain problems of society and the yearnings and frustrations of the individual was an echo of the "sound and the fury" of those troubled times.

Among the first of these playwrights to win theatrical acclaim was New Orleans-born Lillian Hellman Kober, who was quickly recognized as "an earnest, even anxious, student of social and economic conditions and trends, and of world politics."[8] As a student at New York University, she spent her summers in Louisiana with her grandmother and aunts, thus continuing her association with the Deep South. Miss Hellman's first play *The Children's Hour*, is not regional, but it was so significant in heralding her use of the southern social theme a few seasons later (with *The Little Foxes*) that it must be considered here.

Opening at the Maxine Elliott Theatre in New York on November 20, 1934, this impressive play proved highly successful as a realistic and excoriating record of the evil effects of an unfounded accusation of lesbianism. (Incidentally, not too many months later *The Children's Hour* was condemned on the Catholic White List as "completely pernicious" and was banned in Boston and Chicago.) The brilliantly ironic title refers to the action of a pampered and sadistic girl, Mary Tilford, whose malicious gossip and lies about the two young women owners and teachers spread havoc in a private school, already established adjacent to the conservative town of Lancet. Miss Hellman's mastery of material may be seen in her imaginative and original handling of her source—an actual case of slander tried in a nineteenth-century Scottish court. Enhanced by Aline Bernstein's impressive set for the Wright-Dobie School and directed by Herman Shumlin, the play honestly and vigorously treated a timeless theme, the danger of slander to a reputation and the power of public opinion in hastening tragic ruin.

Action is motivated by two abnormal troublemakers: maladjusted Mary Tilford and fuzzy-minded Mrs. Lily Mortar, an aging ex-actress now reduced to monitoring schoolgirls. Both suffer from persecution complexes. Both love the limelight, and both lie in order to achieve their selfish ends. Of the two, Mary, though only fourteen, is the more dangerous. Possessing a strange and abnormal nature and having been overly pampered by a doting and prosperous grandmother, Mrs. Amelia Tilford, the girl is accustomed to getting her way by cajolery and threats. Her skill and obstinacy in lying, her violent temper, her spirit of defiance toward any authority, and, most of all, her capacity for hate enable Mary to move from one despicable triumph to another, until she wrecks both the school and four adult lives. Her worldly wisdom, sheer nerve, and obstinate will insure her success in accusing Karen Wright and Martha Dobie, her teachers, of a homosexual relationship. Young Florence McGee played this role of an evil adolescent with an insight and power well sustained through long acts. (In the screen version, entitled *These Three*, Bonita Granville gave an effective interpretation of this role.)

Of a weaker nature, Mrs. Mortar, played by Aline McDermott, contributes her share toward the wrecking of the school and the eventual suicide of Martha Dobie, the niece who had befriended her. Her fuzzy-mindedness is coupled with vulgarity and an irritating tendency to glorify her doubtful stage career, in what Martha ridicules as "the gilded days." Now out of work and dependent upon Karen and Martha's generosity, this silly old has-been feels persecuted in her present role as a study hall monitor. A liar in her own right, she helps spread Mary's sly suggestions about Karen and Martha.

Still another frightening social type sharply ridiculed is the idle upper-class matron, given to ruling the town by her wealth and her shaping of public opinion. Callous Mrs. Tilford at first feels that her granddaughter's devastating lies can be atoned for by a public apology and an explanation and an offer of money to grief-stricken Karen. At last, with some remorse and an unaccustomed feeling of humility, she recognizes her tragic error in accepting a teen-ager's lies as the truth. But her recognition comes too late. Martha lies dead, and Karen's plans for marriage and a happy life with a young doctor are wrecked. At the finale, Karen denounces Mrs. Tilford, saying: "A public apology and money paid, and you can sleep again and eat again. That done and there'll be peace for you. . . . But what of me? It's a whole life for me. A whole God-damned life."[9] Here, indeed, is a keen awareness of a theme Miss Hellman was to use again: the exposure of social conditions in which, at the end, villainy seemingly triumphs.

Miss Hellman's achievement in creating memorable townspeople, such as the Hubbard clan, and her keen sense of social facts, such as the conditions attendant on the industrialization of small towns in the South, caused her plays to rank among the best theatrical accomplishments of the period. While she has continued to turn out superbly constructed plays, Miss Hellman, after completing the two-part history of the rapacious Hubbards in 1946-47, has not again so brilliantly dramatized small-town social and economic conditions in the South. On the other hand, *Toys in the Attic*, which opened on February 25, 1960, at the Hudson Theatre in New York, has its roots in Miss Hellman's own past and her experience in the Deep South. With its unpleasant theme of family degeneration and its harrowing story, this candid play about Carrie, Anna, Julian, and Lily Berniers of New Orleans is very similar in theme to various small-town plays which hinge upon the exposure of carefully hidden family skeletons.[10]

"Not About Nightingales"

"Not since Eugene O'Neill," wrote Richard Watts, Jr., in 1958,

have we possessed a playwright of [Tennessee] Williams' power and tragic insight. Although I don't think he has the monumental stature of O'Neill in *Long Day's Journey into Night, The Iceman Cometh* and possibly *Mourning Becomes Electra*, he is superior in one important way. He writes with a gift for sheer lyric beauty of which O'Neill, whose words tended to be earth-bound while his dramatic compositions soared, was incapable.[11]

Certainly the world of Williams' plays, except for occasional comic lights, is "dark, tormented, and haunted by evil." With rare understanding of lost souls, he has created out of his native environment—contemporary Mississippi—a microcosm crystallizing universal human experience. As with Henry Adams earlier," . . . he projects his life as a pattern for the frustrations and satisfactions of modern man."[12] While moved by man's struggles in a chaotic world, Williams differs from some of his contemporaries in not being a playwright of social protest. His poetic strain, rich in lyricism and symbolism, has kept him from making the woes of society his primary concern. Rather, he has become a stunning writer for the theater by the exercise of a highly personal art. "There was never a moment," he has confessed, "when I did not find life to be immeasurably exciting to experience and to witness, however difficult it was to sustain." To a great extent, as Nancy M. Tischler has expertly shown, his dramas of despair and hope, of drift and purpose, have developed from his own early experience with small-town living in Mississippi.

Certainly the environment of his youth was ideal as a springboard for his memorable creation of a panorama of small southern communities in which his diverse characters live. In "Facts About Me,"[13] Williams, born Thomas Lanier Williams, tells of his birthplace, the Episcopal rectory in Columbus, Lowndes County, Mississippi, itself an old town on the Tombigbee River in the northeastern part of the state. Here in 1911 aristocratic and bookish William E. Dakin, his liberal-minded grandfather, was clergyman for a dignified, reserved Episcopalian congregation. Young Tom's convivial father, with "the formidable name" of Cornelius Coffin Williams, was descended from early settlers of Nantucket Island, Massachusetts, and from Tennessee pioneers. Genteel and prim Edwina Dakin, Tom's mother, was Puritan by temperament. During their early married life the couple lived for a time in Gulfport, an area later dramatized in *The Rose Tattoo*. Until Tom was about twelve, when the father moved his family to a near-tenement section of St. Louis, the boy and his beloved sister Rose—a lovely but mentally frail girl, later reincarnated as Laura Wingfield in *The Glass Menagerie*—enjoyed childhood pleasures in small towns where the family was respected.

By the time Tom had begun his schooling, the Reverend Mr. Dakin had gone to another assignment in Clarksdale on the Mississippi and the Sunflower Rivers. Here in this outwardly lovely and quiet agricultural town in Coahoma County were picturesque scenes and Delta people, who later in fictional representation were to become symbols, both pleasant and unpleasant, good and evil, of the memories of his youth amidst provincial surroundings. In remembering this fertile cotton-growing community behind the Mississippi levee, Williams was to find the originals for the Blue Mountain, Glorious Hill, Two Rivers, and other little places of his plays. Here, too, was the native environment of two ill-fated heroines, Blanche Dubois and Amanda Wingfield. Big Daddy's plantation and other holdings belonged to this area, as did the scenes for some of Williams' early one-acters. Indeed, the Delta was to become a symbol of the artist's yearning and search for the "sweet bird" of his youth. At the same time, Williams has portrayed this provincial world by so many symbols of corruption and violence that some critics, such as Herbert Gold, have regarded him as the "Uglifier."[14]

Williams' long prelude to maturity began quite early. As he has noted, "At the age of 14 I discovered writing as an escape from a world of reality, in which I felt acutely uncomfortable."[15] His romantic teen-age effusions ("my place of retreat, my cave, my refuge") climaxed in his first published work, a violent tale of sadistic Queen Nitocris of the Egyptians, printed in 1928 in *Weird Tales*. As he has said, his first four plays "were correspondingly violent or more so." When Williams was twenty-five and a senior at Washington University, two of these plays—*Candles to the Sun* and *Fugitive Kind*—were performed by a small, offbeat theatrical group in St. Louis, the Mummers, under the "electrical" direction of Willard Holland. "Dynamism was what The Mummers had, and from . . . about 1935 to 1940 . . . they burned like one of Miss Millay's improvident little candles—and then expired."[16] While revealing Williams' growing sense of theater, these apprenticeship plays were far from professional. As Williams himself admits, "The plays I gave them were bad . . . amateurish and coarse and juvenile and talky." Nevertheless, two more plays—*Spring Storm* and *Not About Nightingales*—emerged from his later dramatic work at the University of Iowa, where he completed his degree in 1938.

In 1939, while living as a bohemian in New Orleans' Vieux Carré, Williams entered his four long plays, together with a collection of one-acters called *American Blues,* in a drama contest sponsored by the Group Theatre of New York. That summer in Los Angeles he joyfully received a special award of $100 for his short plays. Another collection of one-act plays had a faint beginning in St. Louis during his association with Washington University writers. From a tenuous plot idea about the seduction of a very fat blond woman by a small and wiry ginner on a southern plantation there developed "27 Wagons Full of Cotton," itself one of the keys for a screenplay called *Baby Doll* (1956). Williams' pursuit of his furies, in relation to the "ogre country" of the Delta towns, may be said to have started with this title story of *27 Wagons Full of Cotton and Other One-Act Plays* (1945).

Of the thirteen plays in this collection, nine portray misfits and outcasts living in urban areas. ("The Purification" stands apart as a lyrical play set in western ranch lands over a century ago.) Reflecting Williams' nomadic years in New York, St. Louis, and New Orleans, these nine dramatize, with nostalgic pain, the longings of impoverished or maladjusted city dwellers for "the big things in life." Mostly such misfits dream wistfully and vaguely of finding in the country or in a small town some sort of peace and economic freedom. Almost overpowered by the dull routine of labor in industrialized cities, some of these lost souls endure a painful loneliness reminiscent of the unhappiness of the three Wingfields in *The Glass Menagerie*. Williams' sympathy for society's unfortunates is evidenced in his protagonists' struggles with "the hard-knuckled hand of need" and "the cold iron fist of necessity."

A few of these urban one-acters touch upon those darker forces of society determining the lives of "Quarter rats, half-breeds, drunkards, degenerates, who try to get by on promises, lies, delusions!" The tragically toned "Portrait of a Madonna," set in a cheap boardinghouse in the Vieux Carré, foreshadows the later treatment of Blanche Dubois's breakdown. A lonely and addled old maid, Miss Lucretia Collins, imagines herself pregnant. Her bewildered sadness, as her mind sinks back into illusion, parallels Blanche's memories of her native Delta town. Pitiable Miss Lucretia, in ladylike manner, recalls with pride that "my father was Rector of St. Michael and St. George at Glorious Hill, Mississippi. . . . I've literally grown up right in the very *shadow* of the Episcopal Church. At Pass Christian and Natchez, Biloxi, Gulfport, Port Gibson, Columbus, and Glorious Hill!"[17] Miss Collins' churchly background equates with the later rectory upbringing of puritanical Alma Winemiller.

Three plays—"27 Wagons Full of Cotton," "The Last of My Solid Gold Watches," and "This Property is Condemned"—touch upon the dreams, temptations, and frustrations of people of small importance in a small world. All portray the inescapable facts of a new order rising in the decadent South. Subtitled "A Mississippi Delta Comedy," the first play opens with a glimpse of the oddly mated Meighans, who occupy a "doll's house," a cottage of Gothic design on a small plantation quite near the town of Blue Mountain. The episodic action revolves around the unexpected results of a case of arson. Large, purposeful Jake Meighan, a racist and the operator of a cotton gin, is angered that the owners of the nearby Syndicate Plantation, a symbol of the new order, have dared to employ a foreigner, Italian Silva Vicarro, as their superintendent and operator of a modern gin. One evening Jake sets fire to the Syndicate gin and shortly afterward sadistically forces his huge and stupid wife Flora to tell the Blue Mountain citizens that he "ain't been off th' front po'ch. Not since supper!" The next morning Vicarro brings his twenty-seven wagon loads of cotton to the Meighan gin. Misled by his apparent success over his rival and motivated by greed, Jake makes an odd bargain with Vicarro, "a rather small and wiry man of dark Latin looks and nature." Jake goes away to attend to the ginning, leaving Silva to entertain Flora. Delighted at this opportunity for revenge, Silva taunts simpleminded Flora and tricks her into confessing that her alibi for her husband was a lie. Then, luring her inside the house, he rapes the indolent but now terrified "Baby Doll."

That evening when Flora staggers out on the front porch her appearance is ravaged, her hair disordered, and "the upper part of her body is unclothed except for a torn pink band about her breasts." Jake, now happily returning from ginning the twenty-seven bales, mistakenly thinks of her vacant stare, silly laughter, and dishevelment as the aftermath of a "jag." He refuses to listen to her report of what his act of arson has cost her. Ironically, he even approves of Vicarro's proposed "good neighbor policy," allowing him to gin the Syndicate's cotton and giving him the chance to "entertain" Flora through long, hot afternoons. The playlet ends with Flora's vacant laughter, as she suddenly discards Jake's pet name for her, "Baby," and calls herself "Mama." Cradling her large white kid purse in her arms, the distraught woman slowly comes down the porch steps crooning a foreboding lullaby: "Rock-a-bye-Baby—in uh tree tops! . . . Down will come Baby—cradle—an' all!"

Both this tale and its earlier counterpart, "The Unsatisfactory Supper" (in *American Blues*) culminated in *Baby Doll*, widely denounced as "one of the most unhealthy and amoral pictures ever made in this country." In the several versions racism, twisted sexuality, and other manifestations of southern decadence set a pattern which Williams was to adapt to other provincial plays. The vengeance of Silva Vicarro, a community newcomer and a Latin as well, who seduces the wife of a neighbor, symbolizes the rise of a new stock in a provincial world which, in glorifying its past and its genteel tradition, has been reluctant to adjust itself to social and other changes.

An elderly shoe salesman's lament over the blighting of his secure world of yesteryear by the encroachments of a more impersonal and cutthroat form of merchandising provides the conflict for "The Last of My Solid Gold Watches." In a shabby hotel room in a Mississippi Delta town "Mistuh Charlie" Colton, "the last of the Delta drummers," fails to impress indifferent young Bob Harper, a new type of salesman—a reader of *Superman* comic books—with his anecdotes about "the great days of the road." As "Mistuh Charlie" implies bitterly, the revolution in merchandising has brought in "young squirrels" to fight against "the ole war-horses." The thematic treatment of the loss of youth, later to become a familiar motif in Williams, touches upon the old salesman's wistful recollection of his winning fifteen gold watches, as his company's top salesman for so many years. But his memories do not blind him to the inevitability of change. "The world I know is gone—gone—gone with the wind! My pockets are full of watches which tell me that my time's just about over!" Initiative, self-reliance, independence of character, the sterling qualities which once distinguished one man from another, are "gone with the roses of *yesterday!*" In its place, Harper's new and ill-mannered world is controlled by "the terrible—fast—dark—rush of events . . . Toward what and where and why!"

Other images of a lost provincial world appear in the treatment of lonely youth in "This Property Is Condemned." Near a railroad embankment on the outskirts of a small Mississippi town a large yellow frame house, once a boardinghouse for railroad men, now has a look of tragic vacancy. Its only occupant now is undernourished thirteen-year-old Willie, who has been abandoned by a drunken father and by her mother, who ran away with a brakeman. Loneliness has driven her into the most ridiculous dreams as a means of escaping harsh reality. Throughout the action Willie, in boastful conversation with a boy named Tom, appears as a lover of "pretties." Dressed in "outrageous cast-off finery"—a blue velvet party dress, battered silver kid slippers, and glittering dime-store jewelry—she parades along the railroad track. All the while her artless talk indicates that her dream world was actually the sordid world of prostitution to which her adored and pretty sister, now dead, once belonged. Nevertheless, in her childish thinking "there must've been something wrong with my home atmosphere because of the fact that we took in railroad men an' some of 'em slept with my sister."

At best episodic, these one-acters were but stepping-stones to Williams' further experimentation with longer plays. Both their lessons in form and technique, such as the realistic presentation of fictional experience, and their defects prepared him for a fuller mirroring of a contemporary world. Also, these transitional playlets were constructed around themes, as well as character types, which were to be refashioned later. Themes destined to be raised to new dimensions in full-length plays included the sad effects of one's clinging to the genteel tradition of antebellum times, the influx of disturbing changes ushering into Delta society various disorders and even violence, the evil effect on character of a repressive Puritan strain, escapism through sexuality or through a lyrical outpouring of the individual's longing for love and beauty, social injustice growing out of compulsive racism, homosexuality, and sadism, and the conflicts arising between small-towners and outsiders.

The pressures within this fictionalized milieu kept intruding into the private vision of the playwright. His bohemian existence in New Orleans and his hard experience in California deepened his feeling of kinship for rootless, unhappy provincials. Accordingly, during the summer of 1939, at Laguna Beach, California, he began the writing of "a lyrical play about memories and the loneliness of them." His first draft, finished in St. Louis that fall, gave promise of what he called "a play of human longings, about the sometimes conflicting desires of the flesh and the spirit." But this play, called *Battle of Angels*, was destined to undergo an amazing refashioning over a period of seventeen years.

As the holder of a scholarship at the New School for Social Research, New York, young Williams was guided by John Gassner and Theresa Helburn, of the Theatre Guild, in revising his script. Lawrence Langner recalls reading the play with considerable enthusiasm, with the hope that some rewriting would straighten out its technical defects. Both Langner and Miss Helburn were impressed by Williams' modesty, his poet's sensitivity, his imaginative gift, and his feeling for trenchant dialogue. In short, they thought of him as "the most promising young playwright we had come across in a number of years," and agreed, in behalf of the Theatre Guild directorate, to go into production.[18] In time the play was given a tryout at Boston's Wilbur Theatre, opening December 30, 1940 and, because of censorship and unfavorable audience response, closing on January 11, 1941. The combined talents of Margaret Webster as director ("brimming over with local color"), of Miriam Hopkins as the star, and of Cleon Throckmorton as set designer were not enough to save the production. So, as Langner remembered, "We reluctantly withdrew it." In spite of this, however, he and Miss Helburn, by a public letter addressed to the hostile Boston censor and spectators, "ventured a prophecy, a dangerous pastime." With praise for Williams' genuine poetic gifts and his insight into the Mississippi scene, they foretold the future, commenting, ". . . *The Battle of Angels* turned out badly but who knows whether the next one by the same author may not prove a success?"

In spite of the Boston fiasco, the play was not discarded. In 1945 still another version, with comments by Gassner, appeared in published form; and in a screen version, renamed *The Fugitive Kind*, Marlon Brando acted the role of Val Xavier. By 1957, continued revisions brought into being a new play, *Orpheus Descending*. Though changes had been made, the basic plot and the main characters came from *Battle of Angels*. Both plays display Williams' compassion for society's unfortunates and his insight into basic human needs, as well as his talents for creating realistic folksy dialogue and for interpreting the darker aspects of small-town life.

In truth, *Battle of Angels*, a powerful though uneven play, is a searching exploration and unsparing indictment of the darkness and terror existing beneath the surface of life in a very small and old-fashioned town in the Deep South. Published in 1945, this naturalistic representation of sexuality, alcoholism, and sadism in the cotton-growing community of Two Rivers, Mississippi, opens, by way of a prologue, on an uninviting scene in "the famous Torrance Mercantile Store," which had been converted not long before into a tawdry museum exhibiting souvenirs of the sensational tragedy which had taken place there a year earlier. Two sisters—the only surviving relatives of Jabe Torrance—old Eva and Blanch Temple, gossip to inquisitive tourists about what happened, hinting, too, that the wizard-like Conjure Man, an ancient Negro, "knows some things that he isn't telling."

From this point the three acts to follow offer a flashback dramatization of the tragedy of the year before. An epilogue returns the spectator, or reader, to the "Tragic Museum" or store, now empty of the passionate owners and others who once were there and sinister with its testimony of past violence, resembling "a pillaged temple with the late afternoon sunlight thrown obliquely through the high Gothic windows..." The ragged Conjure Man, sitting in immobile dignity, is like "the Spirit of the Dead Watching." His obeisance before Val's snakeskin jacket, now on vulgar display, not only mocks the avarice of the Temple sisters but exalts the freedom-loving spirit of the lynched wanderer. This lividly mottled jacket, though inanimate, "still keeps about it the hard, immaculate challenge of things untamed."

Who are the people at Two Rivers involved in a tragedy which cost five lives? Although the scene is distinctly Mississippian, two of the leading characters are outsiders and are thus the butt of suspicion. Myra Torrance is the emotional daughter of a Sicilian immigrant who drifted into the community years before as a mandolin player with a gaudily jacketed monkey. Scorned by the natives as a "Wop," he suffered from grueling labor until he had saved money enough to buy a few acres near Moon Lake and develop them into a flourishing orchard. Here he built a casino to which the youth of the town flocked for their drinking and lovemaking. Under these circumstances his own teen-age daughter was able to meet and fall in love with David Anderson, son of an upper-class family. One evening a masked mob of "leading citizens," enraged by the rumor that the "Wop" had served wine to "niggers," callously burned the casino and the lovely orchard. Not one person offered to save the helpless owner from burning to death.

Shortly thereafter woebegone Myra, now pregnant with David's child, is trapped by another emotional disaster. David, having rationalized that wealth and social status are more important to him than love, jilts Myra and marries the daughter of a banker. Myra's lively personality is affected by the resulting trauma, yet her capacity for great tenderness remains, as is shown in her grief over the death of her child. Thus trapped by bitter circumstance, she enters into a state of legal prostitution by a loveless marriage with a local merchant, mean-hearted, selfish old Jabe Torrance, who, as Myra later learns, had been an instigator of the mob action which resulted in her father's violent death.

At curtain rise several gossipmongering women, a sort of chorus of provincial harpies, are gathered in the Torrance store and its adjoining confectionery hyprocritically gabbling about the impending return of Myra and old Jabe from a Memphis clinic. They are bustling about preparing a "Welcome Home" party. When cancer-stricken Jabe finally enters the store, he curses the sentimentally effusive women for their obvious lying about his healthy appearance, and then laboriously climbs the stairs to his bedroom. In that room, out of view of the audience, Jabe, slowly dying, secludes himself from prying citizens until the close of Act III. From time to time, however, he moves into the orbit of the downstairs action by thumping the floor with his cane, the symbol of his impotency.

The second outsider is a guitarist and amateur writer, who is picked up by the sheriff's middle-aged wife, Vee Talbott, "a painter of very peculiar pictures she calls the Apostles but look like men around town." It is Vee who brings into the Torrance store the vagabond hero of the tragedy. About twenty-five years old, Val Xavier "has a fresh and primitive quality, a virile grace and freedom of body, and a strong physical appeal." A writing hobo, Val has emerged from his native swamplands to enjoy the free life of vagabondage. Intermittently he has mined coal in the Red Hills of Alabama, recited his poetry and played his guitar in the honky-tonks of towns and cities, and in his wandering filled a notebook with observations of life to be woven into a book. When Myra reluctantly engages him as handyman and clerk, Val reveals the softer, or Christlike,

side of his nature by his emotional thanks: "God, I—! Lady, you, —!"
The association of himself with the Christ and of Myra with the Virgin
Mary provides two of the oft-repeated symbols in the play. In contrast,
he seems to smug Eva Temple "a shameless, flaunting symbol of the
Beast Untamed."

Also beyond the pale of respectable society is native-born Cassandra
or Sandra Whiteside, "dark and strikingly beautiful" and "one of the
richest girls in the Mississippi Delta." A descendant of one of the oldest
families in the area, Sandra is candidly cynical about her aristocratic
origin. With her strange power of seeing beneath the surface of things,
she resembles the Trojan prophetess in foreseeing woes which will blight
the town. She holds the genteel and convention-bound society responsible
for the cramping of the lives of the natives of Two Rivers. Talking with
the customers in the Torrance store, she disdainfully views "the social
contradictions and tragic falsity of the world she lives in." She defiantly
scandalizes sanctimonious townspeople by driving her fine car at break-
neck speed, "jooking" with tavern companions, boasting of sexual
relationships with sundry lovers, drinking, and privately communing with
the dead on Cypress Hill.

As the only aristocrat among the Torrance customers, Sandra boldly
accuses the gossipmongers there of suffering from "sexual malnutrition."
In rebuttal, they spitefully denounce her as "absolutely de-*grad*-ed!"
From her first meeting with handsome young Val, Sandra appears as a
cynical, restless, and boldly seductive girl, whose nonconformity seems in
tune with "this dark, wild river country of ours." Whatever it is that
hedges her nature in and lowers it is ripe for community attack and
examination. Finally, the aridity of her private Waste Land pushes her
toward suicide. She deliberately drives her car into the Sunflower River
and is drowned—but not because, as Eva Temple gossiped, "she knew
that *decent* people were done with her."

Still another native who is different to the point of eccentricity is Vee
Talbott, branded by the gossips as "a public kill-joy, a professional hypo-
crite." A heavy, fortyish woman, Vee has been so frustrated by externals
that her spirit has turned deeply inward. She has found refuge and sublimation in religion and primitive art. Love-starved and bewildered by
her childless marriage to corrupt Sheriff Talbott, she seeks solace by
decorating her apostolic canvases with gaudy Freudian symbols, which
she claims came to her in visions. Her chance meeting with Val brings on
a vision of him as her model for her proposed masterpiece, a portrait of
Jesus. The finished portrait, garish in design, becomes an obvious
Christ-like symbol of the doom awaiting Val Xavier (Savior): cruci-

fixion on the town's lynching tree, a big cottonwood near the levee. (The reference to Saint Valentine, martyred Roman associated with senti-mental love, is also obvious.) Vee's symbolic "Jesus picture" was "the last thing she painted before she lost her mind."

But, as the Temple sisters remind the tourists in the epilogue, on that fateful rainy day five lives were "tied together in one fatal knot of pas-sion." In addition to the Vee Talbott motif, the main facets of the plot concern that ill-fated foursome: Jabe, Myra, Val, and Sandra. While Jabe's condition worsens, Myra and Val discover a mutual love which flowers briefly. Myra expresses her happiness by redecorating the con-fectionery with symbolic springtime motifs, reminders of her father's Moon Lake casino and of her youthful passion, which now seems to be flaming anew. Each discovers in the other not only passion but a love of beauty and a yearning for freedom.

Myra's joy is but momentary, for Jabe becomes aware of her liaison with his clerk. One day the sheriff comes to arrest Val on a false charge of rape. Remembering a similar experience in Waco, Texas, Val is so terrified that he frantically plans to escape alone, leaving Myra, who is now happy over her new pregnancy. Impetuously "shouting doom at the gates," Sandra, who is enamoured of Val, urges him to leave with her, unaware that the river bridge has been washed out. "You an' me," she pleads, "we belong to the fugitive kind." In another frantic appeal to win her lover's consent to accompany him, Myra again refers to the repeated symbol of a barren fig tree in the casino orchard, which at long last bears fruit. Their argument is cut short by a bit of Gothic action. Ghastly-looking Jabe, resembling a specter of death more than an infuriated cuckold, unexpectedly appears at the top of the stairs. He is livid with hatred. Myra in distraction wildly taunts him with the bitter declaration that he is dead, but that she, now with child, is alive. At this point action piles upon action. Jabe fires a revolver pointblank at Myra, fatally wounding her. He then stumbles out the door to the street shouting against the wind that Val has robbed the cash register and then shot him. As Myra dies and the store is seen to be afire, Val rushes to a rear door, only to be seized by a lynch mob of mill hands and other townsmen.

Throughout this finale the terrific rainstorm heightens the Gothic atmosphere. One recalls prophetic words spoken by Sandra somewhat earlier: "The atmosphere is pregnant with disaster!...A battle in heaven. A battle of *angels* above us! And *thunder!* And *storm!*"[19]

Once Myra remarked to Val that "History isn't written about *little* people!" Nevertheless, *Battle of Angels* itself is an impressive dramatic record of *little* people, whose destinies represent more than mere "marks on rocks called *fossils*." Myra herself, robust and passionate is a memorably conceived character, vitally representing the spirit of nature (in connection with the fertile orchard) and the life force. "Paired with death, in the person of Jabe, she is like earth in winter; joined with Val, she is springtime and fertility."[20] Val Xavier, a Christlike outcast, is a southern re-creation of the nineteenth century's romantic concept of the freedom-seeking artist, who finally is sacrificed in a realistic and violent manner, as much for his nonconformity—shown in his humanitarian concern for the dispossessed, both white and black—as for his sexual appeal to the town's lovelorn women. The citizens of Two Rivers, incited by bigots and hatemongers, thwart his escape to New Mexico, with its great sky and its symbolic Sangre de Cristo Mountains. There is a strong characterization of pitiable Vee Talbott, whose genuine suffering from sexual repression is as much misunderstood by the shallow busybodies as by her sadistic husband. Sandra, an idealist at heart, is woefully misunderstood by her hypocritical, and perhaps jealous, associates. In their own "School of Scandalization" they brand her as a nymphomaniac and an alcoholic, and they fail to grasp her insight into the truth about their narrow world, however much they stand in awe of her "lips touched by prophetic fire."

Williams crowds his stage with secondary characters, some of little significance. Generally, as illustrated by the choral gossips, these are little more than thinly portrayed agrarian southerners of truly obscure destinies, whose roles are those of expositors and shallow social commentators. The mill hands and other inflamed irresponsibles, influenced by the brutal sheriff and his vicious deputies, symbolize not only the destructive power of the mob but the corruption of civil authority as well. Taken as a whole, such minor characters, themselves symbols of lostness, typify community guilt in much the same shocking way as do Mark Twain's corrupted Hadleyburgians.

For all its undeniable power of psychological penetration and occasional poetic effects, the play is symbol-ridden. Its abundant symbolism includes images of a white moth, a barren fig tree, Vee's primitive art, the Cypress Hill graveyard, the architectural details and furnishings for the Torrance store—graphic impressions of aridity and ruin: "the pillaged temple," the lifeless phallic columns, and the dressmaker's dummies— and Val's eye-smiting snakeskin jacket, which indicates the youth's swampland origin and implies that he is temptation personified. The symbolism of nomenclature is fairly obvious, notably in the parallels between "Xavier" and "Saviour"; procreative Myra and the Virgin Mary; Cassandra and the Trojan prophetess of woe; and the weird Conjure Man and folk superstition and the spirit of the dead. Williams' fondness for

Gothic effects is shown in his creation of an atmosphere of foreboding heightened by the slow tolling of bells across the wide, rainy fields, the baying of Talbott's bloodhounds, and the shouts of the angry mob, as well as the sound and visual effects of the thunder, lightning, wind, and rain.

Writing in 1958 about the successive changes made in *Battle of Angels,* Williams explained that "I have never quit working on [it] . . . not even now," adding, "So you see that it is a very old play that *Orpheus Descending* came out of . . ." His persistence in revision, with about 75 per cent new writing, brought forth *Orpheus Descending,* which John Gassner thought "an important venture in failure" and Richard Watts, Jr., called "a fine and darkly beautiful drama." Opening at the Martin Beck in New York on March 21, 1957, with Harold Clurman as director and Boris Aronson as set designer, this new yet old play, though a failure by Broadway standards, held its audience by its violence and the superb acting of Maureen Stapleton as Lady, or Myra, Torrance, Cliff Robertson as Val, Crahan Denton as Jabe, and Joanna Roos as Vee. Relating the play to the emotional record of his own youth, Williams has said, "On its surface it was and still is the tale of a wild-spirited boy who wanders into a conventional community of the South and creates the commotion of a fox in a chicken coop."[21] Here again is the tragedy of provincial misfits, an outgrowth of one of the playwright's favorite themes, the tragedy of "souls too tender in their sensibilities to survive in a world of harshness and cruelty." Community malice, intolerance, and social and moral decadence again lead confused souls to their doom. As in *Battle of Angels,* the central figures of a fairly young wife, here symbolized as the Lady, whose father was murdered by a masked mob (the Mystic Crew), a poetic and compassionate vagrant seeking only peace and friendliness, and a philistine type of husband, aging, impotent, and jealous, are all moved by strong passions and haunted by un-answered questions. Two lesser characters, both drawn with sympathy and warmth, are victims of a narrow society: an idealistic girl, now called Carol Cutrere, given to self-chastisement and promiscuity, and the sheriff's half-crazed wife, haunted and confused by her thoughts about her husband's brutalities as a lawman.

This new play follows its original pattern in offering the same pano-rama of a small Delta town; but it also has richer description of scene and characters, an additional stress on the brutal truth about a limited but chaotic world, and a new depth in the tragedy. The Aronson set, again that of the Torrance Mercantile Store, represents in nonrealistic fashion a general drygoods store with an adjoining confectionery in "a small Southern town." As in *Battle of Angels*, this provincial scene, the time of which is now only a short while before the return of the Torrances from the Memphis clinic, is presented by means of a prologue, a favored frame-device which here becomes an integral part of Act I. (The original museum scene has been deleted.) The two youngish middle-aged women of this prologue, however, resemble the stereotyped and gossipy expositors of *Battle of Angels*. In production Feder's dramatic spotlighting of acting areas allowed the limited use of one of the gossips as a monologuist, who addresses the audience directly, like the Stage Manager in *Our Town*, chattily explaining the complexities of Lady's personal background. Elsewhere the dimming of stage lights marks a division of time.

The original techniques of the flashback and epilogue have been abandoned. Their replacements are three descriptive acts which directly narrate a modern adaptation of several aspects of the tragedy of Thracian Orpheus, whose singing and playing upon his lyre were so sweet that no one and nothing could resist him. In the Williams tragedy there is no Eurydice; but a wandering, guitar-playing folksinger, Val Xavier, proves irresistible to the inhibited women of Two Rivers. Orpheus' fearsome journey into Hades to rescue his beloved Eurydice equates with Val's descent into the "underworld" of a little Mississippi town which is festering with suspicion and weakly controlled violence. The legend of the frenzied bands of Maenads, slayers of the gentle Orpheus, is woven into this small-town history of southern bigotry and violent death. By implication, also, Jabe Torrance, unyielding and selfish, has some kinship with Pluto, whose kingly power controls the destiny of the ill-fated Orpheus and Eurydice.

Critics evaluate Williams' gift for characterization as second to none among our recognized American playwrights. "Neurotic, erotic, pathetic, sympathetic, off-beat, or square, the people who walk the stage of a Williams play have their own validity and vitality regardless of the strange and sometimes ridiculously trumped-up circumstances into which he forces them."[22] So it is with the sharply defined major individuals in *Orpheus Descending*. Facets added to each characterization make for a better understanding of Williams' haunting sense of a group of people who have reached a cul-de-sac. Lady Torrance's tragic past—her social ostracism as "Wop" Romano's daughter, her father's horrible burning, the infidelity of her youthful lover (now called David Cutrere), the loss of their child by abortion, and the slow rot of her marriage to an old man who bought her—has fated her to a death-in-life. She discovers her one chance both for revenge on Jabe and for her own resurrection or release in her love for Val. Her desperate turning to this attractive and virile stranger isolates her even more from the already prejudiced community. To the gossips —"hissing geese"— Lady is "not a Dago fer nothin'." The core of the play, in fact, is to be found in the community's efforts to thwart the individual's, and especially Lady's, groping toward affection and love as the path to self-realization and salvation.

Another favorite idea of Williams', concerning the inexplicability of human beings and human relationships, is illustrated tragically in Val's portrait. In this new characterization thirty-year-old Val, having discarded his book project, becomes more of an Orphic character with his cherished autographed guitar and his emotional release in ballad singing. His character gains depth by the new image of youthful innocence, long exposed to but untainted by corruption. (A case in point concerns his meeting with Carol Cutrere in a New Orleans nightclub.) At the finale, his sincere love for Lady is blighted most tragically when Jabe, enraged at her joyous declaration of her pregnancy, shoots his wife and shouts to the town the lie that Val "shot my wife . . . and is robbing the store." The frenzied mob, with "faces like demons," murders Val, not by lynching but with a blowtorch. Lady's last words, remembered from "Papa" Romano, fittingly testify to the lostness of the lovers: "The show is over. The monkey is dead."

In the long interim between the production failures of *Battle of Angels* (1940) and *Orpheus Descending* (1957), Williams gained wide recognition with the stage successes of *The Glass Menagerie* (1944), *A Streetcar Named Desire* (1947), *The Rose Tattoo* (1951), and *Cat on a Hot Tin Roof* (1955). Except for *The Rose Tattoo*, these plays portray maladjusted plantation families or Delta townspeople tragically uprooted from their native communities and lost in the cities. Little is said, however, about the small town per se. Nevertheless, Williams' interest in the little town as a southern microcosm has not diminished. While *A Streetcar* was being successfully produced, and denounced, he was busily at work revising an early play, *A Chart of Anatomy*, later finished as *Summer and Smoke*, in which he re-created a segment of life in the Delta towns of Glorious Hill and Lyon during the Mauve Decade. (In various plays from *27 Wagons Full of Cotton* onward, there are scattered references to such little places as Glorious Hill, Lyon, Sunset, and Two Rivers.)

In that same year of 1947 he visited with the late Margo Jones, then vigorously promoting her project for a Texas theater-in-the-round. The fruitful aftermath of that visit was Miss Jones's production of five of Williams' plays for the initiation of Theatre '47. Actually, the theater opened on June 3 with a fourteen-performance production of *Farther Off from Heaven* by William Inge, then a newcomer introduced to Margo Jones by Williams himself. Next, on July 8, with herself as director Miss Jones opened a production of *Summer and Smoke* for an unlisted number of performances. Starring Tod Andrews as Dr. John and Katharine Balfour as Alma, this arena venture became a stepping-stone to Miss Jones's staging a Broadway production (1948-49), which, in spite of the praiseworthy acting of Andrews and Margaret Phillips in the key roles, was too mechanically done to prove successful. Earlier in the Dallas arena playhouse Margo Jones had broken new ground with her production of three of Williams' one-acters: "The Last of My Solid Gold Watches," "This Property Is Condemned," and "Portrait of a Madonna." Opening November 17, 1947, these little plays ran for sixteen performances, with Tod Andrews again as one of the principals.[23]

Notwithstanding its limitations, Margo Jones's Broadway staging of *Summer and Smoke*, at the Music Box, lasted for 102 performances, from October 6, 1948, until January 1, 1949.[24] Unfortunately Jo Mielziner's excellent triptych set, enhanced by his skill in increasing, dimming, and coloring the light effects, was more suitable for a proscenium stage than for the Music Box arena. The entire action of the play takes place against a wide expanse of sky, a factor which necessitates, for the interior scenes, the omission of the walls or the barest suggestion "by certain necessary fragments such as might be needed to hang a picture or to contain a door-frame."[25] Of the two fragmentary interior sets, each located in the side areas, one shows the Victorian parlor of an Episcopal Rectory and the other an office in the home of Dr. Buchanan next door to the Rectory. In the Music Box arena these interior sets had to be pushed aside near the wings to allow a space for the main exterior set, elevated to a higher level to show a promontory in a park, or public square, in the town of Glorious Hill. In the center is a fountain in the form of an angel "with wings lifted and her hands held together to form a cup from which water flows, a public drinking fountain." The angel, featured in both the interior and exterior scenes, serves as a symbolic figure of Eternity, brooding over the residents of Glorious Hill. Williams' hope that these three units would form a harmonious whole or complete picture was not quite realized in the crowded Music Box arena. Unity seems to have been lost and an episodic effect produced in the course of dramatizing, as Gassner has noted, "the history of a lost lamb and prodigal son."

It remained for a gifted young director, José Quintero, and his off-Broadway Circle in the Square players to produce a stimulating production, which not only added unity, atmosphere, and lyricism to the play but gave glory to the 1952-53 season. Their competent performances, in a former Sheridan Square nightclub, had the advantage of a rectangular stage, which though small was adapted to an effective utilization of Mielziner's triple set. The result was a theatrical presentation of story, characterization, and atmosphere in keeping with Williams' ideal. Under such conditions his landscape of memory was harmoniously linked with a southern phase of Victorianism during a halcyon period soon to culminate in the outbreak of World War I. From the play's prologue through its twelve scenes, timed from an eventful summer through the winter of 1916, the center of Williams' memory world is the Delta village of Glorious Hill, adjacent to Moon Lake and its casino and not far from the town of Lyon. As another instance of the playwright's portrayal of pathetic southern women, *Summer and Smoke* belongs in trilogic succession with *The Glass Menagerie* and *A Streetcar Named Desire*. In this connection, it has been criticized as a stylized version of a situation comparable to Blanche DuBois's dilemma: her wavering between her ideal of Delta gentility and a pathological impulse towards promiscuity, and her eventual breakdown under the strain. Also, Williams' adaptation of one of the devices often used by O'Neill, the *doppelgänger*, gives a psychological—and even allegorical—touch to the age-old conflict between the flesh and the spirit which deepens Alma Winemiller's unhappiness. In the Circle in the Square revival talented Geraldine Page brilliantly interpreted Alma's disturbing dualism and the irony of her situation.

The story of *Summer and Smoke* is as old, and as hackneyed, as the Middle English "Debate of the Body and the Soul," yet woven into the narrative are those elements of lyricism, background music, and truths which make a Williams play memorable. True, these truths are unsubstantial, as the title implies. But, as Brooks Atkinson has written, from Williams' viewpoint

these are the truths that are most profound and the most painful, for they separate people who logically should be together and give life its savage whims and its wanton destructiveness. Although he is dealing in impulses that cannot be literally defined, the twin themes of his tone poem are clearly stated: spirit and flesh, order and anarchy. He has caught them in the troubled brooding of two human hearts.

These truths are adapted to a special place and time to touch the lives of puritanical Alma Winemiller and fun-loving John Buchanan. Ever since childhood, these two young neighbors, an Episcopalian minister's virginal daughter and a doctor's rebellious son, have felt a mutual attraction. In the prologue, as children lingering in the park, they talk about the meaning of the word "Eternity" chiseled on the base of the fountain. Alma, precocious beyond her age, explains that her own name is Spanish for "soul" and that eternity is "something that goes on and on when life and death and time and everything else is through with." John is unimpressed and scornful and finds more fun in shocking Alma by stealing a kiss and boasting that he would rather be a devil and go to South America on a boat. This is the first opening of the gulf which is to widen between them.

As the prologue action moves forward to Part I, "A Summer," John, grown to manhood and locally gossiped about as a hard drinker and a lecher, has rebelled against Dr. Buchanan's plans for his medical education. At Alma's insistence, he does go back to medical school, graduating with honors and returning to Glorious Hill on the evening of the Fourth of July celebration. He drives into the crowded town square just in time to hear Alma, now a teacher of music, singing "La Golondrina" before the assembled townspeople. (The descriptive details of this community scene correspond to O'Neill's evocation of a similar gala entertainment at the opening of *Ah, Wilderness!*)

As the summer passes, John's wastrel ways continue to disturb his father, a kindly man who has Alma's devotion and who has taken more than a professional interest in her nervous disorders. Dr. Buchanan knows that Alma loves John, but his insight makes him realize the almost unbridgeable gulf between their moral natures. During John's medical school years Alma, though still in her middle twenties, has become prematurely spinsterish. To the other young people of the town she seems to be an old maid, putting on airs and speaking affectedly. Actually her excessive propriety, a mark of her bookish rearing, makes her seem a part of "a more elegant age, such as the Eighteenth Century in France."

When Alma and John renew their companionship, she is too soulful and proper. Instead of accepting John's advances, she tries to please him with a lofty, spiritual friendship. Once, when he takes her to the Moon Lake Casino, she becomes hysterical about the rough characters there and about his reference to "intimate relations."

By summer's end, Alma's situation has grown more and more ironic. Though she succeeds in making John aware of his filial and professional obligations, he turns to other women for sexual satisfaction. Mrs. Ewell, the town's Merry Widow, and voluptuous Rosa Gonzales, a Mexican dancer whose "Papa" operates the casino, prove more exciting for his restless nature than decorous and introverted Alma. Once John berates her as a "white-blooded spinster! You so right people, pious pompous mumblers, preachers and preacher's daughter, all muffled up in a lot of worn-out magic."[26] One of the most satiric scenes, a humorous reminder of Gopher Prairie's Thanatopsis Club meeting, is an exposure of the cultural sterility of small towns of the period. John, overcome by boredom while listening to an arty and stultifying program on William Blake, rushes out of the Rectory parlor, thoroughly shocking the members of Alma's tedious "intellectual gathering." At the casino, cock fights, crap games, and Rosa's crude eroticism are more to his liking.

Once when Alma comes to his office, she cannot explain the sensations which are gripping her: the horrors of being walled in. John, in trying to tell Alma the truth about herself, only puzzles her with his joking about her *doppelgänger*. Later, when his father is dying, John accuses Alma of being afraid to look at "a picture of human insides." Pointing to the office anatomy chart, he shocks her by launching into a lecture on the three natures of man. He ruefully admits, however, that "I'm more afraid of your soul than you're afraid of my body."

Alma's suffering comes, in part, from the frustrations brought about by her "crosses": her spiteful and embarrassingly childish mother, who is a kleptomaniac, and her cold, rigidly puritanical father. These pressures, coupled with the stalemate of her association with John, bring on a long illness and her retirement from the town's activities. Events leading to her breakdown are climaxed in a drunken brawl which John's casino companions have in Dr. Buchanan's home. To thwart John's plan to marry Rosa in order to pay a gambling debt, Alma telephones Dr. Buchanan, urging him to come home from Lyon where he was engaged in helping fight a fever epidemic. Arriving as the party is in its last stage, Dr. Buchanan is shot down by the drunken Gonzales.

In remorse, John volunteers to complete his father's mission in Lyon, is successful in doing so, returns to Glorious Hill as a hero, and finally assumes his father's practice. Though at first he blamed Alma for his father's tragic death, John softens in his feelings toward her and tries to talk with her at the Rectory. Dr. Winemiller sternly denies him entry. Thus repulsed, John soon becomes engaged to vivacious Nellie Ewell, a coquettish teen-ager earlier befriended by Alma, who gave her voice lessons when the respectable townspeople were scandalized by her mother's affairs with drummers. Alma, in a scene both ironic and poignant, learns about the engagement just when, at last, she has decided to offer herself, body and soul, to John. Embarrassed, John expresses his deep gratitude for what she has meant to him; both know, however, that what might have been between them, somehow, cannot be sustained.

Nevertheless, Alma, putting her pride aside, tells John that "the girl who said 'no,' she doesn't exist any more, she died last summer—suffocated in smoke from something on fire inside her." She has won the argument about the chart, but has lost John.

The play closes with a symbol of winter—the winter of the soul and perhaps too great a sense of gloom for Alma. There is a bitter irony in John's conversion to Alma's way of thinking, and in her turning to his. In the twelfth scene, or epilogue, Alma, saddened by the irony of her circumstances, seeks peace by the park fountain, where her story began. Her chance meeting there with a young traveling salesman turns the tables for the preacher's daughter. Lonely and nervous because he is on his first job, the salesman asks Alma what excitement may be found in Glorious Hill after dark. When she suggests Lake Casino, now under new management, he dashes off for a taxi. Alma then faces the stone angel, raises her hand in a valedictory salute, and turns away, with her hand still raised in a gesture of finality. As she and the salesman walk toward the taxi, the wind begins to blow and the dead leaves rustle across the pavement. A phrase of music reinstates the grave mood of the play as the two disappear, leaving the stone angel—Eternity—alone in the darkness.

The story of *Summer and Smoke* is a relatively unencumbered presentation of a single situation; yet its motivating ideas, which Williams has utilized in other plays, movingly express universal needs, mainly sexual. Among such ideas, that of apartness, or loneliness, with its suggestion of barrenness, is related painfully to Alma Winemiller, as to pathetic Laura Wingfield. Her innermost being cries out for genuine friendship, understanding, and love. Alma's relationship with Roger Doremus—a bookworm, a bore, and a "mama's boy"—is a sham. Unhappily, she has grown up in a sheltered environment, mostly in the company of her elders. Years of dull church entertainments and of her father's dreary sermons have brought Alma few contacts with the less inhibited citizens of Glorious Hill. Because of her narrow training, she believes that man's nature is coarsened by an animality which only his spiritual nature can control. Actually she herself possesses a truly deep sexual nature which struggles against her protected, and arid, way of life. On the other hand, "her true nature is still hidden, even from herself." Of all the people of Glorious Hill, John—together, perhaps, with his father—best understands her introverted nature, as when he teases her with the truth: "Miss Alma is lonesome."

For John, too, there is the problem of a ruinous loneliness. An only child, brought up by an elderly and busy father in a motherless home, he resembles Alma in his need for a warm and stimulating association with a loving woman who understands his real temperament. In the first scene he is introduced as a handsome youth of "demoniac unrest," indeed, Nelson says, "a Promethean figure, brilliantly and restlessly alive in a stagnant society." While the appeal of "Miss Alma" to his better nature is impelling, still she fails him in other ways. Their dim realization of a mutual need is not strong enough to produce a meaningful communication between the two. In their mutual plight, an obsession with sexuality, John turns to youthfully vital Nellie, and Alma resignedly seeks fulfilment in other men. One of the obvious flaws in plot and characterization is the lack of plausibility in John's sudden involvement with Nellie, whom he has only recently met. Also, is not his conversion from dissipation to a model life as town hero and practitioner a bit too hasty? Moreover, there is too little dramatic explanation for Alma's throwing aside all her moral standards, which she has accepted from childhood, to go sliding toward prostitution. According to Benjamin Nelson's brilliant analysis, the characterizations of Alma and John tend to become abstractions, as their arguments, or sermonic debates, about the flesh and the spirit draw toward the twelfth scene.[27] Thus, at the play's end falsity of situation is added to falsity of characterization.

Of the different presentations of *Summer and Smoke*, the one offering the fullest evocation of the small-town background, both physical and spiritual, was the screen version of 1961. Achieving astonishingly beautiful color tones, producer Hal Wallis translated this "drama of lostness" before the Technicolor and Panavision cameras for Paramount. The distinguished cast included Laurence Harvey as John; Geraldine Page as Alma; Rita Moreno as Rosa; Una Merkel, excellent as Mrs. Winemiller; Pamela Tiffin as Nellie; John McIntire in one of his best roles as the kindly Dr. Buchanan; and Earl Holliman as Kramer, the timid traveling salesman.

Small towns in the South and the Southwest, especially those located near waterways, are generally populated by a variety of ethnic groups, in addition to the native whites and the Negroes. The more familiar foreign strains include the French, Portuguese, Italian (including the Sicilian), Mexican, Cuban, and Puerto Rican. Like actual communities with their motley citizenry, Williams' dramatized Mississippians, from play to play, include Latins: Vicarro, Myra-Lady, "Papa" Romano, Rosa and Señor Gonzales, and Val Xavier. In both one-acters and longer plays, from *American Blues* to *Night of the Iguana*, crosscurrents of good and evil, of hope and despair, of kindness and brutality, of carnality and young love give substance and credibility to Williams' stories about individuals of foreign extraction. This interest in the Latin nature brought Williams, in 1951, to the Broadway presentation of another memorable portrait for his gallery of women, created this time in a dramatic form as much a departure for him as *Ah, Wilderness!* was for O'Neill: folk comedy. In *The Rose Tattoo*, a powerful drama of passion and illusion, he re-created, with vivid reality, the "comic and honestly lusty, sweet, and healthy" aspects of life in a clannish Sicilian fishing village "somewhere along the Gulf Coast between New Orleans and Mobile." More specifically, the play offers the story of recently widowed Serafina delle Rose, a passionate Sicilian-American seamstress for whom love proves stronger than death. As Gassner has said, here Williams makes a fuss "about the sexual career of his torrid Sicilian heroine," whose bizarre conduct marks her as the first in a line of "never-say-die females." More importantly, the characterization of Serafina offers evidence of Williams' versatility. She is his answer to those critics who felt that his portraits of women were limited to delicate and faded southern aristocrats.

Williams' inspiration for this sexual comedy, or tragicomedy as some critics have labeled it, first came from afar. A pleasant sojourn in Rome, from the winter through the summer of 1948, aroused in him an enthusiasm for the charm of the city and the friendliness of its people. The cordial, easygoing Italians reminded Williams of southerners without their inhibitions. The Italian nature, poetic and unrepressed, moved him to create "a warmer and happier play than anything I've written . . . " In short, from "the warmth and sweetness of the Italian people" came the illumination needed for the creation of his transplanted Sicilians in *The Rose Tattoo*. (Later, and closer to home, the neighborhood of his Key West frame cottage became the main scene filmed for the movie version.)

During his Roman holiday Williams did considerable rewriting as well as new writing, including a new play about an Italian heroine, at first titled *The Eclipse of May 29, 1919*. The second draft became *Eclipse of the Sun*, which by a fourth draft was called *The Rose Tattoo*. When Williams returned to Rome in the summer of 1950, he met Anna Magnani, whose talents seemed perfectly suited to the fiery, difficult Serafina role. Actually he had written his comedy with her in mind for the key part. Miss Magnani refused his offer of the stage role but agreed to undertake the screen part, provided the Broadway premiere proved a success. It was successful enough to warrant a fine film version, in which Anna Magnani and Burt Lancaster, as Alvaro, gave magnificent performances. When he returned to New York, Williams discovered in Maureen Stapleton, then an untried actress, a gifted interpreter for the role of

Serafina. Producer Cheryl Crawford and director Daniel Mann were fortunate in their choice of other talented players: Eli Wallach as Alvaro, Serafina's truck driver lover; Phyllis Love as Rosa, Serafina's teen-age daughter; Don Murray as Jack Hunter, the young sailor who falls in love with Rosa; and Ludmilla Toretzka as Assunta, the comforting neighbor. These were the leading members of a distinguished cast when the play opened at the Martin Beck Theatre on February 3, 1951. (A first production by Cheryl Crawford was given at the Erlanger Theatre in Chicago on December 29, 1950.)

This tragicomedy about Serafina delle Rose and her neighbors grows out of the lives of "plain folks," who though colonized in the Gulf Coast area are still governed by their Sicilian loyalties. Although these Latins in their semi-tropical village have become partially Americanized, they still cherish their native customs and believe in the superstitions of their Sicilian forebears. They are passionate and highly emotional people, as quickly excited by the trespasses of a neighbor's bleating goat as by the music of their folk singers or by the rumors about the smuggling secretly engaged in by local drivers of banana trucks. Their religious nature best expresses itself in their reverent attitude toward kindly Father de Leo and, more particularly, in Serafina's yearning vigil before a lighted figurine of the Madonna, worshiped as a symbol of fecundity. Excitement over the local high-school commencement exercises and American Legion celebrations reflects the community pride of a naturalized group which is slowly adapting itself to American ways. Williams himself liked not only their quaint folk speech with its poetic rhythms but also their native humor, which he used expertly to lighten the tone of the more serious happenings. Also adding to the reality of the scene are the noisy neighborhood children and the black-shawled wives. Both groups, in their remarks about fragments of Serafina's story—her woeful double loss of her baby and her husband—serve as choruses.

In his production notes Williams vividly describes Serafina's dilapidated frame cottage, stipulating that the interior must be "exclamatory in its brightness like the projection of a woman's heart passionately in love."[28] A small wall shrine, consisting of a prie-dieu, a blue-robed statue of the Madonna, and a vigil light in a ruby glass cup, is a reminder of Serafina's childlike belief in the mysteries connected with the Madonna. Here, as in other instances, symbols of love and lovers take the form of multi-fashioned images of roses. Rose-patterned wallpaper is matched by a rose-colored carpet. In fact, the key to the protagonist's passionate nature may be found in the roseate images plentifully scattered throughout the play. Serafina herself is Mrs. delle Rose; her loving but unseen husband, Rosario, perfumes his hair with rose oil and has a rose tattooed on his chest. Later another truck driver, Alvaro Mangia-cavallo, in an effort to impress Serafina, has himself tattooed with a rose motif. At the opening of the first act there is a great bowl of roses upon the supper table. Serafina herself, overjoyed with the knowledge that she is again pregnant, is resting while eagerly awaiting Rosario's return from his final delivery of bananas—and dope. Dressed to please Rosario, she resembles "a plump little Italian opera singer in the role of Madame Butterfly." Her high pompadour, with her hair glittering like wet coal, is adorned by a rose held in place by jet hairpins. "Her voluptuous figure is sheathed in pale rose silk." Even the yellow paper fan which she holds in her plump hands is decorated with a painted rose. Serafina tells Assunta that "on the very night of conception" she discovered on her left breast a prickly rose tattoo exactly like Rosario's. Even Estelle Hohengarten, a blackjack dealer from Texas and Rosario's paramour, has a rose design tattooed on her chest to please "this man . . . wild like a Gypsy." Under ironic circumstances, Estelle boldly asks the innocent Serafina to make a rose silk shirt "for a man I'm in love with." Finally, Estelle calls Serafina's teen-age daughter Rosa "a twig off the old rose-bush." This plethora of flowery images is enough to clarify the thematic interest for even the dullest spectators.

As Williams has explained, the imagery of the rose signifies "the Dionysian element in human life, its mystery, its beauty, its significance . . . and although the goat is one of its most immemorial symbols, it must not be confused with mere sexuality. The element is higher . . . the limitless world of the dream. It is the *rosa mystica*."[29] Thus *The Rose Tattoo*, with its overly elaborate symbolism and rather naïve view, is a dramatized tribute to the sexual relationship as a universal cure-all. Alvaro's reproof of Serafina's argument that there are no roses for a widow touches upon the central motif of the comedy: "It's always for everybody the time of roses! The rose is the heart of the world like the heart is—the heart of the—body!"[30]

The plot, criticized as one of Williams' weakest and most contrived, presents in its two-level story a mixture of comedy and pathos. The principal story belongs to Serafina, whose pride in being the wife of "a barone" (a small landowner in Sicily), intense devotion to woman-chasing Rosario, and simple belief in his purity are at odds with the truth. Rosario's sudden death during an encounter with the police as he is bootlegging dope removes him from the scene physically; yet so strong is the effect of his wild nature upon Serafina, Rosa, Estelle, and others that for them he seems to live. In a sense, says biographer Benjamin

Nelson, Rosario "is the Dionysus whose death means rebirth, and the plot of the drama is the joyful rebirth, symbolized by the rose and climaxed by Serafina's announcement [at the finale] that she is [again] with child."[31]

Serafina herself is to experience a series of horrors: her loss of both husband and baby, her chance discovery of Rosario's infidelity, and an unnerving telephone bout with Estelle. As three years pass, she degenerates physically and spiritually, to the point of neglecting pretty Rosa, now ready for high school graduation. In a subplot which offers more conflict, Serafina's slovenly appearance and antisocial manner almost spoil Rosa's sudden love affair with Jack Hunter, a young and almost unbelievably pure sailor. Her old-world feeling about this relationship and her stern questioning of Jack to find out his motives nearly bring about a break between mother and daughter. Eventually, however, she consents to Rosa's staying with Jack during the last hours of his shore leave.

This change of heart comes about because of Serafina's accidental acquaintance with another truck driver, Alvaro Mangiacavallo, who, while courting her, joins with Father de Leo and the neighbors in convincing Serafina that she should stop mourning for Rosario. When she learns of her husband's year-long affair with Estelle, Serafina wrathfully throws the urn containing his ashes across the room and blows out the vigil light before the Madonna's statue. During a most comical courting scene with the awkward Alvaro, Serafina belittles him as the grandson of a village idiot. Though she thinks his body as beautiful as Rosario's, Alvaro arouses her contempt because of his clown's face. At last, feeling that the tattooed Alvaro is symbolically connected with her dead husband, she goes to bed with him and conceives another child. At the play's end Serafina joyously confesses to Assunta that she has felt the burning and prickly rose on her breast for the second time.

In spite of certain inadequacies—the strained resolution of the action, the overemphasis on the sexual act, and excessive, artificial symbolism —The Rose Tattoo is rare among our provincial plays in its realistic portrayal of a village peopled largely by lusty Latins. As members of a Catholic community, these Sicilian-Americans are often irritated at having their cherished European folkways challenged by brash and unpleasant native Americans. The latter are generally satirically portrayed as unflattering symbols of our social crudity. A traveling salesman who deliberately threatens Alvaro's physical and economic well-being becomes a symbol of coarseness and inhumanity. Others, like the noisy, merrymaking Legionnaires, a Texas blackjack dealer in a cheap cabaret, and the two floozies who use Serafina's services as seamstress typify those unattractive townspeople, who, in Williams' view, belittle the status of a community. While among Serafina's neighbors most of the children and the housewives, "chattering at once like a cloud of birds," are sketched casually for choral purposes, their folk speech and their names—Guiseppina, Peppina, and Violetta—give a touch of local color to the picture of this neighborhood.

Several, who play more significant roles, are better individualized. The cronelike Strega, superstitiously regarded as a witch, is the wild-haired owner of an obstreperous goat whose appearances and reappearances suggest to most people a note of lechery—although, as we have noted, Williams has said that the goat symbol must not be confused with mere sexuality. Miss Yorke, a spinsterish high-school teacher who recognizes Rosa's brightness, comes from an outside world of law and decorum and serves as a foil to Serafina's disorderly world. ("Let's not have any more outbursts of emotion.") Assunta, "an old woman in a gray shawl" and a practitioner of "a simple sort of medicine," symbolizes the wise and comforting neighbor. And so does Father de Leo, who tries to bring the authority of the church to bear on the peaceful settlement of domestic problems. In general, the lives of these villagers are marked by a warmth, a vitality, and a spontaneous joie de vivre quite in contrast to the more conventional ways of the Anglo-Saxons in the neighborhood. Hilarity and ribaldry, as in the goat chases and Alvaro's bumbling efforts to master the art of courtship; pathos, as in Serafina's loss of her baby; and tenderness, as in the romance of the young lovers are some of the factors which contributed to the success of *The Rose Tattoo* in production.

Since the beginning of his career, Williams has experimented constantly in the imaginative reconstruction of both native and foreign places which he knows and likes. For instance, the Gulf Coast landscape of *The Rose Tattoo* reappears, with a shift in vicinity, in *Sweet Bird of Youth* (1959). On the other hand, a more sophisticated way of life than that lived in Serafina's village characterizes the politically and socially minded citizens of St. Cloud, a sizable town situated "somewhere along the Gulf Coast." The main scene—parts of "an old fashioned but still fashionable hotel," somewhat vaguely styled as "Moorish" and beautified by balconies, terraces, and a palm garden—is complemented by comfortable Victorian residences from whose wide verandas, terraces, and gardens the owners may view the limitless expanse of the Gulf. Activities of the country club set, owners of fine cars, boats, and other property symbolizing status, mark the town as peopled by affluent citizens and tourists. "The girls are young matrons, bridge-players, and the boys belong to the Junior Chamber of Commerce and some of them, clubs in New Orleans such as Rex and Comus and ride on the Mardi Gras floats"—a narrow and boring routine which to Chance Wayne, one of the protagonists, seems fit only for that "fat-headed gang," the "snobset."[32]

The reverse of this provincial picture reveals a corrupt and a vicious world, quite in contrast with the luxury of the hotel and the time of the action, an Easter Sunday of recent years. Williams' dramatization of this more violent underside reflects popular concern over such disparate problems as those connected with "Sex, Youth, Time, Corruption, Purity, Castration, Politics, and The South."[33] Chiefly responsible for the prevalence of bigotry and chicanery in St. Cloud is Boss Finley, "the biggest political wheel in this part of the country" who came down from the red hills "as if the Voice of God called me." As a cross between Big Daddy Pollitt of *Cat on a Hot Tin Roof* and Huey Long and "a direct descendent of Jabe Torrance," Finley gradually gains power over gullible constituents by skilful demagoguery in preaching hate and racism, or southern purity. His ruthlessness and overbearing nature have cramped and saddened the lives of his timid wife, now dead, his beautiful daughter Heavenly, and his morally weak son, Tom Junior. With the assistance of Tom and other henchmen, the Boss has transformed St. Cloud and its environs into a sort of "beanstalk country, the ogre's country . . ." And those who disagree with "the big man" suffer painful loss in this "country of the flesh-hungry, blood-thirsty ogre."

More particularly, the "beanstalk country" symbolizes the private worlds in which two derelicts become lost in their frantic search for fulfilment and the fading yet ever so "sweet bird of youth." Each of these drifters—an aging actress once a legend of beauty and talent and a youngish native of St. Cloud still striving to outgrow the obscurity and poverty which shackled his youth—has experienced galling disappointments by the time they come to share a plush bedroom at the Royal Palms Hotels. It is this relationship between Ariadne, or Alexandra, del Lago and Chance Wayne which not only dominates the first act and reappears in the third, but also reveals that Williams is still pursuing some of his favorite theories about sex and love, idealism and reality, loneliness and the need for friendship and communication.

The plight of each of these two lost seekers touches upon their attempts to find a solution in sex. During one of their confidential chats, Chance admits that, though he had done a bit of acting and various odd jobs, his only real—and certainly dubious—profession has been lovemaking. He boosts his waning confidence by confessing that he has "slept in the social register of New York." As a handsome gigolo, he has had intimate affairs with millionaires' widows and wives and with the debutante daughters of socially prominent parents. In spite of his promiscuity, for which he was often paid a fee, he has always enjoyed the illusion of giving pleasure and of being the virile master of the situation. In this regard Chance resembles other purveyors of pleasure, Val Xavier and Christopher, or Chris, Flanders of *The Milk Train Doesn't Stop Here Anymore* (1964).

For her part, Miss del Lago, currently traveling incognito as the Princess Kosmonopolis, wishes mostly for life, "terribly, shamelessly, on any terms whatsoever." Through experience with a rich husband, now deceased, and thereafter with a succession of gigolos, she has concluded that "the only dependable distraction" to make her forget those things which she does not want to remember is the act of lovemaking. Chance, formerly a beachboy who gave her a papaya cream rub in a cabana at a fashionable Palm Beach hotel, is simply a pickup and the most recent of the Princess' escorts. With an ogre's toughness, she forces Chance to make love on demand and without illusion. What the Princess does not at first realize was that Chance plans to use her legend of movie stardom, her money, and her white Cadillac to glorify his return to his hometown, mainly to take the sweetheart of his youth, Heavenly Finley, far away from St. Cloud and her villainous father. For the moment Chance is willing to endure spiritual castration in the hope of recapturing the purity and the promise of his youth by persuading the actress to arrange Hollywood contracts for himself and Heavenly. And what he does not yet know is the tragic truth about Heavenly's hysterectomy and the sworn vengeance of her father.

The del Lago-Wayne liaison pinpoints the terrible intensity of the human dilemma. As the first of the two lines of action which split the plot, this relationship, dominating the opening act, helps to introduce a thematic motif—the ill effects of time and emasculation, real and metaphorical, on the individual—which saves the play from total disunity. This leit-motif is reinforced by an epigraph borrowed from Hart Crane, one of Williams' favorite poets: "Relentless caper for all those who step/ The legend of their youth into the noon." In the course of this symbolical stepping into noon, several characters lose their procreative organs. An unidentified Negro agitator, only casually mentioned in the second act, is mutilated by Boss Finley's "goon squad," and at the play's end Chance, after an appeal to the audience to recognize "the enemy, time, in us all," somewhat unaccountably awaits physical castration at the hands of avenging Tom Junior and his fellow sadists. Earlier, Heavenly, ill from a venereal disease reputedly transmitted by her lover Chance, has to undergo a hysterectomy. The aging Princess reflects upon the futility of temporal satisfactions, such as her movie stardom with its legend of youth. Now reduced to using an oxygen mask, hashish, and assorted sedatives, she laments the castrating effect of age on once-beautiful women of her artistic temperament and professional achievements. Hence the note of pathos in her remark to Chance, now twenty-nine and conscious, like Prufrock, of his thinning hair: "BEAUTY! Say it! Say it! What you had was beauty! I had it! I say it, with pride, no matter how sad, being gone, now."[34]

The second phase of the action, dominating Act II, pushes the personal and sexual plot of the initial act into the background, and the Princess moves into limbo, except for one brief appearance. On this occasion the Princess, coming down into the Palm Garden and the hotel bar, emotionally tells Chance that she has experienced a miracle. She has just recognized in him "that terrible stiff-necked pride of the defeated." His return to St. Cloud, she says, has been equal to the failure of her recent Hollywood comeback picture (which she believes has failed completely). "And I felt something in my heart for you. That's a miracle, Chance. That's the wonderful thing that has happened to me. I felt something for someone besides myself. That means my heart's still alive, . . ."[35] She urges him to go with her at once from this ogre's country, but he refuses to do so until he has seen Heavenly.

As the act moves forward, the second story, or social plot, accentuates the disjointed quality of the play. While not a social tract, it is political in nature, emphasizing Boss Finley and his brutal rule. Certain exaggerated effects—a huge TV screen for a political rally, flashbulbs, a raucous professional claque, and a blaring band, all mingled with a recurring lament which blends with the wind-blown sound of the palms—suddenly change the focus of the action from the personal del Lago-Wayne liaison to a powerful materialistic spellbinder, preaching hate and racial segregation on a nationwide hookup. This phase of the plot, moreover, pursues the deadly conflict between Finley and, in his words, that "handsome young criminal-degenerate . . . Chance Wayne." This struggle becomes, on one level of symbolism, a battle between the dark forces —the Boss's hate, his incestuous desire for Heavenly, and his ruthlessness—and the forces of light, of Chance's preaching and practicing love, however illicit. The dark forces prevail, hastened by the Boss's vengeful hint to Tom Junior as to what Chance's doom ought to be. A corresponding case of the doomed concerns the courageous Heckler, a dissident hillbilly with "the length and leanness and luminous pallor of a face that El Greco gave to his saints." He dares to break into the Boss's television ranting and lying about the purity of southern womanhood. His taunting question—"How about your daughter's operation?"—brings an immediate brutal, but silent, beating from the "goons." In the meanwhile when white-garmented Heavenly, being escorted to the platform by her father, faces Chance, he is stunned. Later, during the struggle with the Heckler, Heavenly rushes down the platform stairs, sobbing, and collapses as the curtain falls. In the Finley scenes the very names of his sycophants—Hatcher, Scudder, and Stuff—satirically reflect their subserviency to the will of the demagogue. Even those who try to show compassion in a world of affliction—Miss Lucy, the Boss's mistress with a "sharp little terrier face," and his soft-hearted sister-in-law, Aunt Nonnie—are slaves to his power.

Having experienced a "miracle," the Princess is aroused from her self-pity and lethargy. Like her mythical prototype Ariadne, she offers to lead Chance out of his present danger to Hollywood as her paid companion.[36] His stubborn refusal only hastens his doom. The final act shifts the focus of interest back to the Princess, who unexpectedly finds again a path to climb alone up the beanstalk. Through a Hollywood columnist she gains a reprieve: news that her last picture, which she had thought a failure, has actually broken box-office records. Nevertheless, she knows that time, with its inevitable changes, will continue to dim the legend of youth which she has outlived. Though she still maintains a grand air, she recognizes that her future course will not be a progression of triumphs. In a moment of resignation and searching self-appraisal, Chance honestly admits to the Princess that now his "life means nothing, except that you could never make it, always almost, never quite . . ." Concluding that "something's still got to mean something," Chance knows that his hope for a loving reunion with Heavenly is gone, together with the likelihood of his securing a movie contract. So, both the Princess and her gigolo are faced with castration, and each knows that time "gnaws away, like a rat gnaws off its own foot caught in a trap, and then, with its foot gnawed off and the rat set free, couldn't run, couldn't go, bled and died . . ."

The play ends awkwardly on a nightmarish and ominous note, with Chance now left alone to face his tormentors. Soon there will be no need for him to continue his searching for the "sweet bird of youth." The enemy, time, will have its triumph. Thus at the finale, as elsewhere in the play, Elia Kazan's staging tended to emphasize man's violent end and to underplay or hasten through the few moments of revelation and beauty in the script. The action is timed to coincide with Easter Sunday; yet there is little stress upon the parallel between the characters' searching for new horizons and the Resurrection. Even the Heckler, the mysterious stranger who philosophized about "the silence of God, the absolute speechlessness of Him," is accorded only momentary attention during his fatal struggle. Instead, the spotlight falls upon Chance, so horrified and stunned that he cannot save the saintlike victim from Tom and his gang. Both the unnamed heckler and Chance return to the obscurity—and persecution—into which they were born.

Critical differences about *Sweet Bird of Youth*, as about Williams' achievements as a playwright, cover a wide range. When the play was produced in 1959 there was an approach to unanimity in the responses of the newspaper reviewers. Most found the play electrifying. Brooks Atkinson, writing for the *New York Times*, regarded it as one of Williams' finest dramas, a poetic play "Powerful—Vivid—Brilliantly played." Walter Kerr reviewed it in *the New York Herald Tribune* as an enormously exciting and thrilling blockbuster: "This is the noise of passion, of creative energy, of exploration and adventure." Richard Watts, Jr., of the *New York Post* termed the production "tremendous," "superb," and "memorable," and John Chapman in the *New York News* praised the "strength and theatrical skill, vigor and clarity" of the writing. Opinions expressed by Williams' biographers and other critics offer marked contrast to such journalistic superlatives. Robert Brustein of Columbia University, writing in the *Hudson Review*, offers a brilliant and disparaging evaluation of "the evasions and contradictions of this inferior work." His scholarly criticism is notably sharp in regard to the "mindless and unreal" quality of the play's segregationist themes. As to the organic disunity of the play, he feels that ". . . the wild and fertile imagination which conceives has far outstripped the mind which shapes." Nancy M. Tischler, in her *Tennessee Williams: Rebellious Puritan*, exposes such flaws as the poverty of the minor roles, the strident melodramatic violence, the purple writing in the poetic passages, the falsity of the political rally scene, the excessive plot complication, and, most of all, Williams' placing of the responsibility for Chance's tragedy upon society. Benjamin Nelson, in *Tennessee Williams: The Man and His Work*, cogently analyzes the play's lack of artistic and philosophical unity which produces the effect of "a kind of three-ring circus." In short, ". . . the tapestry of the drama is a ragbag of conflicting plots, characters and symbols." Also, he finds the political tone "hackneyed and naïve."

Most critics, journalistic and academic, agree that Cheryl Crawford's production, with direction by Elia Kazan and stage design and lighting by Jo Mielziner, owed much to the superb performances of a remarkably talented cast. Geraldine Page, until then associated with the Alma role of *Summer and Smoke*, proved to be a model of virtuosity in combining the elements of raucous humor, dignity, and introspection in the role of Princess Kosmonopolis. If, as Henry Hewes has written, Miss Page tended to overdo the pretensions of the flamboyant Princess, she achieved superb effects through her concentration, discipline, and true humor. Paul Newman's portrayal of Chance, with its mixture of humor and seriousness, was brilliantly successful in projecting a handsome youth who has been romanticizing himself for too long, and who must finally face disillusionment. Rip Torn, as Heavenly's avenging brother, received plaudits for giving spectators "that feeling of controlled power held in reserve which so often heralds a potentially great actor." Sidney Blackmer, assigned to play Boss Finley, one of "the most superficial and implausible characters Williams ever created," showed a wonderful mastery over this demanding and unpleasant role. Diana Hyland presented a sensitive interpretation of Heavenly.

In spite of all of the critical charges levied against him—charges that he has overworked themes of violence, horror, corruption, and death, that he is often wrong, and even naïve, in his interpretation of sexuality, that his plays sometimes exhibit structural formlessness or disunity, and that he is too highly symbolical—Tennessee Williams remains the one contemporary American playwright, second only to Eugene O'Neill, who has written most prolifically and meaningfully about small-town life. His frequent portrayals of southern provincialism, begun with his early one-acters, have extended to his more recent longer plays. Except for *Camino Real* (1953), *Garden District* ("Suddenly Last Summer" and "Something Unspoken," 1958), *Period of Adjustment* (1960), *Night of the Iguana* (1962), and *The Milk Train Doesn't Stop Here Anymore* (1964), all have been set in Mississippi, either in small agricultural towns of the Delta or in coastal towns near the Gulf of Mexico. Williams' manifold images of this provincial world generally bare the unpleasant truth about the undersurface of life in outwardly pleasant communities. As life goes on in his memory world, beauty, justice, and truth get little more than lip service from townspeople whose festering hate and violence of spirit would deny freedom and peace to those who are different in race, creed, or temperament. Hypocrisy, conformism, and the pursuit of pseudo-culture are roundly condemned. His exposures of the "unco guid" and the unscrupulous satirize what Mrs. Goforth of *The Milk Train* dismisses as "the human cats of this world, of whom there is no small number." After all, as Mrs. Goforth says, in these small towns there are "sea-level, those lower-than-sea level, people." And such people follow callings familiar to any southern townsman: preaching, traveling as a salesman or drummer, as did Cornelius Williams, merchandising, sewing, trucking, doctoring, ginning cotton, railroading, working as sheriff and deputy, "houswifery," and even whoring.

Williams' pictures of such representative Mississippi provincials bear the hallmarks of his long interest in romanticism, together with a Lawrencian insistence on sex, experiments with expressionism and realism, and a revelation of his intimate knowledge of the different ethnic groups which exist in the northern and southern parts of his native state. Even in his travels Williams seems to have been observant of people of obscure destinies, such as the characters inhabiting the tropical seaport in *Camino Real* and the Mexican village of *Night of the Iguana* testify. In *The Milk Train*, set against the background of a plush Mediterranean villa, the demented memoirs of Italianate and garrulous Mrs. Goforth suggest that her youth was spent in a small swamp community in Georgia. Her climb up the beanstalk led along a rough path before the beginning of her career as a great international beauty. As she admits, "Hell, I was born between a swamp and the wrong side of the tracks in One Street, Georgia, but not even that could stop me in my tracks, wrong side or right side, or no side."[37] Billed as the Dixie Doxy in a carnival show, she kept moving ahead until, though still in her teens, she reached star billing in the Follies. Further advancement came through several marriages to wealthy men. Thus the small town in Williams' imagined world has served as the native milieu for a rich old expatriate as well as for the unambitious and simple-souled Baby Doll, who never escaped.

For some time now critics have been asking probing questions about Williams' talents as a playwright. Some query: "Is Williams as yet a master of his dreams?" Others ask: "Will he once again bring about the miracle of truly moving spectators, as he did in his best plays (*Cat on a Hot Tin Roof, A Streetcar Named Desire*, and others)?" "In the future will his mature talent—his genius—be better controlled than it appeared to be in *Sweet Bird of Youth*?" "Will he again do justice to his potentialities?" "As his talent deepens, where will his subject and imagination lead?" "Will his creative talent match his imagination?" There have been questions, too, about whether he will continue his thematic treatment of what Gassner has described as "the tragic situation of the artist in the hell of modern society and the crucifixion of the pure male on the cross of sexuality." Perhaps, as a gifted portrayer of southern provincialism, Williams may continue to practice "the truth game," with the full knowledge that, as Chris Flanders of *The Milk Train* puts it, ". . . the truth is

too delicate and, well, *dangerous* a thing to be played with at parties . . .
It's nitroglycerin, it has to be handled with the—the carefulest care . . ."[38]
It seems likely that Williams will continue on his way as a free artist un-
afraid of expressing dissident opinion and frankly assuring his critics
that he does not deny that he uses "a lot of those things called symbols,
but being a self-defensive creature, I say that symbols are nothing but the
natural speech of drama."[39] Moreover, he believes that a live theater, one
meant for seeing and feeling, "has never been and never will be extin-
guished by a bucket brigade of critics, new or old, bearing vessels that
range from cut-glass bowl to Haviland teacup."[40] Whatever his future
artistic commitments may be, Williams has already created with power
and beauty some of the most striking and penetrating dramatizations of
the contemporary southern town which have been seen on the modern
stage. And his achievement owes something to another and older Mississippian, William Faulkner.

"This was Jefferson"

The history of one of the most completely pictured little towns in all
American fiction is summarized in the lengthy, and sometimes lyrical,
prose interchapters which preface the three dramatic portions in one of
William Faulkner's strangest novels. As he says in that novel—*Requiem
for a Nun* (1951)—". . . so weeks and months and years had to be con-
densed and compounded into . . . one soundless roar filled with one word:
town: city: with a name: Jefferson . . ." In the beginning there was
nothing more than "a tiny clearing clawing punily" into the pathless
wilderness. In the course of years and "out of the turmoil of the town's
birthing" an imposing brick edifice, looming in the center of the county
itself, was finally completed: the domed and porticoed white courthouse
which was to serve many generations of Jeffersonians and Yoknapatawphians as "the center, the focus, the hub" of their circumscribed universe.
Here, indeed, was the hub of Faulkner's "mythical kingdom," as Malcolm
Cowley has called this imaginary land. Antedating the courthouse, however, was the jail, in the beginning only a log cabin, which symbolized

the panorama not only of the town but of its days and years until a century
and better had been accomplished, filled not only with its mutation and change
from a halting-place: to a community: to a settlement: to a village: to a
town, but with the shapes and motions, the gestures of passion and hope and
travail and endurance, of the men and women and children in their successive
overlapping generations . . .[41]

Strong in its sense of the past, Jefferson, as pictured in novels, stories,
and drama for more than thirty years of writing, is usually thought to

have been modeled on one small agricultural town. (Faulkner himself has said, "I *invented* all that.")[42] Until recently critics and biographers have generally assumed that Faulkner, in creating Jefferson, memorialized his hometown of Oxford, the county seat of Lafayette County, Mississippi —an area approximately sixty miles distant from the Tennessee Williams country around Clarksdale. Both Malcolm Cowley and Robert Penn Warren have placed the larger locale of Faulkner's fictional Yoknapa-tawpha County—presumably Lafayette County—with its imagined 2,400 square miles and its 15,611 persons, between the northern Mississippi hills and the fertile bottomlands. These lands are near the Yocona River, originally called the Yocanapatafa. In 1961 G. T. Buckley, questioning the assumptions of Robert Coughlan, Irving Howe, Ward L. Miner, and William Van O'Connor that Oxford was the *actual* prototype, meticu-lously presented arguments and statistics in support of his belief that what Faulkner "has generally in mind in my opinion is a composite or abstraction of a half dozen small county seat towns of extreme Northern Mississippi, specifically such places as Ripley [where the Faulkners originated], New Albany [the writer's birthplace], Pontotoc, Holly Springs, and Batesville."[43]

In rebuttal, Calvin S. Brown has argued cogently that "Faulkner habit-ually imagines his characters moving about the square and streets of Oxford and the roads, hills, and swamps of Lafayette County."[44] Also, Brown, an Oxford native, reminds his readers that "Jefferson is a ficti-tious town inhabited by people of Faulkner's creation, no matter how much raw material, local scenes and characters may have supplied to his imagination." Whatever the identity of its geographic prototype, Jeffer-son remains a small trading and cotton center, as well as a county seat, in the Deep South. In novel, story, and drama it has appeared as having the marks of class, occupation, and history. The place takes on an air of reality as Faulkner repeatedly portrays the speech, dress, food, houses, manners, and attitudes of typical Jeffersonians.

Peopled by descendants of the first pioneering families, like the Sartorises, and by intruding newcomers such as ambitious Sutpen, Jef-ferson came also to number among its citizens "the descendants of bush-whackers and carpetbaggers, the swamp rats, the Negro cooks and farm hands, bootleggers and gangsters, peddlers, college boys [like Gowan Stevens], tenant farmers, country store-keepers, county-seat lawyers [Horace Benbow and Gavin Stevens]" and others.[45] As the town moved toward more modern decades, the powerful influence of the encroaching carpetbaggers and the codeless Snopeses, "a new exploiting class de-scended from the landless whites," began to leave deep marks on the local society and economy. These offer but a sampling of Jefferson's motley citizenry, whose varied stories symbolize both man's doom and the manhood, or womanhood, with which an individual, such as Nancy Mannigoe, has to face that doom courageously. Many of the descendants of the older and more aristocratic families, like Gavin Stevens, lack the hardihood and the competency of their pioneering forbears. Their tradition of gentility and of idealistic thinking, weakened during successive generations, proves to be a barrier to their successful competition with an intrusive and ruthless Snopesism and other symbols of modern greed and materialism. Faulkner's literary maps of the county and the town, while criticized by modern commentators, help clarify his descriptions of the geographic spread of these newly entrenched groups, in relation to the holdings of the pioneer families.[46]

In the fall of 1951, more than eight months after *The Rose Tattoo* had opened on Broadway, Faulkner published his *Requiem*, picturing at the opening the pretty but deceptively quiet little town of Jefferson as it was in the mid-thirties.[47] Purportedly composed as a sort of relaxation from his long-sustained writing on *A Fable* (from 1944 to 1953), *Requiem* was written as a sequel, "a little coda," to Temple Drake's horrific story related in *Sanctuary* (1931). A deliberately designed shocker, *Sanctuary* was not only a brilliant handling of the psychology of terror, but also a turning point in Faulkner's literary reputation. During the thirties, as Alfred Kazin has shown, the realistic literature of the era plumbed life to great secret depths—the "depths of terror and sensibility." As a young writer then, Faulkner began not only to create pictures of the Jefferson of his future sagas, but to put down some of the foundations for his thought. One such tenet concerned the bitterness of being a Sartoris — the Mississippi aristocrat *manqué*—in a Snopes world, the constantly enlarging world of small, mean traders, expropriators, and ambitious poor whites.

Also, as he studied the decadence of his native region, while still maintaining his connection with it, Faulkner began to express sympathy with the Negroes. Concurrently, he satirically exposed the lack of charity, the self-righteousness, and other appalling excesses of the Calvinist spirit, Mississippi style. In *Sanctuary*, with its notes of horror and despair, Faulkner early explored the depths of terror and sensibility to produce a pattern of moral evil and social failure which at once gained notoriety for both the novel and the young novelist. At one extreme of interpretation was Henry Seidel Canby's feature article, "The Cult of Cruelty," in the *Saturday Review of Literature*; at the other was Paramount's film version in which the original story, now titled *The Story of Temple Drake*, was so distorted that Temple, played by Miriam Hopkins, was portrayed as "a virtuous maiden, temporarily bemused by the power of evil."[48]

The semi-dramatized case history, or extended problem, of Temple Drake, who becomes Mrs. Gowan Stevens, was not destined to lie dormant in the 1951 version of *Requiem for a Nun*. Years afterward another Mississippian, actress Ruth Ford, sensing in its original form an exciting and compelling story, joined with Faulkner in adapting the novel for stage production. At last the three-act tragedy, under the sponsorship of the Theatre Guild, opened at the John Golden Theatre in New York City, on January 28, 1959. This New York premiere impressed at least one spectator as "a Gothic nightmare," which lost some of its appeal largely because Miss Ford, as the tortured heroine, Temple (Drake) Stevens, was not youthful enough in appearance to create the effect of "the volatility and grace of youth."[49] Though Miss Ford was assisted by an expert cast, including Bertice Reading as Nancy, Scott McKay as Gowan Stevens, and Zachary Scott as Gavin Stevens, the play was so sordid that it aroused little audience sympathy, and Gassner felt that the characters looked "painfully barren on the stage under the merciless glare of the footlights." (The later London production drew superlative press notices.)

The questions raised by critics have emphasized the strangeness of Faulkner's habit of making his scenes all too often "some swamp of the spirit," of choosing subjects of "murder, rape, prostitution, incest, arson, idiocy, with an occasional interpolation of broad country humor almost as violent as his tragedies," and of fashioning "the country of his mind" in the form of "a Mississippi county larger than life, but not visibly related to it."[50] Such strangeness marks *Requiem for a Nun* in an even larger sense, for this bleak play, as if in accord with Eliot's concept, is a sordid and rigidly controlled study of interrelated time: of "Time present and time past," both perhaps being "present in time future." In the play Gavin Stevens philosophizes that ". . . the past is never dead. It's not even past." As to Temple's dilemma, what has been discolors her present life more than what might have been.

This sequence of time is as basic to the organic structure of the play as to the 1951 novelistic version. In the latter, the three inter-chapters present the history of town and county "as a record of man's furious attempts to establish a collective identity, to delegate moral responsibility, and to find security within a system of laws."[51] Each of these chapters is a discursive prologue giving a mark of historicity to the scenes of the three acts: the Nancy Mannigoe murder trial in the courtroom of the Jefferson courthouse; the governor's office in Jackson; and the jail in

Jefferson. At the New York premiere the original scenery by Motley consisted of an adaptable basic design, with an elevation—steps and a great louvered door, at center back—to symbolize variously the elevated tribunal of justice of the Yoknapatawpha County court; the gubernatorial office with its emblazoned seal, a massive desk, and a thronelike chair; the Stevenses' living room; and the black-doored jail. Each scene merges with the next one as stage lights dim, thus accentuating the shifting sequences of time and place.

More significantly, the crisp and unadorned dialogue contains sufficient flashback references to establish the link between Temple's present connection with the underworld, in regard to the murder of her baby, and her first discovery of evil eight (or ten?) years ago, when she was a college girl. This evocation of a past which has haunted her gives credence to W. M. Frohock's note that "Misfortune, catastrophe, and death follow Temple Drake wherever she goes."[52] These dialogue flashbacks provide glimpses of Judge Drake's feckless daughter, who in her teens typified the F. Scott Fitzgerald flapper of the raucous twenties, the 1929 prototype of the modern emancipated woman. In the play, as in *Sanctuary*, this past action is revived largely through the conversation of the contrasting personalities of Temple herself, her husband Gowan, his uncle Gavin, nursemaid Nancy Mannigoe (a murderess just condemned to be hanged), and Mississippi's governor. Such a multiple focus on recall offers a complex review of the nightmarish experiences which lasted for more than six weeks during Temple's seventeenth (or eighteenth?) year.

Her nightmare began when at the instigation of young Gowan Stevens, she left a special train of university students to drive with him to a collegiate baseball game. En route, Gowan's excessive drinking, at odds with his code that a Virginia gentleman should be able to hold his liquor, caused him to wreck his car at Lee Goodwin's place, southeast of Jefferson. This was a ruined plantation house at Frenchman's Bend, which was being used as an isolated hideout for a gang of moonshiners. When Gowan went for another car, leaving the frantic and agonized girl stranded, she became the prisoner of a sinister and sexually impotent racketeer, syphilitic Popeye, and his fellow bootleggers. In semi-hysteria, she erred in using the only weapon at her command, coquetry and flirtation, which was understood well enough in her university world but which was dangerous among perverts and vicious men. Goodwin's common-law wife, Ruby Lamar, while scornful of this respectable girl, took her out to the barn and stayed with her until daylight. Later Temple, terrified in a rat-infested corncrib, was to witness Popeye's callous shooting of Tommy (Tawmmy), one of the moonshiners. Then Popeye outrageously violated her. (In *Requiem* idealistic Gavin Stevens, listening to Temple's sordid recital, declares that Popeye "should have been crushed somehow under a vast and mindless boot, like a spider.")[53]

The nightmare continued when Popeye kidnapped Temple, drove her to Memphis, and there imprisoned her in a brothel operated by a drunken procuress calling herself Reba Rivers. In this bawdy house the girl's escape from the moral obligations of her social caste was hastened by her sexual relations with a tavern bouncer, Red, another of Popeye's henchmen. During her forced confinement Temple developed a growing fascination with violence and other evils and, thoroughly corrupted, fell in love with Red. After Popeye killed Red, Temple finally showed up in Jefferson to testify at Lee Goodwin's trial for the murder of Tommy. Her perjured testimony, perhaps motivated by fear of Popeye or possibly by a concern for family honor, indicated that Goodwin, rather than Popeye, was the murderer. Accordingly Goodwin was judged guilty, but before his sentence could be carried out legally, a mob broke into the jail and burned him to death. To remove her from harm and gossip, Judge Drake took his sullen, unhappy daughter to France, and that winter Gowan and Temple were married in Paris. Such, in part, is the gist of Temple's recital to the governor, during which she postures, pretends, exaggerates, becomes bitter and flippant by turns.

As her story continues in *Requiem*, notably in the scene where she and Gavin Stevens confer with the governor, Temple's nervousness indicates how much she has been troubled by feelings of guilt ever since the Goodwin trial of long ago. Now a new trial, that of Nancy Mannigoe for the murder of Gowan and Temple's baby, has ended with the sentencing of the accused to be hanged on the following thirteenth of March. In an emergency meeting with the governor, Gavin, the trial lawyer, and Temple ask for clemency in Nancy's behalf. Momentarily refraining from admitting her own share in the guilt and the responsibility for the death of her child, Temple explains that she has forgiven Nancy because she was crazy. Acknowledging that the Negro woman was a "whore, dope fiend," Temple suggests that the woman was "hopeless, already damned before she was born." In turn, Gavin adds that Nancy became for the Stevenses "nurse: guide: catalyst, glue . . . holding the whole lot of them together." Still toying with the idea of repressing the truth about her own guilt, Temple reluctantly reveals to the two men how much she has been imprisoned anew, during the past few years, in the role of Mrs. Gowan Stevens, living in a small-town world circumscribed by the worship of conformity. Restlessness has made her hope for escape both from a marriage which has become meaningless and from a cult of respectability which has become a sham. She admits that, ironically, the one confidante with whom she can talk freely about "whore morality" and her past is her children's Negro nurse, Nancy Mannigoe. "Two sisters in sin," she describes herself and Nancy, "swapping trade or vocational secrets over Coca-Colas in the quiet kitchen."

For some time the scene remains the same: the office of state in Jackson. The governor is the interlocutor-listener. The time is two o'clock on the morning of March 12, just hours before Nancy's scheduled execution. Speaking as Mrs. Stevens, Temple deliberately besmirches the character of Miss Drake of eight or more years ago. With Gavin acting as a moral gadfly, Temple reveals a secret. By a reversal of time, to June 13 a year earlier, Faulkner dramatizes, from both Temple's and Nancy's points of view, an unpublicized facet of her sordid past. In this flashback episode Pete, Red's younger brother, boldly comes to the Stevens home with threats to tell Gowan that he possesses the incriminating love letters which young Temple wrote to her lover. Pete, handsome, assured, and ruthless, now uses the letters for blackmail to induce Temple to leave her husband and accept him as a new lover. In spite of Nancy's protests, Temple decides to leave with Pete. Not until later is the full meaning of Nancy's words clear: "I tried everything I knowed." While Temple is completing her packing, Nancy smothers the baby in its offstage nursery. As this scene fades and the lights come on to open scene 3, the time again is early morning on March 12. Gowan now sits in the chair behind the governor's desk. Denouncing his wife as a bitch, Gowan testily admits his own failure to achieve a full understanding with her. Learning that the governor has denied their plea to save Nancy's life, Temple thinks now of the difficulty of saving her own soul—"If I have a soul. If there is a God to save it—a God who wants it—."

Throughout her recital before the governor, Temple has become more and more disturbed as she recalls Gowan's quarreling with her because he had doubts about the paternity of their older child, Bucky. Her dilemma had actually begun just after she and Gowan returned from Paris when each became identified, most ironically, with the town's cult of respectability, to the point of conforming outwardly to its prevailing order. Nervously confiding to the governor and Gavin, Temple cynically unmasks the hypocrisy which she has shared with Gowan: "The Gowan Stevenses, young, popular; a new house on the right street, a country club, a pew in the right church."[54]

Prior to her appearance in Jackson, Temple, driven by her personal Furies, had fled to California, with the hope of regaining mental peace there. At Gavin's summons, however, she returns to Jefferson and the

Jackson conference, where, at his insistence, she grudgingly acknowledges her definite involvement in Nancy's act of murder. At last, when Gowan, as an eavesdropper, has taken the governor's chair, Temple in turmoil of spirit recognizes the need for her own salvation. As Gavin says, one's salvation comes only through suffering. In the third act Nancy, with but a few more hours to live, again comes into sharp focus. Both her simple but deep faith in the Lord and her willingness to pay for her crime contrast dramatically with Temple's reluctance either to acquire faith or to pay for her iniquities in full. Nancy's repeated warning to her mistress, who visits her in the jail, is to "Believe . . . Believe." Nevertheless, at the finale Temple's redemption is uncertain. In a daze, she wonders whether we are all "Doomed. Damned."

Gowan's belated admission that he, too, must share in the guilt hints that mutual trust and understanding may yet grow between his wife and him. Each has been a symbol of social violation and isolation as much as Popeye or even their relative Gavin, whose own search for truth and and justice, even among social misfits and criminals, highlights his non-conformism and idealism. Gavin's marital unhappiness, his secret long-ing for his nubile stepdaughter, and his shocking his widowed sister Narcissa by his nonconformism all combine to bring him—scholar, gentleman, and lover of abstract truth—further unhappiness in a Snopes world. (Faulkner's satire against the meanspirited Narcissa, her unchari-table Baptist "sisters," and their heartless attitude toward Ruby Goodwin offers a priceless bit of folk humor and a cutting arraignment of those smug Jefferson folk who worship social decorum and piously speak in defense of " 'an odorous and omnipotent sanctity.' " Yet "This was Jefferson," also.)

What Faulkner as a creative artist has done with such brilliant imagina-tion to refashion his intimately known source material into a mythical kingdom has been examined critically by many analysts, notably by Ward L. Miner (*The World of William Faulkner*, 1952) and Cleanth Brooks (*The Yoknapatawpha Country*, 1963). Faulkner attempted, as Miner has shown, "to record the real history of a particular region of this country, using material he knows himself and which is a part of him." As is well known, his most widely used forms for his reinterpretation of Mississippi provincial life have been the novel and the short story. Drama he used sparingly, with *Requiem for a Nun* remaining his sole long play. Others, however, have transcribed and refashioned some of his Yoknapa-tawpha fiction into plays for screen, television, and stage. The one adaptation most delineative of Mississippi community life was a prac-tically plotless screen play drawn from the Snopes trilogy. Revamping materials found in the early chapters of *The Hamlet* (1931, 1940), Irving Ravetch and Harriet Frank, Jr. in 1958 created a movie and a television play called *The Long, Hot Summer*. Produced by Jerry Wald for Twentieth-Century Fox and directed by Martin Ritt, the play not only brought much recognition to gifted Joanne Woodward (Academy Award winner), but pictorially re-created an easygoing farm village adjacent to the rich bottom land of southeast Yoknapatawpha County.

As originally described in *The Hamlet*, the scene was the Frenchman's Bend community, peopled mostly by Tennessee settlers, plain folks, somewhat coarse and with no aspirations toward "society," who, though slaveless, vigorously tended their cotton and corn fields and "in secret coves in the hills made whiskey of the corn and sold what they did not drink." Among such sturdy people, Will Varner, owner of a decaying columned mansion called the "Frenchman's place," was "chief man in the country." Varner—farmer, usurer, veterinarian—and his son Jody controlled most of the mortgages in the area and operated farms, a general merchandise store, a cotton gin, and other businesses. Varner signs were everywhere about the town square and along the streets. Bustling Mrs. Varner and teen-age Eula, already somewhat sexy, completed the present family, now housed in the only two-story dwelling in the town. As coarse of mind as of moral fiber, Will Varner, with his Rabelaisian wit and shrewd bargaining power with villagers and farmers, was comfortably affluent. Once too often, however, he and Jody became involved in a losing business deal, this time with an intractable tenant farmer and neighborhood intruder having an unsavory reputation as a barn burner. This was Ab Snopes, a Civil War bushwhacker and horse thief.

Jody's unscrupulous plan to outwit Ab Snopes backfired. He had schemed to permit Ab to sharecrop on a newly acquired farm, until just before harvest time, when he would evict the whole Snopes clan on the charge that Ab was a known arsonist. Much to their astonishment, Will and Jody discovered, too late, that their contract with Ab led to a worse entanglement. They found themselves saddled with Flem, Ab's elder son, as a clerk in their store. Flem's clerking job spearheaded the invasion into Frenchman's Bend, and finally into the whole county, of innumerable Snopeses. Throughout *The Hamlet* Flem's shrewdness and ruthlessness, factors in his economic rise, clearly forecast the whole pattern of Snopesism to be completed in *The Town* and *The Mansion*, with their Jefferson locale.[55]

This village scene and the main characters form the basic materials for the Wald movie, starring Joanne Woodward as Varner's daughter, here renamed Clara and made older than Eula in *The Hamlet*. The original Eula role is now identified with Mrs. Jody Varner, "a scatterbrained sex-pot" portrayed by Lee Remick. Jody, unlike the heavily built bachelor son of *The Hamlet,* is a youthfully slender man whose part was played with empathic feeling by Anthony Franciosa. The Will Varner of the play (interpreted by Orson Welles) not only would bargain away his own children but has an association with a longtime mistress played by Angela Lansbury. Creating conflict within this village group, an itinerant and penniless youth, Ben Quick (Paul Newman's role) corresponds to Flem Snopes. His brashness enables him to worm his way into a clerking job in the Varner store and, after much resistance on her part, into the affections of Clara Varner.

Unlike the original Eula (who was to become Mrs. Flem Snopes), Clara herself appears as a lonely, level-headed, sex-starved girl whose red-neck father has been frightening off all the eligible young men in the area ever since she was old enough to hold hands. Though dominated by Will Varner, she remains independent and unbroken in spirit. At last, when he tries too persistently to force her into marrying the arrogant wanderer Ben Quick, Clara defies her father openly.

Her role contains three cleverly conceived and artistically written sequences: a long, candid chat with a girl of her own age on how it feels to be "still on the green side of twenty-five" without a man; an emotional and passionate rejection of her father's scheme, as she repulses Ben's amorous advances; and a moving and humble appeal for love from a thin-blooded aristocratic neighbor (played by Richard Anderson), at the time her only socially acceptable man. Miss Woodward's depth of feeling and forthright portrayal brought much vitality to the role.

While *The Long, Hot Summer* fails to correspond exactly to Faulkner's hamlet of Frenchman's Bend, the adapters, producer, and director, aided by a strong cast, gave validity to this production by concentrating primarily on the character development of these Yoknapatawphians as they appear under the highly emotional stress of personal circumstances. In the closing scene of the script, the resolution—the burning of Will Varner's huge barn in a way that gives an unexpected twist to Ab Snopes's barn-burning in *The Hamlet*—turns the story too abruptly to exciting community action and away from the character portrayal which gave the play its verisimilitude.

The recent dramatization of *As I Lay Dying* has publicized widely a different facet of the Yoknapatawpha saga: the experience of being lost from the home community that is dramatized in the plight of the Bundren family, poor whites, dirt farmers from across the Yoknapatawpha River, to the southwest of Frenchman's Bend and about forty miles away from Jefferson. The original heartbreaking novel (1930) is structured on a succession of personal angles of vision as fifteen rural and small-town characters reveal their awareness of life and death. Here again Faulkner documented a plain, untutored people, whose painful experiences take them through a number of rural and town-sized places such as Mottson. Their nine-day wagon journey with Addie Bundren's coffin may be absurd, nightmarish, and tribulation-beset; yet it touches upon an acute problem which has been transferred to many small-town plays. The individual's feeling of mental or spiritual desolation at having lost a familiar world offers a theme of alienation applicable to the dilemma of the Bundrens. This sense of lostness is pathetically evident in toilworn Addie Bundren, long lost in the wilderness of isolated and impoverished farms, alienated from her native Jefferson. As she lay dying in their farm shanty, she yearned to have burial in the home cemetery in Jefferson, where her folks had their graves. Following Addie's deathbed wish, the Bundrens begin their grim yet heroic odyssey. The selfish father Anse, who is regarded as one of Faulkner's most brilliantly sketched villains, is accompanied by his secretly pregnant daughter, Dewey Dell, and four sons: practical Cash, a carpenter who made his mother's coffin; Darl of artistic temperament, who went insane; illegitimate and wilful Jewel; and the disturbed child Vardaman. The macabre tale of how they accomplish their strange and difficult task is itself a complex of family hardship, loss, danger, and injury. The novel is a bold and odd combination of many elements—the grotesque and the heroic, the comic and the pathetic, pity and terror—all giving a rich variety of tone.

As the journey continues, the dead mother becomes the central or controlling figure. There are suggestions that Addie Bundren may have been a destructive force, a wicked woman. While they do not understand her nature fully, her husband and children have an awareness of her pathetic alienation from her native community, her loss of language communication, her brooding over such words as "love" and "sin" (in consequence largely of her illicit relationship with the preacher Whitfield, who became Jewel's father), and her endurance of bitterness and frustration because of uncertainty as to the object of her search. Nevertheless, asserts Cleanth Brooks, ". . . she is responsible for whatever of heroic temper the Bundrens achieve."[56] The nature of the heroic deed, the significance of honor, the need of the male to prove himself, and the struggle of women (both Addie and Dewey Dell) to express their yearnings and needs are all important thematic motifs brought into high focus as the creaking wagon, with its stinking burden, slowly moves forward along the road to Jefferson.

The simplicity of Faulkner's plot proved no barrier to Robert L. Flynn's seeing in *As I Lay Dying* enough drama and complexity for the composition of a play. Originally presented in Waco, Texas, during 1960 as a part of the program for the Baylor University Drama School under Paul Baker, Flynn's script was to undergo changes. During the 1962-63 season Baker, by now director of the new Dallas Theater Center, produced and directed the Flynn adaptation at the Kalita Humphreys Theater. By July, 1964, the script was revised and retitled *Journey to Jefferson*, in preparation for the Theater Center troupe's participation in a project sponsored by the *Théâtre des Nations* at the Sarah Bernhardt Theatre in Paris. The State Department approved the offering of "a play of rural American orientation with the folk color stirring the audience to grim laughter and a melancholy denouement also in the foreign convention."[57] Everywhere—in West Germany, Belgium, and France—the production brought ovations and bravos.

According to program notes, Flynn's selection of *As I Lay Dying* for stage adaptation was based upon "the strength of its characters, the beauty of its poetic dialogue, and its fable-like simplicity." As much as possible, he retained the novel's uneven sequence of events, its more than thirty major and minor characters, and its passages of poetic prose, shaping his entire dramatization into three acts with nineteen scenes. The latter represent various places along the route to Jefferson: first, Anse Bundren's rickety farmhouse, then Tull's Bridge and the houses and farmyards of several neighbors, then the agricultural village of Mottson, and again similar places alongside the road to Jefferson. In the last four scenes the virtues and vices of Mississippi folk are dramatized in a context of rural and town relationships, on occasion with country humor. These concluding parts, though shorn of many of Faulkner's highly descriptive and narrative sections, nevertheless in the Kalita Humphreys Theater production effectively portrayed the conflicts between the Bundrens, as peculiar outsiders "from down beyond New Hope," with various types of Jeffersonians. Considerable satire is reflected in the portraits of Moseley, Mottson's pious druggist who refused to sell contraceptives to Dewey Dell ("Me . . . that's kept store and raised a family and been a churchmember for fifty-six years in this town"); Jefferson's Dr. Peabody, who lambasts Anse for encasing Cash's broken leg in cement; the soda jerk Macgowan, who tries to seduce Dewey Dell ("a pretty hot mama, for a country girl," according to Jody Varner); and "the duck-shaped woman . . . with kind of hard-looking pop eyes" whom Anse married shortly after burying Addie and getting new "store teeth" with Dewey Dell's money.

When viewed from a theatrical perspective, the checkered history of Jefferson and Yoknapatawpha County, so variously explored in Faulkner's novels and stories, seems but a fragmented record of the decadence of small-town and rural life in northwest Mississippi. Nevertheless, few though the stage and screen adaptations are, they dramatize the strength of the environmental influence on the experience of imaginary Mississippians of widely different social levels. These several dramatic portrayals, though presenting only selected phases of community life in Faulkner's "mythical kingdom," do convey hints as to the infinite variety of physical backgrounds, of characterizations of both white and Negro Yoknapatawphians, and the cogent themes abounding in other Faulknerian fiction. As pictured in these small-town plays, Jefferson, Frenchman's Bend, Mottson, and New Hope typify, in Faulkner's words, "My own little postage stamp of native soil." In contrast to the "nebulous nightmare" of Williams' plays, the more concretely defined nightmare of William Faulkner is evidenced, in part, in these plays. *Requiem for a Nun*, for example, concretely illustrates the novelist's involvement with the cultural past in relation to the birth, early growth, and modern decay of small-town life in Mississippi. The sordid histories of Temple Drake, Gavin and Gowan Stevens, Popeye and his henchmen, Nancy Mannigoe, and others furnish symbols aplenty of the decay of a frontier vigor and a later cultural growth, shattered by modern industrialized and mechanized times. Furthermore, in the mishaps of the Bundrens, the failures of the Varners, and the sure rise of Snopesism there are unmistakable signs of the universal debasement of modern society, manners, and morals. Yet in this web of dramatized complexity there are further signs, or hints, that "man will prevail" even in decadent towns and rural communities. Like Steinbeck's unforgettable Joads, the Bundrens—and even Nancy Mannigoe—symbolize something heroic among provincial southerners.

In analyzing ambivalences in Faulkner's moral dialectic, biographer Irving Howe notes that the novelist did not relish violence for it own sake. Rather, he was "a fastidious romantic" who shrank "from all that is malformed and vicious; the horror into which his books erupt is a sign of over-reaction . . . As it flames into violence, this conflict between the dream evoked by nature and the reality personified by society gives rise to Faulkner's moral position, his distinctive way of looking upon life."[58]

Altamont Revisited

Thomas Wolfe, that dedicated artist, once defended his writing the truth about those he knew, about "all the forgotten faces," by vigorously claiming that "the artist is not here in life to hurt it but to illuminate it." And the radiance of such illumination touched his own truthful re-creation of small-town life as he remembered it to have been in his native hills of western North Carolina, in Asheville and its environing hill country. As we have seen earlier, Wolfe's first great attachment was to the theater. According to one of his friends, the late Edward C. Aswell, his boyish ambition was to see his name in bright lights on Broadway, a desire he never realized.[59] While the dream lasted, however, young Wolfe prepared himself for future theatrical achievement first by studying dramaturgy with Professor Frederick Koch and working with the Carolina Playmakers and then, after his graduation from the University of North Carolina, joining Professor George Pierce Baker in his experimental 47 Workshop at Harvard. From his several years of lonely apprenticeship at Harvard came his most illuminating plays, truthful reminders of certain unsavory aspects of folk life in "the hills of home." *Welcome to Our City* (1922-23), a fiery satire, and that "groping and uncertain play" entitled *Mannerhouse* (1923, 1948) illuminate various changes wrought by the Civil War in the old relationship between the aristocrats, the poor whites, and the Negroes, and by the greedy worship of material progress and kindred social ills.

Wolfe's ambition to win acclaim as a playwright remained unfulfilled. Nevertheless, for all their unwieldiness, his two long plays are, as we have noted, important if not too actable dramas picturing the complex social developments in North Carolina, in town and country, from antebellum times until the booming twenties. These plays were not professionally produced in this country, though *Mannerhouse*, while rejected by the Theatre Guild and the Neighborhood Playhouse, did have a premiere at Yale University on May 5, 1949 (later there was a professional production in Germany), and *Welcome to Our City*, with its innumerable characters and scenes, did impress the Harvard audience at the 47 Workshop presentation. By the summer of 1926, when he failed to discover a producer for this illuminating exposure of an entire small town, possibly because its structure was too unwieldy, Wolfe admitted that both his temperament and talents were unsuited for the disciplined dramatic form. Yet, as he confessed in his Purdue University speech of 1938, bitter memories remained of the months he spent at New York University, from the spring semester of 1924, "supporting my body teaching school in the daytime, and my soul writing plays at night." In his Purdue speech he pointed out further that the abundance of scenes and characters in his plays, unprofitable for the economic and commercial enterprise of the theater, "showed unmistakably the evidence of my real desire" in writing. "Something in me very strong and powerful was groping toward a more full, expansive, and abundant expression of the great theatre of life than the stage itself could physically compass."[60]

This "something," comparable to the bursting of a pent-up flood, began taking expression as Wolfe experimented with a literary form better suited to his talent for pouring out words: the autobiographical novel. Alone in London in 1926, while he was revising *Mannerhouse*, he began a long novel about "the great processional of the years" (1884-1920) and the impact of time upon the Pentlands and the Gants. This was published in 1929 as *Look Homeward, Angel: A Story of the Buried Life*, to be followed in 1935 by *Of Time and the River*. Wolfe never fulfilled his boast, made in reference to *Welcome to Our City*, that some day he expected to produce a play "with fifty, eighty, a hundred people—a whole town, a whole race, a whole epoch . . ." This he achieved in his massive novels. In the theatrical world his fame lives on through the talents of skilful adapters of these two novels.

In *The Story of a Novel* (1936) Wolfe expressed his pleasure in the popularity of *Look Homeward, Angel*: ". . . what was best of all, as time went on, it continued to make friends among people who read books." Among the many who joined the ranks of those friends was a talented Hollywood scenarist and novelist, Mrs. Ketti Frings, who proved to be not only a discerning and enthusiastic reader of Wolfe's fiction but a consummate craftsman in adapting *Look Homeward, Angel* to the stage. The amazing results of her efforts would have thrilled Wolfe had he been alive in 1958. (To use words taken from *Look Homeward, Angel* for his epitaph, Wolfe departed for "the last voyage, the longest, the best" on September 15, 1938.) Twenty-nine years after the publication of the novel, Mrs. Frings's adaptation was awarded the New York Drama Critics Circle Award and the Pulitzer Prize, and ran for 564 performances on Broadway, with later successes on a nationwide tour. This recognition is a sign of the success of an exciting play made from a novel "written of experience which is now far and lost, but which was once part of the fabric of his [Wolfe's] life."

The task facing Mrs. Frings was the conversion of a teeming, bulky novel, itself only the first part of a proposed series of six novels, into an artistically unified play. To achieve her three-act adaptation, she critically reread *Look Homeward, Angel* several times, avoiding any reading of the critics' appraisals of the novel but listing those impressive passages in it which moved her most deeply and which seemed best suited for stage production. Then, as she says, she spent "a year in the writing and many years in thinking and hoping." Carefully she pruned away extraneous matter from Wolfe's "Monster," as he called the novel, and, with rare understanding of dramaturgy, telescoped a few chapters from the latter portion of the book into an overpowering consideration of seventeen-year-old Eugene Gant's escape from adolescence. Though working with the problem of revamping one of the most overused themes in community literature, the revolt of sensitive youth from a stultifying small town, Mrs. Frings managed, in the opinion of Brooks Atkinson, to raise "the homely affairs of an obscure middle-class family to the level of vigorous literature" and to give "planetary significance to little things."

Look Homeward, Angel, with its veritable torrent of words and its innumerable small-town characters, is exceedingly wide in scope. In its meticulous tracing of family genealogies, the novel begins with the English origins of Oliver Gant's (or Gaunt's) family, progressing from that point to its Pennsylvania Dutch phase and then to its long association with the boomtown of Altamont and the hills of Catawba. After that, the checkered annals of the mountaineering Pentlands, from whom Eliza Gant is descended, are related both to the hill country and to the growth of Altamont. The novel moves slowly forward then, through many chapters descriptive of the lostness and the frustration of individual members of the family of Oliver (W. O.) and Eliza Gant. Much of the original action grows out of the increasing conflict of interests between this ill-mated pair. In time freedom-loving, poetic Oliver, a luckless stonecutter yearning to create a perfect marble angel, almost destroys himself by his Rabelaisian excesses in eating, drinking, and whoring. And all the while his tight-lipped wife Eliza, with her pragmatic outlook on life, becomes so property-minded and penny-pinching that she sparks friction not only with her irascible husband and children but with her boarders at her Dixieland establishment. (Mrs. Julia Wolfe had operated a similar boarding house, "My Old Kentucky Home," in Asheville during her son's adolescence.) The childhood vicissitudes of the Gants' five surviving children and the role of the youngest, Eugene, within this lusty and quarrelsome family help make the Wolfe novel a sprawling but unforgettable exploration of small-town life from the later nineteenth century until 1916. It is this latter year which marks the beginning of the action of Mrs. Frings's play.

The Altamont locale, thus vividly re-created, is more sharply limited than in the novel, with its elaborate display of multiple facets of town and country life. In a total of five scenes, including a brief epilogue, Jo Mielziner's several sets bring into clear focus Eliza Gant's gabled, rambling Dixieland boardinghouse of fifteen drafty rooms (the set for four scenes) and the dusty marble yard and shop, behind the town square, where W. O. Gant displays a cherished marble angel—the set for the

Frank Craven as the Stage Manager in *Our Town* (1938). *Vandamm photograph, Theatre Collection, New York Public Library.*

President-elect Lincoln (Raymond Massey) and Mrs. Lincoln (Muriel Kirkland) leave Springfield for the White House, in the finale of *Abe Lincoln in Illinois* (1939). *Theatre Collection, New York Public Library.*

Little Theatre of Dallas

Season 1940-41

"Where the Dear Antelope Play"

Program cover by Jerry Bywaters, Little Theatre of Dallas production of John William Rogers' *Where the Dear Antelope Play*, February 18-21, 1941.

Above, Wilson Brooks, Carol Goodner, and Rebecca Hargis in premiere of William Inge's *Farther Off from Heaven*, Margo Jones Theatre, July 31, 1947. Right, above, portrait by Barry of Katharine Balfour (as Alma Winemiller) and Tod Andrews (as Dr. John Buchanan, Jr.) in the Margo Jones Theatre '47 premiere of Tennessee Williams' *Summer and Smoke*. Right, below, Gilbert Milton (as the Reverend Jeremiah Brown), Harry Bergman (as Bertram Cates), and Louise Latham (as Rachel Brown) in the first production of *Inherit the Wind*, by Jerome Lawrence and Robert E. Lee, January 10, 1955, at the Margo Jones Theatre. *Margo Jones Collection, Dallas Public Library.*

Lavinia (Alice Brady), Ezra Mannon (Lee Baker), and Christine (Alla Nazimova) in the Theatre Guild production of *Mourning Becomes Electra* (1931). *Vandamm photograph, Theatre Collection, New York Public Library.*

GUILD THEATRE

52nd STREET, WEST OF BROADWAY

PROGRAM
PUBLISHED
BY THE
NEW YORK
THEATRE
PROGRAM
CORPORATION

FIRE NOTICE: Look around now and choose the nearest exit to your seat. In case of fire, walk (not run) to that exit. Do not try to beat your neighbor to the street. **JOHN J. McELLIGOTT, Fire Chief and Commissioner.**

BEGINNING
MONDAY EVENING,
MARCH 12, 1934

MATINEES
THURSDAY AND
SATURDAY

THE THEATRE GUILD, Inc.

PRESENTS

FIRST SUBSCRIPTION PLAY OF THE SIXTEENTH SUBSCRIPTION SEASON

AH, WILDERNESS!

A NEW PLAY

By EUGENE O'NEILL

WITH

GEORGE M. COHAN

THE PRODUCTION DIRECTED BY PHILIP MOELLER
SETTINGS DESIGNED BY ROBERT EDMOND JONES

CAST

NAT MILLER, owner of the
  Evening Globe .... *Played by* GEORGE M. COHAN
ESSIE, his wife .... "   " MARJORIE MARQUIS
ARTHUR, their son .... "   " WILLIAM POST, JR.

(Program Continued on Second Page Following)

♠ - ♦ - ♥ - ♠ - ♣ - ♦ - ♥ - ♠

ELY CULBERTSON

International Bridge Champion

CHALLENGES
CONTRACT BRIDGE PLAYERS

to solve his Brain Twister number two
published elsewhere in this program

1934 program for the first-run production of *Ah, Wilderness!* which opened at the Guild Theatre, October 2, 1933. *Hill Collection, Dallas Public Library.*

Eugene and Carlotta O'Neill, Cap d'Ail, France, 1929. *Theatre Collection, New York Public Library.*

first scene of the second act. Mielziner's scheme of placing the upstairs bedroom scenes on the more accessible downstairs level not only made possible remarkable fluidity in the merging of each scene into the next one, but represented a "bold step away from literalism."[61] His use of a revolving stage, built inside the living room, permitted a speedy shift from that room to a front bedroom. Also, this Dixieland set allowed an easy simultaneous playing of scenes, similar to the scheme which in 1949 Mielziner had adapted to Miller's *Death of a Salesman*.[62] For example, Ben Gant may be seen dying in a small bedroom, while his mother Eliza, distraught and wringing her hands, appears in the kitchen. Also, the set is so adaptable that scenes not occurring inside the house may be presented in front of it. For instance, the assembled boarders, after the dinner hour, may be seen in their favorite rockers on the large veranda to the left side of the house, while the young lovers—infatuated Eugene and Laura James—appear in a scene in the front yard, to the right and in front of the side door, out of earshot of the porch-chair gossips.

It is against this unpleasant physical background that the Gant family's activities are crowded into a few weeks during the early fall of 1916. Mrs. Frings achieved further control over the scope of her raw material by finding within Wolfe's "sprawling and effervescent epic" what she termed "the point of not-blindedness." She explains that "in a play the protagonist should have a blind spot about something. When that blind spot is removed from him, the play is over." Working on this basis, she created a sensitive and moving play, one which Gassner viewed as "a trim but still substantial drama."

Eugene Gant's blind spot is his sensitive feeling that he must dutifully accept the demands of his highly individualized family and be bound to Altamont—and the Dixieland boardinghouse and its eccentric boarders—by ties of family love and necessity. His older brother Ben, himself sensitive, imaginative, and lost amidst his mundane surroundings, heightens young Gene's awareness of their mutual imprisonment within the aggravating family circle and the shabby town. Ben's insistence that Gene must somehow liberate himself, preferably by getting a college education, gives the boy his moment of recognition—of "not-blindedness." Around this moment Mrs. Frings condenses the action of her play into a period of three weeks centering around Ben's death from a short siege of pneumonia. When Ben dies the old bonds begin to break, and the family seems to fall apart. As old Dr. Maguire remarks, "We can believe in the nothingness of life. We can believe in the nothingness of death, and of a life after death. But who can believe in the nothingness of Ben?"[63]

After the funeral, members of the Pentland and Gant clans disperse.

Good-humored Luke, the stuttering son who got away early but who still carries the marks of a distressing childhood, returns to his naval base at Norfolk. Hardworking Helen, who has slaved at the Dixieland while Eliza has sallied forth on real estate prospecting trips, is so worn out by her domestic chores and her periodic efforts to control her drunken father that she and her husband, Hugh Barton, scheme to move into a house of their own. Oliver Gant, constantly raging about all that has been "put upon me, old and sick as I am—," bears little resemblance to his former lusty self. Eliza, still obsessive, is rejected by her dying son Ben. Desolate, she sees her hard work to assure family security crumbling away. Caught in such a web of family change, adolescent Gene suffers deeply from the loss not only of Ben but also of Laura James, a pretty boarder six years his senior, who rejects his fervent proposal of marriage. The boy is sick at heart when he learns from her farewell note that she is engaged to another and must return to Richmond to be married. With his dream shattered, Gene knows that he cannot endure remaining in Altmont. Before hurriedly leaving, Laura has contritely confessed to Eliza her romantic love for Gene, but tried to comfort the distracted mother by urging that she give her "wonderful boy" an opportunity to go to college, to discover room "to expand and grow, to find himself." Laura has also warned Eliza that she, too, will have to let Gene go, for he must not be tied down at this point of his life. "He needs the whole world to wander in . . ."[64]

In a passionate scene, Gene bitterly accuses his mother of utter indifference to his real needs—of wanting to strangle and drown him completely. Eliza reluctantly gives in to his imperative need for escape. She arranges to sell her Stumptown property to provide funds for Gene's expenses at the state university in Pulpit Hill (Chapel Hill). At last Gene is free to leave Dixieland—to turn his back on this "God-damned barn! Thief! Travesty on nature!" as his father calls it—this "miserable, unholy house," as Eliza at last sees it. Yet, just before leaving, Gene is emotionally upset by his mother's plea, "We must try to love one another."

A brief epilogue returns the story to the lost Ben. In a touching communion with Ben's spirit, Eugene admits his puzzlement over the world he is about to enter. *("I want to find the world. Where is the world?")* As the train whistle sounds, Ben's voice answers: "The world is nowhere, Gene. *You* are your world." Gene, reassured about the importance of the buried life, leaves Dixieland without looking back. The new life which he experienced far beyond the hills of Catawba became the subject of Wolfe's exploration in *Of Time and the River: A Legend of Man's Hunger in His Youth.*

Opening at the Ethel Barrymore Theatre on November 29, 1957, Kermit Bloomgarden's production of *Look Homeward, Angel,* under the direction of George Roy Hill, was presented to "an enraptured audience." It was a night of triumph for young Anthony Perkins in the role of Eugene Gant. More correctly, Perkins appeared as a younger Tom Wolfe brought to life. His performance caught all of Eugene's bookish and dreamy nature and his feeling of urgency about escaping from the turbulent and frustrated family life of the Gants. (When the play was produced on tour, a young Swiss-born actor, Michael Ebert, presented in his interpretation of Eugene an appealing portrait of an idealistic youth yearning for escape first through love and then through a college education.) In the premiere Jo Van Fleet, wonderfully effective as Eliza Gant, sensed that this dominant and tenacious woman, for all of her pragmatism, suffered from loneliness and a feeling that all were against her. (On tour, Miriam Hopkins "succeeded in arousing more pathetic sympathy than Wolfe probably intended in his forbidding original. Miss Hopkins shaded her humor broadly in strength and weakness alike and wore her passion for property with an absorbing defiance.")[65] Hugh Griffith played W. O. Gant as a roaring, likable old rapscallion. (In his performance on tour, Gilbert Green was sufficiently brawlsome as the aging and whining father still moved by titanic hatreds and sly tricks.) Arthur Hill's Ben Gant, praised as one of the finer portrayals of the 1957 Broadway season, surpassed in effectiveness Lee Richardson's shallower characterization on tour. In both productions cast members assigned to minor roles helped add pathos and humor, sensitivity, robustness, and truth to this appealing and workable family play.

In the play less use is made of symbolism than in the novel. Nevertheless, symbolical motifs contribute to the legend of man's hunger in his youth. Oliver's dusty marble yard and shabby office suggest the failure of his youthful dreams quite as much as do his frequent visits to Madam Elizabeth's establishment and his drunken sprees with disreputable cronies. ("At heart he is a far wanderer and a minstrel, but he has degraded his life with libertinism and drink.") The sculptured angel, lily in hand, is a Miltonic image of Oliver's own youthful yearning, and failure, to create from the rough marble something beautiful. Now old and sick, Oliver looks upon the angel on his shop porch as an image of his idealistic and buried youth and as a reminder of his present "monstrous fumbling for life." (Apparently Wolfe had in mind the passage from "Lycidas": "Look homeward, Angel, now, and melt with ruth:/And, O ye dolphins, waft the hapless youth.")

Tree-shaded Dixieland—"Altamont's Homiest Boarding House"—and its "batty boarders" suggest the changes brought about in Altamont by the then new tourism. More significantly, they also symbolize the acquisitive nature of Eliza Gant and her moneygrubbing brother, Will Pentland. Eliza's boarders, with their small talk, act as a chorus typifying the mediocrity and sensuality of certain provincial folk. (Only Mrs. Fatty Pert, because of her easygoing nature, pleases Ben.) The shadowy trees and the rustle of leaves on the Mielziner set go beyond creating an effect of the autumn season to suggest the inevitable changes now facing the Gants, Ben and Eugene in particular. Among other symbols adding to the poetic quality of passages of dialogue are the references to trains, favorite symbols with Wolfe, which represent Eugene's gateway to the world beyond Altamont, as the Mississippi steamboats once represented escape for youthful Sam Clemens. The environing hills, on the other hand, suggest that the town is an isolated prison for idealistic youth. Ben's habit of unburdening his soul to the ghost of Grover, his dead twin, offers insight into his buried life, just as Eugene's epilogue colloquy with Ben's ghost gives further keynotes about youth's struggle for freedom. In the finale, Gene begins, as did Wolfe, his search for America, seeking from Ben's spirit the way toward "the lost lane-end into heaven" and the meaning of "a stone, a leaf, an unfound door. Where? When?"[66]

In 1959, at Baylor University in Waco, Texas ". . . all the forgotten faces" of Altamont, with scores of others, were portrayed anew when *Of Time and the River* was pruned for an experimental stage presentation. Unlike Mrs. Frings's play, this one came into being through student participation in a project directed by Paul Baker, Eugene McKinney, and Mary Sue Fridge of the university's drama staff. Intensive group analysis of the novel brought forth a script, heralded as "the very heart and essence of Wolfe," which, following a Waco premiere, became the basis for a final transcription, by Baker and McKinney, staged during the 1960 season at the Kalita Humphreys Theater of the Dallas Theater Center. Under Baker's direction, the forty-six players of the resident repertory company of the Center, aided by Baylor students, enacted this three-act dramatization of Eugene Gant's wide search for an identity. Focused on the flux of events which was to create for him a lifetime of ceaseless struggle, this production touched upon Eugene's efforts to remain at a fixed point or to redirect his course. Thus the scope of the Baker-McKinney script is geographically wide, ranging scenically, as does the novel, from small-town North Carolina to Boston and New York, to England and France. Within this complex structure, Eugene's home town of Altamont is featured in only a few introductory sections of the first two acts.

On the other hand, an understanding of the protagonist's later struggle stems from these early insights into his sensitive and inquiring nature. To enhance this complex and looming portrait, Baker cast actor Ronald Wilcox in the role of the physical Eugene Gant, while five other players were used to personify the five senses through which the youth filters his poetic experience. To clarify the background theme—that of a young and vigorous nation emerging from the Civil War and moving toward the exciting new century—two commentators, Time and Change, were added to retain Wolfe's rhapsodical narratives by converting them into a more succinct dramatic form.

The first act portrays Eliza Gant, Helen and Hugh Barton, and other Altamont folk gathered at the depot to form a small-town scene familiar to those who remember the 1916 era. Family and friends are assembled to say goodbye to Gene, now leaving Altamont again to pursue his education, this time to continue his study of drama at Harvard under Professor Hatcher (George Pierce Baker). This further step along the course of Gene's questing foreshadows his European *Wanderjahre* and his eventual decision to continue his search in America. As in the novel, Gene's return to find an answer on native grounds parallels the boisterous twenties, when America itself was changing "from its tumultuous adolescence to its full powered maturity."[67]

While the wide canvas of this play's scenes excludes it from the category of plays devoted solely to small-town life, the fleeting glimpses given of Altamont indicate that Eugene, though long absent, never wholly forgot "the old familiar faces." While wearying of wandering in strange cities among strange tongues and faces and of not leaving even a single imprint of himself in any town, Eugene remembered his father's death in a Baltimore hospital and the funeral services held in Altamont. Such a typical small-town scene forms in this play a part of the central theme: the conflict between the "I"—Eugene's real self—and the intrusive world. In Mrs. Frings's play, Eugene's enemy was the circumscribed world of Altamont narrowed to the horizon of a dreamy teen-ager. And this enemy took different forms, finding full representation in his mother Eliza with her greed, lovelessness, and endless talk, in the ugly boardinghouse which became a tawdry substitute for a real home, in the family's slow disintegration, and in the souring of his father's once jolly nature. In the dramatized *Of Time and the River*, involving more than seventy players, the rapid changes in scene approach, in spectacular fashion, the epic proportions of Wolfe's novel. Eugene's search in a wider world equates with the loneliness of the artist spirit in a pragmatic America. So, while repeating the lament of "Lost, Lost, forever lost!" Eugene questions anew, "Where shall the weary find peace? Upon what shore will the wanderer come home at last?"

All in all, this noncommmercial production was a stupendous effort to recapture the intellectual, emotional, and spiritual record of five years of a young townsman's life. Unlike the compact Frings version of *Look Homeward, Angel*, this dramatization lost in theatrical effectiveness and character appeal by its unwieldy length and the multitude of characters. In spite of the preliminary pruning, the play reflects something of Wolfe's own passion for accumulation. More positively, it portrays the tribulations of an artistic protagonist, small-town born, who persistently yearned to record America, to assimilate it, and to echo it in himself, as Wolfe had tried to do.

Other Towns Down South

Many small-town plays, as we have seen, have centered interest on situations involving social isolation, loneliness, and personal struggles to find companionship. Often, as in the geographically different cases of Eugene Gant and George Willard (of *Winesburg, Ohio*), the protagonist has been a confused and lonely dreamer, a young man in rebellion against those barriers within his immediate environment which thwart his freedom and ambitions. Sometimes these social rebels, usually awkward misfits, have been quite young girls, suffering in one way or another from introversion, as Lillian Hellman's unhappy Mary Tilford of *The Children's Hour,* whose persecution complex leads to tragedy. Occasionally, among dramatizations based upon child psychology, a fragile little masterpiece will put on stage an unforgettable characterization of an awkward, if not ugly, duckling's search for identity in an adult world which she does not yet understand. Such a play of a youngster's growing pains is Carson McCullers' *The Member of the Wedding*, set in a small Georgia mill town, somewhere near Milledgeville. The play was adapted by Mrs. McCullers from her own novel during the summer of 1948, when she worked at a kitchen table across from her friend, Tennessee Williams, then at work on *Summer and Smoke*.

Usually spoken of as a first-rate comedy of sensibility, this appealing "inward" play is structured largely as a character sketch, or a trio of character sketches, rather than as an intricately plotted narrative. What action there is comes rather explosively after two introductory acts sensitively concerned with atmosphere and nuances of character and feeling. The protagonist is a highly imaginative and lonely twelve-year-old girl, Frankie Addams, whose absentminded father, a widower of many years, looks upon her as something of a brat. Busy with his jewelry store affairs, Mr. Addams leaves impetuous, gangling Frankie to her own devices, and in the company of two other lonely persons: John Henry West, her delicate cousin just seven years old, and a much-married Negro cook, Berenice Sadie Brown, whose experience with the segregation code in a Georgia town gives her a warm sympathy with Frankie's splendid notions of some day becoming "a member of the world." This compulsion to belong to somebody or something, if nothing more than a neighborhood girls' club from which she has been excluded, highlights all the more the terrible unwanted isolation of this motherless, sensitive child.

Frankie is so puzzled by, and even afraid of, the adult world that she impulsively alternates between avoiding it and then dreaming, or ludicrously scheming, about entering it. As she says, "But I'm just twelve. When I think of all the growing years ahead of me, I get scared."[68] She has the obsessive notion that when her brother Jarvis, a soldier, marries on the next Sunday she will be a member of the wedding party and go away romantically into the world with him and his bride Janice. She spends the intervening days indulging in strange fantasies and worrying with questions which give a note of poignancy to her alienation from the town at large: "Who am I? Where do I belong? Where can I belong?" Alternately yearning to be a part of the girls' club and yelling curses at its snobbish members as they cross the Addams yard, Frankie turns her energies and imagination toward the production of backyard plays and the playing of card games which her companion John Henry does not wholly understand. She thinks, too, of her letters to Jarvis, when he was stationed in Alaska, which he never bothered to answer.

Still, Frankie, with her flair for the histrionic, imagines herself as a partner in her brother's adventures, including the forthcoming wedding and honeymoon. With her scrawny and too tall body, her cropped head, her calloused elbows, and her tough big feet, young Frankie is truly an unlikely bridesmaid. Nevertheless, her romantic imagination and her fervent longing to be a member of the wedding party lead the child into buying an orange satin evening dress and silver slippers for the occasion. Her anticipatory joy and excitement about the wedding are pictured through her own reactions, with innocent John Henry and Berenice acting as a domestic chorus. When her romantic myth about accompanying Jarvis and Janice on their honeymoon turns into a realization of the bitter truth, Frankie is profoundly shocked. "There are so many things about the world I do not understand," she exclaims. Earlier Berenice had warned Frankie that her dream about the wedding "is the saddest piece of foolishness I ever knew" and nothing but a "fancy trap to catch yourself in trouble." Ignoring Berenice's warning, Frankie had furiously rebelled: "I can't stand this existence—this kitchen—this town—any longer!" Now forcibly pulled out of the going away car, Frankie sobs, screams, and, grabbing her packed suitcase containing her father's pistol, starts running away—to New York—to Hollywood—to a recruiting station to join the Merchant Marines! She gets no farther than the dark alley back of her father's store, where she bitterly thinks, "It was a frame-up all around."

The concluding action seems marred by the intrusion of odd bits of melodrama: the unprepared-for news that John Henry has died from a sudden attack of meningitis, that Berenice's young foster brother, Honey Brown, has hanged himself in a jail cell, and that a sudden and furious storm has spoiled Frankie's getting away from the despised town. There are suggestions throughout the play regarding the racial problem upsetting the town, though these are not developed. Such disturbing events are topped by Frankie's return home the next morning. Beaten by her own disappointments, she now realizes "for the first time that the world is certainly—a sudden place." Months later she finds more pleasant answers in a new friendship with Mary Littlejohn and a neighborhood boy, Barney MacKean. Her days of loneliness end with Mr. Addams' moving to a new house, to be shared with John Henry's parents. At the end, there is still an atmosphere of sadness, for now it is Berenice, who has quit her long-time job as family cook, who is alone; at curtain fall, impressive irony marks her humming of a favorite song, "I sing because I'm happy . . ."

No retelling of the story can give an adequate idea of the play's essence, for Mrs. McCullers (who died in September, 1967) was an evocative stylist. In her realistic small-town scenes, centered around the Addams kitchen, she invested a familiar family situation and ordinary folk, both white and Negro, with an appealing warmth. When the play opened on January 5, 1950, at the Empire Theatre in New York, a gifted cast brought such magic to the roles that the production lasted through 501 performances. Critical praise went to young Julie Harris as Frankie, her first starring part, and to talented Brandon de Wilde for his unusually convincing portrayal of the lonely little boy, John Henry. Miss Harris used with rare success both her imaginative and her physical resources to interpret Frankie as a child of mercurial temperament, at times fractious, antagonistic, and unreasonable, as ugly in manner as she was uncouth in appearance, and then heroic and romantic in her own dreaming of what she would like to be. Ethel Waters' genuinely emotional saying of her lines, her sense of timing, her joyous laughter, and her gift of telling entertaining stories—as in the mixed comic and pathetic recital of Berenice's marital frustrations—all were wonderfully adapted to her role as caretaker of two disturbed children. Her melodious singing of the hymn, "I sing because I'm happy," deeply moved audiences and keynoted both the irony of Berenice's own lonely condition and her simple faith.

Of other dramatizations involving child psychology and portraying small-town mores in the South and Southwest, several belong to the media of television and motion pictures rather than to the legitimate theater, with which we are principally concerned here. Among these, *Intruder in the Dust* (based on Faulkner's uneven novel about the force of race relationships in Jefferson) was selected by the New York Film Critics as ranking with the film of Robert Penn Warren's *All the King's Men* as one of the best motion pictures of 1949. Handled with superb dramatic balance and comprehension of social realities, this uncompromising picture, filmed in Oxford, Mississippi, delineated the wilful and frightening infection of a lynch mob with a passion to see violence done to a Negro, part-white Lucas Beauchamp, supposedly the murderer of a white man. With manifold implications of ugly truths and as many plot extravagances as in the novel, this film showed the role played by fourteen-year-old Charles (Chick) Mallinson, Jr., in saving Lucas from an undeserved lynching. The step-by-step process of Chick's learning to accept old Lucas as an individual is reminiscent of the relationship between Huck Finn and Nigger Jim.

In 1956 a foremost television playwright, Horton Foote, in a volume of plays entitled *Harrison, Texas*, placed on the theatrical map an imaginary small Texas town, situated in the heart of the state's Gulf Coast and reminiscent of his birthplace, Wharton, Texas, and the people he had known there. As he has said, these eight plays, all written and produced for television between January, 1953, and March, 1954, portray mostly "the very young or the very old" native to "my familiar country."[69] Unified by their Gulf Coast locale, the plays also have in common two themes: a happy or unhappy acceptance of life by the young townsmen and a preparation for death by the old. "A Young Lady of Property," for example, sympathetically characterizes a motherless teenager, Wilma Thompson, who reminds one of Frankie Addams in her yearning to escape small-town life and become a Hollywood movie star. At last Wilma realizes that her real ambition is not to become a star but to remain in Harrison, bring up a large family, and do something about the lonesome look of the empty family home which she inherited from her mother. In "John Turner Davis," an abandoned little boy is shown struggling with his dilemma of loneliness and neglect. With equal poignancy old Mrs. Watts, in "A Trip to Bountiful," is characterized through her efforts to see once more the deserted house where she was born, in the hope that she may regain her lost dignity before dying.

Foote's most widely acclaimed dramatization is his screenplay based upon Harper Lee's Pulitzer Prize novel, *To Kill A Mockingbird*, which when filmed in 1963 brought "a fistful of Oscars" to Foote (for the best screenplay), to producer Alan Pakula, director Robert Mulligan, Gregory Peck (best actor), and nine-year-old Mary Badham (best supporting actress). The author, and the playwright, chose to tell the tale of a somnolent, depression-blighted Alabama town called Maycomb (suggestive of Miss Lee's native Monroeville), through the eyes of two irrepressible children. Ten-year-old Jem (Phillip Alford's role) and Scout, aged eight, are the motherless children of easygoing Lawyer Atticus Finch (Gregory Peck), who in the evenings solicitously reads to them, finding in his newspaper maxims for their moral conduct. Among other things, he teaches them that it is wrong to kill a mockingbird whose only offense is to sing for their enjoyment.

The screenplay, necessarily stripped of the richly descriptive passages in the novel, is a progressive unfolding of Jem's and Scout's reactions to life in a "tired old town" and county seat, as it was during the early thirties. Neighborhood affairs make up a large part of the action: the burning of a neighbor's house, Atticus' skill in shooting a mad dog, the mysterious doings within the "haunted" Radley house and the children's fear of afflicted Boo Radley, and the daily domestic routine managed by Calpurnia, the Negro cook and housekeeper for the Finch household. Gradually the children discover larger and more frightening worlds beyond the sphere of their pleasant neighborhood: their school where other students taunt them by calling Atticus a radical and a "nigger-lover"; the packed county courthouse where Atticus loses the sensational case of a Negro youth, Tom Robinson, who though falsely accused of raping sexy Mayella Ewell, is judged guilty; and the ugly world around the town dump where the vicious Ewells live in filth. Most of all, these childish impressions involve the efforts of a truth-loving father to stem the tide of hatred in the minds of his two motherless children.

Technical innovation characterizes another examination of the emotional experience of growing up in a small town. Eugene McKinney's unconventional comedy, *A Different Drummer* (1955), is the "no-success" story of young Royal Barnhill, which develops thematically Thoreau's idea that "if a man does not keep pace with his companions it is because he hears a different drummer." Like numerous other youthful misfits in the chronicles of small-town America, adolescent Royal strives in vain to free himself from his mother's overly indulged protectiveness and the legend of his dead father's successes in ruling the town. Experimenting with technique, McKinney (in a presentation at the Dallas Theater Center in 1964) used a Royal Chorus to reflect the boy's inner turmoil and desires and an Objective Chorus to explain the action and to present town characters, including possessive Mrs. Barnhill, hypocritical Ella Mae Brainard, and other familiar types of provincial citizens.

During a recent Broadway season still another child of the imagination was presented as being disturbed, in much the same way as was Frankie Addams, by discovering in his provincial circle "so many things about the world I do not understand." Such was the puzzlement vexing a small boy growing up in Knoxville, Tennessee, almost fifty years ago. The tender, wistful evocation of the circumscribed world of Rufus Follet, an inquisitive six-year-old, has come about through varied media: an extraordinary autobiographical novel never quite finished, a Broadway play, a movie of the play, and, quite recently, color photography capturing old-time scenes in Knoxville. In the beginning, Rufus was the central character in a Pulitzer Prize novel, *A Death in the Family* (1957), which brought immediate though posthumous recognition to James Agee (1910-1955) and began a cult that "cherishes his words and attitudes." In many ways young Rufus represented James Agee as a boy, and his poignant story originated in the annals of the Agee family as it was in 1915 when living in small-town Knoxville and the environing Great Smokies. In 1958 Tad Mosel, already recognized for his teleplays, reshaped the Agee novel into a most appealing play, *All the Way Home*, itself destined to win a Pulitzer Prize and the Drama Critics Circle Award as the best drama of the 1960-61 season in New York. Early in 1964 a tragic and emotional film version was produced by David Susskind, shortly after *Life* magazine (November 1, 1963) had featured articles about Agee and superb local color photographs by Ernest Haas recording the scenes which Agee had evoked so vividly. *All the Way Home* (starring Robert Preston, Jean Simmons, and boyish Michael Kearney) was filmed, in part, in the authentic settings in Knoxville and the Great Smoky Mountains, in some of the localities which have remained practically unchanged since Agee's boyhood of forty-five years before.

Mosel's dramatization, his first stage play and a hazardous venture in transcription, gave a memorable portrayal of a slight, reminiscent story which moved through theatrical time (May, 1915) by way of atmosphere rather than of events. In the Belasco Theatre production under Arthur Penn's direction, *All the Way Home* sympathetically chronicled the family life of the Follets in pre-World War I Knoxville. Family stress and strain, as well as happiness, develop in scenes involving Jay Follet (a

young husband and lawyer portrayed by Arthur Hill), his wife Mary
(Lenka Peterson's role), their small son Rufus (as superbly impersonated by Master John Megna), and their in-laws. Questions of different
generations, town and rural backgrounds, religious differences, temperamental biases, conjugal love, and ultimate human separateness arise
through the interaction of the characters. What made the play peculiarly
vital as Americana was the impact upon so many lives of Jay's sudden
death in an automobile accident when he was returning home from an
emergency visit to his supposedly dying father.

The cruel impact of her husband's tragic death upon Mary Follet,
pregnant with her second child, furnished the play with an effective climax from which the action quickly moved downward. Jay's death at
once revealed in the others oddly contrasting character strains: the refinement of Mary, often at odds with Jay's nature and his unorthodox views
about religion and moral conduct; the common sense of Aunt Hannah
Lynch (Aline MacMahon's part); the vulgarity and Rotarian spirit of
Jay's alcoholic brother Ralph, forever boasting about his undertaking
establishment and new car; family pride as manifested in matriarchal
Great Great Granmaw's mysterious rapport with young Rufus; and the
boy's wonderment at the beauties of nature revealed to him by his father.
Jay's death shook the family badly, making "secret doors fly open, and
inconsistency raise its honest face."[70]

All the Way Home, like Agee's novel, offers a story of much human
interest involving both a little boy whose childhood happiness ends unexpectedly at his father's death and his anguished mother, who becomes
as lost as the child and begins living in a sort of dream world. Further,
the play depicts the pressures which she endures from the two families,
the Follets and the Lynches (her parents and brother). Ultimately she
emerges from her private world to face hard realities for the sake of
young Rufus and the unborn child. Mosel's skilful adaptation of regional
folk speech and attitudes and his use of personal mannerisms add a
touch of humor which offsets the tragic scene and the overly long ending
of the play. Audience laughter was uproarious when deaf Grandma
Lynch, inimitably interpreted by Lillian Gish, played the piano silently,
in order not to waken Rufus, using various flourishes but never touching
the keys. Possibly the most obvious flaw in an otherwise truthful transcription was Mosel's reliance upon scenes lacking outward drama rather
than upon Agee's inner force. More appealing are the scenes where a
small boy's eyes transform a grimy small-town depot and a hand-cranked
automobile into gateways to the great, unknown outside world.

In recent years dramatizations of southern novels, for screen and stage, have proliferated. In another "best" movie of 1949, *All the King's Men*, the political and social turmoil of a southern small town and the nearby state capital was dramatized from Robert Penn Warren's Pulitzer Prize novel of 1946. The screen play exposed political rottenness closely paralleling the disturbances of the Huey Long regime. In its strong picturing of the steady ascendancy of a spellbinder, the movie in its early portions delineated realistically the small-town environment—the Mason City milieu—of an awkward farm boy named Willie Stark, later to emerge as "the B-b-b- Big B-B-Boss," the governor of Louisiana. Broderick Crawford's portrayal of the demagogue has been praised as "a dynamic tour de force." A dozen years after its publication Warren's novel was to undergo another transformation, this time as a three-act dramatization made by Warren in collaboration with Dallas director Aaron Frankel. Entitled *Willie Stark: His Rise and Fall*, this version, under Frankel's direction, was premiered at the Margo Jones Theatre in Dallas on November 25, 1958.

In an essay called "The Old and the New of It," Warren has written concerning his longtime meditations about Willie Stark and the evolution of *All the King's Men* from his own observations of that once "instructive melodrama which was Louisiana politics."[71] More than twenty years earlier he had thought about the inner drama associated with the rise and eventual fall of a demagogue. As he wrote, ". . . my man had to be . . . an idealist caught in the corrupting process of his own gift of power." From this early view of his ill-fated protagonist Warren created a verse play, "Proud Flesh," completed in Rome during the perilous winter of 1939-40. Later putting aside this play, Warren made a novel, *All the King's Men*, out of the same material. In time a dramatization, with the same title as the book, went out into the world. Finally, motivated by Frankel, Warren revamped this play into an entirely new script, *Willie Stark: His Rise and Fall*.

From the novel the coauthors retained Jack Burden, confidential assistant to Governor Stark and a uniting character serviceable as an expositor in the play's prologue and epilogue, as elsewhere. Flashbacks suggest the provincial Mason City background, where farm boy Willie Stark ploddingly read law books by night and peddled household wares in the back country by day. Jack Burden's habit of recall emphasizes youthful Willie's attempts to provide social betterment for his town, in spite of the chicanery of Main Street politicians. Small-town living appears also through Jack's remembering Willie's early marriage to Lucy, a provincial schoolteacher, self-effacing and blessed with "a kind of domestic sweetness." The three full-bodied acts, localized largely in the state capital

(Baton Rouge), portray the effects upon the Stark family of its removal
from its native town to a strange world of conniving politicians and their
henchmen. Here Willie Stark got the power of a dictator but at last was
assassinated in the very capital which had been the scene of his political
triumphs. By the end of the epilogue Warren's politician had been portrayed as a former provincial whose personal motivation had been, in
one sense, idealistic, who in many ways actually served the cause of social
betterment, but who was eventually corrupted by power, even by power
exercised against corruption.

The new freedom of expression which the twentieth century has
brought to southern writers in general is particularly applicable to those
modern playwrights who have portrayed small-town life in the South.
No longer compelled to subscribe to the conventional opinions long prevalent in their region, these moderns have added new facets to existing
patterns of provincial literature. Most of all, they have shown anew that
twentieth-century life in southern towns, as elsewhere, is by no means a
simple affair. Freely exposing the manifold difficulties of small-town
living in Louisiana, Mississippi, Alabama, and other states in the South
and Southwest, these playwrights have repeatedly broken the mold of
tradition by their naturalistic techniques and exploitation of themes once
taboo. Perverts, degenerates, rootless minstrels, red-necks, political ha-
ranguers, Negroes, Latin types, fading aristocrats tenaciously clinging to
the romantic tradition, confused children and groping misfits, sadistic
sheriffs and constables, and other townsmen tainted in one way or another by crime and violence—all of these, and more, have been dramatized as an integral part of community life in the modern South. On
stage and screen successful plays have drawn attention to the significant
place which the South, once disregarded, now holds in our national
literature.

Some theatrical recorders have been outsiders; but most have been
native small-towners who have had full knowledge of and no little sympathy for the unfortunate provincials of their own locales. Observing the
wide differences, from class to class, in political, economic, racial, educational, and religious faiths, southern playwrights have found abundant
material. Their regional plays reflect a keen awareness of the ominous
economic, political, and moral problems which southerners have had to
face during the last several decades. In such plays, as in modern community dramas about other regions, the force of rebellion, largely on the
part of young people, has often been used as a motif in exposing out-
moded social conventions and in shattering traditional ideals. Youth's
dilemmas and difficulties in coming of age amidst stultifying, and even

hostile, provincial societies, mostly in small agricultural towns, play an important role in these southern exposures. On the other hand, though usually the way is dark and difficult for both youthful and aging protagonists, glimmers of hope and occasional folk humor save these community portraits from utter drabness and overwhelming futility. In these plays there are occasional signs of a return to the dramatization of those more traditional human values and American ideals proclaimed by William Faulkner in his bold declaration at Stockholm: ". . . I decline to accept the end of man . . . because he has a soul, a spirit capable of compassion and sacrifice and endurance." As for our stage representations of southern provincialism, there is a measure of truth in the thought that, though Flem Snopes and his ruthless counterparts seem to triumph, less materially successful folk, such as the Bundrens, manage to endure.

XI. Our Vanishing Towns: Modern Broadway Versions

"This Impossible Modern Life"

SOME OBSERVERS FEEL that modern technology has just about made an anachronism of the American small town's democratic way of life, in spite of the fact that the spirit of its native citizens has resisted the disturbing patterns of change. In order to dramatize the recent frustrations and anger of provincial people bitterly contesting the fate imposed upon them by a changing technology, NBC telecast, on September 18, 1964, a Project 20 Special aptly titled "Smalltown, U.S.A.: A Farewell Portrait." The producer-director of this color special, Eugene S. Jones, quite succinctly described our rapidly vanishing community life: "It used to be The American Way of Life, but now the small town is dying. We want to take a look at its life and its occasional death."[1] By picturing five towns—Cimarron, Kansas; Brandenton, Florida; Bossier City, Louisiana; Greenville, Maine; and Hellier, Kentucky—his show featured regional differences, violent clashes, and contrasts symbolizing the floodtide of change. Actor Frederick March's narration emphasized the small townsman's new conflicts with the old verities: with God, mystery, nature, and, more recently, the economics of survival. The pictorial record revealed anew that during the last several decades citizens in small towns, once happy in self-sufficient isolation, are now having to share with city-dwellers the multiple problems of "the Age of Anxiety," as W. H. Auden has called our troubled times.

Other recent studies, some in the form of seminars sponsored by the Brookings Institution, have been raising comparable questions about the nature of technological change in relation to the American city. In the clash between two cultures—the one provincial, traditionally static, individualistic, and the other urban, dynamic, collectivistic—will the small town be swallowed by the leviathan? Is it feasible for modern municipal leaders to think of a city in almost medieval terms? Is not their planning far outdated when it "inheres from the vague assumption that a city, in its essence, is still a self-contained entity, neatly walled and moated, with green fields labeled 'country' just beyond the outer rim?"[2] Is the modern city merely a mapping of skylines, or of concentric rings, or of zones for housing, industrial plants, and retail stores? Is it a metropolitan area, suburbia, or sprawl? If the demographers are correct, by the year

2000 our nation's population will double. "All but 10 or 15 per cent of the 400 million population will live in some megalopolis, bees that swarm in high-rise hives. From the air, the eye will see but one vast subdivision."[3] For some time such auguries and similar predictions have affected the thinking of Americans concerned about the absorption of the country in a heightened materialism. One cannot help wondering how many may have wished that they could take yesterday and bottle it.

Actually the manifold community changes of more recent times, from the twenties onward, have been fully analyzed by critics and creative writers alike. For several decades some of our most thoughtful playwrights have joined with novelists, short-story writers, and poets in interpreting social change in relation to the decline of the more traditional patterns of American small-town life. Especially in relation to New England and the Midwest, stage versions and other representations of the small town have expressed a kind of nostalgia for our grass-roots heritage, now so rapidly being lost as many small towns are enveloped by sprawling urban expansion. Among our several regions the West, once fully dramatized, has been least represented in recent playwriting, possibly because its vast expanse has been a factor in saving its more isolated communities from revolutionary change. Western and southwestern small-town life, though earlier re-created in twentieth-century plays by Robert Finch, E. P. Conkle, Lynn Riggs, Virgil Geddes, and other regionalists, more recently seems to have been relegated to musical comedies such as *The Unsinkable Molly Brown*.

In general, the modern American town, when subjected to the scrutiny of both factual recorders and imaginative playwrights, has seemingly been out of line with those more laudable aspirations associated with the past. Some interpreters have seen our small towns of more recent times as all but overshadowed by the gigantic complex of a heavily industrialized society. Hence, their stress on our "vanishing towns" and on the continuing emergence of new suburbia, automation, and other familiar symbols of modernity. "The oppressing world," expanding in line with a new conformism inimical to the traditional and more individual ways of the small town, has imposed an inescapable conflict upon those moderns who desire a more peaceful community life. On the one hand, industrial man "and his creature, the machine," symbolize modern homage to a gospel of wealth, to mechanical ingenuity, and to material progress. Caught within this framework, the errant individual, determined to resist popular preachments of "togetherness" and kindred shibboleths, must pay a price for his devotion to the simpler and more obvious truths of individual freedom.

Certain twentieth-century playwrights, disturbed by "this impossible modern life," as Jacques Barzun has called it, have turned to the small town of earlier times in an attempt to find answers to, or to stimulate thinking about, modern social problems. Some of their plays have presented counter-images of past serenity, community trust, self-confidence, and self-reliance. Thornton Wilder's *Our Town,* for example, offers "a glow of relief" from our more modern pressures, frustrations, and anxieties. How, then, did the best of these playwrights chart the past, with its human realities, its probable values, and its flaws?

Grover's Corners, New Hampshire, and Towns Beyond

Among the more experimental modern playwrights who have created vivid community images to counterbalance those of the "uglified" town and the alluring city, Thornton Wilder (1897–   ) has successfully brought into theatrical focus memorable small places, past and present, in New Hampshire, New York, and New Jersey. His daring departures from conventional realism in stories, novels, and plays have stemmed both from his unusually original mind and from his international upbringing, which afforded him wide acquaintance with humanity. The shaping influences on his art have been many. His New England parents, his birthplace (Madison, Wisconsin), his boyhood schooling in Hong Kong, Shanghai, and later in California, his youthful service in the Coast Artillery Corps, his college years at Oberlin, Yale, and Princeton, and his archeological studies in Rome all helped foster in him an unusual detachment and freedom from entangling coteries (though it is true that for a while the New Humanists did regard him as their "golden boy"). A self-reliant thinker, Wilder has explored in his studies the cultures of various epochs and lands, discovering in them different manifestations of a favorite theme: the essential dignity of the human spirit. Apparently the timeliness of such a theme has had much appeal for him. In *The Skin of Our Teeth* the Fortune Teller, speaking about Man's sleeplessness because of worry about his past, asks of Sabina: "What did it mean? What was it trying to say to you?" She warns: "If anybody tries to tell you the past, take my word for it, they're charlatans!" Nevertheless, in his various forms of fiction, Wilder has tried repeatedly to tell the past, often dramatizing it in its relation to the disorders and confusions of the present.

Wilder began his rather curious career with novels, *The Cabala* (1926) and the Pulitzer Prize winning *The Bridge of San Luis Rey* (1927); yet the drama had always fascinated him, even in adolescence. In his preface to a collection of early one-act plays, *The Angel That Troubled the*

Waters (1928), he notes that he composed the first of more than forty one-acters when he was only fifteen. These "three-minute plays for three people" were followed by a second group published in 1931 as *The Long Christmas Dinner and Other One Act Plays*. Although little more than youthful "literary exercises in compressed expression," these playlets reveal his bent toward experimentation as well as his efforts "to capture not verisimilitude but reality." His portrayal of a stage manager in "Pullman Car Hiawatha" and "The Happy Journey from Trenton to Camden" foreshadows the more ingeniously employed Stage Manager who chattily directs the action in *Our Town*. Also, in "The Happy Journey" he experimented with some success in creating illusion on a sceneless stage. This family sketch reveals his ingenuity in stimulating the imagination to supply both scenery and properties on a bare stage. Ordinary chairs serve as the Kirbys' Chevrolet, while a cot suffices for the indoor furnishings. A repetitive pattern appears in "Pullman Car Hiawatha," in which straight chairs are substitutes for berths.

"The Long Christmas Dinner," describing the Bayard family's Christmas gatherings over a period of ninety years, involves time as a potent force which so fascinated Wilder that his experimentations with that motif extended to *Our Town*, *The Skin of Our Teeth*, and other later fiction. In this playlet the directions for costuming and stage business emphasized Wilder's early striving for a new method. The eating of imaginary food with imaginary knives and forks, as well as the use of wigs of white hair and of shawls, adjusted simply and at indicated moments to suggest the aging of the Bayard women, reflects the young playwright's inventiveness. His growing displeasure, during the twenties and earlier, with what he derided as the "soothing quality" of popular plays—of tragedy without "heat," of comedy lacking "bite," and of social plays without a code of "responsibility"—may have motivated his portrayal of Roderick as an exasperated critic of the town which the Bayards, with their factory assets, helped control. "Great God," Roderick exclaims, "you gotta get drunk in this town to forget how dull it is. Time passes so slowly here that it stands still, that's what's the trouble."[4] Finally, in his dramatic writing at Yale in 1919, when as editor of the *Yale Literary Magazine* he serialized his first play, *The Trumpet Shall Sound*, Wilder gave clear foreshadowing of his later efforts to become, as he once said, "not an innovator but a rediscoverer of forgotten goods and . . . a remover of obtrusive bric-a-brac in the theatre."[5]

However charade-like these early playlets were, they quickened the maturing of Wilder's originality. As the thirties lengthened and he turned more and more toward the theater, Wilder shared in common with other insurgent playwrights a dislike for the "ridiculous, shallow, and harmful" plays which then dominated the commercial theater. Like Maxwell Anderson and Eugene O'Neill, he began in earnest to experiment with the dramatic expression of poetry and imagination, combined with enough realism to bring his plays in touch with the everyday world. Fortunately his development as a playwright coincided with a time of crusading zeal in the theater, in both Europe and the United States. Inspiration for a new theatrical course which was to give strong competition to Broadway's commercialized offerings came from many sources. The emergence of progressive producers like Arthur Hopkins; of the Theatre Guild, Eva Le Gallienne's Civic Repertory Theatre, the Playwrights' Company, and other art groups; of original stage designers, such as Jo Mielziner, Lee Simonson, and Robert Edmond Jones, of gifted actors able to respond to fresh and original roles in the new expressionistic, or constructivistic, plays; and of imported imaginative foreign plays like Hungarian Ferenc Molnar's *Liliom* (1921) and Karel Capek's Czechoslovakian fantasy, *R.U.R.* (*Rossum's Universal Robots*), produced in New York in 1922, contributed greatly to the revitalization of our native drama and theater.

Wilder's temperamental distaste for the popular sentimental play, with its pseudo-realistic terms, and for doctrinaire realism, which conventionally represents the surfaces of life with photographic fidelity, influenced his experimentation with unusual dramaturgic methods. He turned toward the creation of effective patterns of feelings and emotions. The aesthetic principles of repetition and variation, of manners and customs indicative of the passage of time, of dramatic portrayal by unrealistic and nonrepresentational techniques, and of contrasting emotions to avoid monotony all appealed to his imaginative mind. It is no wonder, then, that his best-known and most successful original play, *Our Town* (1938), has been termed a "New England allegory," "a beautiful evocative play," "a tender idyll," "a hauntingly beautiful play," and "less the portrait of a town than the sublimation of the commonplace."[6]

In this appealing play Wilder, largely through the medium of a folksy and interlocutory Stage Manager, shows himself as a whimsical philosopher of the commonplace. Re-creating three periods in the history of Grover's Corners, a placid New Hampshire town, he transmutes, as Brooks Atkinson wrote in the *New York Times*, "the simple events of human life into universal reverie" and gives "familiar facts a deeply moving, philosophical perspective."[7] Eschewing what his generation deemed the ultimate in theatrical art—the box set and the convention of the fourth wall—Wilder chose to stage his play without scenery and with the curtain always raised. By stripping his play of everything extraneous, he succeeded in giving a profound, strange, and unworldly significance to the simple life of a remote New Hampshire township from around 1901 to 1913. Wilder himself, however, has written that he did not offer *Our Town* "as a picture of a New Hampshire village; or as a speculation about the conditions of life after death . . . ," an element which he confesses to have borrowed from Dante's *Purgatory*. Rather, he regarded this play as "an attempt to find value above all price for the smallest events in our daily life." To dramatize and universalize the significance of life's minutiae, he set Grover's Corners against "the largest dimensions of time and place."[8] As he has said, his trick of repeatedly using such words as "hundreds," "thousands," and "millions" tended to universalize Emily Webb's happiness and sorrow—to attune her algebra exercises, her twelfth birthday celebration, and her youthful love for George Gibbs to similar experiences of teen-age girls everywhere.

Though an original and stylized drama, *Our Town* presents the life ritual—the plain, uneventful life in a New Hampshire village—through relatively simple action. Timed for certain days in the serene era of the Mauve Decade, the play shows two young neighbors—George Gibbs, son of a kindly doctor, and Emily Webb, whose father edits the Grover's Corners *Sentinel*—growing up amidst a friendly circle of parents, George's sister Rebecca, Emily's brother Wally, neighbors, schoolmates, and townspeople in general. As the first act begins the audience sees a half-lighted empty stage, devoid of either curtain or scenery. Soon the easy-going Stage Manager, "hat on and pipe in mouth," comes on stage and begins to address the spectators in a folksy, friendly manner. (This role was superbly enacted by Frank Craven when the play began its New York run at the Henry Miller Theatre on February 4, 1938.) While he chats about the time—dawn on May 7, 1901—and the history of the town and township, the Manager acts in the dual role of property man and *raisonneur*. He pushes into place a few chairs, tables, ladders, and planks, which with two arched trellises make up the only realistic properties. Serving as a one-man chorus, he genially comments on the plan of the town, with its Polish Town across the tracks as well as its Main Street. After identifying the churches, the town hall, the post office, and the stores, he describes the Gibbs and Webb families, their homes, the neighbors, and local affairs in general. As the action progresses he answers questions asked, from time to time, by the spectators, actually actors planted in the audience, who quiz him about the town's culture and its attitudes toward social injustice, inequality, and drinking. On occasion he assumes the roles of minor characters, male and female.

The organic structure of the almost plotless three acts has frequently been analyzed in relation to the ways in which Wilder telescoped births, everyday living, deaths, and time.[9] Basically each act is structured on the double plan of a street scene followed by an enactment of family life within either the Gibbs or the Webb household. In each street scene the folksy conversation, involving a milkman, a newsboy, a constable, and various other citizens, helps build up an atmosphere of neighborliness and explain the homely nature of each family group. Thus the first act, after a spotty tracing of local history and a review of one full day of community activity, portrays the ordinary routine in the two adjoining homes in which George, played by John Craven, and Emily, played by Martha Scott, are growing up. From this act onward most of the stage business is through pantomime, as when Dr. Gibbs, returning home after an early morning call, "sets down his—imaginary—black bag" and Mrs. Gibbs, busy in the kitchen, goes "through the motion of putting wood in the stove, lighting it, and preparing breakfast." Acts II and III, again offering a combination of street and family scenes, with a final scene at the town's hillside cemetery, have a new focus: the courtship and the marriage of George and Emily and Emily's death in childbirth. Throughout the play Wilder, by abandoning scenery and relying to a great extent on nonexistent properties, tried to revive some of the Elizabethan techniques which gave greater importance to the actor, unencumbered by realistic scenery and properties.

The somberly toned third act, a poignant scene in the graveyard above the town, takes on a rainy day in the summer of 1913. Umbrella-laden townspeople have climbed the hill to attend the burial service for young Emily. Here, as throughout the action, the real protagonist, as Edmond Gagey has shown, seems to be the town of Grover's Corners, with an emerging narrative thread expressing the happiness, and now the sorrow, of a young farm couple over a period of nine years. As Emily joins Mother Gibbs and other townsfolk in the graveyard, these community dead appear indifferent to what is still happening in the town below. As the Stage Manager comments, "They get weaned away from the earth" and are waiting for "the eternal part in them to come out clear." In the conclusion the relationship between life and eternity also touches upon everyday living and its potentialities, the latter too often tragically overlooked by many. Emily's last speech, which gives a moving re-creation of her happy experiences on her twelfth birthday, philosophically implies as much. As the vision of this birthday fades, Emily sobs, "We don't have time to look at one another . . . Oh, earth, you're too wonderful for anybody to realize you. Do any human beings ever realize life while they live it?—every, every minute?"[10] The play ends as casually as it opened. The Stage Manager announces that it is late evening and though "most everybody's asleep in Grover's Corners," the stars are still "doing their old, old criss-cross journeys in the sky." Then he draws a dark curtain across the scene.

Thus imbued with homeliness of action and characterization, *Our Town*, the Pulitzer Prize play for 1938, is reminiscent of the pilgrimage depicted in *Everyman*. As a twentieth-century morality play, it traces the journeying of ordinary people, telling, without sensationalism, "the way we were . . . in our living and in our dying." It reveals Wilder's creative use of the theater. And, as he has said, it was written "out of a deep admiration for those little white towns in the hills . . ." Further, it memorializes—and idealizes—the hill-encircled and custom-bound village of Grover's Corners as a type of once flourishing and neighborly American village now vanished from our national scene. In Wilder's words, it presents "the life of a village against the life of the stars." Such a "sublimation of the commonplace" was to appear again, with style and distinction, in another medium. On June 6, 1947—"the day when televised drama was really born," according to Gassner—NBC featured a telecast of *Our Town*, under the auspices of the Theatre Guild and with Raymond Massey acting as the Stage Manager. Later an excellent revival of the play by José Quintero enriched the production list of his off-Broadway theater, the Circle in the Square.

The Skin of Our Teeth, winner in 1942 of a third Pulitzer Prize for Wilder, is a drama which presents, with experimental technique, the survival of the human race in spite of the periodic catastrophes of glaciation, deluge, and war, and its conflict with ignorance, folly, and the general malaise through which our civilization was passing at the time the play was written. While not primarily a small-town study, this panoramic play begins in the town of Excelsior, New Jersey. Also, though the action moves rapidly backward and forward in time and place, as does James Joyce's *Finnegans Wake* or T. S. Eliot's *The Waste Land*,[11] this "greatest comedy of the age," as Alexander Woolcott has called it, bears some resemblance to *Our Town*. The daily lives of the main characters—Mr. and Mrs. Antrobus, their children Gladys and Henry, and Lily Sabina, the maid—resemble those of the Grover's Corners villagers in that they all furnish the key to the destiny of the human race. Also, Emily in the graveyard felt the tug of the past; in *The Skin of Our Teeth* the world of the past keeps challenging the worlds of the present and the future. Moreover, the Announcer of the first act parallels, in a technical sense, the Stage Manager of *Our Town*.

Wilder's audacious disregard for dramatic conventions and realism brought him no end of difficulty in his attempts to stage *The Skin of Our Teeth*. Rejected by various producers in New York, including the Theatre Guild, this expressionistic chronicle of man's precarious survival was accepted at last by Michael Meyerberg and inventively directed by Elia Kazan. The play was first given a tryout performance in New Haven, at the Shubert Theatre on October 15, 1942. When it finally opened in New York on November 18, 1942, at the Plymouth Theatre, the brilliant cast included Frederic March and Florence Eldridge as the Antrobuses, Tallulah Bankhead as Sabina, Montgomery Clift as Henry, Frances Heflin as Gladys, E. G. Marshall as Mr. Fitzpatrick, and Florence Reed as the Fortune Teller. The play was mystifying even to some of the players, including Miss Bankhead, and baffled and infuriated critics, some of whom dismissed it as "a comic variety show," "a dramatic fantasy," and "a morality play without moral ardor." What some critics missed was the fact that in this small-town family may be found various symbols of home life threatened by forces both from within and from without. The parent-child relationship, the husband-wife association, the threats to family solidarity posed by destructive social forces, including war, and other familial factors undergird the comedy. Furthermore, at a time of real crisis in our modern history Wilder was presenting, among other facets of man's struggles, a challenging revival of the story of Cain in Henry, the man of violence who must remain a member of society.

The Antrobuses, whose name suggests the Greek *anthropos,* "human being" or "man," are middle-class representatives of the race in its long, checkered history. In the beginning their symbolically named hometown, Excelsior, New Jersey, is the confused scene of Nature's impersonal, destructive glaciation. Later, in Act III, it is the background for the return-to-normalcy activities associated with the aftermath of man's own catastrophic folly, world war. With their home environment symbolizing man's constant upward climb, Mr. and Mrs. Antrobus represent, in a series of panoramic scenes, the hard history of human indestructibility, extending from geologic time (Act I) through biblical periods (Act II) and onward through recorded history until the close of World War I (Act III).[12] Before the opening of the first act George Antrobus—Adam and the Eternal Male—had already invented the wheel and the lever, and he has almost completed the multiplication table and the alphabet when suddenly his labors are cut short by a radio announcement that a great mass of ice has been discovered moving slowly toward the vicinity of Excelsior. In the midst of community panic and disruption

Mrs. Antrobus—Eve, "that gracious and charming mammal"—adheres to her watchword: "Save the Family." For her part, Mrs. Antrobus has long been as creative as her husband, having invented the apron, the gusset, the gore, and frying in oil, all achievements symbolizing her main purpose in life: to save her home and keep her children safe. Hence, Lily Sabina—Lilith and the Other Woman—the discontented maid and perennial seducer of man, is eventually overwhelmed by the ever-watchful wife and is returned to the kitchen. It's no wonder that Mrs. Antrobus understands the ways of the Sabinas; in the spring she and George will be celebrating their five thousandth wedding anniversary.

These, then, are the main characters who, together with the daughter Gladys, her father's hope for the future, and the undisciplined son Henry (Cain), appear in both serious and satirically comic scenes as "a typical American family." Typifying humanity's abiding types, all of the characters express Wilder's theories about the relationship between modern Americans and destiny. As Sabina early intimates, this destiny is all the more difficult to envision because the Antrobuses and their neighbors happen to live during a troubled time when "the world's at sixes and sevens." Nevertheless, they and the refugees who have crowded into Excelsior and other towns have "managed to survive for some time now, catch as catch can, the fat and the lean." Although Sabina still has fears that the dinosaurs will trample folk to death and that the grasshoppers will devour their garden stuff, she knocks on wood, hoping that all will live "to see better days" and survive calamities "by the skin of our teeth."[13] Yet she is puzzled by the odd fact that "here it is the coldest day of the year right in the middle of August . . ." Pessimistic and unimaginative, Sabina lacks George Antrobus' insight into society's dangers and complexities, which he reveals in a bit of moralizing at the play's end: "How can you make a world for people to live in, unless you've first put order in yourself?" Profiting by a faith based on experience, George understands far better than Sabina that "living is a struggle . . ." He knows, too, with a kind of worried optimism, "that every good and excellent thing in the world stands moment by moment on the razor-edge of danger and must be fought for . . ."[14] At the finale, all he asks for is a chance "to build new Worlds and God has always given us that." Most of all, Man must first establish order in himself.

While the Antrobuses and their Excelsior neighbors experience the hardships which have confronted Everyman in all ages, from first to last they remain abstractions illustrating Wilder's method of humorous surrealism. They could well serve as theatrical counterparts to Elmer Rice's symbolical Mr. and Mrs. Zero, Mr. and Mrs. One, and other similarly named couples in *The Adding Machine*. The Gibbs and Webb families of Grover's Corners are far more reminiscent of the plain people who inhabit little towns and rural communities than are the Antrobuses, whether they be in Excelsior trying to save their home or in Atlantic City (in Act II) sharing the excitement of a convention—"the anniversary convocation of that great fraternal order—the Ancient and Honorable Order of Mammals, Subdivision Humans." Nevertheless, however allegorical the Antrobuses and their associates may appear, they share in the social enterprises characteristic of modern American townsmen. Numerous zany scenes showing their delight in bingo parlors, fortune-telling, the hullabaloo of conventions, school and P.T.A. affairs, and similar community activities offer a hilarious satire on comparable interests of provincials everywhere.

Wilder's brilliant success in this play stems in part from the expression of philosophic and poetic ideas, culminating in Antrobus' affirmative declaration: "My friends, we have come a long way, in spite of difficult times." Successful, too, were his diverse technical experimentations: his employment of a chatty stage manager, of a symbolic mammoth, of leaning or suddenly disappearing flats representing the Antrobus bungalow, of lantern slide projections and radio broadcasts, and of bursts of music. Further signs of unconventionality and theatricalism which attracted attention include the device of having actors step out of their roles, either to gossip among themselves about their personal difficulties, or to chat with members of the audience concerning their views about old-fashioned playwriting or the peculiar production problems associated with this play. By such daring means Wilder succeeded in communicating one of his favorite beliefs: "that the artistic validity of a play depends to a degree upon the acknowledgment that its pursuit of truth is via make-believe."[15]

For his final venture into community dramatization, Wilder in *The Matchmaker* (1954) moved imaginatively far beyond the regional limits of Grover's Corners—to Yonkers, fifteen miles north of New York City, during the early 1880's. The small-town action of this carefree farce is limited to the opening act, which takes place in the cluttered living room of Horace Vandergelder, a crusty widower whose domestic quarters are located over his hay, feed, and provision store. If *The Skin of Our Teeth* in substance resembles Edouard Dujardin's 1932 *Le Retour éternel,* a dramatization of humanity's survival as symbolized by the destiny of a greatly harassed family, *The Matchmaker* is also an outgrowth of a foreign prototype: Johann Nestroy's comedy *Einen Jux will er sich Machen* (Vienna, 1842), itself derived from John Oxenford's original *A Day*

Well Spent (London, 1835).[16] In the beginning Wilder's Americanized
adaptation was entitled *The Merchant of Yonkers*. Under this title it was
produced by Herman Shumlin, directed by Max Reinhardt, and originally performed at Boston's Colonial Theatre on December 12, 1938.
Its New York premiere was at the Guild Theatre on December 28 of the
same year. *The Merchant* was destined to undergo changes for performance during the Edinburgh Festival in the summer of 1954, when Tyrone
Guthrie directed it, under the title of *The Matchmaker*, for the opening
of the Royal Lyceum Theatre at Edinburgh, on August 23. London and
New York runs began in 1954 and 1955 respectively. During 1964 and
1965 Wilder's entertaining farce reappeared in the form of a musical
comedy, *Hello, Dolly!* with delightful music and lyrics by Jerry Herman
and the book by Michael Stewart. Originally starring Carol Channing,
Hello, Dolly! owed much of its success to redoubtable and inventive
Gower Champion, who was both director and choreographer for the
crowd-drawing performances at the St. James Theatre, New York.

Act I of *The Matchmaker* offers a humorous portrayal of the informal
relationship which once existed between the proprietor and his clerks in
in an old-fashioned provision store, of a type common in American
small towns during the horse and buggy era. Much of the fun to follow
stems from Horace Vandergelder, played by Loring Smith—"sixty,
choleric, vain, and sly"—who is never tired of declaring that most of the
people in the world are fools, women most of all. As he admits, "There's
nothing like mixing with women to bring out all the foolishness in a man
of sense." Nevertheless, he is thinking of marrying again, and to this end
asks the advice of a longtime friend, Mrs. Dolly Levi, a sprightly but
impoverished widow who works at being a marriage arranger. Throughout the action, his experiences with women—including Mrs. Levi, Mrs.
Irene Molloy (a New York milliner), and his sentimental niece and
ward, young Ermengarde—not only nearly make a fool of Mr.
Vandergelder, but remove the Yonkers characters to nearby New York
City, where they become involved in hilarious escapades. At the finale
"the right amount of adventure" quickens Mr. Vandergelder's decision
to marry Dolly Levi, played by Ruth Gordon, and to sanction the marriage of Ermengarde to Ambrose Kemper, her impecunious artist-lover.
After all, Mr. Vandergelder shrewdly regards "marriage as a bribe to
make a housekeeper think she's a householder." Sprightly dialogue and
direct addresses by various characters to the audience help create humorous relationships based upon local scenes and manners. Though one
critic has called *The Matchmaker* "an amiable piece of tomfoolery,"
there is an occasional note of serious reflection, as in Dolly Levi's solilo-

quy on marrying for money, in which she muses that ". . . there comes a moment in everybody's life when he must decide whether he'll live among human beings or not—a fool among fools or a fool alone."[17]

New Salem and Springfield, Illinois
and Other Towns from the "Usable Past"

In the very season when the Grover's Corners citizens first made their stage appearance, other provincial plays, by their emotional dramatization of the American way of peace and goodwill, offered dramatic rebuttals to the then current totalitarian glorification of war and the brutal enslavement of free peoples. Such rediscovery of Americanism during days of world peril gave an impetus to a fresh re-examination of certain national heroes who, during past crises, had courageously met personal dilemmas comparable to modern challenges and decisions. Among these rediscoveries, the Lincoln legend offered "the story of a man of peace who had to face the issue of appeasement or war. He faced it." Biographical drama, one of the successful dramatic patterns of the troubled thirties, reached a climax during the 1938-39 season when the Pulitzer Prize was awarded to *Abe Lincoln in Illinois*, a "complete triumph on stage and screen," written by Robert Emmet Sherwood (1896–1955). As the first production to be sponsored by the newly established Playwrights' Company,[18] this vital Lincoln play expressed one of Sherwood's absorbing interests: the gradual growth of Lincoln's greatness and the fascinating mystery of his mind. Directed by Elmer Rice with stage designs by Jo Mielziner, the production at the Plymouth Theatre offered a superb acting vehicle for Raymond Massey as the young and unsure Abe Lincoln, who, gradually overcoming his fears, rises from the lowly rank of a tall, gangling, uncouth backwoods villager to the status of president-elect on the ticket of the new Republican party.

In his copious notes, "The Substance of *Abe Lincoln in Illinois*," Sherwood wrote at length about the attraction which Lincoln's extraordinary character had for him, especially during the uncertain times when Europe was engaged in war under nazi pressures. In Sherwood's view, Lincoln's life

was a work of art, forming a veritable allegory of the growth of the democratic spirit, with its humble origins, its inward struggles, its seemingly timid policy of "live and let live" and "mind your own business," its slow awakening to the dreadful problems of reality, its battles with and conquest of those problems, its death at the hands of a crazed assassin, and its perpetual human need for it.[19]

Accordingly, Sherwood, in his work notes, equates Lincoln's achievement with "the solidification of the American ideal": the rise of the common man. Nevertheless, this play was his attempt, in twelve scenes, to dramatize "the solidification of Lincoln himself—a long, uncertain process" marked by influences both from within the man's own reasoning mind and from without.

The action of the twelve scenes, set in the era from 1833 to 1861, re-creates the spirit of the young and boisterous Middle West in which Lincoln grew up. Drawing inspiration from Carl Sandburg's *The Prairie Years*, the Herndon and Weil biography (1899), and other authentic sources, Sherwood dramatized innumerable facets of Lincoln's spirit and life during the years when he lived first in log-cabined New Salem and later in Springfield, Illinois. For Lincoln it was a burgeoning time of great personal transformation: of a maturing process quickened by his contacts with a new and exciting world. With the help of such friends as Mentor Graham, the neighborhood schoolmaster who tutored him in the fundamentals of grammar and turned his interests toward reading of the classics, Joshua Speed, a New Salem merchant of good family and superior education, Bowling Green, justice of the peace and leading citizen, and aristocratic Ninian Edwards, gangling Abe Lincoln gradually changed from an uncertain backwoodsman into a townsman, practicing law in Springfield with Billy Herndon and eventually marrying Mary Todd, who came from a genteel Kentucky family.

As the scenes move forward, the play becomes a brilliant analysis of a maladjusted, unhappy man forced into unwilling action, partly by the ambition and singlemindedness of Mrs. Lincoln and partly by Lincoln's own acute insight into the social and moral problems of his time. In the first act the village world of New Salem furnishes the semi-frontier scenes of Lincoln's unsuccessful young manhood, a time of drifting. If he failed as New Salem's storekeeper and postmaster, he profited from Mentor Graham's patient teaching and from the encouragement given by Green and Edwards. His own growing awareness of the promise of the virgin lands to the west is dramatized in scene 7, a fictionalized prairie meeting with the Oregon-bound Gales, which symbolizes Lincoln's change from an uncertain and self-doubting youth to a man of passionate conviction, firm in the belief that the survival of America is tied up with his feeling of kinship with his migrating friends and the sense of responsibility which he at last has for them. Sherwood's consummate skill in evoking the New Salem episodes creates graphic pictures of frontier village life: of the Rutledge Tavern and Abe's love for Ann Rutledge, whose death produced a melancholy which almost wiped out his former comical self;

of the roistering Jack Armstrong and the rowdyism of the Clary Grove boys; of radical firebrands and other early political types; and of the general feeling about manifest destiny that an ambitious man could start "up the ladder in a nation which is now expanding southward, across the vast area of Texas; and westward, to the Empire of the Californias on the Pacific Ocean."

In Act II Springfield, a thriving political center during these years, symbolizes the wider world of affairs for young lawyer Lincoln. Ever widening horizons bring new contacts and a steadily deepening insight into the demands and intricacies of society. His heated debates with the "Little Giant" (Stephen A. Douglas) in 1858, his arguments with his hotheaded abolitionist partner Billy Herndon, his unpopularity in opposing the Mexican War, his awkward courtship of and postponed marriage to genteel Mary Todd, and, in general, his braving the decorum of Springfield's elite circle—all of these experiences and more heightened Lincoln's tragic sense of life, his sincere liberalism, and his sense of social justice. During these "laboratory years," as Sherwood has said, "a philosophy was slowly developing, a philosophy relentless in its thoroughness." Blessed with the soul of a poet and the mind of a pure scientist, Lincoln more and more strove to reflect on all the implications behind and beyond life's many patterns. In meditative moods, he tried to be one "who saw life steadily, and saw it whole." Nevertheless, during these momentous years he appeared, in Herndon's words, "restless, gloomy, miserable, desperate."

Finally, his return to Mary Todd, whom he at first rejected, symbolizes his reluctant acceptance of his destiny. Act III, therefore, shows Lincoln's slow emergence as a Republican "dark horse," as he temporarily shed his negativism. His spirited debates, dramatized with considerable verisimilitude, not only emphasize Lincoln's slow affirmation of American ideals, but also furnish a prelude to the exciting presidential election of November 6, 1860. Lincoln's gloom on the night of the election about the prospect of his victory and his impatience with Mary and her ambitions contrast dramatically with the mounting excitement throughout Springfield. The final scene, set against the background of the yards of the railroad station at Springfield, offers a stirring re-creation of the happenings of February 11, 1861, when Lincoln, in the presence of his neighbors and supporters, calmly delivered his farewell speech from the rear platform of the train which was to carry him and his family to their uncertain future in Washington. In this closing scene Sherwood's artistry is masterly. Blending several of Lincoln's utterances, he created a moving farewell speech which, in part, is highly poetic, as in the sad acknowledgment, "not knowing when or whether ever I may return." The final touch to Lincoln's development during these Illinois years is expressed in words written by Thomas Brigham Bishop and not, as many people suppose, by Julia Ward Howe: "His soul goes marching on." At the last the shrill screech of the engine whistle is matched in sound by the band's playing and the crowd's singing "John Brown's Body" and "Glory, Glory Hallelujah."

As this play reveals, uncertainty was the keynote of the early life of Abe Lincoln; just such a note of irresolution is suggested at the conclusion. The real truth of the play is implied not in a *spoken* line but in the familiar refrain of a song. In the solemn note of this triumphant refrain, "His soul goes marching on," Sherwood intimates that throughout all of Lincoln's uncertainties—private as well as public—there was a slow growth of certainty about the first rights of men: justice, truth, and freedom. Nevertheless, there is an indeterminate ending. Will democracy go marching on? As Lincoln stands on the threshold of greatness, waving to the cheering townspeople from the observation car, the climbing aboard of a military guard sounds a faint note of foreboding. As Sherwood has written, "There is no exaggeration in the suggestion that Lincoln's life was constantly threatened after his election, or that he himself was unresponsive to the attempts to guard him from assassination."[20]

During the turmoil-ridden thirties some of Sherwood's contemporaries also explored the past to discover dramatic parallels for present ills. Two of the more distinguished plays dealing with the relatively distant past are by Maxwell Anderson: *Night Over Taos* (1932), which was discussed in Chapter V, and another poetic and symbolic period tragedy, *The Wingless Victory* (1936), in which Anderson continued his exposure of American materialism by means of "a universal and bitterly timeless story of race prejudice" set in Salem, Massachusetts, during the 1800 era. After seven years in the Orient Nathaniel (Nat) McQueston, a vagabond sailor, returns to his native town as captain and owner of *The Wingless Victory*, a five-master "loaded to the gunnels with spices from the Celebes." Although at first pleased at the prospect of Nat's restoring the family's diminishing fortunes, the intolerant McQuestons later are shocked when they learn that Nat has brought with him to code-bound Salem a Malayan wife, beautiful Princess Oparre, their two children, one called Durian, and their native nurse Toala.

Greedily evaluating Nat's holdings, his narrow-minded mother and his "unco guid" brother, the Reverend Phineas McQueston, permit the prodigal son to bring his family ashore. But only freethinking Ruel, a younger brother, is honest enough to welcome darkskinned Oparre and her half-breed children with any show of sincerity. Governed by religious bigotry and shameful hypocrisy, the Salemites in general reject Oparre and the children as despised outsiders or pariahs. As the days pass certain schemers, including the sanctimonious Phineas, by borrowing and sheer chicanery, get control of Nat's money and straightway bring charges of piracy against him, finally forcing him to consent to returning Oparre and his children to Malaya, "to live out their lives in the brothels of the East." Although he loves Oparre, Nat, now once again under the repressive influence of the Puritan code, begins to view her as an alien and to regard his relations with her as disreputable. Alone in a strange land, Oparre, who had once regarded the Christian doctrine as something beautiful, now sadly realizes that she has been misled. Berating the townspeople for their bigotry and meanness of spirit, she asks hopelessly: "Is there nowhere a kingdom that would count us equals?"

Meanwhile Nat, commercially bound again to the family chandlering business and influenced anew by the Puritan code, knows that he cannot sail away with her and their children. On the other hand, he despises Phineas as a money changer and a pilfering churchman, bent on schemes to ruin him unless Oparre is sent away in *The Wingless Victory*. Oparre, sick of the "white witless faces" and the coldheartedness of the Salemites, turns again to her Malayan gods—in Phineas' eyes, "the ancient witchcraft by which she lives . . ." Her anguish of soul in trying to escape from the hated town parallels action in the Medea story. After being sent to a cabin aboard *The Wingless Victory*, the wretched princess resorts to a native custom by giving hemlock poison to the children, her faithful servant Toala, and herself. Before she boarded the ship her anguish had deepened as she vehemently denounced the Salemites, who wreak vengeance on "all save their chosen," for their rigid Puritan pride and pitiless Christian inhumanity. Brokenhearted, she has now come to think of Christ's doctrine as one "written for beggars," who would do better to remember that "The old gods are best, the gods of blood and bronze and the arrows dipped in venom."[21]

In a somewhat melodramatic finale Nat, overcome by his love for Oparre, rushes into the cabin, but too late. As she dies, confessing to Nat that she loves him and has chosen suicide because of her love, Oparre is momentarily comforted by Nat's embraces and his declaration that he has murdered her. Thus she ends her association with a hated town, thinking, as she told Ruel earlier, that "this Christ of peace" has come too soon. Maybe, men will be ready for him after "another hundred thousand years . . ." Both Nat and Ruel denounce their narrow town and plan to accompany the dead when the ship sets sail on the morrow.

In spite of its note of melodrama at the end and the occasional irregularity of its verse, *The Wingless Victory* is a moving study of the travail of a man's soul when he is faced with a sudden choice involving dishonor and loss of respectability. Katharine Cornell gave an emotionally stirring portrayal of the dusky Oparre in the Broadway production, and the play's theme of intolerance and racial hatred appealed to audiences for its relevance to the nazi doctrine. For the present decade this cogent theme remains tragically topical.[22]

As we have seen, the persistence in American thought and drama of pictures of the folksy small town has left us many images of hometowns and old homesteads. During the thirties and forties such picturing is occasionally linked with the kind of satiric and comic exposure which one may enjoy in dramatizations of the available past of Sidney Howard, A. M. Drummond, and Robert E. Gard. Basing *The Late Christopher Bean* (1932) upon *Prenez Garde à la Peinture* by René Fauchois, Howard transformed the original French scene into a provincial New England town, not far from Boston, of many years ago. First titled *Muse of Work*, this three-act comedy, as produced by Gilbert Miller, opened at Ford's Theatre in Baltimore on October 23, 1932, and then transferred to Henry Miller's Theatre in New York on October 31. Aline Bernstein's realistic stage design featured the dining room of an old house occupied by a rural physician, Dr. Haggett, played by Walter Connally; his silly and pseudo-citified wife, played by Beulah Bondi; and their daughter Susan. In this provincial household the "muse of all work" is a Yankee village woman named Abby, aged vaguely somewhere between youth and maturity. As the leading character, Abby was created for Pauline Lord. The portrayal of the Haggetts offers delightful satire exposing the false judgments of a family who had once known an impoverished young painter, Christopher (Chris) Bean, but had dismissed him as worthless. After his death, the Haggetts find only a few dirty canvases to pay the doctor for his medical services.

Accordingly, Dr. Haggett and his equally undiscerning family are surprised when later one of Christopher's old-time friends calls to pay the medical bill and take away a few paintings as mementoes. A still greater surprise comes when another old friend turns up for a similar purpose. The greatest shock is administered, however, by a distinguished New York art critic, Maxwell Davenport, when he arrives to pay his respects to the dead artist. During all the household furor which ensues it appears that the only person who had understood Christopher Bean was the housemaid Abby, who astonishes everyone by the disclosure that she is Mrs. Christopher Bean and is thus the rightful owner of the artist's paintings. (The disappointing finale of the Fauchois play ends with the awarding of the pictures to the selfish, dishonest doctor.) Much humor stems from the shock experienced by the Haggetts when they learn that Christopher's "daubs" are worth a fortune. In their scurrying around to locate the paintings, they discover one in a chicken coop and another canvas almost ruined by showy flowers which Susan has painted on its back. Their astonishment increases when they find out that their servant girl Abby has in her room a heretofore undiscovered treasure, Bean's portrait of herself. In the midst of all the mad scramble and turmoil of action, Abby, with her lovable simplicity, has her memories of distant happiness with the lost Christopher.

Howard's skill is best displayed not only in his evocation of a New England provincial locale, which he knew well, but in his gradual revelation of the undercurrent beneath the surface of amusing household turmoil: the deep and abiding love of a hired girl for her departed lover. Of all the people in this custom-bound little town, Abby alone understood Christopher's ideals and aspirations and was truly close to him. Her wistful thoughts of him and her faithfulness to his memory offset the mercenary interests of the art dealers and the stupidity and narrow spirit of the townspeople.[23]

Alien Corn, first performed at the Belasco Theatre on February 20, 1933, is another appealing, if inconclusive, play in which Howard again dramatizes a sensitive artist's conflict with a provincial milieu. Here the stultifying atmosphere of a narrow midwestern community complicates the struggle of a music teacher in a small college. Gifted Elsa Brandt, played by Katharine Cornell, gives up her dream of becoming a concert pianist because of her love for the already married college president. When their affair ends, Elsa stifles her feelings and resigns herself to continuing her teaching.

In 1934 Howard, in a skilful adaptation of Sinclair Lewis' novel *Dodsworth*, created still another rebellious protagonist warring with his pragmatic environment. Though not primarily set in a small town, *Dodsworth* reflects, in its first two scenes especially, the lack of real culture in the prosperous manufacturing center of Zenith, in the Middle West. The flight of Samuel Dodsworth, a recently retired automobile manufacturer from Zenith to Europe not only suggests Henry James's Christopher Newman in search of a satisfying cultural life abroad, but also parallels the questing of rebellious escapists featured in many dramas of small-town life. Walter Huston's memorable acting in the Dodsworth role furnished a brilliant portrayal of the education of a provincial American.

In old-fashioned communities of long ago, where entertainment was limited, widespread excitement was quickly aroused by the arrival of wagon-drawn circuses (often merely small menageries), patent medicine vendors in gaudily decorated wagons, itinerant thespians and even wrestlers, and other outside entertainers. In such villages and towns, symbolic of an America now largely vanished, shrewd tricksters, or funsters, sometimes played on the gullibility of the natives. As Mark Twain long ago sardonically demonstrated in *The Man That Corrupted Hadleyburg* (1898), an entire citizenry could fall under the spell of a hoax or a trumped-up marvel. This theme gives direction to a lusty folk play, *The Cardiff Giant* (1949), derived from what has been called "New York State's greatest hoax, perhaps the greatest hoax of a nation of tall-story tellers." Recognizing the dramatic possibilities for a regional comedy in a bit of Onondaga Valley history written by Cornell's former president Andrew D. White,[24] Professors A. M. Drummond of Cornell and Robert E. Gard of Wisconsin fashioned a "show" about a fake petrified giant, buried to be dug up, which once drew excited crowds to the Cardiff neighborhood, near Syracuse. Using many native citizens as well as outsiders, colloquial speech, and numerous scenes, these collaborators show "how most folks acted in 1869 when they heard a giant was dug up over to Cardiff."

The "friend of the show" is a casually dressed Narrator, "a friendly soul of the countryside" serving much the same function as the Stage Manager in *Our Town*. His purpose is to express homely philosophy on the Cardiff Giant yarn as a chapter in human folly and superstition. He also serves to "sort of keep things moving" and to guide both country folks and city visitors on "the Big March to Cardiff." His chatty observations addressed to the audience suggest that "things are humming" throughout Onondaga Valley. In fact, as the days pass everybody keeps "getting all het up about the wonder" and flock "to Cardiff like flies to a sugar barrel." The scene at the Newell farm, near Cardiff village, begins to resemble a county fair. Throughout the simple action the big tent covering the excavated giant is crowded with "home folks" jostling against visiting professors, scientists and pseudo-scientists, preachers and skeptics, newspaper reporters, and other curious onlookers. That great American showman, Phineas T. Barnum, who tried to buy the giant, skeptical Colonel Robert Ingersoll, aggressive Mrs. Bloomer, and David Harum, shrewd "hick town horse swapper" and banker, join with other spectators in having their say about this "showcase for human folly . . . this superstitious hokum." By the time that the humbug is exposed, the perpetrators of the hoax have filled up their cash box many times over.

Cardiff Giant is a lively expression of the time sense motivating writers of the thirties and later, as various regional playwrights belonging to academic circles revealed a disposition toward dramatizing the vanishing phenomenon of small-town life. Among the more creative campus organizations, the Carolina Playmakers and the players at Wisconsin have been noted in earlier discussions of Thomas Wolfe, Zona Gale, and others. Since 1938 a third group associated with the Cornell University Theatre and sponsored by the Rockefeller Foundation and the National Theatre Conference has been drawing dramatic material from the color and atmosphere, lore, legend, song, and story of their provincial communities. Under the direction of Professor Drummond, the Project for New York State Plays has resulted in the writing and production of regional plays, mostly short enough for little theater productions and those of other amateur groups in rural and small-town communities and schools in New York.

Like most of the dramatizations made by the Carolina Playmakers, the student-written plays published in *More Upstate New York Plays* and other collections frequently re-create village and farm life of the past. Arthur Lithgow's "The Big Cheese," for example, offers an amusing picture of a provincial entertainment popular in the 1830's: a public auction conducted by a Colonel Thomas S. Meacham, a born showman with a predilection for the grandiose, who entertained villagers and farmers in Sandy Creek, Oswego County, New York, by his vulgar buffoonery and publicity stunt in auctioning a gigantic cheese. Professor Drummond and Phyllis Murray's "A Little House in Angelica" provides "whimsy spiced with sentiment" in bringing to life the somewhat diminutive charm of a western New York village of years past. "Unpaved Roads," by E. L. Karmack and J. J. Haberman, is set in a small dairy town in Madison County, not too far from the Cherry Valley Turnpike.[25] A realistic playlet dramatizing the desertion of younger villagers to the urban areas, "Unpaved Roads" portrays also the plight of overworked Dr. John Palmer, an elderly country veterinarian in need of help from his son. As one comedy of "courtin' " reveals, the problem of love and marriage on the early frontier could often be reduced to the simplest terms: there were no girls to marry. Lauren Williams, in "Over Fourteen: and Single" (1942), tells the story of how five young bloods organized, during the summer of 1820, a "Confederacy" to lure eligible maidens to Farmersville Village, in present Cattaraugus County. Robert Gard's little play, "Let's Get On with the Marryin' " (1942), centers his plot around the duties of a parson in the frontier settlement of Laketown. Such plays as these typify the village material appearing in some of the more than sixty plays produced at Cornell since 1938.

Once Upon a Yesterday

The successful playwright whose dramatic scope is never outwardly wide, whose characters are as commonplace as old shoes, and whose subject matter rarely rises above the ordinary routine of small-town life, necessarily must possess compensating gifts. William Motter Inge, native of Independence, Kansas, has an abundance of such gifts. Possessed of extraordinary perception, sensitivity, and compassion, he has the rare and admirable trait of expressing the frustrations and dilemmas of the so-called little man "without being patronizing and without the sentimentalist's knack of killing him with a dubious sort of kindness, à la Saroyan."[26] His dramatic aim, as expressed in a series of midwestern and southwestern community plays, is modest but almost invariably true. As the creator of a large number of well-realized, though ordinary, men, women, and children, Inge has portrayed the fortunes and misfortunes of their domestic lives with integrity and sympathy. Beginning with his first Broadway production, *Come Back, Little Sheba*, which the Theatre Guild presented in New York on February 15, 1950, Inge's career has revealed him as "the modest poet of the American landscape of failure and near failure."[27] Although limited in range and depth of technique and style, Inge's stagecraft has captivated both stage and motion picture audiences by its familiar realism.

Come Back, Little Sheba, which introduced Inge to Broadway as an original playwright and virtually made a star of comedienne Shirley Booth, is honest Americana. As a bare, almost clinical characterization of a middle-aged and intellectually mismated couple, the play exhibits a young playwright's genuine concern for hapless people, beset by secret frustrations and dreams of a better life—for small-town natives who, transplanted to a small midwestern city, live lives "of quiet desperation," knowing in themselves that their narrow world will not improve, yet clinging to hope. The nucleus of this regional play is a graphic picture of "little, repressed people living, with all their inhibitions, moral confusion, awry ideals and profound isolation, in a kind of Middletown heartbreak house."[28] The atmosphere—"a drab spiritual desert"—is somewhat lightened by an element of tenderness, notably at the finale. Though Lola Delaney, a slatternly yet good-natured wife, goes about mournfully calling for her lost dog Sheba while her husband Doc, his hope of finishing medical school having long since faded, lives as a lonely chiropractor who once had been a dipsomaniac, in the end they come to rely upon each other. Veteran actor Sidney Blackmer brought real distinction to his sensitive portrayal of Doc. His feeling of empathy seemed especially strong in his understanding not only of the desperation which drives Doc berserk, but also of the quiet desperation revealed by Doc upon his return home from the City Hospital. Shattering though this crisis is, both Doc and Lola survive, by learning something fundamental about their years together. At the end a renewed feeling of mutuality faintly suggests a more stabilized future for these two.[29]

In short, according to a first report on the play cited by Phyllis Anderson, associate producer, on February 8, 1949, here is

a play that at first seems to be almost nothing. But then it grows on you by its little touches and its effects gained by indirection until, by the end, you are genuinely moved. It is impossible to convey in a report the little touches of pity and understanding that make up the texture of this play. In a sense, it illustrates Thoreau's "All men lead lives of quiet desperation . . ."

With the Guild production of this painful play, at the Booth Theatre in 1950, Inge began to be associated with Tennessee Williams and Arthur Miller as an important "new voice."

Come Back, Little Sheba, its meaning deepened by the skilful direction of Daniel Mann, obviously was the creation of a talented playwright. Nevertheless, it was a bit bare and restricted. Just three years later Inge broke through into a much wider world with a new play titled *Picnic: A Summer Romance*, a moving drama about a young drifter and a new group of Kansas townspeople who, during a brief summer association, learn a lot of simple yet profound things about each other. This penetrating comedy was presented first by the Theatre Guild at the Music Box Theatre, in New York City, on February 19, 1953. As Richard Watts, Jr. observed in the *New York Post, Picnic* was "a dramatic hit of vast proportions," with Joshua Logan staging it "with all of his remarkable flair and theatrical knowledge." Jo Mielziner's lighting and set design—". . . the porches and . . . the yards of two small houses that sit close beside each other in a small Kansas town"—and the acting of a brilliant cast made this hit production, in Brooks Atkinson's opinion, "a dramatic achievement of first rank." Moreover, this play won for Inge the Drama Critics' Circle Award, the Pulitzer Prize for 1953, and the firm establishment of the career launched with *Come Back, Little Sheba*.

The background action, pivoted around a traditional form of small-town entertainment, concerns an entire citizenry's enjoyment of an annual Labor Day picnic, held in a river park. The primary action, in the view of Walter Kerr, "is a whisper of a play." Several lonely women, as seen against the background of the Mielziner setting (two porches leaning lazily across a backyard) seem to be marking time, as if expecting some fulfilment which has never been realized. In desperation they plan picnics to give themselves an excuse—to let something thrilling change the monotony of their lives. Widowed Flo Owens, who rents rooms to eke out a living, worries about the future of her two teen-age daughters: beautiful, nubile, but not too intelligent Madge, played by Janice Rule, and alert, tomboyish Millie, played by Kim Stanley, who loves to read fiction and art history. Neighborly Helen Potts, "another but older widow lady," has devoted her life to a now aged and invalid mother, a shrew who earlier broke up Helen's youthful marriage. Fortyish Rosemary Sydney, inimitably portrayed by Eileen Heckart, is Flo's roomer and a schoolteacher, anxious to get married but not too happy over her romancing with Howard Bevans, a pragmatic and permanently smiling storekeeper, small, thin, and rapidly approaching middle age. Rosemary's fellow teachers, also spinsterish and frustrated, strive to create excitement by having an occasional lunch with other "girls" at the local hotel. An agonizing and climactic scene occurs when unfulfilled Rosemary and the two dispirited widows, gathered on the Owens porch to depart for the Labor Day picnic, watch Madge and Hal Carter as they begin to dance, moving together in ecstatic rhythm. Their graceful dancing seems to suggest that the boy and girl are destined for each other. The life-hungry women watch in longing, helpless before the fact of their mischances in youth.

Youth also has its frustrations. Millie, at home in her private world of books, envies her sister Madge because of her beauty and her way with boys. In turn, Madge, who barely finished high school, is afraid of the town's affluent college crowd, even though for the summer she has enjoyed a romance with Alan Seymour (Paul Newman's role), member of a well-established family. She yearns to leave her job as a dime-store salesgirl to find happiness in Kansas City. Her dilemma becomes all the more confusing when Hal (played by Ralph Meeker), a brawny and penniless young vagrant, chances to stop by Mrs. Potts's house "willing to do a few chores in exchange for breakfast, and exuding the sort of animal vitality calculated to stir a few fires." Inge wrote a double resolution of Madge's problem. In the original conclusion, she does not follow her new lover to the city, but resigns herself to remaining in the town, still mindful of her mother's earlier warning that if she did not marry Alan, "first thing you know, you'll be forty, still selling candy in the dime store."[30] Yielding to Director Logan's persuasion, Inge created a more optimistic Broadway version wherein Hal leaves alone, but shortly afterward Madge, disregarding warnings and taking little heed of her mother's own bleak existence, follows her lover to the city.

There has been criticism of Inge's sacrifice of sensitivity and pathos for the sake of calculated effects. Sometimes the comedy lines seem contrived; and, as Kerr felt, "characters pose, prance, pause, and writhe with alarming mathematical efficiency."[31] Also, is the language of the play poetic enough for the wistful ambitions of the characters? Nevertheless, in *Picnic* Inge achieved a rueful sense of comedy in his authentic portrayal of the upsetting of the even tenor of small-town routine by the arrival of a vital and semicollegiate drifter. The "tragical-comical" excitement which broke out in the neighborhood provides a fluid drama flowing with provincial life—humorous, casual, honest.

On March 2, 1955, Inge's phenomenal success in the area of Broadway entertainment skyrocketed with the premiere of his new comedy, *Bus Stop*, at the Music Box Theatre. Although its three acts are held together by an external and arbitrary situation, the stalling of a bus when a blizzard blocks a Kansas highway, *Bus Stop* offers events, characters, and personal revelations of greater variety than those to be found in *Picnic*. The play's levels of interest are more diverse also, ranging from farce to pathos, from normal conduct to poignant abnormality. A Broadway hit, it was "lusty and sad, extravagant and sober, ordinary and extraordinary, deceptively banal in situation and curiously original in treatment."[32] While some of the characters—a Kansas sheriff, a husky bus driver, a scholarly derelict, and a rough-and-ready cowboy—were stock figures, Harold Clurman's effective staging of the play highlighted Inge's fresh treatment of familiar small-town material.

These various levels of interest arise from a restricted action which takes place in a street-corner restaurant in a country town about thirty miles west of Kansas City. For a limited time—from one until five on a bitter cold morning—the stranded passengers, a motley group, are sheltered and fed in the dingy, but cozy and warm, restaurant. The operator is a fortyish and seasoned grass widow, Grace Hoylard (Elaine Stritch's role), who is assisted by a part-time waitress, Elma Duckworth. As played by Phyllis Love, this idealistic high-school student is all too easily impressed by the impromptu Shakespearean recitals and sentimental avowals of love by a middle-aged passenger, Dr. Gerald Lyman. Elma does not recognize the truth that Dr. Lyman actually is an alcoholic derelict, who for years has been unable to fulfill either his marital responsibilities or his college teaching appointments.

Dr. Lyman's plight, alcoholism coupled with nympholepsy, is matched by the dilemmas of other minor characters: by Grace's loneliness since her husband "skipped town" and the secret longing for personal fulfilment which plagues Virgil Blessing, a guitar-playing cowboy, now in his forties, who "was just gonna take bein' lonesome for granted." Having spent his life acting as a father to young Bo Decker, a loudmouthed cowboy from Timber Hill, Montana, "Virge" now finds himself without family and rootless. The principal searchers for personal happiness include the disturbed nightclub singer Cherie, played by Kim Stanley, and her abductor, rambunctious Bo Decker, played by Albert Salmi, whose bizarre love affair furnishes an element of comic theatricality tempered by a note of yearning for fulfilment. In the end, however, Bo's lonesomeness disappears when Cherie's prediction comes true: "And somewhere deep down inside me, I gotta funny feelin' I'm gonna end up in Montana." Inge's expertness in portraying minor characters is further displayed in his realistic characterization of the hefty and jovial bus driver Carl, who has an affair with Grace, and huge, saturnine Will Masters, who admires Grace. Both are scornful of easterners like Dr. Lyman, who "don't know anything about any of the country west of the Hudson River."

On June 3, 1947, Margo Jones opened her Dallas theater-in-the-round with a performance of Inge's *Farther Off from Heaven*, a thoughtful provincial play which ten years later (on December 5, 1957) opened at the Music Box in New York City under the new title of *The Dark at the Top of the Stairs*. As presented by Saint-Subber and Elia Kazan, this perceptive and tender portrayal of ordinary humanity is a study in contrarieties, with contrasting approaches to the central force of fear and disillusionment. Inge, in a *New York Times* statement reprinted in the original program, noted the play's symbolism: "The dark at the top of the stairs may represent any number of things to any number of people. To me it represented a fear of the future." Remembering his own childish dread about how he would meet life when he grew up, Inge tried to bring back into this play the very personal values which a group of Oklahoma townspeople sifted from their own existence and cherished against odds. In short, his conviction that man, in the midst of modern confusion and frightening change, needs faith in personal value is a significant part of the corpus of the play. As he has written, "I have tried to bring back into my play some very sustaining memories of people, in their sad, funny, courageous, and frightened ways of meeting life and trying to cope with it."

A penetrating drama of small-town ways, *The Dark at the Top of the*

Stairs offers a searing and fascinating examination of family love and strife in the oil-boom country of Oklahoma in the early 1920's. Inge observantly presents the violence and the domestic tirades, the humor and the tenderness and the tears in the small-town home of Rubin Flood, a harness salesman, and Cora, his wife to whom he has been married for seventeen years. Because of his bluff and crude ways, including a taste for "rotgut," Rubin at first suggests the stock Hollywood conception of a westerner of the period. As portrayed by Pat Hingle, however, Rubin becomes an individualized extrovert, whose emotional problems are masked, none too successfully, behind this bravado. Rubin's ways are not too fully understood by his wife, a handsome but rather prim young woman more concerned about their two children's emotional life. With good reason, too, for sixteen-year-old Reenie, though attractive, is painfully shy and introspective, while ten-year-old Sonny has retreated defiantly into a tinsel world of motion-picture stars, whose photographs he collects. Clearly the family ties are strained, as the parents' rifts have a devastating effect upon their children.

In the second act Inge concentrates on the elements of contrariety, portraying some other provincials who are getting no better than a draw in the battle with their painful realities. Cora's expansive older sister, Lottie Lacey, who also works defensively at being an extrovert; Morris Lacey, her sensitive husband, an Oklahoma City dentist who has the resigned gravity of a meek and defeated man looking back on his bachelorhood; and Sammy Goldenbaum, a Jewish cadet from a neighboring military academy who has suffered from both prejudice and lack of parental care, are all afraid of "the dark at the top of the stairs." Each seems to have the need for sympathetic understanding and forbearance in conquering his fears, prejudices, and problems. Their unhappiness finds a parallel in Rubin's tension, which stems from his inability to express his anxieties to Cora and from her failure to realize her usually confident husband's fear of the future. Their quarrel, resulting in Rubin's leaving home and turning for sympathy to his pool-hall pals and to Mavis Pruitt in Ponca City, serves to highlight the children's maladjustments, especially Reenie's sense of guilt over Cadet Goldenbaum's suicide. (Elia Kazan's strenuous direction pointed up the one time when the play seemed to lose its grip on its modest subject: the "only time the play is tragic—when the cadet finally has found the dark too forbidding to go on making the climb, and we learn, has become a suicide.")[33] In an all too facile resolution of the main action Rubin, having found a new job, returns home, quickly becomes reconciled with Cora, sends Reenie and Sonny to a movie, and draws his wife up the stairs. The implication is that this comedy of domestic relations is best resolved by love, the real master of the dark at the top of the stairs.

Regardless of its several flaws, *The Dark at the Top of the Stairs* is a moving, perceptive, and striking drama of the impact of the changing times of the twenties upon southwestern townspeople, as well as upon the town itself. As Rubin finally admits, "Times are changin', Cora, and I dunno where they're goin'." With the discovery of oil, the old and more democratic town life began to disappear. New school buildings, churches, modern stores, movie theaters, and a country club changed the physical appearance of the town. And all the while men were becoming millionaires overnight, "drivin' down the street in big limousines, goin' out to the country club and gettin' drunk, acting like they was the lords of creation." Under these new conditions Rubin, while acknowledging his fright, confessed that "a fellow's gotta get into the swim. There's nothing else to do."[34]

In his vigorous presentation Kazan had the services of designer Ben Edwards, who contributed a single set representing the harness man's home: "one of the scenic high points of the season—an authentic and wonderfully atmospheric horror," as one critic saw it. The excellent cast included, in addition to Hingle, Teresa Wright as Cora Flood, Charles Saari and Judith Robinson as the children, Eileen Heckart as Lottie Lacey, Frank Overton as her husband, and Timmy Everett as Sammy Goldenbaum.

By the 1959 season Inge had had four resounding successes in as many attempts on Broadway and had gained, within nine years, recognition as a leading playwright. Failure in the New York theater was something unknown to him. Nevertheless, by January, 1960, Inge freely acknowledged that the New York production of his new play, *A Loss of Roses*, was "a complete failure," although he regarded the script as timely and "the best play I've ever written."[35] Largely because of Shirley Booth's replacement by Betty Field and certain script changes, *A Loss of Roses* suffered from inadequate production. Its initial run, from November 28 to December 19, 1959, at the Eugene O'Neill Theatre ended after only twenty-five performances and at considerable financial loss.

As the realistic setting by Boris Aronson suggested, the action of the play takes place in the small and poor bungalow of widowed Mrs. Helen Baird, in a small town outside of Kansas City. The year is 1933, when both town and countryside are touched by the depression. While Inge gives attention to the bad effects of the depression on the community in general, the plot primarily offers a psychological study of Mrs. Baird, a tired-looking nurse in her middle forties who no longer strives to make herself sexually attractive, and her restless son Kenny, who has just arrived at manhood. Dissatisfied with both his home life and his routine chores at a local garage—where, however, his expertness as a repair mechanic brings him the patronage of the town's richer citizens—Kenny resents his mother's puritan and bossy ways and fusses about their mutual struggle against poverty. He seeks relief by drinking with neighbor "Jelly" Beamis and having clandestine affairs with "the trashiest girls in town." To insure Kenny's independence, and to allay her suspicion that she loves him too ardently, Helen urges her son to get married to a "nice" girl and go off to Wichita and a good job in an airplane factory.

Eventually Kenny does leave for Wichita, but not until his worldly and sexual experience has been widened by a momentary affair with a small-time tent-show actress in her early thirties. Years before, in an Oklahoma town, Lila Green had lived with the Bairds as a sort of friend and household servant. Now jobless because of the depression, she begs refuge in the Baird cottage until she can find a new job. (The part of the mother was played, in turn, by Miss Booth and Miss Field. Kenny's role was portrayed by Warren Beatty, while the older actress with whom he was too intimate was played by Carol Haney.) At first resentful of Lila's being assigned to his bedroom, Kenny at last reacts against his mother-fixation. Falling under the spell of Lila's gaiety and her voluptuousness, he goes to bed with her, while Helen is on night duty at the hospital. No doubt the production failure of the play stemmed in part from the resolution of the action, involving Kenny's quickly freeing himself of his sexual desires, after this single experience, by refusing to marry Lila. Her subsequent hysteria and attempted suicide are only a prologue to her final "loss of roses" by returning to Ricky Powers, a tent-show lover who wants her services as a model for pornographic photography. Helen's attempt to find solace in attending a revival meeting is followed by her reconciliation with Kenny just after he announces his decision to seek a better life in Wichita.

Unlike many small-town plays, A Loss of Roses offers no dramatization of class or race struggles. Rather, as Inge himself has explained, "It deals with individuals who, like people today seeking an inner peace in the midst of terrifying change, must come to deal with evil in their lives, either to be destroyed or to find themselves strengthened." Lila, trapped by circumstances, tries to find consolation in remembering a bouquet of roses which she had once given to a sadistic teacher in the knowledge that "when I gave away lovely presents, I couldn't expect to get them back . . ." And she sadly concludes that she never learned that lesson very well. As for Helen, she knows that whereas Lila's sins have been acknowledged, "Other people have lots of sins you never hear about."

In the words of his friend Tennessee Williams, Inge in his small-town plays has "uncovered a world within a world, . . . a secret world that exists behind the screen of neighborly decorum . . . [the world beneath] the genial surface of common American life."[36]

"Give us something different!"

Broadway will seemingly try anything in its search for oddities, but even an oddity has to be good for the best chance of success. Relevant to this interest in the unusual are various characterizations in more recent times of small-town nonconformists and occasional eccentric interlopers who appear on our stage as modern counterparts to quixotic Yankees and other village oddities of past eras. Sometimes these more recently created provincials are simple souls expressing the resistance, or the compliance, of native folk to disturbing patterns of social and personal change. Again, they may be odd or perverted intruders whose presence upsets the otherwise even tempo of community life. This modern return to the idea of small-town dwellers and their peculiarities has been effected both by established playwrights and by gifted newcomers.

Frequently much use of satire characterizes the modernists' laughter not only at the quiddities of the past, but also at amusing provincial situations of a later date. Such an interpreter appeared in the twenties and thirties in the person of George S. Kaufman, whose flip treatments of fools and philistines made him a leading creator of satiric comedy in America. His full expression of the native comic spirit is grounded upon his keen insight into human behavior, his skilful manipulation of character distortion, and his inventiveness in creating dialogue, costumes, sounds, pantomime, and situations designed to provoke laughter.

His early comedy written in collaboration with Marc Connelly, *To the Ladies!* (1922), is a hilarious American counterpart to Barrie's *What Every Woman Knows*. Elsie Beebe, though only a simple young housewife of Nutley, New Jersey, becomes the guiding spirit of the household in an effort to insure the business success of her somewhat stupid and self-important husband, Leonard. In a satirically pictured public banquet scene, Leonard, who is relying upon a trite speech which he has memorized from a speech manual, is paralyzed with stage fright when he hears his business rival responding to their pompous employer, Mr. Kincaid, with the identical speech. Quickly sensing the embarrassing situation, Elsie, when the time comes for Leonard to speak, rises and explains that her husband is suffering from laryngitis and that she will try to speak from his notes. Much to Leonard's relief, Elsie cleverly makes her little talk so thoroughly appealing in its human warmth and naturalness that Kincaid gives Leonard a coveted promotion. Beneath its lightness of tone this comedy presents a more serious idea. Elsie, remarkably well played by Helen Hayes, learns that a young wife who saves her husband from being scorned by his associates gains glory for herself.[37]

Among the Kaufman satires *The Man Who Came to Dinner*, a 1939 collaboration with Moss Hart, is the most brilliant. Truly a masterpiece of invective, the comedy exposes an intruder in the home of well-to-do Mr. and Mrs. Ernest W. Stanley in a midwestern small town, Mesalia, Ohio. Raising the technique of insult to a fine art, the collaborators plotted hilarious action in friendly parody of the lecture tours of Alexander Woollcott, to whom the play is dedicated. An accident confines Sheridan Whiteside, egocentric lecturer and broadcaster, to the Stanley home, where in the course of a lecture engagement he has been an unwilling dinner guest. Here, confined to a wheelchair, he becomes a most irritating intruder, who takes over the house, insults his hosts, interferes with the affairs of their children, orders their servants about, entertains convicts and greets the press, accepts gifts of penguins and cockroaches, broadcasts his customary sentimental Christmas program for the Cream of Mush Company, monopolizes the telephone, and breaks up a love affair between his long-suffering secretary Maggie and a local newspaper editor. An insufferable *enfant terrible*, middle-aged Whiteside so maliciously disturbs a decorous household, and the entire town as well, that the play, like Restoration comedy, becomes a comedy of bad manners. "In the New York production Monty Woolley 'out-Woollcotted' his original endowing Whiteside with a malice less petulant and more demoniac."[38]

In *The Bicycle Rider of Beverly Hills* William Saroyan (1908-   ) offers a glimpse of his early glowing vision of the world and its wonders: "It is the dirt of the world with the sun shining on it that astonishes a poet when he is a boy." Nevertheless, his boyhood spent in Fresno, his birthplace in California's beautiful San Joaquin Valley, was not an easy existence. His parents were natives of Bitlis in Turkish Armenia, the father being a Presbyterian preacher and writer, educated in an American mission at Bitlis. When the father, turned California grape-grower, died in 1910, William, then only two, was placed in an orphanage so that his impoverished mother could work in a cannery. Five years later the boy, reunited with his family and beginning his school years, started hawking newspapers, wandering about the Fresno streets, sitting through evening movies, working as a telegraph messenger (after just two years of high school training), and eventually laboring in the vineyards and trying other jobs. Oddly enough, such a hard, disorganized life failed to dim young Saroyan's *joie de vivre*. In *The Bicycle Rider* he has frankly confessed his youthful enjoyment of the most ordinary scenes, events, and people: "In the most common-place, tiresome, ridiculous, malicious, coarse, crude, or even crooked people or events I had to seek out rare things, good things, comic things, and I did so . . ." A note appended to his most successful play, *The Time of Your Life* (1939), also suggests his optimism and zestful spirit: "In the time of your life, live—so that in that good time there shall be no ugliness or death for yourself or for any life your life touches. Seek goodness everywhere, and when it is found, bring it out of its hiding-place and let it be free and unashamed."[39]

Goodness seems to have fascinated Saroyan. Modern questers, he believed, should try to "discover in all things that which shines and is beyond corruption." In his own youthful questing along streets, in honky-tonks and other popular hangouts, he early observed life's paradoxes, such as ". . . certain failures seemed to me the greatest men in town." His ebullience and optimism, however, seem matched by his deep concern about the sorrow caused by the shame and the terror of the world, by its evil and ungodliness. In his small-town plays, as elsewhere, he exhibits a compassionate tolerance of both the good and the bad, in much the same manner as did one of his favorite poets, Whitman. His early dramatic experiment began modestly in a simple story, "The Man with the Heart in the Highlands," which first appeared in a privately printed book titled *Three Times Three* and released in December, 1936. A one-act play bearing the title of this story was published in the *One-Act Play Magazine*, edited by William Kozlenko, who suggested that the story contained a play. From this germ came a long one-act play, a surrealist fable retitled *My Heart's in the Highlands*, which, under the direction of Robert Lewis, was offered as a Group Theatre production at the Guild Theatre in New York City on April 13, 1939. Critical reaction to the five performances was quite varied, with most of the critics bewildered by the play's vague messages not only about the misery and sorrow of the world but about its infinite delights and mysteries as well.[40] (A similar spirit pervades Saroyan's widely known novel, *The Human Comedy*, later made into a movie.)

Remembered for its symbolic, surrealistic *mise en scène*, *My Heart's in the Highlands* calls to mind the multiple sets of medieval miracle plays by showing simultaneously on stage "an old white, broken-down, frame house" and Mr. Kosak's grocery store on San Benito Avenue in Fresno. Timed from August to November, 1914, and plotted without indicated act-divisions, the artless story dramatizes the frustrations of the impoverished Alexander family living in this dilapidated house: nine-year-old Johnny, a newsboy "overwhelmed at the glory of ice cream in the world"; his penniless and talentless father Ben, whose poems have been rejected by the *Atlantic Monthly*; and an aged grandmother who speaks only Armenian. The protective little boy worships his father as a genius fighting against an unappreciative world. In spite of their living by theft or fraud, these three welcome to their home white-whiskered Jasper McGregor, a retired Shakespearian actor who has escaped from a home for the aged. A dreaming Scot, McGregor emotionally stirs his hosts and their neighbors by playing Robert Burns's "My Heart's in the Highlands" as a plaintive bugle solo. In return, the neighbors bring gifts of fruits and vegetables, enough for a feast.

Eighteen days later, as he is being taken back to the home by guards, McGregor praises Johnny and Ben for their lofty, pure, and delightful spirit. By November the Alexanders face eviction because of their failure to pay their rent. Although understanding Mr. Kosak cancels their grocery bill, Ben attempts to meet his obligations by gifts of his poems to young Esther Kosak, who weeps because they are so beautiful. As they prepare to vacate their house for the new renters, the Alexanders suddenly hear bugle notes. Again independent McGregor has eluded his caretakers. Just as the guards reappear, the dauntless actor recites jumbled Shakespearian passages and then dies, while the little boy, looking on, thinks that he is simply playing King Lear. For the boy, the poet, and the grandmother the bugle sounds, reverberating in the distance, give a symbol of hope. Still they remain homeless.

At the finale Saroyan attempts to strengthen the playlet's emotional appeal by emphasizing the misfortunes of the sensitive artist or poet in a philistine world. Finally realizing that they no longer have a home, young Johnny remarks, "I'm not mentioning any names, Pa, but something's wrong somewhere." All the while, the father has the kind of courage implied by his consoling words to Johnny: "There will always be poets in the world!" Regardless of whether critical opinion classified this experiment as "a parable of beauty," "a fascinating crackpot comedy," "a bit of virtuoso scribbling," "the freest of fantasias," or the "madcap saga of a poet," Saroyan's simple story may be remembered as "a play filled with affection for small people, for the innocents of this world who long dimly for a beauty they but vaguely understand." In his portrayal of this Fresno family and their associates, Saroyan, fully sympathetic with the plight of the dispossessed, was apparently trying to show "how starved, yet constant, is mankind's love for beauty." Moreover, this little play expresses Saroyan's feeling "that the great people of the earth are not the 'big' men whose greatness is measured by the number they have slain but the little men who rise to greatness by the gallantry with which they meet their privations and sustain their dreams."[41]

Saroyan has the talent of simply glimpsing a few human beings and evoking from them moods and situations of compelling emotion. This he does again in a later play, *Hello Out There*, manipulating the theatre "as frankly as a musician pulling out the sob-stops on the Music Hall organ . . . " Written in early August, 1941, this superb one-acter was first presented at the Lobero Theatre in Santa Barbara on September 10, as the curtain raiser to Shaw's *The Devil's Disciple*.[42] In September, 1942, Eddie Dowling, who had starred in *The Time of Your Life* (1939), presented the new play in New York, in conjunction with a revival of G. K. Chesterton's *Magic*. Emotionally stirring performances by Dowling and Julie Haydon added much to Saroyan's reputation as a playwright of marked sincerity.

Like Williams' *Orpheus Descending*, *Hello Out There* dramatizes, with directness and deep emotional force, the cruelty of a mob in action against a falsely charged drifter. In this instance the lonely and frightened victim is a young gambler hounded by bad luck, whose months of vagabondage bring him to "this God-forsaken broken-down town" on the southern boundary of the Texas Panhandle. At a lunch counter there he is approached by a whore, who after inviting him to her home, threatens to make trouble if he does not give her money. When the youth fails to comply, the slut accuses him of rape and stirs the mob spirit in the town of Wheeling. At this point, the youth is spirited away by officers to the jail in nearby Matador, county seat of sparsely settled Motley County. At curtain rise the youth, restless in his cell and suffering from a head wound, is kidding the world by calling out dramatically: "Hello—out there!" The only answer is a very sweet and soft "Hello," spoken in a girl's voice.

This chance meeting, furnishing the core of the play, brings together two victims of loneliness: the unnamed prisoner and Emily Smith, cook and janitress for the jail. For a brief time these two hard-pressed young people enjoy a feeling of mutuality, as they talk about their personal problems, such as their "trying for the best all the time and never getting it." The girl remembers her own beauty-starved existence. "It's so lonely in this town," she says. "Nothing here but the lonesome wind, lifting the dirt and blowing out to the prairie." In this plain but sympathetic girl, herself imprisoned in an unhappy home and unfeeling town, the youth momentarily satisfies his need for companionship, which he regards as the way to good luck. For a little while he forgets the "little punk people" who "rape everything good that ever was born." He even hopefully proposes that the two of them escape to San Francisco, with its "cool fogs and sea-gulls," its "ships from all over the world," its "seven hills," and "little streets [that] go up and down." But such yearning, expressed in poetic rhythms, ends in utter futility as the cowardly husband of the whore, urged on by the mob outside the jail, fires three times into the cell, killing the young prisoner. Callously the whore slaps the girl, calling her a "little slut," as the young man's body is carried away.

Hello Out There drew plaudits from the critics. Its simple expression of human feeling, its poetic passages, and the intensity of its social implications made this little play one of Saroyan's best—"compassionate, direct, throbbing with suspense, and lighting a sordid situation with beauty."

During the forties and fifties, as folklore societies and their publications began stimulating widespread interest in regional life, folkways and traditions were discovered and interpreted anew by many creative writers throughout the country. Among these, certain playwrights, contemporaries of Wolfe, Green, Williams, Faulkner, and others discussed earlier, took advantage of the literary possibilities of the southern folk tradition to fashion plays delineating both the tragic and the comic aspects of human experience in small towns and the environing countryside.

Such plays have a common thread of interest not only in the portrayals of quirky characters but in the picturing of meeting places familiar to any townsman: boardinghouses, modest hotels (often run-down mansions), an occasional café, general merchandise stores, and, in one instance, a courtroom. For example, George Batson's *Magnolia Alley* (presented at the Mansfield Theatre in New York in April, 1949) is a three-act comedy centering around Laura Beaumont, a kindhearted pleasure-loving landlady, and her boarders in a small southern town. Julie Harris, Jessie Royce Landis, and Jackie Cooper had featured roles. Two years later Lillian Hellman's *The Autumn Garden*, under the direction of Harold Clurman, was presented by Kermit Bloomgarden at the Coronet Theatre in New York. Experimenting with a somewhat loose form of dramaturgy, Miss Hellman achieved a somber portrayal of social degeneration and marital failure, set against the background of the Tuckerman boardinghouse in a resort town on the Gulf of Mexico, a hundred miles from New Orleans. The time is the end of the season, in September, 1949, when the regular summer boarders are preparing to return to their homes. Already the signs of autumn are visible in the Tuckerman garden, symbols of the autumnal elements marring the happiness of individual lives within the group.

And this motley group of boarders and staff exhibits Miss Hellman's keen perception of the strength and the weakness of human nature. Moreover, her evocation of scene is highly artistic. The town itself, though now a resort place, offers a cross section of southern town life, with its old families dominating the social scene, inviting to their receptions and teas only the most acceptable of the summer visitors. Set against this exclusive background, the commodious Tuckerman place, now a summer guest house with its former elegance somewhat faded, symbolizes the better days once enjoyed by handsome Constance Tuckerman, former New Orleans socialite turned landlady. Her paying guests, mostly in family groups, suggest once again a familiar small-town conflict, the inevitable clash between the "Ins" and the "Outs." Mrs. Mary Ellis, still sprightly though in her seventies, is a New Orleans *grande dame*, wielding strong influence over her daughter Carrie and the latter's bookish son Frederick. (There is the faint suggestion that Fred has had a homosexual relationship with an older man.) Family snobbishness stands in the way of Fred's complete happiness with his fiancée, Sophie Tuckerman, Constance's German-born niece who assists with the housework. General Griggs, a good-looking man of fifty-three, is so bored with his socially ambitious and shallow wife Rose, "ex-pretty, soft-looking and about forty-three," that he plans to divorce her and seek happiness alone. Florence Eldridge was superb as Rose Griggs, who actually was suffering from a serious illness.

Fortyish Edward Crossman (Kent Smith's role), once a member of Constance's social set, at the last wearily tells her that he no longer loves her. Then there is Constance's excitement about the expected arrival of the town's expatriate and her former lover, portrait painter Nicholas Denery (Frederic March) and his chic wife Nina (Jane Wyatt). In one way or another, all these summer folk are decadent; but the most surprising of all, in the end, is young Sophie, who breaks her engagement and succeeds in blackmailing the Denerys for a large sum of money to defray her return to Germany. A concluding autumnal note returns the story to Constance. Her eventual disillusionment, occasioned by Nick's philandering with Sophie and her realization of his lack of real talent as a painter, causes Constance to regret "all these years of making a shabby man into the kind of hero who would come back some day all happy and shining."[43] At curtain fall, when Crossman rejects her proposal of marriage, Constance finds some consolation in believing that "most of us lie to ourselves, darling, most of us."

In this dramatized microcosm of resort town society, "Miss Hellman, perhaps striving for a symbolic representation of the failure of society, made her indictment too general to be wholly effective, and her tough-fibred resolution too dubious to be gratifying."[44]

In 1951, the same year that saw the staging of Miss Hellman's story of decadent "autumn garderners," Carson McCullers, in *The Ballad of the Sad Café*, was bringing to life a strange lot of earthy inhabitants of a small Georgia mill town. Here, as in *The Member of the Wedding*, her vision of folk experience is exceedingly rich in memorable community types. Eleven years later and only a few seasons after the Broadway production of his "absurd drama" *The American Dream*, young Edward Albee (1928-   ) converted Mrs. McCullers' haunting novella into a folk play "flecked with weird, halting poetry." Critically received as "a spectacular tour de force" and "a shimmering poem of dark beauty," Albee's play—also called *The Ballad of the Sad Café*—was recognized from its opening on October 30, 1963, at the Martin Beck Theatre as a notable addition to contemporary drama. Under Alan Schneider's direction, *The Ballad* won plaudits as a haunting and potent drama, called by Henry Hewes, *Saturday Review* critic, "the most fascinating and evocative piece of work by an American playwright (or perhaps one should say by two American playwrights) this season."

Albee's gift for stunning dramatic power first appears in his choice of a flashback type of central structure, the device of recall somewhat suggestive of the technique in *The Glass Menagerie* or in *Orpheus Descending*. At intervals throughout the action an unnamed Narrator recalls the strange events which for a period of years agitated the simple folk in a "not very old cotton mill town" in swampy Georgia back-country. While this action takes place in a southern mill town, Negroes were not involved; yet Schneider (with Albee's approval) diverted attention from the principal characters by assigning Roscoe Lee Browne, a Negro, to the role of Narrator in a play restricted to whites.

Told without an intermission, this tale of "a lonesome town—sad—like a place that is far off and estranged from all other places in the world" begins on a hot August afternoon with the Narrator's recital about a two-storied boarded-up house alongside a miserable main street. Eight years earlier this large house had been the center of the town's activity, when its owner, Miss Amelia Evans, operated a general store and a café on its first floor. As the play opens, the house, with its shut-

tered windows, seems a place of the dead. Rather, it has become Miss
Amelia's self-chosen prison, where, like O'Neill's Lavinia Mannon, she
now lives alone alienated from the gossipy town which she once dominated. As the Narrator recalls, there are two stories to be told about
this shuttered house: how the café began and how it died, thus silencing
the "great gatherings on Saturday evenings."

Later in the action a thoughtful query from the Narrator—"But what
sort of thing is love?"—suggests the core of the play and an answer to
the seemingly peculiar actions of the outlandish folk in the town's recent
history.[45] Answering his own question, the Narrator offers "the curt truth
that, in a deep secret way, the state of being loved is intolerable to
many"—an echo of Albee's obsession with sterility. So it must have been
with mannish Miss Amelia, who was "so big: you more like a man."
(The nearest counterpart to her in modern drama is oversized Josie
Hogan in *A Moon for the Misbegotten*.) In the violent conflicts of the
plot, three principal characters, in different ways, are subject to the
condition of love: land-greedy Amelia Evans, played by Colleen Dewhurst; her homosexual Cousin Lymon Willis, an imperious hunchbacked
dwarf and whining mischief-maker; and handsome Marvin Macy, a
loom-fixer at the mill who, after an awkward courtship marries Miss
Amelia in her nineteenth year. As the Narrator reports, no good ever
came of the loves of these three.

And the worst of all was Miss Amelia, whose lonely condition subjected her to several forms of love. As a motherless child, she knew love
of kin through her close relationship with her father, who taught her how
to operate his store and a nearby still for profit. Thus early acquiring a
greed for money, Amelia, after her father's death, began demanding cash
for all purchases, including liquor. Also, she gained control of cotton
land by foreclosing mortgages and domineered over her simple neighbors
as she sold them secretly compounded cures for the croup and other
ailments. Most of all, some quirk in her nature wrecked her marriage.
She even sold Marvin's courtship gifts. On their wedding night she
caused village tongues to wag by spending the hours going over the
store's account books. Thereafter, during the ten days of their life
together, she refused to become a wife to him. Desperately trying to win
her favor, Marvin at last deeded his ten acres of timberland to her.
Amelia's response shocked him. Accepting the deed, she still refused to
endure the act of sex. In the ensuing quarrel, she "cracked" Marvin on
the jaw hard enough to break a tooth, and, loading her shotgun, ordered
him to leave her house, never to return. Marvin's parting threat, in the
form of an abusive letter, was that "I gonna come back some day an' kill

you!" Thus impoverished emotionally and financially, Marvin turned to wandering and youthful wildness, which at last ended when he was given a penitentiary sentence.

Left alone then in her private domain, Miss Amelia one evening receives the strangest of visitors—a travel-stained dwarf claiming to be her Cousin Lymon from Cheehaw. He quickly ingratiates himself into the favor of this lonely, unruly woman. Now again the love of kin reasserts itself in Amelia's heart. In time her close companionship with the "broke-back runt" scandalizes the neighbors, but eventually it leads to the opening of a café in one part of the store. Soon the café becomes the town's chief entertainment spot, for lively talk, the drinking of Miss Amelia's home brew, and the eating of her fried chicken and other good food. All the while Cousin Lymon, circulating among the café patrons, puts on more and more airs, while Miss Amelia pockets money. The growing but sterile love between these two oddly paired cousins is peculiar enough to cause acidulous Emma Hale and other male and female gossips, a scandalmongering chorus, to predict some bad end. So it comes to pass, on "a night of terrible importance."

Unleashed and primitive violence, of the sort often featured in popular balladry, climaxes a series of events which results in calamity and great sadness and in Amelia's closing her café. The first of these events turns a certain Saturday night, when things are "swinging" at the café, into an "unholy holiday." Marvin's return from prison, after four years of detention, not only disrupts the folk hilarity at the café, but also marks the beginning of his revenge upon Amelia. First, he designedly wins the affections and admiration of Lymon, thus leaving Miss Amelia alone. Then his deliberate and defiant return to living quarters upstairs above the store and his lordly airs in the café climax in a brutal fight with Amelia. The struggle ends in utter defeat, in both body and spirit, for Miss Amelia, who is most broken by Lymon's puny efforts to assist Marvin. As she licks her wounds, the two men wreck the store, take what money there is in the café, pocket Miss Amelia's trinkets and jewelry, and leave town together, never to be heard of afterward. "The cafe, of course, never re-opened, and life in the town was that much drearier." After three years of watching for their return, while business in the store declined, ". . . Miss Amelia went indoors one night, climbed the stairs, and never again left her upstairs rooms."

So this is the absorbing ballad of a sad café, which, in Albee's adaptation, is replete with both dark tones and occasional folk humor, with compassionate insight into the needs of lonely people for love, and with entertaining portraits of the secondary characters. For sheer gusto and an intermingling of the serious and the ridiculous, the violent fight is difficult to match in fiction, though it calls to mind elements of Molly Segrim's mock-heroic fight in the graveyard, in Fielding's *Tom Jones.* But this fight, with all its brutality and vulgarity, goes beyond the mock-heroic. According to the recent appraisal of Allan Lewis, "The physical contact of the greased bodies, in a struggle to the death, is the substitute for the marriage act. Contact does not arouse sexual passion but ceremonial hate. Violence and destruction replace any joy of human association."

European visitors have repeatedly criticized the United States as a highly pragmatic nation, quite overlooking a different facet of our national character: our apparent fondness, especially as theatergoers, for impracticality and eccentricity. In the theatrical world, "Broadway, so generally the haven of routine stage art, is actually hungry for uninhibited, if not indeed bumptious, individuality."[46] Since the brief reign of Saroyan from 1939 to the early forties, the "familiar tribe of American stage simpletons," customarily identified with "pure in heart, the salt of the earth, and the democratic majority," has been augmented by various adolescents, retarded or repressed individuals, and naïve dreamers. In the history of native drama based upon "small town stuff," innumerable playwrights have experimented with the creation of impractical village eccentrics and discontented misfits. Truman Capote's first play, *The Grass Harp,* a delicately beautiful and imaginative dramatization of one of his novels, is one of the most esoteric of these plays of village eccentricity.

Opening at the Martin Beck Theatre on March 27, 1952, with Saint Subber as producer, *The Grass Harp,* a two-acter, proved to be a box office failure. Nevertheless, Saint Subber regarded his production as "an honorable failure" and a success as an important venture in the theater. In fact, the play's simplicity, honesty, and wholesomeness in its statement of basic truths in human relationships caused the young producer to become deeply involved in its production. Feeling strongly that there was good theater in this universal play about universal people, with something to say to everybody, he was proud to introduce young Capote (1925-   ) as a new theater talent.[47]

The first scene, opening the action in a small southern town on a Sunday afternoon in late September, is embellished by Cecil Beaton's extremely stylized painted drop of the full-tinted, two-story Talbo house. Within a few minutes another part of the drop begins to light up, revealing a dining room whose overdone elegance suggests that the Talbo sisters "nearly own this town." Catherine Creek is seated at the table trying to work a jigsaw puzzle. A chunky and rough-voiced Negro woman proud of her Indian heritage, she takes the liberties of a longtime servant to discuss the two Talbo sisters with Collin Talbo, their teen-age ward. Dressed as for a party, Catherine voices her dislike of Verena, the bossy "That One" who manages the family store; her love for delicate Dolly, "Dollyheart" who learned long ago from the gypsies how to brew a marketable "homemade dropsy cure that beats all"; and her distrust of Verena's dinner guest, Dr. Morris Ritz, a Chicago pharmacist who is eager to commercialize Dolly's secret formula. Dolly's shocked reaction to her sister's share in the scheme to market her cherished remedy as "The Gypsy Queen Dropsy Cure" is expressed in her unconventional rebellion, which suggests the play's theme.

This age-old theme, involving a quest for one's real self, is summed up by spinsterish Dolly, played by Mildred Natwick. A somewhat daffy dreamer and searcher, she has the urge to "find out what we truly are" and the desire "to be seen as this person . . . this woman that I am . . ."[48] In a peculiar manner she impulsively tries to break away from Verena's nagging and domination in order to save her precious remedy and, most of all, to discover, quite apart from family restrictions, the nature of her real self. Her escape ruse is simple. With the help of Catherine Creek and young Collin, Dolly escapes from the unendurable situation in their spacious home by seeking refuge in a childhood haunt, a tree house in "the River Woods down past the field of Indian grass." The conspiracy of these two rebellious and resolute women against "That One" leads to their meeting with various wanderers in the woods, including kindly Charlie Cool, a retired and widowed judge who is also trying to find himself. The second scene offers a realistic portrayal of town gossips as they comment on this scandalous escapade of Dolly's taking up residence in a roofless tree house. The second act concludes with a disappointing resolution of the action, making Dolly's rebellion appear as "much ado about nothing." Although she is offered the chance of happiness with a kindred spirit who enjoys listening with her to the grass harp—the music created by the wind as it causes the grass to tremble and the leaves to sway near the tree house—Dolly in the end rejects Judge Cool's proposal of marriage and returns to Verena, now somewhat chastened.

Under the theatrical conditions of the early fifties, theater patrons, lamenting the mediocrity of Broadway shows, were given various offerings of run-of-the-mill characters, stock situations, and formula plays. "Most of us," wrote Gassner in 1952, "would gladly check any rationality at the door of the theatre if we were sure to find relief from humdrum stage exercise." The circumstances of the time fostered a tendency to overpraise eccentric production "out of a sense of gratitude it affords." In some measure, discontent with *The Grass Harp* "stemmed from our feelings that he did not go far enough in the direction of carefree improvisation and iconoclasm." Opening the action with a small band of likable Louisiana eccentrics, Capote sent them away to a secluded tree house, left them there briefly for an amusing bout with windmills, and at the finale "restored the equilibrium of narrow small-town life by bringing them back to their former life after some humdrum contrivances."[49] There remains, however, Capote's artistry of style, which in the nature passages breaks into poetic prose.

Other contemporaneous experiments with iconoclastic provincial characters included *The Remarkable Mr. Pennypacker* (1953), *No Time for Sergeants* (1955), and *The Ponder Heart* (1956). Quite apart from its intrinsic merits as a theater piece, *Mr. Pennypacker* was not only Liam O'Brien's first Broadway play and Alan Schneider's first major directing assignment in New York, but also the initial offering of the newly founded Producers Theatre. Interested in using the best of existing talents, the Theatre's founders, Roger L. Stevens, Robert Whitehead, and Robert Dowling, also took an active interest in discovering and developing new talents. These aims were fulfilled in the successful *Pennypacker* production. Opening at the Coronet Theatre on December 30, 1953, this hilarious play gave a professional Broadway showing to a new playwright, a new director, and six new actors. It had the benefit of scenery and period costumes by Ben Edwards and a cast with two major stars, Burgess Meredith as Pa Pennypacker and Martha Scott as Ma Pennypacker, as well as highly respected featured players, Thomas Chalmers, Glenn Anders, Una Merkel, Phyllis Love, and Michael Wager.[50]

The play's successful run stemmed not only from a good script—an amusing satire on resistance to social change during the nineties—and a superior production, but also from O'Brien's evocation of Delaware's past in his delightful pictures of sedate Wilmington in the late spring of 1890. Set in the red brick home of the affluent Pennypackers, the four scenes remind one of the family pictures of this charming, maple-shaded town so vividly recalled by Henry Seidel Canby in his autobiographical *American Memoir*. In the Pennypackers' heavily corniced and cupola-capped house, family living centers around a cheerful, inviting parlor, a golden oak-trimmed octagonal room typifying Pa's idea of "something different." (Pa rails at the usual deliberately formal Delaware parlors of the time, with their gloomy walnut trims and funereal atmosphere.) More than his house, however, Pa—Horace J. Pennypacker, Jr. —is indeed "something different." As a freethinker, whose eight children adore him for his spirited show of self-reliance and his insistence that they, too, must think independently, Pa constantly irritates his decorous and socially established father, a successful manufacturer, horrifies his respectable wife, Ma Pennypacker, and scandalizes those conservative citizens of Wilmington who preach a boring small-town respectability.

An ardent reader of Thoreau's "Civil Disobedience," Pa has engaged in some remarkable and anti-Victorian activities "to stand sleepy old Wilmington on its head." He has waged campaigns in behalf of Darwinism, Henry George and the single tax, Shaw's "new woman" ("League for the Emancipation of the Female"), and other unorthodoxies. Although busily engaged in such causes, for twenty years Pa has kept secret his most remarkable escapade, his "cherishing" two wives. The sudden appearance of young Horace Pennypacker III at the Wilmington home baffles the household. All are shocked when Horace claims Pa as his father and reveals the startling news that he is the oldest of nine children. In short, for years Pa has been a bigamist, happily maintaining two households, one in Wilmington and another in Philadelphia. Pa's admission that Zeralda, his Philadelphia wife, died eight years ago helps Ma Pennypacker to become reconciled to her nonconforming but lovable husband. To the end, he remains remarkable, declaring that he deserves "*twice* the respect, *double* the admiration you give the ordinary, one horse power, model American husband."[51] And he refuses to give up wearing knickers, in imitation of his idol, George Bernard Shaw.

Devotees of both the theater and the cinema may well remember the agricultural community of Callville, Georgia, the hometown of Will Stockdale, a brand new inductee into Air Force routine. Will, a good-natured country boy was first brought to popular attention in *No Time for Sergeants*, an amusing provincial novel by Mac Hyman, a native of Cordele, Georgia. (William Faulkner described Hyman's tale as "one of the funniest stories of war or peace I ever read.") This novel, whose folk humor and use of the vernacular have been compared to the styles of Mark Twain and Ring Lardner, was dramatized by New Yorker Ira Levin as a two-act comedy. As a Maurice Evans production directed by Morton da Costa, this adaptation, which opened at the Alvin Theatre, New York, on October 20, 1955, made a star of Andy Griffith, himself a southerner, cast as the indestructible "cornfed" Will. Using the technique of an enveloping action, Levin opened his wonderful bit of modern folklore with a citizens' assembly at the Callville Township Meeting Hall in honor of "Callville's favorite son in uniform—Will Stockdale," who entertains the natives by a folksy recital of his experiences as an upstart private at an Air Force basic training center, and elsewhere on maneuvers. Now wearing a private's uniform and facing his fellow citizens, Will announces that he will talk on "How I Won My Medal." His casual lecture about "this medal that I got in the draft and I'm supposed to tell how I won it" is presented in the form of a flashback describing his ridiculous performance in the service; his nonplussed officers, including the greatly irritated Sergeant King; his buddies, especially "peewee" Ben Whitledge, inimitably portrayed by Roddy McDowall; his baffling the head psychiatrist and other testing experts at the Classification Center; and his beloved dog Old Blue.

As Will's drawled talk unfolds, it is obvious that Levin's comedy, "an almost continuously hilarious joke," is actually a set of variations on an overused small-town theme: the experiences of a raw village lad who gets his lumps in the world outside, this time in the Air Force rather than in the large city. Although this central motif is hackneyed, the story of Will's escapades and his return to Callville as a hero is broadly funny. The liveliness of the action is a tribute to director da Costa, who succeeded in achieving a farcical flow of events, working from a series of comic episodes. In the uniformly fine cast Roddy McDowall was most effective as the raw private eager to transfer to the Infantry, while Myron McCormick made out of Sergeant King at least a two-dimensional character rather than the usual stereotype. Don Knotts as the Callville preacher acting as master of ceremonies for Will's talk had only a minor role, but was amusing later as the Second Classification Corporal. Andy Griffith was such a natural for the role of Will Stockdale that the *New York Times* critic described his flair for characterizing the indigenous as "the most authentic dish of black-eyed peas, side meat and collard greens to be served up on the legitimate stage in a parcel of years."[52]

"When two principal characters of a modern-dress comedy address each other, in all seriousness, as 'dear heart,' . . . that comedy will be either hopeless or hilarious." *The Ponder Heart* is hilarious. Neither in the script nor on the stage does the comedy make much sense. Nevertheless, the Playwrights' Company's production, opening at the Music Box on February 16, 1956, introduced the "most benign comedy of the season" in the three-act adaptation made by Joseph Fields and Jerome Chodorov from a subtly comic story by Eudora Welty. The Music Box production, with Ben Edwards' designs of the Beulah Hotel, the Ponder home, and a small courthouse, disarmed spectators by its charm and its good-natured portrayal of one section of the South which Tennessee Williams overlooked.

The action is identified with the leisurely and neighborly life in and around Clay, a small town in a Deep South hinterland during the forties. The plot is as errant and wispy and filled with wanderlust as its principal character, Uncle Daniel Ponder, whose inheritance of cotton lands and other properties has freed him from the necessity to work. In him David Wayne found a showpiece perfectly suited to his flair for comedy. Affluent Uncle Daniel, though held in check somewhat by Edna Earle, his sorely tried niece and operator of the Beulah Hotel, is "a blissful, gracious and overly big-hearted lunatic whose capacity for childish happiness challenged the normal code of 'sane' behavior."

His most outlandish and irresponsible act is to marry, on a ninety-day trial basis, barefoot and vacuous Bonnie Dee Peacock, a silly country girl who resembles an Al Capp caricature. Bonnie Dee, an extravagantly naïve crossroads belle, is obviously just the kind of girl childish Uncle Daniel needs. Her delight in pistachio ice cream, in even the most ordinary of wedding gifts, and in a variety of the latest electrical appliances is matched by her engaging daftness in installing the refrigerator in the parlor of the Ponder mansion, an old-fashioned place not yet equipped with electricity. Edna Earle ridicules the girl's vacuity, saying: "She looks like she could sit all day and wonder how the C got through the L in the Coca-Cola sign." On the other hand, Edna Earle defends her uncle with considerable asperity, as she refutes the criticism of a gossipmonger: "People marry beneath them every day and I don't see a sign of the world comin' to an end. Don't be so *small town!*"[53]

In a little while Bonnie Dee, Uncle Daniel's "little fairy creature, . . . light and dainty," finds married life so strenuous that she flees from her dream house. Later she returns, willing to make another attempt at adjustment. Again admitting failure, she is ready to go back to her folks in the country when Daniel suggests a compromise. He proposes to live at the Beulah Hotel, allowing Bonnie Dee the privilege of living alone at the Ponder house and limiting his own visits to Saturdays when he will deliver her allowance and allow her to indulge in the hobby of cutting his hair.

Alas, on the first Saturday of this arrangement, a sudden storm blows over the town. Bonnie Dee, alone in the big house except for the frightened Negro woman Narciss, dies in a swoon of terror as "a big ball of fire comes slidin' down de air!" In time Daniel is charged with his wife's murder, and the last act is devoted to his most unconventional trial, an ordeal which he survives in his own indestructible fashion. During the trial scene, one of the funniest of court episodes, the defendant Daniel wanders in and out in the midst of the legal proceedings. He speaks out of turn, compliments the prosecuting attorney, and is unruffled when one of the witnesses, a village simpleton, refuses to leave the stand until he has been tipped a dime. Directed by Robert Douglas and enacted, in addition to David Wayne, by Una Merkel as Edna Earle, Sarah Marshall as Bonnie Dee, Juanita Hall as Narciss, and others, *The Ponder Heart* was well-directed whimsy.

New Glimpses of "the Groves of Academe" and Other Towns

In more recent years, the world of education has received vast coverage in newspapers, magazines, books, and other media. A veritable behemoth—our sprawling new "multiversity"—has come to dominate the educational scene, almost blotting out the older and more familiar image of the long-established preparatory school or college set down in a picturesque little town. While the "multiversity" has been looming larger and more complex, novels, stories, and plays about American school life have proliferated. Among such fictional interpretations, several plays have focused attention upon facets of preparatory school and collegiate life in the American small town.

As early as 1925 college life during the Jazz Age gave J. C. Nugent, an old-time popular actor, and his son Elliott, an alumnus of Ohio State, raw material for a humorously satiric dramatization of midwestern university activities. In *The Poor Nut* these collaborators poked fun at a timid, maladjusted youth lost in the rah-rah world of Ohio State, in Columbus. This "poor nut," unaccustomed to the hullabaloo associated with football heroes, cheerleaders, frat brothers, and sorority beauties, becomes an easy mark for more sophisticated undergraduates. A visiting beauty queen, "Miss Wisconsin," greatly confuses the ingenuous hero when she analyzes his sex life in terms of Freudian psychology. Much to his confusion, he finds himself unwillingly engaged to her. Luckily another coed frees him from this embarrassing predicament, so that in the end he begins to dream of a happy marriage and an instructorship in biology. Glimpses of the antics of collegians in a pre-"multiversity" world are given with good humor and a satiric touch.

In 1940 Elliott Nugent, by now an actor, collaborated with a former Phi Psi fraternity brother at Ohio State, that "puckish genius" James (Grover) Thurber, in the composition of one of the best modern college comedies. With their sophisticated wit, these friends created in *The Male Animal* a broad satire lampooning the anti-intellectualism which once stirred up a hubbub in an imaginary Ohio college town, presumably Columbus. After Herman Shumlin's production of the comedy at the Cort Theatre in New York City, Brooks Atkinson, in his *Times* review on January 10, 1940, invited his readers to "imagine one of Mr. Thurber's limp cartoons [from the *New Yorker*] translated into three acts of insane hubbub and you have a fair idea of the lark Mr. Nugent and he have pushed on the stage." The general background scene is a midwestern college town when the annual football game with Michigan ushers in a season of pandemonium, with alumni appearing everywhere: at the fraternity and sorority houses, the professors' homes, and the classrooms. The more domestic scene is the living room of the pleasant, inexpensive little house occupied by a young associate professor of English, Thomas or Tommy Turner and his wife Ellen, an extremely pretty and completely feminine woman of about thirty, who always acts from an emotional, rather than an intellectual, stimulus. Their twofold story, related in the anti-heroic manner of Thurber's solemn drawings and his whimsical realism sheathing a deadly satire, first concerns an ordinary uproar in Professor Turner's domestic life. Beyond this more private confusion, there arises a crisis concerning the professor's daring views on academic freedom.

A mentally active and complicated young man, Tommy Turner, played by Elliott Nugent, is, alas, physically unheroic. Soon he is perplexed by dilemmas. First, there is an "unofficial call" by the head of the English department, "tall, thin, distinguished-looking" Dr. Damon, who comes by the Turner home to give the couple a friendly warning about a student editorial in the *Literary Magazine*, scheduled to be circulated the next day when the campus is crowded with football fans. Strongly protesting the recent dismissal of several professors "because they have been ignorantly called Reds," the editor, one of Professor Turner's brightest students, condemns the college as "little more than a training school for bond salesmen, farmers, real-estate dealers, and ambulance-chasers." Branding the faculty as subservient to the trustees and the trustees as followers of a political belief closely resembling fascism, the editorial ends with a fervent note of thankfulness that "we still have one man left who is going ahead teaching what he believes should be taught." And this gentleman, none other than Turner, is lauded for promising to read before his classes Bartolomeo Vanzetti's moving declaration of faith, his last statement, along with Lincoln's letter to Mrs. Bixby, as models of good prose.

Inevitably the "hounds of bigotry and reaction" at once "set upon the trail of this courageous teacher." Thus unexpectedly brought to bay, Professor Turner, in spite of Ellen's pleas and the threat of losing his job, decides that he must fight for something much larger: the individual's right to free thought and speech in a repressive world. He realizes that he must read the Vanzetti letter as planned, though originally he had no thought of a crusade. The test of his courage comes when Turner, in his own home, reads the letter to bigoted Ed Keller, prosperous realtor and the college trustee with "the biggest voice and the strongest hand" in firing nonconforming faculty members.

While he meets this academic situation as a man of strong principle and intelligence at last moved to immediate and courageous action, Turner has still another problem to face. His second challenge concerns Ellen, whose anger at his unorthodox attitude leads her to contemplate an affair with Joe Ferguson, who during the days when he was a football hero was "sweet on her." Now back in town for the game, Joe at thirty-five is so big, handsome, successful, and appealing that Ellen yields to a reminiscent kiss. Later she shocks her husband and others by calmly announcing that she and Joe are going away together. Before the finale of the play, however, there is much comic appeal centering around Professor Turner's wavering, blundering effort to play the hero. A terrific binge with Michael, the radical editor of the *Literary Magazine*, offers a scene of considerable hilarity as Tommy broods on the fact that "a woman likes a man who does something." Finally spurred on by recalling that "even the penguin . . . stands for no monkey business where his mate is concerned," Tommy explains to Michael, in his best professional manner: "There it is, in us always, though it may be asleep. The Male animal. The mate." Tommy's ensuing fight with brawny Joe Ferguson leads to his reconciliation with Ellen. All in all, the genial tone of *The Male Animal* emphasizes that the college world of this era was "more mad than bad."

Undergirding the comic portrayal of the excitement stirring the people of this college town is the note of seriousness suggested by Professor Turner's pursuit of truth. Throughout the action delightful satire belittles those wealthy stadium builders and other self-important donors who try to reshape university standards by the dollar sign. Against this powerful force the young professor balances the greatness of ideas. In effect, Professor Turner was struggling against the Ed Kellers to preserve academic freedom of the kind which Emerson envisioned long ago for his "Man Thinking": "Gowns, and pecuniary foundations, though of towns of gold, can never countervail the least sentence or syllable of wit. Forget this, and our American colleges will recede in their public importance, whilst they grow richer every year."[54]

On the American stage during the early fifties a few community plays shifted interest from collegians in a razzle-dazzle world to confused teenage students, temporarily out of step with their small-town companions. The often used motif of youth's painful search for a true identity furnishes the core for both comic and more serious dramatizations of the standardized school as a microcosm unsuited to the needs of the sensitive nonconformist. For example, Ronald Alexander's much revised *Time Out for Ginger*, which opened at New York's Lyceum Theatre on November 12, 1952, four years after its composition as *Season with Ginger*, humorously portrays a series of domestic crises which disturb the usual harmonious relationship between Agnes and Howard Carol, upper-middle-class residents in a typical small town. Their daughters of high school age—Joan, Jennie, and Virginia, or Ginny—upset family routine with their high-spirited ways. The domestic furor grows mainly out of the girls' individual rebellions against dull school routines and restrictive rules. Neither Joan nor Jennie wants to do the required gym work; so Joan, in order to be excused from her gym class, manages to get the title role in the school's production of *Victoria Regina*. When, to her chagrin, she discovers that the role would require her to assume the part of an aging queen, she cleverly persuades Jennie to take the assignment. At fourteen pert Ginny, enacted by Nancy Malone, differs from her more ladylike sisters in her delight in displaying her athletic prowess. Her rebellion stems from her disappointment in not being a boy and her present failure to persuade her boy friends to acknowledge her as their equal. Her father, Howard, sorry that redheaded Ginny was not the son for whom he had always longed, ruefully admits: "Virginia seems to have discovered a new sex—boys, girls, and equals."

As a banker in a straitlaced town, Howard, portrayed by Melvyn Douglas, has always been something of a nonconformist, frequently creating dilemmas for himself and his family by his creative outlet through tactless speechmaking. Action in the town really begins when Howard, in "a simple little speech on manners" at a high school assembly, censures the whole educational system, to the utter delight of his daughters and other students. He does not reckon on the consequences. His insistence that none of the high school "kids should be forced to do anything that infringes on their dignity as human beings" and that they "should be allowed the freedom of being themselves, of making their own decisions" makes him for once a hero to the "kids" but a "dangerous" meddler to the orthodox superintendent. His daughters, approving of his progressive ideas, immediately put their father's theories to the test, with startling results. Joan resigns from the Victoria role, after the drama coach agrees to permit Jennie to act in her place. The most difficult of the girls to keep in line is tomboyish Ginny, stubbornly bent upon proving her physical equality with the males in her class.

At this juncture Howard discovers the necessity of taking "time out for Ginny." His own stubborn determination, in regard to his advocacy of freedom of action for students, "not [to] retract any statement I ever made" and to "say whatever I like, whenever I like" bears a close resemblance to Professor Turner's stand on academic freedom. At any rate, Howard secretly enjoys taking time from his banking duties, at the risk of being fired, to support Ginny's decision to try out for a place on the football team. Admitted to the scrub team, Ginny shocks the town even while "putting it on the map" when she is featured in *Life* magazine as an anomaly: "The new look in football." When a trumped-up trick by her male teammates allows Ginny, in the last few minutes of a big game, to make a touchdown, Howard is elated that, at last, there is a football expert in the family. As for Ginny, her growing pains have reached the peak, for now she wants her friend Tommy to recognize her not only as his equal but as a pretty girl.

The cross-section views of life in a small town are presented lightly and entertainingly, yet with realism enough to make the high-school scenes, the family discussions, the images of a small-town bank and the local drugstore, popular gathering place for teen-agers, and other aspects of provincial experience approximate what actually has gone on in smug and provincial communities whose inhabitants "get worked up over" any deviation from ordinary daily routine. As for Howard, the president of his bank sums up his situation: "Any man who can construct a whole crusade on absolutely nothing is either crazy or so far ahead of his time, none of us understands him."[55]

In the flux of theatrical presentations during the early fifties several plays by Robert Anderson brought him critical recognition as one of the most masterful craftsmen among our younger American playwrights. His first Broadway production, *Tea and Sympathy*, began its run at the Barrymore Theatre on September 30, 1953, as the season's first hit play. His earliest written drama, however, was *All Summer Long,* the story of a loveless family adopted from Donald Wetzel's moving first novel, *A Wreath and a Curse* (1950). As Anderson has explained, the task of making this adaptation, started in 1951, "was hard work all the way," for since the Wetzel novel provided "little plot or story to carry the play along, every moment had to carry its own reward." It was difficult to create story patterns, "just a thread here and there in the beginning, but finally a working together into a whole." Director Alan Schneider "practically picked the play from the wastebasket, organized an Equity reading of it in New York, then directed it at Zelda Fichandler's Arena Stage in Washington."[56]

Finally Schneider staged the play for the Playwrights' Company, opening at the Coronet Theatre in New York City on September 23, 1954, for a run of eight weeks. In terms of public reaction the play proved a failure, though the setting and lighting by Jo Mielziner, the clothes designed by Anna Hill Johnstone, and the incidental music by Albert Hagler all combined to help create what Brooks Atkinson in his *New York Times* notice called "a poignant and beautiful play . . . the first piece of art this year." As he saw the production, "Inside a lovely though withered sketch of an old house by Jo Mielziner, Alan Schneider has staged a soft, pulsing performance that speaks the truth consistently all evening." Moreover, "such shining work" was further enhanced by a superb cast, with Clay Hall as the appealing eleven-year-old Willie Mumson, gifted John Kerr as the crippled older brother Don, June Walker—in real life Kerr's own mother—as the Mother, Ed Begley as irascible Dad, Carroll Baker in the role of the sister Ruth, and John Randolph as her husband Harry. Young Daniela Boni, in the role of the little Italian neighbor Theresa, completed the talented cast. While counted a box office failure perhaps because of its depressing and drifting story, *All Summer Long* should be accorded an even distribution of praise and blame: praise which is deserved for some excellent characterization and feeling, but blame that must be placed for the overstressed lessons of family irresponsibility and for a general mildness of action and characterization.[57]

Timed about 1950 and set in the outskirts of a small midwestern river town, the play is actually a series of detailed vignettes of the lower-middle-class Mumson family. The story, opening with a lengthy establishment of mood and character, presents this family as beset by neurotic bitterness, during the course of a hot summer when their very existence is threatened by river seepage under the foundations of their house. The maple-shaded house, continuously occupied by members of Mrs. Mumson's family for over a hundred years, is built on the edge of a steep bank, which has gradually crumbled with each flood stage. The conflict dramatizes "the family counterpointed against the river."[58] Unfortunately this main motif is weakened by the intrusion of too many side issues. As vignette succeeds vignette, Ruth, angry because she is pregnant, tries to bring about an abortion by throwing herself against an electrically charged fence; her husband, Harry, a well-meaning but not overly bright mechanic, spends his leisure hours in a barn workshop; Dad, a none too successful bookkeeper, centers his interest on the fence which, with Harry's help, he has erected to electrocute neighbor Parmesis' trespassing chickens; the cynical older son, Don, crippled in an automobile accident because of his father's negligence, broods about his inability to return to college as the basketball champion he had been; the Mother, with quiet resignation, suffers real agony of spirit because of her husband's irascibility and lack of understanding; and adolescent Willie, who zealously tries all summer long to build a retaining wall to save their house, reaches his twelfth birthday both fascinated and repelled by sex.

These characters, separated by their several private agonies or immediate concerns, fail to heed Don's demands that they face the fact of the river. All through the summer Dad simply reiterates, "We'll wait and see." His reaction to the daily encroachment of the swift current is paranoiac. Declaring that it is the state's responsibility to build a retaining wall, he procrastinates about writing to his congressman. Mother Mumson, sweet, wistful, and forever shocked by the family bickering, is an ineffectual woman always declaring her reliance on God. Ruth, beautiful but vain and obtuse, longs to escape from her cramped surroundings. Vain about her physical attractiveness, she is driven to distraction by the discovery that she is pregnant. In the end young Willie's summer-long labor in trying to build a wall of small stones is not enough. The storm-swollen river, a symbol of natural violence, at last forces the family to flee as their house threatens to topple.

If the river and its threat never came alive for some viewers, if the family plight aroused neither pity nor terror for the Mumsons, and if Mielziner's backdrop of "a river snaking through green countryside" seemed little more than "a painted river upon a painted land," *All Summer Long* had compensating merits. Much of the play's appeal centers around the relationship developing between the two brothers. As Don, with his bitterness toward society, faces an uncertain future, he regards his eleven-year-old brother Willie with affection and shows warm sympathy for the youngster's growing up in a bewildering world. It is Don who helps Willie adjust to his father's nagging, though the task is hard. After all, there is the happiness of the neighboring Parmesis family. As Willie observes, "They're all the time laughing together . . . and kissing. It looks like they're having fun."

With *Tea and Sympathy*, a moving play of greater depth than *All Summer Long*, Anderson again returned to a small-town milieu, presumably to Exeter, Massachusetts, where he himself was once a student at Phillips Academy. Beginning its Broadway run under the sponsorship of the Playwrights' Company, the play succeeded beautifully under the effective direction of Elia Kazan and with the distinctive setting and atmospheric lighting by Jo Mielziner.

An intensely dramatic and illuminating interpretation of several attitudes toward love, this appealing three-act drama is the story of three insecure people: a seventeen-year-old student, misunderstood because he is idealistic and sensitive; the warmhearted and sentimental wife of a schoolmaster, whose emotions overpower her common sense; and her athletic husband, who is unsympathetic and even brutal because of his own feeling of insecurity. A select and long-established boys' school in a New England town provides the circumscribed backdrop for a series of embarrassing situations making up the community entanglements. The main action stems from a false charge of homosexuality, with its unfortunate psychological impact upon the principal characters: adolescent Tom Lee, the accused student; his harshest judge and persecutor, housemaster Bill Reynolds; and the latter's misunderstood and neglected wife Laura, whose duty toward the schoolboys, according to her husband's instructions, is largely restricted to that of a bystander. Occasionally, however, she graciously offers tea and sympathy to her husband's adolescent charges. Among them, Tom seems the most lonely, troubled, and appealing.

". . . while I was writing it," Anderson has written of *Tea and Sympathy*, "I kept thinking of it as a love story which I hoped would be tender and a little ironic." It is that, but the plot also involves an even larger theme. Anderson is most effective in portraying the dangerous and hurtful aftereffects of false accusations which damn the innocent. Like the innocent victims of Miller's *The Crucible*, young Tom is charged on flimsy rumor. By chance he is seen on a beach near the school with David Harris, a faculty member suspected of homosexuality. On unproved report Tom is immediately judged, or misjudged, as being a pervert. Thus begins for the gifted boy a period of heartbreak and agony wherever he appears: in classes, at the drama club, on the playing field, or in his small room. Even his graceful way of walking, his failure to wear a crew cut, his delight in good music, and his assignment to the part of Lady Teazle in the school play are all taken as proof of his perversion.

Elia Kazan, directing with good taste and discrimination, worked with an admirable cast. John Kerr played the role of Tom Lee with restraint and empathy. In his portrayal Tom, when in the presence of schoolmates who accuse him of lacking manliness, appears sullen and seems hostile toward the bullying schoolmaster. The child of a broken marriage, the boy scarcely knew his mother and once had a crush on a sympathetic high-school teacher; in his present dilemma he characteristically turns toward an older woman, understanding Laura Reynolds.

Kazan, pacing the play to bring out the conflicts and the tensions of character, visually symbolized the loneliness separating Tom from his fellow students by his narrow room, with its door shut against intruders and well-wishers alike. Also, Kazan directed with the effective use of stage silences as in Tom's hesitant talk and manner when he comes to tea with Mrs. Reynolds and in the slowly building, pulsating end of the play.

Loneliness is a key motif for the other characters also. Though aggressively masculine, Bill Reynolds, a role interpreted with keen insight by Leif Erickson, gives the merest hint that he is unable to achieve with his lovely wife a fulfilment that he dare not seek with the boys in his house or when he takes them on camping trips. Laura's unhappy situation parallels Blanche Dubois's failure with her young husband in *A Streetcar Named Desire*. An attractive, warm, and sweet woman, Laura, having met Bill on a vacation trip, married him in the belief that he needed her. After their return to the school, she discovers her inability to fill this need and fails him. Obsessed by this discovery, she herself is motivated by the need to prove to herself that she is capable of giving to another this fulfilment which she has been unable to give to her husband. Therefore, throughout the action she thinks about Tom and his cheerless room, where in the finale he reassures himself, after an unfortunate experience with the town prostitute, that he is a man, and Laura reasserts her womanhood. In a particularly poignant speech earlier, Laura, overcome by her marital loneliness, movingly but fruitlessly appeals to Bill to prevent their growing apart. In her first American role, Deborah Kerr as Laura won acclaim for her radiant performance, with its variety in voice, gesture, and movement, all rounded out with innumerable subtle facial expressions.

Also touched by loneliness, Herbert Lee, Tom's father and a successful alumnus of the school, furnished a role played most skilfully by John McGovern. A pragmatic business man, Herbert querulously asks, "Why isn't my boy a regular fellow?" Ironically his own lack of sympathy has helped create the present predicament. By keeping Tom in boarding schools and camps, by berating him as a failure, and by denying him the joy of a father-son companionship which the boy needed most desperately, Lee himself has motivated his son's turning to others. His narrow-mindedness appears at its worst when he reprimands Tom with the warning, "It is not what you are that matters, but what people think you are." The important thing to the father is not whether his son is a homosexual, but the fact that people in the community *think* he is one.

Even Al, Tom's friendly, athletic roommate, is ruled by public opinion. As portrayed with understanding by Dick York, Al makes awkward attempts to teach Tom to walk in a more masculine way. But Al is unable to withstand public opinion alone. While he desires to help Tom clear himself of the false charge, Al knows that he, too, will be called a pervert if he champions Tom's cause.

Concerning the origin of this play, Anderson has singled out several key fragments which finally fused during the creative process. From a young girl friend living in a theatrical boarding house he learned that her landlady on occasion "had the girls down for tea and sympathy." Then in 1947 a trip to his old school at Exeter, when he visited the dormitory in which he had lived during his miserable first year, gave the playwright a second clue. He found the place "quite transformed with a semiprivate room for the young boys presided over by a charming woman who told me that many tears were shed in that room by the younger boys . . ." A final idea came from his reading of *Walden*, in which he marked this cogent passage: "If a man does not keep pace with his companions, perhaps it is because he hears a different drummer. Let him step to the music which he hears, however measured or far away." These suggestions, added to the nature of the playwright, resulted finally in the conception of "a play about responsibility, that each of us had to give the other person more than sympathy and tea."[59]

The Mielziner stage design, artistically combining the living room, a tiny hall, and Tom's room, served the dual purpose of providing for a flow of action on different levels and of reflecting the character of the occupants of the separate rooms. The warm, firelit living room, so appropriate for Laura, is sharply contrasted with Tom's gray-toned, narrow room with only one window, which once a day provides a forbidden view into an adjoining house. Finally, at the play's conclusion, when Laura comes to offer herself to Tom, "Mielziner dramatically and symbolically suffuses the boy's room with the warmth and glow with which he formerly lit Laura's room; but this time the radiance is not from the fireplace but from the sun."[60]

In London during the bleak, cold winter of 1958 Anderson completed another New England play, which, he has said, "had been on my mind for some time." Set against the background of a colonial inn in a quiet village, *Silent Night, Lonely Night* is another expression of Anderson's ability to portray, with sympathy and insight, the terrible loneliness which wells up in two bereft strangers, both "lonesome and sick inside." Unencumbered by plot complexities, this dramatic "exercise in restraint" presents a Jamesian "special case" of two lonely adults, who, stranded

at the inn on a snowy Christmas Eve, find each other that evening only
to go their separate ways the next morning. On Christmas Day John
Sparrow must return to his mentally ill wife at the village hospital, while
Katherine Johnson, like James's Isabel Archer, must accompany her
thirteen-year-old son, just released from the infirmary of a local boys'
school, to London to rejoin her unfaithful husband. During their brief
hours together each of these two stranded adults has "the desperate
impulse to reach out a lonely hand to touch someone." And each finds
in the other momentary "protection against the horrors of the night."
According to a recent critic, "The Christmas background implied the
religious approval of resurrection through adultery."[61] While the play,
as produced by the Playwrights' Company at the Morosco Theatre in
New York City, beginning on December 3, 1959, was appreciated by
only a minority of the critics, Anderson had words of praise for those
chiefly involved: "Obviously the gathering together of Henry Fonda [as
John], Barbara Bel Geddes [as Katherine] and Peter Glenville [director]
was worth the effort."[62] And so was the set, Katherine's room at the
inn, designed by Jo Mielziner.

The opening production of Anderson's latest play ushered in a new
project, proposed several summers ago by playwrights Jerome Lawrence
and Robert E. Lee, at a conference of the American Educational Theatre. Designated as the American Playwrights Theatre, this project was
proposed to break the stereotyped pattern which for a long time has
forced theaters outside New York City to wait interminably after a
Broadway production of a play to perform it. This new project, with its
substantial guarantees to playwrights for the production of each unproduced play in fifty or more tryout towns and cities, offers the participat-
ing theaters in these communities the exclusive production rights to each
play for one year.[63]

The play chosen to initiate this project was *The Days Between*, and
the first theater to produce it, in May, 1965, was the Dallas Theater
Center, with its resident professional company. On the Center's huge,
semicircular stage designed by Frank Lloyd Wright, designer David
Pursley constructed a complex setting which allowed the play's succession of domestic scenes an uninterrupted flow from area to area. Various
levels, juxtapositions, lights, and props created the effect of diversified
yet simultaneous action. This multiple arrangement, simulating several
rooms in a faculty home in a New England college town, an adjoining
garden, and a guest room over a converted barn, was designed to reveal
simultaneously such scenes as those of a self-centered associate professor of English, David Ives, typing a novel in an attic room, and of his

wife Barbara talking with Roger or Roge, their ten-year-old son, and
Mrs. Walker, her nagging mother, in the kitchen.

This flexible stage construction provided the background for a painful
story of crisis in an intellectual's relation to himself and to his wife and
boy. David's agonizing search for his real identity is entangled with his
marital difficulties. Once the young man of hopeful dreams after Korea,
David, during years of teaching, of measuring "out my life in examination books and dedications and . . . crud," has changed into a brooding
figure. Domestic tensions have made him brood about "betrayal, compromise and death!" and his frustrated attempts (during a dearly won
summer leave) to finish a second novel, ten years after his first one,
have made him resentful of his best students who seem to have gained
the literary recognition denied him. As the summer wanes, David's preoccupation with his killing creative effort deteriorates into a process of
self-destruction. Although professionally regarded as a successful teacher
of creative writing, David doubts his own ability to create. His neglect
of his nonintellectual wife and his unwanted son steadily increases. He
thus suffers self-punishment, as a sort of academic flagellant, in trying
to prove himself capable of fulfilling the high creative principles which
he has imposed upon his students. Questions beset him. Has he com-
promised too long and wasted his youthful talent in trying to provide for
the family, including an indigent mother-in-law? Has he used Barbara
and Roger as an excuse because of self-delusion about his writing ability? Or is his once bright dream of achieving fame simply his desire to
be freed from onerous tasks of teaching?

Opposition from Barbara and little Roger furnish an antagonizing
situation, especially critical when David, weary of "dragged-out murdering compromises," announces that he must go away. He is no longer
able to stand the burden of Barbara's "understanding and patience and
self-sacrifice." In turn, Barbara's reaction raises questions. Why does
this self-effacing wife contribute toward her husband's destructive process to the point of withholding information about her pregnancy and
quietly having an abortion in order not to upset his plan for the finishing of his novel? Why, too, does she invite Ted Sears, whose wife has
recently died of cancer, to be their houseguest, when she knows of
David's contempt for the "successful, sentimental trash" which has enriched Sears? (David's hatred of mediocrity stems from his youthful
dreams of himself as "a bright and shining hero just back from the war,
. . . [who] was going to be a bright and shining success.")

In an agonizing scene, Barbara, who has almost given herself to Sears,
hysterically accuses David of having "crucified us all on this dream of

yours!" His ignorance of life, she cries out, thwarts his desire to achieve distinction as a novelist. "You hate life . . . this life, this ugly but only life." Barbara's declaration that he "cannot write from hate, only from love" and her crying out that she still loves him at last awaken David. Bitterly he admits his longtime awareness that his talent is limited. Still stung by his need to be a success, he recognizes the impossibility of living "the days between" and humbly declares, "I am going *to try to live now*." He vows to think of himself henceforth as a good teacher, "as something to be valued."[64]

In the Center's premiere, Mary Sue Fridge as Barbara Ives powerfully sustained a difficult role which called for unstinted mental torment, while Ryland Merkey's David realistically characterized the troubled professor's frustrated and self-condemnatory nature. If this new play impressed some spectators as emphasizing unrelieved tensions, nevertheless it illuminates anew Anderson's rare talent for dramatizing lonely townspeople, "torn," as David says in this play, "with tensions and anxieties and needs."

During the 1962-63 New York season the New England small town was again given theatrical prominence with the staging of *Calculated Risk* and the winner of the New York Drama Critics Circle and Tony Awards, *Who's Afraid of Virginia Woolf?* Suggestive of the conflicts in Herne's *Margaret Fleming* of long ago, *Calculated Risk*, by Joseph Hayes, which opened at the Ambassador Theatre on October 31, 1962, with Robert Montgomery as director, is plotted around both an economic crisis threatening the security of a long-established family of millowners and the marital tensions plaguing the president of the Armstone Mills.

Like the Flemings, the Armstones had for several generations dominated the town—presumably in Connecticut—and profitably operated their textile mills. But now change is in the air. In emergency sessions, from a Tuesday through the following Thursday, in the board room of the Armstone Mills, the directors try to ferret out why Armstone stock is being actively traded all of a sudden. This unexpected flurry in the market brings together the Armstone brothers, Julian (played by Joseph Cotten) and Quentin, their wives Helen and Rita, and others owning controlling interest in the mills.

In heated sessions they discover that an unscrupulous stock raider, William Medlow, using "the fine art of blackmail," has been engaged in raiding not only the Armstone corporation, to which he owes nearly a million dollars, but similar companies as well. Suspecting a spy from within, president Julian Armstone exposes banker Harrison Bellows, a mill director, as a secret collaborator playing hand in glove with Medlow.

By boldly taking a "calculated risk" with his own fortune, Julian shrewdly thwarts Medlow. When Rourke, a wily speculator himself, agrees to sell him one of Medlow's notes, Julian saves the family mills from liquidation.

In contrast with modern dramatizations of southern mill towns upset by violent strikes, *Calculated Risk* pictures a vanishing provincial way of life. A portrayal of industrial change, the play deals with threats made against the older economic order of a mill management dating back to old Lucas Armstone, founder of the corporation, who always operated successfully by a sort of paternalistic relationship with his mill hands. Throughout the play references are made to the dependence of the workers and other townspeople upon the mills. In the present crisis Medlow's threat to level the mills into the dust and the expected loss of the Armstone tradition of excellence foreshadow economic death for the townspeople, high and low. The conflict between Medlow (symbol of "a new kind of American business man," the notoriously successful corporate raider) and the Armstones with their inherited wealth suggests that modern intrusive and destructive forces may bring ruination to a whole town. By the closing moments of the action, however, Julian's firm resolution of the Medlow crisis saves the directors from bankruptcy, assures the workers their livelihood, and reunites the Armstone family and friends. A parallel thread of interest concerns Shep, Helen and Julian's prep-school son who, at fifteen, suffers from too much money and too little parental love and companionship. At the last, there is the hint that happier days are ahead for all three.[65]

The idea of immorality as a force affecting family life in manufacturing towns, as in the world at large, is not new in the theatrical history of the small town. Medlow's secret and ruthless manipulation of factory stock parallels somewhat the tragic consequences of an airplane manufacturer's lack of integrity in *All My Sons*, Arthur Miller's first successful play and the winner of the Drama Critics Circle Award in 1947. Both Medlow and his collaborator Harrison Bellows are equally guilty with Miller's Joe Keller in their avoidance of "a kind of responsibility. Man for man." Set naturally, with much realistic detail, in the backyard of the Keller home on the outskirts of an American town, *All My Sons*, like the later *Calculated Risk*, is a family drama, one involving the disturbing impact upon two families—the Kellers and the Deevers—of war profiteering in the sale of defective airplane motors. But Joe Keller's deed, including his throwing the blame on his partner, Deever, goes beyond his having been the cause of the death of American Pilots, including his own son Larry, in World War II. As Miller has explained, this deed obscures the other kind of morality in which the play is primarily interested. Morality is probably a faulty word to use in this connection, but what I was after was the wonder in the fact that consequences of actions are as real as the actions themselves. . . . Joe Keller's trouble is not that he cannot tell right from wrong but that the cast of his mind cannot admit that he, personally, has any viable connection with his world, his universe, or his society.[66]

Thus Keller lives in darkness, unable to understand the import of sensitive Dr. Jim Bayliss' warning: "Every man does have a star. The star of one's honesty. And you spend your life groping for it, but once it's out it never lights again."[67] Keller, at last convinced of his guilt by his surviving son Chris, in expiation kills himself. Finally, there is the hint in this conventionally constructed thesis play that the realistic portrayal of one guilty man may be extended to symbolize an evil characteristic of our pragmatic society.

Albee's New Carthage: The Decay of an American House of Intellect

Edward Albee, one of the most controversial and promising among the "New Wave" playwrights, has been recognized quickly as a satirist without peer among his contemporaries. As the creator of some of the most shattering and satiric dramas of the fifties and sixties—*The Zoo Story* (1958), *The Death of Bessie Smith* (1959), *The Sandbox* (1959), *The American Dream* (1960), and *Who's Afraid of Virginia Woolf?* (1961)—young Albee has elicited extremes of praise and condemnation for his excoriating examinations of the American scene and his unflattering images of human relationships. His patterns of provincial life in the United States are at odds with the interpretations given in numerous other dramatizations of the ways of native townspeople. The world of the family, in which countless Americans, both real and fictional, find happiness and consolation, has little to offer in Albee's plays. *The American Dream*, for instance, is a vitriolic parody of American family life, belittling its togetherness and physical fitness as sentimental middle-class ideals. The loveliness of the natural world, so often linked with the fictional portrayal of village life, is almost totally missing in Albee's work, except in scattered laments about the once promising but now lost world of vigorous pioneers. Albee's dark vision of provincial America contains places of ugliness and decay, usually of a wasteland of moral vacuity; hence, for him contemporary decadence is fit raw material for satiric exposure. In his philosophy of despair, emptiness, and sterility the familiar solid values of folk living, so often pictured realistically or romantically glorified in small-town plays, have no place. Rather, "Albee's American family undergoes anxiety and terrible barrenness as it staggers into decay. A few fugitives detach themselves and seek solutions in aesthetics. They watch a historical dream wither." The core, then, of Albee's views is sterility.

The generations move away from practicality toward emasculation; away from the energetic but amoral use of power toward an amoral but inoperative use of power. A frightened populace creating illusory values; a country afraid to articulate its genuine but shoddy rules of conduct; and a handful of males stimulated to imaginative activity of high order.[68]

Although Albee has a poet's insight, his sardonic outlook offers little hope for the solution of our national dilemma, except, perhaps through an escape into the world of imagination, the best means of survival among people living with false values. The materials, all symbols of social decay, with which Albee has created stage sensations in his "stand against the fiction that everything in this slipping land of ours is peachy-keen" include macabre love affairs, latent homosexual relations, self-annihilation, themes of love-hate, failures in communication, the substitution of artificial for real values in our society, complacency, cruelty, emotional sterility, vapidity, and materialism.

From 1958 until 1960 Albee's reputation as playwright, based upon his four innovational one-act plays, rested largely upon the reception given by limited avant-garde audiences in off-Broadway theaters. A turning point in his career may be dated from October 13, 1962, when his first ful-length play—*Who's Afraid of Virginia Woolf?*—began its fantastically successful run at the Billy Rose Theatre, New York. The following season further acclaim came when his adaptation of *The Ballad of the Sad Café* was produced on October 30 at the Martin Beck. Now, his plays, in addition to their American productions, have been presented in Berlin—where *The Zoo Story* had its premiere, in German translation, on September 28, 1959—London, Tokyo, Buenos Aires, Istanbul, Stockholm, and Dublin. Such performances, in the opinion of Henry Watts, Jr., place Albee "high among the important dramatists of the contemporary world theatre."

Offering criticism germane to Albee's spreading reputation, historian Marshall W. Fishwick recently diagnosed the American dream in the light of dramatic interpretations characteristic of this present "age of disorder." "The play's the thing: it holds the mirror up to man. What, in our time and culture, does it show?" Plays by iconoclasts—Samuel Beckett, Eugene Ionesco, Jean Genet, Albee, and other moderns—present "a distorted picture of a world that has gone mad—in order to break the old mold of language and narrative sequence in the theatre and to emphasize the mystery of truth." In dramatizing the plight of modern man, such playwrights see a world devoid of spirit and humanity. Albee himself has this to say: "Man attempts to make sense out of his senseless position in a world that makes no sense. The social structures man has erected to 'illusion' himself have collapsed." What remains? "Haunted by the gnawing passion to thwart meaninglessness, man gravitates toward ruts, pigeonholes, and fantasies."[69] Such, in part, is the social plight worked out in complex variations in *Who's Afraid of Virginia Woolf?*

In this social satire the action begins with deceptive casualness and simplicity. A realistic living room setting in a faculty home on the campus of a small New England college is used throughout the three acts. The hour at curtain rise is two o'clock on a Sunday morning, and the room is dark. Suddenly there is a crash against the front door, then a woman's boisterous laugh is heard as the door opens, and lights are switched on. The light reveals a middle-aged pair, now a bit drunk, returning to their darkened home from the college president's annual party honoring new faculty members. The wife, a large, boisterous woman of fifty-two, is the president's daughter Martha; her forty-six-year-old husband, George, is an associate professor of history, a man of "dashed hopes and good intentions." George satirizes the changes in his position as "Good, better, best, bested," since through the years he has been forced to recognize that "Martha's father expects his . . . staff . . . to cling to the walls of this place, like the ivy . . . to come here and grow old . . . to fall in the line of service."[70]

Immediately this mismated couple begins "an orgy of verbal sado-masochism" which continues until five that morning. Quarreling over utterly trivial things, they "swill down more liquor than even full professors can afford, . . . [and] seem more interested in fighting and hurting one another than they are in whatever they find to quarrel about."[71] Martha irritates George with her surprise announcement that she has invited two faculty newcomers for a nightcap: a young—and good-looking—biology instructor named Nick and his wife Honey, "a mousey little type, without any hips, or anything." After Nick and Honey arrive the nightcap is prolonged until daylight, with Martha raucously singing "Who's afraid of Virginia Woolf?" at every opportunity. As George ruefully admits to Nick, "It isn't the prettiest spectacle . . . seeing a couple of middle-aged types hacking away at each other, all red in the face and winded, missing half of the time." For years, however, George has been trying "to clean up the mess I made" by resorting to "accommodation, malleability, adjustment," but with little success. He seems doomed, and

in self-mockery he says: "I am a Doctor. A.B. . . . M.A. . . . Ph.D.
. . . ABMAPHID! Abmaphid has been variously described as a wasting
disease of the frontal lobes, and as a wonder drug. It is actually both."[72]

As the drinking marathon continues throughout the early morning
hours, George and Martha, largely at the latter's instigation, harrow
each other in venomous sex dueling. Nick and Honey, unequal to such
bitter warfare, are bewildered and helpless. It is this struggle for domination, with each participant cruelly penetrating the weaknesses of the
other, which gives the play its threefold division. In Act I, ironically
titled "Fun and Games," the hosts and guests return to childhood diversions and games of fantasy, the latter tending to stimulate sexual excitement and personal confessions as the drinking grows heavier. The first
of these ruthlessly-played games is called "Humiliate the Host." It ends
with Martha's triumph, for with abusive name-calling she rips away
every protective layer of dignity from George, until at last when she
begins taunting him about his early novel he goes berserk and tries to
kill her. The second game, "Get the Guests," gives George an opportunity to burst Honey's dream bubble, the result of too much brandy,
and unsettle her simple mind by suggesting unpleasant truths about her
husband.

George and Martha's bitter bickering about their mythical son leads
directly to the second act, the "*Walpurgisnacht*," wherein the third game,
"Hump the Hostess," is played out, in part, as an offstage charade. This
campus game of "musical beds" results in voluptuous Martha's attempt
to commit adultery with Nick, whose potency is questionable, while
George downstairs is fully aware of their "game." Meanwhile, Honey, a
"sort of a simp" who has refused to grow up, has "tooted brandy [so]
immodestly" that she is in a nauseated condition and is lying on the bath-
room tiles peeling the label from a brandy bottle.

Act III, "Exorcism" (the title originally chosen for the play), introduces the final painful game, "Bringing up Baby," wherein George at
last triumphs over domineering Martha. After twenty-three years of trying to adjust himself to her bickering and her taunts about his failures,
George has his revenge by playing a painful game of killing their son on
the day of his maturity. Thus by exorcising from their lives the imaginary
son, George destroys the unrealities of the fantasy in which they have
indulged privately all these years. Now both must face the reality of their
sterility, for the violent old games, which had served them as sex-sub-
stitutes, are gone. In the state of a strange peace following the exorcism,
both George and Martha seem to realize that now only new games are
possible. An ironical note closes the play, with George, singing the title

song, lulling Martha to sleep, as she confesses one of her inadequacies: fear of Virginia Woolf.

The play has varied ramifications. Beyond George and Martha's marital struggle to differentiate between truth and illusion and the younger couple's bewilderment and ineffectuality, there remains the academic community, traditionally the "House of Intellect" alive with ideas and cultural values. Its present phase, coincident with the passing of Daddy's generation, dramatizes the plight of the American intellectual and suggests that a new direction is needed to save campus life from the impotency symbolized by the prevalence of "fun and games," of dancing, drinking, and sexual perversions. Unfortunately George, once regarded as Daddy's heir-apparent, resembles MacLeish's "Irresponsibles." His year-by-year insistence upon his individual rights has unfitted him for a leading role as an organization man. Martha's insulting nagging—"You didn't *do* anything; you never *do* anything; you never *mix*. You just sit around and talk"—emphasizes the dilemma of the sensitive, imaginative man caught in the vise of organizational pragmatism. In his predicament he could survive only by freely choosing futility. His imaginative nature finds a shabby outlet in his jeering at Martha's adulation of her Daddy and belittling the town of New Carthage—the "nouveau Carthage" with its "respected, conservative institution" afraid of new creative talent. He is in quiet, or restrained, rebellion against the narrow views of the townspeople, who gossip about the affairs of others, such as Martha's open attentions to every new man on campus. Even she admits that it is "Just a gigolo, everywhere I go, people always say . . ." In his satiric appraisal, "the women around here are no better than putas—you know, South American ladies of the night. . . . Well they stand around on the street and they hiss at you, like a bunch of geese. All the faculty wives, downtown in New Carthage, in front of the A & P, hissing away like a bunch of geese."[73]

There remains also the chronological context in which the play is cast. Albee undergirds the superstructure of his play with time symbols, somewhat suggestive of Whitman's "filaments of time" and T. S. Eliot's concern with continuity. In "The Theatre of Edward Albee" playwright and critic Lee Baxandall presents Albee's three symbolic time symbols as Then, Now, and Nowhere. In retrospect the dynamic past, as symbolized by the exciting early history of New Carthage's college and the pragmatic achievement of its now aging president, becomes an expression of individual vision and power coupled with community vigor. But most of this pioneer assertiveness has vanished. What remains is an aging Daddy, symbol of the weakening dynamism of a once active *paterfamilias*, who now is merely a remote, superpowered official to whom the whole faculty, for its survival, must pay homage. George satirizes his father-in-law as "a God, we all know that," presiding pompously over "Parnassus," his campus mansion. Though the time has come for change, Daddy still "*is* the college." Carefully guarding his hegemony, Daddy is cautious about allowing new ideas to prevail on campus, as suggested by his—and Martha's—"killing" or suppressing George's first novel, because it was unsuited to the institution's code of respectability. Such conformism, George argues, will allow "the ants to take over the world" by its destruction of the diversity of cultures and races. Thus history will lose "its glorious variety and unpredictability." As "order and constancy" come to rule society, "the surprise, the multiplexity, the sea-changing rhythm of . . . history, will be eliminated," along with the "race of glorious men."

The present has become "an age of deformity," as Grandma, in *The American Dream*, succinctly described twentieth-century conditions. It is a time of spiritual loss and intellectual decadence, as exemplified in the plight of George and Martha. Instead of becoming an active doer in a pragmatic world of board and committee meetings, George has tried to escape Daddy's preachments and Martha's withering insults by creating imaginative worlds full of meaning. Martha's "ugly talents" and "hideous gifts" of insult are an offset of her barrenness. Her strong sexual desire does not bring her the joys of motherhood. Furious at her own sterility, she contributes malicious ridicule toward the destruction of George's brain child, his novel. In the end, with Martha subdued and crushed, Albee leaves these two uncompromising victims cleansed but without purpose.

The future, both of the academic community and of the nation at large, is foreshadowed as being bleak and directionless, leading Nowhere. As typified by the wave-of-the-future couple—Nick repressed by his conformist attitudes and naïve Honey afraid of the demands of maturity—American collegiate society in the years ahead appears intellectually arid, and the academic town a wasteland center. On the other hand, all life does not turn toward sterility. While the rules of George and Martha's silly games dehumanized them, the stripping away of their false myths may enable them to face the future, still clinging to life, still groping for meaning. According to Allan Lewis, the vague implication at the end concerning Martha's fear of Virginia Woolf may be a pun on "Who's afraid of the big bad wolf?" or, perhaps, a reference "to the distinguished English writer herself and the search for freedom, the consciousness of woman's role, and the need for the 'separate room.' " At any rate, as Lewis has noted, the four characters in this plan re-enact the "life of Dionysus, god of theatre and debauchery, who, cut to bits and boiled in the cauldron, returned to life."[74]

In its Broadway premiere, Alan Schneider's easy direction caught the play's satiric—and at times savage—humor, its shifting rhythms, and its painful characterizations of college people whose anguish of spirit occasionally shone through their cold, calculating battle of the sexes. Arthur Hill skilfully expressed George's pleasure in the world of the imagination as well as his almost overpowering sense of desperation and his anger at being trapped by his pragmatic milieu. Uta Hagen won acclaim for her uproariously funny performance as strident-mouthed and boisterous Martha. Cast as the faculty newcomers, George Grizzard and Melinda Dillon realistically expressed the materialism and vapidity of the younger generation. William Rittman's set was designed to combine symbols of the past and the present. The comfortable living room, with its recessed bookcases, hi-fi, an impressionist painting, and other modern equipment, also contained furnishings reminiscent of the eighteenth-century "Age of Enlightenment": Early American pieces, oak beams, a wrought-iron eagle of colonial design, and an American flag oddly reversed.

The Theater of the Absurd, in the opinion of Alan Pryce-Jones, has offered one way of combating the present inertia in theatrical circles, which has developed from the rehashing of the familiar. Nevertheless, there is urgent need for the exploration of something newer, something more original. Thus far, except for the Broadway musical and an occasional expression of an American mood by an American playwright, the recent springs of native drama have been eclectically drawn from Europe. For example, *Who's Afraid of Virginia Woolf?* "is incontrovertibly an American expression of an American situation, but in form, texture, technique, shock potential, it draws on the kind of European hate play of which Strindberg is the obvious master."

During 1966 the film adaptation of *Who's Afraid of Virginia Woolf?* stirred much controversy. Before releasing the film Warner Brothers subjected it to the critical scrutiny of administrators of the National Catholic Office for Motion Pictures as well as to that of the officials of the self-censoring Motion Picture Association. As a result, the movie was classified as an A-4 film "morally unobjectionable for adults, with reservations." In the beginning Warner Brothers had assigned the task of adaptation to producer-screenwriter Ernest Lehman, adapter of *The Sound of Music*, and Broadway director Mike Nichols, who made his movie-directing debut with this film. These two, in an attempt to retain the spirit of Albee's play, rejected the idea of cutting or softening the earthy, uninhibited dialogue, for they felt, as Nichols has noted, that "the language of *Woolf* is essential; it reveals who the people are and how they lived." They decided that the searing dialogue had to remain as the main weapon with which the film's two couples verbally slash each other to exhaustion. The characters' coarse words, exposing terrible truths about marital emotion and delusion, must be used virtually unrestricted on the screen as on the stage. With this working plan, Lehman and Nichols produced a film adaptation which emerged as an honest, corrosive portrayal of great power and final poignancy.

Obviously the film sets produced a more diversified scenic effect than the single set used on the stage. The tavern scene, the exterior as well as interior views of George's and Martha's home, and the views of the campus offer a wider pictorial portrayal of New Carthage. True to the play, the film relates how George, a middle-aged and disillusioned professor brilliantly portrayed by Richard Burton, and his harridan of a wife, a role unusual for Elizabeth Taylor, entertain a new instructor, Nick, played by George Segal, and his wife Honey, played by Sandy Dennis, during a nightlong drinking bout. George and Martha take the younger couple to a roadhouse. In the sexually symbolic scenes following, all contrary to the rules of Hollywood propriety, Martha, smarting from her husband's frequent insults, coarsely taunts him not only with shocking language but by dancing with Nick and embracing him suggestively, while Honey, befuddled by too much liquor, watches in disbelief. It is thus that in almost three hours of movie action the young newcomers to the faculty are initiated by the college faculty's "first family."

Musicals and Other Broadway Shows

Even a casual study of the schedules of New York productions for seasons of the past decade or more reveals the domination of the Broadway scene by musicals, adaptations, suspense dramas, imported attractions, shallow comedies, and other superficial forms of entertainment. Recently well-known critics have been moved to wonder "whether this represents the hopeful stir of genuine creativity, or whether producers are merely grabbing at sub-standard material to fill a void left by writers who are either discouraged or too rich . . ."[75] At any rate, the origin of a number of recent musicals in adaptations of novels, plays, and movies suggests that at present "our writers are in a period of vigorlessness, brought on by the disastrous Broadway economy." The debasing theatrical effect of the "Broadway touch" is revealed in the tendency to do things considered safe for show business at the expense of artistic dramaturgy and cogency of thought. Underneath a current hit, says Alan Thompson, there may be "deserts of vast vacuity." Hence, serious playwrights have been turning more and more to the resident companies springing up in New York. The Actors Studio Theatre, for example, produced James Baldwin's polemical first play, *Blues for Mr. Charlie*, and the Lincoln Center Repertory Company introduced *After the Fall*, Arthur Miller's first new play since 1956 and a starring vehicle for Jason Robards, Jr. While he does not call this pattern a trend, critic Henry Hewes has expressed the fear that "the prevailing odds against commercial success for a serious play on Broadway may well be driving our better playwrights to a kind of theatre with more continuity or artistry, a theatre that can keep their plays alive longer by performing them in repertory." One answer may be found in such experiments as the one recently launched by the American Playwrights Theatre at the Dallas Theater Center.

What has happened on Broadway, explains lyricist Alan Jay Lerner, is that "The musical has been elected by default to serve in the absence of a poetic theatre, a romantic theatre, a heroic theatre, a moral theatre, and a theatrical theatre."[76] Many spectators, unable to respond to the drabness and tragic anxieties of life so often portrayed in modern serious drama, find momentary escape from their own routine worlds in the tinsel realm of gaiety, fun, or fantasy. Moreover, such patronage of "a make-shift species of showmanship" enables producers to meet present-day inflated production costs.

Among the diversions which have held the modern stage, some musicals and related forms have interpreted, in a more elementary kind of dramatization, certain aspects of small-town life already featured in serious drama. If not essentially lyric or artistic in the best sense, these entertainments generally appeal through extravaganza and spectacle. Nevertheless, elaborate stage designs, bright costuming—often for period effects—vivacious choreography, skits, and lilting songs, however appealing to the emotions, offer no new vistas for the theater. Rather, so far as the reinterpretation of the American small community is concerned, a few musicals have succeeded merely in activating popular interest in a vanished provincial life. However lively their picturing in native musicals, the nineteenth-century California mining town and later agricultural villages, a Pennsylvania Amish settlement, midwestern farming centers, and other little communities are fictionalized more with sentiment than with the hard core of reality and genuine satire that has often in the past been at the center of artistic dramatizations of the small town.

Among the musicals of scattered merit which have flourished throughout the fifties and into the sixties is *Paint Your Wagon*, with book and lyrics by Alan Jay Lerner, which had its beginning in 1947 after Lerner's first success with *Brigadoon*. It was then that he began thinking about the possibility of plotting a story about the illusion of success. His original visualization of two painted wagons—one going hopefully to the gold country and the other coming back in despair—eventually led him to write "the life and death of a ghost town, and to do it in a serious tone."[77] Lerner's much rewritten script finally came to completion as a two-act story about Ben Rumson, a wandering middle-aged miner who has a dream of success and pursues it to the Far West in 1853-54. As a rugged pioneer compelled to follow his deepest impulses "in goin' a-westering," Ben dreams of a success which will enable him to educate his teen-age daughter to be a lady, as her mother was. A lucky strike "due west of Sonora" leads Ben to the founding and ruling of the Gold Rush town of Rumson. For a while his dream is fulfilled, until the gold vein plays out and Rumson Town becomes a shabby ghost settlement, as its motley population is lured away by rumors of new strikes in neighboring camps. The "boys meets girl" motif reappears in Jennifer's romantic love for a handsome young Mexican miner, a self-styled Castilian named Julio Valveras.

This somewhat episodic story of a rugged individualist "born under a wand'rin star" opened at the Shubert Theatre in New York City on November 12, 1951. Under Daniel Mann's direction, the musical, in Lerner's opinion, gave "an honest reproduction of life on the musical stage." The music was by Frederick Loewe, the choreography by Agnes De Mille, the typical mining town sets by Oliver Smith, and the costumes by Motley. In its successive versions, *Paint Your Wagon*, though marked by a confusion of style, is remembered best for its stellar role of Ben Rumson, played first by James Barton and thereafter by Eddie Dowling and Burl Ives.

Another stage re-creation of traditional folk customs, *Plain and Fancy*, at first failed to impress some of the critics, but audiences were plentiful and enthusiastic from the time of its premiere on January 27, 1955, at the Mark Hellinger Theatre, New York. This amusing regional musical represented the joint efforts of a number of journeyman craftsmen— librettists Joseph Stein and Will Glickman, lyricist Arnold B. Horwitt, and composer Albert Hague—and of little-known actors, rather than the work of star performers and technicians. With its action set "in and around Bird-in-Hand, a town in the Amish country of Pennsylvania," the story basically concerns the differences between two ways of life.

The Yoders, Zooks, Lapps, Rebers, and other Amish families have traditionally led a peaceful, though disciplined, life, delighting in their bountiful crops and profitable sales of their produce in nearby Lancaster. Proud of their good earth, they sing joyfully about "Plenty of Pennsylvania/Where anything grows."[78]

Disagreements between the "plain people" and "fancy" urbanites begin with the arrival of two sophisticated New Yorkers. At the outset Dan King, a magazine writer, and Ruth Winters, his wisecracking girl friend, are interested solely in their mission to sell the river farm which Dan has inherited from his Amish grandfather, old Joshua Koenig. As events develop, they remain to help an Amish girl escape the fate of an arranged match. The likeliest buyer of Dan's farm is Papa Yoder, bent upon having his daughter Katie marry Ezra Reber, a crude, muscular, and industrious farmer of the Bird-in-Hand community. Yoder covets the farm as a wedding present and future home for the young couple. Katie, however, loves Ezra's sensitive brother Peter, who is regarded by Papa Yoder as a troublemaker who is more inclined toward fighting than toward farming.

Amidst the stir of preparations for the wedding feast, Peter, who has been exiled for brawling, suddenly returns to the village. Resentful of Ezra's taunts, Peter scuffles with him. Then a fire destroys the huge barn on Dan's farm, and Papa Yoder charges Peter with hexing the place. At once shunned by all the Amish folk, Peter remains in bad repute in spite of Dan's protests and Katie's pleas. Unwittingly Ruth gets Ezra drunk, thus motivating his going to a carnival in Lancaster, where he disgraces himself in the eyes of his Amish neighbors. The love story of Katie Yoder and Peter Reber ends happily after they overcome Papa Yoder's objections to Peter. The latter's efforts at the carnival to keep Ezra out of trouble at last convince stubborn Papa Yoder that the right man for Katie is Peter, now all the more welcome because Dan has sold the youth his farm. A secondary thread of plot interest concerns another Amish maiden, outspoken Hilda Miller, who becomes infatuated with Dan. At the finale, Dan persuades Hilda to marry within her sect; he, himself, belatedly awakens to the attractiveness of Ruth, who had about given up hope on that score.

In this musical, as in *The Most Happy Fella*, American folkways are celebrated in song, dance, and folksy dialogue. Local color abounds in scenes picturing an entire community's excitement over the wedding festivities, a neighborhood barn raising, the superstition of the Amish about hexing, their habit of wearing plain, buttonless clothes, and their sanction of bundling. Such rural vignettes reveal how much the simplicity of life in secluded Bird-in-Hand contrasts with the worldliness of the big city.

During the New York season of 1956-57 a California small-town locale of the recently vanished past was re-created by means of musical comedy. In *The Most Happy Fella*, Frank Loesser as composer, lyricist, and librettist, moved in the direction of opera by refashioning, with considerable accuracy, Sidney Howard's 1924 Pulitzer Prize play *They Knew What They Wanted*. When his musical adaptation was first presented by Kermit Bloomgarden at the Imperial Theatre on May 3, 1956, a question arose as to whether Loesser knew what *he* wanted. He had cast about two-thirds of the work in operatic form, retaining the Broadway pattern of spoken dialogue most of the way but including a certain amount of recitative. (At the time of the premiere Loesser's music was considered as close to operatic level as anyone in the popular musical field had come since Gershwin, excluding Menotti and Blitzstein.)[79] In spite of its being something of a hybrid lacking an overall unity of style, the musical won the New York Critics Circle Award as the best musical for 1956-57. This success, no doubt, owed much to the superb singing and acting of operatic and concert baritone Robert Weede in the exacting role of "the most happy fella," matrimonially inclined Antonio (Tony) Esposito.[80]

Loesser was fortunate in finding an operatic book in the Howard comedy. A strong drama with universal emotional appeal, the play also has sweep, earthy flavor, local color, and some ribald humor growing out of the courtship and marriage of Toni Patucci, a middle-aged Italian-American owner of a vineyard near Napa, California. While the Tony of *The Most Happy Fella* is not expressly the Italian bootlegger he was in the Howard original, he remains middle-aged, profane, and lonely, finding more irritation than comfort is his too sisterly sister, Marie. He remedies his lonely situation and his longing for *bambini* by courting a young San Francisco waitress he calls Rosabella, impulsively mailing her a picture of the handsome, virile foreman of his vineyards, Joe, in place of one of himself. The girl's dream of love and security is almost destroyed when, on arriving in Napa, she discovers this deception. Finally Rosabella agrees to go through with the misrepresented match, mostly out of pity for Tony, who has been badly injured in a highway mishap when he was speeding to the Napa depot to meet her. When Tony is immobilized in a wheel chair, wayfaring Joe changes his mind about leaving Napa Valley. Attracted to Rosabella, he decides to remain at the Esposito vineyards. On her wedding night Rosabella gives herself to Joe. Presently Rosabella is both pregnant and repentant. At first enraged at the news, Tony eventually forgives her and, out of his desire for children, generously declares that the child will be recognized as his own. Joe, a natural wanderer, hits the road again. All accept the situation with no thought about the moral code.

The wide variety of lyrics ranges from the more seriously toned "My Heart is So Full of You," "My Rosabella," and "Pretty Bambini" to some lyric lines burlesquing Italian opera. Of the strictly popular songs, "Standin' on the corner,/Watching all the girls/Go by" (a quartette by vineyard workers) wittily describes a typical small-town street scene on Saturday during the twenties, when young men delightedly ogled the passing belles. Realism is added by a Mielziner set depicting the main street corner of Napa, against the distant scene of the rolling California grape lands bathed in sunlight. Other catchy tunes, in addition to the title song, include the haunting "Joey, Joey, Joey" and the briskly sung "Big D," an amusing tribute to Dallas, Texas. Dania Krupska's choreography is quite vigorous. Pure Americana, it is in the form of lively dances by typical Napa townspeople, lusty vineyard workers, and others of the 1927 era.

On December 19, 1957, the 1912 era came gaily alive on stage at New York's Majestic Theatre, as a kerosene-lamped day coach on the Rock Island line slowed down for the next stop: River City, a little tank town in Iowa. The passengers, mostly a fraternity of card-playing drummers, have been discussing a wily charlatan about whom they have heard on their travels: "A neck-or-nothin' rip-roarin', ever'time-a-bull's eye *sales*man, that's Professor Harold Hill." As they speak this first-scene lyric in fuguelike patterns, they do not know the identity of the stranger who has just hit the jackpot in their card game. Actually he is that same Harold Hill, a gabbing confidence man destined to enliven the dull routine of River City's "neck-bowed Hawkeyes" by his shenanigans as a quick-tongued salesman of band equipment.

The "Professor," protagonist of Meredith Willson's prizewinning *The Music Man*, "blows into town" on the Fourth of July, 1912. Full of grandiose talk about rescuing River City's youth from the temptations of Mayor Shinn's pool parlor, this slick spellbinder proposes to organize them into a boys' band, for which he will supply the instruments, uniforms, and instruction books—all for a sizable fee, of course. In reality Hill cannot read a note of music or play a single instrument; but, as he sings a confidence-game number titled "Ya Got Trouble," this ear-catching, dream-making, fast-talking charmer casts a spell over the townspeople. In the beginning he has no intention of lingering in the town to deliver the goods, or to betray his ignorance of music. His scheming called for a quick getaway, once he had the citizens' money safely secreted in his cardboard suitcase. His experiences as a spellbinder are familiar ones, like those of the charlatan in N. Richard Nash's *The Rainmaker*. Professor Hill had not reckoned on the influence of a good woman. A demure but high-spirited music teacher and librarian, Marian Paroo, recognizes the better side of his nature and persuades him to confess his fraud by facing a sort of public trial in the high school assembly room. At curtain fall the Professor wins both exoneration and Marian for his efforts, however originally dishonest, to transform River City into a singing and dancing community.

This turn of events is commonplace, sentimentally nostalgic, and corny; yet so brilliant was Morton Da Costa's direction and the combined talents of Herbert Greene as musical director and vocal arranger, Onna White as choreographer, Howard Bay as stage designer, and Paoul Pené du Bois as costume designer that the production, by Kermit Bloomgarden, won multiple prizes and unanimous critical scoring as "one of the best musical comedies of our time." Talented Robert Preston, as the original Harold Hill, employed a variation of the talking-to-music perfected by Rex Harrison, and from the beginning made a wonderful thing of "Ya Got Trouble." One of the most memorable scenes was the colorful one of the band ensemble as it marched to the rousing tune of "Seventy-six Trombones." Still another big production number was "Marian the Librarian," along with "Pickalittle," a delightful satire on gossipy women, and "The Shipoopi," a new dance step the Professor taught the "kids." Barbara Cook as Marian and little red-haired, freckled Eddie Hodges, as lisping Winthrop Paroo, added much to the spirited singing and dancing, as did the townsmen forming a barbershop quartet. Yet for all of its ebullient good humor, quick footwork, and inventive scoring, *The Music Man* has been criticized as lacking something approximating the freshness and individuality of Meredith Willson's native state that inspired it.

Barbershop quartets and girls in middies and bloomers, standard athletic choreography that passes for Americana, a time-tested story line and a prevailing air of determined cuteness may all be sure-fire ingredients for commercial success on Broadway, but they add up to a stage picture that is slick and formula-ridden when it should be full of native vitality and spontaneity.[81]

In other words, postcard quaintness is no substitute for true regionalism.

In the history of the actual American small town, census records and other surveys offer ample evidence about the relationships existing between the small town, the surrounding countryside, the county seat, and the nearest city. Often closeness of association stems from economic, legal, medical, and other needs, particularly if a small place is located

near a trading center such as a county seat or an easily reached city. Relationships, also, may develop from cultural and entertainment desires,
depending upon the interest of townspeople in metropolitan social affairs, concerts, plays, movies, and operas. On occasion the relationship
may be reversed, notably when city-dwellers seek relaxation in those
small places whose peaceful routine offers them relief from the hurly-
burly of the city.

Reflections of such relationships sometimes appear in musicals, as in
the serious drama of the small town. For example, the plot of Meredith
Willson and Richard Morris' *The Unsinkable Molly Brown*, a Theatre
Guild production which opened on November 3, 1960, at New York's
Winter Garden, begins with small-town life, moves far afield, and eventually returns to the town. As the rags to riches theme develops, action
moves from Hannibal, Missouri, to Leadville, Colorado, thence to Denver, to Paris, and back to Denver and Leadville.

At the turn of the century Shamus Tobin, "a big Irishman with a flush
of bourbon," was living in a Hannibal hovel with his teen-age red-haired
daughter Molly and his several sons. While she is scuffling with her
husky brothers, Molly sings her fighting song, "I Ain't Down Yet," which
foreshadows the entire action. Lustily singing, "There'll come a time
cause/Nuthin' ner/Nobody wants me/Down like I wants me/Up/Up
where the people are . . . ," Molly self-reliantly reassures herself that "I
am important to/Me I ain't no/Bottom to no pile." Soon afterward
Molly, like her brothers, "goes a-westering" as far as Leadville, Colorado, where she encounters a burly miner by the name of Johnny Brown.
With the hope of improving her hand-to-mouth existence, she marries
Johnny.

When he hits pay dirt, Johnny buys Molly a life of opulence in Denver
and abroad. Motivated by her social aspirations, Molly moves from the
Saddle Rock Saloon and Flophouse in Leadville to hard-won leadership
in Denver and European circles. Her fight with "the beautiful people of
Denver" leaves Molly unsinkable, for by her determination, wits, and
Irish humor she at last triumphs over Mrs. McGlone, "a regal-looking
grande dame, the czarina of Denver society." In Paris Molly becomes
the toast of the international set, from whom she learns tricks to astound
Denver's elite, now "only in its second generation." A sensational episode, the sinking of the transatlantic ship on which she is a passenger,
not only suggests the horror of the *Titanic* disaster but gives Molly an
opportunity to prove her capacity for heroism, and eventually to return
to Johnny in Leadville. In the Guild production Tammy Grimes's many
talents in interpreting the role left no doubt about Molly's eventual hap-

piness and the fun poked at the social pretensions of the *nouveau riche* of the mining camps in the era from about 1900 to 1912. After all, Molly had "Tobin guts and Brown luck—with that combination who wouldn't be unsinkable?"[82]

Another musical tangential to the drama of the small town of past years is *Hello, Dolly!* Under the direction of Joseph Anthony, this became the outstanding box office success of 1963 and since then has been pleasing thousands both in David Merrick's New York production and on the road. As mentioned earlier, Michael Stewart's libretto originated in Thornton Wilder's *The Matchmaker*. The play's touching passages tell of the blooming of a repressed Yonkers clerk, Cornelius Hackl, and the return to happiness of widowed Dolly Levi, who at last recognizes that her husband is dead but that, after all, a second marriage is not out of the question. The musical's only interruptive passages seem to be those where the trite theme of the triumph of love is interpolated, "even though the climactic number, where Dolly Levi whams into the Harmonia Gardens Restaurant 'Back Where She Belongs' was a kind of bacchanal of second birth." In its fusion of all the arts, including the tuneful music and catchy lyrics of Jerry Hyman, the musical has proved a livelier dramatic vehicle than Wilder's comedy. All in all, with its leading role of Dolly Gallagher Levi, *Hello, Dolly!* is a delightful expression of uninhibited exuberance and a showcase for the strident genius of Carol Channing. Ginger Rogers, who gave quieter but enthusiastically applauded performances, took Miss Channing's role in the New York production in the summer of 1965. The fast-moving action, shifting from small-town Yonkers, as it was in the 1880's, to New York City, offers another sprightly fictionalization of the close relationship which once existed between provincials and urbanites.

The continuing present-day popularity of themes involving close interrelation between the small town and adjacent areas is reflected once more in N. Richard Nash's 1964 revision of his most successful play, *The Rainmaker*. Rewritten as a musical titled *110 in the Shade*, this adaptation shifts its action from a farmhouse, presumably in the arid Southwest, "somewhere west of a line running through Beaumont, Fort Smith, and Kansas City", to a nearby farm village and back again. The combined talents of Nash, lyricist Tom Jones and his fellow Texan, composer Harvey Schmidt, and choreographer Agnes De Mille produced another southwestern folk musical highly suggestive of the locale and the conflict between good and evil popularized in *Oklahoma!* Starbuck, the con man, bamboozling susceptible villagers and farmers by his witty ballyhoo, at last awakens to a world of love and beauty a repressed and supposedly plain farm girl, who blossoms in response to his charm and his lovemaking. The premiere of this musical featured Robert Horton (as Starbuck) in his Broadway debut, with Inga Swenson.

Contributing to the shaping and reshaping of theatrical images of the small town, modern interpreters and adapters have offered new kinds of entertainment: poetized narrative and the dramatic anthology. In 1951 folklorist and poet Ralph Alan McCanse, using smoothly flowing rhythms, chronicled the life and death of a historic county seat in the picturesque Ozarks of Camden County, Missouri. His *Waters over Linn Creek Town* tells the moving story of the submerging of a quiet little town once peopled by sturdy Missourians who cherished equally their old homesteads and their traditional folkways. When in 1931 the waters of the gigantic Lake of the Ozarks—a man-made inland sea—flooded the peaceful valleys of five counties in Central Missouri, Linn Creek Town and all that its simple folk held dear were swept away forever. This idyll of the Ozarks, with its authentic human situations related to the destruction of humble life in the name of a delusive material prosperity, is one of our most poetic and emotionally stirring versions of our vanishing small towns. Its sympathetically narrated stories, such as those of keen old Dr. Franklin Barr and his rustic patients, of a village preacher conducting "baptizin'" rites at a roadside creek, and of an unsophisticated girl's love affair, go beyond memorializing the little people of Linn Creek, whose old-time associations are obliterated by a huge corporate enterprise. In prefatory words Professor Robert L. Ransay calls this appealing regional poem also "a veritable assault of Leviathan."

In keeping with the pervasive disenchantment of the world of the sixties, *Spoon River*, a 1963 stage adaptation of Edgar Lee Masters' verse portraits created by Charles Aidman, represents a late twentieth-century acknowledgement of hate, love, dissimulation, and lust in village life of long ago. It was a considerable gamble to bring to New York a compilation of dramatic excerpts from the Masters *Anthology*, which originated as readings by a group of reciters associated with the Theatre Group, University Extension, UCLA. The success of the recent Broadway production at the Booth Theatre may have come from Aidman's choice of a book unique in the annals of American poetry, which was as much a sensation of its time (1914-15) as *Leaves of Grass* had been in the late 1850's. Under the brilliant direction of Aidman, who also acted some of the parts, three other players, or reciters—Robert Elston, Betty Garrett, and Joyce Van Patten—showed much versatility in interpreting multiple roles. They were supported by two folk singers, Naomi Caryl

Hirshhorn and Hal Lynch, "singing to a plaintive—and charming—twangle of accompaniment."

The Aidman dramatization indicated that Masters, while always aware of the unpleasantness of early Illinois village life, also acknowledged the presence of loyalty, love, and spirituality in the average town and portrayed some characters as the happy conquerors of circumstances. As the poet once described it, his *Anthology* was meant to be

. . . the interwoven history of a whole community, a village, a city, or whatever you like to call it. . . . I had a variety of things in mind in the writing of the anthology. I meant to analyse character, to satirize society, to tell a story, to expose the machinery of life, to present to view a working model of the big world. . . . And I had in mind, too, the creation of beauty and the depiction of our sorrows and hopes, our religious failures, successes, and visions, our poor little lives . . .[83]

As most readers know, the original anthology, deprecating the hypocrisy of the conventional tombstone inscription, purports to be composed of epitaphs in the Spoon River graveyard. The background and key to the entire work, probably suggested by Masters' memories of the deserted cemetery at New Salem, Illinois, are provided in the prologue—"The Hill"—descriptive of the village dead.[84] In most uncompromising terms each buried man and woman—"the weak of will, the strong of arm, the clown, the boozer, the fighter"—is made to speak from the tomb his or her retrospect of life. Thus is acknowledged the presence of lust, greed, and sordidness, as well as beauty and commendable vitality, in this midwestern village. The secrets of the entire citizenship are laid bare; few reputations are left undisturbed.

In the staged readings given by Theatre West, as the Aidman group describes itself, as each player in turn acted out a separate poetic epitaph, gradually the entire village along the Spoon River came to life. In keeping with Masters' purpose, the village, as dramatized, became provincial America everywhere and the villagers the counterparts of people in everyday life. By their sense of conviction in their presentation of folksy vignettes, these California players brought a much-needed freshness to the Broadway scene.[85]

XII. Afterword

"ONE OFTEN HEARS," wrote Herman Melville concerning his struggles with the immensity of his findings on whales and whaling when he was writing *Moby-Dick*, "of writers that rise and fall with their subject, though often it may seem but an ordinary one. How, then, with me writing of this Leviathan?" One feels an empathy with him in writing of the drama of the American small town, a subject which, while not so monumental as Melville's, has greatly widened in scope over the two centuries of its history. Some observers may regard our native community life as too ordinary, too dully commonplace a subject for the imaginative writer; but the truth is that the little town has been re-created in dramatic form by some of our best playwrights. And the time span from Colonel Munford's politically slanted comedy of 1770, *The Candidates*, and Royall Tyler's socially satiric *The Contrast* (1787) to the 1962-63 productions of *Who's Afraid of Virginia Woolf?* and the 1967-68 presentation of *Spofford* is quite wide enough to allow any literary historian to "rise and fall" with the subject.

Undeniably, certain aspects of small-town material, notably the sense of "togetherness" existing in the small town, its narrowness of spirit, and the desire to escape from it, have been overworked. What choices of untried dramatic material and fresh production methods remain, then, to challenge the creative dramatist and appeal to the public as well? In spite of the efforts of the "New Wave" playwrights and other iconoclasts, there is today a body of criticism stressing the need for new horizons and new techinques to rescue the American theater from the seasonal influx of stereotyped, stale plays, unoriginal ones about the small town included. Hemingway, in his "Monologue to the Maestro," stated the problem clearly: "There is no use writing anything that has been written before unless you can beat it. What a writer in our time has to do is to write what hasn't been written before or beat dead men at what they have done."

The artistic dramatizer of the small town will do well, in the future, to search for "what hasn't been written before." One area in which this may be found is American interpretation of foreign small-town life, which has been relatively neglected by our playwrights. True, Godfrey's *The Prince of Parthia* (1767) was set in Parthia's small capital, Ctesiphon. Later, with the rise of the romantic plays, Robert Montgomery Bird, with *The*

Broker of Bogota (1834) reopened the foreign field in his dramatization of small-town affairs in the capital of New Granada (Colombia). Shortly thereafter his fellow romantics Nathaniel Parker Willis, in *Bianca Visconti* (1837) and *Tortesa the Usurer* (1839), and George Henry Boker, in *Francesca da Rimini* (1855), recreated the past of Milan, Florence, and Rimini respectively. But these were isolated instances.

In more recent times, American awareness of other cultures has obviously been deepened by new confrontations brought about by increased tourist travel, wartime movements, economic links with other nations, the exchange of professors and students, the sending of Peace Corps workers to needy areas, and other occasions for encounters with people beyond our borders. Nevertheless, too few American playwrights seem to have recognized the fact that our "homemade provincial wares no longer startle and amaze the world." Except for widely traveled writers like Thornton Wilder, Americans have written only a small number of artistic plays about foreign small towns. A few plays, however, have represented successfully the struggles of the peoples of other nations. For example, views of the effect of modern war on European townspeople are reflected in several stage hits. Robert Sherwood's *There Shall Be No Night* (1940), set at the time of the Russo-Finnish War of 1939, championed a small democracy fighting for survival. In 1942 John Steinbeck's *The Moon Is Down* dramatized the effect of the Nazi occupation on the inhabitants of a small town in Norway. Paul Osborn's artistic adaptation in 1944 of the John Hersey novel *A Bell for Adano* dealt with the way in which democracy was made to work in an Italian village during the World War II American occupation.

During the fifties a few foreign provincial locales were featured on the American stage, each in response to some phase of world unrest. John Patrick's delightful adaptation from Vern Sneider's novel *The Teahouse of the August Moon* (1953) was an amusing picture of naïve charm and native cunning in an Okinawan village occupied by a small American force. During the same season Tennessee Williams' philosophic *Camino Real*, a melancholy study of wayward souls miscast in a decadent modern society, was set in "an unspecified Latin-American country," possibly Mexico, which also furnished him with a specific locale, near Puerto Vallarta, for *The Night of the Iguana* (1961).

As our society continues to be disrupted more and more by all sorts of violent upheavals, the theater may become a forum for the further representation of community reaction to grave domestic issues, old injustices, and new social forces. Public complacency in regard to ethnic problems and social strife may be challenged in entirely new ways in the small-town dramas of tomorrow. Already, in addition to the plays we have discussed in Chapters VII and X, there have been dramas which contain scenes attacking the intolerance shown by small-town society toward minority groups. Robert Ardrey's *Jeb*, *Deep Are the Roots* by Arnaud d'Usseau and James Gow, and Lillian and Esther Smith's dramatized *Strange Fruit* (1945) are such plays. In 1964 James Baldwin's first play, the fiery but awkwardly constructed *Blues for Mr. Charlie*, bared the tragic truth about the inequality separating two groups of American townspeople: the favored dwellers in Whitetown and the "Have-Nots" in Blacktown—both parts of Plaguetown, U.S.A., where "the plague is race, the plague is our concept of Christianity." Unfortunately, in the Actors Studio production the polemics of this play overshadowed the art. Perhaps these plays, and others like them, are only preludes to future and more universally appealing dramatizations of folk material symbolizing the struggles for racial identity in American towns of every region.

One thing is certain: the knowledgeable playwright of the future, moved by an interest in folkways, needs to be, as Henry James advised, an imaginative person "on whom nothing is lost." Possibly new frontiers —Cuba, Vietnam, Latin America, and other areas of war and unrest— may beckon to him. Most of all, however, as Wright Morris has observed, we have on the American theatrical scene today "a need, however illusive, for a life that is more real than life. It lies in the imagination. Fiction would seem to be the way it is processed into reality." In these angry days, new and different vistas of both American and foreign communities would bring fresh vigor to the drama of Smalltown, U.S.A.

Notes

CHAPTER I

1. Phillips Bradley, ed., *Democracy in America* (New York: Alfred A. Knopf, 1954), 1:319.

2. Howard Mumford Jones, ed., *A History of American Literature: 1607-1765* (Ithaca: Cornell University Press, 1949), pp. 85, 88.

3. Perry Miller, *The Puritans* (New York: American Book Co., 1938), p. 19. Cf. "The New England Way," in Miller, *Orthodoxy in Massachusetts* (Cambridge: Harvard University Press, 1933); Miller, *The New England Mind: From Colony to Province* (Cambridge: Harvard University Press, 1953) and *Errand into the Wilderness* (Cambridge: Harvard University Press, 1957); William Warren Sweet, *Religion in Colonial America* (New York: Charles Scribner's Sons, 1942); V. L. Parrington, *The Colonial Mind: 1620-1800* (New York: Harcourt, Brace & Co., 1927); "The New England Way" and "Molders of New England," in Joseph Dorfman, *The Economic Mind in American Civilization: 1606-1865* (New York: Viking Press, 1946), 1:29-59, 60-74.

4. Miller, *The Puritans*, p. 4.

5. Miller's analysis, "The Marrow of Puritan Divinity," in *Errand into the Wilderness*, pp. 49-98, clarifies the Calvinistic views of the original settlers of New England, who generally did think of man and the universe much as did Calvin; yet "they learned the Calvinist theology only after it had been improved, embellished, and in many respects transformed by a host of hard-thinking expounders and critics."

6. Carl Sandburg, *Remembrance Rock* (New York: Harcourt, Brace & Co., 1948), pp. 37-38.

7. *Ibid.* Cf. William Haller, *The Rise of Puritanism* (New York: Columbia University Press, 1938), p. 187.

8. Moses Coit Tyler, in Jones, ed., *History of American Literature*, p. 91.

9. Charles and Mary Beard, *The Rise of American Civilization*, one vol. ed. (New York: Macmillan, 1930), 1:69, 143. An older survey, Rufus M. Jones, *The Quakers in the American Colonies* (London, 1911), and Sweet's more recent *Religion in Colonial America* (1942) discuss in full the tensions associated with Quakerism.

10. See Helen A. Clarke, *Longfellow's Country* (New York: Baker and Taylor, 1909), pp. 147 ff., for a partial reprinting of Longfellow's chief sources: Joseph Besse, *A Collection of the Sufferings of the People Called Quakers for the Testimony of a Good Conscience . . . 1650 to the . . . Act of Toleration . . . in the Year 1689*, 2 vols. (London, 1753); John Norton, *The Heart of New England Rent at the Blasphemies of the Present Generation* (Cambridge, 1659); and George Bishop, *New England Judged by the Spirit of the Lord* (London, 1703).

11. Jules Michelet, *Satanism and Witchcraft: A Study in Medieval Superstition*, trans. A. R. Allinson (New York: Citadel Press, 1939), pt. 1. For a full analysis, with 250 illustrations, see "The Devil," "Witchcraft," and "Diabolic Rites," in Kurt Seligmann, *The Mirror of Magic* (New York: Pantheon Books, 1948), pp. 216 ff., 238 ff., 290 ff.

12. George Lyman Kittredge, *Witchcraft in Old and New England* (Cambridge: Harvard University Press, 1928), p. 338. Chap. 18, "Witchcraft and the Puritans," fully describes colonial attitudes toward demonology.

13. *Ibid.,* p. 335.

14. An enlargement of an earlier work, Joseph Glanvill, *Some Philosophical Considerations Concerning the Being of Witches and Witchcraft* (1666).

15. Cf. Michelet, *Satanism and Witchcraft,* and "The People Who Became Witches" and "The Sabbats" in Pennethorne Hughes, *Witchcraft* (London: Longmans, Green & Co., 1952), chaps. 6, 10.

16. Sweet, *Religion in Colonial America,* p. 99.

17. Miller, *Errand into the Wilderness,* pp. 71 ff.

18. Randall Stewart, *Nathaniel Hawthorne: A Biography* (New Haven: Yale University Press, 1929), p. 258.

19. A departure from the somber tone prevailing in Puritan village plays has been made by students of Professor Frederick Koch in a volume of four one-act plays on colonial themes, from the *Dakota Playmaker Series* (Boston: Walter H. Baker Co., 1923). Although written primarily for the Pilgrim Tercentenary of 1921, these one-acters are not restricted to the Plymouth locale. For instance, John E. Grinnell's *John Bargrave, Gentleman,* based on records of the Virginia Company, portrays Williamsburg during 1720. There is much roguish merriment in Cotton Mather's daughter, Betty, the heroine of Beulah Bomstead's farcical *The Diabolical Circle.* Puritan Betty, outwardly demure, is inwardly rebellious against the strict conventions of her Boston household, and uses her own clever trick to get a wedding ring. (In the opinion of her learned father, the ring is "a diabolical circle for the devil to dance in.") Rose C. Meblin's *Dowry and Romance,* picturing Boston of 1720, is a comedy sketch based on the familiar episode in Samuel Sewall's diary of the judge's persistent courtship of Dame Winthrop.

20. Kittredge, *Witchcraft in Old and New England,* pp. 370-71.

21. Miller, *Orthodoxy in Massachusetts,* p. 161.

22. Paul H. Musser, *James Nelson Barker* (Philadelphia: University of Pennsylvania Press, 1929), pp. 92, 215 (full list of sources).

23. Cf. Samuel Longfellow, *The Life of Henry Wadsworth Longfellow* (Boston: Houghton Mifflin, 1886), 2:312, 319, 323, 3:123; T. W. Higginson, *Henry Wadsworth Longfellow* (Boston: Houghton Mifflin, 1902), p. 239; Herbert S. Gorman, *A Victorian American* (New York: Doran, 1926), p. 280.

24. Arthur Miller, *The Crucible* (New York: Viking Press, 1955), p. xi.

25. Musser, *James Nelson Barker,* pp. 138 ff., a reprint of the comedy.

26. *Ibid.,* p. 87. Cf. Arthur Hobson Quinn, *A History of the American Drama from the Beginning to the Civil War* (New York: Crofts, 1944), p. 147.

27. Quinn, *American Drama Beginning to Civil War,* p. 150.

28. Musser, *James Nelson Barker,* p. 92.

29. Marion L. Starkey, *The Devil in Massachusetts: A Modern Inquiry into the Salem Witch Trials* (New York: Alfred A. Knopf, 1949), p. 28, describes the Reverend Samuel Parris (an excellent prototype for Ravensworth) as having something in his composition "to which so dramatic a struggle with the powers of darkness made a direct appeal."

30. Albert Mordell, ed., *Notorious Literary Attacks* (New York, 1926), pp. 129-37. Randall Stewart, in his scholarly *Nathaniel Hawthorne,* pp. 96 ff., surveys both the favorable and the unfavorable aspects of the critical evaluation first given *The Scarlet Letter.* Earlier Henry James, *Hawthorne* (London: Macmillan & Co., 1879), chap. 5, evaluated *The Scarlet Letter* in a far more judicial manner than that used by Coxe and other hostile critics who violently opposed what they considered the pronounced immorality of the novel. Contrasting Hawthorne's novel with a similar treatment of a rigidly Calvinistic society, John Gibson Lockhart's *Adam Blair,* James points out that the history of a passion in the latter work throws into relief the *passionless* quality of *The Scarlet Letter.*

31. H. J. Eldredge, comp., *The Stage Encyclopaedia: A Bibliography of Plays* (London: "The Stage," 1909), p. 399. Nina E. Browne, *A Bibliography of Nathaniel Hawthorne* (Boston: Houghton Mifflin, 1905), p. 100, lists an opera in three acts, with words by George Parsons Lathrop and the vocal score by Walter Damrosch (Leipzig: Breitkopf & Hartel, 1896); and a dramatization by Joseph Hatton, presented in 1892 by Richard Mansfield, with no record that it was published.

32. Cf. Kittredge, *Witchcraft in Old and New England*, pp. 366-69.

33. For biographical data see Evert A. Duyckinck and George L. Duyckinck, *Cyclopaedia of American Literature* (New York: Charles Scribner, 1856), 2:645-49; for critical summary of *Witchcraft* see Quinn, *American Drama Beginning to Civil War*, p. 276. For more detailed evaluation consult Margaret Fuller, "American Literature, Its Position in the Present Time, and Prospects for the Future" (from *Papers on Literature and Art*, 1846), in Mason Wade, ed., *The Writings of Margaret Fuller* (New York: Viking Press, 1941), pp. 367-69.

34. Cornelius Mathews, *Witchcraft: A Tragedy, in Five Acts* (New York: Samuel French, 1852), p. 10.

35. *Ibid.*, p. 31.

36. *Ibid.*, p. 98.

37. Fuller accounts appear in Longfellow, *Longfellow*, 2:312, 319, 323; 3:83, 102, 122, 173; Higginson, *Henry Wadsworth Longfellow*, pp. 229 ff.; Gorman, *A Victorian American*, pp. 280, 305; Clarke, *Longfellow's Country*, pp. 147-73.

38. Rufus M. Jones, *The Quakers in the American Colonies* (London, 1911).

39. *John Endicott*, in Henry Wadsworth Longfellow, *The New England Tragedies* (Boston: Ticknor and Fields, 1868), Act IV, sc. 5, p. 81.

40. *Giles Corey of the Salem Farms*, in Longfellow, *The New England Tragedies*, p. 101.

41. *Ibid.*, Act IV, sc. 2, p. 157.

42. Samuel G. Goodrich, *Recollections of A Lifetime: Or Men and Things I Have Seen* (New York: Arundel Print, 1856), pp. 56-57.

43. Mary E. Wilkins Freeman, *Giles Corey, Yeoman: A Play* (New York: Harper & Bros., 1893), Act I, p. 88.

44. Although Starkey, *The Devil in Massachusetts*, pp. 7, 17, 119, shows that the Bayley name, especially that of the Reverend James Bayley, was well known in Salem, I have not found a reference to a real Paul Bayley.

45. Miller, *Errand into the Wilderness*, p. 239.

46. Winfield S. Nevins, *Witchcraft in Salem Village in 1692* (Salem: North Shore Publishing Co., 1892), p. 104.

47. Freeman, *Giles Corey*, Act V, pp. 95-96.

48. *Ibid.*, pp. 71-72.

49. *Ibid.*, pp. 65-68.

50. *Ibid.*, pp. 70-71.

51. *Ibid.*, p. 94.

52. "Salem and *The Scarlet Letter*, 1846-1850," in Stewart, *Nathaniel Hawthorne*, chap. 2, gives full publication data, as does Browne, *Bibliography of Nathaniel Hawthorne*, pp. 62-68, in listing early editions of the novel.

53. Quinn, *American Drama Beginning to Civil War*, p. 482. Joseph Jefferson, *The Autobiography of Joseph Jefferson* (New York: Century, 1890), p. 151, refers to Andrews as comedian; the title page of Andrews' version indicates his work as a comedian, as well as the dramatizer of *The Count of Monte Cristo*.

54. In "The Early New England Village in Literature," chap. 2 in Ima Honaker Herron, *The Small Town in American Literature* (Durham: Duke University Press, 1939), from which the above quotation is taken, I fully analyzed *The Scarlet Letter*; hence, the omission of such analysis in this study.

55. George H. Andrews, *The Scarlet Drama: A Drama in Three Acts from

N. Hawthorne's Celebrated Novel (Boston: Charles H. Spencer, Agent, 1871); Elizabeth Weller Peck, *Nathaniel Hawthorne's Scarlet Letter Dramatized* (Boston: Franklin Press, 1876); Gabriel Harrison, *A Romantic Drama, in Four Acts, Entitled The Scarlet Letter, Dramatized from Nathaniel Hawthorne's Masterly Romance* (Brooklyn: Harry M. Gardner, Jr., 1876); and James Edgar Smith, *The Scarlet Stigma: A Drama in Four Acts. Founded upon Nathaniel Hawthorne's Novel The Scarlet Letter* (Washington, D.C.: James J. Chapman, 1899).

56. Alice Felt Tyler, *Freedom's Ferment* (Minneapolis: University of Minnesota Press, 1944), pp. 78 ff. *Vide* Dr. A. Maclister, "Stigmatization," in *Encyclopaedia Britannica*, 11th ed., 15:917-18, for a brief historical sketch of the infliction of stigmata (especially concerning the "irresponsible self-infliction of injuries by persons in the hystero-epileptic condition"). For a contemporary account see "Spiritualism," in T. L. Nichols, M.D., *Forty Years of American Life*, 2d ed. (London: Longmans, Green, & Co., 1874), chap. 28. (First edition, 1864).

57. Smith, *The Scarlet Stigma*, Act I, sc. 1, p. 11.

58. *Ibid.*, p. 14.

59. Cf. Peck, *Nathaniel Hawthorne's Scarlet Letter Dramatized*, Act III, sc. 1, p. 35, Arthur's soliloquy:

> How poor a thing is life! How terrible
> When twin errors—remorse and pain—
> Drive talons deep with every heart-beat! . . .
> I will no longer bear it; but forth
> On the pillory's shameful height I'll cry my shame,
> And bare by branded breast to a world
> That joys that evil liveth.

60. Oscar F. Adams, *A Dictionary of American Authors* (Boston: Houghton Mifflin, 1904), p. 172.

61. Montrose J. Moses, "A Plea for Folk Basis in American Drama," *North American Review*, 243 (January, 1931): 84.

62. Percy MacKaye, *Epoch: The Life of Steele Mackaye, Genius of the Theatre* (New York: Boni & Liveright, 1927), *passim*. See also "Percy Mackaye and the Drama of Spectacle," in Arthur Hobson Quinn, *A History of the American Drama from the Civil War to the Present Day* (New York: Crofts, 1943), chap. 13. Valuable, too, is the essay on *The Scarecrow* in Montrose J. Moses and Joseph Wood Krutch, eds., *Representative American Dramas* (Boston: Heath, 1941), pp. 191 ff.; Wisner P. Kinne, *George Pierce Baker and the American Theatre* (Cambridge: Harvard University Press, 1954), chaps. 12-27, for general background.

63. Moses and Krutch, *Representative American Dramas*, p. 194. *Feathertop*, first published in the *International Magazine*, February-March, 1852, was included in *Mosses from an Old Manse*, 1854.

64. Percy MacKaye, *The Scarecrow* (New York: Macmillan Co., 1908), preface.

65. *Ibid.*, Act I.

66. *Ibid.*

67. *Ibid.*, Act IV.

68. Kinne, *George Pierce Baker*, p. 130, nn., in connection with Winthrop Ames's experiments at his "New Theatre" in New York, the February, 1910, production of Herman Hagedorn's *The Witch*, a Sardou-like adaptation of a Scandinavian play to the conditions of the Salem trials, long antedating *The Crucible*.

69. John and Alice Griffin, "Arthur Miller Discusses *The Crucible*," *Theatre Arts*, 37 (October, 1953): 34. See also "*The Crucible*," in Sheila Huftel, *Arthur Miller: The Burning Glass* (New York: Citadel Press, 1965), chap. 7, for cogent analysis.

70. Jay Williams, *The Witches* (New York: Random House, 1957).

71. Joseph Wood Krutch, *American Drama since 1918*, rev. ed. (New York: George Braziller, 1957), p. 325. Cf. George Jean Nathan, "Henrik Miller," *Theatre Arts*, 37 (April, 1953): 24-26, who feels that the parallel is not only obvious, but quite harmful to Miller's dramatic art.

72. Griffin and Griffin, "Arthur Miller Discusses *The Crucible*," p. 33.

73. Van Wyck Brooks, *On Literature Today* (New York: E. P. Dutton, 1941), pp. 13-15.

74. Nathan, "Henrik Miller," pp. 25-26.

75. This scene, a sequence added to Act II, was first staged in the new production of July, 1953, and first printed, with photographic illustration, as part of the complete text in *Theatre Arts*, October, 1953.

76. Nevins, *Witchcraft in Salem Village*, p. 130.

77. Arthur Miller, *The Crucible: A Play in Four Acts* (New York: Viking Press, 1955), p. 33. The earlier version was copyrighted under the title of *Those Familiar Spirits*.

78. *Ibid.*, p. 145.

CHAPTER II

1. Arthur M. Schlesinger, Jr., *The Age of Jackson* (Boston: Little, Brown & Co., 1945), p. 368.

2. Arthur Hobson Quinn, *A History of the American Drama from the Beginning to the Civil War* (New York: Crofts, 1944), p. 292.

3. Schlesinger, *The Age of Jackson*, p. 369.

4. *Ibid.*, p. 370.

5. "How Americans Choose Their Heroes," in Dixon Wecter, *The Hero in America: A Chronicle of Hero-Worship* (New York: Charles Scribner's Sons, 1941), chap. 18.

6. Brander Matthews, "The American on the Stage," *Scribner's Monthly*, 18 (July, 1879): 321-22.

7. *Ibid.*

8. "Corn Cobs Twist Your Hair," in Constance Rourke, *American Humor: A Study of the National Character* (New York: Harcourt, Brace & Co., 1931), chap. 1.

9. *Ibid.*, p. 17.

10. Jennette Tandy, *Crackerbox Philosophers in American Humor and Satire* (New York: Columbia University Press, 1925), p. 2.

11. "The Yankee," in Richard Moody, *America Takes the Stage* (Bloomington: Indiana University Press, 1955), p. 110. A recent book-length study is Francis Hodge, *Yankee Theatre: The Image of America on the Stage, 1825-1850* (Austin: University of Texas Press, 1964).

12. Montrose J. Moses and John Mason Brown, eds., *The American Theatre as Seen by Its Critics: 1752-1934* (New York: Norton & Co., 1934), pp. 24-25. William Dunlap, *A History of the American Theatre* (New York: J. & J. Harper, 1832), pp. 71-72, evaluated the portrayal of Jonathan, as follows:

"The Contrast" ranks first in point of time of all American plays, which had been performed by players. It is extremely deficient in plot, dialogue, or incident, but has some marking in the characters, and in that of *Jonathan*, played by Wignell, a degree of humour, and knowledge of what is termed Yankee dialect, which in the hands of a favorite performer, was relished by an audience gratified by the appearance of home manufacture—a feeling which was soon exchanged for a most discouraging predilection for foreign articles, and contempt for every home-made effort. This comedy was given by the author to Wignell, who published it [in Philadelphia] in 1790 by subscription.

13. William Clark Tyler, *The Contrast*, in Allan Gates Halline, ed., *American Plays* (New York: American Book Co., 1935), Act III, sc. 1, p. 27.

14. Woodrow Wilson, "Character of Democracy in the United States," *Atlantic Monthly*, 64 (November, 1889): 579.

15. Tyler, *The Contrast*, in Halline, *American Plays*, Act III, sc. 1, p. 28.

16. Halline, *American Plays*, pp. 5-6.

17. "The Comic Countryman (1775-1839)," in Tandy, *Crackerbox Philosophers*, chap. 1. Other helpful parallel studies include Mary Alice Wyman, *Two American Pioneers: Seba Smith and Elizabeth Oakes Smith* (New York: Columbia University Press, 1927) and Edwin Harrison Cady, *The Gentleman in America: A Literary Study in American Culture* (Syracuse: Syracuse University Press, 1949). In the latter, chap. 3 ("'Fine' Gentleman vs. Christian Gentleman") gives a cultural contrast between Billy Dimple's Europeanism and Manly's native American gentility.

18. Dunlap, *History of the American Theatre*, p. 72.

19. *Ibid.*, p. 75.

20. Arthur Hornblow, *A History of the Theatre in America* (Philadelphia and London: Lippincott, 1919), 1:172. See also Tandy, *Crackerbox Philosophers*, pp. 3-5, and Quinn, *American Drama Beginning to Civil War*, pp. 65-66, for fuller data.

21. Dunlap, *History of the American Theatre*, pp. 72, 74, 77, 85.

22. The most familiar portion of Sydney Smith's "Review of Adam Seybert's *Statistical Annals of the United States*," *Edinburgh Review*, 65 (January, 1820): 79-80.

23. See Ima Honaker Herron, *The Small Town in American Literature* (Durham: Duke University Press, 1939), pp. 28-32, for fuller data. Benjamin T. Spencer, *The Quest for Nationality: An American Literary Campaign* (Syracuse: Syracuse University Press, 1957), is an indispensable history of native efforts to foster a national literature.

24. For complete coverage consult Dunlap, *History of the American Theatre*, p. 78; Quinn, *America Drama Beginning to Civil War*, pp. 129-32; Louis M. Eich, "The Stage Yankee," *Quarterly Journal of Speech*, 27 (February, 1941): 16-25; for a reprint of *Tears and Smiles*, Musser, *James Nelson Barker*, pp. 138-207; and Moody, *America Takes the Stage*, pp. 63, 66, 115, 116, 241, n. 6.

25. George O. Seilhamer, *A History of the American Theatre* (Philadelphia: Globe Printing House, 1891), 3:150-51, 164, 171, 221, 244, 284-85, 303, 311, 372. Dunlap, *History of the American Theatre*, p. 324, nn.: "On the 22nd of October, 1804, the theatre of New York was opened with the Clandestine Marriage, and Village Lawyer, . . ."

26. Rourke, *American Humor*, p. 17.

27. This comedy and many other plays mentioned in the earlier chapters of this study are now easily available in a two-volume Readex Microprint collection of early American dramas. The Yale University copy (Readex Microprint, 1955) is a presentation copy, with the inked inscription, "John Trumbull, 1816," but with no date imprinted on the title page, which reads as follows: "*The Yankey in England, A Drama, in Five Acts* by General Humphreys." An introductory letter of appreciation to the British satirist and critic, William Gifford, who had read *The Yankey* in manuscript, bears the note, "Written from Humphreysville, Sept. 1, 1815." Further internal evidence regarding the date of composition appears on p. 111 in a brief account of the presentation of the comedy by young actors for a Humphreysville, Connecticut, manufacturing establishment. Finally, the long quotation describing "Yankey peculiarity" is a small part of Humphreys' "Sketches of American Characters," a critical preface (pp. 11-16) to his comedy. Humphreys, dissatisfied with the vague applications of the term "Yankee" to Americans in general, in his comedy limits it to "the inhabitants of the interior parts of New

England, as distinguished by a peculiar idiom and pronunciation, as well as by a peculiarity of character."

28. See Amos Herold, *James Kirke Paulding, Versatile American* (New York: Columbia University Press, 1926), *passim*; Halline, *American Plays*, pp. 77-80.

29. *The Bucktails*, in Halline, *American Plays*, Act I, sc. 2.

30. *Ibid.*

31. Montrose J. Moses, ed., *Representative Plays by American Dramatists, From 1765 to the Present Day* (New York: Dutton, 1925), 2:382.

32. *Ibid.*

33. *Ibid.*, p. 383.

34. *Ibid.*, p. 388.

35. Joseph S. Jones, *The Silver Spoon: A Character Sketch in Four Parts* (Boston: Walter H. Baker & Co., 1911), introductory notes. (Original production: Boston Museum, February 16, 1852.)

36. "The American Stage Negro," in Laurence Hutton, *Curiosities of the American Stage* (New York: Harper & Bros., 1891), pp. 87-144; Carl Wittke, *Tambo and Bones* (Durham: Duke University Press, 1930); and "Negro Minstrelsy," in Moody, *America Takes the Stage*, pp. 32-60, discuss and illustrate the history of Negro minstrelsy.

37. A. P. Herbert, introduction to *The Beggar's Opera* (New York: Heritage Press, 1937), pp. vii-viii. Cf. Oral S. Coad, "The Plays of Samuel Woodworth," *Sewanee Review*, 27 (April-June, 1919): 164; O. G. T. Sonneck, *Early Opera in America* (New York: Schirmer, 1915); and Sol Smith, *Theatrical Management in the West and South* (New York: Harper & Bros., 1868), p. 238. Smith recalls:

The OPERA has no permanent home in New York, but, broken into fragments, scatters itself into the interior towns and cities, where, with scant orchestra and a chorus of eight or ten cracked voices, IL TROVATORE, IL BARBIERE DE SEVIGLIA, and all the other *Ils* of the Italian repertoire, are given to the worthy citizens of Peoria and Detroit at a dollar admission, children half price, and no charge extra for securing seats; while the Academy of Music in Fourteenth Street stands with its doors closed, except . . . for a complimentary benefit.

38. From the title page of Micah Hawkins, *The Saw-Mill* (New York: J. & J. Harper, 1824). The Library of Congress copy (registered December 16, 1824) is available in Readex Microprint, 1953.

39. New York State, after long delay, began the construction of the Erie Canal in 1817, but it was not opened to commerce until 1825, shortly after the composition date of *The Saw-Mill*.

40. Joseph N. Ireland, *Records of the New York Stage from 1750 to 1860*, 2 vols. (New York: T. H. Morrell, 1866), chap. 2.

41. Samuel Woodworth, *The Forest Rose: or American Farmers* (Readex Microprint, 1954, of the University of Pennsylvania copy), prefatory note.

42. Coad, "Plays of Samuel Woodworth," calls attention to the omission of the music in later performances. The opera, he says, was repeated until 1866.

43. Woodworth, *Forest Rose*, p. 9.

44. *Ibid.*

45. *Ibid.*, pp. 15-16.

46. Coad, "Plays of Samuel Woodworth," pp. 166, 168.

47. What Herbert Ross Brown has traced most wittily for the novel, in *The Sentimental Novel in America: 1789-1860* (Durham: Duke University Press, 1940), in general applies to *The Forest Rose* and other village plays as they reflect the level of taste of this period.

48. For the cityward movement, so much reflected in our fiction and poetry, see "Modern Trends," in Herron, *Small Town in American Literature*, pp. 22 ff.

For economic backgrounds see Carl Fish, *The Rise of the Common Man, 1830-1850* (New York: Macmillan Co., 1939). Arthur M. Schlesinger's *The Rise of the City, 1878-1898* (New York: Macmillan Co., 1933) deals with the 1870's and later.

49. Moody, *America Takes the Stage*, pp. 28-29. Hornblow, *History of the Theatre*, vol. 1, chaps. 12, 13, gives much attention to first hand reports of the size and accommodations of American theaters during what he calls "the golden era of the American stage," the twenties and thirties.

50. Perkins Howes, *New England Drama* (Dedham, 1825), p. 12. Available in Readex Microprint, 1952, of an original copy in the Harvard University library.

51. *Ibid.*, p. 11.

52. Mary Carr, *The Fair Americans* (Philadelphia, 1815), p. 7. Available in Readex Microprint, 1954, of an original copy in the New York Public Library. Perly Isaac Reed, *The Realistic Presentation of American Characters* (Columbus: Ohio State University, 1918), p. 147, lists this comedy as *The Fair American*, in manuscript, and as produced at the John Street Theatre, New York, in 1789, the same season in which Dunlap's comic sketch of an Irish villager, *Darby's Return*, was played at the New Theatre.

53. *Ibid.*, p. 30.

54. Printed as Samuel Benjamin H. Judah, *A Tale of Lexington* (New York: Dramatic Repository, 1823). Readex Microprint, 1952, of a copy in the Harvard University Library. George C. D. Odell, *Annals of the New York Stage* (New York: Columbia University Press, 1927), 3:29-30, considers the hasty composition of this comedy as ridiculous and says of *The Rose of Arragon* (a "romantic gem" which Judah wrote in about *two* days), "A sillier piece was never penned in America, or elsewhere." Joseph Ireland, *Records of the New York Stage*, 1:400, 413, offers no criticism, merely listing the dates of performances and the players.

55. Ernest E. Leisy, *The American Historical Novel* (Norman: University of Oklahoma Press, 1950), p. 3.

56. *Metamora and Other Plays*, in Eugene R. Page, ed., *America's Lost Plays* (Princeton: Princeton University Press, 1941), 14:110. Conway, an experienced man of the theater, is mentioned as the author of a similar play, *New York Patriots: Or, The Battle of Saratoga*, first performed at Barnum's Theatre, New York, June 6, 1856. I have not seen this play, but since there were two battles (the first near Stillwater on September 19, 1777 and the second near Saratoga village on October 7, 1777), *New York Patriots* is either a reworking of the first comedy or a sequel to it.

57. H. J. Conway, *The Battle of Stillwater*, in *America's Lost Plays*, 14:120.

58. H. J. Conway, *Hiram Hireout: Or, Followed by Fortune* (New York: French, n.d.), The Minor Drama, no. 170, pp. 6-7.

59. Arthur Herman Wilson, *A History of the Philadelphia Theatre: 1835 to 1855* (Philadelphia: University of Pennsylvania Press, 1935), p. 63, cites as the new plays of American character produced in Philadelphia in 1837 *The Star Spangled Banner: Or the American Tar's Fidelity*, W. T. Moncrieff's *A Down East Bargain*, written especially for "Yankee" Hill, and Logan's *Yankee Land*. Elsewhere (pp. 661-62, 670) he lists five plays with "village" in their titles and twenty-nine Yankee plays produced in Philadelphia during the thirties and later. There are dramatizations of Yankee travelers—in Tripoli, Spain, China, England, France, and Mississippi—and Down East duelists, servants (valets and footmen), watchmen, dentists, wool peddlers, farmers, and tars.

60. Robert E. Spiller, ed., *James Fenimore Cooper*, American Writers Series (New York: American Book Co., 1936), pp. 170-71.

61. Preface to *Home as Found* (1838), in *ibid.*, p. 304. For a modern critical reappraisal of the problems of nationalism, see M. F. Heiser, "The Decline of Neoclassicism, 1801–1884," in Harry Hayden Clark, ed., *Transitions in American Literary History* (Durham: Duke University Press, 1953), pp. 93-159.

62. William Dunlap, *A Trip to Niagara: Or, Travellers in America* (New York: E. B. Clayton, 1830), preface. Oral S. Coad, "The American Theatre in the Eighteenth Century," *South Atlantic Quarterly*, 17 (July, 1918): 190-97, calls attention to the growing importance of the scene painter, by the 1790's a recognized member of a theater's staff. Whereas earlier scenery had been largely neglected, with reliance on all occasions upon cheap canvases age-blackened, by the time of Dunlap's early career new scenes were customarily painted for the more notable plays and suitable descriptions of special scenery were featured modes of advertising. "Romanticism in Stage Design," in Moody, *America Takes the Stage*, chap. 4, fully discusses the techniques involved in scenic displays by means of the diorama (transparencies), the panorama (a continuous, nonchanging picture), and the cosmorama, involving use of magnifying lenses and even wax figures set against a panoramic scene.

63. Dunlap, *Trip to Niagara*, p. 7.

64. *Ibid.*, p. 43.

65. *Ibid.*, p. 47.

66. See Quinn, *American Drama Beginning to Civil War*, pp. 298-99, 450 (for reference to an anonymous play, *Green Mountain Boys*, which was presented at the Park, February 22, 1822). A once widely read novel on the same subject is Daniel Pierce Thompson, *The Green Mountain Boys: An Historical Tale of the Early Settlement of Vermont* (Boston: Caldwell, 1840).

67. Moses, *Representative Plays by American Dramatists*, 2:381 ff., says that Owens changed Jones's manuscript without permission, made from $200,000 to $300,000 from the role, but sent Dr. Jones only a $500 check.

68. Matthews, "The American on the Stage," p. 331. Cf. Hutton, *Curiosities of the American Stage*, p. 40.

69. Joseph Stevens Jones, *The People's Lawyer*, in Moses, *Representative American Plays*, 2:421.

70. *Ibid.*, p. 422.

71. The original title was *The Silver Spoon: Or Our Own Folks: A Joiner's Job in Four Parts* (1852). The long-lasting popularity of the comedy is suggested by the edition used in this study: William Warren Edition of Standard Plays, Revised and Reconstructed, with a listing of the original cast at the Boston Museum, 1852 (Boston: W. H. Baker & Co., 1911). In introductory quotations from an article by John Bouve Clapp appearing in the *Boston Transcript* for Friday, December 30, 1910, attention is called to successful revivals, featuring Warren, on March 5 and 10 of 1883; to the not so popular sequel titled *Batkins at Home: or Life in Cranberry Centre* (performed at Boston Museum, May 10, 1858); and to the extension of the original play into a novel, published in 1871 by A. Loring as *Life of Jefferson S. Batkins, Member from Cranberry Centre. Written By Himself*. Finally, the 1911 edition bore the full title of *The Silver Spoon: Character Sketch in Four Parts*.

72. Joseph Stevens Jones, *Yankee Land, A Comedy in Two Acts*, one of eight plays in Spencer, *Boston Theatre: A Collection of Scarce Acting Tragedies, Comedies, Dramas, Farces and Burlettas* (Boston: William V. Spencer, n.d.), vol. 19. According to the schedule of production listed, *Yankee Land* was produced at the Park, 1834; the National, Boston, 1842; in Providence, 1843; at the Tremont, Boston, 1843; at the Walnut Street Theatre, Philadelphia, 1844; the Federal Street Theatre, Boston, 1848; and again at the National, 1854. Quinn, *American Drama Beginning to Civil War*, pp. 301, 496, lists a production at the Pennsylvania, Philadelphia, January 4, 1837, as well as an altered version, *Hue and Cry*, by Leman Rede, in 1846.

73. Comedian Don Marble first played in *The Vermont Wool-Dealer* in Cincinnati on June 4, 1838. Hodge, *Yankee Theatre*, p. 232.

74. See Oscar Sonneck, *Report on "The Star-Spangled Banner," "Hail*

Columbia," "*America,*" *and* "*Yankee Doodle*" (Washington, D.C.: Government Printing Office, 1909), pp. 79-95, for explanations of the etymology of the term "Yankee."

75. "Cuff," "Cuffy," and variants appeared in early writing as nicknames for the Negro, or Negro characters. Whitman uses "Cuff" in one of his catalogues in "Song of Myself," line 109.

76. Lawrence LaBree, *Ebenezer Venture,* in The Minor Drama, no. 174, pp. 10-11.

77. Henry Watterson, ed., *Oddities in Southern Life and Character* (Boston: Houghton Mifflin & Co., 1883), p. vii. For fuller analysis see "Village Scenes in the Old Southwest," in Herron, *Small Town in American Literature,* pp. 288-307.

78. Franklin J. Meine, ed., *Tall Tales of the Southwest* (New York: Alfred A. Knopf, 1930), pp. xv-xvi.

79. Herron, *Small Town in American Literature,* pp. 289-90.

80. *A Collection of Plays and Poems, By the Late Col. Robert Munford of Mecklenburg County, in the State of Virginia Now First Published Together* (Petersburg: William Prentis, 1798).

81. For two complete critical evaluations see Jay B. Hubbell and Douglass Adair, "Robert Munford's *The Candidates,*" *William and Mary Quarterly,* 3d ser., 5 (April, 1948): 217-57, with a reprint of this rare play; and "Robert Munford," in Jay B. Hubbell, *The South in American Literature* (Durham: Duke University Press, 1954), pp. 142-48. *The Patriots,* ed. Cortlandt Canby, has been republished in the *William and Mary Quarterly,* 3d ser., 6 (July, 1949): 437-502. Readex Microprints of the original in the Library of Congress are now available. More recently "The Politics of a Literary Movement," in Kenneth S. Lynn, *Mark Twain and Southwestern Humor* (Boston: Little, Brown & Co., 1959), chap. 3, has given further consideration to Munford's contribution to the tradition of humor developed in the Southwest before Twain.

82. Published in Washington, 1824, but apparently not produced. Cf. Quinn, *American Drama Beginning to Civil War,* pp. 160-61 and Reed, *Realistic Presentation of American Characters,* p. 93. Comparable to these early satires on Virginia politics is "a comic opera or, political farce" appearing just four years after the publication of *The Candidates.* A Yale graduate, Chester Leonard, in his *Federalism Triumphant in the Steady Habits of Connecticut Alone: Or the Turnpike Road to a Fortune* (1802), extended through six acts a violent attack on the office-holding class, assembled in "body politick" at Hartford (Readex Microprint of a copy in the New York Public Library).

83. James F. Brice, *A Country Clown: Or Dandyism Improved: A Dramatic Medley in One Act* (Annapolis: J. Weber, 1829). Readex Microprint of the original owned by the American Antiquarian Society.

84. Isaac I. Jewett, "Themes for Western Fiction," *Western Monthly,* 1 (1833).

85. Morris Barnett, *Yankee Peddler: Or Old Times in Virginia,* in The Minor Drama, no. 154, dated listing of performances and the several casts.

86. James E. Heath, *Whigs and Democrats: Or Love of No Politics* (Richmond: T. W. White, 1839), pp. v-vi. Printed anonymously, but attributed to Heath.

87. See W. P. Trent, *Southern Writers* (New York: Macmillan Co., 1905), pp. 252-53; John D. Wade, *Augustus Baldwin Longstreet: A Study of the Development of Culture in the South* (New York: Macmillan Co., 1924), p. 166; Napier Wilt, *Some American Humorists* (New York: T. Nelson & Sons, 1929), pp. 56-57; and Hubbell, *The South in American Literature,* pp. 669-72. Hubbell notes that the only known extant copy of the first edition of *Major Jones' Courtship* (Madison, 1843) is now in the Duke University Library.

88. *Major Jones' Courtship, With Other Scenes, Incidents, and Adventures in a Series of Letters by Himself,* rev. ed. (New York, 1872).

89. *Major Jones' Courtship* . . . (Savannah: Edward J. Purse, 1850). Produced at Barnum's Museum, Philadelphia, December 22, 1851. As noted earlier, a similar village dramatization, the anonymous comedy, *Major Jack Downing: Or, The Retired Politician*, was produced at the Park Theatre, May 10, 1834.

90. Thomas Bailey Aldrich, *From Ponkapong to Pesth and An Old Town by the Sea* (Boston: Houghton Mifflin & Co., 1897), p. 258. *An Old Town by the Sea* was written in 1883.

91. For fuller analyses of *Neighbor Jackwood*, see Reed, *Realistic Presentation of American Characters*, pp. 113-14, and Quinn, *American Drama Beginning to Civil War*, pp. 289-90. For the Swayze play see the Standard Drama, Acting Edition, 226 (New York: French, 1859).

92. Beecher to Robert Bonner, January 3, 1886, in Henry Ward Beecher, *A Legend of Norwood: Or Village Life in New England* (Boston, 1895), prefix.

93. Arthur Hobson Quinn, *A History of the American Drama from the Civil War to the Present Day* (New York: Crofts, 1943), 1:129. See, too, a sequel to *Joshua Whitcomb*, Denman Thompson, *The Old Homestead* (Boston: Walter H. Baker Co., 1927), *passim*. Perhaps the most successful of these rural plays, *David Harum*, a dramatization of Edward Noyes Westcott's popular novel (1898), opened at the Garrick Theatre, New York, October 1, 1900. Starring William H. Crane and produced by Charles Frohman, this comedy, according to Hornblow, "netted half a millon dollars for its promoters."

94. Both Quinn, "Herne and the Realism of Character," in Quinn, *American Drama Civil War to Present*, vol. 1, chap. 6, and Julie A. Herne, *Shore Acres and Other Plays*, rev. ed. (New York: French, 1928), biographical note, give analyses and full data about the genesis of *Shore Acres* and other plays.

95. Herne, *Shore Acres and Other Plays*, p. xxviii.

96. For confirmation of the independence and the strength of these nautical folk see Edmund Gilligan, "The Dorymen," *Atlantic Monthly*, 202 (July, 1958): 28-33, a very artistic tale by a native of Gloucester, Massachusetts, familiar with the lives of dorymen since his boyhood.

97. Benjamin T. Spencer, *The Quest for Nationality: An American Literary Campaign* (Syracuse: Syracuse University Press, 1957), p. 138.

98. T. L. Nichols, *Forty Years of American Life*, 2d ed. (London: Longmans, Green & Co., 1874), pp. 320-21.

99. Ralph Waldo Emerson, "Self-Reliance," in Frederic I. Carpenter, ed., *Ralph Waldo Emerson* (New York: American Book Co., 1934), p. 106.

CHAPTER III

1. William V. Spencer, *Boston Theatre*, New Series (Boston, 1855), no. 9. Scholarly confirmation of the romantic tastes suggested by the Spencer advertisements may be found in William Stanley Hoole, *The Ante-Bellum Charleston Theatre* (Tuscaloosa: University of Alabama Press, 1946). His full "Annual Chronological Records, 1800-1861," pp. 65-153, and his "Play List," pp. 154-206, offer an index to antebellum theatrical tastes in Charleston. Plays whose performances were advertised in Charleston newspapers and recorded elsewhere tally with many of the romantic titles advertised in the *Boston Theatre*.

2. For a discussion of a localized use of Gothic painted drops of the Rhine, by John Russell Smith, for *The Naiad Queen: Or the Mystery of Lurlei Berg*, see Arthur Herman Wilson, *A History of the Philadelphia Theatre, 1835 to 1855* (Philadelphia, 1935), pp. 68-69. Also, Sol Smith, *Theatrical Management in the West and South* (New York: Harper & Bros., 1868), p. 161, recalling his work at the St. Francis Theatre, New Orleans, notes the "showy pieces" painted in "the most extensive and expensive manner" for "*The Naiad Queen, Napoleon, Dick Turpin*, and other grand dramas, . . ." The scenic painter was Joseph Foster.

3. See "The English Village Transplanted," in Ima Honaker Herron, *The Small Town in American Literature* (Durham: Duke University Press, 1939), pp. 32-43, for a documented analysis of early village poetry. Lewis Leary, *That Rascal Freneau: A Study in Literary Failure* (New Brunswick: Rutgers University Press, 1941) and Benjamin T. Spencer, *The Quest for Nationality: An American Literary Campaign* (Syracuse: Syracuse University Press, 1957), chaps. 1, 2, offer definitive interpretations of this restless period.

4. For population distribution, see *The Fifteenth Census of the United States,* 1:6; *A Century of Population Growth, 1790-1900,* p. 20; Charles Francis Adams, Jr., "Genesis of the Massachusetts Town," *Proceedings of the Massachusetts Historical Society,* 2d ser., 7 (1891-92): 172 ff.; Anne Bush MacLear, "Early New England Towns," *Studies in History and Public Law,* vol. 29, no. 1 (New York, 1908).

5. Harriet Martineau, *Retrospect of Western Travel* (London, 1838), 2:78.

6. I am indebted to Wolfgang Born, whose *American Landscape Painting* (New Haven: Yale University Press, 1948) offers a brilliantly written and fully illustrated history of ideas on American landscapists. His first three chapters—"The European Heritage," "Sentiment of Nature," and "The Panoramic Style"—show various interrelations between the arts, especially those of landscape painting, landscape poetry, and scenic design as applied to commercial panorama, the *tableau mouvant,* and other kindred devices. Related works include Alexander Eliot and the editors of *Time* magazine, *American Painting* (Chicago: Time, Inc., 1957); "Romanticism and Materialism," in Elie Faure, *History of Art,* trans. Walter Pach (New York: Dover Publications, n.d.), vol. 2, chap. 7; Edgar Preston Richardson, *American Romantic Painting* (New York: E. Weyhe, 1944); John Francis McDermott, *The Lost Panoramas of the Mississippi* (Chicago: University of Chicago Press, 1958), describing five extravaganzas ("paintings by the mile") which served viewers a century ago as travelogue-movies; "The Federal Era—1790-1830" and "The Mid-Century—1830-1860," parts 4 and 5 of Virgil Barker, *American Painting* (New York: Macmillan Co., 1950).

7. "To Cole, the Painter, Departing for Europe" (1829), in Tremaine McDowell, ed., *William Cullen Bryant: Representative Selections* (New York: American Book Co., 1935), p. 70. Their friendship is further commemorated in Doughty's landscape, "Kindred Spirits," a tribute painted after Cole's death in 1848. See also "Bryant's Cedarmere," with illustration, in Theodore F. Wolfe, *Literary Haunts & Homes* (Philadelphia: Lippincott, 1898), pp. 136-43.

8. For the amply illustrated story of this enterprise see Colin Simkin, ed., *Currier and Ives' America* (New York: Crown, 1952).

9. For a scholarly and illustrated analysis of the architectural role played by Italians in America see Clay Lancaster, "Italianism in American Architecture before 1860," *American Quarterly,* 4 (Summer, 1952): 127-48.

10. John S. Hart, *The Female Prose Writers of America* (Philadelphia: E. H. Butler, 1857), p. 113.

11. *Ibid.,* p. 114.

12. Andrew Jackson Downing, *Rural Essays* (New York: G. P. Putnam & Co., 1853).

13. Lancaster, "Italianism in American Architecture," p. 137.

14. For full analysis see Arthur Hobson Quinn, *A History of the American Drama from the Beginning to the Civil War* (New York: Crofts, 1944), chaps. 6, 7, 9, 12; for the spirit of the times see Vernon Louis Parrington, *The Romantic Revolution in America: 1800-1860* (New York: Harcourt, Brace, 1927), *passim.*

15. Allardyce Nicoll, *British Drama: An Historical Survey,* 4th ed., rev. (London: George G. Harrap, 1949), p. 325.

16. See citations from Seilhamer, chap. 2, n. 25.

17. O. G. T. Sonneck, *Early Opera in America* (New York: Schirmer, 1915), pp. 67, 72, 73, 76.

18. Smith, *Theatrical Management West and South*, pp. 115-16, recalls his successful impersonation of Kit Cosey when *Town and Country* was performed at the Park Theatre, September 26, 1835. He cites the full cast and includes a flattering criticism, "Old Sol's Benefit," which appeared in William T. Porter's *Spirit of the Times*. Francis C. Wemyss, *Chronology of the American Stage from 1752 to 1852* (New York: Taylor, 1852), p. 125, presents Solomon Franklin Smith as "the favorite Low Comedian of all the south-western Theatres" and mentions his first appearance on the New York stage, at the Park Theatre, as a star in 1835.

19. Quinn, *American Drama Beginning to Civil War*, p. 133.

20. John Minshull, *Rural Felicity with the Humour of Patrick and Marriage of Shelty* (New York: printed for the author, 1801), pp. vi-viii. (Readex Microprint.)

21. See Hoole, *Ante-Bellum Charleston Theatre*, pp. 111, 115, 194, 209, 225.

22. Leary, *That Rascal Freneau*, p. 423.

23. For foreign backgrounds see Edith Birkhead, *The Tale of Terror: A Study of the Gothic Romance* (New York: Dutton, 1931); Eino Railo, *The Haunted Castle: A study of the Elements of English Romanticism* (New York: Dutton, 1927). "The Gothic and the Revolutionary," chap. 2 of Lillie Loshe, *The Early American Novel* (New York: Columbia University Press, 1907), and Harry R. Warfel, *Charles Brockden Brown: American Gothic Novelist* (Gainesville: University of Florida Press, 1949), trace the influence of Gothic fashions upon early American fiction.

24. See Harry R. Warfel, "Charles Brockden Brown's German Sources," *Modern Language Quarterly*, 1 (1940): 357-65.

25. For an interesting treatment of the Gothic influence on Poe, see N. Bryllion Fagin, *The Histrionic Mr. Poe* (Baltimore: Johns Hopkins Press, 1949), chap. 5.

26. Whitman Bennett, *Whittier: Bard of Freedom* (Chapel Hill: University of North Carolina Press, 1941), pp. 56, 59, 131.

27. From Jones's "Editorial Remarks" prefacing *Moll Pitcher: Or The Fortune Teller of Lynn* (Spencer's Boston Theatre, 1855, New Series, no. 1, in French's *The Standard Drama*, acting edition).

28. See "American National Literature" (1891) in Malcolm Cowley, ed., *The Complete Prose of Walt Whitman* (New York: Pellegrini & Cudahy, 1948), p. 501.

29. Charles H. Moore, "Materials for Landscape Art in America," *Atlantic Monthly*, 64 (November, 1889): 671, 673.

30. Joseph Jefferson, *Autobiography* (New York: Century Co., 1890), pp. 223 ff.

31. Montrose J. Moses, ed., *Representative Plays by American Dramatists, 1856-1911*, New Popular Edition (New York: E. P. Dutton & Co., 1925), p. 17.

32. *Ibid.*

33. William Winter, *The Jeffersons* (Boston: James R. Osgood & Co., 1881), p. 188.

34. Accessible today are Winter's *The Jeffersons* and his illustrated *Life and Art of Joseph Jefferson* (Macmillan, 1894); Moses, *Representative Plays*; Quinn, *American Drama Beginning to Civil War*. Also, Jefferson, *Autobiography*, which gives a very personal account of various versions, is now available in a new, revised edition (with an introduction by Eleanor Farjeon, Jefferson's granddaughter), published by Appleton-Century-Crofts, 1949.

35. The "J. Jefferson," named in a printed announcement of the cast, is identified by Winter, *Joseph Jefferson*, p. 306, as the third Joseph Jefferson and by Moses,

Representative Plays, p. 19, as John, talented brother to Elizabeth (Mrs. Sam Chapman) and son of Joseph Jefferson III.

36. See Winter, *The Jeffersons*, pp. 305 ff., for a listing of the early casts of *Rip Van Winkle*; Quinn, *American Drama Beginning to Civil War*, p. 328. The Readex Microprint of an original at the University of Pennsylvania cites the title as follows: John Kerr, *Rip Van Winkle* (Philadelphia, 1829).

37. Quoted as part of a long sketch of Hackett in Winter, *The Jeffersons*, pp. 212-13.

38. Winter, *The Jeffersons*, p. 308.

39. *Ibid.*, p. 309.

40. The full title of Burke's undated version is *Rip Van Winkle, A Legend of the Catskills: A Romantic Drama in Two Acts, Adapted from Washington Irving's Sketch Book by Charles Burke*. Moses, *Representative Plays*, pp. 29 ff., reprints both the Kerr and the Burke versions for purposes of comparative study.

41. Jefferson, *Autobiography*, pp. 109-10.

42. John B. Thompson, "The Genesis of the Rip Van Winkle Legend," *Harper's New Monthly*, 67 (September, 1883): 617-22.

43. Lucy C. Lillie, "The Catskills," *Harper's New Monthly*, 67 (September, 1883): 521-38. Copious photographs of the area.

44. See Francis Wilson, *Joseph Jefferson: Reminiscences of a Fellow Player* (Scribner's, 1906), pp. 79-82, 84-86; Nathan Haskell Dole, *Joseph Jefferson at Home* (Boston: Estes & Lauriat, 1898), *passim*, for intimate and illustrated accounts of Jefferson as a landscapist. The *Autobiography* is filled with references to Jefferson's delight in nature and in painting various natural scenes.

45. Quoted by L. Clarke Davis, "At and After the Play," *Lippincott's*, July, 1879.

46. Winter, *Joseph Jefferson*, p. 174. Winter also mentions, p. 309, a well-liked opera on the Van Winkle story, with music by George Bristow and libretto by J. H. Wainwright, which was performed by the Pyne and Harrison Opera Company on September 27, 1855. He does not cite the theater.

47. *Ibid.*, p. 175; Gilbert A. Pierce, "A Good-by to Rip Van Winkle," *Atlantic Monthly*, 52 (November, 1883): 695-703, for data on Jefferson's later appearance as Rip. Quinn notes that Jefferson continued acting until less than a year before his death on April 23, 1905, at Palm Beach, Florida.

48. For a contemporary evaluation of Boucicault, see Brander Matthews and Lawrence Hutton, eds., *Actors and Actresses of Great Britain and the United States: The Present Time* (New York: Cassell, 1886), pp. 77-94. A recent reappraisal appears in Albert Johnson, "Fabulous Boucicault," *Theatre Arts Monthly*, 37 (March, 1953): 26 ff.

49. George William Curtis, "Editor's Easy Chair," *Harper's New Monthly*, 62 (March, 1871): 615. Cf. Clarke L. Davis, "Among the Comedians," *Atlantic Monthly*, 19 (June, 1867): 750-61, for an excellent contemporary contrast of John E. Owens as Solon Shingle and Jefferson as Rip. Also interesting is J. Ranken Towse, "Joseph Jefferson as 'Caleb Plummer,'" *Century*, 27 (January, 1884): 476-77.

50. Curtis, "Editor's Easy Chair," p. 616.

51. Pierce, "Good-bye to Rip Van Winkle," p. 696.

52. *Rip Van Winkle*, Jefferson ed. (New York: Putnam, 1870) contains eleven engraved illustrations by notable artists (including Darley) and five photographs by the Sarony photographers (1869), showing Jefferson costumed as both the young and the old Rip.

53. Winter, *Joseph Jefferson*, p. 180.

54. Matthews and Hutton, *Actors and Actresses*, p. 154. Another character actor, James A. Herne, during his period as stage manager at Maguire's New Theatre in San Francisco about 1874, also made a stage version of *Rip Van Winkle*,

"highly praised by David Belasco for its fidelity to the Dutch quality in the character," notes Arthur Hobson Quinn in *A History of the American Drama From the Civil War to the Present Day* (New York: Crofts, 1943), 1:130.

55. Percy MacKaye, Preface, in Percy MacKaye and Reginald DeKoven, *Rip Van Winkle: Folk-Opera in Three Acts* (New York: Alfred A. Knopf, 1919), pp. v-vi.

56. MacKaye and DeKoven, *Rip Van Winkle*, p. 73.

57. *Ibid.*, p. 80.

58. Gerald Carson, "Get the Prospect Seated ... But Keep Talking," *American Heritage*, 9 (August, 1958): 40-41.

59. Brandler Matthews, "The American on the Stage," *Scribner's Monthly*, (July, 1879), p. 333.

CHAPTER IV

1. "Roosevelt and the Pioneer Spirit," in Stewart Edward White, ed., *The National Edition of Roosevelt's Works* (New York: Charles Scribner's Sons, 1926), 2:xvi.

2. *Ibid.*, p. xiii.

3. Illustrative of the many conceptions and records of the taming of the Oregon wilderness are Washington Irving; *Astoria: Or Anecdotes of an Enterprise Beyond the Rocky Mountains* (Philadelphia: Carey, Lea & Blanchard, 1836), describing John Jacob Astor's fur-trading empire; Francis Parkman, *The Oregon Trail*, first published in the *Knickerbocker Magazine*, 1848; Joaquin Miller's *Overland in a Covered Wagon: An Autobiography* (New York: Ray Whitaker & Co., 1909). William Cullen Bryant, "The Prairies," 1832, in *Poems* (New York: Harper & Bros., 1840), p. 50, romantically reviewed the Illinois prairies as "the gardens of the Desert ... the unshorn fields, boundless and beautiful."

4. Lewis Mumford, *The Golden Day: A Study in American Literature and Culture* (New York: W. W. Norton & Co., 1926), p. 56.

5. Bernard De Voto, *The Year of Decision: 1846* (Boston: Little, Brown & Co., 1943), p. 4.

6. Theodore Roosevelt, "The American Wilderness," in White, *Roosevelt's Works*, 2:4.

7. *Ibid.* For full treatment see Walter Prescott Webb, *The Great Plains* (Boston: Houghton Mifflin, 1931); De Voto, *The Year of Decision: 1846.*

8. Alonzo Delano, *Life on the Plains and Among the Diggings* (New York: Miller, Orton & Co., 1854), pp. 286-89.

9. Issued in 1936 as *Across the Plains and Among the Diggings.*

10. Letter 12, from Ottawa Bar, Feather River, March 22, 1850, in Irving McKee, ed., *Alonzo Delano's California Correspondence: Being Letters Hitherto Uncollected from the Ottawa (Illinois) Free Trader* (Sacramento: Sacramento Book Collectors Club, 1952), p. 52.

11. See Alonzo Delano, *Pen-Knife Sketches: Or Chips of the Old Block* (San Francisco: Grabhorn Press, 1934), *passim*, and *Old Block's Sketch Book*, with original drawings by Charles Nahl and a foreword by Marguerite Eyer Wilbur (Santa Ana: Fine Arts Press, 1947), *passim*. The modern edition of the *Pen-Knife Sketches* (foreword by G. Ezra Dane) is a series of letters dedicated to Delano's fellow Forty-Niners and reprinted from the only edition of 1853. The illustrations by the German-born Nahl, once popularly called the "California Cruikshank," have been praised for their accuracy of technique.

12. Henry Van Brunt, "Architecture in the West," *Atlantic Monthly*, 64 (December, 1889): 772.

13. Delano, *Life on the Plains*, p. 286.

14. Joaquin Miller, *First Fam'lies of the Sierras* (Chicago: Jansen, McClurg & Co., 1876), p. 118.

15. George Augustus Sala, *America Revisited* (London: Vizetelly & Co., 1883), 2:138.

16. *Ibid.,* pp. 145, 147.

17. *Ibid.,* p. 153.

18. *Ibid.,* p. 155. Cf. Sala's satiric observations with Mark Twain's wild charges against Scott's fiction and its debilitating influence on the architecture of Baton Rouge and other Mississippi River towns, "Castles and Culture," chap. 40 of *Life on the Mississippi.* Both Sala and Clemens, ridiculing architectural falsity in 1882 and 1883 respectively, early foreshadowed Sinclair Lewis' animadversions about the sham building designs along Main Street in Gopher Prairie.

19. For earlier British views of "the full madness of the Rush" see Max Berger, *The British Traveller in America: 1836-1860* (New York: Columbia University Press, 1943), *passim.*

20. W. G. B. Carson, *The Theatre on the Frontier: The Early Years of the St. Louis Stage* (Chicago: University of Chicago Press, 1932), pp. 1, 15. Cf. Ralph Rusk, *The Literature of the Middle Western Frontier* (New York: Columbia University Press, 1926), 1:358, 381 ff.

21. John Francis McDermott, "Culture and the Missouri Frontier," *Missouri Historical Review,* 50 (July, 1956): 355-70, gives many details about the cultural interest of citizens in St. Louis, Potosi, Franklin, Cape Girardeau, and other frontier towns. Cf. Francis C. Wemyss, *Chronology of the American Stage from 1752 to 1852* (New York: Taylor, 1852), p. 12, regarding the first theater in St. Louis.

22. Joaquin Miller, *Overland in a Covered Wagon: An Autobiography* (New York: Appleton, 1930), p. 92.

23. Francis Parkman, *The Oregon Trail* (New York: Ginn & Co., 1910), p. 21.

24. Theodore Roosevelt, "Ranch Life in the Far West," *Century,* 35 (February, 1888): 495-510. For further discussion see Roosevelt, "In Cowboy Land," in White, *Roosevelt's Works,* 2:325-52. The *Century* articles, extending through the March and April issues, were profusely illustrated by Frederic Remington, whose art graphically recorded life at the home ranch, at roundup time, in the cattle towns, and elsewhere on the plains.

25. Roosevelt, in White, *Roosevelt's Works,* 2:235.

26. "Old America," in Van Wyck Brooks, *America's Coming-of-Age* (New York: Macmillan Co., 1917), p. 106.

27. Joseph Francis Daly, *The Life of Augustin Daly* (New York: Macmillan Co., 1917), p. 106.

28. Letter 30, August 1, 1851, San Francisco, in McKee, *Delano's California Correspondence,* p. 123, published in the *True Delta,* September 16, 1851.

29. Subtitle of *The Frontier Settlement: A Play in Three Acts* (New York: Francis Clarke, 1846). Arthur Hobson Quinn, *A History of the American Drama from the Beginning to the Civil War* (New York: Crofts, 1944), 1:287, noted that *A Trip to the California Mines* (starring Charles Burke, possibly its author, and staged at Philadelphia's Arch Street Theatre, January 10, 1849) was "probably the earliest of the California plays of which we have record."

30. G. Ezra Dane, Foreword, in Delano, *Pen-Knife Sketches,* p. vii.

31. Second subtitle: *A Local Play in Two Acts* by Old Block. Published as The Minor Drama, no. 130 (New York: Samuel French, 1857).

32. Delano, *Pen-Knife Sketches,* p. xii.

33. In the headnote to his comedy, Delano identifies various characters and explains the origins in real life of several scenes.

34. De Voto, *The Year of Decision: 1846,* pp. 138-39.

35. MacMinn, *The Theatre of The Golden Era in California* (Caldwell,

Idaho: Caxton Printers, 1941), p. 208. Cf. Quinn, *American Drama Beginning to Civil War*, pp. 286, 466. Ronald L. Davis, "They Played for Gold: Theater on the Mining Frontier," *Southwest Review*, 51 (Spring, 1966): 169-84, offers a recent graphic discussion.

36. Thomas Dunn English, *The Mormons: Or, Life at Salt Lake City* (New York: Samuel French, 1858), p. 14.

37. *Ibid.*, p. 3.

38. According to Ray B. West, Jr., *Kingdom of the Saints: The Story of Brigham Young and the Mormons* (New York: Viking Press, 1957), p. 368, the first notable anti-Mormon book, based upon affidavits obtained by a Mormon apostate, Philastus Hurlbut, in 1833, was Eber D. Howe, *Mormonism Unveiled* (Painesville, Ohio, 1834). During the next several decades anti-Mormon feeling was often heightened by prejudiced reports by newspapers. Thomas English based his characterization, no doubt, upon current hostile reports of the murder of Elder Pratt in 1857. According to newspaper accounts, Pratt was killed in Arkansas by Hector McLean, the former husband of one of the Elder's wives. For full details see the authentic account in West, *Kingdom of the Saints*, p. 234.

39. English, *The Mormons*, p. 13.

40. Quoted by Sala, *America Revisited*, p. 304, from Burton, *The City of the Saints* (1862).

41. For a strong expression of anti-Mormonism see C. C. Goodwin, "The Mormon Situation," *Harper's New Monthly*, 63 (October, 1881): 756-63; for an authentic account of the Danites, see West, *Kingdom of the Saints*, *passim*; for a thoroughly humorous approach to "the Mormon question," see Mark Twain, *Roughing It*, chaps. 13-17.

42. Cf. M. M. Marberry, *Splendid Poseur: Joaquin Miller—American Poet* (New York: Thomas Y. Crowell, 1953), p. 158; Edmond Gagey, *The San Francisco Stage: A History* (New York: Columbia University Press, 1950), p. 141; Richard Moody, *America Takes the Stage* (Bloomington: Indiana University Press, 1955), pp. 181-83.

43. Joaquin Miller and P. A. Fitzgerald, *The Danites*, in Allan Gates Halline, ed., *American Plays* (New York: American Book Co., 1935), Act II, p. 389.

44. Published in San Francisco, 1882.

45. Included in *Poems*, 8 vols. (San Francisco: Harr Wagner Publishing Co., 1910-20), vol. 6.

46. Gagey, *San Francisco Stage*, p. 85; Franklin Walker, *San Francisco's Literary Frontier* (New York: Alfred A. Knopf, 1939), p. 21.

47. Felix Sper, *From Native Roots* (Caldwell, Idaho: Caxton Printers, 1948), p. 234.

48. Walker, *San Francisco's Literary Frontier*, p. 118.

49. Sper, *From Native Roots*, p. 235.

50. According to George R. Stewart, Jr., the country of the Forty-Niners "offered the most unrestrained and flamboyant experiment in American naming." For an entertaining discussion see "Melodrama in the Forties," chap. 30 of his *Names on the Land* (New York: Random House, 1945).

51. Gagey, *San Francisco Stage*, pp. 3, 107.

52. George R. Stewart, Jr., *Bret Harte: Argonaut and Exile* (Boston: Houghton Mifflin Co., 1931), p. 231.

53. Daly, *The Life of Augustin Daly*, p. 234.

54. Moody, *America Takes the Stage*, p. 184.

55. Stewart, *Bret Harte: Argonaut and Exile*, p. 232.

56. Brander Matthews, "The American on the Stage," *Scribner's Monthly*, 18 (July, 1879): 328. Other contemporary appreciations of Raymond's acting in the

Sellers role may be found in "The Stage American in the Character Play," in Laurence Hutton, *Curiosities of the American Stage* (New York: Harper & Bros., 1891), sc. 4, and in Brander Matthews and Laurence Hutton, eds., *Actors and Actresses of Great Britain and the United States: The Present Time* (New York: Cassell, 1886), pp. 229-46. Characteristic of the critical appreciation of Raymond's gifts is William L. Keese's praise on p. 230:

> "There's millions in it!"—words devoid of wit;
> But loud the laugh from gallery and pit
> When Raymond gives them speculative tone,
> And clothes them with a humor all his own.
> *Sellers* gleams faintly on the printed page,
> As drawn by Clemens in the "Gilded Age,"
> But dominates, in Raymond, all the stage.
> Long may we live to see before us stand
> That humorous figure with uplifted hand.

57. Walter Blair, *Mark Twain & Huck Finn* (Berkeley: University of California Press, 1960), p. 154.

58. Stewart, *Bret Harte: Argonaut and Exile*, p. 234, notes that "no copy of the text seems to exist."

59. Bartley Campbell, *The White Slave & Other Plays*, ed. Napier Wilt, *America's Lost Plays* (Princeton: Princeton University Press, 1941), 19:xi.

60. *Ibid.*, p. xii. Cf. Gagey, *San Francisco Stage*, pp. 139-41.

61. Campbell, *White Slave and Other Plays*, p. xxxviii.

62. *Ibid.*, pp. xxxix, lxxv.

63. Wilt notes that *My Partner*, first produced at the Union Square Theatre, New York, from September 16 to October 18, 1879, was later presented on tour at Hooley's Theatre in Chicago in 1880; in Berlin in 1883; in London in 1884; and finally on stage in Chicago in 1904. A motion picture version was released in 1909.

64. Lucius Beebe and Charles Clegg, eds., *The American West* (New York: E. P. Dutton, 1955), pp. 242-46.

65. For various critical appraisals see *Theatre Arts Monthly*, 42 (January, 1958): 25.

66. Some of the best criticism of *The Girl* appears in Craig Timberlake, *The Life & Work of David Belasco: The Bishop of Broadway* (New York: Library Publishers, 1954), pp. 283 ff., and Montrose J. Moses, ed., *Representative Plays by American Dramatists, 1856-1911* (New York: Dutton, 1925), pp. 49 ff.

67. Timberlake, *David Belasco*, p. 285.

68. *The Girl of the Golden West*, in Moses, *Representative Plays*, Act I, p. 57. Quinn notes that the minstrel Jake Wallace and his folk songs provided the theme of the Italian composer Puccini's *La Fanciulla del West*, the first grand opera to originate from American material. Cf. "David Belasco and His Associates," in Arthur Hobson Quinn, *A History of the American Drama From the Civil War to the Present Day* (New York: Crofts, 1943), pp. 192-93. Puccini's opera was produced at the Metropolitan Opera House, December 10, 1910. Not long after, in 1911, Grosset and Dunlap published Belasco's novelized version of *The Girl*.

69. *The Rose of the Rancho* (New York: Samuel French, 1909), Act II, p. 61.

70. Maxwell Anderson, *Night Over Taos* (New York: Samuel French, 1932), Act I, p. 51.

71. *Ibid.*, p. 90.

CHAPTER V

1. Cf. Frederick Jackson Turner, *The Frontier in American History* (New York: Henry Holt & Co., 1920), pp. 9 ff.; "The Range Country," in Ima Honaker Herron, *The Small Town in American Literature* (Durham: Duke University Press, 1939), pp. 273-85. Highly detailed treatments, of course, are in Walter Prescott Webb, *The Great Plains* (New York: Ginn & Co., 1931); J. Frank Dobie, *The Longhorns* (Boston: Little, Brown & Co., 1941); Mari Sandoz, *The Cattleman from the Rio Grande Across the Far Marias* (New York: Hastings House, 1958).

2. Cf. "The Cattle Kingdom" and other essays, in Foster Rhea Dulles, *The United States Since 1865* (Ann Arbor: University of Michigan Press, 1959), pp. 43-51; and R. R. Dykstra, *The Cattle Towns* (New York: Alfred A. Knopf, 1968), pp. 3 ff.

3. Augustin Daly, *Horizon*, in Allan Gates Halline, ed., *American Plays* (New York: American Book Co., 1935), Act II, opening directions, p. 348.

4. Joseph Francis Daly, *The Life of Augustin Daly* (New York: Macmillan Co., 1917), p. 106. This is generous praise, for in the 1870's Palmer, at the Union Square Theatre, was a rival manager to Augustin Daly, then managing the Olympic.

5. Daly, *Horizon*, Act II, p. 348.

6. *Ibid.*, Act I, p. 346.

7. *Ibid.*, Act II, p. 352.

8. *Ibid.*

9. *Ibid.*, Act IV, p. 365.

10. *Ibid.*, Act I, p. 343.

11. For a fuller account of Hoyt's abilities as a legislator, see "Charles Hoyt," in Montrose J. Moses, ed., *Representative American Dramas: National and Local* (Boston: D. C. Heath & Co., 1941), pp. 3-5.

12. John Chapman and G. P. Sherwood, eds., *The Best Plays of 1894-1899* (New York: Dodd Mead & Co., 1955), p. 3.

13. Douglas L. Hunt, ed., *Five Plays by Charles H. Hoyt*, in *America's Lost Plays* (Princeton: Princeton University Press, 1941), 9:x. Hunt, "The Life and Work of Charles H. Hoyt," *Birmingham-Southern College Bulletin*, 39 (January, 1946): 30, notes that Will Rogers starred as Maverick Brander in the motion picture version of *A Texas Steer* made by Metro-Goldwyn-Mayer in 1928.

14. F. L. Pattee, *The New American Literature: 1890-1930* (New York: Century Co., 1930), p. 105.

15. *The Wallet of Time* (New York: Moffat, Yard & Co., 1913), 2:530. Chap. 16 of this volume, "The Plays of Augustus Thomas," is useful for contemporary evaluation.

16. William Dean Howells, "The Recent Dramatic Season," *North American Review*, 122 (March, 1901): 468-70. Pt. 4 of this article offers a full contemporary analysis of the New York production of *Arizona*.

17. Augustus Thomas, *The Print of My Remembrance* (New York: Charles Scribner's Sons, 1922), pp. 351-52. Chap. 19, "Some Experiences in Arizona," fully records Thomas' search for dramatic material in Arizona.

18. Augustus Thomas, *Arizona: A Drama in Four Acts* (New York: Robert Howard Russell, 1899), Act III, p. 124.

19. Montrose J. Moses, *The American Dramatist* (Boston: Little, Brown & Co., 1917), p. 160.

20. Thomas, *The Print of My Remembrance*, pp. 359-61.

21. *Ibid.*, p. 358.

22. These two plays, still in typescript, may be found in the Theatre Collection, New York Public Library. Both reveal Thomas' use of large casts of characters, incidental music such as miners' songs featured in *Colorado*, and detailed stage directions.

23. "To Colorado for New Material," chap. 21 of Thomas, *The Print of My Remembrance*; Isaac Marcosson and Daniel Frohman, *Charles Frohman: Manager and Man* (New York: Harper & Bros., 1916), p. 210.

24. Montrose J. Moses, ed., *Representative Plays by American Dramatists, 1856-1911* (New York: Dutton, 1925), p. 452.

25. Augustus Thomas, *In Mizzoura*, in Moses, *Representative Plays*, Act I, p. 249. The play was originally published in 1916 by Samuel French.

26. *Ibid.*, Act II, p. 492.

27. Produced by John D. Williams at the Shubert Theatre, New York, the play had a run of 120 performances (beginning on February 18, 1918), largely because of Lionel Barrymore's inspired acting as Milt Shanks and the patriotic feeling then running high.

28. Augustus Thomas, *The Copperhead*, in Helen Louise Cohen, ed., *Longer Plays by Modern Authors* (New York: Harcourt, Brace & Co., 1922), pt. 1, Act I, p. 117.

29. *Ibid.*, pt. 2, Act IV, pp. 160-61.

30. Thomas, *The Print of My Remembrance*, p. 214.

31. Frederick Mayer, "India and the Western Mind," *Saturday Review*, 43 (July 30, 1960): 11.

32. Fanny Kemble Wister, *Owen Wister Out West: His Journals and Letters* (Chicago: University of Chicago Press, 1958), p. 3.

33. *Ibid.*, pp. 11-12, a quotation from Owen Wister, *Roosevelt: The Story of a Friendship* (New York: Macmillan Co., 1930).

34. "Disaster and Transition," chap. 7 of Ernest Staples Osgood, *The Day of the Cattleman* (Chicago: University of Chicago Press, 1929), *passim*.

35. *Ibid.*, p. 240.

36. Owen Wister, *The Virginian: A Horseman of the Plains* (New York: Macmillan Co., 1902), p. 12.

37. Wister's Journals (Wyoming and Yellowstone Park, June-September, 1891) record his impressions of such frontier towns as Douglas and Buffalo, Wyoming. "The town of Buffalo ... is something horrible beyond words. ... A general litter of paltry wood houses back to back and side to back at all angles that seem to have been brought and dumped out from a wheelbarrow." Of Douglas, in the "midst of empty desolation," he records: "The town, board houses standing at all angles, with the unreal look of stage scenery, always that same artificial soon-to-be-changed-for-something-else look." Cf. Fanny Kemble Wister, *Owen Wister Out West*, pp. 100 ff.

38. Owen Wister and Kirke La Shelle, *The Virginian: A Play in Four Acts*, with an introduction and notes by N. Orwin Rush, mimeographed (Tallahassee, Florida, 1958), Act II, pp. 32-33.

39. Wister, *The Virginian: A Horseman of the Plains*, p. 399.

40. Fanny Kemble Wister, *Owen Wister Out West*, p. 225.

41. *Ibid.*, p. 2.

42. Moses, *The American Dramatist*, p. 15.

43. Olivia Howard Dunbar, *A House in Chicago* (Chicago: University of Chicago Press, 1947), p. 208.

44. *Ibid.*, pp. 58-59.

45. *The Great Divide*, in Thomas H. Dickinson, ed., *Chief Contemporary Dramatists* (Boston: Houghton Mifflin Co., 1915), Act I, p. 288.

46. Cf. Arthur Hobson Quinn, *A History of the American Drama from the Civil War to the Present Day* (New York: Crofts, 1943), 1:273-74; Burns Mantle and G. P. Sherwood, eds., *The Best Plays of 1899-1909* (New York: Dodd, Mead & Co., 1947), pp. vi, 2, 358.

47. Moses, *Representative Plays*, p. 527.

48. Archie Bell, *The Clyde Fitch I Knew* (New York: Broadway Publishing Co., 1909), pp. 58-59.

49. *Ibid.*, p. 76.

50. From a typed prompt copy in the Theatre Collection, New York Public Library.

51. Data drawn from the typescript of a prompt copy (dated 1901) in the Theatre Collection, New York Public Library.

52. In this series are *Wolfville* (1897), *Sandburrs* (1900), *Wolfville Days* (1902), *Wolfville Nights* (1902), *Wolfville Folks* (1908), and *Faro Nell and Her Friends* (1913), all marking Lewis as one of the pioneers in the interpretation of the range town. See Louis Filler, ed., *Old Wolfville* (Yellow Springs, Ohio: Antioch Press, 1968).

53. Moses, *The American Dramatist*, p. 180.

54. Alfred Henry Lewis, *Wolfville* (New York: Stokes, 1897), p. 218.

55. Clyde Fitch and Willis Steell, "Wolfville: A Drama of the South West," typescript subtitled "A New Play," with penciled notes, n.d., Theatre Collection, New York Public Library, Act IV, p. 10.

56. Cf. "Long Ago on the Rio Grande," in Alfred Henry Lewis, *Wolfville Nights* (New York: Stokes, 1902), p. 306.

57. The true spirit of southwestern cow towns is further preserved in Charles Wilkins Webber, *Tales of the Southern Border* (New York, 1852) and Thomas A. Janvier, *Santa Fe's Partner: Being Some Materials of Events in a New Mexico Track-End Town* (New York, 1907).

58. Chapman and Sherwood, *The Best Plays of 1894-1899*, p. 4.

59. Cf. "Plays Produced in New York," in *ibid.*, pp. 83-260, and Marcosson and Frohman, *Charles Frohman*, pp. 421-40, for listings of popular productions during this era.

60. For a full tracing of many types of regional movements, as these affect native drama, see Felix Sper, *From Native Roots* (Caldwell, Idaho: Caxton Printers, 1948); see also Frederick J. Hoffman, Charles Allen, and Carolyn F. Ulrich, *The Little Magazine: A History and a Bibliography* (Princeton: Princeton University Press, 1946).

61. Robert Finch, *Plays of the American West* (New York: Greenberg, 1947).

62. Jack Shaefer, "Real Heroes of the West," *Holiday*, 22 (December, 1957): 76. For a contrasting type, the bad man, see Peter Lyon, "The Wild, Wild West," *American Heritage*, 11 (August, 1960): 32-48. Both articles are richly illustrated.

63. "The Work of E. P. Conkle," Foreword, Barrett H. Clark, *Crick Bottom Plays* (New York: Samuel French, 1928), pp. ix-x.

64. Ellsworth Prouty Conkle, *The Shadow of a Rock* (New York: Samuel French, 1936).

65. "Drama of the Southwest," in George Sessions Perry, ed., *Roundup Time* (New York: Whittlesey House, 1943), pp. 366-67. Two related regional articles in this volume are Henry Nash Smith, "The Southwest: An Introduction," and Rebecca W. Smith, "The Southwest in Fiction."

66. Published by Samuel French, 1924; republished in *Southwest Review*, 10 (October, 1924): 3-23, and in Elizabeth Matchett Stover, ed., *Son-of-a-Gun Stew* (Dallas: University Press in Dallas, 1945), pp. 173-85.

67. For the first play see *One-Act Plays for Stage and Study*, Ser. 5 (New York: Samuel French, 1929). *Westward People*, first appearing in *Southwest Review*, 20 (Autumn, 1934): 87-109, was published by Samuel French, 1935. The quotation from J. Frank Dobie is from his *Guide to Life and Literature of the Southwest* (Dallas: Southern Methodist University Press, 1952), p. 186.

68. Cf. James T. DeShields, *Cynthia Ann Parker* (St. Louis: Charles B. Woodward, 1886) for a recognized early treatment of this captivity.

69. John William Rogers, Jr., *Roam Though I May* (Boston: Walter H. Baker Co., 1933). *Where the Dear Antelope Play* appears in *Three Southwest Plays* (Dallas: Southwest Review, 1942).

70. Frederick J. Hoffman, *The Twenties* (New York: Viking Press, 1955), p. 216.

71. Albert Riebling, "A Playwright's Theatre," *Theatre Arts Monthly*, 15 (July, 1931): 549-51. This entire issue, containing production pictures of many provincial plays, is devoted to "The Tributary Theatre."

72. Virgil Geddes, *Native Ground: A Cycle of Plays* (New York: Samuel French, 1932), p. vii. Born on a farm in Dixon County, Nebraska, in 1897, Geddes attended country schools, later worked at small jobs in Boston and Chicago, and for four years proofread for an American newspaper in Paris.

73. "Virgil Geddes," Foreword, in Barrett H. Clark, *The Earth Between and Behind the Night* (New York: Samuel French, 1930), p. xii.

74. Helen Louise Cohen, ed., *More One-Act Plays* (New York: Harcourt, Brace & Co., 1927), pp. 89-90.

75. Dan Totheroh, *One-Act Plays for Everyone* (New York: Samuel French, 1931), pp. 67-83. This play was first published in *Ten Minute Plays* (New York: Brentano's, 1923). Totheroh's *One-Act Plays* contains also "Good Vintage" and "The Great Dark."

76. "Seeing the Elephant," in *America in Action* (New York: Crowell, 1941), p. 143. First published by Dramatists Play Service, 1939.

77. For full details see Burns Mantle, ed., *The Best Plays of 1924-25* (Boston: Small, Maynard & Co., 1925), pp. 384-417.

78. *Ibid.*, p. 423. The idea for *Wild Birds* came to Totheroh while he was trouping through small-town and rural Nebraska.

79. Mildred Adams, "A Roster of New Playwrights," *Theatre Arts Monthly*, 17 (April, 1933): 296.

80. A playlet, "The Lonesome West" (1927) has seen neither printing nor footlights, according to Miss Adams. The same is true of "The Son of Perdition" (1923).

81. Both of these plays were published by Samuel French. *Big Lake*, popular with little theater audiences, was first produced by the American Laboratory Theatre, New York, on April 8, 1927.

82. Published by Samuel French in 1930.

83. See "Story of Oklahoma!" in the Guild's illustrated program. For an adverse review of *Green Grow the Lilacs* as presented by the Theatre Guild see Richard Lockridge, "Lynn Riggs' Southwest," *New York Sun*, January 27, 1931.

84. Lynn Riggs, *Green Grow the Lilacs*, in Barrett H. Clark and William H. Davenport, eds., *Nine Modern American Plays* (New York: Appleton-Century-Crofts, 1951), sc. 4, p. 120. (The play is divided into six scenes.)

85. *Ibid.*, sc. 6, p. 133.

86. *Ibid.*, sc. 2, p. 100.

87. David Belasco, *The Theatre Through Its Stage Door* (New York: Harper & Bros., 1919), p. 229.

CHAPTER VI

1. Van Wyck Brooks, "The Critical Movement in America," *Freeman*, 4 (October 12, 1921): 118-19. (Reprinted in *Sketches in Criticism*, 1932, pp. 11-25.)

2. Meredith Nicholson, *The Valley of Democracy* (New York: Charles Scribner's Sons, 1919), p. 2.

3. "The Age of Confidence," pt. 1, of Henry Seidel Canby, *American Memoir* (Boston: Houghton Mifflin Co., 1940), p. 33.

4. Sherwood Anderson, *Home Town* (New York: Alliance Book Corp., 1940), p. 33.

5. Willard Thorp, *American Writing in the Twentieth Century* (Cambridge: Harvard University Press, 1960), p. 11.

6. See The Easy Shopper, "Country and General Stores," *Holiday*, 21 (June, 1961): 165 ff. Included is a photograph of two New England men playing a leisurely game of checkers on the cracker barrel of a Maine country store, to be compared with a photograph (p. 29) of the cluttered general store in San Augustine, Texas, one among the many small-town illustrations used in Anderson, *Home Town*.

7. Introduction by Julie A. Herne in Mrs. James A. Herne, ed., *Shore Acres and Other Plays* (New York: Samuel French, 1928), p. xvi. Also, for a detailed analysis, with a full-page portrait of Herne, see "Herne—The First Collaborator," chap. 9 of Craig Timberlake, *The Life & Work of David Belasco: The Bishop of Broadway* (New York: Library Publishers, 1954).

8. Herne, *Shore Acres and Other Plays*, p. xvi.

9. *Ibid.*, p. xvii.

10. For a full account of Herne's development as a playwright see H. H. Waggoner, "The Growth of a Realist: James A. Herne," *New England Quarterly*, 15 (March, 1942): 62-73.

11. Herne, *Shore Acres and Other Plays*, p. xix.

12. *Ibid.*

13. *Ibid.*, p. 16.

14. *Ibid.*, pp. 17-18.

15. *Ibid.*, p. 30.

16. *Ibid.*, p. xx.

17. Arthur Hobson Quinn, *A History of the American Drama from the Civil War to the Present Day* (New York: Crofts, 1943), chap. 6.

18. *Margaret Fleming*, in Arthur Hobson Quinn, *Representative American Plays*, 7th ed. (New York: Appleton-Century-Crofts, 1953), Act III, p. 540.

19. See Quinn, *History of the American Drama*, pp. 144-46, for Mrs. Herne's views on these two conclusions.

20. "Mr. and Mrs. Herne," *Arena*, 4 (October, 1891): 543.

21. Douglas L. Hunt, ed., *Five Plays by Charles H. Hoyt*, in *America's Lost Plays* (Princeton: Princeton University Press, 1941), 9:x.

22. *Ibid.*, p. viii.

23. *Ibid.*, p. 51.

24. Douglas L. Hunt, "The Life and Work of Charles H. Hoyt," *Birmingham-Southern College Bulletin*, 39 (January, 1946): 14.

25. Preface to *A Temperance Town*, in *America's Lost Plays*, 9:149.

26. Hunt, "Charles H. Hoyt," p. 17.

27. *Ibid.*, pp. 17-18.

28. Preface to *A Milk White Flag*, in *America's Lost Plays*, 9:193.

29. Montrose J. Moses, *The American Dramatist* (Boston: Little, Brown & Co., 1917), p. 92.

30. Montrose J. Moses, "Cobwebs of Antiquity: A Plea for Folk Basis in American Drama," *North American Review*, 231 (January, 1931): 81-82.

31. For more complete staging details about *Old Jed Prouty* and other plays listed in this connection, see John Chapman and G. P. Sherwood, eds., *The Best Plays of 1894-1899* (New York: Dodd, Mead & Co., 1955) and Mantle and Sherwood, eds., *The Best Plays of 1899-1909*.

32. Undated in the typed prompt copy in the Theatre Collection, New York Public Library.

33. Isaac F. Marcosson and Daniel Frohman, *Charles Frohman: Manager and Man* (New York: Harper & Bros., 1916), pp. 208-9.

34. Their full names are James Ripley Wellman Hitchcock and Mrs. Martha Wolcott (Hall) Hitchcock. In the Theatre Collection, New York Public Library, Frohman's personal prompt book—copyrighted in 1898 by Hitchcock—is a bound volume of three copies in typescript, each with penciled production notes and deletions. Another volume, very large, contains two typed copies of the comedy "as we played it in 1901." Helen Sargent Hitchcock holds the copyright on the acting version published in 1938 by Samuel French.

35. Fred C. Kelley, *George Ade, Warmhearted Satirist* (Indianapolis: Bobbs-Merrill, 1947), p. 175.

36. *Ibid.*, p. 176.

37. Dorothy Ritter Russo, *A Bibliography of George Ade, 1866-1944* (Indianapolis: Indiana Historical Society, 1947), p. ix.

38. *Ibid.*, p. 174.

39. George Ade, *The County Chairman* (New York: Samuel French, 1923), *passim.*

40. Kelley, *George Ade, Warmhearted Satirist*, p. 186.

41. James Woodress, *Booth Tarkington: Gentleman from Indiana* (Philadelphia: Lippincott, 1954), pp. 34-36, 82-83.

42. Grant Overton, *Authors of the Day: Studies in Contemporary Literature* (New York: Doran, 1924), p. 113.

43. Woodress, *Booth Tarkington: Gentleman from Indiana*, pp. 189-90, notes that since its creation in 1914-15 Tarkington's *Seventeen* has been dramatized, but never by the novelist himself, as a silent movie, stage play, musical comedy, talking movie, and in 1951 as another musical.

44. For complete analysis see August Derleth, *Still Small Voice: The Biography of Zona Gale* (New York: Appleton-Century, 1940), with Miss Gale's unfinished *Autobiography.*

45. Derleth, *Still Small Voice*, p. 93.

46. Zona Gale, *Friendship Village Love Stories* (New York: Macmillan Co., 1909), p. 6.

47. Derleth, *Still Small Voice*, p. 117.

48. Published in 1920, by B. W. Huebsch, as *The Neighbors*, and in 1921, by Walter H. Baker Co., as *Neighbours.*

49. Zona Gale, *Uncle Jimmy* (New York: Baker, 1922), p. 25.

50. Quoted in Overton, *Authors of the Day*, p. 140.

51. Derleth, *Still Small Voice*, pp. 114-15.

52. Mantle and Sherwood, *The Best Plays of 1909-1919*, pp. 352-53, 634. Samuel French is the publisher of *Lightnin'* (1918).

CHAPTER VII

1. Augustus Thomas, *Alabama: A Drama in Four Acts* (Chicago: Dramatic Publishing Co., 1898), p. 1. Maurice Barrymore is listed as playing the role of the mysterious Captain Davenport, ostensibly a Northern railroad man, but actually a native of Talladega. William Stanley Hoole, " 'Alabama': Drama of reconciliation," *Alabama Review*, 19 (April 1, 1966): 83-108, fully evaluates this drama about Talladega, Alabama.

2. Jay B. Hubbell, *The South in American Literature, 1607-1900* (Durham: Duke University Press, 1954), p. 720.

3. Grant C. Knight, *The Critical Period in American Literature, 1890-1900* (Chapel Hill: University of North Carolina Press, 1951), p. 36.

4. Edward Brewster Sheldon, *"The Nigger": An American Play in Three Acts* (New York: Macmillan Co., 1910), Act. I, p. 33.

5. *Ibid.,* Act II, p. 172.

6. "English 47," in Wisner Payne Kinne, *George Pierce Baker and the American Theatre* (Cambridge: Harvard University Press, 1954), p. 105.

7. "Keeping the Negro in His Place," in Allison Davis, B. B. Gardner, and M. R. Gardner, *Deep South* (Chicago: University of Chicago Press, 1954), pp. 44-49.

8. Sherwood Anderson, *Dark Laughter* (New York: Boni & Liveright, 1925), p. 16.

9. Edd Winfield Parks, "Southern Towns and Cities," in W. T. Couch, ed., *Culture in the South* (Chapel Hill: University of North Carolina Press, 1935), p. 515. Cf. Carey McWilliams, *Brothers under the Skin* (Boston: Little, Brown & Co., 1943), pp. 288 ff.

10. Gilbert W. Gabriel, "Rhapsody in Red," in Montrose J. Moses and John Mason Brown, eds., *The American Theatre as Seen by Its Critics* (New York: W. W. Norton & Co., 1934), pp. 311-13. Originally a review in the *Telegram-Mail*, January 13, 1925.

11. Hallie Flanagan, "A Theatre is Born," *Theatre Arts Monthly*, 15 (November, 1931): 911.

12. John Howard Lawson, *Processional: A Jazz Symphony of American Life* (New York: Albert & Charles Boni, 1925), Act IV, last lines.

13. John Gassner, *Theatre at the Crossroads* (New York: Holt, Rinehart & Winston, 1960), p. 58.

14. John Wexley, *They Shall Not Die* (New York: Samuel French, 1934), Act III, p. 146.

15. Data from printed program for the performances at the Playmakers Theatre, Chapel Hill, on December 10, 11, and 12, 1931. See "The Consequences of the Crash," in Edmund Wilson, *The Shores of Light* (New York: Vintage Books, Random House, 1952), pp. 497-98, for a report on the bitter and violent Gastonia strike of the Carolina textile workers, from the spring to September, 1929. This strike "was the first major battle conducted by a Communist union."

16. Elizabeth Nowell, *Thomas Wolfe, A Biography* (Garden City, N.Y.: Doubleday & Co., 1960), pp. 46-47.

17. Richard Walser, *Thomas Wolfe* (New York: Barnes & Noble, 1961), pp. 25-26.

18. Nowell, *Thomas Wolfe, A Biography*, pp. 57, 62-63. "Young Faustus," Bk. 2 of *Of Time and the River*, contains a frank evaluation of Baker as "Professor Hatcher," his conduct of the Workshop, and the student dramatists, for the most part "lost Americans" whose plays were "unreal, sterile, imitative, and derivative."

19. Nowell, *Thomas Wolfe, A Biography*, p. 68.

20. Thomas Wolfe, *Welcome to Our City*, abridged, *Esquire*, 48 (October, 1957): 58-82.

21. Editorial note, *ibid.*, p. 58.

22. Lawrence Langner, *The Magic Curtain* (New York: E. P. Dutton, 1951), pp. 158-59.

23. Wolfe, *Welcome to Our City*, p. 58.

24. Paul Green, *In the Valley and Other Carolina Plays* (New York: Samuel French, 1928), p. 3. A later collection of Green's plays, *Out of the South* (New York: Harper & Bros., 1939), contains *Potter's Field*.

25. *Johnny Johnson*, in John Gassner, ed., *Twenty Best Plays of the Modern American Theatre* (New York: Crown, 1939), p. 190.

26. Langner, *The Magic Curtain*, p. 226. Cf. editorial note, *"Porgy*: The Play That Set a Pattern," *Theatre Arts*, 34 (October, 1955): 33-34.

27. DuBose and Dorothy Heyward, *Porgy*, Theatre Guild Acting version (New York: Doubleday, Page & Co., 1927), p. 3.

28. *Ibid.,* Act IV, p. 203.

29. Langer, *The Magic Curtain,* p. 158.

30. Ollie Stewart, "An American Opera Conquers Europe," *Theatre Arts,* 34 (October, 1955): 30-33, 93-94. Illustrated.

31. DuBose and Dorothy Heyward, *Mamba's Daughters* (New York: Farrar & Rinehart, 1939), Act I, p. 31.

32. *Ibid.,* Act IV, p. 174.

33. DuBose Heyward, *Brass Ankle* (New York: Farrar & Rinehart, 1931), Act I, p. 14.

34. *Ibid.,* p. 41.

35. The phrase is the title of John Spencer Bassett's controversial essay, first published in the *South Atlantic Quarterly,* 2 (October, 1903): 297-305.

36. Heyward, *Brass Ankle,* Act III, p. 131. When *Brass Ankle* was first performed (at the Masque Theatre, New York, April 23, 1931), Alice Brady played the role of Ruth Leamer and Ben Smith appeared as Larry.

37. Dorothy Dudley, *Dreiser and the Land of the Free* (New York: Beachhurst Press, 1946), p. 441.

38. Theodore Dreiser, *The Hand of the Potter* (New York: Boni & Liveright, 1918), Act I, p. 27.

39. Dudley, *Dreiser,* p. 323.

40. Theodore Dreiser, *Plays of the Natural and the Supernatural* (New York: John Lane Co., 1916), p. 10.

41. Edgar Lee Masters, *Across Spoon River* (New York: Farrar & Rinehart, 1936), pp. 330-31.

42. Data from the typed play list (dating from 1947) in the Margo Jones Theatre Collection, Dallas Public Library.

43. Jerome Lawrence and Robert E. Lee, *Inherit the Wind,* in John Gassner, ed., *Best American Plays, 1951-1957* (New York: Crown, 1960), Act I, p. 406.

44. Another small-town play wherein the protagonist is a young fellow shut up in a jail cell is William Saroyan's one-acter, "Hello Out There," from his *Razzle-Dazzle* (New York: Harcourt, Brace & Co., 1942). The sympathetic acting by Eddie Dowling and Julie Haydon, in the roles of the prisoner and the girl, highlighted Saroyan's belief in the man's showing "a compassionate tolerance of all, good or bad, that walk the earth."

CHAPTER VIII

1. Alice Brown, *Children of Earth* (New York: Macmillan Co., 1915), Act IV, p. 207.

2. Susan Glaspell, *Alison's House* (New York: Samuel French, 1930), Act III, p. 149. The play was produced by the Civic Repertory Theatre, New York, on December 1, 1930, under the direction of Eva Le Gallienne, with scenery and costumes designed by Aline Bernstein.

3. August Derleth, *Still Small Voice: The Biography of Zona Gale* (New York: Appleton-Century, 1940), p. 146.

4. Cf. Alan S. Downer, *Fifty Years of American Drama: 1900-1950* (Chicago: Henry Regnery Co., 1951), p. 54.

5. R. C. Benchley, Foreword, in Zona Gale, *Miss Lulu Bett: An American Comedy of Manners* (New York: D. Appleton & Co., 1921), p. xv.

6. Gale, *Miss Lulu Bett,* Act I, sc. 2, pp. 54-55.

7. Carl Van Doren, *Contemporary American Novelists, 1900-1920* (New York: Macmillan Co., 1922), p. 166.

8. Zona Gale, *Mister Pitt* (New York: Appleton, 1925), Act III, pp. 186-87.

9. Zona Gale, *Faint Perfume: A Play with a Prologue* (New York: Samuel French, 1934), p. 125.

10. Booth Tarkington, *Alice Adams* (New York: Doubleday, Page & Co., 1921), pp. 433-34.

11. Included with the published play, Elizabeth Trotter, *Alice Adams* (Boston: Baker's Plays, 1921).

12. Cf. James Woodress, *Booth Tarkington: Gentleman from Indiana* (Philadelphia: Lippincott, 1954), p. 318.

13. Introduction to *The Detour*, in Montrose J. Moses, ed., *Representative American Dramas: National and Local* (Boston: D. C. Heath & Co., 1941), p. 492.

14. Cf. Owen Davis' autobiography, *I'd Like to Do It Again* (New York: Farrar & Rinehart, 1931), for data about his early background.

15. Owen Davis, *The Detour*, in Moses, *Representative American Dramas*, Act I, pp. 498, 504.

16. *Ibid.*, Act II, p. 509.

17. Cf. Owen Davis, *My First Fifty Years in the Theatre* (Boston: Baker Co., 1950), pp. 83-84.

18. Stage directions, Act I, Owen Davis, *Icebound*, in Allan Gates Halline, ed., *American Plays* (New York: American Book Co., 1935), p. 621. Davis, *First Fifty Years*, p. 91, notes that "when the play opened no actor in the cast was very well known, but after that Robert Ames, Phyllis Povar and Edna May Oliver [excellent as Hannah, the family servant] were firmly established."

19. Davis, *Icebound*, in Halline, *American Plays*, Act II, p. 637.

20. *Collected Poems of Edwin Arlington Robinson* (New York: Macmillan Co., 1937), pp. 900-901.

21. Edith Wharton, *A Backward Glance* (New York: Appleton-Century-Crofts, 1934), pp. 293-94.

22. Owen and Donald Davis, *Ethan Frome: A Dramatization* (New York: Charles Scribner's Sons, 1936), Act I, sc. 1, pp. 23-24.

23. Alfred Kazin, *On Native Grounds* (New York: Reynal & Hitchcock, 1942), pp. 80-81.

24. Foreword, January, 1936, Edith Wharton, *Ethan Frome: A Dramatization*.

25. Cf. *TV Guide*, 8, no. 7 (February 13, 1960): A-33-A-34.

26. John Howard Lawson, *Roger Bloomer*, in A. R. Fulton, ed., *Seven Modern Plays* (New York: Holt, 1946), Act I, p. 223.

27. Lionel Trilling, "Winter Day in Town," in Paul Rosenfeld, ed., *The Sherwood Anderson Reader* (Boston: Houghton Mifflin Co., 1947), p. 510.

28. James Schevill, *Sherwood Anderson: His Life and Work* (Denver: University of Denver Press, 1951), p. 96.

29. *Ibid.*, p. 94.

30. *Ibid.*, p. 97.

31. Eugene P. Sheehy and Kenneth A. Lopf, comps., *Sherwood Anderson: A Bibliography* (Los Gatos, California: Talisman Press, 1960), pp. 22-23, 46.

32. Henry Hewes, "Do Books Make the Best Theatre?" *Saturday Review*, 41 (February 8, 1958): 26-27. Cover page portrait of Miss McGuire.

33. Cf. "Terrible Town," *Time*, 72, no. 3 (July 21, 1958): 67. Photograph by Radford Bascome.

34. Sherwood Anderson, *Plays: Winesburg and Others* (New York: Charles Scribner's Sons, 1937), p. 3.

35. Rosenfeld, *The Sherwood Anderson Reader*, p. xii.

36. *Ibid.*, pp. xxi-xxii.

37. *Winesburg, Ohio*, in Anderson, *Plays: Winesburg and Others*, sc. 4 (epilogue), p. 152.

38. *Ibid.*, p. 81.

39. Cf. Epifanio San Juan, Jr., "Vision and Reality: A Reconsideration of

Sherwood Anderson's *Winesburg, Ohio,*" *American Literature*, 35 (May, 1963): 153.

40. Christopher Sergel, *I'm a Fool* (Chicago: Dramatic Publishing Co., 1942), p. 7.

41. *The Hero*, in Arthur Hobson Quinn, *Contemporary American Plays* (New York: Charles Scribner's Sons, 1923), Act III, p. 296.

42. *Ibid.*, p. 275.

43. Sidney Howard, *Ned McCobb's Daughter* (New York: Charles Scribner's Sons, 1926), p. v, lists full cast and other details about the Guild production.

44. Frank Hurburt O'Hara, *Today in American Drama* (Chicago: University of Chicago Press, 1939), p. 84.

45. Lillian Hellman, *Another Part of the Forest*, in E. B. Watson and B. Pressy, eds., *Contemporary Drama* (New York: Charles Scribner's Sons, 1956), Act II, p. 225.

46. Lillian Hellman, *The Little Foxes,* in Richard A. Cordell, ed., *Twentieth Century Plays* (New York: Ronald, 1947), Act III, p. 251. In 1950 Marc Blitzstein made an attempt at American opera on Broadway with his *Regina*, a musical version of *The Little Foxes*.

47. Cf. Mark Schorer, *Sinclair Lewis: An American Life* (New York: McGraw-Hill Book Co., 1961), *passim*.

48. Sinclair Lewis, "The Long Arm of the Small Town," in H. E. Maule and M. H. Cane, eds., *The Man from Main Street* (New York: Random House, 1953), pp. 271-72.

49. Lloyd Lewis, "The Title," in Sinclair Lewis and Lloyd Lewis, *The Jayhawkers* (New York: Doubleday, Doran & Co., 1935), p. ix.

50. Sinclair Lewis, *Dodsworth* (New York: Harcourt, Brace & Co., 1934), sc. 2. The play, with Walter Huston in the titular role, opened at the Garrick Theatre in Philadelphia on February 5, 1934, and at the Shubert Theatre in New York on February 24, 1934.

51. Sinclair Lewis, *It Can't Happen Here: A Novel* (New York: Doubleday, Doran & Co., 1935), pp. 57-58.

52. *Ibid.*, pp. 433-34.

53. On September 18, 1936, the Play Bureau of the Federal Theatre Project, New York, issued the play as a Federal Theatre Playscript, Publication no. 1. In this mimeographed form the title page bore the authors' names as John C. Moffitt and Sinclair Lewis. Cf. Schorer, *Sinclair Lewis: An American Life*, p. 264, n., regarding the omission of Moffitt's name.

54. *It Can't Happen Here*, Act II, sc. 4, pp. 8-9.

55. Sherwood Anderson, *Memoirs* (New York: Harcourt, Brace & Co., 1942), pp. 295-96.

56. "The American Small Town," from *Towns, Ho!* pt. xiii in Paul Rosenfeld, *The Sherwood Anderson Reader* (Boston: Houghton Mifflin Co., 1947), pp. 747-48.

57. "Introduction to *Main Street*," in Maule and Cane, *The Man from Main Street*, p. 214. Cf. John Bartlow Martin, "The Changing Midwest," *Saturday Evening Post*, 230 (January 11, 1958): 17 ff.

CHAPTER IX

1. Eugene O'Neill, *The Straw* (New York: Random House, 1928), Act I, sc. 2, p. 361.

2. Barrett H. Clark, *Eugene O'Neill: The Man and His Plays* (New York: Dover Publications, 1947), p. 18.

3. *Ibid.*, p. 20.

4. Arthur and Barbara Gelb, *O'Neill* (New York: Harper & Bros., 1962), p. 250.

5. *Ibid.*, p. 233.

6. Doris M. Alexander, *The Tempering of Eugene O'Neill* (New York: Harcourt, Brace, & World, 1962), p. 184.

7. Gelb and Gelb, *O'Neill*, p. 234.

8. Gladys Hamilton, "O'Neill's Debt to Clayton Hamilton," in Oscar Cargill, N. B. Fagin, and W. J. Fisher, eds., *O'Neill and His Plays* (New York: New York University Press, 1961), p. 22.

9. Cf. Cargill, Fagin, and Fisher, *O'Neill and His Plays*, pp. 19-20.

10. Gelb and Gelb, *O'Neill*, p. 52.

11. Croswell Bowen, *The Curse of the Misbegotten: A Tale of the House of O'Neill* (New York: McGraw-Hill Co., 1959), p. 38.

12. Joseph Wood Krutch, *American Drama Since 1918*, rev. ed. (New York: George Braziller, 1957), p. 115.

13. John Gassner, *Theatre at the Crossroads* (New York: Holt, Rinehart & Winston, 1960), p. 73.

14. Self-description, in O'Neill to Nathan, Provincetown, June 20, 1920.

15. Interview with Malcolm Mollan, "Making Plays with a Tragic End," *Philadelphia Public Ledger*, January 22, 1922, magazine section.

16. Oliver M. Sayler, "The Real Eugene O'Neill," *Century Magazine*, 103 (January, 1922): 351-59.

17. Eugene O'Neill, *Abortion*, in *Lost Plays of Eugene O'Neill* (New York: New Fathoms, 1950), pp. 19-20.

18. Eugene O'Neill, *The Rope* (New York: Random House, 1928), p. 580.

19. From Woollcott's review in the *New York Times*, November 11, 1921.

20. O'Neill, *The Straw*, Act III, p. 394.

21. *Ibid.*, Act I, sc. 2, pp. 358-59.

22. Eugene O'Neill, *Diff'rent* (New York: Random House, 1933), Act II, pp. 542-43.

23. Doris V. Falk, *Eugene O'Neill and the Tragic Tension* (New Brunswick: Rutgers University Press, 1958), p. 72. For a detailed analysis, see Edwin A. Engel, *The Haunted Heroes of Eugene O'Neill* (Cambridge: Harvard University Press, 1953), pp. 29-36.

24. "The Culture of Industrialism," in Van Wyck Brooks, *America's Coming-of-Age* (Garden City, N.Y.: Anchor Books & Doubleday Co., 1958), pp. 104-5.

25. "Mencken's Democratic Man," in Edmund Wilson, *The Shores of Light* (New York: Random House, 1952), pp. 296-97.

26. Alfred Kazin, *On Native Grounds* (New York: Reynal & Hitchcock, 1942), p. 196.

27. *Ibid.*

28. Cf. "O'Neill's New Play," *American Mercury*, 8 (August, 1926): 499-505.

29. Eugene O'Neill, *The Great God Brown*, in *The Plays of Eugene O'Neill*, 3 vols. (New York: Random House, 1941), 3:278, Act I, sc. 3.

30. For full description, see Gelb and Gelb, *O'Neill*, pp. 88-89.

31. O'Neill, *The Great God Brown*, Prologue, p. 260.

32. *Ibid.*, Act IV, sc. 2, p. 322.

33. "Eugene O'Neill Writes About His Latest Play, *The Great God Brown*," *New York Evening Post*, February 13, 1926.

34. Eugene O'Neill, *The Plays, Strange Interlude*, 1:199, Act IX. All other quotations from the play have been from this edition.

35. Cf. Gelb and Gelb, *O'Neill*, p. 648, for a full discussion. Also, one of the most brilliant criticisms available for *Strange Interlude* appears in "Everywoman" in Engel, *Haunted Heroes*, pp. 199-229.

36. Quotations from the memorandum received by the Guild officials from O'Neill and quoted in full in Lee Simonson, *The Stage Is Set* (New York: Harcourt, Brace & Co., 1932), pp. 117-18.

37. *Ibid.*, p. 461.

38. An early copy of this letter, which Nathan published in *American Mercury*, may be found attached to a typescript prompt copy of *Dynamo* in the Theatre Collection, New York Public Library.

39. Letter printed on the original Theatre Guild program (February 11, 1929), a copy of which is in the Theatre Collection, New York Public Library.

40. Eugene O'Neill, *The Plays, Dynamo*, 3:477, Act III, sc. 1.

41. Eugene O'Neill, "Working Notes and Extracts from a Fragmentary Work Diary," in Barrett H. Clark, *European Theories of the Drama*, rev. ed. (New York: Crown, 1947), p. 530. Originally published in the *New York Herald-Tribune*, November 3, 1931, as "O'Neill's Own Story of 'Electra' in the Making." Cf. Aeschylus, *Oresteia: Agamemnon, The Libation Bearers, The Eumenides*, trans. and with an introduction by Richmond Lattimore (Chicago: University of Chicago Press, 1953).

42. O'Neill, "Working Notes," pp. 531-32.

43. Eugene O'Neill, *The Plays, Mourning Becomes Electra* (1942), 2, *Homecoming*, Act I, sc. 1, pp. 6-7.

44. Lawrence Langner, *The Magic Curtain* (New York: E. P. Dutton, 1951), p. 279.

45. Cf. Lionel Trilling, "Eugene O'Neill: A Revaluation," *New Republic*, 377 (September 23, 1936): 127-40.

46. Langner, *The Magic Curtain*, pp. 282-83.

47. *The Plays of Eugene O'Neill*, Wilderness Edition (New York: Charles Scribner's Sons, 1934-35), 3:xi-xii.

48. Eugene O'Neill, *The Plays, Ah, Wilderness!* 2:298, Act IV, sc. 3.

49. Arthur Ruhl, "A Minor Poet of Broadway: George M. Cohan," *New York Herald-Tribune*, October 15, 1933. In 1935 Metro-Goldwyn-Mayer released a film version with Wallace Beery cast as Uncle Sid and Lionel Barrymore in the role of Nat Miller.

50. Langner, *The Magic Curtain*, pp. 284-85.

51. Gelb and Gelb, *O'Neill*, pp. 774-75.

52. *Ibid.*, pp. 81 ff., for a full discussion.

53. Jordan Y. Miller, *Eugene O'Neill and the American Critic* (Hamden: Archon Books, 1962), p. 129. In "Two Projected Cycles," *ibid.*, pp. 129-31, Miller explains the order of the nine plays eventually planned for this cycle.

54. Gelb and Gelb, *O'Neill*, p. 801.

55. Miller, *O'Neill and the American Critic*, p. 130.

56. Engel, *Haunted Heroes*, p. 278.

57. Karl Ragnar Gierow, "Eugene O'Neill's Posthumous Plays," in Cargill, Fagin, and Fisher, *O'Neill and His Plays*, p. 379. See O'Neill, *More Stately Mansions*, adapted by Karl Ragnar Gierow, Donald Gallup, ed. (New Haven: Yale University Press, 1964).

58. Eugene O'Neill, *A Touch of the Poet* (New Haven: Yale University Press, 1957), Act IV, p. 147.

59. *Ibid.*, Act I, p. 11.

60. Gassner, *Theatre at the Crossroads*, pp. 238-39.

61. O'Neill, *A Touch of the Poet*, Act IV, p. 171.

62. *Ibid.*, Act IV, pp. 168, 171.

63. *Ibid.*, Act I, p. 25.

64. See Tom Prideaux, "A Shining Return for Ingrid," *Life*, 63 (October 13, 1967): 63-68, for a fully illustrated review of the opening of the Ahmanson

Theatre in Los Angeles with a production of *More Stately Mansions* starring Ingrid Bergman as Deborah Harford, the mother; Colleen Dewhurst as Sara (Melody) Harford, the wife; and Arthur Hill as Simon Harford, her husband.

65. Quoted in full in Gelb and Gelb, *O'Neill*, pp. 6-7.

66. Printed as a dedicatory letter in Eugene O'Neill, *Long Day's Journey Into Night* (New Haven: Yale University Press, 1956), p. 7.

67. Seymour Peck, "Talk with Mrs. O'Neill," *New York Times*, November 4, 1956.

68. Gelb and Gelb, *O'Neill*, p. 81.

69. O'Neill, *Long Day's Journey Into Night*, Act I, p. 44.

70. Gilbert Seldes, *"Long Day's Journey Into Night," Saturday Review*, 34 (February 25, 1956): 15, review of the published play before its New York production.

71. O'Neill, *Long Day's Journey Into Night*, Act IV, pp. 153-54.

72. Cf. Henry Hewes, "O'Neill 100 Proof—Not a Blend," *Saturday Review*, 34 (November 24, 1956): 30.

73. O'Neill, *Long Day's Journey Into Night*, Act II, sc. 2, p. 87.

74. *Ibid.*, Act IV. p. 153.

CHAPTER X

1. Benton McKaye, *The New Exploration* (New York: Harcourt, Brace & Co., 1928), p. 151.

2. Henry Hope Reed, Jr., *The Golden City* (Garden City, N.Y.: Doubleday & Co., 1959), p. 101.

3. Cf. "The Invisible City," in Joseph Hudnut, *Architecture and the Spirit of Man* (Cambridge: Harvard University Press, 1956), and "The Spreading City," in Robert Moses, *Working for the People* (New York: Harper & Bros., 1956).

4. Frederick J. Hoffman, *The Twenties* (New York: Viking Press, 1955), p. 123.

5. Author's Note, Marc Connelly, *The Green Pastures*, in Montrose J. Moses, ed., *Representative American Dramas: National and Local* (Boston: D. C. Heath & Co., 1941), p. 826.

6. Carl Carmer, *"The Green Pastures," Theatre Arts Monthly*, 14 (October, 1930): 897-98.

7. From a review by Joseph Wood Krutch, *Nation*, 130 (March 26, 1930): 376.

8. Richard A. Cordell, ed., *Twentieth Century Plays: American* (New York: Ronald Press, 1947), p. 215.

9. Lillian Hellman, *The Children's Hour*, in John Gassner, ed., *20 Best Plays of the Modern American Theatre* (New York: Crown, 1947), Act III, p. 597.

10. The complete text of *Toys in the Attic* appears in *Theatre Arts*, October, 1961. The play won the New York Drama Critics Circle Award as the best play of the 1959-60 season.

11. Richard Watts, Jr., "Orpheus' Ascending," *Theatre Arts*, 42 (September, 1958): 26.

12. Nancy M. Tischler, *Tennesee Williams: Rebellious Puritan* (New York: Citadel Press, 1961), p. 15.

13. Autobiographical essay appended to the initial program for *A Streetcar Named Desire* (1947).

14. Herbert Gold, "Fiction of the Fifties," *Hudson Review*, 12 (Summer, 1959): 201. Regarding Williams' own views on themes of violence in his plays, see Lewis Funke and John E. Booth, "Williams on Williams," *Theatre Arts*, 46 (January, 1962): 17 ff.

15. Tennessee Williams, "Well of Violence," reprint from the *New York*

Times, later used in the New York program (1959) for *Sweet Bird of Youth* and as a preface to the published play.

16. "Something wild . . . ," Preface, Tennessee Williams, *27 Wagons Full of Cotton* (Norfolk, Conn.: New Directions, 1945, 1953), p. ix.

17. "Portrait of a Madonna," in Williams, *27 Wagons Full of Cotton*, p. 97.

18. See Lawrence Langner, *The Magic Curtain* (New York: E. P. Dutton, 1951), pp. 331-33, for a full account of this production.

19. *Battle of Angels*, in Tennessee Williams, *Orpheus Descending with Battle of Angels* (Norfolk, Conn.: New Directions, 1955, 1958), Act III, p. 216.

20. Tischler, *Tennessee Williams: Rebellious Puritan*, p. 77.

21. "The Past, the Present, and the Perhaps," in Williams, *Orpheus Descending*. p. x.

22. Arthur Knight, "Where There's a Williams . . . ," *Saturday Review*, 47 (July 18, 1964): 22.

23. Cf. typed list of plays, with annotations, in the Margo Jones Theatre Collection, Dallas Public Library.

24. Cf. *Theatre World*, 5 (1948-49): 26-27, for production data and photographs of players and set.

25. Author's Production Notes, in Tennessee Williams, *Summer and Smoke* (Norfolk, Conn.: New Directions, 1948), p. viii.

26. *Ibid.*, pt. 2, sc. 8, p. 93.

27. Benjamin Nelson, *Tennessee Williams: The Man and His Work* (New York: Ivan Obolensky, 1961), pp. 125 ff. Cf. Esther Merle Jackson, *The Broken World of Tennessee Williams* (Madison: University of Wisconsin Press, 1965), pp. 137-38.

28. Author's Production Notes, Tennessee Williams, *The Rose Tattoo* (Norfolk, Conn.: New Directions, 1950), pp. xiii-xiv. See also Arthur Knight, "The Magnificent Magnani," *Saturday Review*, 38 (December 10, 1955): 25-26, for a criticism, with illustrative photographs, of the screen version.

29. Tennessee Williams, *Vogue*, March 15, 1951.

30. Williams, *The Rose Tattoo*, Act II, sc. 1, pp. 99-100.

31. Nelson, *Tennessee Williams: Man and Work*, p. 160.

32. *Sweet Bird of Youth*, in *Three Plays of Tennessee Williams* (Norfolk, Conn.: New Directions, 1964), Act I, sc. 2, p. 374.

33. Cf. Robert Brustein, "Williams' Nebulous Nightmare," *Hudson Review*, 12 (Summer, 1959): 255.

34. Williams, *Sweet Bird of Youth*, Act I, sc. 2, p. 374.

35. *Ibid.*, Act II, sc. 2, p. 425.

36. Cf. Henry Hewes, "Tennessee's Easter Message," *Saturday Review*, 42 (March 28, 1959): 26. See also James Baldwin, "Geraldine Page: Bird of Light," *Show*, 2 (February, 1962): 78-79, for appraisal of Miss Page's rehearsal interpretation of the role of the Princess.

37. Tennessee Williams, *The Milk Train Doesn't Stop Here Anymore* (Norfolk, Conn.: New Directions, 1964), sc. 5, p. 65.

38. *Ibid.*, p. 72.

39. Tennessee Williams, *Camino Real* (Norfolk, Conn.: New Directions, 1959), p. x.

40. *Ibid.*, p. xii.

41. Quotation from the interchapters to William Faulkner, *Requiem for a Nun* (New York: New American Library, 1961), *passim*.

42. Cf. Robert Coughlan, "William Faulkner," *Life*, 35 (September 28, October 5, 1963), for detailed report of conversations with Faulkner.

43. Cf. G. T. Buckley, "Is Oxford the Original of Jefferson in Faulkner's Novels?" *PMLA*, 76 (September, 1961): 447-54. See Coughlan, "William Faulk-

ner"; Irving Howe, *William Faulkner, A Critical Study* (New York: Random House, 1952); Ward L. Miner, *The World of William Faulkner* (Durham: Duke University Press, 1952); William Van O'Connor, *The Tangled Fire of William Faulkner* (Minneapolis: University of Minnesota Press, 1954).

44. Calvin S. Brown, "Faulkner's Geography and Topography," *PMLA*, 77 (December, 1962): 652.

45. Robert Penn Warren, "William Faulkner," *New Republic*, 115 (August 12, 1946): 176. This criticism, extended into the August 26 issue, forms a brilliant appraisal of Malcolm Cowley's introduction to *The Portable Faulkner* (New York: Viking Press, 1946).

46. Cf. the map which Faulkner made for the endpapers of Cowley, *The Portable Faulkner*, and a more detailed one published with *Absalom, Absalom!* (New York: Modern Library, Random House, 1951).

47. "Since the events of *Sanctuary* occurred in 1929, those of *Requiem for a Nun* can thus be dated either 1937 or 1934." Cleanth Brooks, *William Faulkner: The Yoknapatawpha Country* (New Haven: Yale University Press, 1963), p. 395.

48. See O'Connor, *Tangled Fire*, p. 56, for a full survey of the critical reception accorded this novel.

49. John Gassner, *Theatre at the Crossroads* (New York: Holt, Rinehart & Winston, 1960), p. 166.

50. Kazin, *On Native Grounds*, p. 465.

51. Olga W. Vickery, *The Novels of William Faulkner* (Baton Rouge: Louisiana State University Press, 1959), p. 115.

52. W. M. Frohock, *The Novel of Violence in America* (Dallas: Southern Methodist University Press, 1957), p. 159.

53. William Faulkner, *Requiem for a Nun* (New York: Random House, 1959), Act II, sc. 1, p. 57.

54. *Ibid.*, p. 62.

55. Cf. artist Doug Anderson's satiric sketches of the predatory Snopeses and James H. Meriweather, "The Snopes Revisited," in *Saturday Review*, 40 (April 27, 1957): 12-13.

56. Brooks, *William Faulkner: The Yoknapatawpha Country*, p. 152.

57. John Rosenfield, "Faulkner Tale on Stage Again," *Dallas Morning News*, June 6, 1964, section 3, p. 6. Cf. Kent Biffle, " 'Jefferson' Troupe Got Rave Reviews," *Dallas Morning News*, July 20, 1964, section 4, p. 3.

58. Howe, *William Faulkner: A Critical Study*, p. 202.

59. Edward C. Aswell, "Thomas Wolfe: The Playwright Who Discovered He Wasn't," Preface to Ketti Frings, *Look Homeward, Angel* (New York: Charles Scribner's Sons, 1958), p. vii.

60. Cf. Elizabeth Nowell, *Thomas Wolfe, A Biography* (Garden City, N.Y.: Doubleday & Co., 1960), pp. 102-3.

61. Cf. Henry Hewes, "Thomas Wolfe's 'Angel,' " *Saturday Review*, 40 (November 23, 1957): 27-28.

62. Cf. Robert Edmund Jones's set for O'Neill's *Desire Under the Elms* (1924).

63. Frings, *Look Homeward, Angel*, Act II, sc. 2, p. 152.

64. *Ibid.*, Act III, p. 166.

65. Rual Askew, review of the Broadway Theatre Alliance, Inc. production, *Dallas Morning News*, May 8, 1960, section 1, p. 14.

66. Excerpt from Wolfe's symbolical epigraph prefacing *Look Homeward, Angel* (New York: Charles Scribner's Sons, 1929).

67. Cf. the program booklet issued by the Dallas Theater Center for the 1960 season.

68. Carson McCullers, *The Member of the Wedding*, in Jordan Y. Miller, ed., *American Dramatic Literature* (New York: McGraw-Hill, 1961), Act I, p. 431.

69. Horton Foote, *Harrison, Texas* (New York: Harcourt, Brace, 1956), pp. vii-viii. The long plays were presented on the Philco-Goodyear Playhouse and the short ones on the Gulf Playhouse. Later *The Trip to Bountiful* was presented on Broadway as a three-act play. *A Young Lady of Property* was staged on March 15, 1963, by the staff of Theatre Three in Dallas. Foote's first full-length play, *Texas Town*, was completed in 1941.

70. Louis Kronenberger, ed., *The Best Plays of 1960-61* (New York: Dodd, Mead & Co., 1961), p. 9. Cf. John Rosenfield, "Warming Story of Americana," *Dallas Morning News*, January 31, 1964, section 1, p. 12. See also the Haas photographs and a personal essay about Agee by Richard Oulahan, in *Life*, 45 (November 1, 1963): 57-72.

71. Program for the twenty-four performances at Theatre '58 from November 25 to December 14, 1958, Margo Jones Theatre Collection, Dallas Public Library. In this collection one may find a typescript of the acting version of the play, as well as numerous photographs of John McQuade, a New York actor imported for the Willie Stark role. The Margo Jones Theatre Collection has varied materials about other provincial plays produced, generally for the first time, by Miss Jones: Owen Crump's *Southern Exposure*, Irving Phillips' *One Foot in Heaven*, and others.

CHAPTER XI

1. *Weekly TV Magazine*, 5 (August 23-29, 1964): 16. Cf. *Show*, 4 (September, 1964): 77. For a recent book-length treatment of such community changes see Thomas C. Wheeler, ed., *A Vanishing America: The Life and Times of the Small Town* (New York: Holt, Rinehart & Winston, 1964), an illustrated symposium.

2. James J. Kilpatrick, "Changing Cities Present Problem," *Dallas Morning News*, October 24, 1964, section 4, p. 3. Cf. "A Business Civilization," chap. 18 of Foster Rhea Dulles, *The United States Since 1865* (Ann Arbor: University of Michigan Press, 1959), pp. 287-302.

3. Kilpatrick, "Changing Cities . . ."

4. Thornton Wilder, *The Long Christmas Dinner and Other One Act Plays* (Yale University Press and Coward-McCann, 1931), p. 133.

5. Thornton Wilder, Preface to Travis Bogard, ed., *Three Plays: Our Town, The Skin of Our Teeth, The Matchmaker* (Harper & Row, 1957), p. xiii.

6. Brooks Atkinson, review of *Our Town*, *New York Times*, February 5, 1938, following the play's opening on February 4.

7. *Ibid.*

8. Wilder, Preface, in Bogard, *Three Plays*, pp. xi-xii.

9. Cf. Bernard Grebanier, *Thornton Wilder* (Minneapolis: University of Minnesota Press, 1964), p. 25. For full analyses see Rex Burbank, *Thornton Wilder* (New York: Twayne, 1961), pp. 88-97; Edmond Gagey, *Revolution in American Drama* (New York: Columbia University Press, 1947), pp. 107-8; John Mason Brown, "Wilder: *Our Town*," *Saturday Review of Literature*, 32 (August 6, 1949): 33-34.

10. Thornton Wilder, *Our Town* (New York: Coward-McCann, Inc., 1938), pp. 124-25.

11. See Joseph Campbell and H. M. Robinson, "The Skin of Whose Teeth?" *Saturday Review of Literature*, 25 (December 19, 1942): 3-4, and 16 (February 13, 1943): 16-18, for their charges of plagiarism against Wilder for his indebtedness to *Finnegans Wake*. Bennett Cerf's rebuttal may be found in "Trade Winds," *Saturday Review*, 26 (January 19, 1943): 12-13.

12. Cf. Burbank, *Thornton Wilder*, p. 104.

13. Wilder, *The Skin of Our Teeth*, in Bogard, *Three Plays*, Act I, p. 533.

14. *Ibid.*, Act III, p. 576.

15. Grebanier, *Thornton Wilder*, p. 38.

16. Bogard, *Three Plays*, p. 256.

17. Wilder, *The Matchmaker*, in *ibid.*, Act IV, p. 395.

18. This company, organized for the production of their own plays, was formed in 1938 by Sherwood, Maxwell Anderson, Sidney Howard, S. N. Behrman, and Elmer Rice. *Abe Lincoln in Illinois* was presented first at the National Theatre in Washington on October 3, 1938. Its long run (472 performances) at the Plymouth Theatre, New York, opened on October 15.

19. See E. B. Watson and B. Pressey, eds., *Contemporary Drama* (New York: Charles Scribner's Sons, 1941), p. 110. See, also, John Mason Brown, "The Worlds of Robert E. Sherwood," *Saturday Review*, 48 (August 14, 1965): 19-20, 63-64, as a preview of the first volume of a biography, entitled *The Worlds of Robert E. Sherwood: Mirror to His Times, 1896-1939* (New York: Harper & Row, 1965). A second volume, "On A Larger Stage," is now in preparation. Chap. 28 of *Worlds of Sherwood* tells in full the story of the composition of *Abe Lincoln in Illinois*.

20. "The Substance of *Abe Lincoln in Illinois*," in Watson and Pressey, eds., *Contemporary Drama*.

21. Maxwell Anderson, *The Wingless Victory: A Play in Three Acts* (Menasha, Wisconsin, 1936), Act II.

22. Thomas F. Gossett, *Race: The History of An Idea in America* (Dallas: Southern Methodist University Press, 1963), offers a recent book-length exploration of "how ideas of race have affected currents of thought in America."

23. See Sidney Howard, *The Late Christopher Bean: A Comedy in Three Acts* (New York: Samuel French, 1932), *passim*.

24. "The Cardiff Giant: A Chapter in the History of Human Folly—1869-1870," in Andrew D. White, *Autobiography* (New York: Appleton-Century-Crofts, Inc., 1904, 1905).

25. See A. M. Drummond and E. L. Karmack, eds., *More Upstate New York Plays* (Ithaca: Cayuga Press, 1950), *passim*.

26. Cf. editorial comment, *Theatre Arts*, 42 (February, 1958): 20.

27. John Gassner, *Theatre at the Crossroads* (New York: Holt, Rinehart, & Winston, 1960), p. 307.

28. Cf. Harold Clurman's review, *New Republic*, March 13, 1950.

29. *Come Back, Little Sheba*, in Brooks Atkinson, ed., *New Voices in the American Theatre* (New York: Modern Library, Random House, 1955), Act III, sc. 3, pp. 295-99. See also Phyllis Anderson, "Diary of a Production," *Theatre Arts*, 34 (November, 1950): 58-59, as well as 59-88, for the complete text of *Come Back, Little Sheba*, a portrait of Inge, and pictures of Howard Bay's distinguished set. (Phyllis Anderson, head of the Play Reading Department of the Theatre Guild for many years, was associate producer of this play.)

30. William Inge, *Picnic* (New York: Random House, 1953), Act I, p. 16. For an account of the development of *Picnic* from "the second play I ever wrote, which I first called *Front Porch*," see William Inge, "From 'Front Porch' to Broadway," *Theatre Arts*, 38 (April, 1954): 33 (portrait of author also). The same issue contains the script of *Picnic*, with photographs of the set and players by Alfredo Valente.

31. Review in the *New York Herald-Tribune*, February 20, 1953.

32. John Gassner, ed., *Best American Plays, Fourth Series 1951-1957* (New York: Crown, 1958), p. xx. For full page photographs of the Music Box cast see *Theatre Arts*, 34 (June, 1955): cover, 30-31. *Theatre Arts*, 40 (October, 1956): 57-59, offers a collection of pictures drawn from the Cinemascope film of the screenplay by George Axelrod. Directed by Joshua Logan, the screen version featured Broadway players Betty Field, Arthur O'Connell, and Eileen Heckart. The romantic principals were Marilyn Monroe and Don Murray.

33. Review of the Music Box premiere, *Theatre Arts*, 42 (February, 1958): 21.

34. William Inge, *The Dark at the Top of the Stairs* (New York: Random House, 1958), Act III, p. 100.

35. Foreword, *A Loss of Roses* (New York: Random House, 1960). See also Jack Balch, "Anatomy of Failure," *Theatre Arts*, 44 (February, 1960): 10-11, for notes on his interview with Inge.

36. Introduction to Inge, *Dark at the Top of the Stairs*, pp. vii-viii.

37. *To the Ladies!* is included in Arthur Hobson Quinn, ed., *Contemporary American Plays* (New York: Charles Scribner's Sons, 1923), pp. 300 ff.

38. Gagey, *Revolution in American Drama*, p. 220. *The Man Who Came to Dinner* is included in Allan G. Halline, ed., *Six Modern American Plays* (New York: Modern Library, Random House, 1951), pp. 118 ff.

39. "Note Appended to *The Time of Your Life*," in M. W. Steinberg, ed., *Aspects of Modern Drama* (New York: Henry Holt & Co., 1959), p. 349.

40. See "How the Play Was Received in New York," in *My Heart's in the Highlands* (New York: Harcourt, Brace & Co., 1939), pp. 109-25, a collection of reviews.

41. *Ibid.*, p. 116 (excerpt from a review by John Mason Brown, in the *New York Post*). See Lawrence Langner, *The Magic Curtain* (New York: E. P. Dutton, 1951), pp. 320 ff., for a full account of production difficulties connected with *My Heart's in the Highlands*. Philip Loeb played the poet, while young Sidney Lumet was very good as his son. The settings were by Herbert Andrews, and the music ("a little weird") was by Paul Bowles.

42. The play, with production notes, may be found in William Saroyan, *Razzle Dazzle* (New York: Harcourt, Brace & Co., 1942), pp. 347-87.

43. Lillian Hellman, *The Autumn Garden* (Boston: Little, Brown & Co., 1952), Act III, p. 137.

44. Gassner, *Theatre at the Crossroads*, p. 133.

45. See Albee, *The Ballad of the Sad Café* (Boston: Houghton Mifflin Co., 1963), p. 116. See also Robert S. Phillips, "Painful Love: Carson McCullers' Parable," *Southwest Review*, 51 (Winter, 1966): 80 ff.

46. John Gassner, "Give Us Something Different," *Theatre Arts*, 36 (June, 1952): 86, and *Theatre at the Crossroads*, p. 151.

47. Saint Subber, "I'd Do It Again," *Theatre Arts*, 31 (September, 1952): 32-33. *The Grass Harp* was directed by Robert Lewis; the music was composed by Virgil Thomson; and the beautiful scenery and costumes were designed by Cecil Beaton.

48. Truman Capote, *The Grass Harp* (New York: Dramatists Play Service, 1952, 1954), Act II. p. 57.

49. Gassner, "Give Us Something Different," pp. 86-87.

50. Roger L. Stevens, "Show Businessmen of Broadway," *Theatre Arts*, 34 (April, 1955): 33-34.

51. Liam O'Brien, *The Remarkable Mr. Pennypacker*, in *Theatre Arts*, 34 (April, 1955): 56.

52. Ira Levin, *No Time for Sergeants*, is included in Gassner, *Best American Plays*, pp. 572 ff. See *Theatre Arts*, 34 (December, 1955): 28-29, for an illustrated review of the Maurice Evans production for October 20, 1955.

53. Joseph Fields and Jerome Chodorov, *The Ponder Heart* (New York: Random House, 1956), pp. 39-40.

54. From "The American Scholar." A similar small college town of the Midwest is the setting for *The Happiest Years*, a domestic comedy by Thomas Coley and William Roerick, which opened at the Lyceum Theatre in New York City on April 25, 1949, for only eight performances.

55. The entire text for *Time Out for Ginny* is published in *Theatre Arts*, 38 (February, 1954): 36-64. See in the same issue Alexander's play-by-play account of the years separating completion of his first draft and the final production, in "It Needed Work," pp. 33-35.

56. Anderson, "A Postscript . . . Not a Post-Mortem," *Theatre Arts*, 34 (August, 1955): 33. The complete text of *All Summer Long* is printed in this issue.

57. Cf. Gassner, *Theatre at the Crossroads*, p. 291.

58. Cf. Maurice Zolotov, "The Season On and Off Broadway," *Theatre Arts*, 38 (December, 1953): 90.

59. Anderson, "Draw Your Own Conclusions," *Theatre Arts*, 38 (September, 1954): 33. (This identical passage from *Walden* gave the thematic note to Gene McKinney's *A Different Drummer*, already discussed.) The complete text of *Tea and Sympathy* may be found in this issue. See also Gassner, *Best American Plays*.

60 Cf. *Theatre Arts*, 37 (December, 1953): 19.

61. Allan Lewis, *American Plays and Playwrights of the Contemporary Theatre* (New York: Crown, 1965), p. 156.

62. Cf. Anderson's headnote to the complete text of the play in *Theatre Arts*, 45 (December, 1961): 26.

63. Henry Hewes, "Aptitude Test," *Saturday Review*, 48 (June, 19, 1965): 28.

64. *The Days Between* (Random House, 1965), Act III, p. 119.

65. The complete text of *Calculated Risk* appears in *Theatre Arts*, 47 (December, 1963): 20 ff.

66. For Miller's full analysis of *All My Sons*, see his *Collected Plays* (New York: Viking Press, 1957), pp. 12-22 .

67. *All My Sons*, in Gerald Weales, ed., *Eleven Plays: An Introduction to Drama* (New York: W. W. Norton, 1964), Act III, p. 74.

68. Lee Baxandall, "The Theatre of Edward Albee," *Tulane Drama Review*, 9 (Summer, 1965): 25.

69. Marshall W. Fishwick, "Diagnosing the American Dream," *Saturday Review*, 46 (October 21, 1963): 8.

70. Edward Albee, *Who's Afraid of Virginia Woolf?* (New York: Pocket Books, Simon & Schuster, 1964), Act I, pp. 32, 41.

71. Henry Hewes, "Who's Afraid of Big Bad Broadway?" *Saturday Review*, 45 (October 27. 1962): 29.

72. Albee, *Who's Afraid of Virginia Woolf?* Act I, p. 37.

73. *Ibid.*, Act II, pp. 113-14.

74. Lewis, *American Plays and Playwrights*, pp. 93-94.

75. Henry Hewes, "Broadway Postscript," *Saturday Review*, 45 (September 8, 1962): 27. Cf. Elizabeth Hardwick, "The Theatre of Decadence," *New York Review of Books*, 6 (April 28, 1966): 8-9; and John Simon, "The Tragedy of the American Theater," *Holiday*, 39 (March, 1966): 76-83 (illustrations).

76. See "The Musical Theatre," chap. 13 of Lewis, *American Plays and Playwrights*, and Gassner, *Theatre at the Crossroads*, pt. 2, chap. 5, for discussions of this popular form of entertainment.

77. Armand Aulicino, "A Musical that Kept on Growing," *Theatre Arts*, 36 (December, 1962): 32. The complete text of *Paint Your Wagon* is in this issue; it has also been published by Coward-McCann, New York.

78. *Plain and Fancy* appears in full in *Theatre Arts*, 40 (July, 1956): 33 ff.

79. Cf. "On Broadway," *Theatre Arts*, 40 (July, 1956): 18.

80. Irving Kolodin, "From Tonio to Tony (in Twenty Hard Years)," *Saturday Review*, 34 (May 5, 1956): 30-31. The full text of *The Most Happy Fella* is printed in *Theatre Arts*, 42 (October, 1958).

81. Cf. "On Broadway," *Theatre Arts*, 42 (March, 1958): 11. *The Music Man* was published in 1958 by G. P. Putnam's Sons, New York.

82. The complete text of *The Unsinkable Molly Brown* may be found in *Theatre Arts*, 47 (February, 1963).

83. C. E. Wisewell, "An Interview with Masters," *Current Opinion*, 58 (May, 1915): 356.

84. *Spoon River Anthology* (New York: Macmillan Co., 1915), p. 1. Cf. Ima Honaker Herron, *The Small Town in American Literature* (Durham: Duke University Press, 1939), pp. 354-62.

85. Aline Jean Treanor, "A Chat with Joyce Van Patten," *Theatre Arts*, 47 (December, 1963): 17 ff., gives information about the activities of Theatre West.

Selected Bibliography

ALL REFERENCE MATERIALS are documented fully in the chapter notes, which indicate the writer's considerable indebtedness to authorities of various classifications: to theatrical and dramatic historians, to historians of American life and letters, to biographers and autobiographical recorders (including diarists), and to innumerable critics interpreting American community life as well as the dramas about that life. Also documented in the notes are stage encyclopedias, playbills, checklists, anthologies (including the valuable *America's Lost Plays*), and many pertinent articles about small-town drama. None of these references, therefore, are repeated here.

The following titles are offered as selections from the large number of plays which have been used in the preparation of this volume. Ordinarily the writer has consulted first editions. In certain instances, photostats, films, Readex Microprints, prompt copies (in typescript, from the New York Public Library's Theatre Collection), old prints and playbills, newspapers, and plays printed in *Theatre Arts* have been most useful. Where theater names and dates are included, these indicate place and time of first production.

CHAPTER I

AIKEN, G. L. *The Scarlet Letter* (dramatization of the Hawthorne novel). Barnum's Museum, New York, February 24, 1858.

ANDREWS, GEORGE H. *The Scarlet Drama: A Drama in Three Acts from N. Hawthorne's Celebrated Novel.* Boston: Charles H. Spencer, 1871. Boston Theatre, December 28, 1857.

BARKER, JAMES NELSON. *Tears and Smiles.* Philadelphia: printed by T. & G. Palmer for G. E. Blake, 1808. Reprinted in PAUL H. MUSSER, *James Nelson Barker, 1784-1858.* Philadelphia: University of Pennsylvania Press, 1929. "The Theatre Philadelphia," March 4, 1807.

———. *Superstition: Or, The Fanatic Father.* Philadelphia, 1826. Reprinted in A. H. QUINN, ed., *Representative American Plays.* New York: Century Co., 1917. Chestnut Street Theatre, Philadelphia, March 12, 1824.

BOMSTEAD, BEULAH. *The Diabolical Circle.* In Dakota Playmakers Series. Boston: Walter H. Baker Co., 1923. Produced in 1921.

FREEMAN, MARY E. WILKINS. *Giles Corey, Yeoman: A Play.* New York: Harper & Bros., 1893.

GRINNELL, JOHN E. *John Bargrave, Gentleman.* In Dakota Playmakers Series. Boston: Walter H. Baker Co., 1923. Produced in 1921.

HARRISON, GABRIEL. *A Romantic Drama, in Four Acts, Entitled The Scarlet Letter, Dramatized from Nathaniel Hawthorne's Masterly Romance.* Brooklyn: Harry M. Gardner, 1876.

LONGFELLOW, HENRY W. *The New England Tragedies.* Boston: Ticknor & Fields, 1868. Includes "John Endicott" (first drafted as "The Old Colony" and redrafted as "Wenlock Christison") and "Giles Corey of the Salem Farms."

MacKAYE, PERCY. *The Scarecrow.* New York: Macmillan Co., 1908. Middlesex Theatre, Middletown, Conn., December 30, 1910; Garrick Theatre, New York, January 17, 1911.

MATHEWS, CORNELIUS. *Witchcraft: Or, Salem Village.* London, 1852. Simultaneously published in New York by Samuel French as *Witchcraft: A Tragedy in 5 Acts.* Billed in Philadelphia, 1846, as *Witchcraft: Or The Martyrs of Salem.* Walnut Street Theatre, Philadelphia, May 5, 1846.

MATTISON, H. B. *The Witch: Or A Legend of the Catskills.* Chatham Theatre, New York, May 24, 1847.

MEBLIN, ROSE C. *Dowry and Romance.* In Dakota Playmakers Series. Boston: Walter H. Baker Co., 1923. Dakota Playmakers, 1921.

MILLER, ARTHUR. *The Crucible: A Play in Four Acts.* New York: Viking Press, 1955. Earlier version copyrighted under title of *Those Familiar Spirits.* Martin Beck Theatre, New York, January 22, 1953.

PECK, ELIZABETH WELLER. *Nathaniel Hawthorne's Scarlet Letter Dramatized.* Boston: Franklin Press, 1876.

SMITH, JAMES EDGAR. *The Scarlet Stigma: A Drama in Four Acts, Founded upon Nathanial Hawthorne's Novel The Scarlet Letter.* Washington, D.C.: James J. Chapman, 1899.

SMITH, R. P. "The Witch." Holographic MS, dated October 1, 1827, in the Harvard Library.

CHAPTER II

BARKER, JAMES NELSON. *Tears and Smiles.* Philadelphia: printed by T. & G. Palmer for G. E. Blake, 1808. Reprinted in PAUL H. MUSSER, *James Nelson Barker, 1784-1858.* Philadelphia: University of Pennsylvania Press, 1929. "The Theatre Philadelphia," March 4, 1807.

BARNETT, MORRIS (?). *The Yankee Pedlar [Peddler]: Or Old Times in Virginia.* New York: Samuel French, n.d. (1853 penciled in on frontispiece). Park Theatre, New York, September 6, 1834. First-version authorship unknown.

BEACH, LAZARUS. *Jonathan Postfree: Or, The Honest Yankee.* New York, 1807.

BICKERSTAFFE, ISAAC. *Love in a Village.* Southwark Theatre, Philadelphia, c. 1766; John Street Theatre, New York, December 15, 1794.

BRICE, JAMES F. *A Country Clown: Or Dandyism Improved, A Dramatic Medley.* Annapolis: J. Weber, 1829, Readex Microprint of American Antiquarian Society's copy.

CARR, MARY CLARKE. *The Benevolent Lawyers: Or Villainy Detected.* Philadelphia, February 23, 1823.

————. *The Fair Americans.* Philadelphia, 1815. Readex Microprint, 1954, of New York Public Library's copy. Produced in 1799.

CONWAY, H. J. [DAWES, RUFUS?]. *The Battle of Stillwater: Or, The Maniac.* MS in New York Public Library. Also in EUGENE R. PAGE, ed., *America's Lost Plays.* Princeton: Princeton University Press, 1941, vol. 14. National Theatre, Boston, March 16, 1840.

————. *Hiram Hireout: Or, Followed by Fortune.* New York: Samuel French, [1852]. Chicago Theatre, Chicago, 1851.

————. *New York Patriots: Or, The Battle of Saratoga.* Barnum's Museum, New York, June 2, 1856.

————. *Our Jemimy: Or, Connecticut Courtship.* New York, n.d. Chestnut Street Theatre, Philadelphia, May 9, 1853; Broadway Theatre, New York, July 15, 1853.

DALY, AUGUSTIN. *A Legend of Norwood: Or, Village Life in New England.* Adapted from novel by HENRY WARD BEECHER. Privately printed, 1867. New York Theatre, New York, November 11, 1867.

DUNLAP, WILLIAM. *The Modest Soldier: Or, Love in New York.* 1787.

————. *A Trip to Niagara: Or, Travellers in America, a Farce in Three Acts.* New York: E. B. Clayton, 1830. Bowery Theatre, New York, November 28, 1828.

GLOVER, CAPTAIN STEPHEN. *Banished Provincials: Or, Olden Times.* American Theatre, New Orleans, April 29, 1833.

HACKETT, JAMES H. (?). *Down East: Or, The Militia Training.* Alternate title, *The Militia Muster.* Park Theatre, New York, April 17, 1830.

HAWKINS, MICAH. *The Saw-Mill: Or, A Yankee Trick.* New York: J. and J. Harper, 1824. In Readex Microprint from Library of Congress copy. Chatham Garden Theatre, New York, November 29, 1824.

HEATH, JAMES E. *Whigs and Democrats: Or, Love of No Politics.* Richmond: T. W. White, 1839. (Printed anonymously but attributed to Heath.) Walnut Street Theatre, Philadelphia, October 12, 1839; Arch Street Theatre, Philadelphia, October 31, 1844.

HERNE, JAMES A. *Sag Harbor.* In *Shore Acres and Other Plays*, rev. and ed. by MRS. JAMES A. HERNE. New York: Samuel French, 1928. Park Theatre, Boston, October 23, 1899.

————. *Shore Acres.* In *Shore Acres and Other Plays*, rev. and ed. by MRS. JAMES A. HERNE. New York: Samuel French, 1928. Under title of *Shore Acres' Subdivision*, McVicker's Theatre, Chicago, May 23, 1892.

HITCHCOCK, J. R. W., and HITCHCOCK, MARTHA (HALL). *David Harum: A Comedy in 3 Acts.* New York: Samuel French, 1938. Dramatization of novel by EDWARD NOYES WESTCOTT, 1898. Garrick Theatre, New York, October 1, 1900.

HOWES, PERKINS. *The New England Drama.* Dedham, Mass., 1825. Readex Microprint, 1952, of Harvard Library original.

HUMPHREYS, DAVID. *The Yankey in England: A Drama in Five Acts.* Readex Microprint, 1955, of Yale University copy. Presented by amateurs, Humphreysville, Conn., January, 1814(?).

JONES, JOSEPH STEVENS. *Batkins at Home: Or Life in Cranberry Centre* (sequel to *The Silver Spoon*). Boston Museum, May 10, 1858.

————. *The Green Mountain Boy.* New York, [1860]. Chestnut Street Theatre, Philadelphia, February 25, 1833.

————. *The Liberty Tree: Or, Boston Boys in '76.* Warren Theatre, Boston, June 17, 1832.

————. *Moll Pitcher: Or, The Fortune Teller of Lynn.* Boston, 1855. National Theatre, Boston, May 20, 1839.

————. *The People's Lawyer.* New York, n.d.; Boston: William Spencer, 1856. Reprinted in MONTROSE J. MOSES, ed., *Representative Plays by American Dramatists*, vol. 2. New York, E. P. Dutton & Co., 1925. Park Theatre, New York, December 17, 1842.

————. *The Silver Spoon.* Boston: Walter S. Baker Co., 1911. Boston Museum, February 16, 1852, under the title of *The Silver Spoon: Or Our Own Folks: A Joiner's Job in Four Parts.*

JUDAH, SAMUEL BENJAMIN H. *A Tale of Lexington.* New York: Dramatic Repository, 1823. Readex Microprint, 1952, of Harvard Library original. Produced at Park Theatre, New York, July 4, 1822, as *The Battle of Lexington.*

LA BREE, LAWRENCE. *Ebenezer Venture: Or, Advertising for a Wife.* New York: Samuel French, n.d. Buffalo Theatre, Buffalo, N.Y., September 18, 1841.

LEONARD, CHESTER. *Federalism Triumphant in the Steady Habits of Connecticut Alone: Or, The Turnpike Road to Fortune.* N.p., 1802. Readex Microprint of New York Public Library original.

LINDSLEY, A. B. *Love and Friendship: Or, Yankee Notions.* New York: D. Longworth, 1809. Park Theatre, New York, 1807-8 season.

LOGAN, CORNELIUS AMBROSIUS. *The Vermont Wool-Dealer.* New York: Samuel French, n.d. Bowery Theatre, New York, April 11, 1840.

————. *Yankee Land: A Comedy in Two Acts.* Boston: William Spencer, *Boston Theatre,* vol. 9, n.d. Park Theatre, New York, 1834. An alteration by REDE LEMAN was produced in 1846 under the title of *Hue and Cry.*

Major Jack Downing: Or, The Retired Politician. Park Theatre, New York, May 10, 1834.

The Moderns: Or, A Trip to the Springs. [By a Gentleman of New York.] Park Theatre, New York, April 18, 1831.

MUNFORD, COLONEL ROBERT. *The Candidates: Or, The Humours of a Virginia Election.* 1770. In *A Collection of Poems and Plays.* Petersburg, Virginia: William Prentis, 1798. Reprinted in *William and Mary Quarterly,* 3d series, 5 (April, 1948) and in Readex Microprint.

————. *The Patriots.* Philadelphia, 1776. In *A Collection of Poems and Plays.* Petersburg, Virginia: William Prentis, 1798. Reprinted in *William and Mary Quarterly,* 3d series, 6 (July, 1949) and in Readex Microprint.

O'KEEFFE, JOHN. *World in a Village.* John Street Theatre, New York, April 9, 1794.

PAULDING, JAMES KIRKE. *The Bucktails: Or, Americans in England,* in *American Comedies.* Philadelphia, 1847. Reprinted in ALLAN GATES HALLINE, ed., *American Plays.* New York: American Book Co., 1935. First produced in 1812.

————. *The Lion of the West.* Park Street Theatre, New York, April 25, 1831.

The Politician Outwitted. Written 1788. Published 1789 as "by an American." Attributed to SAMUEL LOW.

ROBINSON, J. *The Yorker's Stratagem: Or Banana's Wedding.* New York, 1792. Produced by the Old American Company, John Street Theatre, New York, April 24, 1792.

SAWYER, LEMUEL. *Blackbeard.* Washington, 1824.

SWAYZE, MRS. J. C. *Ossawattomie Brown: Or The Insurrection at Harper's Ferry*. New York: Samuel French, 1859. Bowery Theatre, New York, December 16, 1859.

THOMPSON, DENMAN. *The Old Homestead*. Boston: Walter H. Baker Co., 1927. Boston Museum, April 5, 1886.

THOMPSON, WILLIAM TAPPAN. *Major Jones' Courtship: Or Adventures of a Christmas Eve, by Major Jones*. Savannah, Georgia: Edward J. Purse, 1850. Barnum's Museum, Philadelphia, December 22, 1851.

TROWBRIDGE, JOHN TOWNSEND. *Neighbor Jackwood*. Boston, 1857. Boston Museum, March 16, 1857.

TYLER, ROYALL. *The Contrast*. Philadelphia: Prichard & Hall, 1790. Dunlap Society Edition, 1887. First acted by the American Company, John Street Theatre, New York, April 16, 1787.

The Village Lawyer: Or Ba! Ba! Ba! Old American Company, New York, December 15, 1794. (Later attributed to WILLIAM MACREADY.)

WOODWORTH, SAMUEL. *The Forest Rose: Or American Farmers*. New York, 1825; Boston: William V. Spencer, n.d. [*ca.* 1855]. Readex Microprint, 1964, of the University of Pennsylvania copy. Chatham Garden Theatre, New York, October 7, 1825.

CHAPTER III

BARKER, JAMES NELSON. *Superstition: Or, The Fanatic Father*. Philadelphia, 1826. Reprinted in A. H. QUINN, ed., *Representative American Plays*. New York: Century Co., 1917. Chestnut Street Theatre, Philadelphia, March 12, 1824.

BOUCICAULT, DION. *Rip Van Winkle*. New York, 1895. Adelphi Theatre, London, September 4, 1865.

BURKE, CHARLES. *Rip Van Winkle: A Legend of the Catskills. A Romantic Drama in Two Acts*. Adapted from WASHINGTON IRVING, *Sketch Book*. In MONTROSE J. MOSES, ed., *Representative Plays by American Dramatists, 1856-1911*. New York: E. P. Dutton & Co., 1925. National Theatre, New York, January 7, 1850.

CARR, MARY CLARKE. *The Fair Americans*. Philadelphia, 1815. Readex Microprint, 1954, of New York Public Library's copy. Produced in 1799.

CONWAY, H. J. *The Battle of Stillwater: Or, The Maniac*. MS in New York Public Library. Also in EUGENE R. PAGE, ed., *America's Lost Plays*. Princeton: Princeton University Press, 1941, vol. 14. National Theatre, Boston, March 16, 1840.

HERNE, JAMES A. *The Minute Men of 1774-1775*. In EUGENE R. PAGE, ed., *America's Lost Plays*, vol. 7. Princeton: Princeton University Press, 1940. Chestnut Theatre, Philadelphia, April 6, 1886.

HOWES, PERKINS. *The New England Drama*. Dedham, Mass., 1825. Readex Microprint, 1952, of Harvard Library original.

JEFFERSON, JOSEPH. *Rip Van Winkle*. New York, 1895. In A. H. QUINN, ed., *Representative American Plays*. New York: Century Co., 1917. Olympic Theatre, New York, September 3, 1866.

JONES, JOSEPH STEVENS. *Moll Pitcher: Or The Fortune Teller of Lynn*. Boston, 1855. National Theatre, Boston, May 20, 1839.

JUDAH, SAMUEL BENJAMIN H. *A Tale of Lexington*. New York: Dramatic Repository, 1823. Readex Microprint, 1952, of Harvard Library original. Produced at Park Theatre, New York, July 4, 1822, as *The Battle of Lexington*.

KERR, JOHN. *Rip Van Winkle: Or, The Demons of the Catskills!!!* Philadelphia [1830-35]. In MONTROSE J. MOSES, ed., *Representative Plays by American Dramatists, 1856-1911*. New York: E. P. Dutton & Co., 1925. Tottenham Street Theatre, London; Walnut Street Theatre, Philadelphia, October 30, 1829.

———. *Rip Van Winkle: A Legend of Sleepy Hollow*. Rev. by T. H. LACEY. London, n.d.

MACKAYE, PERCY. *Rip Van Winkle: Folk-Opera in Three Acts*. New York: Alfred A. Knopf, 1919.

MATHEWS, CORNELIUS. *Witchcraft: Or Salem Village*. London, 1852. Simultaneously published in New York by Samuel French as *Witchcraft: A Tragedy in 5 Acts*. Billed in Philadelphia, 1846, as *Witchcraft: Or The Martyrs of Salem*. Walnut Street Theatre, Philadelphia, May 5, 1846.

MINSHULL, JOHN. *Rural Felicity with the Humour of Patrick and Marriage of Shelty*. New York: privately printed, 1801. Readex Microprint. Bedlow Street Theatre, New York, January 15, 1805.

Rip Van Winkle: Or, The Spirits of the Catskill Mountains. South Pearl Street Theatre, Albany, May 26, 1828.

WAINWRIGHT, J. H. *Rip Van Winkle*. New York, 1855. Niblo's Garden, New York, September 27, 1855.

WOODWORTH, SAMUEL. *The Forest Rose: Or American Farmers*. New York, 1825; Boston: William V. Spencer, n.d. [*ca.* 1855]. Readex Microprint, 1964, of the University of Pennsylvania copy. Chatham Garden Theatre, New York, October 7, 1825.

CHAPTER IV

ANDERSON, MAXWELL. *Night Over Taos*. New York: Samuel French, 1932. Forty-eighth Street Theatre, New York, March 9, 1932.

BELASCO, DAVID. *The Girl of the Golden West*. New York: Samuel French, 1933. Belasco Theatre, Pittsburgh, October 3, 1905.

————. *The Rose of the Rancho*. New York: Samuel French, 1909. A revision of *Juanita*, by RICHARD WALTON TULLY. Majestic Theatre, Boston, November 12, 1906.

————, and HERNE, JAMES A. Produced as *Chums*, Baldwin Theatre, San Francisco, September 9, 1879; as *Hearts of Oak*, Hamlin's Theatre, Chicago, November 17, 1879.

BURKE, CHARLES (?). *A Trip to the California Mines*. Arch Street Theatre, Philadelphia, January 10, 1849.

CAMPBELL, BARTLEY THOMAS. *How Women Love: Or, The Heart of the Sierras*. 1876. In EUGENE R. PAGE, ed., *America's Lost Plays*. Princeton: Princeton University Press, 1941, vol. 19. Arch Street Theatre, Philadelphia, May 21-26, 1877.

————. *My Partner*. Copyrighted 1880. Union Square Theatre, New York, September 16, 1879.

————. *The Vigilantes: Or, The Heart of the Sierras*. Another version of *How Women Love*. Grand Opera House, New York, July 1, 1878.

DELANO, ALONZO ("Old Block"). *The Frontier Settlement: Or, Scenes in the Far West: A Play in Three Acts*. New York: Francis Clarke, 1846.

————. *A Live Woman in the Mines: Or, Pike County Ahead! A Local Play in Two Acts by Old Block*. New York: Samuel French, 1857.

DENSMORE, G. S. *The Gilded Age*. California Theatre, San Francisco, April 23, 1874. Unauthorized version.

Deseret Deserted: Or The Last Days of Brigham Young. New York, [1858]. Wallack's Theatre, New York, May 24, 1858.

ENGLISH, THOMAS DUNN. *The Mormons: Or, Life at Salt Lake City*. New York: Samuel French, 1858. Burton's Theatre, New York, March 16, 1858; Maguire's Opera House, San Francisco, early summer, 1858.

HALE, RUTH HUDSON. *Handcart Trails*. Salt Lake City: Mutual Improvement Association, 1940.

————, and HALE, NATHAN. *It Shall Keep Thee*. In *Book of Plays*. Salt Lake City: Mutual Improvement Association, 1941. Vol. 3.

HARTE, BRET. *The Luck of Roaring Camp*. Dramatization of the story. Frohman production, Empire Theatre, New York, May 14, 1894.

————. *Two Men from Sandy Bar*. Boston: Houghton Mifflin Co., 1882. Dramatization of "Mr. Thompson's Prodigal." Union Square Theatre, New York, August 28, 1876.

HARTE, BRET, and PEMBERTON, T. EDGAR. *Sue.* Dramatization of Harte's "The Judgment of Bolivas Plain." Hoyt's Theatre, New York, September 15, 1896.

HARTE, BRET, and TWAIN, MARK. *Ah Sin.* National Theatre, Washington, D.C., May 7, 1877.

HITCHCOCK, FRANK (MURDOCK, FRANK H.). "Davy Crockett," rev. by FRANK MAYO. In *Favorite American Plays of the Nineteenth Century.* Princeton University Press, 1943. Rochester, N.Y., September 23, 1872.

MILLER, JOAQUIN (MILLER, CINCINNATUS HEINE). *Forty-Nine: An Idyl Drama of the Sierras.* San Francisco: California Publishing Co., 1882. Haverley's Theatre, New York, October 1, 1881.

————. *Tally Ho!* and *An Oregon Idyll.* In *Poems*, vol. 6. San Francisco: Harr Wagner Publishing Co., 1910. Unproduced.

————, and FITZGERALD, P. A. *The Danites: Or, The Heart of the Sierras.* Based on *First Families of the Sierras*, 1876. San Francisco: California Publishing Co., 1910. Broadway Theatre, New York, August 22, 1877.

NUNES, JOSEPH A. *Fast Folks: Or, Early Days in California.* Philadelphia: Barnard & Jones, 1861. American Theatre, San Francisco, July 1, 1858.

PALMER, ANNIE D. *The Rescue. Book of Plays.* Salt Lake City: Mutual Improvement Association, 1929. Salt Lake City, 1927.

RHODES, WILLIAM H. *The Mormon Prophet.* In *The Indian Gallows and Other Poems.* New York: E. Walker, 1846.

TWAIN, MARK. *The Gilded Age.* Park Theatre, New York, September 16, 1874.

CHAPTER V

CONKLE, ELLSWORTH PROUTY. *Crick Bottom Plays.* New York: Samuel French, 1928.

————. "Forty-nine Dogs in a Meat House." MS, n.d.

————. *In the Shadow of a Rock.* New York: Samuel French, 1936.

————. *Loolie and Other Short Plays.* New York: Samuel French, 1935.

DALY, AUGUSTIN. *Horizon.* Privately printed, 1885. In ALLAN GATES HALLINE, ed., *American Plays.* New York: American Book Co., 1935. Olympic Theatre, New York, March 21, 1871.

FITCH, ROBERT. *Plays of the American West.* New York: Greenberg, 1947.

FITCH, WILLIAM CLYDE, and STEELL, WILLIS. *The Cowboy and the Lady.* Typed prompt copy, n.d., in Theatre Collection, New York

Public Library. Knickerbocker Theatre, New York, December 25, 1899.

———. *The Girl and the Judge.* Typed prompt copy, dated 1901, in Theatre Collection, New York Public Library. Lyceum Theatre, New York, December 4, 1901.

———. *Wolfville: A Drama of the South West.* Dramatization of AL-FRED HENRY LEWIS, *Wolfville* (New York: Stokes, 1897). Typescript, n.d., in Theatre Collection, New York Public Library. Broad Street Theatre, Philadelphia, October 23, 1905.

GEDDES, VIRGIL. "As the Crow Flies." In *Native Ground.* New York: Samuel French, 1932.

———. *The Earth Between.* New York: Samuel French, 1930. Provincetown Players, March 5, 1929.

———. "The Plowshare's Gleam." In *Native Ground.* New York: Samuel French, 1932.

HOYT, CHARLES HALE. *A Texas Steer: "Money Makes the Mare Go."* In MONTROSE J. MOSES, ed., *Representative American Dramas: National and Local.* Boston: D. C. Heath & Co., 1925. Chestnut Street Theatre, Philadelphia, September 29, 1890; Bijou Theatre, New York, November 10, 1890.

———. *A Trip to Chinatown.* In EUGENE R. PAGE, ed., *America's Lost Plays.* Princeton: Princeton University Press, 1941, vol. 9. Chestnut Street Theatre, Philadelphia, January 26, 1891.

MOODY, WILLIAM VAUGHN. *The Great Divide.* New York: Macmillan Co., 1909. In T. H. DICKINSON, ed., *Chief Contemporary Dramatists.* Boston: Houghton Mifflin, 1915. Princess Theatre, New York, October 3, 1906. As *A Sabine Woman,* Garrick Theatre, Chicago, April 12, 1906.

RIGGS, LYNN. *Big Lake.* New York: Samuel French, 1927.

———. *Green Grow the Lilacs.* New York: Samuel French, 1931. Theatre Guild, New York, January 26, 1931.

———. *Knives from Syria.* New York: Samuel French, 1928.

———. "A Lantern to See By." In *Two Oklahoma Plays.* New York: Samuel French, 1928.

———. "Reckless." In *One-Act Plays for Stage and Study.* New York: Samuel French, 1928.

———. *Roadside: Or Borned in Texas.* New York: Samuel French, 1930. Little Theatre of Dallas, June 8, 1936.

———. "Sump'n Like Wings." In *Two Oklahoma Plays.* New York: Samuel French, 1928.

ROGERS, JOHN WILLIAM, JR. *Judge Lynch*. New York: Samuel French, 1924. Originally published in *Southwest Review*, 10 (October, 1924): 3-23. Dallas Little Theatre, 1923.

―――. "The Rescue of Cynthia Ann." In *One-Act Plays for Stage and Study*. New York: Samuel French, 1929.

―――. *Roam Though I May*. Boston: Walter H. Baker Co., 1933.

―――. *Westward People*. New York: Samuel French, 1935. Originally published in *Southwest Review*, 20 (Autumn, 1934): 87-109.

―――. *Where the Dear Antelope Play*. In *Three Southwest Plays*. Dallas: Southwest Review, 1942.

THOMAS, AUGUSTUS. *Arizona: A Drama in Four Acts*. New York: Robert Howard Russell, 1899. Hamlin's Grand Opera House, Chicago, June 12, 1899; Herald Square Theatre, New York, September 10, 1900.

―――. *Colorado*. Typed MS in Theatre Collection, New York Public Library. Wallack's Theatre, New York, November 18, 1901.

―――. *The Copperhead*. In HELEN L. COHEN, ed., *Longer Plays by Modern Authors*. New York: Harcourt, Brace, 1922; New York: Samuel French, 1922. Parson's Theatre, Hartford, Conn., January 22, 1918.

―――. *In Mizzoura*. New York: Samuel French, 1916. Hooley's Theatre, Chicago, August 7, 1893.

―――. *Rio Grande*. Typed MS in Theatre Collection, New York Public Library. Lyric Theatre, Allentown, Pa., February 26, 1916.

TOTHEROH, DAN. "Good Vintage." In *One-Act Plays for Everyone*. New York: Samuel French, 1931.

―――. "The Great Dark." In *One-Act Plays for Everyone*. New York: Samuel French, 1931.

―――. *Seeing the Elephant*. New York: Dramatists Play Service, 1939. In *America in Action*. New York: Thomas Y. Crowell Co., 1941.

―――. *Wild Birds*. New York: Samuel French, 1930.

WISTER, OWEN, and LA SHELLE, KIRKE. *The Virginian*. Mimeographed copy, with introduction and notes by N. O. RUSH, Tallahassee, Fla., 1958. Dramatization of 1902 novel by OWEN WISTER. Manhattan Theatre, New York, January 5, 1904, after Boston tryout.

CHAPTER VI

ADE, GEORGE. *The College Widow*. New York: Samuel French, c. 1924. Garden Theatre, New York, September 20, 1904.

————. *The County Chairman*. New York: Samuel French, 1923. Wallack's Theatre, New York, November 24, 1903.

BARNARD, CHARLES, and BURGESS, NEIL. *The County Fair*. New York: Samuel French, 1922. Proctor's Twenty-third Street Theatre, New York, March 5, 1889.

DAZEY, CHARLES TURNER. *Home Folks*. New York Theatre, New York, December 26, 1904.

————. *In Old Kentucky*. Privately printed, 1894. Detroit: Fine Book Circle, 1937. Grand Opera House, St. Paul, Minn., June, 1893.

————. *The Suburban*. Prompt copy, n.d., in Theatre Collection, New York Public Library.

GALE, ZONA. "Neighbors." In T. H. DICKINSON, ed., *Wisconsin Plays*. New York: Huebsch, 1914. As *Neighbours*, New York: Walter H. Baker Co., 1921.

————. *Uncle Jimmy*. New York: Walter H. Baker Co., 1921.

GILL, WILLIAM, and GOLDEN, RICHARD. *Old Jed Prouty: The Man from Maine*. Union Square Theatre, New York, March 13, 1889.

HERNE, JAMES A. *Drifting Apart*. Rev. of *Mary, the Fisherman's Child*. People's Theatre, New York, May 7, 1888.

————. *Margaret Fleming*. In A. H. QUINN, ed., *Representative American Plays*. New York: Century Co., 1930. Tryout, Lynn, Mass., July 4, 1890; Chickering Hall, Boston, May 4, 1891.

————. *Sag Harbor*. In *Shore Acres and Other Plays*, rev. and ed. by MRS. JAMES A. HERNE. New York: Samuel French, 1928. Park Theatre, Boston, October 23, 1899.

————. *Shore Acres*. In *Shore Acres and Other Plays*, rev. and ed. by MRS. JAMES A. HERNE. New York: Samuel French, 1928. Boston Museum, February 20, 1893. Under title of *Shore Acres' Subdivision*, McVicker's Theatre, Chicago, May 17–30, 1892. As *Uncle Nat*, McVicker's Theatre, Chicago, May 30–June 11, 1892.

————, and BELASCO, DAVID. *Chums*. Baldwin Theatre, San Francisco, Sept. 9, 1879. Refashioned with Belasco's collaboration as *Hearts of Oak*. In MRS. JAMES A. HERNE, ed. *Shore Acres and Other Plays*. New York: Samuel French, 1928. Hamlin's Theatre, Chicago, November 17, 1879.

HIGGINS, DAVID, and WALDRON, GEORGIA. *Up York State*. Fourteenth Street Theatre, New York, September 16, 1901.

HITCHCOCK, J. R. W., and HITCHCOCK, MARTHA (HALL). *David Harum: A Comedy in 3 Acts*. New York: Samuel French, 1938. Garrick Theatre, New York, October 1, 1900.

HOYT, CHARLES HALE. *A Midnight Bell*. In EUGENE R. PAGE, ed., *America's Lost Plays*. Princeton: Princeton University Press, 1941, vol. 9. Bijou Theatre, Boston, November 10, 1889.

————. *A Milk White Flag*. In EUGENE R. PAGE, ed., *America's Lost Plays*. Princeton: Princeton University Press, 1941, vol. 9. Wilkes-Barre, Pa., December 23, 1893.

————. *A Rag Baby*. MS, 1884. In EUGENE R. PAGE, ed., *America's Lost Plays*. Princeton: Princeton University Press, 1941, vol. 9. Haverley's Theatre, Philadelphia, August 16, 1884.

————. *A Temperance Town*. In EUGENE R. PAGE, ed., *America's Lost Plays*. Princeton: Princeton University Press, 1941, vol. 9. Chestnut Street Theatre, Philadelphia, March 28, 1892; Madison Square Theatre, New York, September 18, 1893.

————, and EDOUIN, WILLIE. *A Bunch of Keys: Or The Hotel*. In EUGENE R. PAGE, ed., *America's Lost Plays*. Princeton: Princeton University Press, 1941, vol. 9. Newark, N.J., December, 1882.

IVES, ALICE E., and EDDY, JEROME H. *The Village Postmaster*. Fourteenth Street Theatre, New York, April 13, 1896.

KIDDI, EDWARD E. *Peaceful Valley*. Produced in 1894.

PARKER, LOTTIE BLAIR. *Way Down East*. Manhattan Theatre, New York, February 7, 1898.

PRESBREY, EUGENE W. *New England Folks*. Fourteenth Street Theatre, New York, October 21, 1901.

ROSE, EDWARD E. *Alice of Old Vincennes*. Dramatization of novel by MAURICE THOMPSON, 1900. Fourteenth Street Theatre, New York, December, 1902.

————. *Eben Holden*. Dramatization of novel by IRVING BACHELLER, 1900. Fourteenth Street Theatre, New York, October, 1902.

————. *Penrod*. Dramatization of novel by BOOTH TARKINGTON. Globe Theatre, New York, September 2, 1918.

SMITH, WINCHELL, and BACON, FRANK. *Lightnin'*. New York: Samuel French, 1918. Gaiety Theatre, New York, August 26, 1918.

STAMHE, H. S., and MEARS, S. *Seventeen*. Dramatization of novel by BOOTH TARKINGTON. Booth Theatre, New York, January 22, 1918.

TARKINGTON, NEWTON BOOTH. *The Gentleman from Indiana*. Liebler & Co., English's, Indianapolis, 1905. Dramatization of 1899 novel.

THOMPSON, DENMAN, and RYER, GEORGE W. *Joshua Whitcomb*. As variety sketch, Harry Martin's Varieties, Pittsburgh, February, 1875; as play, National Theatre, Washington, D.C., April 3, 1876.

————. *The Old Homestead*. Walter H. Baker Co., 1927. Boston Museum, April 5, 1886.

CHAPTER VII

BAILEY, LORETTO CARROLL. *Job's Kinfolks: A Play of the Mill People.*
In FREDERICK H. KOCH, ed., *Carolina Folk-Plays.* New York: Henry
Holt & Co., 1928.

————, and BAILEY, J. O. *Strike Song.* Playmakers Theatre, Chapel
Hill, N.C., December 10-12, 1931.

BEIN, ALBERT. *Let Freedom Ring.* New York: Samuel French, 1936.
Dramatization of GRACE LUMPKIN, *To Make My Bread.* Broadhurst
Theatre, New York, November 6, 1935.

BLITZSTEIN, MARC. *The Cradle Will Rock.* New York: Random House,
1938. Mercury Theatre, New York, summer, 1937.

DREISER, THEODORE. "The Blue Sphere." In *Plays of the Natural and
the Supernatural.* New York: John Lane & Co., 1916.

————. "The Girl in the Coffin." In *Plays of the Natural and the
Supernatural.* New York: John Lane & Co., 1916.

————. *The Hand of the Potter.* New York: Boni & Liveright, 1918.

GREEN, PAUL. *In the Valley and Other Carolina Plays.* New York:
Samuel French, 1928. Title changed in 1931 version to *Potter's Field.*
In *Out of the South,* New York: Harper & Bros., 1939. Plymouth
Theatre, Boston, April 16, 1934.

————. *Johnny Johnson: The Biography of a Common Man.* New
York: Samuel French, 1937. Group Theatre, New York, November
19, 1936.

————. *Roll, Sweet Chariot: A Symphonic Play of the Negro People.*
Revision of *Potter's Field.* New York: Samuel French, 1935. Cort
Theatre, New York, October 2, 1934.

HEYWARD, DUBOSE. *Brass Ankle.* New York: Farrar & Rinehart, 1931.
Masque Theatre, New York, April 23, 1931.

————. *Porgy and Bess.* Theatre Guild-sponsored folk opera, 1935.
Lyrics by IRA GERSHWIN, score by GEORGE GERSHWIN. Alvin Theatre, New York, October 10, 1935.

————, and HEYWARD, DOROTHY. *Mamba's Daughters.* New York:
Farrar & Rinehart, 1939. Dramatization of DUBOSE HEYWARD's 1929
novel. Empire Theatre, New York, January 3, 1939.

————. *Porgy: A Four-act Folk Play.* New York: Doubleday, Page,
1927. Dramatization of DUBOSE HEYWARD's 1925 novel. Theatre
Guild, at Republic Theatre, New York, October 10, 1927.

HURLBUT, WILLIAM. *Bless You, Sister.* 1927.

————. *The Bride of the Lamb.* New York: Boni & Liveright, 1926.

————. *Salvation.* 1928.

————. *The Strange Woman.* 1913.

KEARNEY, PATRICK. *An American Tragedy*. Dramatization of THEODORE DREISER'S 1925 novel. Longacre Theatre, New York, October 11, 1926.

LAWRENCE, JEROME, and LEE, ROBERT E. *Inherit the Wind*. In JOHN GASSNER, ed., *Best American Plays, 1951-1957*. New York: Crown Publishers, 1960. Margo Jones Theatre, Dallas, January 1, 1955. National Theatre, New York, April 21, 1955.

LAWSON, JOHN HOWARD. *Processional: A Jazz Symphony of American Life*. New York: Boni, 1925. Theatre Guild, New York, January 12, 1925.

PHILLIPS, IRVING. *One Foot in Heaven*. Script, Margo Jones Collection, Dallas Public Library. Margo Jones Theatre, Dallas, December 12, 1951.

SHELDON, EDWARD. *"The Nigger": An American Play in Three Acts*. New York: Macmillan Co., 1910. New Theatre, New York, December 4, 1909.

THOMAS, AUGUSTUS. *Alabama: A Drama in Four Acts*. Chicago: Dramatic Publishing Co., 1888. Madison Square Theatre, New York, April 1, 1891.

————. *Colonel Carter of Cartersville*. Boston: Houghton Mifflin Co., 1892. Dramatization of Negro stories by FRANCIS HOPKINSON SMITH, 1891. Palmer's Theatre, New York, March 22, 1892.

WEXLEY, JOHN. *They Shall Not Die*. New York: Samuel French, 1934. Royale Theatre, New York, February 21, 1934.

WOLFE, THOMAS. *Mannerhouse*. New York: Harper & Bros., 1948. First titled *The Heirs: Or The Wasters*, 1920.

————. *Welcome to Our City*. Abridged in *Esquire*, 48 (October, 1957): 58-82. First titled *Niggertown*, 1922. Accepted by the Theatre Guild, but withdrawn by Wolfe, 1923.

CHAPTER VIII

ANDERSON, SHERWOOD. *Plays: Winesburg and Others*. New York: Charles Scribner's Sons, 1937. Dramatization of stories from *Winesburg, Ohio: A Group of Tales of Ohio Small Town Life*, 1919. "Winesburg," Jasper Deeter's Hedgerow Theatre, Moylan-Rose Valley, Pa., 1934. "The Triumph of the Egg" (with Raymond O'Neil), Provincetown Players at Playwrights' Theatre, New York, December 27, 1920. "Mother," Johns Hopkins University Players, n.d. "They Married Later," unproduced.

BROWN, ALICE. *Children of Earth*. New York: Macmillan Co., 1915. Booth Theatre, New York, January 12, 1915.

DAVIS, OWEN. *The Detour*. Boston: Little, Brown & Co., 1922; New York: Samuel French, 1922. Astor Theatre, New York, August 23, 1921.

————. *Icebound*. Boston: Little, Brown & Co., 1923. Harris Theatre, New York, February 21, 1923.

————, and DAVIS, DONALD. *Ethan Frome: A Dramatization*. New York: Charles Scribner's Sons, 1936. Based on novel by EDITH WHARTON, 1911. Garrick Theatre, Philadelphia, January 6, 1936.

EMERY, GILBERT (POTTLE, EMERY). *The Hero*. In A. H. QUINN, ed., *Contemporary American Plays*. New York, Charles Scribner's Sons, 1923. Longacre Theatre, New York, March 14, 1921.

GALE, ZONA. *Faint Perfume: A Play with a Prologue*. New York: D. Appleton-Century, 1934. Dramatization of the novel, 1932.

————. *Miss Lulu Bett: An American Comedy of Manners*. New York: D. Appleton, 1921. Dramatization of the novel, 1920. Belmont Theatre, New York, December 27, 1920.

————. *Mister Pitt*. New York: D. Appleton, 1925. Dramatization of the novel *Birth*, 1918. Thirty-ninth Street Theatre, New York, January 22, 1924.

GLASPELL, SUSAN. *Alison's House*. New York: Samuel French, 1930. Civic Repertory Theatre, New York, December 1, 1920.

HELLMAN, LILLIAN. *Another Part of the Forest*. New York: Viking Press, 1946. New York, November 20, 1946.

————. *The Little Foxes*. New York: Random House, 1939. National Theatre, New York, February 15, 1939. Musical version by MARC BLITZSTEIN, *Regina*. Produced in New York, 1950.

HOWARD, SIDNEY. *Ned McCobb's Daughter*. New York: Charles Scribner's Sons, 1926. Theatre Guild, at John Golden Theatre, New York, November 22, 1926.

————, and LEWIS, SINCLAIR. *Dodsworth*. New York: Harcourt, Brace, 1934. Dramatization of novel by SINCLAIR LEWIS, 1929. Garrick Theatre, Philadelphia, February 5, 1934; Shubert Theatre, New York, February 24, 1934.

LAWSON, JOHN HOWARD. *Roger Bloomer*. New York: T. Seltzer, 1923. Equity Theatre, New York, March 1, 1923.

LEWIS, SINCLAIR, and LEWIS, LLOYD. *The Jayhawker*. New York: Doubleday, Doran, 1935. National Theatre, Washington, D.C., October 14, 1934; new opening at Cort Theatre, Washington, November 5, 1934.

————, and MOFFITT, JOHN C. *It Can't Happen Here*. New York: Bureau of the Federal Theatre Project, September 18, 1936 (mimeo-

graphed). Simultaneous production in eighteen cities, October 27, 1936.

SÀDDLER, DONALD. "Dance Drama" based on SHERWOOD ANDERSON, *Winesburg, Ohio.* Jacob's Pillow, Massachusetts, Dance Festival, July 17, 1958.

SERGEL, CHRISTOPHER. *I'm a Fool.* Chicago: Dramatic Publishing Co., n.d. Dramatization of story by SHERWOOD ANDERSON.

————. *Winesburg, Ohio.* Dramatization of story by SHERWOOD ANDERSON. New York, February 5, 1958.

TROTTER, ELIZABETH. *Alice Adams.* Dramatization in 1921 of novel by BOOTH TARKINGTON. Gloucester, Mass., August 17-18, 1945; Indianapolis Civic Theatre, March 7, 1946.

CHAPTER IX

O'NEILL, EUGENE GLADSTONE. *Abortion.* Written in 1913-14. In *Lost Plays of Eugene O'Neill.* New York: New Fathoms Press, 1950; New York: Citadel Press, 1958. Unproduced.

————. *Ah, Wilderness!* Written in 1932. New York: Random House, 1941. Guild Theatre, New York, October 2, 1933.

————. *Beyond the Horizon.* Written in 1918. New York: Random House, 1928. Morosco Theatre, New York, February 2, 1920.

————. *Diff'rent.* Written in 1920. New York: Random House, 1928. Playwrights' Theatre, New York, December 27, 1920.

————. *Dynamo.* New York: Random House, 1941. Martin Beck Theatre, New York, February 11, 1929.

————. *The First Man.* Written in 1921. New York: Random House, 1928. Neighborhood Playhouse, New York, March 4, 1922.

————. *The Great God Brown.* Written in 1925. New York: Random House, 1928. Greenwich Village Theatre, New York, January 23, 1926.

————. *Long Day's Journey Into Night.* Written in 1939-41. New Haven: Yale University Press, 1956. Helen Hayes Theatre, New York, November 7, 1956.

————. *More Stately Mansions.* Written in 1935-38; 1939; 1940; 1941. New Haven: Yale University Press, 1964. Shortened version by KARL RAGNAR GIEROW, Royal Dramatic Theatre, Stockholm, November 9, 1962.

————. *Mourning Becomes Electra.* Written in 1929-31. New York: Random House, 1941. Guild Theatre, New York, October 26, 1931.

————. *The Rope.* Written in 1918. New York: Random House, 1928. Playwrights' Theatre, New York, April 26, 1918.

———. *Strange Interlude*. Written in 1926-27. New York: Random House, 1941. John Golden Theatre, New York, January 30, 1928.

———. *The Straw*. Written in 1918-19. New York: Random House, 1928. Greenwich Village Theatre, New York, November 10, 1921.

———. *A Touch of the Poet*. Written in 1935-42. New Haven: Yale University Press, 1957. Royal Dramatic Theatre, Stockholm, March, 1958. Helen Hayes Theatre, New York, October 2, 1958.

CHAPTER X

BAKER, PAUL, and MCKINNEY, EUGENE. *Of Time and the River*. Adaptation of THOMAS WOLFE'S 1935 novel. Script, Dallas Theater Center Library. Baylor University, Waco, Texas, 1959; Kalita Humphreys Theater, Dallas, 1960 season.

CRUMP, OWEN. *Southern Exposure*. Script, Margo Jones Collection, Dallas Public Library. Margo Jones Theatre, Dallas, April 3, 1950.

CONNELLY, MARC(US). *The Green Pastures*. New York: Rinehart & Co., 1930. Adaptation of ROARK BRADFORD, *Ol' Man Adam an' His Chillun*, 1928. Mansfield Theatre, New York, February 26, 1930.

FAULKNER, WILLIAM. *Intruder in the Dust*. Screenplay, 1949. Based on the 1948 novel.

———, and FORD, RUTH. *Requiem for a Nun*. New York: Random House, 1959. Theatre Guild production at John Golden Theatre, New York, January 28, 1959.

FLYNN, ROBERT L. *Journey to Jefferson*. Adaptation of WILLIAM FAULKNER, *As I Lay Dying*, 1930. Script, Dallas Theater Center Library. Baylor University, Waco, Texas, 1960; Kalita Humphreys Theater, Dallas, 1962-63.

FOOTE, HORTON. *Harrison, Texas*. New York: Harcourt, Brace, 1956. Short plays presented on the Philco-Goodyear Playhouse and the Gulf Playhouse: "Texas Town" (1941), "The Trip to Bountiful" (later on Broadway), and "A Young Lady of Property," Theater Three, Dallas, March 15, 1963.

———. *To Kill a Mockingbird*. 1963. Screenplay based on HARPER LEE'S novel.

———. *A Trip to Bountiful*. Theatre Guild and Fred Coe production, Henry Miller's Theatre, New York, November 3, 1953.

FRINGS, KETTI. *Look Homeward, Angel*. New York: Charles Scribner's Sons, 1958. Dramatization of novel by THOMAS WOLFE, 1929. Ethel Barrymore Theatre, New York, November 29, 1957.

HELLMAN, LILLIAN. *The Children's Hour*. In JOHN GASSNER, ed., *Twentieth Century Plays*. New York: Crown Publishers, 1947. Maxine Elliott Theatre, New York, November 20, 1934.

————. *Toys in the Attic*. In *Theatre Arts*, 45 (October, 1961). Hudson Theatre, New York, February 25, 1960.

MCCULLERS, CARSON. *The Member of the Wedding*. Norfolk, Conn.: New Directions, 1951. Dramatization of the 1946 novel. Empire Theatre, New York, January 5, 1950.

MCKINNEY, EUGENE. *A Different Drummer*. Written in 1955. New York: Samuel French, 1967. Dallas Theatre Center, 1964.

MOSEL, TAD. *All the Way Home*. New York: I. Obolensky, 1961. Dramatization of the JAMES AGEE novel, *A Death in the Family*, 1957. Belasco Theatre, New York, 1960-61.

PHILLIPS, IRVING. *One Foot in Heaven*. Script, Margo Jones Collection, Dallas Public Library. Margo Jones Theatre, Dallas, December 12, 1951.

RAVETCH, IRVING, and FRANK, HARRIET. *The Long, Hot Summer*. 1958. Film and teleplay adapted from WILLIAM FAULKNER, *The Hamlet*, 1931, 1940.

WARREN, ROBERT PENN, and FRANKEL, AARON. *Willie Stark: His Rise and Fall*. Dramatization of Warren's novel, *All the King's Men*, 1946. Script, Margo Jones Collection, Dallas Public Library. Margo Jones Theatre, November 25, 1958. (A screenplay, *All the King's Men*, appeared in 1949.)

WILLIAMS, THOMAS LANIER (TENNESSEE). *American Blues*. New York: Dramatists Play Service, 1948.

————. *Battle of Angels*. In *Orpheus Descending with Battle of Angels*. New York: New Directions, 1955; 1958. Wilbur Theatre, Boston, December 30, 1940. (A screenplay, *Fugitive Kind*, appeared in 1945.)

————. *Camino Real*. Norfolk, Conn.: New Directions, 1953. Martin Beck Theatre, New York, March 19, 1953.

————. *The Milk Train Doesn't Stop Here Anymore*. Norfolk, Conn.: New Directions, 1964. Morosco Theatre, New York, January 10, 1963.

————. *The Night of the Iguana*. New York: New Directions, 1962. Royale Theatre, New York, December 28, 1961.

————. *Orpheus Descending*. New York: New Directions, 1958. Martin Beck Theatre, New York, March 21, 1957.

————. *The Rose Tattoo*. New York: New Directions, 1951. Erlanger Theatre, Chicago, December 29, 1950; Martin Beck Theatre, New York, February 3, 1951.

————. *Summer and Smoke* (first titled *A Chart of Anatomy*, 1947). Norfolk, Conn.: New Directions, 1948. Margo Jones Theatre, Dallas, July 8, 1947; Music Box Theatre, New York, October 6, 1948.

————. *Sweet Bird of Youth*. New York: New Directions, 1959. Martin Beck Theatre, New York, March 10, 1959.

————. *27 Wagons Full of Cotton and Other One-Act Plays*. Norfolk, Conn.: New Directions, 1945; 1953. "The Last of My Solid Gold Watches" and "This Property Is Condemned," Margo Jones Theatre, Dallas, November 17, 1947. "27 Wagons Full of Cotton" filmed as *Baby Doll*. New York: New Directions, 1956.

CHAPTER XI

AIDMAN, CHARLES. *Spoon River*. Written in 1963. Adaptation of *Spoon River Anthology*, by EDGAR LEE MASTERS, 1915. Booth Theatre, New York, September 29, 1963.

ALBEE, EDWARD. *The American Dream*. New York: Coward-McCann, 1961. Broadway production early in 1961.

————. *The Ballad of the Sad Café*. Boston: Houghton Mifflin, 1963. Adaptation of novella by CARSON McCULLERS, 1951. Martin Beck Theatre, New York, October 30, 1963.

————. *The Sandbox*. In *Three Plays*. New York: Coward-McCann, 1960.

————. *Who's Afraid of Virginia Woolf?* New York: Atheneum, 1962. Billy Rose Theatre, New York, October 13, 1962.

ALEXANDER, RONALD. *Time Out for Ginger* (originally titled *Season with Ginger*). In *Theatre Arts*, 38 (February, 1954): 36-64. Lyceum Theatre, New York, November 12, 1952.

ANDERSON, MAXWELL. *The Wingless Victory: A Play in Three Acts*. Menasha, Wisc., 1936.

ANDERSON, ROBERT. *All Summer Long*. Dramatization, 1951, of DONALD WETZEL, *A Wreath and a Curse*, 1950. In *Theatre Arts*, 39 (August, 1955): 34 ff. First produced at Zelda Fichlander's Arena Stage, Washington, D.C. Playwrights' Company, Coronet Theatre, New York, September 23, 1954.

————. *The Days Between*. New York: Random House, 1965. Kalita Humphreys Theater, Dallas, May, 1965.

————. *Silent Night, Lonely Night*. In *Theatre Arts*, 45 (December, 1961): 26 ff. Playwrights' Company, Morosco Theatre, New York, December 3, 1959.

————. *Tea and Sympathy*. In *Theatre Arts*, 38 (September, 1954): 34 ff. Barrymore Theatre, New York, September 30, 1953.

BATSON, GEORGE. *Magnolia Alley.* Mansfield Theatre, New York, April 18, 1949.

CAPOTE, TRUMAN. *The Grass Harp.* New York: Dramatists Play Service, 1952; 1954. Martin Beck Theatre, New York, March 27, 1952.

DRUMMOND, A. M., and GARD, ROBERT E. *The Cardiff Giant.* Ithaca: Cornell University Press, 1949. Willard Straight Theatre, Cornell University, Ithaca, May 20, 1939.

DRUMMOND, A. M., and KARNACK, E. L., eds. *More Upstate New York Plays.* Ithaca: Cayuga Press, 1950. Produced at Cornell University.

FIELDS, JOSEPH, and CHODOROV, JEROME. *The Ponder Heart.* New York: Random House, 1956. Dramatization of story by EUDORA WELTY. Playwrights' Company, Music Box Theatre, New York, February 16, 1956.

HAYES, JOSEPH. *Calculated Risk.* In *Theatre Arts*, 47 (December, 1963): 20-54. Ambassador Theatre, New York, October 31, 1962.

HELLMAN, LILLIAN. *The Autumn Garden.* Boston: Little, Brown & Co., 1952. Coronet Theatre, New York, March 7, 1951.

HOWARD, SIDNEY. *Alien Corn.* Belasco Theatre, New York, February 20, 1933.

———. *The Late Christopher Bean: A Comedy in Three Acts* (first titled *Muse of Work*). New York: Samuel French, 1932. Ford's Theatre, Baltimore, October 23, 1932; Henry Miller's Theatre, New York, October 31, 1932.

———, and LEWIS, SINCLAIR. *Dodsworth.* Adaptation of the Sinclair Lewis novel, 1929. Shubert Theatre, New York, February 24, 1934.

INGE, WILLIAM. *Bus Stop.* Written in 1955. In JOHN GASSNER, ed., *Best Ameircan Plays, 1951-1957.* New York: Crown Publishers, 1958. Music Box Theatre, New York, March 2, 1955.

———. *Come Back, Little Sheba.* In BROOKS ATKINSON, ed., *New Voices in the American Theatre.* New York: Modern Library, Random House, 1955. Theatre Guild, February 15, 1950.

———. *The Dark at the Top of the Stairs.* New York: Random House, 1958. Titled *Farther Off from Heaven*, Margo Jones Theatre, Dallas, 1947. Music Box Theatre, New York, December 5, 1957.

———. *A Loss of Roses.* New York: Random House, 1960. Eugene O'Neill Theatre, New York, November 28-December 19, 1959.

———. *Picnic: A Summer Romance* (originally titled *Front Porch*). New York: Random House, 1953. Theatre Guild, at Music Box Theatre, New York, February 19, 1953.

KAUFMAN, GEORGE S., and CONNELLY, MARC. *To the Ladies!* In A. H. QUINN, ed., *Contemporary American Plays.* New York: Charles

Scribner's Sons, 1923. Lyceum Theatre, Rochester, N.Y., February 13, 1922; Liberty Theatre, New York, February 20, 1922.

KAUFMAN, GEORGE S., and HART, MOSS. *The Man Who Came to Dinner*. Written in 1939. In ALLAN GATES HALLINE, ed., *Six Modern American Plays*. New York: Modern Library, Random House, 1951.

LERNER, ALAN JAY. *Paint Your Wagon*. New York: Coward-McCann, n.d. In *Theatre Arts*, 36 (December, 1952): 37-60. Shubert Theatre, New York, November 12, 1951.

LEVIN, IRA, and HYMAN, MAC. *No Time for Sergeants*. In JOHN GASSNER, ed., *Best American Plays, 1951-1957*. New York: Crown Publishers, 1958. Dramatization of Hyman's novel. Alvin Theatre, New York, October 20, 1955.

LOESSER, FRANK. *The Most Happy Fella*. In *Theatre Arts*, 42 (October, 1958): 26-53. Musical version of SIDNEY HOWARD, *They Knew What They Wanted*, 1924. Imperial Theatre, New York, May 3, 1956.

McCANSE, RALPH ALAN. *Waters Over Linn Creek Town*. New York: Bookman Associates, Twayne Publishers, 1951. Unproduced.

MILLER, ARTHUR. *All My Sons*. In GERALD WEALES, ed., *Eleven Plays*. New York: W. W. Norton & Co., 1964. Coronet Theatre, New York, January 29, 1947.

MORRIS, RICHARD. *The Unsinkable Molly Brown*. In *Theatre Arts*, 47 (February, 1963): 25-56. Theatre Guild, at Winter Garden, New York, November 3, 1960.

NASH, RICHARD N., JONES, TOM, and SCHMIDT, HARVEY. *110 in the Shade*. Musical version of Nash's *The Rainmaker*, 1954. Broadhurst Theatre, New York, October 24, 1963.

NUGENT, ELLIOTT, and THURBER, JAMES. *The Male Animal*. Written in 1940. In JOHN GASSNER, ed., *Best Plays of the Modern American Theatre*. New York: Crown Publishers, 1947. Cort Theatre, New York, January 9, 1940.

NUGENT, J. C., and NUGENT, ELLIOTT. *The Poor Nut*. 1925.

O'BRIEN, LIAM. *The Remarkable Mr. Pennypacker*. In *Theatre Arts*, 39 (April, 1955): 56 ff. Coronet Theatre, New York, December 30, 1953.

REED, DANIEL. *Spoon River Anthology*. Dramatization of poems from book by EDGAR LEE MASTERS. Brooklyn Academy of Music, Brooklyn, N.Y., January 22, 1954.

SAROYAN, WILLIAM. *Hello Out There*. In *Razzle Dazzle*. New York: Harcourt, Brace, 1942. Lobero Theatre, Santa Barbara, Calif., September 10, 1941.

————. *My Heart's in the Highlands.* New York: Harcourt, Brace, 1939. Dramatization of the story, "The Man with the Heart in the Highlands," 1936. Group Theatre at the Guild Theatre, New York, April 13, 1939.

SHERWOOD, ROBERT. *Abe Lincoln in Illinois.* In HARLAN HATCHER, ed., *Modern American Dramas.* New York: Harcourt, Brace, 1941. National Theatre, Washington, D.C., October 3, 1938; Plymouth Theatre, New York, October 15, 1938.

STEIN, JOSEPH *et al. Plain and Fancy.* In *Theatre Arts,* 40 (July, 1956): 33 ff. Mark Hellinger Theatre, New York, January 27, 1955.

STEWART, MICHAEL, and HERMAN, JERRY. *Hello, Dolly!* Musical version of *The Matchmaker,* by THORNTON WILDER. St. James Theatre, New York, 1964-65.

WILDER, THORNTON. *The Long Christmas Dinner and Other Plays in One Act.* New York: Coward-McCann, 1931.

————. *The Matchmaker.* Edinburgh Festival, Edinburgh, Scotland, summer, 1954. Royale Theatre, New York, 1956.

————. *The Merchant of Yonkers.* New York: Harper & Bros., 1939. Colonial Theatre, Boston, December 12, 1938; Guild Theatre, New York, 1938.

————. *Our Town.* New York: Coward-McCann, 1938. McCarter's Theatre, Princeton, N.J., January 22, 1938; Henry Miller Theatre, New York, February 4, 1938.

————. *Three Plays: Our Town, The Skin of Our Teeth, and The Matchmaker.* Ed. TRAVIS BOGARD. New York: Harper & Row, 1957. *The Skin of Our Teeth,* Shubert Theatre, New Haven, Conn., October 15, 1942; Plymouth Theatre, New York, December 13, 1942.

WILLSON, MEREDITH. *The Music Man.* New York: G. P. Putnam's Sons, 1958. Majestic Theatre, New York, December 19, 1957.

CHAPTER XII

ARDREY, ROBERT. *Jeb.* Martin Beck Theatre, New York, February 21, 1946.

BALDWIN, JAMES. *Blues for Mr. Charlie.* Actors Studio, New York, 1964.

NASH, RICHARD N. *A Handful of Fire.* Martin Beck Theatre, New York, October, 1958.

OSBORN, PAUL. *A Bell for Adano.* New York: Dramatists Play Service, c. 1945. Adaptation of 1944 novel by John Hersey. Cort Theatre, New York, December 6, 1944.

PATRICK, JOHN. *The Teahouse of the August Moon.* New York: G. P.

Putnam's Sons, 1954. Adaptation of novel by VERN SNEIDER, 1951. Martin Beck Theatre, New York, 1953-54.

SHERWOOD, ROBERT. *There Shall Be No Night*. New York: Charles Scribner's Sons, 1940. Playwrights' Company and Theatre Guild, 1940.

SHUMLIN, HERMAN. *Spofford*. ANTA Theatre, New York, 1967-68.

SMITH, LILLIAN, and SMITH, ESTHER. *Strange Fruit*. 1945. Dramatization of Lillian Smith's novel, 1944. Royale Theatre, New York, November 29, 1945.

STEINBECK, JOHN. *The Moon Is Down*. New York: Viking Press, 1942. New York, April 7, 1942.

USSEAU, ARNAUD D', and GOW, JAMES. *Deep Are the Roots*. New York: Charles Scribner's Sons, 1946. Fulton Theatre, New York, September 26, 1945.

WILLIAMS, THOMAS LANIER (TENNESSEE). *Camino Real*. Norfolk, Conn.: New Directions, 1953. Martin Beck Theatre, New York, March 19, 1953.

————. *The Night of the Iguana*. New York: New Directions, 1962. Royale Theatre, New York, December 28, 1961.

Index